TRANSPARENCY IN POSTWAR FRANCE

Cultural Memory

in

the

Present

Hent de Vries, Editor

TRANSPARENCY IN POSTWAR FRANCE

A Critical History of the Present

Stefanos Geroulanos

STANFORD UNIVERSITY PRESS

STANFORD, CALIFORNIA

Stanford University Press
Stanford, California

©2017 by the Board of Trustees of the Leland Stanford Junior University.
All rights reserved.

Printed in the United States of America on acid-free, archival-quality paper

Library of Congress Cataloging-in-Publication Data available upon request.

ISBN 978-0-8047-9974-4 (cloth)
ISBN 978-1-5036-0459-9 (paper)
ISBN 978-1-5036-0341-7 (ebook)

Typeset by Bruce Lundquist in 11/13.5 Adobe Garamond

Contents

List of Illustrations

Acknowledgments

I should like to acknowledge the rights holders who granted me permissions for the research that went into this book: Monique Lévi-Strauss, especially for allowing me to reproduce two images from Claude Lévi-Strauss's typescript of *Tristes tropiques*; Jocelyne Rouch for the unpublished photograph from the test screening of *Chronique d'un été*; Bernhard Canguilhem, for permitting citations from Georges Canguilhem's archive; and Daniel Métraux, for access to the archive of his father, Alfred. I am grateful to New York University for providing financial support for my research through a Goddard Fellowship and a Provost's Global Research Initiative fellowship in 2011–12. Librarians and archivists at every site where I carried out research were extremely helpful, especially Guillaume Fau, Marion Abélès, Marie-Dominique Mouton, Frédéric Doubois, and Claire Guttinger.

My essays "Theoscopy: Transparency, Omnipotence, Modernity," published in Hent de Vries and Lawrence Sullivan, eds., *Political Theologies: Public Religions in a Post-Secular World* (2006), and "Transparency Thinking Freedom," in *Modern Language Notes* 122 (5): 1050–78 (2007), played a role in my conceptualization of the project. I have also presented parts of the book at Stanford's French Culture Workshop; the Freie Universität Berlin; the Columbia University Global Center in Paris; a meeting of the BIOS Center of the London School of Economics in conjunction with the University of Aarhus; the Political Theory Workshop at Yale; Université Paris 1 Panthéon-Sorbonne, the European History Workshop at Princeton; the École normale supérieure in Paris, twice; the History Department, Mellon Vitalism Workshop, and Society for the Humanities at Cornell University; the 2014 Society for French Historical Studies Annual Meeting held at MIT; and the Instituto de Humanidades at the Universidad Diego Portales in Santiago, Chile. I am indebted to my hosts at each of these institutions for their generous invitations and to many participants for discussions and recommendations that offered great opportunities for refinement.

At Stanford University Press, I thank above all Emily-Jane Cohen, who engaged, nurtured, and fought for this book, and who also pushed for its improvement. I am also deeply grateful to my production editor Jessica Ling, as well as to Manuela Tecusan and Peter Dreyer, who edited and enriched the manuscript so ably as to make it effective and beautiful. For the convenience of the English-speaking reader, I have opted to quote English editions of French books whenever available; I have also retranslated passages as I saw fit.

I started this book as an experiment, and I am immensely grateful to colleagues and friends for their intellectual support, friendship, sustained conversation, and criticism. I want to thank by name those whose contributions have directly improved the book: Emmanuel Alloa, Emily Apter, Alexander Arnold, Aner Barzilay, Giuseppe Bianco, Julian Bourg, Françoise Coblence, Katherine Fleming, Juan-Manuel Garrido, Peter Gordon, Vanessa Gubbins, Nicolas Guilhot, Dagmar Herzog, Nicole Jerr, Ben Kafka, Jair Kessler, Wilmot Kidd, Jacob Krell, Ruth Leys, Mark Mazower, Eric Michaud, Sam Moyn, Molly Nolan, Knox Peden, Jamie Phillips, Andy Rabinbach, John Raimo, Pamela Reynolds, Andrew Sartori, Danilo Scholz, Maria Stavrinaki, Judith Surkis, Adam Tooze, Claudia Verhoeven, Tony Vidler, Hent de Vries, Molly Warnock, and Frédéric Worms. I am especially grateful to my co-conspirators Richard Baxstrom, Zvi Ben-Dor Benite, Dan Edelstein, Todd Meyers, Camille Robcis, Natasha Wheatley, and Larry Wolff, who have turned my writing of this book and our projects together into a joyous exercise in friendship and intellectual invention; it is because of our work together that I could continue to engage in this one.

Finally, I want to acknowledge the continued encouragement, playful eye rolling, and love of my parents, Maria and Nikos; my sister, Sarra; and my children, Isabelle and Leon—especially their Kikuchiyo defiance toward my working habits and this project. This book is dedicated to my brilliant wife, Rania. I wrote it, with a glance and a smile, for the one in my life who, again and again, brings forth moments of transparency as moving as they are delicious.

TRANSPARENCY IN POSTWAR FRANCE

Introduction

The Matter with Transparency

The role of philosophy is not to discover what is hidden but to render visible precisely what is visible, that is to say to make appear what is so close, so immediate, so intimately linked to us, that as a result we don't see it.

Michel Foucault, "The Analytic Philosophy of Politics" (1994a, 3: 540)

It's my inclination when I compose to be crystal clear in the sense that sometimes the crystal reflects yourself and other times you can see through the material. So the work suggests a hiding and opening at the same time. And what I want most to create is a kind of deceiving transparency, as if you were looking in very transparent water and couldn't make an estimate of the depths. If you're a complicated self you express yourself in more complicated terms.

Pierre Boulez, "On New Music" (1984)

The Crystalline Self, or, The Best of Masks: Starobinski, Rousseau, Rorschach

In 1957, the literary theorist Jean Starobinski published his *thèse ès lettres*, a reading of Jean-Jacques Rousseau's body of work, with the Paris publisher Plon.[1] Starobinski, who had just defended this dissertation in Geneva, subtitled his book *La Transparence et l'obstacle*: "transparency and obstacle," or, in Arthur Goldhammer's translation, *Transparency and Obstruction*. He centered on the persona that Rousseau created for himself, above all in his later works, the *Confessions*, the *Dialogues: Rousseau, Judge of Jean-Jacques*, the *Reveries of a Solitary Walker*. Rousseau, this isolated, pure, sincere, truthful

Jean-Jacques, hounded by self-dissimulating creatures of the shadow realm of false arts, oppressive mores, and enchaining lies generated by a long history of divergence from nature—which is to say, everyone around him.

Starobinski's argument on transparency follows two movements in Rousseau's thought. The first is Rousseau's quest to render himself transparent and to conceive of a society that returns to the unmediated "Nature," uncontaminated by human design, that preceded social obfuscation. Calling on his readers to return to a prehistoric age of transparency themselves,[2] Rousseau appealed to a state of nature in order to imagine the possibility of a pure society.[3] As he made clear in *The Social Contract* (1762), across history "evil is veil and veiling."[4] Identifying his childhood with this innocent time, he cast himself as a soul "transparent as crystal,"[5] a crystal he was presenting to the world uncovered and unchipped.

Starobinski contends that Rousseau's logic of identifying himself with purity generated an ever-compounding series of external obstacles, which Rousseau gradually came to perceive as insurmountable. Rousseau in other words succumbed to a second movement in his thought, one that followed from the very *success* of his pursuit of personal and ethical transparency. Having declared himself transparent, he found the masks, separations, and veils he had banished from his soul all now rising up everywhere around him, bringing back the opacity he had sought to overcome and rendering it an external threat. His transparency radicalized this world of lurking shadows in paranoid fashion; it guaranteed that the persecution he felt would become a cage welded shut.[6] In Starobinski's view, once Rousseau "achieved" his intention of becoming pure, he developed a "secret desire" to *not* act, to *not* be responsible for his life.[7] Purity led to the projection of all action and all guilt onto others: Rousseau could maintain transparency in his self-affection only by treating it as contaminated by worldly action among those others who imprisoned him in an "impregnable asylum" of solitude and dispossession.[8] Step by step, this countergesture immobilized the transparent soul, making inevitable the increasingly solipsistic, paranoid, haunted self that Rousseau famously became.

Rousseau's claim to purity had already been a matter of debate and exasperation among his contemporaries. But Starobinski's idea that this purity was itself responsible for generating the epistemological, ethical, and political *obstacles* that debilitated it was new. Original here was the identification of the two movements and, specifically, the conviction that it was the pursuit of transparency that led directly to Rousseau's paranoia about an overbearing world of infinite obstacles. Rousseau's search for transparency expanded from his self-depiction into an interpretation of problems as wide-ranging as social organization, ethical relationships, human history, and the likelihood of political remedy. Starobinski identified Rousseau's politics with a commitment to liberation from the ornamentation and masking that defined aristocratic society, and that was exemplified by the theater—the "world of opacity" decried in Rousseau's *Lettre à d'Alembert sur les spectacles* (*Letter to D'Alembert on the Theater*).[9] Famously, Rousseau counterposed the festival, an ecstatic, ultimately democratic event, in which masks could not survive, to the theater. A few years after his dissertation, in 1964, Starobinski presented Rousseau's antitheatrical festival as his principal influence on the French Revolution:

The festival that Rousseau envisaged was an assembly of people aware that their own presence was the basis of their fervor: they could look at one another with a joyful sense of their shared freedom. . . . They would celebrate a new transparency: hearts would hide no more secrets, communication would be completely free of obstacles. Since everyone present would be simultaneously audience and actors, they would have done away with the distance which, in the theater, separated the stage and the auditorium. The spectacle would be everywhere and nowhere. Identical in everyone's eyes, the image of the festival would be indivisible—and it would be the image, multiplied indefinitely, of man meeting man in absolute equality and understanding. . . . The system of façades, screens, fictions, alluring masks which dominated the world of aristocratic culture could no longer be retained: they were condemned to disappear, for they were felt . . . to be simply inert elements, harmful obstacles.[10]

Transparency, under Starobinski's pen, became Rousseau's supreme mask: a mask first of all ethical but also epistemological and political, a mask that might efface itself perfectly if it did not also project inner anxieties onto the outside world and devolve its author's search for sovereignty into a precarious solitude.

This was not merely a matter of literary criticism.[11] For someone involved in psychological and medical debates like the ones Starobinski wrote about in Georges Bataille and Eric Weil's journal *Critique*, this mask exposed a truly contemporary problem of the modern phenomenological, psychological, and political subject. In an essay published in *Critique* shortly after *Jean-Jacques Rousseau: La Transparence et l'obstacle* appeared in 1957, Starobinski took on the theory behind the Rorschach test with an eye to questions about sincerity and dissimulation, interiority and masks. He mocked the claims made for the test by its practitioners, presenting its practice as an exemplary case of psychology-as-policing: the underlying theory was so inadequate that "everything remains to be done." Anticipating by several years Michel Foucault's paradigm-setting *Folie et déraison* (1961; *History of Madness*), Starobinski denounced this policing as ever present in a modernity where "society no longer burns witches and the possessed, it puts them under care as 'abnormals.'"[12] In his view, "contemporary psychology does not in the least like the notion of depth," and the Rorschach test constituted the perfect reduction of interiority: it erased consciousness by ignoring all the complex operations of interpretation, expression, and communication in favor of two purified moments—the test subject's perception and the test administrator's unmediated translation of the test subject's claims:

While the test appeals to the immediacy of perception, this immediacy is quickly lost and compromised, first because the subject must *say* what he perceived, and thus interpret in the "tribal language" what he has sensed; and following, because the psychologist must comment, in his science's language, on the "naïve" speech in which the subject has held forth.[13]

This betrayed a conception of the mind as flat, mechanistic, and transparent. It allowed the psychiatrist to claim the status of an impersonal interpreter of scientific data and the test to typify "all the sadism that the psychiatrist disavows: a sadism . . . analogous to the machine Kafka describes in *In the Penal Colony*."[14]

In Starobinski's view, only one Rorschach theorist stood apart from this smothering of consciousness and intersubjectivity: the existential psychoanalyst Roland Kuhn, who wrote at length on patients who interpreted the blots as masks or saw masks in them.[15] In his *Phénoménologie du masque à travers le test de Rorschach* (1957), published with an admiring preface by Gaston Bachelard, Kuhn identified the perception of masks in Rorschach blots with the patient's dissimulating behavior and his or her willingness to project the mask onto others. Studying between 200 and 400 cases (42 of them in depth),[16] Kuhn treated the practice of interpreting the blot as a mask as a sign of severe psychosis. The patient who saw masks everywhere transformed external reality into constant danger, and became at once guiltless in his/her own mind and unable to reason in harmony with others (see fig. 0.1 and 0.2).

Dessin de Kuno, cas n° 3, représentant son père.

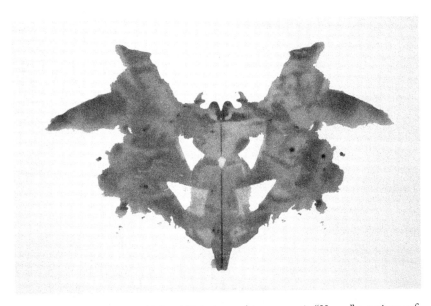

FIGURES 0.1 AND 0.2 Roland Kuhn's case history no. 3: "Kono," a patient suffering from schizophrenia, identified the first card of the Rorschach test (below) with the face of his father, and specifically with a drawing of his father's face (above) that, as a child, he had made to "cut to wear as a mask" (Kuhn 1957: 21, 23).

SOURCE: Fig. 0.1: Kuhn 1957. Fig. 0.2: Hermann Rorschach, *Psychodiagnostik: Tafeln* (Bern: Huber, 1921), card 1, https://commons.wikimedia.org/wiki/File:Rorschach_blot_01.jpg.

Both Bachelard and Starobinski interpreted Kuhn's Rorschach masks as potentialities of being, and hence as fundamentally future-oriented. In his preface, Bachelard—who had invented the concept of the "epistemological obstacle" that Starobinski was using in his reading of Rousseau—went so far as to claim that Kuhn's interpretation of masks was an essential complement to a Freudian interpretation of dreams.[17] Starobinski treated the argument on masks as profoundly consequential for any phenomenology of depth, depersonalization, and dialogue.[18] Wherever transparency laid its claim, dissimulation reigned; to dive into masks was to deny psychologistic reductionism, to engage questions of human existence in earnest rather than police them away. Going one step beyond Bachelard, who largely identified the desire for dissimulation as a pathological condition, Starobinski suggested that the human being "remains *always* possessed by a troubled desire of obscurity and depth."[19]

It is hard to miss the parallel between Starobinski's treatment of Rousseau and his interest in the Rorschach test and its masks. And yet readers of *Jean-Jacques Rousseau: Transparency and Obstruction* usually place Starobinski in the camp of lucidity and transparency. His colleague and mentor Georges Poulet wrote of his "intellect as being analogous to Rousseau's, yearning for an immediate transparence of all beings."[20] Robert Darnton (who pronounced the book a true classic of eighteenth-century scholarship), Judith Shklar (who called it the "second best book" on Rousseau, after Rousseau's own *Confessions*), and Martin Jay have focused on the impulse *to* transparency.[21] Still, Starobinski's attachment was much more to masks, obstacles, and opacity than to their banishment; for him transparency was itself such a mask—a supremely forceful one. This is how he would later on describe his own intellectual concerns of the time, retracing his Rousseau book

back to the time of [World War II], to the anxiety aroused in me by the fanaticism in uniform whose irrational imperatives had unleashed a worldwide conflict, and to the astonishment I felt at the seductive power exerted by leaders whose "charisma" stemmed essentially from their knowing how to make use of a certain kind of mask. My interest centered on modern ways of using masks and their powers of fascination. Meanwhile, in literary history, I was obliged to take note of a literary tradition of denouncing masks. . . . My first project . . . [was] to write a history of the use of masks in terms of the most typical examples, coupled with a history of the kinds of accusations that had been leveled at masked behavior. I wanted to combine a history of mystifying alienation with a history of demystification.[22]

Starobinski had offered a version of this project in an essay titled "Interrogatoire du masque" (1946; Interrogation of the Mask).[23] That "interrogation" engaged in half-literary-historical, half-philosophical-political fashion with a Europe riveted by a proliferation of masks, lies, and veils: "The new masks that we have now seen at work are the expression of the lie of the will to power."[24] He still hoped that the human dependence on masks could be overcome:

We know today how certain masks are impressive and shallow, and what it costs to prefer them to the truth of our own face. Still, we are not finished yet with masks. As long as this sour dissatisfaction that refuses to accept the servitudes of our carnal identity remains alive within us, as long as we suffer from our own incompleteness, the mask will remain this strange promise of a *healing through metamorphosis* for us. As long . . . as we dream of being stronger or better than we are, the mask will tempt us the way Mephistopheles tempted Faust. It all happens as if our truth could never be for the now, as if we needed to quest eternally after the human face.[25]

So dreamt the younger Starobinski—of an unmasking that would penetrate to the true human face, and shaping this hope into both an urgent political demand and an ever-receding possibility. The change of attitude between 1946 and 1958 is astonishing. A dozen years after "Interrogatoire du masque," Starobinski argued in *Jean-Jacques Rousseau* that the transparency of the self had proven to be little more than a particularly dangerous mask. The shift helps us delineate the intellectual and political claims of that book and brings into relief Starobinski's demand that a modicum of opacity, dissimulation, and masking remain essential to subjectivity.

Any effort to enforce absolute transparency—on oneself, others, or society at large—was bound to fail and primed to recreate, perhaps in a far more paranoid form, the very shadows and masks it sought to banish. Starobinski's reconstruction of Rousseau as a thinker whose obsession with transparency ended up by projecting outside the opacities he could not bear within would prove exemplary of the postwar concern with the term "transparency" and its implications. A transparent society, like a transparent ethics, comes with a price: a redeployment of masks, which results not from the failure but from the realization of one's intentions.

Fold upon Fold: The Development of the
Critique of Transparency in Postwar France
Object

During the three decades after World War II, French philosophers, psychoanalysts, filmmakers, anthropologists, poets, historians of science, and politically engaged intellectuals from Jean-Paul Sartre to Jean-François Lyotard consigned the hopes associated with transparency to an armory of destructive modern illusions. They treated the concept highly critically, even dismissively, and relegated its corollaries—both ideas and ideals—to a past that most of them considered obsolete. Until "now," they claimed, "to be transparent" had been a synonym for surviving free of sin and secrecy, for revealing and taming hidden motivations, for living an ethical life unburdened by lies and bias. To make the world transparent had meant knowing it without illusion and without intermediary. To make the social and political realms transparent had meant cleansing them of injustice, corruption, superstition, and oppression from authority and capital. To make the visible transparent had meant purging it of false images and reaching to its supposed essence. But not any more.

The tightly wound web of the concepts, ideals, and goals these figures linked to transparency had been central to ethics, politics, and epistemology at least since the Enlightenment. Rousseau was only one of the more famous names in the modern idealization of transparency; a list of his precursors and followers would be long indeed. It begins perhaps with Descartes and his *cogito* and features Comte's ideas of the flawlessness of a world perceived through positivist science; the young Marx promoting revolution in the *Communist Manifesto*; Nietzsche and the perspective of the *Übermensch*; Léon Brunschvicg equating mathematics and idealism; and Heidegger and the authenticity of being-toward-death—but also Robespierre in his famous speeches from Year II on political morality and on revolutionary government; the nationalist uses, from Rivarol through Renan, of the French language as a paragon of clarity; and Napoleon, with his dream of a perfect police. Throughout the history of European philosophy, philosophers and scientists had repeatedly introduced the concept of transparency into the formulation of social goals and treated it as a foundation of knowledge or as a premise in human beings' interaction with their world. Interpersonal transparency often appeared as a prerequisite for sharing meaning, and self-transparency as a subjective ideal, or even as an ethical desideratum. Specifically, it had been possible to claim

- that the self could be transparent to itself, and that achieving a pure, crystalline self was the very purpose of ethics;
- that the mind could know the world and could have an unimpeded encounter with it;
- that relations between individuals could be pure, not dissimulated—that a "meeting of the hearts" between two individuals was possible, desirable, ethical;
- that society could be open, transparent to its members and/or to the state.

Such claims were no longer tenable. Postwar French thought built tool after tool for dismantling them:

- The presumed transparency of the self—in Rousseau's terms, a transparent soul; in Verlaine's, a transparent heart—became a central target of critiques of "the subject" that denied the capacity for self-knowledge and the homogeneity of the self and dissected it until unconscious codes, norms, and the alterity of the other could explain both how this self is fragmented and constructed and how it is articulated as singular and absolute.

- Epistemological transparency, an enigma for philosophers and scientists already in the 1930s, came simply to be dismissed as a fantasy of scientific positivism and idealism, tendencies that had not appreciated what an abyss separated the mind from the world. The question became how the positivist shortcut could be obviated or shown to be staged, how obstacles and especially social and mental structures could be studied, if science was to be rethought and this fault overcome.

- The rise of notions of separation, *the other*, abnormality, and masking specifically targeted the overbearing romantic idea of a "meeting of the hearts." Like the transparency of the self, transparency in ethics (and the impulse to it) could appear as a delusion.

- A "transparent" society was now synonymous with a completely *homogenized*, indeed totalitarian society. Against this threat, changing concepts of *norms*, *the other*, *alienation*, *complexity*, and *information*, like the new figures of the *résistant* and the gangster, the lacuna in the subject, the maladjusted adolescent, and the student revolutionary offered a sense of the individual's need to become irreducible to state and social standards.

In a word, transparency had become suspect. It represented dated, even oppressive promises. It was mercurial—slippery and poisonous. It held up a false mirror to the self, to society, to knowledge, proffering a misguided belief in the purity of self. The world was not transparent, because it was complex, layered, structured, filled with heterogeneity. To appeal to transparency and related ideas was to pretend that this complexity did not exist.

Transparency thus wilted to become dead weight. Until World War II, it had supposedly composed a unitary worldview, masking and oppressing rather than revealing and liberating. Recoiling from its illusion also meant rejecting an opacity hidden "within" it and rendered unreachable: each danger seemed to give quarter to the other and to a foggy, mystical self-loss that pompously announced authenticity or enlightenment. Forms of otherness, concepts of structure, codes for information and power could hold off homogenization. They could serve for retrieving the minute, the a-normal, the oppressed, the different, and for using them as an interface through which philosophy could mitigate a better-theorized knowledge and a more just, more hybrid view of reality. A different world, dynamic and cognizant of difference, could perhaps arise.

⟨∾⟩

This book draws up the history of these concepts and ideals from the standpoint of postwar thought; it reconstructs this evolving critique and, with it, the quiet role of transparency in earlier systems. My purpose is to trace the steps and shifts—at times disparate, incremental, recursive, or convulsive—that exemplified a major revaluation of ideals. It is also to recompile the arsenal of hermeneutic, historical, and political weapons and counterideals that emerged from under the penumbra of transparency and promised a better understanding of the world, society, information, and the self.

Of course, transparency had occasionally been written up with a potentially critical eye before, notoriously by Paul Valéry in the *Log-Book of Monsieur Teste*, in an ironic 1903 passage on transparency and self-narration:

So direct is my vision, so pure my sensation, so clumsily complete my knowledge, and so fine and clear my reflection, and my understanding so perfected, that I see through myself from the farthest end of the world down to my unspoken word; and from the shapeless thing desired on waking, along the known fibers and organized centers, I *follow* and *am* myself, I answer myself, reflect and reverberate myself, I quiver to the infinity of mirrors—I am made of glass.[26]

For all this irony, however, the rhapsodizing of transparency continued.

The first systematically critical uses of "transparency" as word, concept, and figure appeared in the skeptical moment of the immediate postwar period—the subject of Parts I and II of this book—and had a sociopolitical component. Phenomenologists and scientifically minded epistemologists were the first to inscribe this critique into their approaches. The political climate, with its calls for ideological purity doubled by the state's attempts to reach into grey zones of control over private and social affairs, gave it a certain currency that was not immediately apparent. Intellectuals presented the postwar condition as one in which perception and reality were differently juxtaposed from how they had been before the war: the philosophical or ethnological gaze had been confounded, its totalizing scientific claims thwarted to such an extent that it needed to start anew. Squirming in its limited ability to control economy and society at the end of the war, increasingly corporatist, and encumbered by a forceful but all too autonomous police, the French state posed an intellectual as well as an everyday problem. The state's effort to rule over its citizens, to purge society of collaborators, and to reach into private and public life without constantly confronting elusive grey zones, in which citizens, economic forces, and sociopolitical formations stood apart, created a duplicitous and tricky relationship and sparked some limited forms of resistance to state power, which were often understood as a refusal of state-imposed transparency.

Jean-Paul Sartre was perhaps the first to dismantle traditional approaches to perceptual, phenomenological, and ethical transparency systematically, even if he eventually resorted to a morality of "engagement" that recovered meaning or truth only in the transparent, authentic act by which human beings bear the world on their shoulders. Others went further, notably Maurice Merleau-Ponty, who opted for "ambiguity," Georges Canguilhem and Alexandre Koyré, who waged war on positivism and intellectualism, and Daniel Lagache and Jacques Lacan, who sought to save psychiatric care from a state-led ideal of a normative, standardized selfhood. They and the likes of Lucien Febvre, Emmanuel Levinas, and Georges Friedmann involved themselves in identifying the perils of a transparent gaze, especially when that gaze was attached to a communist or statist politics. Anthropologists—notably Michel Leiris, Claude Lévi-Strauss, and André Leroi-Gourhan—similarly served as protagonists of a discipline that, shedding its earlier aims at totalization, now became a leading opponent of racism and advocate for others subjugated or denatured by the West.

By the mid-1950s, the critique had spread across new social and ethical theories that rethought (a) foundational *concepts* such as separation, individuality, alienation, identity, alterity, and the human, and (b) *relations* such as those between science and the human being, the subject and the absolute, the normal and the aberrant, the state and society. Transparency was involved and invoked in the major conceptual shifts of the 1950s, which constitute the subject of Part III, in many ways the backbone of this book: the fast and wide dissemination of the idea of "the other," from phenomenology and anthropology to ethics and psychoanalysis; the rethinking of norms as constructed, not natural, and as structurally violent toward human difference; the prioritization, among structuralists, of language as fundamentally exceeding the speaker's grasp; and the antihumanist attention to *both* the limitations *and* the overbearing force of human access to the world. Separation, others, obstruction, heterogeneity, doubts, masks, ambiguity, dialectical remainders, abnormality, and the circumvention of reductionisms became the central tropes and themes of the conceptual web. Thanks to these displacements, it became possible in the 1950s to discard the epistemological and ethical pretense to transparency, to pull back its skin and peek at a messy tissue composed of things, signs, thoughts, and problems formerly undisclosed—all now in need of study and understanding.

Most of the frontal assaults on "transparency" launched earlier had aimed at the preceding philosophical generation, typically accusing it of ironing out the "folds of experience," and its relations to the state and politics. From the 1950s on, the attack could be directed at one's peers: it was Lévi-Strauss against Sartre, Canguilhem and Lacan against the psychologists, Derrida against Lévi-Strauss. As new, systematic, and rigorous philosophical languages emerged around the tropes of the norm, the other, and the symbolic, these languages motivated a search for new ways of thinking. They aimed at factoring ineradicable complexity and otherness into thought and intellectual engagement, and they all encoded a refusal to grant transparency new philosophical possibilities. Transparency represented a *faux* humanistic urge, to be left behind. As Jacques Lacan warned, truth throwing off its mask and ostensibly revealing itself meant that it merely "[took] on another and even more deceptive mask."[27]

By this stage in the 1950s, transparency was a word, a concept, and an image in relatively broad and quite univocal employ. It had clear epistemological, ethical, and political domains of application and fairly straightforward uses. Once the 1960s set in, the refusal of transparency could be taken for granted: transparency now was an illusion that required its own history, a problem invoked to mobilize the search for complexities. It could be used for slander. Rather than unfold pleats and marvel at the bright flat panes that would supposedly appear in their stead, philosophers focused on uncovering ever-multiplying fissures, opacities, forces, and obstacles. Far more acutely aware of the conditions in which these forces had emerged, philosophers also became profoundly invested in historicizing the establishment, course, achievements, and ills of modernity.

Part IV, which deepens the book's analysis of conceptual debates, focuses on the structuralist generation—Claude Lévi-Strauss, Jacques Lacan, André Leroi-Gourhan, and especially Michel Foucault and Jacques Derrida. The crystallization of new philosophical concepts and priorities—such as cybernetics, discursive history, difference, and the origin of modernity—accelerated the rethinking of the history of philosophy and modernity, of the control of information, and of the status of the present moment. By the mid-1960s, ideas of a self-transparent self, transparent communication, and a "crystalline" community were not only relegated to an earlier age—an age hypothesized as having *perhaps* ended—but were routinely marked as a fundamental characteristic of modernity. Transparency was identified with the establishment of modernity, notably in Descartes and Rousseau, as well as with its ills: it served as an operator or signifier that grounded both the strengths and the weaknesses of thought and life in the twentieth century. It profoundly affected the present time and, for any better future to become thinkable, it had to be replaced with the image of a non-human and antihumanist complexity. Language, information, and their regulation seemed particularly consequential for moving away from the pretense that communication between two people or integration into society could be complete. As a philosophical act, their endorsement was decisive for the course of philosophy, in that the relentless criticism and re-dating of transparency forced rethinking of the past and the present. The present became less and less the vanishing point of the past, and more a crossroads through which information management, normativity, and the deconstruction of selfhood cut new paths, beyond modernity and the limitations it imposed on society.

These shifts paralleled a widening gulf between state and society, which was exacerbated and highlighted in and after May 1968. The anti-transparency phenomenon had heretofore aligned philosophy's animus toward a transparent self with society's conflict with the state. Now the critique became forked. In one direction, the philosophical and structuralist critique of transparency was in the process of wording new sciences of language, society, and representation and of turning them into the tools for something new, dynamic, more hybrid. In a different direction, a revival took place, of the unitary agent of history, now explicitly aimed against a homogenizing and too-powerful state. This agent was the conglomerate of student and proletarian movements, which, defined above all in its opposition to the state, became a decisive force in political opposition: the whole philosophical tine of the critique of transparency was sidelined as an abstract matter of discourse and epistemology. In other words, the varieties of Marxism that dominated the period 1966–75 absorbed structuralism well, as Althusserians and Maoists showed. However, their opposition to the state and its norms now defined a new generation, and political and revolutionary activity let slide the forms of complexity and multiplicity that were being elaborated by philosophers. "May '68," as a confrontation, turned the public's rapt attention to a much more immediate politics of the Left, which prioritized very different lineages, images, and tropes. The state-society conflict, rather than complementing the promises of philosophy, largely sidelined the non-humanist future as vague.

In the mid-to-later 1970s, even those intellectuals who kept their distance from *gauchisme* shifted their attention to a critique of transparency that was political first, targeting information and its neoliberal commodification (Jean-François Lyotard), the disciplinary power and purposes of government (Michel Foucault), or totalitarianism and the chances of democracy (Claude Lefort and his collaborators). Lefort in particular identified transparency with totalitarianism and helped turn it into the explicit target of political philosophies concerned with democracy and power. "Transparency of society to itself; transparency of the instituting to the instituted; of the idea to the real, of the project to its concretization, of the will to what it wills, of freedom to its goal"—this was the decisive modern mirage and persistent threat, the phenomenologist Marc Richir argued in a passage that intentionally conflated phenomenology, the Terror of 1793–74, and the Soviet regime.[28] Part V of this book follows the period 1968–85 right up to the development of new languages favoring transparency in the 1980s, which sidestepped the critiques and brought France closer to the admiration for transparency typical of other Western societies.

Why Postwar France?

Part of the appeal of the concept of transparency is the significant disparity between its uses and meanings in postwar France and those developed in other Western societies after World War II, which have largely led to the current dominance and celebration of this concept.

Today, transparency is usually conceived of in the Popperian framework of an "open society," where good government is identified with open leadership and respect for privacy. On January 20, 2009, in an inaugural memorandum titled "Transparency and Open Government," U.S. president Barack Obama proclaimed: "My Administration is committed to creating an unprecedented level of openness in Government. We will work together to ensure the public trust and establish a system of transparency, public participation, and collaboration. . . . *Government should be transparent.* Transparency promotes accountability and provides information for citizens about what their Government is doing."[29] In this kind of idealization, the roots of transparency extend back into history, and it is given a linear rise to prominence. It is promised as a human right in a world dominated by information management, bureaucratic administration, and the inscrutability of power; it becomes a slogan and fuels the distribution of praise and blame (*you* should be more transparent; *this* government is more transparent than any before it). It pretends to mirror, in government, a heightened acceptance and aestheticization of personal exposure among the citizenry, and it promises governance as a "collaboration." Secrecy and privacy require justification and become matters of negotiation. As a result of contributions to public discourse by organizations like Wikileaks and by whistleblowers such as Edward Snowden—to say nothing of the systematic dissembling of Donald Trump—the *pursuit* of transparency usually bypasses critical examination, and resistance seems somehow nefarious.[30] In postwar France, its uses and problems were diametrically opposite. A first question, then, is: Why did transparency come "under fire" *precisely* then and there, especially given that it had served as an intellectual and political ideal until World War II? Why did the French experience differ so radically from that of other countries, languages, and cultures? Why did France take a path that still remains so alien to the dominant pursuit of transparent institutions today?

Throughout the twentieth century, transparency had very different sets of meanings in Germany, Russia, and the Anglo-American world. In Germany, it has consistently functioned as a national and public ideal, easily adaptable to political circumstances. For the German National Socialists, transparency was, simplistically put, a matter of purification that would allow for race and socioeconomic organization to correlate; it is in this sense that Hitler declared, at the opening of the 1937 Great German Art Exhibition, that "to be German is to be clear."[31] The term's postwar democratic career began with Karl Jaspers's complaint that Germans continued to live beneath a mask they had to shed.[32] It continued throughout the 1960s, expressed by Jürgen Habermas's valorization of the public sphere and by a culture of holding the older generation responsible not only for Nazism but for failing to work through the past and produce a truer social space.[33]

"They who build transparently build democratically," the motto went. Transparency has long been a mainstay of modernism in architecture and art; modernity, as Anthony Vidler beautifully put it, "has been haunted by a myth of transparency: transparency of the self to nature, of the self to the other, of all selves to society, and all this represented, if not constructed, from Jeremy Bentham to Le Corbusier, by a universal transparency of building materials, spatial penetration, and the ubiquitous flow of air, light, and physical movement."[34] But in Germany during the latter part of 1940s, and again from the 1970s on, transparency became a central political-architectural metaphor, a performance of the accountability of government itself.[35] Even critics—for instance, Hans Blumenberg, whose anthropology of rhetoric granted that there is no pure self-relation and no pure Habermasian communication—credited the very thinkers whom the French dismissed (thus Blumenberg praised Kant) and did not construct the present's relation to the past by celebrating complexity at the expense of transparency.[36]

In late imperial Russia, transparency was already a catchword for administration and governance around the turn into the twentieth century.[37] After the Revolution, the project of "tearing off the masks" attracted revolutionary fervor, particularly in the early Soviet years, and this led to self-inventions designed to show how individuals were *becoming* true in order to fit into a revolutionary system.[38] In the USSR, the construction of communist selves in the 1930s involved speaking a Stalinist language that regulated what was acceptable public discourse and how individual attempts at privacy or escape could be handled.[39] East of the Iron Curtain, in the decades after 1945, the persistence of non- or precommunist norms in private life (not least those of non-communist art) and the problem of non-socialist *résistants* and, later, dissidents, became important concerns in the production of an official history of the regime and of the proletariat's triumph. In East Germany, the fear that the new regime lacked adequate support and could be clandestinely undermined by either Nazi sympathizers or (especially) partisans of the (West-German) Federal Republic was paramount.[40] Then, in the late 1980s, the Soviet motto of *glasnost* ("openness") promoted a version of greater governmental transparency to enable *perestroika* ("rebuilding").

In the United States, after World War II, despite occasional efforts to question the claim to transparency by placing the dramatic aspect of everyday life and selfhood center stage, political and economic thought called consistently for "more" transparency, at the level of both institutions and social divisions. Among intellectuals, too, for every Erving Goffman who critiqued the pretense to transparency and for every Hannah Arendt who worried that the social had ruined the democratic potential of a strict private-public divide, there would be a Lionel Trilling who chose a version of transparency—in Trilling's language, sincerity—as a norm-setting ethic, over modern "authenticity."[41] For all the analytical power that a Michael Fried would put into demonstrating that minimalist theatricality was destroying the very possibility of modernist absorption and of genuine aesthetic experience, a phalanx of other critics would celebrate intentional, authorial, and artistic transparency.[42] The political force of the Freedom of Information Act and the Watergate effect in America in the 1970s strengthened the liberal, Popperian, and also libertarian suspicion that closed-doors government was either poor or manipulative.

∾

So, rather than provide a systematic comparativist account of the uses of the term "transparency" across different languages and cultures

(*Durchsichtigkeit*, *Transparenz*, transparency, *glasnost*, and so on), I propose to make a close examination of the French conceptual web in which transparency played its part. In some of the chapters that follow I reconstruct the multiple parallel prehistories where postwar thought ruptured. But here it is important for this conceptual history to emphasize how the aftermath of World War II down to the 1970s created a structurally different intellectual regime, so that the French case stands apart.

With France's defeat in 1940, the generational divide of the 1930s—which had already pitted younger, more radical intellectuals against a university cohort of older Dreyfusard idealists—became institutionalized. This put an abyss between the postwar period and earlier ideals of social harmony or claims that the state could improve society. The war—or rather the occupation and the Vichy government—hung over France long after the Liberation, especially as projects of political, social, and national regeneration proved disappointing (as in the case of communism) or tiresome (as in the case of *résistants*' emphasis on their purity).

The transparency concept deployed and modulated the weight of these histories. With the Liberation, France seemed to experience a "year zero": the world appeared decidedly different from that which had preceded the war, and the French Enlightenment and republican and revolutionary traditions needed to be rethought as a whole. Distance from state policies and political alternatives was coupled with the state's mistrust of society itself—the same society that came out for Pétain in 1940 and for the barely more palatable de Gaulle four years later—such that the corporatist and welfarist efforts that followed, weighed down by the collapse of the French empire stage by stage, identified few chances at substantive internal change. A parallel opening, in anthropology, to the racial, colonial, or indigenous other coincided with the anticolonial movement and opposed governmental ideologies of national and cultural integration. As elsewhere in Europe and especially in Great Britain, during the late 1940s, and then again in the late 1950s and 1960s, the state treated society as pliable: state intervention in everyday life, although intended to deal with problems like crises in policing, the end of the occupation, the persistence of economic devastation, or the influx of French Algerians, and to offer a rational expansion of the welfare state and of the university system, nevertheless generated a whole arsenal of criticisms of state overreach. New dreams of humanity were possible only at a remove from the state and its work toward economic normalization and advancement. State-society relations often hinged precisely on the issue of transparency, notably in cases concerning the purge of Vichy collaborators in 1944–45, police activity, the anti-tax *poujadiste* movement, the black market, the government's relation to the army (especially in the context of Algeria), the status of the French language, postwar urban planning, the adaptation of children and adolescents to society, the status of the *pieds-noirs*, and, in the 1970s, what has now come to be known as the *banlieue*.[43]

Eradicating the blind spots of French state power generated resistance to rules and policies perceived as excessively normative or as enforcing social transparency. If anything, the violent war in Algeria and the difficult management of the influx of French Algerians after Algeria's independence only solidified the sense that social space, already shaded by political division and now also by revolts of the youth, was changing into an incomprehensible realm of shadows. In the absence of a revolution, society remained epistemologically grey. Institutional, generational, and intellectual developments became encoded into what we might call an epistemology of everyday life and its structures: existentialism and structuralism offered solutions to questions developed politically and philosophically for a world that seemed unable to move away from the terrain that was politically on offer. Just as, with the gradual distancing of left-wing intellectuals from the Soviet Union, "alienation" became systematized into a premise of consumption that embraced all social life, "structure" elevated the present temporal moment—at the expense of continuities built by modernity—into a new conceptual and historical form. While elsewhere such developments put pressure on opening a public sphere and on making government more responsive, in France, for much of the intellectual world, the chasm between society and state seemed absolute by 1970, as in Pierre Clastres's famous title *La Société contre l'ètat* (1974; *Society against the State*). May 1968 had changed the equation, radicalized this contrast, and made revolution and antistatist transformation into major political and intellectual goals.

Some celebrations of transparency emerged, for example, in the promised overthrow of "spectacular" capitalism, and in the mass politics and "general will" of the Chinese proletariat. But, more important, May '68 hung over the Left throughout the 1970s, notably in the debates of the Gauche prolétarienne party and its milieu, not least because it developed a new "regime of historicity": it refused the static tensions of the earlier 1960s, resurrected agents of history, and pitched revolution as a dynamic force in political activity and thought.[44] Preoccupations with the state and transparency reflected a new set of concerns: the potential of May and its interpretations among Maoists and other radicals, the danger of totalitarianism, the needs of democracy (highlighted by Claude Lefort), and emerging worries over "neoliberal" economics.

The dust of such tensions settled in the 1980s, the end point of this study. Through televised debates over state violence and terrorism that continued in West Germany and Italy, through public scandals (domestic and foreign) such as Watergate and the stir created by publication in French translation of Aleksandr Solzhenitsyn's *L'Archipel du Goulag, 1918– 1956* (1974–76; *The Gulag Archipelago*), the late 1970s promoted a growing awareness of the need for institutional and governmental openness. A resurgent republican universalism settled into intellectual consensus. Soviet *glasnost*, European economic integration, and Anglo-American small-government politics during the Reagan years only contributed to making the French case seem exceptional. The new concerns consigned the erstwhile dominant anxieties about transparency to the margins of intellectual life. Anxiety about the state, which had fed the critique of transparency, was largely replaced—especially in the Mitterrand government, after its 1983 economic volte-face—by a full-throated advocacy of modernization and transparent information. Republican universalism became the prevalent rhetoric of the Left in the 1980s and swept aside the pursuits and pressures of the preceding generations, giving the conceptual web a new structure, which prevails to this day.

When the classicist and historian Paul Veyne refused causal and contextualist lines of reasoning in favor of an approach that resembled "a polygon with an indefinite number of sides," his goal was

to reveal the unpredictable contours of this polygon, which no longer has the conventional forms or ample folds that make history into a noble tragedy, and to restore their original silhouette to events, which has been concealed under borrowed garments. The true forms are so irregular that they literally go unseen. . . . If, then, history proposes to lift the cloth and make what-goes-without-saying explicit, it ceases to be explanatory and becomes a hermeneutic.[45]

The silhouette I am trying to assemble from the "contours" created by the backdrop above is akin in spirit to Veyne's. I am talking about a hermeneutics of conceptual events that allows us to discover a non-causal but continually reorganized relationship between concepts and history. Whereas elsewhere in the West a certain continuity of traditions of openness and transparency *could* be reconstructed that supposedly dated back variously to Luther, Descartes, or the American Revolution, tensions in postwar France generated a sense of break with such traditions and spurred a radically different approach to transparency in its relation to society and selfhood. Epistemology and the human sciences contributed to governance, but some intellectual strands in them contributed even more to a vehement critique of that governance and postwar society more generally. Ever since the 1960s, the intellectuals discussed in this book have offered tools, some of them used today in a renewed critique of transparency, in a manner not matched by, say, British or German social science of the period. The *positive* aim of the critiques of transparency was to step beyond the exhaustion of historical progress.[46] Thus this book is also an episodic history of postwar France itself, at least insofar as postwar French thought involved major attempts to overcome the limitations and violence of modernity and to remold thought and society drastically and swiftly.

Method

To approach the word and concept of transparency as well as the figures associated with it, the book takes its first cues from Ludwig Wittgenstein's focus on the *uses* rather than *meanings* of words and from Georges Bataille's remark: "A dictionary begins when it no longer gives the meaning of words but their tasks."[47] Insofar as the philosophers, anthropologists, psychiatrists, and political thinkers who treated transparency with great suspicion (and even wielded the critique against each other) often shared little by way of schools of thought, political stripes, or particular projects, my focus here is on the word and figure of "transparency," and on how it was rendered into a "master code" almost coordinating the web of concepts that dominated the 1945–80 period. The idea is to unleash a phantom concept that held a particular value and was a well-connected and important, if mostly quiet, operator in systems of thought in order to outline the critical, creative, dispersed, yet forceful conceptual disarrangements and rearrangements that occurred during the *trente glorieuses*, the thirty years of quite swiftly rising living standards in France from 1945 to 1975.[48] Perhaps a better term for the intellectual history I am attempting is semiotic history: to pull historically relevant meaning out of the uses of an idea that seemed minor on its own terms yet was meticulously woven into the fabric of postwar life and thought, an idea phrased always in terms of a critique that gained momentum and became emblematic of the period itself. Starting from here, this project experiments in three methodological directions.

Historical Epistemology and Entangled Microhistories

The first direction involves my use of practices common in historical epistemology for a history of non-scientific concepts.[49] I have organized this book around problems or objects. Each of the twenty-two chapters engages a particular object and the particular conditions under which this object could be asserted, elucidated, known, dismantled, refuted, or overcome. Particular objects recur over several, mostly non-consecutive chapters. Some of them concern high philosophical discussions that require me to study a text or a set of concepts at length; others, the anthropological and psychiatric production of knowledge; others still, a basic social sensitivity and suspicion of state practices. In other words, anxieties regarding privacy, the open society, and the fear of state intervention are contrived alongside philosophical articulations of particular concepts and alongside efforts to retheorize the meaning of science and information. These different objects relate through mimetic and conflictual relationships because, for reasons that will gradually become clearer, philosophical activity, especially in epistemology and the human sciences, functions as a social practice in a manner that both connects with and negates social activity.

This methodology is possible thanks to the extraordinary work carried out in recent years in postwar French history: it relies on the arguments and innovations of a new generation of intellectual historians.[50] It also follows the path laid out twenty-five years ago by Martin Jay's monumental *Downcast Eyes: The Denigration of Vision in Twentieth-Century French Thought*, even though, as will become clear, transparency in my reading was a concept that all but bypassed *vision*, and the story I tell is quite different.[51]

As a result of the epistemological approach I pursue, there are several things I avoid. Although at specific moments I look at particular "prehistories" from the vantage points of the postwar period, I have intentionally not offered an overarching linear history of transparency from the ancients to contemporary France, so to speak, partly to avoid causal and contextualist reduction, partly to retain the integrity of the more detailed objects of study, and partly because a long sequential prehistory would have made little sense to postwar French thinkers. Only some elements of this past did make sense *within* the postwar conceptual web of transparency. Also, the book certainly does not claim to cover the postwar waterfront. I do not cover histories of gender (Julia Kristeva's, Luce Irigaray's, and Chantal Ackerman's work can be productively engaged in this context) and decolonization (though Aimé Césaire, and especially Édouard Glissant, with his "right to opacity," could well be marshaled in strong support of my account).[52] The net I should cast to cover these adequately would be too wide, the argument would wear thin; besides, my sense is that the logics of the feminist movement and decolonization cannot be properly synthesized around the figure of transparency.[53] Instead of setting up separate lines or inserting token "representatives," I refer to questions of gender and colonialism only where they directly impact the dismantling of the transparency dream.

Nevertheless, by virtue of its historical-epistemological priorities, the book does cast a wide net. It dissects matters in greater detail than intellectual histories focused on individual thinkers or ideas can; and it proposes directions for further research. For this reason, it proceeds in rhizomatic rather than linear fashion: readers could focus on the problem of psychiatry and norms through chapters 5, 9, 11, and 17, look at the rise of structuralism in 11, 13–14, 16–19, and 22, track the critique of Rousseau (further to the opening discussion above) in 14, 16, and 20, the problem of difference in 3, 6–7, 11–12, 14, 18, and 21, and the rise of computing and information in 5, 13, 19, and 22, or pick up the more political chapters 2, 6, 7–10, 15, and 20–22. The same goes for themes like representation, identity, homogeneity, and worldhood. These at times unrelated, at times overlapping discussions brought transparency to the fore at particular moments and compounded to produce far more elaborate syntheses and affirmations.

A Web as a Model for Conceptual History

Second, in this book I experiment with developing a model for studying the structure of concepts and their embeddedness in social life and thought. To do so, let me begin by expanding on Clifford Geertz's note that "man is an animal suspended in webs of significance he himself has spun."[54] Imagine a web made of strings. At each point where two or more strings intersect, they are tied together into a knot. Sometimes only a couple of strings cross at an intersection point, at other times there are many, a thicker knot; some strings begin at one knot and end at the next, others begin at one knot and go through several others before being tied at the last. As they extend between different knots, strings sometimes get tangled. Many strings allow some leeway: you could pull a string or a knot, and watch other strings tighten or move; you could effect a different threading, or even break a part of the web.

The web need not look two-dimensional: as you perceive a seemingly horizontal web from above, some points appear to be tied to others suspended further away, which you may or may not discern; and those points may in turn be tied to others through strings that produce hidden tensions. The web need not be singular or closed; the strings need not be of equal thickness and sturdiness; nor need two points be united by a single string only. The web is certainly not suspended in a vacuum: it is always enveloped in a medium whose enigmatic density allows it to be pliable enough to be moved around by these strings, to let some knots brighten up in its midst, to be torn or remolded by the tightened strings. Were the medium thick as mercury, we could sense its warping and forces surrounding each string as it moves; were it jello, we would see the strings tear right through; were it earthy, we would see the ground shift in uneven chunks.

Concepts are the points or knots of this web. They are tied one to another. To write their history is to address the way in which they are strung together, pulled, yanked sometimes in one direction, sometimes in another. Now they come close enough to us to be visible, now they fade out of focus. New strings appear, others loosen and vanish in the tangle. I call "intellectuals" those who engage, create, give new shape to the web or manage, sometimes by themselves, to pull certain points together or force them apart. When they write, whoever they might be, they create articulations, and along with the knots and strings they weave into their text they also drag others, often unconsciously. Like competing puppeteers, they raise some of these knots to prominence and alter their meanings. In this sense, intellectuals are epistemologists of their time who nurture, express, and promulgate conceptual tensions. Whoever they are—artists, scientists, letter writers, functionaries, lawyers, philosophers, filmmakers, diarists—they give us a sense of the political, philosophical, ethical, and everyday problems and tensions of their milieu, whether they understand and express them well or not. They are also controlled by the very strings they believe themselves to hold at their fingertips: their thought, refined out of particular uses of these strings, can often be pulled back into the web. Intellectual revolutions, too, warp the web in particular ways, like new networks introduced in it. The tension they bring in may shift or reconfigure a section of the web; over time, these networks mutate and fall apart, leaving ever weaker marks across longer distances—and also broken strings in their wake.

Regardless of how they are puppeteered, concepts strung together in a given space have a temporality and a life of their own, one not quite attached to specific intellectuals, or to social-political circumstances and events. More often than not they structure, clothe, stage these circumstances and events in manners that historians are often eager to ignore. Concepts do not rest among clouds, to be stared at, "contextualized," or "historicized" from the "real" vantage point of society; rather they thread together the experience of knowledge, reading, speech, and belief. They cannot be experienced in the absence of this articulation, "without strings," apart from one another. Nor are they felt the same way across social or other divisions—and this is why the web cannot be flat. Social life, that enveloping aether, mercury, or jello, holds the web in place and is at times moved around by particular ways of replaying and recasting concepts and their use. A level of uncertainty remains essential to the structure: Can we ever be sure how tight a knot is, or when a string has snapped and the world of a concept has irrevocably changed?

As the knot around which the aperture tightens in this project, transparency is strung, tautly or loosely, to other knots—perception, self, other, objectivity, norm, representation, information, the thickness (or opacity) of society—and these can take center stage. Reading transparency through the syncopation of discourse facilitated by this conceptual web helps elucidate the period better than alternative methods do: certain figures, terms, words, and problems yield an essential pattern of a period's self-understanding, of its different thematics, theories, and genres.[55] They are a central force present in various expressions and practices, yet do not seem to form easily identifiable spaces or objects of research. Thus too metaphors of a transparent society—metaphors of light, openness, homogeneity, reach, but also of obscurity, opacity, clandestinity, refusal of state-driven norms, inadaptability—are frequent actors' categories in state-society relations. Without claiming for transparency the status of a motor of conceptual and cultural change in postwar France, I do mean that through it we can give voice to broadly felt concerns about aspects of French society and literate culture. Precisely because transparency is tied to other concepts, it is reflected or expressed together with them, in moments of social and cultural tension;[56] and it, in turn, expresses, relays, short-circuits these tensions. In France, transparency played this mirroring, mimetic, and distortive role both at the epistemological and at the sociopolitical level.

A History of the Present

A final methodological experiment in which this project is engaged concerns the problem of confronting a contemporary conceptual problematic with an earlier one. In recent years, the pendulum swung toward a rhapsodizing of the open society, exposure, and governmental transparency.[57] We traded the fear of a society pried apart for an aesthetics of exposure, and for a suspicion that privacy tends toward conspiratorial secrecy.[58] (This is perhaps a reason why we find it so surprising in 2017 to see the givenness of this dream fall apart so easily.) Given the significant difference between the semantics and changing fantasies of postwar France and our own, this book should fall under the rubric of a critical history of the present.[59]

The predominance of our own understanding of transparency makes it difficult to recall that its current meaning is the temporary result of a social and theological negotiation rather than the culmination of a long tradition of celebrating the open public sphere, criticizing governments, and overcoming grey zones.[60] Besides, these matters are not confined to directly political or social questions: transparency is of considerable significance in medicine and psychiatry, and there too, *for the time being*, the impetus toward privacy is fading.[61] Transparency—this hall of mirrors where freedom of information allows us to see, and see ourselves, from every distorted angle, as if we were simply exposed from the outside—is often reflexively decried as neoliberal, or as a collateral effect of postmodernity.[62] Some recent critics of trends "favorable" to transparency—including Byung-Chul Han in *Transparenzgesellschaft* (*The Transparency Society*)—construct a far too vague and easy target.[63] These and other less theorized critiques, which identify transparency with neoliberalism in order to denounce the one through the other, fall prey to a magical thinking according to which transparency works everywhere in the same way and can be rejected uniformly across different domains that involve a dialectical interplay of opposites. Subtler critiques of a "transparency of the self," such as Judith Butler's warning that "to acknowledge one's own opacity or that of another does not transform that opacity into transparency," remain largely underappreciated.[64] By and large, these approaches are directly contrastive.

This book proceeds otherwise: it confronts the recent celebration not with a contrastive alternative but with the dialectic of an evolving conceptual matrix, captured in its historical development. The French articulation of images, terms, temporalities, complexities, and futures in the half-century after 1940 allows us to unleash a series of questions related to the contemporary fantasy of transparency from a historical and philosophical perspective. What *is* a transparent life? On what grounds is a morality premised on transparency (of the state as well as of the individual) defensible? Does it mean anything to be ethically pure, or to engage others in a way that makes recognition possible? Is that really desirable? Epistemologically, how does knowledge relate to the crevices within it and to the conflicts it creates? How would abstraction and normativity avoid erasing the difference between experiences? Politically, what are the implications of calling for a transparent society or of pursuing a transparent domain of communication and power? What claims can privacy lay on the public sphere? How do values like liberty, justice, community, fraternity, or openness forge human relations today, and what kinds of opacity, complexity, and concealment thrive within them? What are the alternatives?

Such questions are present in this study and at times criticized for their limitations and tendency to reinforce a partial, even delinquent critique. I am at any rate moved by the need to raise afresh, in question form, the solutions pursued by French postwar thinkers in their rejection of transparency. Perhaps their solutions merit renewed attention today. Where transcendence had reigned, obstacles and mediation promised to create a hybrid existence that accounted for the complexity of information, language, and power. Identity was displaced by alterity and by a conception of individuality as shattered; splits, counternorms, pathologies, constructedness, and hidden forces took the place of self-sufficiency and dislocated its luminous subjectivity. If norms had quietly mediated between the natural and the human, for these thinkers they became signifiers of social organization and domination, themselves in need of being examined. Modernity's lights seemed to extinguish the shadows; but then new fissures had appeared that would not be healed by these lights. Most conspicuously, the scientificity bestowed by humanism came into great doubt, as humans and science became near opposites.

The liberation of language promised to offer tools, even entire sciences, for grappling with the power of a dehumanized information boom and its undemocratic consequences. It was essential, however, while peeling away, to *not* reduce veils, filters, norms, layers, obstacles, and the infractions forced by language. How these veils, obstacles, and language were rendered visible and how they, surprisingly, lit up an entire intellectual world is the play of this book. As an idea, transparency seemed destined for the realm of dreams unexamined; it inhabited a past whose battles and tragedies left behind wreckage and ghosts as well as room for improvement. Its place was to be invaded by the secret, difference, separation, the opaque, the private, the spectacle, the power of uncontrollable information, the transience of becoming, the obscure objects of desire, the counternorms of those ill-adapted to normality, the small heterogeneities of life.

PART I

LIFE IN THE FOLDS

Perception, Consciousness, and Knowledge Displaced

Was Transparency an Optical Problem?

A Short History

Thanks to common usage and etymology, transparency is usually taken to be mainly a visual matter. The noun *transparentia* did not exist in classical Latin; it is a medieval creation, formed in calque of the ancient Greek διαφάνεια—a derivative of compounds like the verb διαφαίνω ("show through," "allow the light to pass") and the adjective διαφανής ("translucent," but also "manifest," "conspicuous," and even "red-hot"): *trans-* rendered δια-, while the main part of the word was formed on the Latin counterpart of the Greek φαίνω ("bring to light, cause to appear," etc.): *pareo, parere* ("appear/be visible"). The *Oxford English Dictionary* concentrates on two definitions: "(1a) The quality or condition of being transparent; perviousness to light; diaphaneity, pellucidity," and "(2a) That which is transparent; a transparent object or medium."

Yet we should recall that the optical meaning has never been predominant or self-sufficient. As early as Plato, the notion of transparency was used in inquiring about the purity of the soul; in late antiquity, by Saint Augustine's time, it had become replete with religious connotations. Transparency is more than *visual* transparency.

The visual field has been a privileged site for the concept of transparency, but the latter is neither restricted to nor metaphorically derivative of it. Furthermore, transparency poses conceptual rather than simply visual problems. What we mean by "transparency" affects (and is affected by) the way sensation, objects, and materiality—not to mention mediation, objectivity, light—are constructed within a system of thought: were we to press the point, we would have to admit that transparency is a concept that has made sensation, perception, mediation, and knowledge *possible*. "Manifestation" and "showing through" are conceptual, epistemological, and not simply visual issues. The dragonfly that struggles against a glass ceiling, like the bird that flies into a window, suffers from a surfeit of the visual and lacks a concept of transparency, a way of managing *what* shines through, and *through* what it shines. Still, this dependency on the visual requires a demonstration: a few words on the history of *visual* transparency and its enmeshing with epistemology, phenomenology, and ethical prerogatives are in order. I focus on four reference points—Aristotle, Descartes, Newton, and the French Enlightenment—from the specific perspective of postwar France.

The inaugural text for Western theories of transparency as a visual concept is Aristotle's *De anima* (*On the Soul*), which treats transparency as a positive quality of objects—a quality that some have to a greater degree than others.[1] It is an actuality that, thanks to the texture and consistency of an object, facilitates the absorption and retransmission of color. Its positivity resides in the property of a body to be revealed thanks to the color of other bodies. The diaphanous is here in conceptual interplay with color, light, and the nature of the thing itself. Aristotle argues:

> There is, surely, something transparent. And I call transparent what is visible, not strictly speaking visible in itself, but because of the colour of something else. Of this sort are air, water, and many solid bodies; for it is not *qua* water or *qua* air that these are transparent, but because there exists in them a certain nature which is the same in them both and also in the eternal body above. Light is the activity of this, the transparent *qua* transparent.[2]

At issue here is the structure of perception; perception links transparency to light and to the experience of the world in a way that would remain definitive for subsequent treatments of the problem all throughout the Roman period, and again in the high and later Middle Ages, around Thomas Aquinas.[3] Indeed light appears thanks *only* to the transparent.[4] Only through this medium does it allow one to see and to see through. Light is, perhaps astonishingly for us, premised on the transparent and impossible without it: it is transparency become "active."

The later tradition of treatises on optics is replete with considerations of transparency that bind it to these conceptual operators: light, color, thinghood.[5] In Aristotle's definition, "space" is latent in "light," given the scaffolding provided by air (which, again, is *not* transparent *as* air, but is air *because* it is transparent), but by the early modern era, space would become independently meaningful.

Postwar thinkers, following a long tradition, credited Descartes with joining optical transparency to ethics and clarity of thought. In his first work, *The World, or Treatise on Light*, originally published in 1632, Descartes famously called air a "body" that the senses do not perceive unless affected by wind, cold, or heat; its exemplary transparency was a matter of the interaction between light and the senses.[6] He also began to use light as a metaphor for the absolute certainty and clarity that mark and guide the philosopher's thought and ethical life. His *lumen naturale*, "natural light," became the decisive figuration of human reason: natural light, "the faculty of knowledge which God gave us . . . cannot encompass any object which is not true, insofar as it is encompassed by this faculty, that is, insofar as it is clearly and distinctly perceived."[7] In 1926, André Lalande's seminal *Vocabulaire technique et critique de la philosophie* still defined *lumen naturale* as a "synonym of *reason*, a totality of the truths that are *immediately* and *without doubt* evident to the mind as soon as it attends to them."[8]

Descartes further used *clair* ("clear") and *obscur* ("obscure") to motivate important movements in his thought. "Clear" or "clear and distinct" accompanied the ideas and knowledge that facilitate the cogito's (transparent, correct) understanding of the world,[9] while "obscure" gestured toward ideas and manners of thought that hampered clear thinking.[10] Natural light guaranteed an object's transparency to the mind through a movement that emanated from God and was experienced and mediated by the mind. Here is the full translated title of Descartes's incomplete work *La recherche de la vérité par la lumière naturelle* (*The Search for Truth*):

The Search for truth by means of the natural light that, all pure and without recourse to religion or philosophy, determines what opinions an *honnête homme* should hold on any matter that may occupy his thought, and penetrates into the secrets of the most recondite sciences.[11]

By making the quest for certainty the cornerstone of his thought, by pinning his hopes on universal logic, by pursuing a universal natural language, and by fastening these efforts securely to his own persona as *honnête homme*, Descartes instituted clarity as the basis of a philosophical perception of the world and of an ethics that would culminate in *les lumières*—

"the lights," or the Enlightenment. In this tradition, the self-transparency of thought became an extension of the *lumen naturale*, but also the necessary requirement for any possible meeting between—or knowledge of—the mind and the object of its contemplation.

Descartes's approach to air as a transparent body was important to a second scientific tradition as a result of the way in which it attached sensation and perception to the environment. Like Descartes,[12] Newton refused to believe that air could be a vacuum. To explain how transparent air could transmit light, he posited that the refraction of light required an all-pervasive ether that was present in, and "much subtiler" than, air; indeed this ether was present not just in the air but in "the eye, the nerves, and into the muscles."[13] Newton's theory of ether became an essential premise in subsequent theories of space and environment precisely because it denied the existence of vacuum. It postulated a minimal environmental presence where there appeared to be an absence and situated organisms and things within their surrounding worlds, even if their interplay depended on, and hence fostered, a seeming transparency.[14] From Descartes and Newton onward, space, air, light, and the environment—and the perception, experience, and knowledge of these presences—became entangled with the definition and experience of the transparent.

The transparent is thus a figure of epistemological as much as visual import. Diaphaneity has had a part in every phenomenology: the transparent was a concept and a metaphor for the presence and materiality of the world to the perceiver. It made the world available and promised clarity and comprehensibility. It was made comprehensible only by an author's way of describing the world. Nor was the visual element of "transparency" separate from, or prior to, social, political, or ethical concerns. Part of a broader apparatus for understanding the world, transparency in the eighteenth century became a purpose of philosophy, for the *lumen naturale* was not a politically neutral but a strategic, even combative concept, whose exercise aimed at particular kinds of "clarification."

Epistemological, ethical, and political transparency would become standard fare during the Enlightenment, which wove together the scientific needs of optics with an extensive use of concepts such as clarity, purity, and light. The brief, unsigned article on "transparency" in Diderot and d'Alembert's *Encyclopédie* stuck to summarizing Aristotle, Descartes, and eighteenth-century scientists on how the "rectitude of an object's pores" allowed light to pass through it.[15] However, the major article *"Lumière"* (Light), which d'Alembert wrote himself, engaged precisely the shared syntax of transparency and light, offering a detailed presentation and criticisms of the Aristotelian and Cartesian optical theories of light. *Lumière*, of course, also made for a major subject of d'Alembert's "Preliminary Discourse," which identified natural light and human reason.[16]

By the 1789 Revolution, the ethicopolitical diction of transparency had drowned the optical one. Jean-François Féraud's *Dictionnaire critique de la langue française* (1787–88; Critical Dictionary of the French Language) cited figurative uses, notably a passage from Louis-Antoine Caraccioli about men becoming "transparent" to a perceiver).[17] As the historian of science Theresa Levitt has noted (echoing Michel Foucault, Hans Blumenberg, and Jonathan Crary), the rise of optics as a science in nineteenth-century Paris followed the collapse of the apotheosis of light and transparency around the Revolution. Without that phenomenon, modern optics would neither have acquired its own sociopolitical meaning nor developed into the science we know.

In the first years of the nineteenth century, the symbolic power of light took on a specifically modern configuration . . . attendant in the creation of a modern visual culture. Gone was the firm security in light that guaranteed a connection between subject and object. Opacity emerged to take its place alongside illumination. . . . With the dream of complete transparency gone, visibility became a form of discipline. No longer was there the hope that *everyone* would see *everything*. Rather, strict control determined who saw what.[18]

It may come as a surprise that after 1945, scientific optics would play virtually no role in the debate on transparency. After the decline of the utopia of light and reason, the light–vision–space triangle came to be understood much better through the study of the polarization of light in early nineteenth-century Paris, then through Hermann von Helmholtz's influential studies of the eye, and finally through the discovery of X-rays, which rendered the body transparent and displayed its internal functions undisturbed.[19] Yet the twentieth-century sociopolitical tradition saw little reason to register these developments, inasmuch as the metaphor of light remained largely the same as in the eighteenth century. Its invocation continued to follow the same rules—in Georges Canguilhem's words, "the motor of history is light. Progress is the illumination of shadows."[20] French thinkers in the interwar and postwar periods increasingly viewed the nineteenth century as a Comtean "positive age," overwhelmed by scientific determinism and by educational projects that advanced "truth" at the expense of metaphysics and outdated beliefs. The persistent image of truth as reliant on the progress of transparency, clarity, and light was annexed to the belief that the human mind had sought to chart the entire world. Auguste Comte, and especially apostles like Émile Littré, had renewed trust in transparency and had marshaled an influential identification of progress with a purified scientific gaze and future social harmony.

Scientific optics was not the only major development bypassed as a result of attitudes to light and transparency. French thinkers by and large neglected the enrollment of perception into psychological theory in the later nineteenth century and the elaborate debates that followed. Particularly striking is the case of Gestalt psychology, which treated light, space, color, and transparency at considerable length.[21] In German thought from Johann Gottlieb Fichte and G. W. F. Hegel through Edmund Husserl and Hans-Georg Gadamer, transparency was a matter of consciousness and self-consciousness; these thinkers showed virtually no interest in the visual component.[22] And yet, in Germany, Gestalt theory sparked broad interest in psychological perception. Erwin Panofsky used it as the intellectual ground for his 1927 "Perspective as 'Symbolic Form,'" sharply criticizing the naturalism of visual perspective in the Renaissance as a manifestation of anthropocentrism in the spatial domain.[23] In France, by contrast, the polemical and theoretical value of psychological theories was generally discarded (with the exception of Merleau-Ponty).

Martin Jay has argued that vision was subsequently deposed from its position as hegemon over the senses.[24] However, it was not a decline, but a *renewal* of attention to perception around 1930–45—coupled with the recognition that vision classically conceived of could not generate epistemic transparency (something widely accepted across Europe around 1930)—that gave rise to a displacement of vision's centrality in analysis. Jean Wahl set the stage for a shift in the understanding of perception when he noted: "Perception fails in its explanation of the world . . . we should not make use of perception so as to explain; perception presents, it does not explain."[25] Wahl contended that perception involved, not a direct continuity with the world, but a form of representation to oneself that allowed for a better understanding of the human being's halting access to the real. Otherwise his claim was not particularly provocative or controversial. Bergson had long dissociated perception from knowledge,[26] and a similar idea was seemingly important to Gaston Bachelard, who in his discussion of the notion of philosophical obstacle used a visual metaphor to cast doubt on the epistemological possibility of perfect knowledge: "knowledge of the real is a light that always casts a shadow somewhere."[27] Marcel Mauss deplored the insufficiency of the observer-participant's localized perception when he called for "a bird's-eye view" in the form of extensive photo and cinematographic recordings of groups under ethnographic study.[28] At that point, Merleau-Ponty, influenced by the phenomenologist Aron Gurwitsch, mobilized Gestalt psychology to challenge the self-sufficiency traditionally accorded to perception.[29]

A change in the relation between reality and perception had consolidated by the mid-1940s. In 1950, Wahl registered a "new climate" in his account of "The Present Situation and Present Future of French Philosophy": "French philosophical thought directs itself more and more toward the concrete aspects of imagination and perception, and of the world in general."[30] Attention turned from visual transparency to the counterconcepts of distortion and opacity. In 1955, the medievalist Jurgis Baltrušaitis published a study that bridged philosophy and art history through anamorphoses, distorted representations, as "visionary mechanisms" belonging to the rational as much as to the optic domain. He focused on their capacity to obstruct, displace, and undo forms that emphasized the abstract coherence of reason and perspective: "The anamorphosis bursts into the vertigo of abstraction which balances, to a certain degree, the speculative and semantic reasoning that gravitates around the same forms."[31] From Jacques Lacan's discussion of anamorphoses (famously in Hans Holbein's painting *The Ambassadors*) through Baltrušaitis's later works, the studies of trompe l'oeil and simulacra undertaken by his fellow medievalist Pierre Charpentrat, and Louis Marin's study of the "tombs" of absolutism and subjectivity in painting, it appeared that the pretense to transparency in art led directly to a distortion that was not merely visual but symptomatic of broader subjective and phenomenological problems.[32]

Light, too, could no longer unify experience and claim the power of a *lumen naturale* that clarified the world: it now pointed to its opposite—darkness and night. In other words, the claim that old theories of perception had been misguided gained credibility alongside the mistrust of vision and the turn to studying the empirical and the concrete, as the emerging "new climate," new status quo, or "new age" brought new requirements for perceiving and understanding the world. What had appeared as transparent seemed now to paper over the folds and furrows of the empirical.

To attend to optical questions is also to accept firmly that, throughout its history, transparency has served them as a *concept* and not as a mere fact—as part of a matrix that combined ethics, self-knowledge, epistemology, and politics and was not reducible to vision alone. The sense of transparency reached around 1945 can serve us as an analytical perspective as well. Nothing is simply visually transparent; transparency has no ontological standing. It is the result of a way of looking at the world and identifying objects and media. As a concept, it denotes—at times by way of optical metaphors—a concurrent presence and absence, or presence alternating with absence, which allow something to *appear across*: something that generally does not interfere unless itself foregrounded, something that is there but absents itself in a way that it makes one aware of its presence, something that is *not* present in the same way as that which it lets appear. At the end of World War II, these positions gained force from a persistent sense that the war had deformed both reality and perception.

ing the constructed and polemical character of modern life. The postwar world was to be experienced through different eyes, which recognized that human beings were not as they had seemed. Marking this transformation, Merleau-Ponty described this new phenomenology of perception as a realization about ontology and the future:

consciousnesses have the strange power to alienate each other and to withdraw from themselves . . . they are outwardly threatened and inwardly tempted by absurd hatreds, inconceivable with respect to individuals; and . . . if men are one day to be human to one another and the relations between consciousnesses are to become transparent, if universality is to become a fact, this will be in a society in which past traumas have been wiped out and the conditions of an effective liberty have from the first been realized. Until that time, the life of society will remain a dialogue and a battle between phantoms—in which real tears and real blood suddenly start to flow.[17]

A recognition of separation, of the difference between minds, of the impossibility of any transparent society was now imperative. The future society of transparent selves was but a remnant of the prewar "Cartesian" past, and a dangerous dream that required habituating oneself to violence. Achieving the dream was by no means guaranteed, but this violence was. In 1945, this gave Merleau-Ponty a new sense of politics, made up of a peculiar Marxism (he thought Marxism "had to be thought anew, for it threatened to confirm our prewar prejudices")[18] and of a specific conception of existing in the present ("We are in the world, mingled with it, compromised with it").[19] This amounted to a continuing hope in transparency, *mingled with the conviction that transparency was impossible*, Merleau-Ponty suggested. Against "the solitary Cartesian," who does not believe in the reality of classes, nations, and empires and "does not see his shadow behind him projected onto history as onto a wall,"[20] Merleau-Ponty proposed a dual commitment: first to a theoretical Marxism that would "bind together" subjective and objective factors in history,[21] making it possible to understand that "values remain nominal and indeed have no value without an economic and political infrastructure to make them participate in existence";[22] and, second, to an emphasis on this existence, where mundaneness, struggle, and the multiple relationships between real living beings grounded and structured social and personal values, expressions, and beliefs. "Outside this unique fulguration of existence there is nothing," he concluded. Interpersonal transparency was an unrealizable dream, irrelevant to human reality, and to battle toward "effective liberty" was to move away from such an ideal.[23]

Levinas and the Light

The interplay between the jarring transformation of the contemporary world and the visual and epistemological mediation involved in transparency was even more clearly at issue in Emmanuel Levinas's first postwar book, *De l'existence à l'existant*, which opens as follows:

> Expressions such as "a world in pieces" or "a world turned upside down," trite as they have become, nonetheless express a feeling that is authentic. The rift between the rational order and events, the mutual impenetrability of minds opaque as matter, the multiplication of logical systems each of which is absurd for the others, the impossibility of the *I* rejoining the *you*, and consequently the unfitness of understanding for what should be its essential function—these are things we run up against in the twilight of a world, things which reawaken the ancient obsession with an end of the world.[24]

In this "feeling" about the current "twilight of a world," folds, rifts, and breaks were visible everywhere, and acknowledging them was imperative, even urgent, if the work of thought was to begin afresh. Rifts had appeared between the rational order, different systems of thought, and contemporary events; they had also appeared between different minds—each of them "*opaque* as matter." It became necessary to rethink existence and individual beings from this perspective of separation. In a clause that could be said to underwrite his better-known later work, Levinas treated the "impossibility of the *I* rejoining the *you*" as a fact: this broken tie may have existed but was now irretrievable. The recalibration of perception in its relation to the world perceived now motivated the study of existence as much as that of the history of philosophy.

De l'existence à l'existant articulated these problems via the concepts of *light* and *night*. With "light," Levinas pointed back above all to the Aristotelian, Cartesian, and Enlightenment traditions of *natural light*, which he placed in phenomenological perspective. "Light illuminates and is naturally understood: it is comprehension itself":[25] alongside clear vision, clarity, and illumination, light belonged to a tradition that, from Plato through Heidegger, treated it as "a condition for all beings."[26] Levinas articulated this position phenomenologically—light is "a condition for phenomena, that is, for meaning"—but proceeded to explain that this is so because light guarantees my separation from the others I encounter in the world: it creates the inside–outside distinction. Light offers objects to "us," divulges them within "our" horizon, sets up this horizon by itself: "due to the light, an object, while coming from without, is already ours in the horizon which precedes it; it comes from an exterior already apprehended and comes into being as though it came from us, as though commanded by our freedom."[27] This dense passage equates light with anticipation, with the "horizon" of our grasp: light makes possible our understanding and "possession" of objects, our sense that they are given to us. But the passage also indicates that it is *our* comprehension that makes them possible and available. Crucially, by the same move, light guarantees our *separation* from objects: natural light, *lumen naturale*, does *not* establish the unity between thought and world, as it does in empiricism and Cartesianism, but their separation: it causes pleating, greyness, and furrows. There is none of the unmediatedness or immediacy between light as such and the "light" cast by consciousness; light allows us to turn inward, to distance ourselves from objects, to avoid getting lost among them. "Light is . . . the event of a suspension, an *epochē*, which consists in not compromising oneself with the objects or the history with which one relates or which one realizes, in always remaining outside of those objects and that history."[28]

In other words, although light guarantees illumination, it does so through separation and irreducibility, not through an object's transparency to its perceiver. On the contrary, light allows the perceiver the possibility of not being engulfed by that object, of keeping it at bay, within her horizon. To perceive a world *through the light* was, for Levinas, to be aware of this structure of perception—to double back and wonder at it.

Now if light was a precondition of both grasp *and* separation, this was only because it was itself bracketed by "the night." For Levinas, the night presented an outside to this horizon, and one that binds "us" to our being (because in his view we always seek to leave being behind or aside). The night's emptying of light was not a mere loss of intelligibility; it pointed to a different kind of experience, "if the term experience were not inapplicable to a situation which involves the total exclusion of light."

The loss of "the world" corresponded to the subject's loss of self in an anonymity of being.

When the forms of things are dissolved in the night, the darkness of the night, which is neither an object nor the quality of an object, invades like a presence. In the night, where we are riveted to it, we are not dealing with anything. But this nothing is not that of pure nothingness. There is no longer *this* or *that*; there is not "something." . . . The mind does not find itself faced with an apprehended exterior. The exterior—if one insists on this term—remains uncorrelated with an interior. It is no longer given. It is no longer a world. What we call the I is itself submerged by the night, invaded, depersonalized, stifled by it. . . . There is a nocturnal space, but *it is no longer empty space, the transparency which both separates us from things and gives us access to them, by which they are given.* Darkness fills it like a content; it is full, but full of the nothingness of everything.[29]

Like Merleau-Ponty, who similarly rejected the inside–outside divide,[30] Levinas moved away from the illumination and whatever "transparency" remained in the light, toward accounting for its limited spectrum and for the primacy of a desubjectifying darkness. Being qua being, pure, unqualified, was captivity, argued the officer in the camp; it was the erasure of the subject's particularity and thought, its staggering within a generalized horizon of sameness.[31] Pure being was not, as in Heidegger, something that can be experienced in a "clearing": it was the night, the realm where things and their intelligibility recede and vanish, but their presence persists. If light and meaning were to be tied to transparency and intersubjectivity, night tended in the opposite direction. It confirmed the deficit of transparency as a phenomenological given, its limitations, dependence, and even regression away from the mind. Night denies understanding by concealing the "world" that is necessary for experience. And now that this denial had been certified, was it still possible, when in the light, to perceive things without being aware of their nocturnal dissolution? Could light be understood as an unquestioningly present force that sets "us" on a path to reason, intelligibility, and transparency? Levinas had already doubted this; and he persisted in his doubt.

Did people *see* differently in the wake of World War II? Many other texts confirm that we can answer in the affirmative: recall Albert Camus's emphasis on "the absurd," and his famous depiction of the sun as an oppressive force in *L'Étranger* (1942; *The Stranger*); or André Malraux's presentation in *Les Noyers de l'Altenbourg* (1943/48; *The Walnut Trees of Altenburg*) of gas warfare as an unprecedented form of destruction that clouded efforts to think the course of Western culture. In 1953, Georges Bataille, too, would liken his contribution to philosophy to a senseless light: "this light is blinding, perhaps, but it announces the opacity of the *night*; it announces night alone."[32] Did *reality itself* shift along with its perception? Yes. Political thinkers registered unprecedented options. Merleau-Ponty went on to operationalize the change from a deluded prewar intellectual regime in sociopolitical language. Historians like Febvre also participated in the new "regime of historicity," which required a different set of tools, both for the past and for the present.

Philosophers thought that perception needed to be rethought, and texts such as those by Levinas and Deleuze discussed here hint at something that was debated and broadly accepted in the early postwar period. The spread of phenomenology during and after the war (including in the work of Levinas and Sartre), with its emphasis on perception, separation, and existential anguish, was symptomatic of a perceived insufficiency of previous modes of being in the world. The cycle of war, occupation, resistance and collaboration, and liberation disrupted standard philosophical categories: they no longer appeared efficient. At this point, "perception" failed to confront "reality" in the same way, and experience seemed to have opened up to depths hitherto untouched.

The World's Opacity to Consciousness

Sartre and Merleau-Ponty

Transparency emerged as an important philosophical problem thanks to the rise of phenomenology and existentialism in France. Phenomenology's effort to abandon idealism and reach "the concrete," begun in the 1930s,[1] quickly identified limitations of consciousness and focused on making them the object of philosophical endeavors. It was Jean-Paul Sartre who most firmly established the opacity of the world to consciousness as a necessary premise of phenomenological ontology. This move to separate consciousness from the world constituted a definitive expansion of earlier efforts in epistemology and the theory of perception and, as the public explosion of Sartre's thought and persona began an intellectual revolution, the revision of philosophical principles about transparency that he offered in his magnum opus *L'Être et le néant* (1943; *Being and Nothingness*) became central to the post-Liberation period.

The "new French philosophy" (as it was often called) that started with *Being and Nothingness* was highly respected, even among its more vociferous philosophical critics, on the grounds that it set a new standard in the conceptualization of the relationship between humans and the world.[2] Besides, Sartre's ebullient critique of prewar philosophy was paralleled by the widely read work of his partner Simone de Beauvoir and received additional philosophical force from Maurice Merleau-Ponty's *Phénoménologie de la perception* (1945; *Phenomenology of Perception*). Sartre's proposed new phenomenological and ethical priorities were promulgated by a fast-growing number of partisans.

The new philosophy flatly renounced the idea that the world is readily available to the mind and that thought can map, articulate, or model the universe, facing it without mediation. The separation of mind from the world became instead an essential ingredient in the entrapment, solitude, and anguish of human beings. In *Being and Nothingness* as in the other phenomenological and existentialist works of the later 1940s, the term "transparency" occurs time and again as code for outdated philosophies that depict the place of human beings among other creatures in the world as theologically, politically, or socioeconomically harmonious. By exiting an ostensibly pure realm of consciousness, the human subject of existential phenomenology engaged with a world that was profoundly alien to his or her desire to render it transparent; in this world, the subject encountered even herself as fundamentally opaque. This phenomenological and interpersonal opacity spurred some of Sartre's collaborators, notably de Beauvoir and Merleau-Ponty, to plant the notion that there was an ineradicable ambiguity at the heart of human existence. For Sartre, at first sight paradoxically, transparency's ontological unavailability forced its return as an *ethical* desideratum, an urgent (if unbearable) demand for human freedom.

Sartre's Use of Transparency in *Being and Nothingness*

Being and Nothingness attempted to refound philosophical investigation. Sartre introduced "transparency" as a problem right from the opening pages and carried it into some of the most famous sections—on "objective" knowledge, on "bad faith," and on the ungraspability and elusiveness of the other. Central to his use is the distinction between operations that occur only "within" consciousness and remain transparent to it, and operations involved in being in this world, where such "internal" transparency fails utterly.

What was phenomenology? Sartre introduced it as a way to overcome philosophies that had failed to think the fundamental disjunction between consciousness and what it encounters in the world, namely, neo-Kantianism and realism, which he thought distinguished between being and appearance in such a way as to make appearance effectively belong to the subject. We do not relate to phenomena in such a way that the movement of our perception is in unbroken continuity with the objects perceived, nor are phenomena available to this perceiver simply because he or she covers their noumenal essence or true being. Sartre defined consciousness by postulating a chasm between it and the world. Recalibrating Husserl's "transcendental reduction"—that is, the claim that consciousness "reduces" and reorganizes the world—and giving it a more manageable form, Sartre accentuated the breach between the world and consciousness's perception of it:

A table is not *in* consciousness—not even in the capacity of a representation. A table is *in* space, beside the window, etc. The existence of the table in fact is a *center of opacity* for consciousness; it would require an infinite process to inventory the total contents of a thing. To introduce this opacity into consciousness would be to refer to infinity the inventory which it can make of itself, to make consciousness a thing and to deny the cogito. The first procedure of a philosophy ought to be to expel things from consciousness and to reestablish its true connection with the world, to know that consciousness is a positional consciousness of the world. *All consciousness is positional in that it transcends itself in order to reach an object, and it exhausts itself in this same positing.*[3]

By separating consciousness from the world, by describing the two as operating in parallel, and by attributing to the former a specific effort to "transcend itself in order to reach an object," Sartre deployed as fundamental the idea that entities in the world hold back from the attempt to grasp and interpret them, and so does the world. Consciousness became a movement of constant self-exertion, a "void" that would not "get filled" by "reality" but remained incomplete as a result of this self-transcending gesture toward the world and its objects. What Husserl had defined as the "transcendental reduction," Sartre now formulated in terms of an inner transparency that confronted the opacity of any external object—say, the table (an example of what he would later call the *in-itself*). The hard fact is that the world's exteriority and opacity vis-à-vis consciousness oblige the later to force itself on this elusive world in order to explain it, judge it, handle it.

That consciousness is transparent to itself when considered on its own was a point Sartre insisted on time and again: the expression "transparency of consciousness" always appears associated with modifiers such as "total"[4] or "necessary."[5] Consciousness, from its very beginning—that prereflective latticework of "non-thetic consciousness" out of which its particular intentions and movements emerge—is transparent to itself, so that its knowledge, however mistaken or based on unexamined beliefs, can form a self-same unity, not constantly threatened by doubt:

> non-thetic consciousness is not to know. But it is in its very translucency at the origin of all knowing.[6]

> To introduce into the unity of a pre-reflective cogito a qualified element external to this cogito would be to shatter its unity, to destroy its translucency; there would then be in consciousness something of which it would not be conscious and which would not exist in itself as consciousness.[7]

Whether cogitative or affective, as in Sartre's accounts of pleasure and pain,[8] the phenomenological operations of consciousness *must* remain transparent to themselves. But the world resists this transparent cogito and gives it no room in its reality. Husserl had ostensibly presented the ontological independence of phenomena as "unreal"; Sartre postulated that the world's resistance was philosophy's propulsive task. How can philosophy "preserve at once the opaque resistance of things and the subjectivity of thought?"[9]

   Sartre had staged this self-transparent consciousness against an opaque world as early as 1935, in an essay that distinguished between an *impersonal consciousness* and *the I*—the person-specific, active, merely empirical self of that consciousness. Were the I transcendental, it "would tear consciousness from itself; it would divide consciousness; it would slide into every consciousness like an opaque blade."[10] No such opacity could slide in: "the Transcendental Field, purified of all egological structure, recovers its primary transparency. In a sense, it is a nothing, since all physical, psychophysical, and psychic objects, all truths, all values are exterior to it."[11] In Sartre's novel *La Nausée* (1938; *Nausea*), the narrator, Roquentin, appeals to the transparency of thought as a cleansing device: "I must wash myself clean with abstract thoughts, transparent as water."[12] Sartre insists no fewer than four times in *L'Imaginaire* (1940; *The Imaginary*) that "a consciousness is always transparent to itself";[13] images and the world, on the other hand, are fundamentally opaque.[14] Yet the transparency of consciousness is not without limits: along with transcendence, Sartre rejected the identification of spontaneity with the ego.[15] Instead, he located spontaneity, which for Henri Bergson and Léon Brunschvicg characterized the thinking subject's automatic relationship with the world, on the rim of the self-transparent consciousness, where it marked its tensions with the world.[16]

Sartre's sense that the world remained oblique and opaque was essential to a critique of neo-Kantian idealism and of then-prevalent theories of knowledge, which found no discontinuity between subjective consciousness and objectivity. In the interwar era both idealism and realism presented an idealized notion of truth, reliant on a progressive, in principle unproblematic, spread of knowledge as it filled the world's crevices and folds. Idealism located this truth in the mind, to which the world was largely available and in any case decipherable, while scientific realism conceived of a reality replete with truth, which the mind would come to mirror.[17]

That transparency was essential to the relationship between consciousness and ideas and hence a decisive characteristic of modern rationalism was emphatically foregrounded by Léon Brunschvicg, arguably the most important academic philosopher of the interwar years. The idealism Brunschvicg endorsed as his own at the end of his magnum opus *Le Progrès de la conscience dans la philosophie occidentale* (1927; *The Advance of Consciousness in Western Philosophy*), was one of consciousness and reason, in which the mind becomes transparent to spirit "thanks to the deepening of reflection on its radical principle."[18] Brunschvicg was not alone in this theorization, but he was doubtless the most significant, coherent, and brilliant proponent of a progressive synthesis of science, knowledge, and the advancing human mind. These, for him, became enmeshed in a movement toward clarity and rational abstraction; and transparency was the mind's goal, as already revealed at the birthplace of modern rationalism—Cartesian analysis.[19] A "perfect transparency of the mind to the idea" had reemerged with Spinoza, allowing him "to construct a new definition of psychic reality and consciousness, founded on the adequation of the idea and the development of truth that is immanent to it."[20] What is more, Brunschvicg credited Spinoza with the novel idea of a transparency shared between consciousness and mathematical truth. This led to the union of mathematics with Kantian rational morality, which Brunschvicg regarded as the twin decisive achievements of the Western mind.[21] Mathematical philosophy asserted the possibility of freedom, and the success of objective, transparent, mathematically formulated knowledge grounded the universality of moral action. Praising Kant's ethics at the conclusion of *The Advance of Consciousness*, Brunschvicg noted that,

if "salvation is in us," this is because the "Promised Land" is before us: the idea of a humanity reconciled with itself, a republic of souls which, raised to the same level of disinterest and sincerity, would finally become transparent to one another, without hurtling themselves at the curse of the Tower of Babel, the duality of the external Word against the internal Word.[22]

Whereas Sartre's fixation on transparency testifies to Brunschvicg's influence,[23] Merleau-Ponty took aim exactly at fantasies like Brunschvicg's republic of transparent souls when he wrote that, before the war, "we had not understood that consciousnesses have the strange power to alienate each other." For Sartre, too, nothing could be *less* evident to the alienated, threatened, world-resisting subject than Brunschvicg's borderless liquidity of consciousness.[24] Nothing could be more violent than the self's subsumption of a supposed universal, which it "morally" inflicted onto a world ripe with the achievements of Western thought. Sartre's Cartesian insistence on the transparency of a consciousness alienated in an opaque world turned Brunschvicg's conception on its head. Sartre did this in three arguments: one on *science, subjectivity and objective knowledge*; another on *bad faith*, especially that faith of sincerity; and the third on *the experience of others*, which founds his ethics of freedom.

Objective Knowledge

Central to Sartre's concerns in *Being and Nothingness* was the embeddedness of the human being (a "for-itself") in the world and its experience of subjectivity, that is, its awareness of the opacity of others (including objects) as it incorporated them into its own being. This gap between consciousness and "my" being—the being of a for-itself whose existence consists in negating its own static nature and in embracing itself as one upsurge among others in the midst of an opaque world—inspired many of Sartre's critiques of objectivity, knowledge, and abstraction; and some of these took the form of a rejection of all-too-easy transparencies. Approaches that established a "false" continuity—the sciences, and especially psychology—would come under criticism for the same reason as Kantian and Husserlian idealism.

Sartre used the crystalline lens of the eye to demonstrate the difference between objective knowledge and a being "for-itself" as "one upsurge among others." In a speculative history of a science of the eyes, he proposed that the scientific approach, aimed as it was at "technical" objectivity,

offered nothing but a proof that the world and scientific knowledge inter-
fered between me and my eye:

The problem of sense knowledge is raised on the occasion of the appearance, in the
midst of the world, of certain objects which we call the senses. First we established
that the Other had eyes; later as physiologists dissected cadavers, they learned the
structure of these objects; they distinguished the cornea from the crystalline lens
and the lens from the retina. They established that the object, crystalline lens, was
classed in a family of particular objects—lenses—and that they could apply to the
object of their study those jaws of geometric optics which concern lenses. More precise dissections, effected progressively as surgical instruments were perfected, have
taught us that a bundle of nerves leave the retina and end up in the brain. With the
microscope we have examined the nerves of cadavers and have determined exactly
their trajectory, their point of departure, and their point of arrival. The totality of
these pieces of knowledge concerned therefore a certain spatial object called the
eye; they implied the existence of space and of the world. In addition they implied
that we could see this eye, and touch it; we are ourselves provided with a sensible
point of view on things. Finally, between our knowledge of the eye and the eye itself
are interposed all our technical knowledge (the art of making our scalpels, our lan-
cets) and our scientific skills (e.g., geometric optics, which enables us to construct
and use microscopes). In short, between me and the eye which I dissect there is interposed the whole world such as I make it appear by my very upsurge.[25]

In other words, neither *a* lens nor *my* eye itself are themselves crystalline,
certainly not because objective, scientific knowledge tells "me" as much. To
know the crystalline quality of the lens is to enmesh "my" involvement in
the world—my capacity to see and reveal this knowledge—in the historical and technical elaboration of a science that takes itself to be objective.
Through "my upsurge" I interfere with and confirm objective knowledge.
This works the other way round as well: objective knowledge intercedes
where I bring myself to believe that I see simply through my eyes. Similarly, my body's ostensible immediacy to me is belied by its extension into
the world and by its being mediated by the world ("the bomb which de-
stroys my house also damages my body insofar as the house was already an
indication of my body"),[26] by my knowledge of my body as *a* body, and so
on. I do not experience my body without this mediating knowledge and,
conversely, I do not have such knowledge without experiencing my body.
Neither a phenomenalist experience of the world nor an abstracted objectivity can aspire to transparent truth.[27]

Psychology was a particularly troubling case in the empiricist expansion of this view, for it presupposed a continuity between my experience of objects and the objects themselves. For example, psychological experiments pretend to bracket a world that the *I* never forgets or misunderstands, even as the experimenter believes to have reduced the "for-itself" to a subject homogeneous with all others.[28] Fuzzy concepts that create a continuity between *me*, this subject that supposedly *represents* me, and *objectivity* complete the empiricist distortion; a case in point was psychologists' dependence on sensation.[29]

But if Sartre was extending Husserl's critique of psychologism, his attack on scientific objectivity did not spare phenomenology, whose formalization or idealization of the world depended on erasing a "coefficient of adversity." Sartre had borrowed this term from Gaston Bachelard to denote the resistance of the world, the effect of things not going quite as the transparent consciousness assumes.[30] He also criticized the idea of independence related to scientific objectivity on the grounds that it considered "the structures separately by isolating them from the whole; hence they appear with other characteristics. But in no case do we get out of an existing world."[31]

Bad Faith

Few sections of *Being and Nothingness* are as well known as the long description of "bad faith"—that "evanescent phenomenon" through which Sartre establishes that the self is *not* identical to itself (an "in-itself," as objects are), but is rather a "for-itself," a nothingness that fundamentally negates or transforms one's "given being," determination, and identity.[32] As a "for-itself," the human being is pure negation of what is, a "nothing" when compared to the fully determined objects it encounters in the world.

What consciousness has to be in the mode of being of the For-itself is not-being-the-chair. For its "not-being-the-chair" is, as we shall see, in the form of the consciousness (of) not-being (i.e., the appearance of not-being) for a witness who is there only to bear witness to this not-being. The negation then is explicit and constitutes the bond of being between the perceived object and the for-itself. The For-itself is nothing more than this translucent Nothing which is the negation of the thing perceived.[33]

The for-itself is transparent only in that it resists, negates determination, and alters everything it encounters. It exists in the world as a negation: the transparency of its consciousness and, by extension, of it as negation are not something it "owns" as a subject but something it constantly effects by exercising its freedom. As a result, any attempt to enforce one's identity amounts to an act of self-delusion; anxiety is its marker, and bad faith emerges as the main mechanism through which the subject can generate self-identity and sincerity while veiling and dividing itself. The first inkling of this mechanism comes in a discussion of how anxiety stimulates efforts toward its own avoidance:

we can not overcome anxiety, for we *are* anxiety. . . . We can hide an external object because it exists independently of us. For the same reason we can turn our look or our attention away from it . . . henceforth each reality—mine and that of the object—resumes its own life, and the accidental relation which united consciousness to the thing disappears without thereby altering either existence. But if I am what I wish to veil, the question takes on quite another aspect. I can in fact wish "not to see" a certain aspect of my being only if I am acquainted with the aspect which I do not wish to see. . . . I must indicate this aspect in order to be able to turn myself away from it; better yet, I must think of it constantly in order to take care not to think of it.[34]

To maintain the transparency of consciousness and of the for-itself's negating action in the world, Sartre has to address the ways in which this self may veil itself by lying, and in particular by lying to itself. Since consciousness is self-transparent, "hiding a displeasing truth or presenting as truth a pleasing untruth"[35] amounts to bad faith. If the for-itself is constant negation, then to perform or pronounce oneself self-identical amounts to giving oneself an identity, a labored self-reduction. This means pretending that one is merely an in-itself, rather like the chair. Sartre's famous examples of bad faith included a woman on a date who acted as if she did not know her date's intentions, lying to herself as well as to him, and a waiter who "performed" his job with overwrought zeal, as a way of declaring himself superior to it and recovering himself in it.[36]

But the worst and most perverse of all forms of bad faith was *sincerity*, that ideal of purity toward oneself and others.[37] A transparent consciousness thinking of itself cannot determine its being: "in introspection, I try to determine exactly what I am, to make up my mind to be my true self without delay . . . but what does this mean if not that I am constituting myself as a thing?"[38] Sincerity in this argument becomes "a task, impossible to achieve, whose very meaning is in contradiction with the structure of my consciousness. To be sincere . . . is to be what one is. That supposes that I am not originally what I am."[39] It is for this reason that bad faith, the illusion of self-identity, comes to define sincerity, transforming it into an "affection of being."[40] Bad faith is the capacity to claim that one is fundamentally one's "essence" or one's ideal rather than a free, unstable nothing. Sincerity reveals its structural derivativeness from bad faith: each one renders the other possible and valorizes it:

in order that the concepts of bad faith can put us under illusion at least for an instant, in order that the candor of "pure hearts" (cf. Gide, Kessel) can have validity for human reality as an ideal, the principle of identity must not represent a constitutive principle of human reality and human reality must not be necessarily what it is but must be able to be what it is not. . . . If candor or sincerity is a universal value, it is evident that the maxim "one must be what one is" does not serve solely as a regulating principle for judgments and concepts by which I express what I am. It posits not merely an ideal of knowing but an ideal of being; it proposes for us an absolute equivalence of being with itself as a prototype of being. In this sense it is necessary that we make ourselves what we are. But what are we then if we have the constant obligation to make ourselves what we are, if our mode of being is having the obligation to be what we are?[41]

So much for the transparency of the heart-to-heart: Sartre dismisses in passing that tradition of the ethical romanticism of sincere hearts and concentrates on the fallacy of guiding oneself to sincerity. This proves to be a particularly flawed attempt to enforce a subjective transparency that denies precisely what it achieves, and does so in the very process of achieving it.

Who cannot see that the sincere man constitutes himself as a thing in order to escape the condition of a thing by the same act of sincerity? . . . The essential structure of sincerity does not differ from that of bad faith since the sincere man constitutes himself as what he is *in order not to be it.* . . . Total, constant sincerity as a constant effort to adhere to oneself is by nature a constant effort to dissociate oneself from oneself.[42]

The rejection of self-identity as a destructive falsehood becomes the ground for equating freedom with a constant negation, destruction, and transformation of the given—including of oneself.

The Weight of Separation: The Other and Freedom

For Sartre, our relations with others are the work not of intimacy, but of labor over and against the dominant separation within the world. *Love*, for example, "is infinitely heavier, more solid than that absolute transparency" of a self-consciousness or psyche.[43] No relation can be transparent toward an "other." In the well-known commentary on Hegel, Husserl, and Heidegger that introduces the chapter "The Other" in *Being and Nothingness*, Sartre used the three thinkers as stepping-stones, to build distance from the classic intellectualist and realist positions that falsely promised to make "the other" accessible and real to oneself. A "decentralization of the world which undermines the centralization which I am simultaneously effecting," this "other" was the decisive element that denied my capacity to experience the human world as transparent to me.[44] Objects, we have seen, always elude our perception; we are not self-same, despite our efforts at bad faith; other subjects are even more oblique to us—absolutely different from our sense of them. Only Hegel offered true inspiration down this philosophical path: his dialectical thought presupposed the existence of an *other* in order for *the self* or *the same* to be even possible. Moreover, dialectics brimmed forever with an inexhaustible dynamism, which sustained the phoenix-like return of otherness. Just as God, in Kafka's *The Trial*, is "the concept of the other pushed to the extreme," so, in living amid a world of others, one faces a "total opacity [that] can only be felt as a presentiment across total transparency."[45]

Up to this point I have attended to the way in which Sartre, after limiting transparency to the relation of consciousness to itself, proceeds to raise obstacles all around it, as if to emphatically confirm that perception fails in its effort to capture the world, that bad faith lurks in indecision, that others are inaccessible to us and even disruptive.

Freedom, too—the concluding and definitive problem of *Being and Nothingness*—is constructed as if Sartre could not bring himself to argue that, in each free act, the subject imposes itself on the world and enforces a certain transparency. The same for-itself that is unable to render transparent the objects, practices, affects, and people it encounters is nonetheless free, because it remains capable of an act: "to act is to modify the shape of the world."[46] And yet, for now, "inasmuch as it is not our actual possibility but the foundation of possibilities which we are not yet," our freedom "constitutes as a sort of opacity in full translucency, something like what

[Maurice] Barrès called 'the mystery in broad daylight.'"[47] Because at every moment our freedom recasts our past existence, "our actual conduct is both totally translucent (the pre-reflective *cogito*) and at the same time totally hidden by a free determination which we must wait for."[48]

In other words, given a chance to impose self-identity in freedom, Sartre demurs, adopting a language of "transparency and opacity" where freedom denotes both an inner transparency (freedom from determination) and a troubled temporal and historical existence (whose consequences cannot be fathomed). Responsibility forces him to pick sides: in the lyrical pages of "Freedom and Responsibility," Sartre would finally weigh in on this ambivalence, pursuing a limited transparency in ethics. The famous line about "man being condemned to be free carries the weight of the whole world on his shoulders; he is responsible for the world and for himself as a way of being"[49] makes no mention of transparency, yet the impact of Sartre's decision was clear: his advocacy of praxis "still dreamt of a radical revolution that borrowed from the pathways of transparency."[50] From representing a human being's freedom in terms of obstacles to be confronted, Sartre shifted sharply to ethical subjectivism and voluntarism, in order to make clear that, as far as the *I* or the *me* is concerned, nothing stands in the way of its imposition onto the world.

we must understand first of all that I am always equal to what happens to me *qua* man, for what happens to a man through other men and through himself can be only human . . . the situation is *mine* because it is the image of my free choice of myself, and everything which it presents to me is *mine* in that this represents me and symbolizes me. Is it not I who decide the coefficient of adversity in things and even their unpredictability by deciding myself?[51]

For Sartre, *I* am always at once responsible for the whole world and entirely free to act, not *as if* the situation were *mine*, but *because it is*. The shadows of others, situations, and the world recede, as *I* am called upon to act and take over without allowing obstacles to *my* freedom. Sartre complemented his critique of classic and recent uses of transparency by redeploying it in a recursive moment of the subject's coincidence with itself: the free act. Transparency came to involve the reassertion of selfhood and was essential to freedom, as much to the possibility of philosophy as to a way of life. Existentialism would be based on the tension between the absence of transparency in the world and the possibility of, indeed the need for, recapturing it.

Merleau-Ponty's *Phenomenology of Perception*

Even more than Sartre, it was his friend and colleague Merleau-Ponty who pulled transparency and subjectivity apart; and he did so by constructing an original phenomenology, steeped in anxieties and ambiguities over a human being's situation and "natural attitude" in a world of obstacles and opacity. In his magnum opus *Phénoménologie de la perception* (1945; *Phenomenology of Perception*, Merleau-Ponty was more explicit than Sartre on the problem posed by transparency, using the term in a technical sense and roundly rejecting any notion that human consciousness could be transparent at all—not only to others (as Sartre also denied), but even to itself. Merleau-Ponty also relegated transparency to the all-too-abstract, outdated, and irrelevant philosophical systems of idealism and intellectualism.[52] These offered the misguided notion of an "entirely transparent" consciousness, which rids the world of its "opacity."[53] A consciousness transparent to itself and capable of reducing the world's opacity to a clear and coherent set of sensations and objects was an intellectualist invention of Leon Brunschvicg's and Jules Lachelier's, philosophers whom Merleau-Ponty blamed as theoretically and politically obsolete, despite his earlier studies under Brunschvicg. He expanded what looked like an academic quibble into an elaborate retheorization of the place of ideas of consciousness and the mind. In his model, I, like any other being that I encounter, am a being "outrun" by the world as well as by you.[54] "I am never quite at one with myself": the future I can see before me will always exceed my predictions, forcing me to "reflect upon the element of opacity in my present" as an element I could not overcome.[55] By contrast, "a logically consistent transcendental idealism," particularly Lachelier's and Brunschvicg's varieties, had produced continuities that "rid the world of its opacity and its transcendence."[56] "Insofar as intellectualism purifies consciousness by delivering it of all opacity . . . the coming together of this thing [that the mind senses] and the mind becomes inconceivable."[57]

When Merleau-Ponty sought a way of understanding the subject as an *embodied perceiver*—one whose experience and thought were defined by being embodied in this world—he reacted against this purely formal and extrinsic conception of the relationship between consciousness and the objects in its horizon.[58]

This involved a critique and an advocacy of Husserl, both akin to Sartre's. An advocacy, because it replayed Husserl's assault on "psychologism" and targeted the reduction of consciousness through scientific objectivity:

When science tries to include my body among the relationships obtaining in the objective world, it is because it is trying, in its way, to translate the suturation of my phenomenal body onto the primordial world. At the same time as the body withdraws from the objective world, and forms between the pure subject and the object a third genus of being, the subject loses its purity and its transparency.[59]

Yet a critique insofar as the primacy of consciousness and the "transcendental reduction" of Husserl's phenomenology ran the danger of replicating idealism's mistakes:

For a long time, and even in recent texts, the reduction is presented [by Husserl] as the return to a transcendental consciousness before which the world is spread out in an absolute transparency, animated through and through by a series of apperceptions which it is the philosopher's task to reconstitute on the basis of their result.[60]

Why does the "embodied perceiver" lose any chance of being transparent to herself? The primary "suturation" between the body and the world, the contact between the two as they "outrun" each other, organizes their interplay and constant pressure against each other, which in turn situate us in the world and preclude any approach to us unmediated by this situatedness.

If we are in a situation, we are surrounded and cannot be transparent to ourselves, so that our contact with ourselves is necessarily achieved only in the sphere of ambiguity.[61]

Consciousness is not an eternal subject perceiving itself in absolute transparency, for any such subject would be utterly incapable of making its descent into time, and would, therefore, have nothing in common with our experience: it is the consciousness of the present.[62]

These claims would remain foundational for Merleau-Ponty's phenomenological project well beyond the *Phenomenology of Perception*. During the late 1940s, Merleau-Ponty would use them to construct a history of the "obscure" fusions of body–mind and body–soul in modern philosophy, fusions he would contrast with his own, ostensibly proper suturing of

embodied experience.[63] "Ambiguity" and the "consciousness of the present" would become major technical terms for Merleau-Ponty's political
ethics throughout the decade following the *Phenomenology of Perception*.
This was most visible in his political essays, from the infamous "defenses"
of the Soviet Union in essays collected in 1947 in *Humanism and Terror* and
in the 1949–50 essay "The Days of Our Lives," co-authored with Sartre, to
the equally famous 1955 essay "Sartre and Ultra-Bolshevism," which followed his rupture with Sartre. All of these texts argued for a political ethics
of ambiguity: an ambiguity opposed to transparency and premised on the
impossibility of knowing the future. In his 1949 "Note on Machiavelli,"
Merleau-Ponty made this particularly explicit, rejecting humanism as "a
philosophy of the inner man which finds no difficulty in principle in his
relationships with others, no opacity whatsoever in the functioning of society, and which replaces political cultivation by moral exhortation" and
advocating—with Machiavelli, in humanist spirit—"a philosophy which
confronts the relationship of man to man and the constitution of a common situation and a common history between men as a problem."[64] The
"problem" was not that a Sartrean, existential choice needed to be made
but that the right ambiguity had to be chosen. Ambiguity was essential to
any conceivable present and future of philosophy:

> We must not say that I continually choose myself, on the excuse that I might con-
> tinually refuse what I am. Not to refuse is not the same thing as to choose. We
> could identify drift and action only by depriving the implicit of all phenomenal
> value, and at every instant arraying the world before us in perfect transparency,
> that is, by destroying the world's "worldliness."[65]

Even taking one's chances with a moral transparency identified as constant
choice, freedom, and obligation, as Sartre was doing, would not do.

　　Far more than the faculty and history of vision was at stake in
the phenomenological treatments of the failure of transparency: the experience of a fragmented world, in which the self could find no standing ground; the sense yet to be made of perception and experience;
the importance of dissonance and obstacles, raised high by situations
that were much more visible in the light of progressivist defeat, occupation, and violence; the untrustworthy entwining and separation
of human beings amid a world where the former promise of transpar-

ency no longer made sense. For Sartre, transparency had to be reimposed at the moral and political level; for Merleau-Ponty, it would still be defeated by ambiguity. It is hard not to interpret the phenomenologically derived existentialism of *Les Temps modernes*—as expressed by Sartre, Merleau-Ponty, Simone de Beauvoir, or even Raymond Aron—as fundamentally attached to a theorization *against* transparency. Such a theorization—which was premised on a critique of the capacity of consciousness and knowledge to offer a complete, or even an adequate representation of the world—pervaded the major claims that existentialists saw as novel: that the world has no pregiven meaning; that the human being finds itself abandoned in an opaque universe, unable to comprehend it; that the individual is bound to attempting to resolve his or her ethical situation and must commit to a political and anthropological project that aims to serve the whole of humanity. In subsequent decades the problem of encountering and absorbing the world, of handling this dissonance and these obstacles would resurface time and again with reference to this moment of upheaval in philosophy.

Much more emphatically than in Germany, where it originated, phenomenology in France focused on the subject–world divide as fundamentally dissonant and troubled. Simone de Beauvoir gendered it; for Catholics like Gabriel Marcel, Paul Ricoeur, and Michel Henry the existentialists' incapacity to control the world gave new impetus to theology; Marxists who were invested in phenomenology—like Tran Duc Thao, Jean-Toussaint Desanti, or Jean-François Lyotard—negotiated the survival of the individual thinker in a class-divided world that could only be described objectively by Marxist science. The obstacles to consciousness brought up by Sartre and rendered irresolvable by Merleau-Ponty built many of the roads and roadblocks of postwar subjectivity.

4

The Image of Science and
the Limits of Knowledge

Of existentialism's many challengers, in the 1940s and 1950s the most philosophically powerful and consequential one was French epistemology—a real doppelgänger. Its protagonists, the historian-philosophers Gaston Bachelard, Georges Canguilhem, and Alexandre Koyré, are rightly credited with inaugurating a systematic study of reason, scientific concepts, and history that, in short, reshaped the understanding of modernity and science. But at first—*pace* claims that have been commonplace since the advent of Althusserian Marxism in the 1960s, and especially since Michel Foucault's 1984 essay on Canguilhem—epistemology was far from hostile to the ideology displayed in the existentialist journal *Les Temps modernes*;[1] on the contrary, it lent existentialism something of a helping hand.[2] It also received from it contributions toward a critique of transparency, which for epistemologists was related to the status of science, reason, and the concept of mind.

How did a problem with transparency emerge in the history and philosophy of science, and to what end? Differently put, what was "science," how were limitations to it established, and how did the premises of scientific inquiry come to be examined in order for a non-positivist and non-existentialist philosophical approach to the concept to develop? This chapter considers three reassessments that were central to the development of an epistemology of concepts and scientific rationalities from the 1930s on and became particularly significant, in French philosophy, to the development of a persistent critique of traditional humanistic practices, including the postulate of transparency:

- first, *the marginalization of idealism*, which forced a series of reinterpretations of the relationship between mind and world, and eventually led epistemologists to the dismissal of existentialism;

- second, *the critique of scientific determinism*, which redefined "science" in terms of the limits of human knowledge;

- third, *the disparagement of the claim that progress constituted the motor of science and reason.*

Under the pressure exerted by these three reassessments, it became possible to refuse to knowledge the capacity of mirroring the world (as existentialism had done with consciousness), to admonish existentialism's ostensibly subjectivist limitations, and to discredit the belief that progress and determinism offered a regulative ideal. A new generation of philosophers came of age, all concerned with showing how concepts like "subject," "consciousness," "history," "science," "form" were far from satisfactory. The writings of Georges Canguilhem, more often praised than appreciated for their place in postwar thought, form a partial guide through these three problematics.

The Marginalization of Idealism: Antifoundational Realism and the Relationship of Science to Philosophy

Crises in the relation between philosophy and science were routinely diagnosed throughout the Third Republic; in the 1870s, philosophers roared about "joining" their discipline with the sciences (especially the physical sciences), complaining that a growing separation trimmed philosophy's wings and weakened scientific conceptualization.[3] At the turn of the century Henri Bergson, Pierre Duhem, and Henri Poincaré led the pack by questioning the totalizing expectations of the exact sciences. In the 1920s most philosophers still retained a Cartesian streak in treating "science" as *the* model for knowledge.[4] Léon Brunschvicg's treatment of mathematics and Kantian idealism as *the* two parallel histories of the human mind was an obvious effort to reconstruct a relationship between the two. So was Henri Bergson's more contentious effort to revise, across vitalism, the grounds of philosophy and scientific truth.[5] Developing in parallel, phenomenology and the new philosophy of science of the 1930s held hands in rejecting the philosophical establishment of Brunschvicg and Bergson; yet they, too, were profoundly interested in the horizons of science.

In the early 1930s a shift occurred away from the positions established in the dominant realism–rationalism debate and toward an "antifoundational realism"—a realism that was openly hostile to investing truth in reality itself.[6] "Antifoundational realists" denied human beings any kind of transcendent exteriority vis-à-vis the reality that both entraps and elides them. They attributed to "the human" a partial constitution of this reality, but they also represented humans as powerless when it comes to changing it. This brand of realists included some important innovators in the philosophy of the 1930s: Bachelard, Jean Wahl, and Koyré—but also Jean-Paul Sartre and Emmanuel Levinas. In the work of otherwise very different thinkers, both idealism and realism became targets for an argument that epistemology was unable *either* to extricate consciousness from the world *or* to immerse it so perfectly as to allow for a continuous movement between it and its objects. No longer was the mind's ability to map the world a possibility; the givens were the *limits* and *obstacles* to the mind's hermeneutic and representational force, which now rendered the world structurally opaque and obliquely plastic. It resisted being transformed. As Bachelard put it, "experience that is ostensibly concrete and real, natural and immediate presents us with an obstacle."[7] Transparent scientific knowledge was limited; unmediated experience, exceptional and shocking to the mind. Thought and knowledge tethered consciousness and subjectivity to life, experience, world, reality, folding each within the other: the subject was now a being that emerged into the world, largely conditioned by it; it also experienced in a way that involved reconfiguring that world in a partial, slanted fashion. Human knowledge was not capable of mapping the world transparently, and it profoundly affected those parts that it interpreted. The two sides—world and mind—were fundamentally contaminated by each other. To use Richard Rorty's expression regarding a different tradition, the mind could no longer pretend to be a mirror of nature.[8]

Thus epistemologists, notably Gaston Bachelard and Alexandre Koyré, painted modern science in distinctly antipositivist hues: no longer a force of human activity that would eventually allow a precise translation of the world, "science" strained to master this world. Its aim could not be perfect intelligibility—what positivists had dreamt up and other philosophers still sought—but rather a systematic conception of the world that recognized its own limitations and dependence on metaphysical and religious premises.

By 1940 Bachelard moved gradually toward an "applied rationalism" he had hoped to use in order to undermine the rationalism–realism split. His "non-Cartesian epistemology," which dated from the early 1930s, was central to the suspension of epistemological transparency.[9] As Mary Tiles observes in contrasting the positions of Descartes and Bachelard,

> if it can be presumed that the medium through which one is looking is perfectly transparent and non-distorting, there is no problem in sorting out what part of what is seen is due to the medium and what to the object viewed through it; it can be assumed, with the naive realist, that things are just as they are seen to be. If it cannot be presumed that the medium through which one is looking is perfectly transparent and non-distorting, one cannot extract from what one sees information concerning the shape, size, color or surface features of the objects viewed through it without learning what the characteristics of the medium are.[10]

Bachelard, who represents this second position, did not content himself with repudiating the idea that mind has unmediated access to nature. He also complained about the scientist's reduction of phenomena to their easily determined basic constituents: such practices amounted to a "repression" of the scientific "unconscious," namely, of those aspects of the scientific imagination that were irreducible to physics or chemistry.[11] Fire, for example, was not just a product of physical–chemical reactions: in the Western world it was related to a series of myths or "syndromes" that ran from Prometheus to Novalis and Hoffmann and shaped it for every practicing scientist. No rationalism could "clean up" nature for the scientific observer, or ignore this world of metaphors.

In an undated manuscript of the 1930s, Alexandre Koyré contrasted Brunschvicg's adoption of Kantian *noumena* to the attitude of the philosopher of science Émile Meyerson, Brunschvicg's near contemporary:

> Meyerson insists on the reality of the irrational, which is impenetrable and opaque to thought to the degree that it is foreign to it; Brunschvicg, by contrast, strives to show that this opacity and impenetrability to reason belongs to the products of reason themselves. After all, for him, all objects of our knowledge are products of thought in which "the mind that knows finds itself in the complete work of

knowledge, yet it finds there also something opaque and impenetrable for it, which one calls the beginning of things."[12]

Conceived this way, the clash between Brunschvicg and Meyerson is one between a pure philosophy, committed to mathematical ideals for which the opaque is a resolvable problem, and a philosophy of science that recognizes a fundamental irrationality in the world; and we can take these two names as a metonymy for an even broader clash. Koyré saw himself as participating in this conflict and, despite holding that thought is not finite, belonged decidedly in the camp of those for whom the mind could not bridge distances and completely penetrate the world that had engendered it.[13]

World War II solidified the opposition to approaches that directly confronted mind and world. In *Sur la logique et la théorie de la science*, which he wrote in 1942 while imprisoned by the Germans for resistance activity, the philosopher of mathematics Jean Cavaillès offered a forceful critique of Edmund Husserl's "philosophy of consciousness," which it abjured for "a philosophy of concepts." Thinking *against* theories of the mind could now "provide a doctrine for science" and an explanation of its promise and pursuits.[14]

In subsequent years the philosophy of science insisted on idealism's failure and on the need to treat thought and reality as interwoven, impossible to extricate from each other. In the process it limited and at times disallowed phenomenology's claims to have overcome this problem. Georges Canguilhem began his book *La Connaissance de la vie* (1952; *Knowledge of Life*) with a manifesto staging just these concerns. He proposed that knowledge, with its deterministic and normative tendencies, scrapes against but does not quite reach the world, reality, or life—in a word, those things that contain yet surpass the human being. Writing that "intelligence can apply itself to life only if it recognizes life's originality" (that is, life's way of sneaking out of epistemic bounds), Canguilhem argued against both "a crystalline (i.e., transparent and inert) intellectualism and a foggy (at once active and muddled) mysticism."[15] The attack on the former (and note the characterization of intellectualism) marks Canguilhem's distance from Brunschvicg, who had given prominence to mathematics as the ideal domain for reason: "to do mathematics," Canguilhem ironized, "it would suffice that we be angels. But to do biology, even with the aid of intelligence, we sometimes need to feel like beasts [*bêtes*] ourselves."[16] The critique of the latter—the "foggy" mysticism—guards against classic vitalism, and perhaps against existentialism too, both of which eschewed scientific determinism altogether: in noting that "knowledge can only be deterministic," Canguilhem rejected the idea that life is simply a true reality that is ultimately unknowable.[17]

As was quickly recognized, this way of opposing life—"the formation of forms"—to knowledge—"the analysis of in-formed matter"—allowed Canguilhem to dismiss a core idea of positivist epistemology: the expectation that the world was fundamentally knowable and the conviction that science was making it known.[18] If the tissue of this world is dense because the world is woven into our knowledge of it, then the purpose of knowledge is to make this opaque density manageable, declaw it, explain its richness and its capacity to elide human conceptualizations—and also single out science as the mode available to humans for theorizing all this richness.

Critiques of Scientific Determinism

That historians and philosophers of science insisted so strongly on a critique of French Kantian intellectualism is a valuable indication of the salience of the problem of scientific determinism, especially in the post–World War II period. Bluntly put, it is all fine and good for existentialists to describe reality as elusive and threatening and to derive from it a tragic conception of the subject; but when philosophers of science speak critically of determinism and foreground the limits of progress, this has altogether different consequences.

The critique of determinism and progress was not specific to the postwar climate. Already in in 1906 the physicist Pierre Duhem argued that theories were underdetermined by facts, meaning that facts could support multiple theories. Even if a particular theory seemed proven, it was merely one of several possible options; as a result, the relationship between theory and experiment was due for reevaluation.[19] Social scientists were even more concerned with scientificity. Sociologists of the Durkheimian school, who had been derided as unscientific, were at pains to refute that accusation and developed a claim to scientificity that was based on ethnology's ability to offer totalizing systematizations of social facts, rituals, behaviors, and so on. Mauss labeled it the pursuit of "the total man."[20] Yet it gradually became clear that indeterminacy had to be factored into the argument; toward the end of his massive 1943 study of technology *Évolu-*

tion et techniques, André Leroi-Gourhan emphasized the constitutive role of this indeterminism:

> It is pointless to hide that the same facts which we have used lend themselves at times to the exactly opposite considerations; maybe, one day, using the same materials, I might have to contradict the current work; reality can only be grasped partially and it is superfluous to be obstinate about attaining, by a two-dimensional tableau, its complete and living representation.[21]

If problems of determinism and theory could be identified in physics and sociology, they were just as evident in Canguilhem's epistemology of the life sciences, which hovered somewhere between the two.[22] After the publication of his thesis *Essai sur quelques problèmes concernant le normal et le pathologique* (*The Normal and the Pathological*) in 1943, Canguilhem, who had fought in the Resistance, made the epistemological and historical status of systematic worldviews the central theme of his output. He was then teaching epistemology and general philosophy at the University of Strasbourg; in 1948 he became *inspecteur général* for the instruction of philosophy and began a parallel, twenty-year career as an examining magistrate for state examinations—a position of tremendous institutional consequence, which allowed him to support the entire philosophical revolution of the 1960s, from Foucault and Deleuze to Badiou and Derrida.[23] The dual question of *scientific determinism* and of the *limits of human knowledge* quickly became the major problem in his teaching and writing.

Canguilhem was particularly interested in determinism-related endeavors that were ambiguous, notably in technology, medicine, and biology. For him, scientific determinism concerned how systems relate to nature and to human subjectivity, given the success of science (1) at determining and reducing natural phenomena and (2) at offering human subjects values and norms through which they could experience and think. In an agonistic passage that draws the implications of *The Normal and the Pathological*, he described the pressure and failure of norms to determine existence as follows:

> A norm, or rule, is what can be used to right, to square, to straighten. To set a norm, to normalize, is to impose a requirement on an existence, a given whose variety, disparity, with regard to the requirement, present themselves as a hostile, even more than an unknown, indeterminant. It is . . . a polemical concept which negatively qualifies the sector of the given which does not enter into its extension while it depends on its comprehension.[24]

The problem of the limits of human knowledge was much the same as that of norms: both concerned the capacity of science to analyze and reveal the world. The two themes recur throughout Canguilhem's lectures for the *agrégation* exam and underlie his engagement with the major themes of his research.

Already in a February 1945 course titled "Determinism and Indeterminism," Canguilhem noted the significance of the challenge to classic determinism that the Copenhagen school of quantum physics represented—particularly Werner Heisenberg's uncertainty principle.[25] All the way from Louis de Broglie and Alexandre Kojève to François Châtelet and Évelyne Pisier-Kouchner in 1980, quantum physics "renewed the question of the unity of physics and the transparency of science."[26] Working from an offprint of de Broglie's 1929 talk at the Société française de philosophie, Canguilhem noted the significance of the author's emphasis on the inability of physics to predict, deterministically rather than statistically, what particles would do, what "nature" would choose. In a passage highlighted by Canguilhem, de Broglie argued:

The future will tell if this new way of conceiving Physics is definitive or if we come to return in some way to determinism. But from today on, we are right to reflect on the consequences of these new ideas. It is up to philosophers to see whether these ideas can contribute, to a certain degree, to bridging the gap that until now seemed to separate artificially the material world from the moral world, in whose case the idea of a rigorous causal determinism appears so difficult to apply.[27]

Next to this passage, Canguilhem scrawled and underlined "*enorme!!!*"[28]— a word whose capacity to undermine "the norm" he knew well (and later probed explicitly).[29] Canguilhem went on to radicalize de Broglie's suggestion, offering a *Begriffsgeschichte* of determinism in chemistry, biology, physiology, and philosophy, with a cast of characters that included Pierre-Simon Laplace, Claude Bernard, Émile du Bois Raymond, and Henri Bergson. Closing with Werner Heisenberg's dispute with Albert Einstein and Paul Langevin, Canguilhem gave pride of place to the "crisis of determinism" in physics under debate in the 1930s[30] and arrived at what was for him the pressing epistemological question. This crisis had a specific "benefit" for philosophy in that, through it, "determinism ceases to appear as a *thing* so as to appear as a *form* or, better yet, a *norm* of knowledge."[31] When he qualified determinism as a "norm," indeed shortly after his critique of classic norms in *The Normal and the Pathological*, Canguilhem distinguished it from natural causality, as the human interpretation of causation. "Causality, that is, productivity, can only be authentic if it is not entirely reducible to a knowable object . . . *knowledge can only be deterministic, but knowledge does not suffice to account for experience.*"[32] Knowledge is incapable of operating non-deterministically; it is internally structured to generate obstacles regardless of its successes in approximating natural causation through nomothetic determinism: "what creates uncertainty is knowledge itself. This is an insufficiency of knowledge."[33] Indeterminism, Canguilhem went on to argue, revealed the mediating and refracting force of norms for determination and causation that, while making knowledge possible, heighten its non-coextensiveness with nature and life.

The contrast generated by the limits of determinism halted any deterministic claim to epistemological transparency. This argument would lead Canguilhem to a series of further claims: that "progress" is a matter of values,[34] that—in an untypical endorsement of existentialist language— the finite "human existential situation" is the foundation of all knowledge,[35] and, above all, that the major issue with knowledge is the "limits of its ambitions, the limits of its dreams . . . the limits of its technique."[36] It is not excessive to claim that upholding indeterminism against the modern promises of determinism fueled Canguilhem's project and secured continuity between the subjects of his research. In the 1960s he could claim that the history of science would either be epistemological or be meaningless progressivism. Unlike the history of science carried out by scientists, which is "transparent, liquid in the sense that the time of this history flows fluidly," the history of science carried out by philosophers, despite the ideal of collaboration and cooperation with the scientists themselves, would have to be "opaque and viscous."[37] Knowledge could be adjudicated through a history of science because "the history of science concerns an axiological activity, the search for truth. It is at the level of questions, of methods, of concepts, that scientific activity appears as such."[38] This axiology could never overcome indeterminism. Studying historical discontinuities in scientific systems could instead show how these systems competed with one another, how they reconstructed life to develop different human possibilities:

knowledge consists in the search for security via the reduction of obstacles; it consists in the construction of theories that proceed by assimilation. It is thus a general method for the direct or indirect resolution of tensions between man and milieu. Yet to define knowledge in this way is to find its meaning in its end, which is to allow man a new equilibrium with the world, a new form and organization of his life . . . to help man remake what life has made without him, in him, or outside of him.[39]

Progress

A third site joining phenomenological with epistemological anxieties over science was the reinterpretation and critique of progress. Here, too, the impetus came from a series of parallel engagements that in the 1930s and 1940s congealed into the suspicion of a naïve, sweeping concept of progress. In 1922–32, the Société française de philosophie published the massive *Vocabulaire technique et critique de la philosophie* under André Lalande's editorship, after twenty years of collaborative efforts and terminological debates. The definition of *progrès* there followed general understanding: "(a) forward march, movement in a definite direction . . . (b) transformation toward the better, either in a limited domain or in the totality of things." But Lalande added a point of censure to the second branch of this definition:

progress, in this sense, is an essentially relative term, because it depends on the opinion professed by someone who speaks about a ladder of relevant values. "Progress," understood in absolute terms, is an expression that is used very frequently: one often makes of it a sort of historical or cosmic necessity, sometimes even a real power that acts on individuals, a collective finality that is made manifest by the transformations of societies. The difficulty is to give precise content to this formula, in other words, to determine the direction and meaning of this movement.[40]

Lalande's *Vocabulaire* was explicitly inspired by a Cartesian hope of a transparent, agreed-upon language and meaning and a universal knowledge from which all advancement would be linear, direct, and evolving naturally from the *Vocabulaire* itself. According to Brunschvicg, the purpose of the *Vocabulaire* was "to render thought transparent to itself" by not only clarifying, but indeed *fixing* the relations between a word and its meanings.[41] Lalande's approach to progress involved a generalization of positivism that dated back to Auguste Comte, for whom progress moved invariably toward positive scientific knowledge and (as Lalande quoted him saying) toward the development of order.

Somewhat more ambivalent was an exchange organized in 1929 by the Fondation pour la science at the Centre international de synthèse on the word and idea *civilisation*, which included presentations by Lucien Febvre, Marcel Mauss, and Louis Weber.[42] Febvre's presentation, which traced the "evolution of a word and a group of ideas," addressed the intertwining of *civilisation* with *progress* and dated the emergence of the former to the late eighteenth century; the latter would be part of the vocabulary of moral and social improvement. The key term for Febvre was not *civilization* but, in anticipation of Foucault, *police*: just as around 1800 "advanced" European nations were called *nations policées*; the civilized person from Rousseau and the young Turgot on, the person of good education (*Bildung*) according to Wilhelm von Humboldt, was the well-disciplined, well-policed person.[43] Progress was plausible within the strict limits of discipline and police. Mauss, for his part, poured suspicion on progress by emphasizing that the "progress of humanity" was a commonplace in philosophy and politics, now that "civilization" denoted both an ideal future state and a normative take on reality.[44]

Progress was of course far from being specific to science; to index famous and available critiques, one need only reference Max Nordau and the racial argument on degeneration that followed him, Friedrich Nietzsche, and Oswald Spengler. No less significant were domestic attacks on the theme, envisioned especially in Catholic and conservative circles. Influential neo-Thomists like Jacques Maritain often described the Renaissance as the beginning of a centuries-long diversion that led the human creature away from God, into spiritual decline; conservatives from Gustave Le Bon through the Action Française and the right-wing nonconformists of the 1930s amalgamated a refusal of trust in scientific progress with political concerns about French decline, with Catholicism, and with a general disgust at the republican regime. But philosophers were a different bunch, largely attached to the Third Republic and its secular progressivism. Lalande's dictionary expressed a morsel of doubt about the relativity of progress, however, and epistemologists, sociologists, and historians would expand on this considerably.

Three figures drove a veritable skeletonization of progress in its late interwar and early postwar "crisis": the Marxist sociologist Georges Friedmann, the historian Lucien Febvre, and the epistemologist Gaston Bachelard. Friedmann's work, begun in the 1930s, centered on industrial management and the relationship of human beings to the machines that had dominated the workplace since the second Industrial Revolution. His 1936 study *La Crise du progrès* was a social, moral, and intellectual history that diagnosed the perils of technical progress and examined the conditions that socialism would need in order to overcome alienation. Friedmann, who identified the technical domination of progress with Taylorism and Fordism, also ventured that this domination invalidated the humanism to which the idea of progress had been attached.[45] Unless buttressed by a *Marxist* humanism, "progress" was bound to result in destruction and dehumanization; establishing the right sort of socialism was imperative because technical transformations had to be prevented from generating alienation. In Friedmann's eyes, Marxism was the most appropriate "technology of human progress."[46]

During the same decade Lucien Febvre became profoundly ambivalent about the role of the "progress of humanity." This was due to the political situation, his judgment that history should not be understood as the record of an advancing Humanity, and his previous participation in the process of historicizing a constellation of concepts around "progress." In line with the Annales school's favor of social and quantifiable approaches over philosophical views of history, Febvre reviewed Friedmann's 1936 book enthusiastically:

Dictatorship in its contemporary form has not passed only over "the putrified cadaver of Goddess Liberty," as . . . one of its two principal representatives [Mussolini] says. It is on the corpse of the god Progress, whose cult men of my generation still saw their parents celebrate back in our adolescence—whose radiance and power, and, Friedmann is right to recall this, the Dreyfus affair instilled among so many. There is no drama in the history of our life that is comparable to the crumbling of such a revered power.[47]

Progress had been a recent and misguided hope, revealed by fascism to be not a permanent movement or improvement but something evanescent, easily trampled or taken over. The killing of this particular god was also an act of contemporary political demythologization; it opened the way for a proper rethinking of "civilization," Europe, and history. These concepts worked together, and perhaps they failed together too. In his 1944–45 course at the Collège de France, Febvre proposed a *longue durée* history of the notion of Europe, asking at the end of it whether "Europe" was a dated concept that had been overcome or a "vital necessity for the progress of the world."[48] Not unlike Adorno or Freud, Febvre was offering an account in which progress enabled new barbarisms and Europe destroyed its own advances, its own "civilization." He ended on a cliffhanger: "Should we dream of Europe or proceed in the economy of this overcome notion?" Disaggregating the Europe–progress duet was imperative.

If Friedmann and Febvre propelled the epistemological revision of industrial management and history respectively, Bachelard did much the same for science as a whole. We might begin with Hans-Jörg Rheinberger's definition and argue that "'progress' in Bachelard's sense . . . means permanent goings-on, a continuous movement of differential reproduction rather than a movement toward a preconceived end, or an approximation of an 'ultimate reality.'"[49] Progress had a heuristic value, which Bachelard often identified with the advancement of science,[50] but otherwise it was, at best, a double-edged sword that hampered epistemologists and even scientists themselves. In his 1938 *The Formation of the Scientific Mind*, Bachelard wrote, in a formulation that could have served to title the present book: "Knowledge of the real is a light that always casts shadows."[51] Such knowledge was never pure—"never immediate, never complete"—it was constructed by factors in the personal and institutional world of the scientist as well as by the philosophical and metaphysical underpinnings of his endeavor. These constituted a psyche of research, which organized new perceptions and possibilities by agglomerating them, whereas research needed to attend to breaks, ruptures with this expected reality. Reality could then be approached by highlighting past failures or errors in the production of knowledge, but the wall separating the scientist from this reality would remain an obstacle: "Empirical thought is clear in retrospect, when the apparatus of reason has been developed. Whenever we look back and see the errors of our past, we discover truth through a real intellectual repentance."[52] Truth and progress were dragnets, *only retrospectively* affirmed and justified. Even then, the old was not simply superseded in a progress to clarity. "Even in a clear mind there are dark areas, caverns still haunted by shades, and traces of the old remain in our new ways of thinking."[53] In a renewed call for the study of the "psychoanalytic foundations" of scientific research, Bachelard cautioned that "clarity of mind" hampered advances by not considering its own foundations, while trust in progress might itself degrade into an obstacle:

As Bergson has so rightly said, "our mind has an irresistible tendency to consider as clearest the idea that serves it most often." This idea thus acquires an abusive intrinsic clarity. With use, ideas become unduly valorized. A value in itself impedes the circulation of values. It is a factor of inertia for the mind. On occasion, a dominant idea polarizes the totality of a mind.[54]

Progress did not guarantee improvement, but rather marked the entrenchment of a particular horizon into an obstacle. Obstacles could only be understood through a "psychoanalysis" of knowledge, of the expectations that underwrite it, so that research advanced in fits and starts:[55]

In fact, crises in the growth of thought result in a total recasting of the system of knowledge. The well-drilled mind must then be remade. It changes species. It sets itself against the previous species through a decisive function. Through the mental revolutions that scientific invention requires, humankind becomes a mutating species, or to put it better still, a species that needs to mutate, that suffers if it does not change.[56]

Bachelard was advancing here, through a protoconcept of epistemological rupture, what Thomas Kuhn was to popularize as a paradigm shift. A similar development would occur in Canguilhem's *The Normal and the Pathological*, which forcefully undermined Comte's theory of progress by equating this notion with that of normality and its failings.[57]

Bachelard's engagement with progress and transparency is perhaps clearest if his emphasis on the obstacle is seen against Émile Durkheim's argument on the place of ideas in crude scientific thought. Durkheim had argued that crude concepts populate scientific study, taking priority over things, such that "the facts intervene only secondarily, as examples or confirmatory proof. Thus they are not the subject matter of the science, which therefore proceeds from ideas to things, and not from things to ideas."[58] Arguing against this kind of science, Durkheim proposed that the study of social facts (the aim of his sociological science) had to rely on a more sound foundation, because

notions formed in this way can only present a roughly appropriate practicality, and then only in the general run of cases. How often are they both dangerous and inadequate! It is therefore not by elaborating upon them, however one treats them, that we will ever succeed in discovering the laws of reality. *On the contrary, they are as a veil interposed between the things and ourselves, concealing them from us even more effectively because we believe to be more transparent.*[59]

It might appear at first that Bachelard was making a similar point in the 1930s. Yet his own claim was that undertheorized concepts and values *always* inflect scientific thought; they cannot be shed, and, for all their inadequacy, they have to be addressed if any reality is to be discovered and any progress to be achieved. Bachelard's domain was very different from Durkheim's, of course, but with Bachelard, the claim to scientificity shifted to include and critique rather than exclude and dismiss the formative role of concepts. If Durkheim saw concepts as extrinsic, as entities to be shed, much like the scales from one's eyes, so that "transparency" might be restored and scientific progress might follow, Bachelard placed obstacles, illusions, and the impossibility of such transparency, at the core of scientific engagement. Progress and revaluation might play out thanks to them and their limitations.

Machines and the Cogito

To better understand the scope and consequence of the matrix of epistemological recalibrations presented in the previous chapter and its relevance to the overall theme of transparency, I will attend here to Georges Canguilhem's arguments against the transparency of knowledge that the Cartesian cogito needs to achieve, and against the transparency of the cogito itself. He articulated these arguments in a text that has been lauded for epitomizing postwar epistemological concerns: his 1947 lecture on "Machine et organisme" ("Machine and Organism"), published in *Knowledge of Life* in 1952.

Canguilhem's text speaks to three concerns relevant to my theme: the postwar displacement and reappreciation of Descartes's thought, which he treats as the generally accepted foundation of the place of science and technology in modernity; the critique of epistemological transparency, which he identifies with the cogito, positivism, and idealism and criticizes for explaining away organismic complexity and failing to understand the place of technical domination;[1] and the postwar critique of the purity of scientific inquiry, where his emphasis is on the historical and conceptual situatedness of the observer. Channeling contemporary fears of "human engineering," Americanization, and atomic destruction, Canguilhem refuses Descartes's postulate that science is pure, systematized, abstract knowledge that is applied technically only at a second remove. Arguing that the Cartesian cogito leads to the technological domination of nature and other people, Canguilhem counters with a theory of science as a human *technique*, which he affiliates to the need for a less violent control of life.

Descartes and the Violence of Mechanism

In "Machine and Organism," Canguilhem revisited Descartes with the intention of delivering a broad-ranging critique of biological mechanism and of rethinking the place and particular theoretical status of organisms and their parts. When he situated Descartes at the root of modern thought and science, Canguilhem was entirely symptomatic of his generation. Nor was there great novelty in his effort to situate Descartes's theory of science at the center of the process through which "determinism" had come to be the base of philosophical and scientific knowledge. Descartes's *mechanism*—the reduction of organisms to machines—and the alternative it generated in the late eighteenth century, *finalism*—the reduction of organic functions to goal-oriented activities—were widely viewed as the key hermeneutic models in the history of biology. For Canguilhem, both were essential to a series of misguided modern scientific premises: that the scientist-observer holds an all-powerful position of objectivity vis-à-vis matter and upholds theories whose truth is the product of the predictability and mechanical nature of matter; that scientific knowledge is prior to and uncontaminated by technique and technology, which are mere applications; and that a living being can be reduced to matter and to the role of a mechanical support for the soul. In his view, both mechanism and finalism ignored that each individual organism always experienced its environments differently. Since organisms *had* interactions—and *singular* interactions at that—they could not be physical–mechanical systems undifferentiated from one another and reducible to their parts.[2] In an anti-Cartesian, anti-determinist, vitalistic gesture of refusing what he saw as the violence done by mechanistic biology to the individual organism, Canguilhem interpreted *technique* as a concept that mediated between "life" and "science" and could offer an ethical and non-reductive alternative.[3] Human knowledge and science could never grasp the totality of life in the transparent manner that the Cartesian cogito promised; continued allegiance to mechanistic principles amounted to a misplaced trust in the transparency and inertness of nature and life and turned a blind eye to the inbuilt violence of scientific thought.[4]

In the immediate postwar period, after a long debate that had roughly equated mechanism with materialism and vitalism with conservative romanticism, mechanism seemed to provide the theoretical foundation for biologists' and biochemists' understanding of tissues and organisms.[5] In mechanistic biology, the organism possessed no level of internal complexity that would not itself be mechanistically formed and deployed. Thanks to mechanism's prioritization of physics and chemistry over biology, and thanks also to the readiness with which vitalist biologists and *Lebensphilosophen* like Hans Driesch and Ludwig Klages had sided (however inconclusively) with National Socialism, vitalism was deeply suspect, politically as well as scientifically, when Canguilhem used his credit as a former *résistant* to attempt its philosophical rescue.[6]

Nevertheless, at the time this state of affairs was not nearly as settled as it appears in hindsight: respected historians of the life sciences like Charles Singer (whom Caguilhem quoted extensively) treated the debate as unresolved,[7] and some subfields of biology and medicine—especially physiology, endocrinology, neurology, and medical and psychiatric therapeutics—also sought intermediary rather than harshly mechanistic forms.[8] Yet in 1953, only a year after the publication of Canguilhem's quasi-vitalist *Knowledge of Life*, James Watson and Francis Crick would present their findings on the double helix structure of DNA in *Nature*,[9] launching a new mechanistic revolution, which would dominate molecular biology over the following thirty years. Their conclusions were partly inspired by Erwin Schrödinger's 1944 account of the statistical basis of the physical laws of life.[10] By proposing this new genetic paradigm, Watson and Crick wiped out classic deterministic mechanism almost as resolutely as they did vitalism. DNA, a program underlying protein synthesis and the basic structures of life, yielded the apparatus thanks to which molecular biology could be mechanistic yet escape the reductiveness associated with traditional mechanism. Although Canguilhem would long remain skeptical of the genetic paradigm as an explanation of life,[11] his denial that life could be reduced to a sum of mechanistic physical–chemical principles belongs to a moment when this biological and philosophical paradigm was itself in flux, even if in the 1960s a new mechanism was to triumph in biology.[12]

Biology was only one leg of Canguilhem's critique of Descartes and Cartesian epistemology; the other was technique and technology. Canguilhem was by no means the only thinker to offer a historically grounded critique of a mechanist and mechanical imagination in the early postwar era; philosophical approaches to technology spanned a wide spectrum. At one end, the technophobic position presented technology as independent of humanity and capable of overwhelming or destroying it, while its counterpart insisted that "technique," the invention and use of technical objects, was a natural and universal human activity. Pieces like Michel Crozier's article on "human engineering" as an effect of Americanization, published in 1951 in *Les Temps modernes* with an introduction by Maurice Merleau-Ponty, tied technology to capitalist exploitation.[13] Martin Heidegger's well-known attack on the effects of Cartesian selfhood in his 1938 lecture "The Age of the World Picture" also appeared in print in the early 1950s. Similar statements were made in more public fora as well: a relevant example is an essay published in *Le Figaro* in December 1949 by the academician André Siegfried that loudly pointed to Descartes as the originator of Taylorism—a practice of industrial organization that was much hated in French culture.[14] At the other end of the spectrum one finds the positions taken by ethnologists like Marcel Mauss and his former student André Leroi-Gourhan, and by the historian Lucien Febvre, who insisted that human activity was—fundamentally, cross-culturally—technical. For Leroi-Gourhan, the study of technical objects was at the root of every comparative study of human cultures. Somewhere between these two extremes came Georges Friedmann's elaborate and influential critique of industrialization and industrial mechanism as dehumanizing.[15] Alexandre Koyré also bridged the two positions when he connected Descartes with the birth of modern technicist civilization and denounced his failure to balance technological innovation with social reform.[16]

For Canguilhem, the modern Cartesian claim that science was a fundamentally pure activity of interpretation while technology was just an application of science was absurd. As early as December 1944, he insisted on the priority of technique over science, writing, for example: "It can no longer be contested that not every technical achievement carries a scientific explanation."[17] Canguilhem cited an array of thinkers—including Friedmann, Mauss, Leroi-Gourhan, and Febvre—on the point that scientific analysis postdates, and often comes in response to, technique.[18] This allowed him to take up a position with *both* "technophilic" and "technophobic" elements. On the one hand, technique had a decidedly positive and as it were "natural" meaning. Technical activity was a creative handling of the milieu. On the other, Cartesian mechanism was not free of connotations related to an industrial perversion of life, experimental brutality, or eugenicist fantasy. While technique was a component of life and human activity, technique in the Cartesian mode resulted in a misunderstanding and deformation of life.

Canguilhem's Long Dance with Descartes

Canguilhem's engagement with Descartes in "Machine and Organism" dates in part to the 1930s. Although Descartes had figured in his studies (Canguilhem's supplementary doctoral thesis was a translation of a Latin treatise on Descartes by Émile Boutroux),[19] his first public engagement with Cartesianism occurred at the 1937 International Congress of Philosophy. The Congress was organized by the French Society of Philosophy and presided over by Henri Bergson and Émile Bréhier and marked the tricentennial of the *Discourse on Method*. There Canguilhem presented a paper titled "Descartes et la technique" and met for the first time two other crucial figures of the new generation of French epistemologists: Gaston Bachelard and Alexandre Koyré. Bachelard's engagement with Descartes and transparency was discussed in chapter 4. For his part, Koyré also played an important role: his 1922 *Essai sur l'idée de Dieu et les preuves de son existence chez Descartes* is frequently (and unironically) believed to have demolished the then prevalent view that Descartes had singlehandedly overpowered scholasticism.[20] In his conference presentation Koyré drew a parallel between Descartes and Galileo: both put an end to the medieval cosmos to the benefit of an "infinite universe" that was to define modern science. Canguilhem's own effort at this early stage was still largely determined by his neo-Kantian studies under Alain and Léon Brunschvicg and aimed at an enlarged Cartesianism, in strong contrast with the other presentation on Descartes and technique that was to take place at the conference—Martin Heidegger's original version of "The Age of the World-Picture."[21] Where Heidegger would have charged Descartes with reducing the world to the picture it offered the subject, Canguilhem attended to Descartes's understanding of invention and construction in order to destabilize from within the sense that technique is a mere application of scientific thought and objective knowledge.

By 1941, when he taught a course on purposiveness in nature, Canguilhem had begun to piece together the image of Descartes that he would present in "Machine and Organism."[22] His thought changed considerably during the war, both toward an engagement with the relations between vitalism, mechanism, and finalism and toward a greater acceptance of Bergson.[23] He emphasized that Descartes set himself up as an opponent of Aristotle's finalism and indeed took himself to have overcome it.[24] The payoff of "overcoming" Aristotle was clear to Canguilhem: "If there is no purposiveness in nature, including among living beings, man can consider all of nature outside himself as means—not as means that are offered to him all ready and opportune by divine providence, but means that he has the obligation to institute as such in order that he may render himself a master and possessor of nature."[25] Descartes's thought thus appeared to Canguilhem to appeal to humanity to use thought and science so as to make the whole of nature its object, its possession, and its slave.

Finally, it is worth noting that, when he first prepared "Machine and Organism," Canguilhem was in the middle of his second attempt at writing a book on Descartes.[26] In the late 1930s he sketched out a book that would expand on his lecture "Descartes et la technique"; of this book only the outline remains.[27] A decade later, Canguilhem accepted an invitation from the publisher Bordas in early 1947 to write a new account of Descartes's overall thought and submitted five chapters (half the manuscript) in March, promising to complete the book in July.[28] In this book Canguilhem offered a rather sympathetic reading of Descartes, emphasizing his distance (indeed "obscurity," as it appeared from the postwar perspective), celebrating his skepticism and even his metaphysics,[29] and insisting that the destruction of the old cosmos led by Descartes (here Canguilhem was following Koyré) could be understood by analogy with what was happening in the present: "In the atomic age, amidst a divided humanity, we have the means to imagine what the cosmic revolution was for a no less divided Christianity." By comparison with this cosmic revolution, he observed, "the Lisbon earthquake, which so shook eighteenth-century thinkers, can pass for a landslide on an anthill."[30] Like the early to mid-sixteenth century, the postwar period was a time when skepticism à la Descartes had returned.

The book on Descartes would remain unfinished; its remains survive in Canguilhem's archive in a folder titled "Descartes interrupted . . ." Ten days before sending off the second half the manuscript to the publisher, Canguilhem presented "Machine and Organism" at Jean Wahl's Collège philosophique as the second in a series of three talks titled "Biology and Philosophy."[31] Canguilhem suddenly took a position at the opposite end from that of Descartes. Whatever his intellectual or institutional reasons for not finishing that book, he now developed plenty of philosophical reasons—and a very different tone when addressing Descartes—as though that note about the dangers of the atomic age compelled a new, *anti-Cartesian* skepticism.

"Machine and Organism":
The Transparency of the Cogito

In his reading of Descartes in "Machine and Organism," Canguilhem made two novel claims concerning the cogito's sovereignty over nature and the body.

Canguilhem's First Claim

The first claim was that "the theory of animal-machines is inseparable from *Cogito ergo sum*."[32] In other words, Descartes's "I think therefore I am" applies by virtue of the human being's possession of a soul (or
thought), but animals—and bodies in general—are entirely mechanical, in
that they have no thought. This claim allowed Descartes to deny animals
thought yet not life, hence to reduce them to breathing machines; and it
also established the sovereignty of a self-transparent cogito over the realm
of the living:

> The theoretical mechanization of life and the technical utilization of the animal
> are inseparable. Man can make himself master and possessor of nature only if he
> denies all natural purpose and can consider all of nature, including, apparently,
> animate nature—except for himself—to be a means.[33]

For the mind to acquire mastery over life, it was essential that organisms
be reducible without remainder to parts identical or analogous with those
of machines, that is, to things that humans *already know* because they have
built them as a means for themselves. To the cogito that asserted its own
plenitude and could understand nature and technology without loss, this
premise confirmed its own mastery and clarity. We find here a sharpening
of the claim that Canguilhem had made in his 1941 course: if Aristotle had
seen nature as purposive, Descartes transplanted this purposiveness into
his own mechanism. Descartes's mechanism did not overcome Aristotelian
finalism and purposiveness, it merely recast it in a way that transformed
all of nature into a machine for the cogito.[34] Linking rather than opposing
Descartes to Aristotle allowed Canguilhem to argue that between mechanism and politics there is a distinct relationship, thanks to which machines
and their analogues appear as servants of certain people capable of abstract
thought.[35] By the same token he could frustrate any Marxist account that
credited modernity and capitalism with the emergence of machines and

mechanism.[36] This part was particularly significant for Canguilhem, inasmuch as it suggested that both a conception of the self that began with the cogito and a Marxist alternative that began with submission through labor amounted to a mechanization of life and to a profoundly problematic politics of mastery and submission.

Canguilhem's Second Claim

The second major claim is linked to the first, but inserted somewhat on the sly: "the human body, *if not man*, is a machine."[37] In other words man himself, not just the body but the entire human being, may be a machine. Only the cogito (and Canguilhem specifically distances the soul from movements and actions of the body)[38] may escape from the order of machines. Canguilhem finds this claim to be implicit in the Sixth Meditation and explicit in the famous discussion of automata at the opening of the *Treatise of Man*:

I might consider the body of a man equipped with and made up of bones, nerves, muscles, veins, blood and skin in such a way that, even if there were no mind in it, it would still perform all the same movements as it now does in those cases where movement is not under the control of the will or, consequently, of the mind.[39]

These men will be composed, as we are, of a soul and a body, and I must first separately describe for you the body; then, also separately, the soul; and finally I must show you how these two natures would have to be joined and united to constitute men resembling us. I assume their body to be but a statue, an earthen machine formed intentionally by God to be as much as possible like us.[40]

At stake then is not only the animal or the body as a machine but the entire human being, God, their creativity and capacity for invention, and the cogito. Canguilhem reads the famous passage on automata as proposing the priority of the fact of life over the actual machines made by God. He then proposes that the Cartesian theory of divine art as imitation grants precedence to the living. At first blush, this seems to be quite an astonishing turn in the argument, insofar as up to this stage all life appeared to be machine. The turn is not real, however; for Canguilhem aims in this direction in order to conversely identify the cogito, with its articulation of knowledge and science, as the bearer of the capacity for abstraction and perfection— of all that stands apart from matter. Whereas nature and God nestle in one another, the cogito, in its self-assertion, produces its own separation from nature.

The construction of the living machine implies, if one reads the text well, an obligation to imitate a prior organic given. The construction of a mechanical model presupposes a vital original. . . . The Cartesian God, the *Artifex Maximus, works to equal the living itself.* The model for the living machine is the living itself. The Idea of the living, which *divine art imitates,* is the living thing.[41]

And the idea that God *imitates* the living itself, producing living machines, and that the human creature is such a machine offers Canguilhem a precise and substantive gain. For *his* Descartes, it is not divine providence that turns the living into a means; humans themselves do that. And thus it is with Descartes that the *modern* style of mastery over nature and others begins in earnest. Aristotle had identified slaves with animate machines,[42] interweaving social with technical domination; yet for Aristotle the first *motor* was the soul.[43] Descartes commits instead to a theory in which the cogito, science, and knowledge combine to make the world "man's due." More radically than Koyré, who thought that "the machine had betrayed the hopes placed in it" by the Cartesian dream,[44] and in a manner at times resembling Adorno and Horkheimer's *Dialectic of Enlightenment*, Canguilhem identified the cruelties against nature and fellow human beings that he regarded as endemic to modernity with this proclamation of the cogito as an all-powerful observer and manipulator of nature, a human technician and a "pure" scientist.[45] Mechanism and the glorification of the cogito led directly to domination because they reduced nature and the living to an agglomeration of machines and parts that can be studied and experimented on. The transparency enforced by the cogito that understands itself as self-transparent necessarily led *directly* to domination and violence.

Parenthetically, one may speculate why Canguilhem could not complete his *Descartes* book of 1948 after this talk. In the outline of that book, the Manichaeism of the Cold War recalled the background against which Descartes's doubt arose. But in "Machine and Organism" Descartes was no longer the skeptic but the founder—no longer the one who found, through doubt, a way out of Protestant–Catholic debates and a new philosophy, but the one who asserted the transcendence and transparency of the cogito and its mastery over the entire physical, biological, and human world.

Intimacy with Life as Canguilhem's Alternative

We thus come to a point where the Cartesian cogito serves as the cornerstone of modernity and explains its violence. But Canguilhem has an alternative to offer on life and technique, and he proceeds to articulate it patiently, along two movements (though their respective purposes are at times difficult to discern).

First he argues, in a historical vein, that, since the late nineteenth century, philosophers concerned with the status of technique have gradually come to see the machine *not* as the structural basis of organisms but as the result of a specifically human technical activity. In a Kantian spirit, these philosophers distanced technology from biological mechanism. In the closing pages of "Machine and Organism," Canguilhem finds inspiration in Kant's theory of technique, even as this tendency clashes with his forceful rejection of Kantian intellectualism, which contributed to the sidelining of Kant as a formative influence on contemporary thought. Tracking recent philosophical and anthropological theorizations, Canguilhem distinguishes the purposive element in machines from the non-purposive and non-programmed existence of living beings. Following Friedmann, he imagines technique—"the development of a technique for adapting machines to the human organism"—as offering an expansion of life that would lead to "an ineluctable revolution."[46] Technological inventions would appear not as reductive models for nature, but as tools tending to inscribe "the technical within the organic," as they had been for early humanity. Historical, sociological, and anthropological studies should move toward such an understanding of technique, and taking a stand against Descartes pointed in this direction.[47]

Second, Canguilhem explicitly argues against placing science, knowledge, and consciousness at the foundation of life—be it human life or life more generally. Life is not reducible: "Life . . . is experience, that is to say, improvisation, the utilization of occurrences; it is an attempt in all directions."[48] Moreover, he claims, against Descartes, that the prioritization of science and of the cogito over life distorts not only life but also its relationship with technique and science:

Science and Technique must be considered not as two types of activity, one of which is grafted onto the other, but as two types of activity, each of which borrows from the other sometimes its solutions, sometimes its problems. The rationalization of techniques makes one forget the irrational origin of machines. And it seems that in this area, as in any other, one must know how to cede a place to the irrational, even and especially when one wants to defend rationalism.[49]

Most striking in this approach is the fluidity between science and technique and the claim that rationalism has to be separated from its own rigid traditions. Technique had to be understood as the use and invention of means for relating to one's world—an activity that characterizes living species in general. Knowledge and science are specific and often derivative forms of human technique. They rely on abstraction and formalization but do not, for all that, ground technique itself. Descartes may have imagined that they confirm the cogito's sovereignty; but, if science is seen as a specific form of the human engagement with the world, then determinism would cease to present the world as belonging to humans. Philosophy, moving beyond Cartesian subjectivism, might come to rethink knowledge, technique, and "life" in terms that might generate continuity and perhaps even harmony between them.

We have proposed that, in spite of initial appearances, a mechanist conception of the organism is no less anthropomorphic than a teleological conception of the physical world. The solution we have tried to defend has the advantage of showing man in continuity with life through technique prior to insisting on the rupture for which he assumes responsibility through science.[50]

If the cogito is a modern, anthropomorphic, and hence humanist invention that appropriates the entirety of life for itself and generates a structure of domination over other human beings, then the joint recognition of the originality of life and derivative status of knowledge can salvage technology from its immediate association with the violence of this humanism. And, since this gesture toward life struggles against the Cartesian (and Husserlian) conception of a self-transparency of the cogito, ending that conception will work against the technological domination of nature and life. Demolishing Cartesianism in science and nestling technique into life are two complementary gestures—one negative, one positive—that produce the same result.

To take stock: in Canguilhem's treatment of Descartes's mechanism we begin to glimpse the value of a new kind of antihumanist scepticism, that of an "atomic age, amidst a divided humanity,"[51] inimical to "transparent and inert intellectualism" or "foggy (at once active and muddled) mysticism."[52] His sense of organic as well as technical complexity thus underscores the impossibility of pure observation and uncontaminated science. While Canguilhem held back from making frequent political claims and despised moralism, it is clear that he did not shy away from associating violence with the scientific determinism that he regarded as resulting from the Descates' mechanistic paradigm and the transparency of the cogito. In *The Normal and the Pathological*, he had argued for a nonreductivist understanding of the pathological experience, which would follow its own norms.

Even more emphatic refusals of deterministic conceptions of life and thought came from Canguilhem in the 1950s, notably the 1958 lecture "Qu'est-ce que la psychologie?" This critique, which tackled the very rationale underlying psychology and decried it as police practice,[53] would later form part of his critique of early neuroscientific reductions of thought to the brain.[54] No less pronounced was his suspicion of cybernetics and of its use in theories of biological and social regulation.[55] Across the texts that developed these insights, Canguilhem's "vitalism" envisioned science as a technique that, rather than appropriate all life, pushed back against reductionism, in a movement of autonomy.

There is no point in avoiding the ethical implications of these novelties, which are as stark as Levinas's in his contemporary critique of Descartes. Without reverting to traditional liberalism, Canguilhem made a strong claim about the complexity of life and technique, the possibility of difference, and the irreducible nature of individuality. Against Marxism's refusal of the category of the individual and equally against the liberal advocacy for it, Canguilhem argued for an individualism that, aware of the rule of reason, of the normalizing tendencies of norms, and of the force of mechanization, still fights for life's priority over an abstract science and appeals to a world that will not be determined. This "proximity to life" was a new epistemological skepticism, against Descartes and against the politics of the early Cold War.

From the Total Man to the Other

UNESCO, Anticolonialism, and
the New Humanism of French Anthropology

The ethnographer parades across his face as pretty a collection of masks as that possessed by any museum.

Marcel Griaule, *Méthode de l'ethnographie* (1957: 14)

Philosophy and the history of science were not the only knowledge systems that moved from a progressivist, totalizing theory toward one foregrounding epistemological and ethical obstacles; social anthropology—more precisely, *ethnologie*—insisted on these obstacles as well and created serious ethical dilemmas out of them. After World War II, ethnologists presented theirs as a young science, or at the very least a profoundly transformed one, opposed to the homogenization caused by the colonial "civilizing mission" and by new governmental policies of "integration" in Algeria, and capable of unsettling a totalizing Western gaze. In the 1920s and 1930s, Marcel Mauss and his leading associates had attempted to chart the human world—an approach that, despite its socialist credentials, remained quite blind to colonialism. But several of the newly preeminent ethnologists of the late 1940s turned their Mauss-trained eyes back to the West, often with open hostility to its universalism. With UNESCO's support and working in part within it, they spearheaded an antiracism campaign through which they could pursue a politics of opposition to the destruction or uniformization of human others, whose alterity they sought to encourage.

This chapter tracks the institutional and discursive transformation of French ethnology to the point where it could assert itself as the only guardian of humanity and "the other." Claude Lévi-Strauss's rise to heights of intellectual and academic power played a great role in this process, although many of his widely heralded arguments—particularly his opposition to the humanist pretenses to transcultural transparency—were common currency among anthropologists. The chapter follows three major themes:

- the path followed in French ethnology from totalization to internationalization that resulted in a praise of alterity and a very different relationship to "home" and to the strictures of post-Durkheimian theory;
- the role of UNESCO and its antiracism campaign in modifying the purview, objects, and rhetoric of anthropology in the early 1950s; and
- the reorganization of the science itself during the decline of the French empire, with changes of course that were often explicitly supportive of decolonization.

Developments along these lines helped fashion ethnology into a "redemptive" project of extraordinary potential.[1] Supposedly, it could resolve humanist and colonial problems, imagine a harmonious world based on difference, and liberate Western knowledge from the transparentist values that had contributed to the domination and homogenization of the world. As Alfred Métraux would write in 1962: "Ethnology seeks to escape the rigid optics of our cultural and social frames."[2] Formerly devoted to the accumulation of colonial knowledge and to the training of officials, it shifted toward the study of "other peoples" and the celebration of human diversity.[3]

The Transformation of French Ethnology
Totalization and Homogenization in the 1930s

In the 1920s, Marcel Mauss began to describe his goal as the capture of the "total man." *Mon cher Maître*, as his students addressed him,[4] had turned toward ethnology by way of guiding fieldworkers to discover strategies for capturing the *entire* worlds and worldviews of the groups they were studying. This "total man" or "total social fact" radicalized and materialized Durkheim's social morphology. Notes from Mauss's posthumously published courses insist on the most thorough pursuit of the tasks of observation.[5] The aim was an all-embracing, utopian epistemology:

Cartography of society, cartography of its content: it does not suffice to say of such or such a tribe that it consists of two or three thousand members, one must locate every one of these three thousand.[6]

Extreme as this claim may seem, it was only a tidbit in a vast database of entry points into each particular society that emphasized bodily techniques—from the manual use of tools or weaponry to juridical–religious rites, the expressions of tears, and breast-feeding styles. Meanwhile, French ethnologists operating from the Musée d'Ethnographie du Trocadéro in Paris (renamed the Musée de l'Homme in 1937) began to present their work, if not as the first human science, then certainly as the broadest. The Musée was involved in massive undertakings, notably the Dakar–Djibouti Expedition of 1931–33 and the production of *L'Espèce humaine* (The Human Species), volume 7 of the *Encyclopédie française.*[7] The Dakar–Djibouti Expedition, led by Marcel Griaule and including Michel Leiris, André Schaeffner, and others, brought a vast collection of materials to the Musée, a "bounty" contemporary newspapers praised and Leiris wrote about in his controversial 1934 memoir *L'Afrique fantôme* (*Phantom Africa*),[8] where he nonetheless also expressed a measure of repentance. The journey sought, at times embarrassingly, to capture as much as could be recorded, and adopted fundamentally colonialist practices (see fig. 6.1).[9] As directed by Mauss, the *expéditionnaires* photographed and filmed African rituals and everyday behavior, using several cameras at a time, to get both different overviews and close-ups of the rituals (see fig. 6.2).[10]

The second major effort, the publication of *L'Espèce humaine* (1937), was directed by Paul Rivet, one of the directors of the Musée, and co-authored by over a dozen ethnologists linked to it, including Mauss students Alfred Métraux and André Leroi-Gourhan. The volume provided an overview of human cultures, grouped by geographic area. To give a sense of this totalizing approach, suffice it to point out that Leroi-Gourhan, then twenty-five years old and with no more than a year's fieldwork in Japan behind him, contributed impressively detailed synthetic chapters on

FIGURE 6.1 Opening credit, by the Ministry of Colonies, for *Sous les masques noirs* (1939), which the subsequent credit line describes as a film "shot in the course of an official mission directed by Marcel Griaule." The circles are radio waves radiating out from Paris; note the sea waves in the ocean and the map of French-ruled Africa.

SOURCE: *Jean Rouch: Une Aventure africaine* (2010; DVD, Éditions Montparnasse).

FIGURE 6.2 The Dakar–Djibouti expedition, October 20, 1931: Marcel Griaule seated under the tripod, filming the funeral of a hunter.

SOURCE: Fonds Marcel Griaule, University of Paris–X (Nanterre), Mission Dakar Djibouti, fmg_E_a_02_L_13_008. Reproduced with permission of the library and its librarian Frédéric Dubois.

culture and society in Europe, the Arctic Circle, India, and the whole of East Asia—Japan, China, and continental Southeast Asia. On conceptual matters, too, the volume showcased the Musée's rejection of race: Henri Neuville, an ethnologist who deemed race a weak category, wrote chapters concerning physical and racial anthropology and undermined classic racial suppositions.[11] The limitations of antiracism in the interwar years did not allow the wholesale rejection of race and ethnic parentage as categories, but contributors used them without according them evidentiary or scientific value.[12] *L'Espèce humaine* held back from fully integrating this criticism of physical anthropology—fundamentally theoretical and methodological— into a broader approach. Editor and contributors were just as hesitant about justifying sociological and ethnological concepts and unities as self-sufficient alternatives.

Two of Mauss's former students, Leroi-Gourhan and Griaule, went on to develop his work into legacy methodologies of their own. Griaule, a crucial figure in Africanist studies in France, became the most established ethnologist of the early postwar period and the one most committed to a Maussian project of the "total man," notably through his long-term study of the Dogon people in Mali.[13] Griaule's methodological innovations, some of which relied on technological superiority (e.g., aerial photography), and others on colonial practices, are particularly interesting in this regard. Taking on the role of an "examining magistrate," Griaule sought to force the natives to relinquish their masks, abandon their theater, and submit to science.[14]

André Leroi-Gourhan's own project was closely tied to a different side of Mauss's work: the problem of technique and technology. In *L'Homme et la matière* and *Milieu et techniques,* two weighty volumes that appeared in 1943 and 1945, Leroi-Gourhan sought to demonstrate not only the place of tools and techniques in particular societies but their fundamental role in human differentiation and history. *L'Homme et la matière* dealt with the fabrication of technical means, *Milieu et techniques* with the processes of acquisition ("hunting, fishing, stockbreeding, and agriculture") and consumption ("alimentation, clothing, habitation"). Together the two books offered detailed hypotheses about the development and interactions of units usually described as ethnic or racial and about the dominance of cultural and technical factors over biological ones. Although he made clear the role of the latter, Leroi-Gourhan treated them as always inflected by the techniques that the group practiced. This process was two-pronged. Leroi-Gourhan advanced a model of the relationship between "nature" and "culture" in which "culture" governed how "nature" was experienced in each group. By the same token, he articulated a system for thinking about similarity and difference within larger groups ("racial unities")—namely, the capacity of technical, political, and religious differences to produce the assimilation of some groups by others.[15]

"[Physical] anthropology still lives to a considerable degree on the idea of races, pure in the past, mixed in the present, and uniform in a distant future," Leroi-Gourhan observed in *Milieu et techniques*, and he swept aside race as "unstable" and "imprecise."[16] What Neuville had not managed to do in overcoming race became Leroi-Gourhan's project: his counterclaim to physical anthropology in *Milieu et techniques* was that techniques, which depend on particular groups' relations to their geographic milieu, constitute the ground or, better yet, the cipher for each culture's modification and control of nature. He could thus propose how the "natural" is reconstituted and mediated via the techniques and tools that groups develop or borrow and modify. His work can be seen as an important contribution to ethnology's ascendancy over the other human sciences, and the new humanism he would later adopt scoffed at European feelings of evolutionary superiority as largely dependent on technique and geography.[17] The conclusion outlined a theory of dynamic cultural transformation, opposed to acculturation as a key colonial practice.

Internationalization and Anthropologization: Beyond Mauss

By 1947, when Mauss's *Manual* appeared, French anthropologists had begun to distance themselves from its sweeping generalizations, showing clearer signs of embarrassment. A "perfect representation" of the peoples under study was no longer at stake, and the Paris-centered international socialism that had underwritten Mauss's politics since the Dreyfus Affair had proven insufficient as a response to the growing awareness of colonialism as a problem.[18]

All this happened because, during World War II, the world of the French anthropologists had broken apart, and it had come back together very differently. Increased contact with American anthropologists dislodged the Maussian approach from its central position; some leaders of the next generation, like Griaule, were politically compromised; others, like Leiris and André Leroi-Gourhan, had suffered or struggled during the Occupation and were sympathetic to political and anticolonial struggles.

French anthropologists and sociologists had experienced dispersal, occupation, and persecution, but for some these brought also a considerable expansion of their intellectual and institutional horizons. Some fled the country, Lévi-Strauss, Rivet, and Roger Caillois among them. In New York, Lévi-Strauss was befriended by American colleagues such as Franz Boas, Ruth Benedict, and Margaret Mead and converted to Roman Jakobson's structural linguistics. The Swiss-born anthropologist Alfred Métraux—a close friend of Leiris and Georges Bataille since the 1920s and a student of Mauss and Rivet—had moved to the Americas to do fieldwork in the mid-1930s. He gradually drifted to Berkeley, where he worked under Robert Lowie's supervision, then to Yale. As of 1941, he was with the Smithsonian Institution; during the war he befriended Lévi-Strauss.[19] Major players at the Musée de l'Homme remained in France under often difficult conditions: Mauss and Marcel Cohen were banned from teaching and as Jews lived a highly precarious existence. The early issues of *Résistance* were printed on the press of the Musée de l'Homme, leading to executions and deportations among the Musée's ethnologists (other scientific institutions, notably of physical anthropologists, were much more sympathetic to the Occupation).[20] Leiris's *L'Afrique fantôme* was banned, and he himself hid Jewish friends at his home. Marcel Griaule's wartime sympathies became a subject of controversy immediately after the war, including among colleagues like Schaeffner, who blamed him for advancing his career (he replaced Cohen after the latter's removal) and for playing a part in the banning of *L'Afrique fantôme*. Supporters retorted that he had been obliged to perform a balancing act by the hostility of Robert Brasillach's collaborationist journal *Je suis partout*; they also highlighted his return to the French air force in 1944.

Those anthropologists who had moved to America looked back with a profoundly changed viewpoint both on Europe and on their own science. In 1937, Métraux had written to Mauss of being "profoundly assimilated" in America, saying, "I love this country."[21] After the war, however, he expressed an "immense nostalgia" for Europe, mollified by a short visit to Germany with the U.S. Strategic Bombing Survey in 1945 to "measure public opinion."[22] Returning through Paris, he missed seeing Leiris and wrote him an extraordinary letter about the Germany he had witnessed:[23]

This journey that I have just completed has been of the highest interest. During three months I traveled around the south of Germany in jeeps and trucks, stopping in all sorts of picturesque locations, either to do nothing, or to question people. . . . The sight of destroyed cities is a spectacle that fascinates me. I take no pleasure in it, but this massive obliteration of urban life, of all that makes our civilization, is something so prodigious that one must observe it in person to understand its impact. Here is a vast country, with a dense population, that has been smashed like a nest of termites. The problem that worries me is to know how people will pull themselves out of it, what will come of all this. Are we really going to witness a total cultural regression? I have realized that I have an immoderate love for old houses and old monuments, and wanted to assure myself that not everything has been entirely destroyed. In the ravaged cities, I developed the passions of the collector for the houses or the views of streets that escaped from the disaster. I cannot give you my impressions of the French Zone by letter. I return from it very anxious and pessimistic. How I have hoped to have a long, honest conversation with you. To tell the truth though, I fear such a conversation, because it might reinforce my pessimism and discouragement. I came to Europe in the hope that I could be useful and might stay, but I think that it is wiser to continue an American career, more modest, less interesting, but more solid. The perpetuation of civilization necessary for us to remain ethnographers may only be possible in the United States and England.[24]

Métraux turns Germany into an ethnographer's object: locations are "picturesque," the spectacle of destruction "fascinating," he has developed a "collector's passion," and old houses that have escaped destruction resemble monuments or temples of Old Europe.[25] The state of the French zone is too awful to be conveyed in a censored military epistle. To see how restoration might be envisaged, he flees Europe altogether, imagining that Britain and the United States are as the only possible academic bases for anthropologists. Europe has itself become a site for ethnography; America, the best place from which to reconstruct knowledge of the world.[26]

The systematic contact of Métraux and Lévi-Strauss with American colleagues that began in New York helped them to introduce American anthropology in France and use it (and their own work) to transform the field. Lévi-Strauss all but called French ethnology provincial: in 1953, in a thirty-page essay titled "Panorama de l'ethnologie," despite several dozen references to recent works, he accorded French ethnology less than one page of discussion, making just two references to Marcel Griaule and Germaine Dieterlen, one to Leiris, one to Schaeffner, and two to Métraux.[27] Métraux was directly responsible for "importing" Mead's and Benedict's work and brought together French and American ethnographers to do fieldwork with him in Haiti.[28] The two New Yorkers also rehabilitated the term *an-thropologie*, as against the prevailing *ethnologie* (Leiris, Leroi-Gourhan, Griaule) and *sociologie* (Durkheim), rescuing it from past associations that were right-wing and often racial.

The Stakes of the UNESCO Campaign against Racism: Métraux and Leiris

New institutional positions—particularly Métraux's job as social affairs officer at the United Nations as of early 1946—opened French anthropology to scientific and cultural–political developments outside France, internationalized it, and gave it considerable influence. Especially once Métraux transitioned into the directorship of the Office of Race Relations at UNESCO—a position of importance when UNESCO began its antiracism campaign in 1950—the new international scope contributed to a culture of difference. Métraux's own position was explicit: contemporary racism was the "stupidest and least poetic myth" in history, "a more ferocious and absurd" barbarism than any "Dark Ages" had been.[29] Thanks to his involvement with UNESCO, he moved back to Paris in 1949, where he began systematically including fellow anthropologists in the networks of scientists on which the legitimacy of UNESCO's work depended.[30]

Historians have begun to study the early years of UNESCO, its rhetoric, and its transnational scientific networks: Chloé Maurel has noted that the original dream of a "unique world culture" model was already abandoned during the tenure of Julian Huxley in the late 1940s, basically to the benefit of a difference-based model, which Huxley's successor, Jaime Torres Bodet, pursued with military rhetoric and fervor.[31] Métraux shared the passion for difference, while French involvement was of great political interest to Paris. Maurel has emphasized a subsequent conflict between "Latin" and "Anglo-Saxon" clans, while Todd Shepard has noted that UNESCO's Paris base "facilitated aggressive attempts to use this forum to reinsert French models and experts into the mainstream of post-1945 intellectual exchange."[32]

In the spring of 1950, Métraux's office launched UNESCO's campaign against racism with a "Declaration of Experts on Questions of Race," published on July 20, 1950. The document was drafted by a team headed by the anthropologist Ashley Montagu (known for his opposition to racial thought) and was signed by Lévi-Strauss, among others.[33] Métraux's department had prepared this declaration as a manifesto, only to see it severely criticized by biologists and physical anthropologists, whereupon it had to be revised. In the words of the historian Michelle Brattain, while the revised version "was clearly a rebuttal to a certain style of scientific racism, it was not the straightforward repudiation of racial thinking that UNESCO planners had initially envisioned."[34]

Already before the first declaration was published, UNESCO had commissioned pamphlet-sized essays from a number of intellectuals, including Lévi-Strauss and Leiris. Lévi-Strauss went on to write "Race et histoire" ("Race and History"), a text that deliberately attacked the notion of indigenous peoples as "primitive" (in the literal sense of less advanced or less complex) and is remembered today as an early critique of imposed economic development.[35] Métraux asked Leiris, who was otherwise a minor figure among the anthropologists, to write a "popularizing brochure of about forty double-spaced typescript pages" on "Race et civilisation" ("Race and Culture") to appear in both French and English, in 1950 and 1951 respectively.[36] Rather than on Lévi-Strauss's better-known essay, which also sparked a heated debate with Roger Caillois in 1954, I focus here on Leiris's contribution, because his composition method gives a clear sense of the newfound influence of American anthropology on his work and demonstrates his advocacy of anthropological findings.

Leiris studied a series of anthropological, sociological, and biological writings on race and copied about a hundred pages of passages by hand, strongly privileging social scientists—anthropologists such as Ralph Linton, Ashley Montagu, Franz Boas, T. T. Waterman, and especially Ruth Benedict (of whom Leiris had thought little only a couple of years earlier).[37] He duplicated these passages on the verso of typescripts from his work—the recto covering all manner of topics that interested him, from bullfighting as an endeavor of artistic subjectivity to the formation of colonial researchers (a central task of the Musée de l'Homme).[38]

Leiris began by discussing National Socialism's foundation in racism, flatly insisting on the contribution of the sciences to the violence of World War II.[39] "Who could forget that the development of *our* sciences, if it allowed *us* to achieve undeniable advances . . . also allowed *us* to perfect to such a degree the means of destruction that have given armed conflicts in the past several decades the character of veritable cataclysms?"[40] He then synthesized the copied passages through a sort of montage, silently paraphrasing, reusing, or redeploying them by rewriting the text as his own.[41] He also reworded and quoted silently almost the *entire* original UNESCO "Declaration of Experts on Questions of Race," including its contentious claims.[42]

Anthropology afforded Leiris a platform for criticizing all reliance on biological and other non-cultural factors in the explanation of racial difference. He went so far as to replicate and rephrase Ruth Benedict's account of Mendelian genetics almost in its entirety, as if to avoid relaying a biologist's version.[43] Although colleagues often cited biologists, psychologists, and sociologists (among his papers on race, Métraux kept folders of quotations organized by discipline), Leiris opted for anthropologists at every turn.[44] Only the psychologist Otto Klineberg and the economist Gunnar Myrdal received entries in the bibliography. And he mentioned only a single work by a biologist, a book that Julian Huxley, then only recently the first president of UNESCO, had co-authored with the anthropologist Alfred Cort Haddon titled *We Europeans* (1936).[45] Huxley and Haddon had argued against the use of "race," to which they preferred "ethnic group"; and, while heading UNESCO, Huxley had become an important contributor to the antiracism campaigns, although he remained interested in eugenicism. Leiris reworked one passage thus:

The essential reality of the existing situation is not the hypothetical subspecies or races, but the mixed ethnic groups, which can never be genetically purified into their original components or purged of the variability which they owe to past crossing. Most anthropological writings of the past and many of the present fail to take account of this fundamental fact.[46]

Perhaps to radicalize the point, Leiris commented in the draft that "the authors do not have reference to preexisting 'pure races' but merely to earlier states of an ancestral group." Pursuing a logic that, again, followed Benedict's, Leiris positioned their argument at the cultural, *not* the biological level, asserting that cultural borrowing was the basis for the impression of singular groups: "So great is the part played by borrowings . . . that we may say the same of cultures as of races, that they are never "pure," and that there is none of them which, in its present state, is not the result of co-operation between different peoples."[47] Out of an argument originally directed against the validity of "race," Leiris fashioned the claim that otherness and cultural interdependence were far more profound than the existence, inexistence, or crossing of "races."

Contrast this approach, for example, to Marcel Griaule's. In 1947–48, Griaule was invited to head an interdisciplinary international UNESCO study on "the originality of cultures," and, while working for the cultural affairs division of the Union française, comfortably made broad claims about "knowing the native" and "the problem of black culture" in texts he wrote in support of African culture.[48] Leiris and Griaule had maintained a hostile but functional relationship after falling out in the mid-1930s, but from the late 1940s on, Leiris's overt anticolonialism highlighted Griaule's utter complacency over colonial practices.[49] Partly because of this mimetic rivalry and his resentment of Griaule's success, Leiris laid into Griaule's comfort with European generalizations made for the benefit of Africans. At the explicit urging of Jean-Jacques Mayoux (an official at UNESCO who was also uneasy about Griaule's claims), Leiris also appended a harsh rebuke of Griaule to his study of sculpture.[50] Eventually he chose not to publish the explicit rebuke, but traces of it remain in his main text.[51] Against Griaule's "Problem of Black Culture," Leiris wrote:

What matters from the point of view of universal culture is neither to annex to our own culture a purely theoretical knowledge of Negro African civilizations nor to preserve an African folklore (which like all folklores would necessarily be closed in on itself) nor even to aid the persistence of certain traits of culture that have been minutely selected by us. It's a matter of allowing these cultures to evolve following their own vocation, that is, in a manner that responds solely to the culture of Africans (which by definition excludes interference, of whatever form, by colonizing powers whose tutelage is not only borrowed from their own particularism but also motivated by it); to allow them on the other hand—following their experience of what appears to us as their originality—to acquire a sufficient technical and political development to remain capable of radiating, influencing in turn the becoming of other civilizations.[52]

Leiris's implication is clear: Griaule's counsel for "African culture" was a homogenizing and dis-authenticating force, which pretended to give back to "Africans" their own originality while aiding colonialism's survival. Against this tendency, Leiris jettisoned much of Mauss's approach in favor of American theory even before Mauss was dead and buried (he passed away in February 1950) and strengthened a culturalist anthropological stance vis-à-vis otherness.

Empire and Ethnology
Anticolonialism

Leiris was not the only anthropologist to proceed in this direction. Germaine Tillon, for example, noted that the Maussian project of mapping a "total man" could not proceed as if the perfection of European science did not entail underhanded support for European control. In his *Introduction à l'œuvre de Marcel Mauss* (1950; *Introduction to the Work of Marcel Mauss*), Lévi-Strauss took a complementary approach and famously updated Mauss to make him seem a protostructuralist, going as far as to call upon UNESCO to follow Mauss's project of cataloguing all the "techniques of the body" around the world. An inventory of bodily possibilities and learned practices would "counter racial prejudices" that take the body as the foundation of the human being at the expense of studying how the human being "makes of his body a product," as Mauss did.[53] But Leiris did spearhead the anticolonial argument well beyond Tillon and Lévi-Strauss. He met Aimé Césaire in 1946, when he had already written about colonialism; he had also expressed guilt, as early as 1934, over the bribery, threats, and theft he and his associates had used in order to remove indigenous sacred objects during the Dakar–Djibouti expedition.[54] The meeting was transformative: he and Césaire became close friends, and Leiris became invested in the cause of Antillean independence. In 1950, shortly before the invitation to write *Race et civilisation*, Leiris gave a public lecture titled "L'Ethnographie devant le colonialisme" ("Ethnography Confronted with Colonialism") to an audience that included Césaire and Lévi-Strauss; this would become famous after its publication in *Les Temps modernes*, where Sartre was heralding Césaire's and Léopold Sédar Senghor's *négritude*.[55]

Even though many ethnologists had followed Mauss down the path of socialism, their political priorities had remained starkly French. Leiris was perhaps the first among them explicitly to depict his discipline as an imperial exercise of knowledge building; he called the ethnographer "a 'collaborator,' of the regime," his quotation marks self-evidently evoking Vichy and offering a direct analogy between the Occupation and colonialism.[56]

Ethnology still relied on primitivist obsessions, he argued, and it falsely claimed the status of a pure science; Leiris compared it disparagingly to entomology.[57] The empire might have been renamed the Union française, but ethnology still worked for it,[58] especially through claims of "educating" "backward peoples" that resulted in a colonial valorization of cultures and in a demand for acculturation and—as Lévi-Strauss would argue as well—homogenization.[59] But, for Leiris, the ethnographer was also the "natural advocate" of colonized societies: the education he or she provided ought to be used as a weapon, not only against crude colonial administrators, but against colonialism and its "underlying cause," capitalism.[60] Given that acculturation had long been going on and that the "petrification" of any culture would be a destructive and no less "colonial" practice, Leiris did not argue for protecting the purity of other cultures.[61] But he could dream of a world in which ethnology became the science that taught other cultures to develop counterethnologies of their own, trained ethnographers to see things through these others, and articulated values accordingly. "For ethnography to contribute to a true humanism," it had to cease being unilateral or European.[62] Such a transformation, which he deemed utopian but pursued nevertheless, would allow the ethnologist to sustain the otherness of cultures even in a dynamic situation defined by relations of power and violence. The interests of the colonized were quickly "converging" with those of the "great masses" within colonizing nations. The ethnologist could be the agent of this convergence and of its resulting politics.[63] Five years before Lévi-Strauss's *Tristes tropiques* (1955), Leiris contended even more forcefully in "L'Ethnographie devant le colonialisme" that the ethnologist shackled to colonial administration could also defect and become a hero. Born of colonialism, he could help overcome it, and racism, in one fell swoop.[64]

The Redefinition of Ethnology and Its New Humanism

Theoretical destabilization was internal to the discipline as well. As recently as 1945, in his opening lecture for a course on "Colonial Ethnography," Leroi-Gourhan—whose proximity to Mauss has been noted—declared:

The terrain of ethnology is unstable: the physicist who appreciates a phenomenon is relatively certain of the nature of the phenomenon and the exactness of his calculations; the ethnologist does not yet enjoy such security. Take the definition[s] of the words "race," "civilization," [and] "people," across a century of ethnological literature, and you will see how loose and contradictory they are.[65]

Leroi-Gourhan continued: "Our science is still young, still in the process of saying good-bye to its heroic age."[66] Although this sense of instability was over by 1950, the notion that anthropology had been reborn in the war and in the resistance to Nazi occupation, and was now combating racism and colonialism, inspired methodological innovation and rendered the politics of anthropology more far-reaching than socialist egalitarianism had in the 1930s.[67] The claim that anthropology was a "young" science became highly strategic; it aimed to free anthropology from of its long racial and colonial past.[68] As Lévi-Strauss and Leiris were committed to redefining the very words that Leroi-Gourhan had called "loose and contradictory," anthropologists came to view their science in terms almost as heroic as those they had abandoned.[69] The "position of ethnology" in modern science and in French culture and empire became the subject of a series of writings for Leroi-Gourhan at least on six occasions,[70] for Leiris four, and for Lévi-Strauss eight.[71] Leiris's and Lévi-Strauss's essays recall time and again the failure of Western humanism and systematically argue that, if any humanism is possible, it will come from anthropology—the one science aware of the violence of the West and of the need for "the other" to replace it.[72] Leroi-Gourhan's definitions, though quite academic, are no less emphatic on these points. Ethnology, "the most human of the human sciences,"[73] was for him not a science but a scientific complex, a synthesis of all human sciences.[74] He declared that "ethnology's pathways are tied at once to physical man, to his mental manifestations, and to his milieu,"[75] and he followed Mauss in suggesting that, as a science, ethnology seeks to know "man in his totality" and to provide a "cultural base for the different aspects of human behavior."[76] Concerning its history and the wrong direction of modern humanism, Leroi-Gourhan wrote:

The liberation of ethnology was slowed down by restrictions of social origin that weighed on its beginnings in implicit rather than explicit fashion. Coming from a Western environment whose specific values merged with the general idea of human perfection within a humanism that was in reality very divided, the material of ethnology could only take the route of racist argumentation, or else turn almost trivially in the direction of curiosity and flow from the peak of the curious down the slopes of the folkloric and the exotic.[77]

Racism in anthropology was thus a function of European humanism and of its goal of human perfection. A new humanism had to proceed from ethnology—but only from one of cultural specificity. Like Lévi-Strauss, Leroi-Gourhan was recalibrating Mauss's priorities, and he grasped contemporary concerns just as forcefully. At a conference on "The Major Movements of Contemporary Thought and the Future of Freedom" held in 1962 at the Fédération nationale des syndicats d'ingénieurs et de cadres supérieurs, the opening speaker—Denis Huisman, a philosopher—gave a presentation on the decline of humanism in contemporary thought and dramatically concluded: "How could we make the idea of *humanism* meaningful once again if we are in the process of making the very existence of man disappear from our little planet?"[78] Leroi-Gourhan began his own presentation by tackling this question: as the title announced, he linked "ethnology and the elaboration of a new humanism."[79] An ethnology of prehistory was vital to developing a broad and appropriate humanism: it offered a thorough historical and comparative interpretation of human activity on the entire planet. Leroi-Gourhan further claimed that the only major transformation since the birth of *Homo sapiens* concerned the experience of distance, the practice of techniques, and the use of the human body; and it had occurred in the past century. The present was characterized by an exteriorization of the nervous system (in modern technology), an elimination of distances, and an ever-complicating entanglement of individuals within societies.[80] As a result, "the creation of ethnic values is an attainment particular to *Homo sapiens*, one that we are in the process of losing."[81] Without a recognition of the vast political consequences of the erosion and elimination of ethnic multiplicity, these transformations would have a catastrophic effect over the next two centuries. For a "conscious humanization" to be possible, a "vital space" had to be preserved, and that was the purpose and domain of ethnology.[82]

Métraux was similarly insistent on the benefits of anthropology and promoted his discipline in the Declaration on Race in the *UNESCO Courier*.[83] In a 1950s talk titled "The Right to Life of Primitive Peoples," he credited anthropology with rethinking concepts of culture that allowed for a new recognition and support for "savage" or "primitive" cultures. "The Protection and Integration of Aboriginal and Other Tribal and Semi-Tribal Populations," he noted,

could not have been prepared without the participation of anthropologists who, in consecrating themselves to the study of primitive peoples, have denounced the abuses these have suffered and the dangers threatening them. . . . Anthropology has also revealed the cultural wealth of peoples called "savage" or "primitive" and has shone a light on the treasures of experience and wisdom contained in the institutions and techniques of apparently miserable populations. Thanks to anthropology we know that every civilization has a complex structure and that we cannot change one of its aspects without affecting the whole; it is not reasonable to want at all cost to mold exotic cultures based on the norms of our own.[84]

Time and again, Métraux attributed to his discipline a beneficial influence on colonial administration: the anthropologist taught the cultural complexity and alienness of "peoples called primitive," underlining the "unforeseen and often catastrophic" consequences of "brutally imposed cultural changes" and emphatically popularizing cultural relativism.[85] Cleansed of its colonial past, anthropology could be identified with the future of humanity—a humanity that this science articulated in terms of cultural difference.

Antiracism, Developmental Economics, and Homogenization

At the turn into the 1950s, then, we find French ethnologists using the arsenal of arguments that Lévi-Strauss would famously deploy in *Tristes tropiques*: an open denunciation of colonialism; the description of the ethnographer as an incarnation of Western power now successfully extricating him- or herself from the embarrassing position of colonial officer; an advocacy of the causes of the indigenous and the colonized; and the reconceptualization of ethnology as the only science untainted by racism and capable of rejecting colonial homogenization and false humanisms. Backed by its leadership in an international campaign against racism, anthropology could indeed recast itself as new and young, the "most human of the human sciences," and the only real source of a new, true humanism of human difference.

The antiracism campaign offers a useful background for understanding the relationship between anthropology and the difficult issues of colonial politics in the 1950s, because in both French Algeria and the "Third World" the promise of ethnological humanism was not nearly as sustained as all this discussion suggests.[86] Shepard argues that the policy of the French government in Algeria benefited considerably from UNESCO's networks, particularly through the intermediary of Jacques Soustelle, the ethnologist turned Gaullist politician who played an important role in the French state's response to the Algerian insurrection after his appointment and the application of the policy of *intégration*.[87] At the other end of the political spectrum, Lévi-Strauss rejected *intégration*—indeed, it corresponded to what he called "homogenization"—and had no qualms about reiterating his "disgust" at French policy.[88] But even he never expressed himself in quite the same forceful terms as Leiris, who went on to sign the "Manifesto of 121" advocating insubordination to military orders in Algeria.[89]

To mark one's political distance from Soustelle (or Griaule) is easy; to think about the complicated politics of economic development and the place of ethnological humanism is far trickier—as Lévi-Strauss noted at the close of his *Race et histoire*. Like Leroi-Gourhan and Leiris, he insisted that cultures were dynamic entities; this explains why, for him, in text after text, the threat they faced was *not* colonialism or industrialization but the *homogenization* that underwrote these phenomena. The gaze that eliminates otherness; the removal of differentials to the benefit of a world mapped and controlled; the "total man" who can be represented without loss: this kind of homogenization is isomorphic with transparency.

The need to preserve the diversity of cultures in a world which is threatened by monotony and uniformity has surely not escaped our international institutions. They must also be aware that it is not enough to nurture local traditions and to save the past for a short period longer. It is diversity itself which must be saved, not the outward and visible form in which each period has clothed that diversity, and which can never be preserved beyond the period which gave it birth. We must therefore hearken to the stirrings of new life, foster latent potentialities, and encourage every natural inclination for collaboration which the future history of the world may hold.[90]

In other words, cross-cultural collaboration, which of course included power dynamics, had to allow for the modification of cultures on their own—or, in a manner closely echoing Leroi-Gourhan's, for "coalitions" of cultures.[91] But the Western development of other societies was destructive through and through:

Grappling with the problems of the industrialization of underdeveloped countries, Western civilization first meets with the deformed image, as if unchanged through centuries, of the destruction that it first had to perpetrate in order to exist. In the same manner, although on a more reduced scale, we would be wrong to believe that the coming into contact of mechanized civilization with those populations that had remained the most alien to it takes place in the abstract. In fact, long before an acknowledged contact occurs, some anticipated effects are felt for many years, and in two ways: either in the form of a second destruction from a distance, or in that of an aspiration, which is also equivalent to a destruction.[92]

Lévi-Strauss's critique of homogeneity amounted to a rejection, not only of integrationist policy, but of all assimilation of an "other" into the self or the same.

Métraux, by contrast, was more favorable to top-down, UNESCO-led developmental economics, because he felt that it was possible to shield it through a new, antiracist humanism. True, he was concerned that humanitarian efforts to improve the lot of others might destroy particularity.[93] Yet problems such as hunger rendered essential the introduction of techniques that facilitated survival even at this price; the role of specialists in this kind of technical transformation and development was largely a positive one. As he wrote in the *UNESCO Courier*, feeding the starving must be balanced against what they would not accept; but feeding them took priority over protecting them from, say, new agricultural techniques.[94] Similarly, Métraux explained that education for indigenous populations had to be understood as a right, which had to be protected precisely in order to protect these groups.[95] In these proposals we see something akin to Leiris's ambivalent project of helping the colonized. But Métraux felt safe going one step further: in a February 1958 article on the emergence of new technical elites—transnational in the sense of belonging to international organizations or of emerging from developing cultures and guiding their development—he pointed out these elites' technical, educational, and even democratic achievements.[96] International cooperation needed new partners in each country, and Métraux did not deem these new elites to be as tainted by neocolonial policies as Lévi-Strauss did.

Conclusion: A New Consensus

The excitement around UNESCO's antiracism campaign should not be taken to indicate a successful overcoming of past or present faults.[97] Decrying racism in this manner was quite safe. The campaign nevertheless contributed significantly to the establishment of a middle- and highbrow consensus against racism and in favor of "respect" for other cultures, which spread quickly to mainstream magazines. In a very different direction, Aimé Césaire made patently clear the implications and importance of the ethnographic shift in his famous *Discours sur le colonialisme* (1950; *Discourse on Colonialism*), in whose revised 1955 edition he defended Lévi-Strauss's *Race and History* from Roger Caillois's Eurocentric attack:

I almost forgot hatred, lying, conceit. I almost forgot M. Roger Caillois. M. Caillois, who from time immemorial has been given the mission to teach a lax and slipshod age rigorous thought and dignified style, M. Caillois, therefore, has just been moved to mighty wrath. Why? Because of the great betrayal of Western ethnography which, with a deplorable deterioration of its sense of responsibility, has been using all its ingenuity of late to cast doubt upon the overall superiority of Western civilization over the exotic civilizations. . . . [His enemy] is those "European intellectuals" who for the last fifty years, "because of exceptionally sharp disappointment and bitterness," have relentlessly "repudiated the various ideals of their culture," and who by so doing maintain, "especially in Europe, a tenacious malaise."[98]

For Césaire, too, ethnology was a science assiduous in inquiring about how societies handle their worlds, and especially about how these worldviews escape European observers, who without it developmentally homogenize and wipe them out. The spectrum of options—care expressed in policies of development; worry over the ongoing destruction and the locking in of humanity into a single manner of life—came to color intellectual politics and even Marxist critiques throughout the 1950s. The new anthropological humanism revealed the blind spots of a traditional humanist gaze, which aimed at intercultural transparency from the Western philosopher's and politician's point of view. Lévi-Strauss's assault on Sartre in his 1962 "History and Dialectic" would make it amply clear that a philosophical anthropology not ethnologically grounded was inadmissible.[99] The new conception of the other and of humanity completed the transformation and redefinition of a science that, handmaiden to colonialism until recently, had now become the first human science of "dissolving Man."[100]

PART II

TRANSPARENCY IN POLITICS

State, Utopia, Grey Zones, 1944–1959

What Is Social Transparency?

A Second Short History

In a text that was also broadcast on the BBC's Radio Londres in December 1944, Jean-Paul Sartre famously described the French resistance as a force of the night, whose truth lay in the purity assaulted by the forces that reigned over the daytime:

To those who were engaged in underground activities, the conditions of their struggle afforded a new kind of experience. . . . They were hunted down in solitude, arrested in solitude. It was completely forlorn and unbefriended that they held out against torture, alone and naked in the presence of torturers clean-shaven, well-fed, and well-clothed, who laughed at their cringing flesh, and to whom an untroubled conscience and a boundless sense of social strength gave every appearance of being in the right.[1]

Sartre raised this imagery of darkness, solitude, and fear to the level of a morality of radical freedom and exhorted the new French government that had emerged into daylight after the liberation of Paris that August to stick to its wartime ideals:

This Republic without institutions, without an army, without police, was something that at each instant every Frenchman had to win and to affirm against Nazism. No one failed in this duty, and now we are on the threshold of another Republic. May this Republic to be set up *in broad daylight* preserve the austere virtue of that other Republic of Silence and *of Night*.[2]

A mystique pervades the clandestine organization—a superior ethics of true freedom. For the solitary individuals who make it up, such a body constitutes a spectral community, a transparency unavailable to the repressive forces that have mastered the daylight. But, when the clandestine comes out into the open and wrests power, it runs the danger of becoming itself oppressive and untrue—a state that would not exist at one with society, in tandem with it, or diaphanously, but would reestablish repressive relations, failing to "preserve the austere virtue" of the "Republic of the Night."

Sartre's dramatic, pointedly unrealistic exhortation was far from fulfilled in the republican regimes that followed the liberation. Yet his text succinctly presents a problem that would remain central to postwar French culture: its conflicting tendencies toward light, transparency, and purge *and also* toward the opposite values of night, privacy, resistance, fantasies of the underground, and social bereftness. To Sartre, social transparency was morally desirable yet coercive: "daylight" was the source of the oppression that violated society. To arise from the shadows was to overwhelm this misleading light with a virtuous one, but one had to worry that the virtue would fade. Sartre quietly asked: Can a transparent society exist in the light? When does the ruling ethics deserve to be the principle of social organization? Who has the right to demand transparency, and who might be forced back in the dark?

Sartre's portrayal of the resistance as an ideal still alive after the Liberation encapsulates the conflicting demand for an ethical transparency that would exist without institutional enforcement. This demand summed up histories and traditions of advocating, but also problematizing, social transparency. Some of them were being countermobilized by the French Communist Party to claim political authenticity and governmental virtue.

The Concern with Social Transparency

The concern with social transparency is not specific to the postwar period or to French culture. Nor is it just an abstract or intellectual concern; it is a vivid and multifaceted political one, which affects a wide range of problems—from the definition of a religious community to the use of language, from ethnic particularity to policing, from norms to social exclusion. Several traditions that concerned transparency in the community, in the individual, and in interpersonal relations of "fusion" (as in love) painted utopias side by side with realities and promised that social and intersubjective transparency either existed or would become possible. This chapter outlines a number of such traditions that were highly visible in postwar France, starting with the Catholic tradition, and reviews motifs of social transparency during the eighteenth and nineteenth centuries and their multiplication and expansion to new domains, such as architecture and urbanism. My intention is not to be exhaustive but to set the stage for the specific criticisms intentionally or collaterally directed against "social transparency" that I discuss in subsequent sections.

But when we ask what social transparency is, or why it came to appear as a synonym for totalitarianism in postwar France even if a Sartrean countertransparency could on occasion still be imagined, we must keep two definitions in check. First, in France the idea that the workings of state institutions need to be transparent to citizens generally postdates the publication of the French translation of Solzhenitsyn's *Gulag Archipelago*[3] in 1974–76 and became common currency only in the mid-1980s. Until then, intellectuals were *not* concerned that the French government was insufficiently transparent and they did not think that a surplus of transparency would improve living conditions, equality, or social policy. In Sartre's "Republic of Silence" the occupation had governed in a "false daylight"; and, at least until 1978, the pretense to transparent government meant very little. Second, although postwar French thinkers tended to equate a "transparent society" with a totalitarian one, one should not imagine that this was in response to some "Orwellian" intrusion into citizens' innermost worlds. Orwellian intrusions were not the only possible consequence of general notions of social transparency or of specific operations of the postwar "rule by experts." Rather, the Orwellian scenario represents one point on the spectrum of options related to the infliction of transparency. In another scenario a secular, transparent society, by overcoming separation, opacity, and absolute difference, can become homogeneous, and therefore entirely plastic and bluntly dependent on the state's shaping of it. A third scenario discloses fears of a static, morally and politically overregulated normative life. Religious claims around the Catholic community, secular instances and visions of a transparent society (notably in the Enlightenment), and organicist utopias had been presented as unifying theories, premised on natural law or egalitarian thought. But after 1945 these visions seemed troubling and were rejected on the grounds of allowing a certain sort of totalitarianism.

Traditions of Social and Political Transparency
The Church

Central to the history of personal and social transparency is western Christianity, for which transparency was a moral as much as a religious duty. Early Christians focused on of the soul's nakedness before God. Thus Augustine, citing Paul's Letter to the Hebrews, writes: "Indeed, Lord, to your eyes, the abyss of human consciousness is naked. What could be hidden within me, even if I were unwilling to confess it to you? I would be hiding from myself, not myself from you."[4] Augustine speaks about the goal of confession: making oneself transparent through God's intermediary (the priest), and thereby participating in a society that banishes concealed intentions and lies. The torment Augustine suffers when faced with the indiscernibility of God's shape dissipates thanks to an imbalance of visibility: God sees Augustine; but God is visible, recognizable, and present *only insofar as* he remains perpetually unseen and therefore ever present.[5] One-sided transparency before the divine would remain crucial throughout the early modern period.[6]

Christian theology held the transparency of the pure self before God to be essential also to any true community of faith. In medieval Catholicism, confession and communion served as techniques designed to ensure the purity of community: one's visibility to God through them legitimized the cohesiveness of this *ekklēsia*. Just as the technique of confession made the faithful pure and transparent to the priest and, through him, to the entire *ekklēsia*, their sharing in Christ's body and blood in communion created a single body of them all. Post-Reformation Catholic intellectuals—all the way up to neo-Thomists like Jacques Maritain—insisted on this past unity as the model for a community.

A different kind of transparency became significant in early modern reformist movements concerned with a life hermeneutically sealed in the shadow of efficacious grace. Calvinism and Jansenism posed particular threats to the French Catholic understanding of soul and community insofar as their organization of transparency was very different.[7] Abandoning confession and communion, they cultivated a direct relationship between oneself and God; in Calvinism, such a relationship was pursued through "works," which never guaranteed the attainment of divine grace; in Jansenism, it imposed a community, in the absence of confession, through a more direct engagement in the purification of the self before God. Scholars have commented on the role of Gallican and Jansenist traditions in the constitution of something like a French national–religious body where the (self-)regulation of the faithful indicated God's great distance from human affairs.[8]

The French Revolution and the Legacy of the Terror

Secular developments in the eighteenth century often maneuvered in and around this theological language. Rousseau's depiction of transparency, his endorsement of festivals of active participation, and his opposition to the theater as an opaque spectacle that corrupted social mores could be read as trailing off Calvinist motifs.[9] During the Enlightenment, transparency began to be associated with hopes in a life unmediated by non-egalitarianism and superstition, with the role of language in a pure "national spirit," and with problems of sovereignty over populations.[10] The utopian tradition relied on and recalibrated paradisiac motifs; cardinal among them, as Bronisław Baczko has argued, was the theme of the utopian city as a "transparent whole." Claude Nicolas Ledoux's architectural designs were as relevant to this new world resplendent with light as were utopias in the style of Louis-Sébastien Mercier.[11]

Hence the 1789 French Revolution grappled at every turn with problems concerning a transparent society, repeatedly postulating it as a social ideal. Article 15 of the 1789 Declaration of the Rights of Man stated: "Every community has a right to demand of all its agents an account of their conduct." (Only a year earlier, Jean-François Féraud's Dictionaire critique de la langue française had cited a passage claiming that "nothing inspires such terror [among the English] as seeing their administration be transparent, its mysteries revealed to foreigners.")[12] With the Revolution, the cry for transparency in society and government resonated widely, from the revolutionary demand that the public be allowed to witness parliamentary debates to the Great Fear, and from the obsessions with secrecy and conspiracy to the Law of Suspects of September 17, 1793. Transparency became a focal point in some of the most forceful episodes of the Revolution: Robespierre's introduction of the "Reign of Virtue," the festivals of 1793–94, and above all the Terror itself.[13] In his famous advocacy of republican Virtue, Robespierre lays out the terms of the continuing negotiation of transparency:

Republican virtue can be considered in relation to the people and in relation to the government; it is necessary in both. When only the government lacks virtue, there remains a resource in the people's virtue; but when the people itself is corrupted, liberty is already lost.[14]

The violent "transparency" of the Terror remains notorious and it would be a staple of later projects to transform society.[15] Revolutionary transparency would matter to nineteenth-century arguments, counterrevolutionary as well as liberal, which attempted to recast the Enlightenment's heritage: Manfred Schneider has described Charles Fourier's utopianism as profoundly involved in the creation of a social transparency that, unlike Robespierre's, would not neutralize individuality but rather recognize the chaotic nature of inner life and transform society so as to harmonize the two.[16]

The French Revolution's engagement with transparency was also the central point of reference in the immediate post-1944 period, and it is worth interrupting the chronological sequence to point out this link. Communists consistently adopted Marx's view that 1789 had been a bourgeois revolution—the first, and one to be followed by the communist revolution, but they also believed that the Terror had sought to keep in check the popular committees and proletarian-led violence that might have made room for a workers' revolution.[17] The intellectual circle of Robert Antelme, Dionys Mascolo, Marguerite Duras, and Maurice Blanchot looked at the Terror as a request for a pure and fraternal community. Writing about Saint-Just in 1946, Mascolo asked about the chances of a new humanism finally emerging from the confrontation with the Terror and its constitutive role in modernity.[18] Blanchot, in his 1948 novel Le Très-Haut (*The Most High*), described a transparent postrevolutionary society in which the narrator-protagonist is utterly immersed in a Hegelian state that fully expresses him:

That everyone was equally faithful to the law—ah, that idea intoxicated me. Everyone seemed to be acting only in their own interests, everyone performed obscure acts, and yet there was a halo of light around these hidden lives: there wasn't anyone who didn't see every other person as a hope, a surprise, and who didn't approach him knowingly. So, I asked myself, what is this State? *It's in me, I feel its existence in everything I do, through every fiber of my body.*[19]

No theory of social transparency could be further-reaching or more perverse than this life lived as literature. That the postrevolutionary moment pervades "every fiber of my body" constituted for Blanchot the very premise of a totalitarian dystopia.[20] No "pure" society was possible, because life lacked the transparency so necessary in revolution and in writing:

Revolutionary action explodes with the same force and the same facility as the writer who has only to set down a few words side by side in order to change the world. Revolutionary action also has the same demand for purity, and the certainty that everything it does has absolute value. . . . [With the Law of Suspects,] no one has a right to a private life any longer, everything is public, and the most guilty person is the suspect—the person who has a secret, who keeps a thought, an intimacy to himself. And in the end, no one has a right to his life any longer.[21]

As we shall see, this *imaginaire* of transparency, totalitarianism, and violence would return with the intellectual circle around Claude Lefort and François Furet.

Marxism and Socialism

A different subtext involving transparency persisted throughout the nineteenth century across nationalist and socialist ideals, and in new practices of the state.[22] Nationalism's claim to the status of a transparent ideology is, of course, a subject of Benedict Anderson's *Imagined Communities*, which has inspired a huge volume of work.[23] Michel Foucault has argued that the century allowed the coalescence of ideals of total surveillance; this had begun with Bentham and his coupling of transparency of the self with panoptic supervision[24] and found expression at the state level in the figure of Napoleon, who "wished to arrange around him a mechanism of power that would enable him to see the smallest event that occurred in the state he governed; he intended, by means of the rigorous discipline that he imposed, 'to embrace the whole of this vast machine' without the slightest detail escaping his attention."[25]

In 1815 Benjamin Constant had observed something similar:

The conquerors of our day, peoples or princes, want their empires to possess a unified surface over which the proud eye of power can wander without encountering any inequality that hurts or limits its view. The same code, the same measurements, the same regulations and, if possible, the same language will proclaim the perfection of the social organization. . . . Above all else, the great word of today is uniformity.[26]

One need not identify this perceptual sovereignty with Napoleon or even prioritize the state and the law as sites of social transparency (as Bentham and Constant imagined) in order to notice its preponderance. Different transparentist hopes came to be attached to nineteenth-century political theories, especially to socialism around the 1848 revolutions, just as authenticity, biological purity, and sincerity became catchwords for the Right. For Marx, especially the young Marx, the ethical purpose of communism had to be conceived in terms of overcoming the mediation that capitalism imposed through alienation. As the famous passage from the *Economic and Philosophical Manuscripts of 1844* has it:

An immediate consequence of the fact that man is estranged from the product of his labor, from his life-activity, from his species being, is the *estrangement of man* from *man*. When man confronts himself, he is confronted by the *other* man. What applies to a man's relation to his work, to the product of his labor and to himself, also holds of a man's relation to the other man, and to the other man's labor and object of labor. In fact, the proposition that man's species-nature is estranged from him means that one man is estranged from the other, as each of them is from man's essential nature.[27]

The later Marx, who was far more reticent about overcoming alienation, still postulated the need to make human relations transparent,[28] and this was an aspect of his thought that French (and not only French) communists would take very seriously in the twentieth century. The idea that Marx had promised, for better or worse, a world in which mediation would be effaced fueled the ethical justification of communist revolutions,[29] and it remained central to the Marxist dream. From the beginning of the twentieth century on, socialists and revolutionary syndicalists in France felt compelled to rethink the demands of parliamentarism and the capacity of parties to mobilize and accurately represent popular will. As the historian Romain Ducoulombier has argued, the left-wing parties of the Third Republic—notably their socialist and revolutionary-syndicalist components, represented by Jean Jaurès, Gracchus Babeuf, and Georges Sorel—played at intimidating the government through the "purity" of their representation of the people.[30] Communism and the Popular Front inherited this technique, which achieved a "general will" politics by criticizing representative government for its clear failure to accommodate popular will.

Or, as Walter Benjamin exclaimed in 1929, "To live in a glass house is a revolutionary virtue par excellence."[31]

Politics and Society

The right had its own glass houses, whether loved or feared. Gustave Le Bon's vision of the crowd as the "last sovereign force of our times" portrayed the crowd leader as hypnotized by the same gestures with which he hypnotized the crowd. When a mass of people was reduced to irrational thinking through a blend of unconscious mimesis and contagion, the leader's role was to pull the right images from the early life of the race in order to conduct the crowd most efficiently: both for the leader and for the racial crowd, transparency arose from this equation between race, crowd, and power. Promising to render social relations harmonious, right-wing movements aimed, in a consistently antibourgeois and antiparliamentary fashion, at the purity of a race, class, or national community.

By 1920 social transparency was an ideal shared by the Right and the Left, in and beyond France, and especially among fascist movements.[32] Soviet communism and the Comintern preached the revolutionary overcoming of capitalism on a journey toward a society unburdened by moral distortions or by social class. In François Châtelet and Évelyne Pisier-Kouchner's felicitous expression, communist society bore in it a tripartite dream of "abundance, transparency, and the repression of all politics and all forms of domination."[33] In Mussolini's Fascist Italy, corporatism promised a political–economic functioning coextensive with society, which would not fall into the feared fragmentation of the bourgeois world. German National Socialism imposed a social transparency specific to the racially purified New Man, with a culture based on its image and force.[34]

It has long been known that, in the main, the progressivist and rationalist philosophers of the French Third Republic committed to a teleological history according to which the human being was gradually coming to understand the world in a purer, more rational, more universalistic fashion.[35] But, as we have seen in Brunschvicg's case, epistemological transparency in late neo-Kantianism requested not only mathematical and intellectual progress but political and communicative openness. Sociology was no less involved in a negotiation of social transparency; indeed, central among the problems that sociologists faced, especially in the Durkheimian school, was the development of modernity as a process that combined "moral density," the effacement of myth, and the emergence of the division of labor. Moral density—which, for Durkheim, grew together with "material density" and the concentration of the population—indicated the entanglement of social relations that followed the overcoming of premodern social segmentation. It offered a rationale for individuation: in the multiplication of entanglements, people found themselves differentiated only alongside threads of entanglement.

Nevertheless, in the 1930s and especially outside professional ethnographic circles, Durkheim's thought was often considered in the light of his own understanding of modernization as a process of demystification and homogenization of society and thought. Here "density" lost the connotation of complexity, because the modern loss of the sacred—according to Durkheim's *Elementary Forms of Religious Life*—amounted to a social homogenization that destroyed not only ecstasy but true difference as well. The Collège de sociologie that Georges Bataille and Roger Caillois co-founded was specifically invested in using Durkheimian sociology to counter this desymbolization and de-differentiation of society, since the effacement of the sacred undermined the egalitarian chances of socialism.[36] Hoping to recapture a primitive, heterogeneous sacredness and to create a new community without succumbing to the danger of fascism, the Collège remained a singular, tense, precarious, and ultimately short-lived endeavor.

Art and Architecture

In 1930s' sociological thought, contradictions in conceptions of society and community could be tied to the political pressures of the decade, from the rise of Nazism to Stalin's constitution. Far more committed to an identification of social transparency with politics and the future was early twentieth-century avant-garde art, particularly art that sought to restart the world, as Kasimir Malevich's *Black Square* of 1915 or André Breton's surrealism. The artist's mind was a refractory out of which the world might be conceived anew; pre-aesthetic reality could be denied and reformed from top to bottom, in a gesture of aesthetic genius.[37] Transparency and the experience of art were already at stake in Albert Gleizes and Jean Metzinger's *Du cubisme* (1912); cubism was invested in an artwork–audience relationship, as Guillaume Apollinaire would emphasize when he called it "extremely lucid and pure."[38] At stake in other movements—for example, Malevich's suprematism—was an ideatic transparency available to the artist and related especially to the power of imposing one's will on the world. Futurism, too, used transparency as a goal: in Giacomo Balla and Fortunato Depero's 1915 pamphlet *Ricostruzione futurista dell'universo* ("Futurist

Reconstruction of the Universe"), the principle of the "futurist reconstruction of the universe" is said to be (1) *astratto* (abstract); (2) *dinamico* (dynamic); and (3) *trasparentissimo* (most transparent: "from the speed and volatility of the plastic complex, which must appear and disappear, most light and impalpable").[39] Francis Picabia presented a theory of transparency in 1930,[40] and René Magritte's famous painting *The Human Condition* (1933) is of a canvas vanishing in front of a window, all but effacing the function of representation.

In architecture, social transparency became an imperative in the early twentieth century, not least thanks to the availability of large glass surfaces, for instance, Bruno Taut's 1914 Glasbau (Glass Pavilion), Pierre Chareau's Maison de verre (1927–31), Mies van der Rohe's planned Friedrichstraße station in Berlin (1921) and his Farnsworth House (1945–51), and, following from rather different premises, Philip Johnson's Glass House (1949) and Tadao Ando's Ishihara House (1977).[41] Influential on Taut and on Le Corbusier, and central to the German culture identifying glass and transparency with political openness was of course Paul Scheerbart's utopian book *Glasarchitektur* (1914), which equates glass ("we can indeed speak of a glass culture") with the new: "The new glass environment will completely transform mankind, and it remains only to wish that the new glass culture will not find too many opponents . . . [we] want to strive after the new, with all the resources at our disposal; more power to them!"[42] In France, the artistic experience was no less significant, no less political, due in part to long-standing concerns with public housing, in part to the development of modernist aesthetics.[43]

Le Corbusier dominated the French engagement with modernization and transparency, calling for architecture to rid itself of tradition and the opaque social and physical structures that hampered modern life, to break the barrier between imagination and creativity, and to become, thanks to technology, a "pure creation of the mind." He wrote ecstatically of how the Parthenon exemplified this spirit and had united Athenians in a community. This begged for repetition today:

[The Parthenon] happened at a moment when . . . a man, stirred by the noblest thoughts, crystallized them in a plastic work of light and shade. . . . Here, the purest witness to the physiology of sensation, and to the mathematical speculation attached to it, is fixed and determined: we are riveted by our senses; we are ravished in our minds; we touch the axis of harmony. No question of religious dogma enters in; no symbolical description, no naturalistic representation; there is nothing but pure forms in precise relationships. For two thousand years, those who have seen the Parthenon have felt that here was a decisive moment in Architecture. We are at a decisive moment.[44]

Although the "right state of mind" for touching the axis of harmony "[did] not exist" in Le Corbusier's day,[45] there was, he claimed, both a technological and an architectural capacity to hypostatize the architect's pure idea. This translation or actualization of the supposedly beautiful mind would then turn homes into triumphs of mass production,[46] combatting, through them, "the cult of family and race,"[47] resolve the fundamental political question of "architecture or revolution" in favor of the former, and realize a postbourgeois transparency in mass-produced, tool-like homes.[48] Against the "sickness" of the city and of the modern mind, Le Corbusier proposed a series of organicist metaphors and a new type of organism,[49] implementing a physical and mental urban hygiene.[50]

⟡

In all these traditions, transparency is a matter of society's clarity, availability, and opening up, *not* a promise of good government. That good government be itself fairly transparent—in the sense of socially responsive and responsible—was an ideal vaguely related to the tradition of natural law and the obsession with constitutions and bills of rights that began in the last quarter of the eighteenth century. Yet there, too, the purpose of constitutions was not to render the processes of government visible to the citizenry but to provide a framework that refused—or at least severely limited—arbitrary power and served as a legal structure of social forms. If these ideals were political, they were fundamentally moral as well. They not only created bonds through images of a crystalline community but generated normative priorities for both the state and its citizens.

Thus we may note that, whereas in recent years the scholarly interest in transparency has been limited to recent, "neoliberal" developments concerning the transparency of government and perhaps the openness of society, transparency as a problem has concerned above all the interweaving and conflicts between state agents and society, their competing dreams and utopias, their norms and pursuits. (As should be clear by now, by "the state" I mean not a monolithic apparatus of governance but the broader system or the framework that, to the society governed by its various agencies, *appears* as a largely unitary apparatus and actor.)

Social Transparency after World War II

Long before World War II, but even more afterward, citizens' and subjects' accessibility to the state was a matter of concern all across Europe. Society had to be *unitary* and its members *available* to the state, to legal rule and everyday management. The urge to identify internal threats—radicalized by interwar fears of communist and fascist infiltration and espionage—was strong in wartime governments *and* resistance movements (which were especially keen to punish traitors) across Europe. Sartre's *résistancialiste* imagery in the "Republic of Silence" testifies to it. Purity was as essential as it was brittle, and the false transparency of Vichy had to be negated and replaced by the true transparency of a new era. At the end of the war some philosophers would go further along this line. Merleau-Ponty decried transparent society as a society of statues; in *The Most High*, Maurice Blanchot described a society and a subjectivity so profoundly permeated by the state that only an epidemic like that described by Albert Camus in *The Plague* could disrupt their union. Transparency often entailed isomorphism between self and society: the purer the self was, the better, more harmonious, more reflective society would be, and the less internally divided or miasmic society was, the more the individual self would have a wholeness of purpose. Of course, accentuating this isomorphism after the war only made its terms appear fantastic or oxymoronic.

At the same time, especially because of the antifascist rhetoric of the Allies and the Soviet Union's facility in persuading outsiders that communist rule was rule by the people itself, it became imperative in western Europe to provide forms of government that displayed a good measure of democratic identification between people and the state. Ever since 1917, when the Bolsheviks had published secret wartime treaties, disrupting the French "enthusiasm" for secret diplomacy, the political danger of being caught in acts of secrecy—a necessary feature of diplomatic work and an important one for French soft power—had been quite clear, though France had carefully insisted on keeping diplomatic work secret.[51] In France, the Third Republic had evidently failed at democratic identification, and the pressure to come up with a superior form of republican rule was doubled by the sense that the Liberation had been not only political but moral. Part of this pursuit was perhaps constitutionally satisfied: as noted in Article 2 of the Fourth Republic's constitution of October 27, 1946, and reiterated in the Fifth Republic's constitution of October 4, 1958, the principle (*principe*) of the Fourth

Republic was *gouvernement du peuple, par le peuple et pour le peuple.* Enshrining this fragment of Lincoln's Gettysburg Address in the constitution gave a semblance of coextensiveness between government and governed, although today it might strike us as a simple formalization of the contrast with Vichy, a recognition of French reliance on American support for liberation, and a convenient expression of republican rhetoric. It had much to do with the need to show the distance between the present and the "secret state" of the nineteenth century.[52] To protest the inapplicability or vagueness of the principle misses the point, namely, that the republican relationship supposedly allowed for this mirroring effect, whereas alternative systems, including communism, Vichy, and the Third Republic, made such government "perish from the Earth."

But there were far more concrete pressures than constitutional flourishes could handle, not least due to the appeal of communist promises. Communist rhetoric contrasted shadowy international trusts and capitalist oligarchies to law and the will of the nation, making short shrift of the pretense to republican coextensiveness of government and governed: "these men whose wealth is created through the sufferings and misery of the people constitute a veritable occult power that keeps legal power in check." Only communism would secure a proper, open space for converting French industrial goods into national wealth, the argument went.[53] Immediate problems relating to collaboration also played a part. The early postwar period was defined on the one hand by a dream for *épuration* ("purification"), commonly known as "the Purge," and, on the other, by the *résistancialiste* repression of the memory of French participation in German and Vichy rule.[54] The title France's attorney general André Mornet gave his 1949 book on the Occupation, *Quatre ans à rayer de notre histoire* (Four Years to Strike Out of Our History), metaphorically seeks to expunge the blight or disease of "rotten," "infested" Vichy from the social body. In fact, of course, such "deleting" of them simply veiled those four years (and Mornet had reasons to want his own record forgotten).[55] The shearing of women's hair for "horizontal collaboration" is a classic reference point for this cleansing: it made these women immediately identifiable, fully visible to the rest of society (and thus obliged them to remove themselves from public view), and at the same time it absolved those "with hair" of any responsibility by suggesting that men and women who participated in social life were clear of the collaborationist stigma.[56]

We can thus identify a series of social tensions between the desire for transformation and the pragmatic difficulties of managing even what was available. Police and the black market, which I consider in the next chapter, provide excellent examples of the creation of such tensions. The historian of urbanism Kenny Cupers has similarly signaled a tension in the mass production of new urban spaces in postwar housing projects, noting that architecture's role in modernization was constrained by the limitations on social engineering imposed by "a liberal capitalist democracy, the impact of private development, and the dynamics of mass consumerism" and led to the production of a new kind of consumer and user, at once designed and private, withdrawn yet socially participating.[57] The French state sought to expand and rationalize its access to the population, and opposition to what was perceived as state intrusion was expressed in different areas of intellectual work. Projects of social transformation would be met with retreat and even derision by an ever more disappointed public. Similarly, in the late 1960s, medical and psychiatric discourse was routinely derided for molding structured subjects pliable to the state, while the antimedicine and antipsychiatry of the 1970s would raise the question (in France and elsewhere) of the kind of therapeutics that might remain immune to enforced subjectivity.[58] Transparency was at stake in a broad range of discussions: the negotiation of what is within the state's purview in everyday life, obstacles and resistance to its intervention, the government's power over family and social or ethnic groups, access to information, the development of spheres of legitimate privacy, the separation of powers and their respective scope, the role and place of the police, the possibility and purpose of planning, the potential of science to improve governance and society, anxiety over excessive intrusiveness, fantasies of anti-establishment resistance or escape. Such engagements, at once moral and political, sometimes elaborate, sometimes trivial, give us an idea of the role and degree of a society's "openness" to the state, which figures as a bureaucratic apparatus seeking to render society transparent and plastic for its own purposes. The state's effort created its own shadows—the various responses to its attempts to deal with the asocial and abnormal.

In the mid-1960s, further problems—ranging from immigration, especially from Algeria, to new information technologies—were casting doubt in the possibility of social transparency. In a 1979 study of poverty among the "urban neoproletariat" titled *On est tous dans le brouillard* (We Are All in the

Fog), the anthropologist Colette Pétonnet examined a social space prefiguring the *banlieues* of the past two decades: the *bidonvilles* of (mostly) Spanish and Portuguese immigrants who mixed with an urbanized French working-class population and with immigrants from Algeria and the Maghreb.[59] New concerns with information and exposure in the 1970s prompted more than one philosopher to prize and advocate secrecy, privacy, and freedom of information.[60] The European Economic Community—and the 1980s' pretense to a shared European culture—similarly became a powerful mechanism for increased and homogenizing transparency.[61] As Jacques Derrida hit back in his 1991 book *L'autre cap* (*The Other Heading*):

> The best intentioned of European [cultural] projects, those that are quite apparently and explicitly pluralistic, democratic, and tolerant, may try, in this lovely competition for the "conquest of spirits," to impose the homogeneity of a medium, of discursive norms and models. . . . Under the pretext of pleading for transparency (along with "consensus," "transparency" is one of the master words of the "cultural" discourse I just mentioned), for the univocity of democratic discussion, for communication in public space, for "communicative action," such a discourse tends to impose a model of language that is supposedly favorable to this communication. . . . Claiming to speak in the name of intelligibility, good sense, common sense, or the democratic ethic, this discourse tends, by means of these very things, and as if naturally, to discredit anything that complicates this model. It tends to suspect or repress anything that bends, overdetermines, or even questions, in theory or in practice, this idea of language.[62]

Or, in the terms offered by the anthropologist Mayanthi Fernando in her discussion of Muslim privacy and its conflicts with French secularism since 1989:

> The desire to bring Islam into the light emerges from a widespread anxiety about so-called underground Islam. . . . The semiprivate existence of this [unregulated] Islam makes secular republicans nervous precisely because it remains out of public view. Muslims must not pray conspicuously in public, but they must not pray too inconspicuously either; they must be neither too visible nor too invisible.[63]

If the social is, in Stanley Cavell's beautiful and relevant phrase, "the scene of mazes of meaning," then it matters to see "transparency"—a crossroad of meanings—not simply as a demand for transparent government or justice, but as *a conflictual negotiation of the accessibility or resistance of social formations to the state and vice versa.* Doing so allows historians to engage much more closely with the cultural interstices of governmental author-ity.[64] As state apparatuses, individuals, scientific organizations, and other social agents negotiated the reach of the state into everyday affairs and the visibility of its subjects, they fundamentally affected the *moral* and nor-mative understanding of a good society along with the *socioeconomic*, and well beyond the legal concern with privacy. Thus fears of a radical intru-sion into citizens' privacy tell only a part of the story—and so do dreams of a pure community, or the idea (which, as we shall see, dates in France to the late 1970s) that a state's workings need themselves to be transparent. In what follows, social transparency will designate a society whose members and organizations are simply *available* to state institutions and do not pro-duce (or appear to produce) grey areas or moral and economic communi-ties that exceed that society's authority and challenge its control.

Between State and Society, I

The Police, the Black Market, and
"the Gangster" after the Liberation

The Problem with the Police

Transparency was not only an ideal but a very concrete norm in practices of governance. Perhaps this should be attributed above all to the establishment of the modern police. Etymologically, the French noun *police*—like its English counterpart—is related to the well-known family of words around the ancient Greek *polis*, especially *politēs* ("citizen") and *politeia* ("polity"): it derives from the medieval Latin *politia*, which was a transliteration of *politeia* and designated the government and its organization of the country.[1] In *Discipline and Punish*, Michel Foucault wrote eloquently of an ideal that dates back to Napoleonic police but continues to the present:

It is an apparatus that must be coextensive with the entire social body. . . . Police power must bear "over everything" . . . the dust of events, actions, behavior, opinions—"everything that happens." . . . With the police, one is in the indefinite world of a supervision that seeks ideally to reach the most elementary particle, the most passing phenomenon of the social body.[2]

Foucault went on to define discipline as "a type of power, a modality for its exercise, comprising a whole set of instruments, techniques, procedures, levels of application, targets," noting its deployment by "state apparatuses whose major, if not exclusive, function is to assure that discipline reigns over society as a whole (the police)."[3] He read the imperatives of nineteenth-century police with the acuity of a military strategist attuned to post-1968 anxieties; and he was not inventing a straw-man ideal to attack. The historian Louis Bergeron, too, declares Napoleon's "primordial interest" in the police "disquieting."[4] Developments in anthropometry with Alphonse Bertillon (1890s) and especially Edmond Locard (1920s) had furthered the highly similar ideal of a complete policing eye: "A perfect police is the mark of a state that has reached the highest point of civilization."[5] Locard's *criminalistique* conceived of crime scenes as spaces filled with fingerprints, chemical traces, and other physical clues, and of the policeman as someone in possession of objective and complete knowledge, whose proof was not troubled by doubt, deception, or error committed in good faith.[6]

Since its inception, the modern French police has been a complicated organization, comprising several bodies: a national police (the Sureté), local police forces, the *gendarmerie*, and policing services in various ministries.[7] How these were to constitute a reliable and competent tool for social order was a permanent concern, not least because its tasks were manifold, far-reaching, often oppressive, yet also quotidian, paperwork-oriented, haphazard.[8]

The identification of the police with the state was institutionally strengthened during the Vichy period, when the various police corps were nationalized for the first time and made to serve the state as a whole. In addition to its despised *milice*, Vichy inaugurated the Groupes mobiles de réserve, designed to fight against the resistance. This contributed to the perception of the police as supercollaborators and embodiments of the regime—a repressive arm of the state. Its porous relation with the army and the *milice* consolidated that impression. As the historian Alain Pinel has noted, "that Vichy deployed the police in a civil war left profound scars on collective memory."[9]

Healing such scars by purging the police would prove no easy task in 1944–45. Nowhere did the Purge trouble state efforts to increase social transparency as deeply as in relation to the police. Presumed to be an unproblematic mediator, the police in fact obstructed state–society relations and confirmed that the former had no sure way of parsing the latter nonrepressively. And, if society was suspect, the police were even more so. Police allegiance to the Fourth Republic seemed doubtful, but the repressive role of the police remained highly visible. It rubbed off on republican governments unable to control the police, yet blamed for its actions anyway.

Attempts at rehabilitation of the police began on August 15, 1944. As the Allies advanced, the groups L'Honneur de la Police, Police et Patrie, and Front national de la Police met, and the Paris police went on strike. It was a significant gesture, which allowed some policemen to fight with the Free French and ballooned to mythical status; police historians would later purport that policemen had made "the highest number of any resistance group" and talk of their *souffrances glorieuses*.[10] But even though some policemen had indeed served the resistance, the rather ridiculous portrayal of the police as a "vanguard" of the Liberation or a "guide and guardian of honor, in war as in peace"[11] persuaded few that this was the kind of institution to (in Sartre's words) "preserve the austere virtue of that other Republic".

Historians have described the chaotic, frequently spontaneous policing that followed the Liberation, and the moral as well as procedural incompleteness of the Purge, which left the basic organizational structure and 70 percent of officers in place.[12] Police cadres were essential to the new regime, not least because they were tasked with carrying out the *épuration* of their own ranks. Many resented it and loudly denied that serving during the Occupation had constituted an act of collaboration *eo ipso*; it only meant doing their duty for the police to "cast its rays all over France" under the regime that ruled the territory.[13]

The police were quickly accused of failing their purpose of securing transparent order and surveillance in the later 1940s. This appears most clearly from the debate over police strikes. After the celebrated strike of August 1944 (which made the liberation of Paris easier), a law in October 19, 1946, granted policemen the right to strike, among other citizens' rights they had not had. Yet it quickly became clear to the *tripartiste*, then to the *troisième force* governments of 1947–48 that this right put them in a bind. Police unions had already threatened work-to-rule strikes in September 1945, then escalated and actually carried out such strikes in December, and then threatened them again in September 1946. After the law was passed, they carried out two more strikes, in March and November 1947; and they threatened to do so again in August 1948.[14] Targeting low salaries and poor working conditions, police unions explicitly invoked their "glorious" strike during the liberation of Paris in August 1944 as a precedent, which clearly implied that they were resolved to improve their standing even at the cost of institutional crisis. The frequency and recursivity of this threat struck at the heart of the government's legitimacy and suggested that it was weak and incapable of consistent rule; in turn, this perception decoupled the government from the police, pitting the state against itself. Police unionization complicated matters further by turning the police into a force whose inner divisions, political priorities, and loyalty were unclear. Since officers were suspected of communist or Gaullist commitments that might threaten the state itself, the idea of a police strike was especially delicate. An article in *France-Dimanche*, not reliable as much as significant for the anxiety it stoked about police disloyalty, claimed: "In the police and the CRS [Compagnies républicaines de sécurité] . . . 30 percent have more or less direct ties with the communists, and 20 percent are Gaullists."[15] The author speculated that violent confrontation between communists and Gaullists would be impossible to control.

At the beginning of the Cold War, the anxiety aroused by threats to a regime's legitimacy was far from pointless. For ministers and *hauts fonctionnaires* (and among the socialists too), the sheer idea of a police strike was incommensurable with a modern European state. In 1948, the socialist president of the Commission de l'Intérieur denounced police strikes on the principle that "in any state deserving of the name, the police is the guarantor of all freedoms, including the right to strike. This is the reason why one cannot in a republican regime conceive of a strike of the police any more than a strike of the legislative or the executive branches."[16] Jules Moch, the minister of the interior, further argued that depriving policemen of the right to strike would not eliminate recourse for grievances; it would only facilitate "the maintenance of public order" by making it "possible to sanction, outside of disciplinary guarantees, any concerted cessation of service and all acts of collective indiscipline by police personnel."[17] (Meanwhile, to win support and enhance their legitimacy, the communists explicitly treated the police as allies of the working class and defended their right to strike.)[18]

The revocation of the right to strike in 1948 left the police even more disgruntled: the loss of a hard-won recourse for quality-of-life grievances added to the mistrust generated by the Purge. Indignities then piled on— including a restriction in the use of weaponry that was experienced as a violent declawing[19] and budget cuts that resulted in cutbacks on provisions and in a considerable shrinkage of the police force itself.[20]

It is worth considering the effect of this double-edged change in the role of the police as an arm of the state. Among the public, the impression persisted that the police was a hostile, prurient, oppressive institution, not one apt to foster social harmony. As the sociologist Jean-Louis Loubet del Bayle sees it, the state suffered from both the image of police *instrumentality*—its status as an apparatus of repression —and that of police *insularity*—its functioning as " an autonomous instrument, resisting external constraints, notably those of the political system," which made it appear as a "state within the state."[21] This image was further damaged by accusations of occasional and systemic incompetence, beliefs that the police longed for Vichy or protected those who had not been purged, mistrust about its unionization, and suspicions of collusion with black marketeering.[22] Under a cloud of scandals (real and imagined), the ministry of the interior attempted to control the dissemination of information that might harm the police.[23] In short, the belief was widespread that the police served goals alien to public order, social openness, and citizen security.[24] Many routinely despised policemen as "dirty cops" (*sales flics*) and Pétainists.[25]

The sense that the government shared this distaste exacerbated both police insularity and public mistrust. Police newspapers complained extensively of "malaise" or "discontent" among policemen about their living conditions, civil status, and treatment—by governments as well as by the public.[26] In 1954, the journal *Police de France* asserted that in ending the right of the police to strike, the government had consciously made promises it could not keep. For police unions of different stripes, too, the role of the police in buttressing the regime justified greater support.[27]

In the 1950s, once Algeria became a national problem, government–police conflicts worsened. The government's failure to protect policemen from indictments over "doing their job" and to put behind it the *épuration* of the police was something that "the Fourth Republic would pay for dearly in terms of abandonment, in other words, treason, by a part of its police force during the last months of its existence," when the police "passed in all essentials to the subversive camp" led by the army.[28]

This was the police drama—so distant from the Napoleonic idealization—that played out after the war in newspapers and the parliament, during police unionization and the Purge. The atmosphere of increasing mistrust suspended the police's capacity to present itself as a disinterested intermediary between state and society and to enforce basic social transparency. This was a failure acutely felt by students and leftist intellectuals, as well as by the police themselves.[29] The problem became most evident in the repression of the black market during the late 1940s and, later, in the policing of delinquent and "maladapted" youth. Different paths to disciplining society opened up and, alongside them, a new ethics of the anti-hero did too.

The Black Market, the Police, and the Gangster Counterhero

In postwar France society was *transparent* when its members and organizations were *available* and *accessible* to governance, detailing, and intervention by state institutions. As indicated by the case of the police, too, *available* and *accessible* are opposed here to *hidden from* or *evasive toward* policing, policy implementation, public health, security, education, taxation, and so on. But if the police, imagined as an apparatus through which the state could render the population visible and accessible, was not only *not* succeeding in this task but becoming a locus of opacity and an obstacle, might one look elsewhere for attempts to open up the social body? Yes: other state agencies attempted to open and rationalize society in a number of ways, and they were often rebuffed. Indeed, among the most storied facets of French culture in the post–World War II era is a forceful antagonism between "state" and "society"—between agents of the state and elements in society that seemingly evaded governmental control. The antagonism often involved a pervasive anxiety that the state was interested in and capable of enforcing a transparent society at the expense of privacy, individuality, even authenticity. To intellectuals, this raised fears of totalitarianism. Yet "society" *had* to be relatively transparent to the state, so that the latter would not struggle against extensive distortions of its authority and plans, and subjects would not produce "grey areas" of any sort. At stake across these situations was not exactly the undermining of private life; nor was this about a "closing" of an "open society." Rather, we can speak of limits to the relationships between the state and the individuals, families, and populations within it, and of how these limits were being probed by state agencies and cultural products. "Negotiation of social transparency" is the key concept here; and it addresses both the pressure from different agents and the relative, non-absolute character of this pressure. Articulating the many ways in which state agencies involve themselves in subjects' lives and, conversely, how opposition to that involvement was expressed, keeps questions of privacy and openness in play, while suggesting that what really mattered for the state was how it sanctioned everyday life.

The situation appears paradoxical. Although the French lived in a highly advanced welfare state, with high regard and legal protections for individual privacy, and with laws that even allowed for a measure of feedback from families and social organizations,[30] whole sectors of French society, intellectual life, and politics inclined nevertheless toward antistatist paranoia—and on occasion even celebrated a stateless society—on account of the state's reach into everyday life.[31]

This paranoia has long been explained away as the product of a Marxist-driven intellectual scene that decried democracy and the state as a violent bourgeois sham (an approach mirrored in *poujadisme*'s denunciation of the machinations of the "corrupted brain" in a "vampire tax state"[32] against the "little," "free," truly French, etc.); as a result of the experience of Vichy and the heroization of the resistance; or as the afterlife of an early postwar hope for a superior political regime—a disappointed hope that returned at crucial moments, like the early 1960s. These approaches mistake particular political constellations for a set of concerns that reached into the grain of private life. The present section proposes instead to explain the antagonism as it was felt both by agents of the state and by those who proposed escape from its clutches. To focus on the complex imagery of transparency negotiated in this conflict, we need to look at how this negotiation, which included problems surrounding the police, spanned from economic sovereignty to the psychological treatment of children. All of this occurred at the level of everyday life as much as in imaginings about the future, putting into question but also fortifying the machines and even the concepts of "state" and "society." Such an approach yields a dynamic picture, which explains the demand of "the state" that the public realm be a transparent, available space for it to act on, and permits us to understand the antistatist animus that its involvement left to "society," that is, to subjects and groups within it.

The Black Market

The post-Liberation Purge was not the only way to "purify" society immediately after the war. No less significant was the effort to eliminate the black markets for basic and luxury provisions, which dated to Vichy

and continued largely unimpeded. Blending supply, rationing, and prosecution, this effort encapsulated the principles of a fresh start for society
and of a new kind of state control, one supposed to pursue equality, openness, and efficiency without becoming oppressive or divisive. This was not
really about collaboration: food rationing was vital to the ability of a state-
driven economy to bring goods to the market and provide for the population. Thus the situation licensed a close involvement of the state in its
citizens' lives down to the end of the 1940s. Since September 1940, the
ministry of supply (*ministère du ravitaillement*) had to organize and distribute supplies and *cartes d'alimentation* (vouchers) and to determine prices.
It continued to perform this task well into 1949, when basic items like milk
and paper were still under its purview.[33]

During Vichy, shortages and rationing had been as exasperating
as foreign and collaborationist rule, and certainly more regularly experienced.[34] The historian Kenneth Mouré has argued that "Vichy's failures [to
provide civilians with enough to eat] eroded popular support for Pétain's
regime and its aspirations to build a New Order in France" and "fostered
structural problems that would continue to plague new governments after
the libération."[35] In wartime poems he later published under the title *Soap*,
Francis Ponge linked scarcity and rationing to authentic poetry: "here are
the first notes, then, which I put down on paper in April 1942, at Roanne,
a small town in central France, where my family and I were . . . refugees.
There we were then in the midst of war, that is to say of restrictions of all
kinds, and soap, real soap, was particularly missed. We had only the worst
Ersätze—which did not froth at all."[36] Standing in for a poetry that was itself reduced to an ersatz, *Soap* speaks of an experience of retreat, hiding and
uncleanliness and of the memory of an open society. This motivated Ponge's
own participation in the postwar purge of literature—the purification of
the literary body.[37]

If the extent of political openness, purge, and reconciliation had
roughly been settled by late 1946, socioeconomic transparency had proved
far harder to achieve and was now pursued more aggressively. The continuing black market—which the occupation had rendered "*inevitable*, given
the combination of shortages and fixed prices"—was a one of the main
reasons.[38] As is well known, political liberation did not circumvent either
the substantial reduction in industrial capacity or the continued need for
rationing—nor could it, given the scale of the destruction of infrastructure

in France. In October 1944 fraud and black marketeering were showcased as results of collaboration and "commerce with the enemy." Even after May 1945, officials of the ministry of supply insisted on the clandestine market's "anti-national" character, both in order to blame Vichy and the Germans, thereby stressing their distance from the old ministry, and in order to forget that this rhetoric of denunciation remained exactly the same across the regime change.[39] The effort to ensure and control the circulation of basic goods revealed continuity between the two ministries, their policies, and their rhetoric: not only did the same language persist, but agents of the ministry were now and then decried as collaborators, and the ministry continued to pursue cases of black marketeering dating from 1942. (But only so long as they did not seem to have benefited the resistance; illegal trafficking for the Maquis was at times accepted as a resistance act, even though the relationship between the resistance and the black market was at best ambiguous.)[40]

After 1944, the "black," "parallel," or "clandestine" market was the object of detailed governmental studies. Its persistence signaled that society did not rely on the state for its provisions, and that the regime's control of the economy and society was rigid and insufficient, even though it appeared excessive. As Mark Mazower has written, "the scope and importance of a black market stand in inverse proportion to the power of the state," and, faced with the phenomenon, the new French state certainly demonstrated its limited sovereignty over the economic structures of everyday life.[41] For example, in 1946 the government managed to control sugar supplies completely in only 25 percent of the French *départements*.[42] The notion that "fiscal justice" should be exercised and economic clandestinity overcome worked in tandem with the plan to organize the economy, to end inflation, and to reverse industrial decline rapidly. Yet it also spotlighted the persistence of black marketeering as a rejection of a state-directed economy. Part of the problem was that, with the Liberation, as the conservative politician Jacques Debû-Bridel shrewdly put it, the black market became "endemic." It could no longer be understood as a side effect of "defeat, occupation, clandestine struggle" but was a "durable phenomenon of the nation's economic, social and moral life."[43] Shortfalls in supply and everyday black and grey markets profoundly troubled the sense of the liberated French that their state was capable of delivering justice and non-oppressive governance to its subjects.[44]

The black market eluded its prosecutors in the ministry conceptually as well as economically. It came to figure in their writings as the dominion of gangsters and gangs, who were responsible for major and petty illegal trafficking alike. Ministry memos often claimed that repressive practices suffered from confusion or poor definition of goals, methods, and targets. In response, governments repeatedly reorganized the ministry, its processes and agencies, as if that were a way of attacking the black market.[45] Unable to control the clandestine markets, frustrated ministry agents ignored the conflicting social interests involved and the trivial, even haphazard reasons for engaging in illegal trafficking—for example the desire to make quick money, or sellers' unwillingness to tolerate the socially targeted minimization of profit.[46] Instead, according to internal documents of the ministry of supply that detailed illegal trafficking practices, agents blamed the black market on the existence of huge networks and even postulated a vast secret conspiracy "on a territorial scale" (*à l'échelon du territoire*)—a single organized "gang." The reach of the gang's maneuvers "was such that it showed the disposal of enormous funds and the assurance of protection from the highest level."[47]

Though factually wrong, such fantastic descriptions were not random exaggerations but consequential efforts to respond to a vicious cycle whereby the black market was perpetuated by structural problems that exceeded the ministry's control. The black market was a grey zone: a fundamental opacity that undercut the state's gaze and reach. The pressures of poverty were aligned with mismatched shortages and provisions (basically, a situation where cash was available to many who were willing to offer much more than the official price), and, worse, with the operational weakness and oppressiveness of the policing of supplies. All this exceeded the government's capacities, yet had to be handled, and conspiracy theories constituted one politically acceptable way to explain the state's limitations. Since the early Vichy years, the system itself had created incentives that worked against the official distribution of adequate supplies, largely by imposing a situation that enticed ordinary citizens to "manipulate" it.[48] The paranoid identification of "the enemy" with a vast "gang" explains *both* the belief that socioeconomic transparency was possible "if only" the black market could be defeated *and* the reasoning of state institutions, at once paralyzed and intrusive, in their attempt to make this transparency a reality.

Yet shedding light on the shadows did not dispel them: it merely multiplied them. Policing was tricky, first of all because the problems of the *épuration* were never more troubling for the state's efforts to impose greater transparency on society than in the case of the police itself. Institutionally, the suspicion spread that police departments (including the existing *police économique*) would not understand "the seriousness of the affairs" of the black market and would not care to follow cases with the necessary attention. This suspicion led some within the government to believe that policing by the ministry of supply itself would be essential.[49] Still, proposing a proper police force for the ministry was "delicate"; a short-lived effort to organize such a force from within the ministry was ended in 1947, and control was yielded back to the same disliked economic police that the ministry deemed incapable of tackling the situation.[50] As for inefficiency and powerlessness, rumors ran wild. An article in the newspaper *L'Aurore* claimed, for example, that economic control "costs 912 millions, mobilizes 8,700 functionaries and is powerless against the triumph of the black market."[51] Just as damaging to the ministry were occasional accusations and arrests of market control agents on grounds of corruption.[52] This seems unsurprising, given the petty payroll of the police itself and the temptations of black market practices. A police commissioner directing the Service économique of the Paris prefecture complained to the press that, unlike in the prewar period, when his service was staffed with "honest functionaries," he now directed "a group of youths" who made little money and lived beyond their means: "To tell you the truth, I need a brigade to surveil their activities and even a second brigade to surveil the first."[53] His interviewer countered that the economic police were not just passively corrupt; they also marketed goods clandestinely themselves, selling aperitifs to restaurant owners at prices of their own choice and blackmailing them over past trafficking. Accusations of incompetence and collusion with criminals and black marketeers thus furthered the impression of a corrupt, insular, incompetent, oppressive apparatus. The 1947 Joanovici Affair—the case of a wealthy black marketeer who had supplied the German army but was protected by the Honneur de la Police group of former police *résistants*— was used as evidence in these critiques. Even higher levels were not spared scandal. The wine scandal (*l'affaire des vins*) of 1946–48 was again blamed on a "vast mob" redirecting large quantities of wine from the legal to the black market and pitted Yves Farge, the minister of supply, against government ministers no less than wine merchants. One of the former was Félix Gouin, de Gaulle's successor as president of the provisional government, whom Farge charged unsuccessfully with corruption.[54]

Thus the survival of the black market came to appear as a sign of the government's failure to provide for its society: it signified mistrust in the government on practical rather than political grounds—an attitude woven into the way people went about their daily lives. In a sense, given the shadow of powerful state intervention and the absence of a real free market, the black market served as a surrogate (if banned) "free" market. It was practiced despite the penalty of prison, introduced in 1946; it involved a large part of society; and it persistently mocked the failure of economic and social rule. "Billions of 'black' restaurants function in Paris and provincial cities. . . . Does economic control wear a blindfold over its eyes?"[55] Social transparency was an important variable in the attempt to reach the primary goal of economic control: ensuring an equitable distribution of goods in short supply so as to prevent starvation. But the general feeling was that economic control missed its own social purpose and made society more elusive, hostile, and impenetrable. Ministry agents in fact pursued this crystallization of a state–society contrast as if to heighten the state's authority. The instructions for agents who policed the supplies highlighted the need to insist on the benefits of the open market, which were not obvious:

You must sanction all guilty practices. With severity, but without losing sight of the fact that repression will not be really efficacious unless you have established, by way of a contrast to the fortunate results of your initiative, the antinational character of practices that steal available alimentary products and commodities from the regular market.[56]

That the line into illegality was fuzzy was also suggested in other ministry memos, one of which noted that "it is no secret to anyone that the greatest part of fraudulent *cartes d'alimentation* are not entirely false" but were rather illegally produced in, or obtained from, legal sources (printing houses or even ministry agents).[57] Nevertheless, the point became one of *enforcing conviction* in the regulated market by contrasting it to the clandestine, "antinational" alternative.

The very fact that repression contributed to the persistence of the black market by trying to force production, supply, and circulation into a rational and egalitarian matrix and yet alienating those with means or reasons to go around it speaks volumes as to the failure of the state to achieve a satisfactory provisioning system and the transparency necessary for this system to function. Given the problems posed by the police itself, this state of affairs also explains, at least in part, the tendency to produce conspiratorial theories to account for the clandestine. Only improved supply thanks to the improvement of economic activity from late 1947 on—and not the repression—facilitated the decline of the black market.

The Gangster and Criminality in Cinema

The widespread need for the black market, combined with hostility to the police, facilitated a certain resistance to state norms and gave prominence to figures antagonistic to state power. Foremost among these figures was the *résistant*, whose heroization continued to haunt police institutions, and cautioned against an imposing state in ways that would be co-opted by intellectual movements such as existentialism. The continuing battle of groups of *résistants* for a social and cultural position they considered appropriate to the memory of their struggle both extended and fatigued the figure's appeal.

A related and morally more complex counterfigure emerged in the late 1940s and persisted into the late 1960s. This was the gangster. Far from being a mere cinematic cliché, the figure of *le gangster* expressed, through its appeal, a mistrust of intrusive police order. From the later 1950s on, it also paralleled *poujadiste* resistance to taxation and embodied a fantasy of escape from state control.[58] While the gangster trope did not put order fundamentally in trouble, it signaled difficulty in identifying with those who ruled. As newspaper articles supportive of the police often complained, even the best-behaved children, "when asked what they want to become, say *gangsters* not *policemen*."[59] How can this desire be understood?

Part of the reason was the highly problematic status of the police. Because it remained unclear to what degree being part of the police during the occupation had constituted an act of collaboration, and because the repressive role of the police remained highly visible (even as its allegiance to the Republic that was purging it remained in doubt),[60] suspicion and hatred of the police persisted. That provisions were policed and the black market persecuted certainly added to this blame.

If mistrust of the police goes some way to provide an explanation, a much more fascinating role was played by the figure of the gangster, whose history in cinema as well as in contemporary criminology helps explain the postwar sociopolitical fantasy of escape associated with it. The words *gangster* and *gang* entered the French lexicon rather abruptly in the mid 1930s. They were Anglophone imports linked to the Al Capone myth and to the rise of the Hollywood gangster film (e.g., *Scarface*, 1932). The term preserved some negative connotations. Yet, from the 1940s through the 1970s, "gangster" became a widely used, near-native term in police thrillers and in pulp literature and changed in flair, if not in meaning. Despite being obviously suspect, the male gangster by no means appeared as a serious threat to social order; he was in fact quite often a sympathetic character. French gangster films of the 1930s, such as *Gangster malgré lui* (*Gangster Despite Himself*) and *Gentleman Gangster* (both 1935), had already presented gangsters not as troublesome destroyers of the social order, but as heroic free agents, men pushed to the brink by society but not lacking in admirable qualities. After World War II, the "good gangster" became a staple. Novels made semi-exculpatory claims or suggested forms of heroization or aestheticization, at times even in their titles: *Monsieur Scrupule, gangster* (1953), *Le Gangster aux yeux bleus* (1950), and *Le Gangster aux étoiles* (1954).[61] Films, including *films noirs*, radicalized this robinhoodism, and the French gangster film quickly established a fairly straightforward pattern of plot and protagonist. Stars such as Jean Gabin (*Touchez pas au grisbi!* 1954) and, later, Lino Ventura (*Classe tous risques*, 1960; *Les Tontons flingueurs*, 1963) played the good, ethical, handsome gangster who has helped others, has paid his debts to society, and is typically involved in one last heist either against his will or for a "good" cause.[62]

Not only was this protagonist the only one capable of inner life and ethical commitment, he was also quite explicitly attempting to establish his individuality against the demands of both state and society—itself little more than a criminal underworld.[63] As a result, audiences were ripe for identification with this solitary counterhero. The director Jean-Pierre Melville made a career out of highly stylized gangster films like *Le Samouraï*, *Bob le Flambeur*, *Le deuxième souffle*, and *Le Cercle rouge*. All of these films were propelled by the same structural premise: the fantasy of a nomad pursuing his freedom via a criminal but ethical rejection of social order—indeed of both state and crime-syndicate orders. Stylistically, in Melville's hands, this became an aesthetic and popular form of cinematic self-construction—a syntax. However, it bears mentioning that, in the work of other directors as well, the genre and its audience appeal were profoundly influenced by the persistent ethics of resistance to police and to economic regulation—in other words, to the state's push for transparency.

A former *résistant* himself, Melville linked gangsters to the resistance quite openly. In his second film on the resistance, *L'Armée des ombres* (1969; *Army of Shadows*), he forced an even stronger collusion between the ethics of the gangster and those of the *résistant*. The film used the particular cinematic syntax Melville had recently developed in *Le deuxième souffle* (1966) and *Le Samouraï* (1967) for the purpose of speaking of the resistance. Slow pacing, aversion to climactic tempos, and long takes emphasizing the unreadability of protagonists' faces contributed—critics argued—to turning the resistance into an affair of gangsters.[64] Although ostensibly ethical, Melville's *résistants* are isolated in the solitude of their group, appear aimless (it is not clear what, if anything, they achieve), and murder their own when necessary; moreover, they conspire, dress, even ambulate just like Melville's gangsters. Melville dismissed this direction of influence:[65] on the contrary, he claimed, the gangster film itself relied on visual codes associated with the historical resistance and with the experience of poverty and illegality. If his cinema "gangsterized" the resistance and "resistentialized" gangsters, this was a result of the complex emergence of the gangster as antihero in the postwar period, a safe fantasy in the service of the moral denial of the state.

The Gangster and Criminality in Criminology and Psychiatry

Two questions persist, however: How was it possible for gangsters to be heroes? To what extent could gangsters be understood as opposing the repressive norms of police and society by subscribing to a superior counterethics? These questions, and even the sheer possibility of a counterethics, were no mere cinematic fantasy; for criminologists and psychologists, they were a staple.[66] In the 1950s the respected psychoanalyst and theorist Daniel Lagache, for example, wrote a series of well-received and influential texts on the ethics of policing and crime. In these studies Lagache considered it widely accepted among his colleagues that crime was not a defect or an antisocial pathology but an *axiological* activity; and he sought to finesse this approach psychoanalytically.[67] He argued that the criminal, particularly the gangster, abandons the "normal" normative world and, with his "adjusting" personality, enters a different one, "perhaps a criminal one."[68]

On this view, the criminal begins from the subjective experience of a world riddled with corruption and crime, which justifies his search for counter-values shared by peers and denied by his parents' normative yet ostensibly flawed world.[69] The gangster resolves the internal psychological tensions generated by parental control by carrying out acts marked by "heroic identification."[70] In a way familiar from police thrillers, he construes himself as a hero and interprets his acts as unproblematic ones, sanctioned by the values of the world he has joined; his non-acceptance by his father's society defines him as a criminal, but also helps him adapt to new norms. Thus he achieves "heroic identification" and resolution of his internal conflict through attacks on social norms that he considers malevolent.[71] If Lagache's views on the axiological foundation of criminality were indeed shared among criminologists, his personal contribution lay in the explanatory import of this psychoanalytical "heroic identification"—a trope especially close to the police thriller.

Other psychologists confirmed this "reversal of values," proposing that gangs offer delinquents "true moral values" opposed to the oppressive ones of policed society.[72] In a 1935 essay on the psychology of the murderer, the influential phenomenological criminologist Étienne de Greeff described the process of passing from the intention to the act of murder as a matter of normal, *not* pathological psychology that involved the rejection of a "'normal' milieu that was susceptible to experiencing this conversion as social treason."[73] Lecturing on group psychology at the 1952 "First International Course on Criminology," where Lagache presented his theory of heroic identification, another psychoanalyst, Serge Lebovici, echoed Lagache's claim that the gang is morally well defined and offered this comment: "a guilty act is . . . explained by the group's acts . . . the initiator de-culpabilizes the initiated," while at the same time "codes of a gang define a new honor that is no less demanding than the moral rules of the superego" that the initiated have to overcome.[74] Going a step further in his "Premises to Any Development of Criminology," Jacques Lacan noted that "these criminals whom we have here called the criminals of the *ego* are the voiceless victims of a growing evolution of the forms that direct culture toward ever more external relations of constraint."[75] His friend Georges Bataille theorized the capacity of crime to produce legends that at once shocked and contributed to systems of thought. Bataille identified crime with "the night" and presented it as "a fact of the human species, a fact of that species alone, but . . . above all, the secret aspect, impenetrable and hidden."[76] Like him, Lacan interpreted the relationship between crime and the law as dialectical, then criticized criminology for making "sanitary" and "dehumanizing" appeals to punishment and ascribed crime to the efforts of an enchained subjectivity, unable to empathize with the world it found itself in.[77]

Criminology and psychology fostered the same sense of crime as the cinema, and their approaches granted a certain "legitimacy" to illegal responses to state-directed society. Where cinema offered antiheroes, psychologists supplied norms and counterethics. Intellectual reactions to crime proposed that such phenomena proved society not to be available to state norms or transparent before state power. Crime and gangs served as conceptual conduits for a refusal of social transparency, for a system of identifications that denied the adequacy of state control and its harmony with society. If police could not be trusted and the black market—supposedly a dominion of gangs—offered an alternative realm to that of state control, the grey area inhabited by the imaginary gangster represented rejection of the state's and mainstream society's power over norms and truths.

Between State and Society, II

*Psychology, Public Health, and
the Rebellion of the* Inadaptés

In the 1950s and 1960s, criminology and psychology contributed to a further set of developments: the medical and psychocriminological efforts to "adapt" children and adolescents to the "normal" mainstream. Just as the police, the black market, and the aestheticized gangster had constituted problems for social transparency, the *inadaptés*—"maladapted" or "maladjusted" children and adolescents—would become a major concern for the state's education and policing of the younger generation from the mid-1950s on. The historians Richard Jobs and Sarah Fishman have shown the importance of juvenile justice for the French state's attempts to create better conditions for its young.[1] Juvenile delinquency, a flashing beacon for penal reform and education, was at the center of social policy both under Vichy and after the Liberation. In the 1950s a new theoretical and diagnostic category, *inadaptation*,[2] addressed children's potential inability to adjust to society's rules. But the category expanded well beyond juridical and educational aspects of juvenile delinquency. It contemplated the threating possibility that a "normal" and relatively transparent society might have little control over its future and might fragment beyond the point of no return.

The 1950s witnessed an explosion of writing on children's and adolescents' relations to their home and school environments and a rise in the scientific and public purchase of this literature. "Adaptation," a concept that criminologists, child psychologists, and education specialists often explicitly adopted from biology, quickly became a crucial concept in school policy, an expression of philanthropic and socially protective state intervention.[3] The category of *inadaptés* was very broad: while some cases concerned specific medical conditions (epilepsy, diabetes, even hydrocephaly), the category was mainly made up of vaguely defined "behavioral problems" like ingratitude, disrespect, aggression, adolescent revolt, refractoriness, even excessive docility, isolation, and mutism.[4] In focus was the stability of the youth's relations with his or her *milieu* (a term of significance in both criminology and behavioral psychology).[5] One author observed that the word *inadaptés* was more "fecund" than synonyms like "'abnormal,' 'irregular,' 'handicapped' and . . . 'backwards' [*arriérés*]," which all had a judgmental flavor.[6] *Inadaptés* was "broader," diagnosed a noxious abnormality related to the equilibrium between individual and environment, expressed "philanthropic" intent, and proposed a causal link between antisocial behavior, criminality, and violence. The category of "inadaptation" was structured hierarchically; it ran from normal to "maladapted" social behavior and treated the latter as a juridical–pathological problem. Thus it offered grounds for conceiving of the *inadapté* as threatening the norms of "normal" society and produced rifts in it that could not be controlled. All this was supposed to bring under the radar an underworld of delinquency, disease, prostitution, and violence that perhaps evaded the state altogether. Because such problems threatened the future of a unified, transparent, and well-administered society, *inadaptation* was in a sense worse than delinquency.

Proposed reasons for *inadaptation* to school norms varied. Most were behavioral: the result of abandonment, familial conflict, or even moral "dissociation." A number of writers blamed the environment, in particular the presence of recently urbanized families and the "dilapidated, degraded, insalubrious" conditions of public housing.[7] The CNRS sociologist Joffre Dumazedier, acting as plenary speaker at a conference on socioeducative equipment held by the High Commissariat of Youth and Sports in 1959,[8] lectured an audience of architects, among them the by then legendary Le Corbusier, on how austere modern buildings, especially HLM (*habitation à loyer modéré*: rent-controlled housing), *caused inadaptation* by making leisure all but impossible. To survey and explain cases of *inadaptation*, the Ministry of Education instructed the Service de santé scolaire et universitaire (SSSU; School and University Health Service) for its officials to ask far-reaching, direct questions about students' "character at home, attitude toward brothers and sisters, sleep, conditions for work at home, agricultural or other work, appetite, attitude toward other pupils and the teacher, toward the mother, and toward animals."[9] Anxieties about privacy that might be raised elsewhere were trumped by the imperative of individual and (especially) public health. The family was seen as crucial in the development of delinquency: one study noted that, among the 55 percent of families deemed "normal" (in that both parents lived with the delinquent child), "we may find a disabled father, a notorious drunkard, an infirm mother; other cases testify to a grave lack of interest in the children: for example, a mother unaware of where her son works even though he lives with her."[10] Sociological studies of delinquency agreed on the importance of the family even when statistical psychological studies declined to offer conclusive support.[11] Childhood traumas experienced during the war were also in focus. By 1960, the children born during the war were aged between sixteen and twenty-one. If one added a few more years at both ends, one could apply the category of *inadapté* to large swathes of an entire generation.

State intervention had distinct targets related to age and the environment. Adolescence was regarded as the critical period for delinquency and crime,[12] and state care had to counter "abnormal" familial situations in order to save the teenager.[13] Explaining the importance of normal development, Jean Piaget, the most influential child behaviorist of the time, concluded that adolescence (roughly, the age around 13–15) is the period when individuals enter the "adult social body," form a personality that transcends earlier egocentrism, construct relations with abstract ideals like "nation" or "humanity," recognize values rather than mere hierarchies, and develop autonomy and a "plan of life."[14] Piaget had used a category of adaptation in the 1930s;[15] now he insisted that the development of abstract faculties resulted in the young adolescent's tendency not only to *adapt to* the environment but to *adapt* the environment to herself. This evolved toward a "sort of messianism" shared by "the most normal, the most modest, the most gentle" pupils; unchecked, these could produce fabulations that would later appear "as signs of pathological megalomania."[16] Piaget made it clear that disturbances in the "normalization" of behavior could have disastrous consequences for society and its organization.

Unsurprisingly, then, governmental agencies were particularly anxious about adolescents who moved in a "pathological" direction. State reports depicted non-normalization and its sequela, delinquency, as two modern social threats that could be remedied, at least in part, through state initiatives to create complete persons.[17] Since situations at home could not really be addressed, schools themselves had to become sites where the grey areas of *inadaptation* could be cleared up.

Leading criminologists such as Jean Pinatel and Étienne de Greeff claimed a place in these discussions as well. Together with other influential colleagues such as Georges Heuyer, they presented their work as a new science, which no longer defined itself through race (Le Bon, Tarde), anthropometrics (Lombroso, Bertillon), biological predetermination or degeneration (Magnan, Dallemagne, Nordau), or social conditioning (Marx).[18] They trumpeted their readiness to enlist their work in the service of preventing antisocial behavior engendered by poor development and inadaptation. De Greeff wrote that "mental hygiene concerned with troubles in children's character can render the greatest of services," because children tended "to search for, or build, *milieux* of criminal allure (gangs)."[19] In other words, failure to treat maladapted adolescents properly was enough to set them on the way to a gangster life that led subsequently to punishment. Together, psychocriminology and public health policy could remove the threat of criminality emerging from areas to which the state had little access.

In other words *inadaptation* represented something opaque to government power, a moral value that threatened to lead to rebellion, a pathological condition with power to contaminate. Ending (or at least limiting) *inadaptation* quickly became an urgent mission for education and public health officials. Their goal was to recreate existing environments, especially schools, to place maladapted children and adolescents in specialized schools or "therapeutic" versions of the English reform school (observational centers, live-in apprenticeships, and so on); this offered them separate spaces and strengthened "normal" schools themselves. The SSSU, which was responsible for health in schools, was tasked with their "amelioration" to combat *inadaptation* and with identifying *inadaptés*. This was a consequential development, because at the time when criminologists and psychologists portrayed childhood intervention as an imperative in the early 1950s, tuberculosis had just stopped being the principal public health threat (universal BCG vaccination in France started in 1947), so the SSSU could make this its main focus. The shift from tuberculosis to *inadaptation* was clearly articulated in directives to school health officials that emphasized the urgency of psychological screening.[20] One guide estimated the number of school-age *inadaptés* at 400,000—8 percent of France's children—and this included "uneducable idiots or imbeciles" (hardly a medical definition) as well as *caractériels contagieux moraux* (morally contagious disturbed individuals).[21]

State health measures in schools thus primarily targeted pupils with behavioral or moral "problems."[22] The use of medical language accentuated an implicit behaviorist determinism: in 1959, SSSU internal documents argued that it was imperative to carry out a *dépistage* (literally, "detection") of *inadaptation*—*dépistage* being the standard term for the screening and eradication of epidemics.[23] In a memo aimed at enlarging the strictly biomedical scope of medical surveillance the direction of social and psychological *dépistage*, Louis Joxe, the minister of education, implored officials to shed light on the causes of this "darkness," so that "the intervention by medico-social crews might become the occasion of a display of all that prevents the normal physical and intellectual development of the child, and of the implementation of all means necessary to facilitate this free development either by acting on the school to adapt it to the child, or by acting on the child to adapt it to the school."[24]

This language of balancing aid with fearful concern pinpointed *inadaptation* as a major inhibitor of education policy.[25] Not screening the students could result in "attacks on the community," whereas screening them would perhaps guarantee that "perverse tendencies" would be spotted as the first symptoms appeared.[26] In passages that, in retrospect, beg for Foucauldian analysis (and explain some of its purchase in the 1970s), another official described schools as ideal research environments analogous to "laboratories," and talked of a school health regime of broadened "surveillance" and its merits.[27] Others opined that adaptation screening created an "avant-garde educational milieu" and recommended placing "maladapted" pupils in vocational schools (*écoles de perfectionnement*) where they would be directed to a new role in society.[28] All these memos slide from concern over public health to the deployment of behaviorist terminology in relation to normality, the development of values, and the proper place of the individual in social environments. Public health officials and criminologists had no qualms about treating the family as detrimental to society, advising the state to classify and "treat" maladapted children, or claiming expertise on the pupil's psyche, on social cohesion, and on the good society.

It is unclear whether screening for *inadaptation* met with opposition beyond the occasional refusal of vaccination efforts. What is clear, however, is that, at least according to the confusing state standards, enough children were *inadaptés* to warrant alarm. The definition was vague enough to allow one to "make up" the kind of subjects that fell under it.[29] Significant resistance to this language appeared in the late 1950s and early 1960s and was expressed in philosophy and the *nouvelle vague* films that were some of the finest products of contemporary French culture.

The *nouvelle vague* in the early 1960s brought with it a celebration of the freedom of childhood and youth as stages of life that reveled in *inadaptation* and were blissfully ignorant of policing and of educational, state, and social rules. François Truffaut's *Les quatre cents coups* (1959; *The Four Hundred Blows*) portrays a child who runs away from limiting environments. Jean-Luc Godard's fame was tied to his innovative film language, but also to his depiction of small rebellions of young characters poorly adapted to social rules: the seemingly spontaneous decision to carry out an easy crime in *Bande à part*, the petty criminality of Jean-Paul Belmondo's character in *À bout de souffle* (*Breathless*), the mad run (against both Algerian gangsters and police) in *Pierrot le fou*, or the student revolutionaries in *Masculin féminin*. In the French cinema of the 1960s, the "maladapted" antisocial adolescent added to and partly replaced "the gangster" as the principal antagonist of the established order.[30] For this younger generation, what was at stake was the cultivation of a space for authenticity, immediacy, and spontaneity—things society failed to understand—rather than the conflict between a moral gangster, depicted almost as a *résistant,* and an oppressive, corrupt, Vichy-like state. This aspect of the student revolts should not be underestimated. Such an imaginary did not promote heightened privacy but rather a wild escape from frames and formations, indeed, from a society whose ostensible openness was premised on oppressive and ultimately violent rules. Differently put, the very idea of an open society seemed predicated upon the formation of well-adjusted individuals, and Truffaut's and Godard's elegies to the *inadaptés* were efforts to unravel this idea.

Philosophers of very different schools also advocated a quasi-personal rebellion against both social inequality and normalization. "Existential Marxism" (a label proposed by Mark Poster) is the tendency to blend elements of subjective existentialism with Marxist sensibilities regarding class, society, and oppression. Its heightened philosophical subjectivism captures the permanent resistance to norms and state involvement in individual life quite well.[31] Critics of Marxism and existentialism, most famously Raymond Aron, sought to make the individual an irreducible source of meaning and experience as against totalitarianism. Scientists and their historians did so as well: in an important 1958 lecture at the Sorbonne titled "What Is Psychology?" Georges Canguilhem presented psychology and psychiatry as policing practices and made the point that the 1950s' language of "adaptation" and "environment" was an instrument for leveling individuality:

Studies of the laws of adaptation and learning, of the relation of learning to aptitudes, of the detection and measure of aptitudes, of the conditions of efficiency and production (whether it be that of individuals or groups) . . . all admit an implicit common postulate: the nature of Man is to be a tool, his vocation is to be put at its place and its task.[32]

The rejection of psychology—the "enlightened" treatment of "unreason"—as a utilitarian and policing tactic is Michel Foucault's big concern in his 1961 *Folie et déraison* (*History of Madness*). But this line of thought is already visible in critiques of psychology such as Jean Starobinski's of the Rorschach test in "Des taches et des masques" (1958), discussed in the Introduction:

Today, almost no important social act remains unaccompanied by a medical certificate or expert's report . . . the more the State sees itself as rational, the more it tends to consider the infraction of laws as an effect of unreason that is susceptible to treatment or "reeducation." The medical diagnosis is a verdict in abeyance.[33]

Some psychoanalysts (most famously Lacan) similarly argued against the use of their science for a social adaptation that emphasized "normal" developmental schemata and criminalized *inadaptation*. This was a profoundly violent process, which caught children and adolescents—whether "adapted" or not—in a conceptual crossfire of social management. Lacan's famous "return to Freud" targeted above all (American) behaviorist psychology, which deformed psychoanalysis in order to enforce "the adaptation of the individual to the social environment"; the state's obsession with *inadaptation* offered a perfect domestic description of what he condemned.[34]

Foucault later referred to Vichy's culture of denunciation and police as a regime that continually breached privacy. This breach inspired his own work: "Our private life was truly threatened. Perhaps that is the reason why I am fascinated by history and by the relationship between personal experience and those events amidst which we find ourselves. I think that this is the point of departure of my desire to theorize."[35] Although Foucault's work hardly amounts to a defense of privacy, it is important to see that the state intervention into private spaces to which he attests did not abate after Vichy. In Foucault—as in Canguilhem, and even in Lacan—the fantasy of an anarchic, wild chance of autonomy persists even as norm-enforcing practices committed to securing society's transparency to the state seek to wipe it out.

Alienation, Utopia, and Marxism after 1956

A Clarity Worse Than the Penumbra

Lest I be accused of writing as if the rejection of transparency was a universal goal of postwar thought, it is time to note again that the thinkers discussed thus far were not representative of something like "postwar French thought," even if many have become canonical. This is not only because no such category existed, but because the critiques of transparency were far from universally accepted—indeed, they were largely extraneous to the two main belief systems of the day: Catholicism and Communism. Both Catholics and party-line Marxists had ways of handling transparency within their respective frameworks and of explaining away the web of theoretical gestures that signaled an impending epistemological and anthropological transformation by chalking them up to the failures of modern bourgeois humanism. For Catholics, transparency was a non-issue so long as society remained distant from the "integral man" of Christianity and thereby without access to transcendence.[1] For communists, transparency belonged to the postrevolutionary world of equals; in the present moment its dearth was the plain consequence of capitalism. That democratic politics was undermined by capitalist and imperial geopolitics, that secret trusts rather than peoples ruled the world, that the economy was skewed even for the petite bourgeoisie—these were ideological givens and promising short-term political strategies: building a transparent society was an obvious corollary of the destruction of capitalism.

Still, if Catholicism had ready-made answers and could look haughtily upon the coalescence of arguments and problems of social transparency, epistemology, and existential doubt, if its theology remained the vanishing point for any engagements with philosophy and the human sciences, Marxism was time and again transformed by debates around transparency and contributed to them in return, even if ambiguously. Gone, already by Stalin's death, were claims like Walter Benjamin's, that "to live in a glass house is a revolutionary virtue par excellence."[2] During the interwar period, socialist realism had pursued the pedagogical line of transporting into the immediate present the utopia of communism's path into the future; but the appeal of this ideology was negligible in postwar France.[3] In the later 1940s, the French Communist Party described itself more as "humanist" than "revolutionary," and its rhetoric was pervaded by the claim that it cared above all for human dignity, even if, as Tony Judt wrote, communism's political language assumed that the "drive to create a 'transparent' society, to overcome the heritage of the 'bourgeois' revolution, must of necessity be at the expense of the claims of the individual."[4] The humanist rhetoric made the revolutionary ideal more palatable and put lower demands on communists. They did not need to endorse every single Soviet or Eastern European practice, nor effect the revolution here and now; they could point out that, if terror was necessary in revolutionary times, this was because such times were exceptional, rare, radically creative. In the late 1940s, once their best chance of radically affecting the French regime had collapsed and normalcy had returned, communists and fellow travelers faced a series of different problems, not least how to behave as an electoral and political force. The international scene, especially behind the Iron Curtain, presented further complications: for example, it was only a matter of time before Walter Ulbricht's assertion, two months into the Berlin Blockade, that there was almost no difference between the East German Communist Party and the proletariat itself was called into doubt.[5] (Nevertheless, it took Merleau-Ponty seven years to mock this claim.)[6]

That clarity and creativity in communist action and politics were ambiguous at best was an ongoing concern: Dionys Mascolo wrote in his unorthodox and highly controversial *Le Communisme* (1953) that "before the communist revolution, Marxist dialectics was clear and distinct, indeed very readable. . . . Ever since revolutionary dialectics was triggered in practice, it has ceased to be clear."[7] Any claim to clear-sighted vision and transparent speech favored the "clarity" "of the clear phantoms of values and ends, which is worse than the penumbra in which realities are found."[8] Mascolo similarly deplored as cheap Camus's pretense, in *The Plague* (1947), to celebrate "clear language,"[9] which he thought only persuaded those who acted of their innocence while allowing the violence of their claims to become invisible. Mascolo endorsed Merleau-Ponty's and Sartre's stance of struggle in a world of ambiguity and political–linguistic opacity. Lucidity in language caused "a great part of the unhappiness of men": it excluded violence, to be sure, but at the cost of not recognizing the complexity of the world.[10] This was also the position of Hoederer, the leader in Sartre's *Les mains sales* (*Dirty Hands*), when he made the classic point that an omelet cannot be prepared without breaking some eggs:

How you cling to your purity, young man! How afraid you are to soil your hands! All right, stay pure! What good will it do? Why did you join us? Purity is an idea for a yogi or a monk. You intellectuals and bourgeois anarchists use it as a pretext for doing nothing. To do nothing, to remain motionless, arms at your sides, wearing kid gloves. Well, I have dirty hands. Right up to the elbows. I've plunged them in filth and blood. But what do you hope? Do you think you can govern innocently?[11]

Publishing right around Stalin's death, Mascolo was not arguing in the middle of a revolution: he was extending the dirty hands principle to all life before a true revolution (but what, he asked, was a *true* revolution?). Neither he nor the imaginary Hoederer were exemplary communists, yet they expressed in plain and certain terms the broadly felt sense that theirs was an age without clarity or purpose; and Mascolo, like Sartre and Merleau-Ponty, emphasized that, even if this were just a stage preceding the end of history, one could not (and probably should not) aim at clarity and transparency, whether linguistic or social. As a disheartened Merleau-Ponty, no longer a communist, would write in 1955, less than a year before Khrushchev's "Secret Speech" at the Twentieth Congress of the CPSU: "This idea of an absolute purification of history, of a regime without inertia, chance, or risk, is the inverted reflection of our anguish and our solitude."[12] This was the heart of the mid-1950s criticism: whereas the basic tenets of generic socialism included the belief that capitalism distorts society, politics, and everyday human relations, the fusion of history, party, and self that was necessary for the destruction of such effects no longer seemed plausible.

At the same time both party politicians and intellectuals with varying degrees of attachment to Marxism were deeply doubtful—partly thanks to the sensitivity of "existential Marxism"—that the broader communist effort to render the self transparent to the force of history made sense or was worth pursuing. Until 1968, when Benjamin's exhortation seemed relevant once again to radicals like Guy Debord's Situationist International group or to the Maoists around the magazine *Tel quel*, Marxism underwent multiple transformations, which further confounded its fraught relationship with historical action and the utopia of transparence.

Marxists expressed renewed doubts from time to time about the very idea of revolution and about a postbourgeois world. The most prominent of these moments was 1956—the period following Khrushchev's Secret Speech and the invasion of Hungary—but waves of disillusionment hit the party every few years from 1948 on. "Disillusionment" itself became central among the tropes of postwar Marxist history. Marxists of nonorthodox varieties were among those who most emphatically scorned the revolutionary hopes for transparency, along with the disillusioned who fled the party. If instances of political violence were for many the proverbial straw that broke the camel's back, this was due to the growing conviction that the only traces of the desired transparent society could be found in these premonitions and promises of terror.

Rather than track the history of Marxist critiques of transparency, I should like to cut three slices of it that were instrumental in the great transformations in the 1950s: the change in Merleau-Ponty's political thought from the late 1940s to his *Les aventures de la dialectique* (1955; *Adventures of the Dialectic*); the development of a theory of alienation and everyday life in Henri Lefebvre's revisionist Marxism and in the journal *Arguments*; and the development of the category of ideology in Althusser's thought, in particular across his reading of transparency in the early Marx.

A Density That Moves: Merleau-Ponty and the Persistent Illusions of Transparency

Already in 1945, in "The War Has Taken Place," Merleau-Ponty had argued that human relations might become transparent only in a future "in which past traumas have been wiped out and the conditions of an effective liberty have from the first been realized." He was fully aware of the improbability of such a future.[13] While before the war it was possible to imagine transparency, the advent of a Marxist way of perceiving the world put paid to it: "We were not wrong, in 1939, to want liberty, truth, happiness, and transparent relations among men, and we are not now abandoning humanism. The war and the Occupation only taught us that values remain nominal and indeed have no value without an economic and political infrastructure to make them participate in existence."[14]

From *Humanisme et terreur: Essai sur le problème communiste* (*Humanism and Terror*) in 1947 until at least "Les Jours de notre vie" ("The Days of Our Lives") in 1949–50—an essay co-signed with Sartre, which essentially supported the Soviet Union against David Rousset's exposure of parts of the network of Soviet camps, yet was increasingly critical of Stalinism—Merleau-Ponty used the politics and philosophy of ambiguity to balance two concerns. One was that the defense of the Soviet Union was essential because Western liberalism intentionally failed to recognize that relations between human beings were socially mediated. In the liberal world this social mediation was violence pure and simple, yet liberalism could not see this violence at its source. The other concern was that the Soviet Union was manifestly failing its mission; Merleau-Ponty was explicit about this in his infamous "defense" of the Soviet Union in *Humanism and Terror*.[15] In "Days of Our Lives," he concurred that the permanence and autonomization of the Soviet repressive apparatus was no longer possible to ignore. Stalin's purge had led to the forced labor and "reeducation" of a twentieth of the Soviet population ("a tenth of its male population," "ten million slaves").[16] Socialism had been traded for domestic colonialism.[17] Utopia had turned from innocence into oppression:

The formulas of the Corrective Labor Code are still those of an edenic socialism: it is not a matter of punishing, but of reeducating; criminals are blind, all that is necessary is to enlighten them; in a society where exploitation is banned, laziness and rebellion are mere misunderstandings. We must bring the antisocial into the shelter of the righteous anger of a unanimous people, and thus make the people safe from his scheming. It is best to put him back to work, explaining with high indulgence the grandeur of the new society. After that, calmed and saved, he will resume its place in the common work. . . . These are nineteenth-century thoughts, which remain touching, and perhaps deeper than we think, because after all we never did till now provide men with comparable chances, since we never tempted them with the good. . . . And so these young ideas begin to grimace like old men, those innocent thoughts become the height of hypocrisy and cunning when one citizen in twenty is detained in their name, when they decorate camps where men die from overwork and starvation, when they cover over the repression of a harshly unequal society, when under pretense of reeducating the lost they are used to break the opponents, when, under the pretext of self-criticism they amount to denial. And then in one stroke their virtue turns into poison. But this is not felt so clearly. Besides the cynical and the perverse, who are everywhere, probably many young Soviet heroes who have never lived in a country without camps side, without a shadow of a scruple, with the party of decency. Have *we* never seen something like this?[18]

The claims made here are astonishing: the transparent Eden of the nineteenth century had degraded into camouflage tactics for hypocrisy (*tartuferie*) and cunning, for justifications of repression. "Reeducation" was an euphemism for the process of breaking the politically undesirable so as to sustain the delusions of young communist heroes. At this point, any defense of the Soviet Union meant refusal of liberalism rather than advocacy for its practices; and from there on Merleau-Ponty advanced steadily toward a stark rejection of the Soviet Union. By the time he wrote *Adventures of the Dialectic*, he had abandoned any kinship with communism. There he spoke of the intellectual anguish and solitude that accompanied the twentieth century's "liquidation" of "revolutionary dialectics," which had identified the proletariat with the course of history only to discover that the problems it seemed to have overcome were reemerging.[19] The proclaimed shortcut to a transparent society was pitiless and ridiculous: Soviet claims made in *Pravda* presupposed, in bad faith, the obliteration of the historical consciousness that mediated relations between human beings and that was necessarily opaque.[20]

Merleau-Ponty also targeted Sartre's emphasis on the transparency of consciousness: not only had it found no equivalent reality in the real political world, but it had perverted the program of *Les Temps modernes* with its coefficient theory of *engagement*, which refused the primacy of critique and dialectics.[21] Time and again, Merleau-Ponty deprecated Sartre's "fantasy" of "pure action." Its critique was urgently needed, and by blending Marx with Max Weber—the ubiquitous postwar reference point for critics of communism, from Aron to Wittfogel—Merleau-Ponty aimed to retain the originality of dialectical and critical thinking in the political realm.

Thus Merleau-Ponty rejected both Sartre and Soviet communism, accusing each of mythmaking. "If, in an opaque history, rationality is created by Party action and you are in conflict with the Party—the only historical agent (all the more so if it eliminates you)—you are historically wrong. If it gets the better of you, it knows better than you do."[22] No room was left for ambiguity, and the pretense to purity, objectivity, and social transparency only resulted in "extreme opacity." Transparency and opacity joined hands high up in the order of evils. "We need, not a world that is, as Sartre says, opaque and rigidified, but rather a world that is dense and that moves."[23] The choices of the French Left revolved around two poles: a density that moved and a rigid opacity that had to be traversed.

Arguments and Henri Lefebvre's Critical Theory

Three journals are generally credited with the development of the French New Left and a theoretical Marxism decidedly opposed to the French Communist Party's submission to the Soviet Union: *Socialisme ou Barbarie*, founded by Cornelius Castoriadis and Claude Lefort in 1949, after their abandonment of the weakened Trotskyist Parti communiste internationaliste (PCI) and continuing until 1965; *Arguments*, founded in December 1956 by Edgar Morin, Henri Lefebvre, Jean Duvignaud, and Roland Barthes, and co-edited from late 1957 until its dissolution in 1962 by Kostas Axelos; and the *Internationale situationniste*, which, edited by Guy Debord, ran irregularly from 1957–58 through 1972. *Socialisme ou Barbarie* is best known for Castoriadis's argument that the Soviet Union was by no means a classless society but had replaced the middle class with a bureaucratic class. The Soviet system pretended to have enabled proletarian universalism when in reality it fused and deformed society much as capitalism had done.[24] This sham proclamation of classless egalitarianism was a barbaric affront to socialism and to the postrevolutionary transparency that populated communist dreams. Castoriadis's writing on bureaucracy translated directly into attacks on the French Communist Party (PCF): French intellectual support for the Soviet Union rested on an ethical–political hypothesis that "real," transparent, and harmonious human relations were possible but only among the PCF and the French intellectual class.

Arguments remains the least studied of the three journals: conceived explicitly as a revisionist "report on research open to all those who place themselves in a perspective at once scientific and socialist,"[25] it operated in parallel with the Italian *Ragionamenti* and helped spawn a number of similar journals across Europe.[26] Growing in size over time (from thirty to about seventy pages), *Arguments* moved from a generic post-1956 revisionism toward the importation of German thinkers and Western Marxism,[27] a political anthropology of Western societies,[28] studies of the "global," "planetary," or cosmological problem,[29] and, echoing *Socialisme ou Barbarie*, bureaucratic technocracy.[30] *Arguments* laid the groundwork for a French version of critical theory[31]—a collage of the Frankfurt School with French sociology, semiotics, and literature—that cast aside the revolutionary imaginary for an enigmatic stance of anticipatory opposition to the political and the techno-economical. A more productive social theory was necessary now that the revolutionary drive had dried up. Under this pressure, the concept of alienation shifted: it could be found not only in labor, but even *in the experience of consumption* and in commodity capitalism more generally. As argued by Georg Lukács's partisans in *Arguments*, generalized alienation was now the permanent condition of capitalist modernity, and its anthropological diction had to be rediscovered.[32]

This undercut Marx's promise of a world in which mediation would disappear; now, theories of revolution concurred. Since 1945, as has been repeatedly argued, revolution and terror—and particularly the 1793 Terror in France—were mobilized to defend the violence of the Soviet Union, as well as a version of history whose dialectical progress inevitably led to a transparent society. Now the decline of trust in revolutionary transformation—of which *Arguments* was perhaps the clearest symptom—paralleled the conviction that other sources of political and cultural legitimacy were needed for the critique of contemporary society. In this respect the journal was deeply indebted to Henri Lefebvre, who had been an early philosophical adherent to communism in the 1930s, instrumental especially in the popularization of Marx's 1844 manuscripts, and by the early 1950s was just as much of an influence on revisionism—a barometer for the generation that sought to negotiate the relationship of Marxist principles to "actually existing communism." The stations in Lefebvre's postwar intellectual trajectory parallel those in the trajectory of transparency. In his major postwar publications *Critique de la vie quotidienne* (1947–62; *Critique of Everyday Life*); *Introduction à la modernité* (1962; *Introduction to Modernity*); and *La production de l'espace* (1974; *The Production of Space*), Lefebvre forsook his earlier orthodoxy to develop new theories of social interaction and eventually of urban space. Through them he placed the dream of ethical and political transparency at the heart of socialism but moved, surely if gradually, away from it.

One of Marx's "projects for the transformation of everyday life," Lefebvre wrote in the second volume of the *Critique de la vie quotidienne*, was "of an ethical order." It implied "the transparency of the relations between men . . . the end of the 'social mystery' . . . of everything which makes the relations between men opaque and elusive, and which conceals these relations from their consciousness and their actions."[33] Lefebvre was evidently referencing the idiom of nature, spontaneity, and transparency in Marx's *Capital*:

The religious reflections of the real world can, in any case, vanish only when the practical relations of everyday life between man and man, and man and nature, generally present themselves to him in a transparent and rational form. The veil is not removed from the countenance of the social life-process, i.e. the process of material production, until it becomes production by freely associated men, and stands under their conscious and planned control. This, however, requires that society possess a material foundation, or a series of material conditions of existence, which in their turn are the natural and spontaneous product of a long and tormented historical development.[34]

In his rendition, Lefebvre was indicating that the pressure the problem of "everyday life" put on Marxism also called into question the binaries surrounding alienation. Alienation was not merely due to the economic activities of a substructure that had to be itself overturned, but an experience of self-division, othering, and non-transparency unavoidable in capitalism. With and against Marx, everyday life had to be celebrated without the easy and false distillation proffered by socialist realism. A year later, in his *Introduction to Modernity*, he described the same project in similar terms, relying now on the early Marx, whose *1844 Manuscripts* he had helped popularize:

Marx announced and prepared the way for total revolution, a historical task by means of which the proletariat would put an end to human alienation, by radical critique and absolute action. No more political and ideological alienation, no more economic alienation, and of course no more religious alienation . . . in one leap, men organized in a free (socialist) society would pass from necessity—and above all from the necessity to accumulate—into aesthetic rapture and ethical transparency.[35]

It is impossible to read this passage without noting the ironic tone in which the absolute terms of the socialist utopia are announced. By this stage, above all in the aftermath of the revelations of Khrushchev's Secret Speech, it was imperative to take a step back, to engage the present time as one of uncertainty even about Marx's dream, and move from adherence to anti-utopian irony:

Even if the beautiful child of our dreams (Communism, the Communism of the utopian and the scientist reconciled at last) may yet be born, would it not still be a good thing to experience uncertainty, to recognize uncertainty so as to enhance our appreciation of this present moment of becoming? We need irony. Without irony, we all become embroiled in acts of faith. Blind trust is sometimes associated with devotion, but mostly it goes hand in hand with stupidity.[36]

Today transparency was an idealist, utopian illusion; claims that social space was somehow transparent presupposed a brutal simplification and impoverishment of the concurrent operations of transparency and opacity in modern life. Lefebvre placed social and ethical transparency in the past—in Marx's thought and in the Paris Commune of 1871. For most French communists, the Commune had been the single most important event in the French Left's revolutionary struggle; Lefebvre agreed, crediting its working-class character, anti-institutional vehemence, and Rousseauian transparency. In his 1965 *Proclamation de la Commune*,[37] the Commune appeared as a revolutionary urban festival—a local political act that erupted into a genuinely democratic expulsion of the bourgeois world of commodities and imagined life in a free city as a life to be lived transparently, regulated by workers' councils and without centralized authority. Yet Lefebvre also saw in the Commune *what could not be repeated*, a topos for a revolution that remained unachieved and the likes of which could not be seen again.

Moving again beyond revolutionary hopes, Lefebvre argued in *The Production of Space* (1974) that "(social) space is a (social) product" and blamed the "illusion of transparency" for scrambling that fact:

The illusion of transparency: Here space appears as luminous, as intelligible, as giving action free rein. What happens in space lends a miraculous quality to thought, which becomes incarnate by means of a *design* (in both senses of the word) . . . the illusion of transparency goes hand in hand with a view of space as innocent, as free of traps or secret places. Anything hidden or dissimulated—and hence dangerous—is antagonistic to transparency, under whose reign everything can be taken in by a single glance from that mental eye which illuminates whatever it contemplates.[38]

Similarly opposing an "illusion of opacity" that aspired to realism, Lefebvre invoked the Marxist insight that modern life was forever opaque and shaped it into an argument that space itself was profoundly unlike a pure and universal condition of experience (a Kantian a priori). Space was the product of capital, labor, consumption.

Lefebvre's formalization of an opposition to the transparency goal was one of the most propulsive sparks in post-1956 Marxism. The conclusion that even space is socially stratified—that it does not offer itself up in an undifferentiated, "pure" state but as part of a socially and politically organized framework for life—perfected this formalization. Yet Lefebvre could also be appropriated by revolutionaries, notably the Situationist International group around Guy Debord, which held a similar view on social space before and during May 1968. Co-opting Lefebvre's treatment of everyday life and his sense of a generalized alienation, the Situationist International denounced "the false sun of spectacular capitalism"[39]—that is, the transformation of modern commodity capitalism into a social system that was hopelessly divided, broken down, and hierarchized. Debord, who liked to think of himself as a new Lenin steering a conspiratorial avant-garde, proposed to replace the "spectacle" that covered for "real life" with the true transparency of an anarchic revolutionary festival à la Rousseau. Here, too, Debord was close to Lefebvre, particularly to his treatment of the Paris Commune (which, according to Debord and the situationists, Lefevbre had plagiarized from them),[40] all the while clashing with him over the belief that the Commune was singular and unrepeatable.[41] Debord's situationists, in contrast to Lefebvre, considered the Commune a historical precursor to the "festival" that would follow the imminent collapse of the contemporary spectacle. The only "true" transparency belonged to the festival and served them *ex negativo*: an anti-architecture targeting the ever-present, multifarious dangers of Western "spectacular" capitalism, in which

the images detached from every aspect of life merge into a common stream in which the unity of that life can no longer be recovered. *Fragmented* views of reality regroup themselves into a new unity as a *separate pseudo-world* that can only be looked at. The specialization of images of the world has culminated in a world of autonomized images where even the deceivers are deceived. The spectacle is a concrete inversion of life, an autonomous movement of the nonliving.[42]

If May 1968 had failed, then declaring it to be an exemplar of this festival and a premonitory moment, forever in contrast with June 1968's violent return to order, allowed the eternal recurrence of the other—the inversion of this spectacle of images and capital.

Althusser: Ideology as (False) Transparency

Louis Althusser, for his part, identified transparency with worse than confusion: it was pure ideology, the failure of critical reflection and of a proper theory of knowledge. In his lexicon, transparency and ideology were synonyms: whenever one term came up, he would use the other pejoratively. Defining ideology in his 1965 book *For Marx*, Althusser wrote:

But what, concretely, is this uncriticized ideology if not simply the "familiar," "well known," transparent myths in which a society or an age can recognize itself (but not know itself), the mirror it looks into for self-recognition, precisely the mirror it must break if it is to know itself?[43]

He continued, in praise of Bertold Brecht:

For him, the total, transparent consciousness of self, the mirror of the whole drama is never anything but an image of the ideological consciousness, which does include the whole world in its own tragedy, save only that this world is merely the world of morals, politics and religion, in short, of myths and drugs.[44]

As is well known, Althusser found in Marx a crucial epistemological rupture between the early "ideological" works (the early writings until about 1848–50), and the mature, post-1848, "scientific" works; Althusser's Marx became "Marx" by abandoning his early utopian socialism and misguided Feuerbachianism. What was dropped in the rupture, to the gain of the theory, was the transparent and humanist basis of the early thought, which had rendered it abstract, false, immaterial.[45] Ideology would stand for Marxism's target, Althusser's opposition to it announcing a revolutionary tendency that would unveil the false transparencies promulgated by the state. In a remarkable passage from his infamous "Ideology and Ideological State Apparatuses," Althusser wrote:

[It is] in ideology, that we "live, move and have our being." It follows that, for you and for me, the category of the subject is a primary "obviousness" (obviousnesses are always primary): it is clear that you and I are subjects (free, ethical, etc. . .). Like all obviousnesses, including those that make a word "name a thing" or "have a meaning" (therefore including the obviousness of the "transparency" of language), the "obviousness" that you and I are subjects—and that that does not cause any problems—is an ideological effect, the elementary ideological effect. It is indeed a peculiarity of ideology that it imposes (without appearing to do so, since these are "obviousnesses") obviousnesses as obviousnesses, which we cannot *fail to recognize* and before which we have the inevitable and natural reaction of crying out (aloud or in the "still, small voice of conscience"): That's obvious! That's right! That's true!"[46]

Attacking the obvious, the transparent, equaled forcing the real conditions of production—including the production of ideology—to reveal themselves; and in this regard the assumption of transparency in one's methodology was a falsehood as well. At the very beginning of *Reading Capital* Althusser mocked the ease with which "we have all read, and all do read *Capital*." An alternative to this "transparent" reading was necessary:[47]

Every reading merely reflects in its lessons and rules the real culprit: the conception of knowledge underlying the object of knowledge which makes knowledge what it is. We have glimpsed this with respect to the "expressive" reading, the open and bare-faced reading of the essence in the existence: and behind this total presence in which all opacity is reduced to nothing we have suspected the existence of the darkness of the religious phantasm of epiphanic transparency, and its privileged model of anchorage: the Logos and its Scriptures.[48]

All the "critical effort" that Althusser saw himself putting in toward a new "theoretical elaboration of Marxist philosophy" that should distinguish "science from ideology" was "indispensable . . . to a reading of Marx which is not just an immediate reading, deceived either by the false transparency of his youthful ideological conceptions, or by the perhaps still more dangerous false transparency of the apparently familiar concepts of the works of the [epistemological] break" of 1845.[49] For Marx to be read anew, for a theory of capitalism and of revolution to be possible, ideology—in Marx and in the present—had to be assaulted, transparency destroyed.

These different directions in theory and praxis offer a trajectory of French Marxism's engagement with transparency. With the publication of *Socialisme ou Barbarie* and the decline of pro-Soviet communism in France in the 1950s, communism became far less committed to a transparent society that might overcome the fog of dialectical history. Other thinkers, including Jacques Rancière and Jean-François Lyotard, would pursue highly similar lines of thought, at times strengthening the place of the dialectics and the irreducibility of alienation, at times negating the possibility or desirability of overcoming them.[50] With the exception of situationism, it was not until *after* 1968, indeed, until the spread of Parisian Maoism in the radical years 1969–73, that an advocacy of transparency would return in Marxist thought and politics.

PART III

NORMS, OTHERS, ETHNOGRAPHY, THE SYMBOLIC

New Languages of Philosophy, 1950–1963

Face, Mask, and Other as Avatars of Selfhood

A Third Short History

How much less hateful men would be if every one of them did not wear a face.

Henri Michaux, *Darkness Moves* (1997: 172)

I am no doubt not the only one who writes in order to have no face.

Michel Foucault, *The Archaeology of Knowledge* (1972: 17)

We also say of some people that they are transparent to us. It is, however, important as regards our considerations that one human being can be a complete enigma to another. One learns this when one comes into a strange country with entirely strange traditions; and, what is more, even though one has mastered the country's language. One does not *understand* the people. (And not because of not knowing what they are saying to themselves.) We can't find our feet with them.

Ludwig Wittgenstein, *Philosophical Investigations* (1986: 223)

The purpose of this chapter is to examine postwar conceptions of selfhood, subjectivity, and identity with the help of a group of concepts that I am treating here as "avatars" of the self. The first part tracks philosophical uses of the face and its masking in the period 1930–60, when the symbolic value of "the face," which was associated with sincerity and wholeness, corroded and was gradually replaced by that of masking and theatricality. The second part engages with the meaning and multiplication of "the other" in discussions of dialectics, homogeneity, and the unconscious, especially as understood by Jacques Lacan.

The Face and the Mask

In *Peau noire, masques blancs* (1952; *Black Skin, White Masks*), Frantz Fanon outlined a psychology of the racism experienced by black African and Caribbean men in contemporary France and the francophone world. Fanon never discussed his famous title in it—the meaning was obvious. Masks imposed by white men parade across the faces of the colonized, fusing with them; and this assemblage is supported by economic substructures that brim with the fantasies of the white other. Famously Fanon writes, "the black is not a man."[1] To explain the interweaving of cultural and economic realities, Fanon emphasized that culture can never be completely masked by economic structures; racism organizes economic power, ensuring the deformation of black selfhood by the same gesture that erases the humanity of the colonized and keeps their voices elusive, incomprehensible—utterly other.

Fanon held up the face as something natural or authentic dissimulated by masks imposed by the other. In this respect he was inverting a fairly common trope of the postwar period. As a signifier of autochthonous identity and selfhood, the face had become unavailable to Fanon's contemporaries; its original purity was lost. If he proposed to restore—or rather grant—a face, it was the face of this colonized other: those denied a face and an identity. In this assault on racism, Fanon turned the subject against itself.

This section focuses on the uses of the concept of face—along with facial damage, masking, and facial restoration. These uses changed considerably from the 1930s through the 1960s. In the 1930s, "face" often served as shorthand for identity and interpersonal transparency. The tropes of facial damage, mask, and desire to restore an original face played a surprising role in promoting an aesthetic and ethical currency in the area of interpersonal relations.

Face and visage

Visage, the common French equivalent for the English "face," designates both the front of the head and the character of the person; it has both a physical referent and an abstract one. In contrast, the French *face* has a more formal and technical use. Diderot and d'Alembert's *Encyclopédie*, which sought to limit *le visage* to physiology, nevertheless defined it as "ex-

heightened subjectivity by imposing its understanding of it on me. Beauvoir's passage closely reflects this formulation. For her, the momentary fantasy of ripping the face off promises an escape from oneself, yet remains a fantasy because of the ultimate transparency of the face. One is oneself only because of one's *visage*, but one's *visage* confirms relations with others without really showing itself. By being visible and human, the *visage* remains (unlike Garbo's face) undistinguishable. It denies any escape and thus confirms that the everyday is undisturbing and bearable because it is not dependent on disguise, masks, or dissimulation but on the transparency of human faces.

Masks also quickly became a standard bearer of postwar identity—and with them the world of shadows and the theater. In a 1948 study of masks, the sociologist Georges Buraud highlighted the tension between the desire for the face of another that is found in the static mask and the desire for sincerity.[22] Jean Starobinski, we have seen, became convinced that masking and dissimulation were essential to modern politics and authenticity. In the 1940s and 1950s, a subtle change in the study of Descartes stressed his theatricalization of identity and masking: quite suddenly, a passage in Descartes's *Cogitationes privatae* drew the mask into a philosophical engagement with identity. This was the famous *larvatus prodeo* passage where Descartes writes: "Masked I advance—like an actor who wears a mask to hide the redness of his face—on the stage of the world, to which until now I was a spectator."[23] Paradoxically, our knowledge that Descartes should be read, not as a paragon of sincerity and certainty, but as someone forever masking himself, bolstered the idea that sincerity was but the most forceful of masks. In his abandoned 1948 book on Descartes, Canguilhem quoted this passage twice, and only once did he mention Descartes's cautious stance toward the authorities, as was the customary interpretation:[24] "the prophet of the intellectual, political, economic, and social revolution remains prudently dissimulated, even if always troubled."[25] The second time *larvatus prodeo* served the more sweeping goal of rendering Descartes, his project, and his accomplishment less obvious, "masked" for all their apparent clarity:

Masked I advance. The masked philosopher? Perhaps, but know then that the possibility of wearing a mask is not for Descartes the artifice that would permit him to dissimulate his contempt for metaphysics, it's the artifice that he raises to the dignity of an instrument of metaphysical analysis."[26]

The cogito was to be understood as masked; and its mask could not be thrown off. Other contemporary readings of the passage also emphasized the mask as a problem: in 1946 Jacques Maritain, who sought to promote his own neo-Thomism, used the passage extensively in order to denounce Descartes: it is "a characteristic of Cartesian thought itself to be a masked thought. Is it deliberately calculated to be so? Obviously not. But thought that is involuntarily ambiguous, therefore ambiguous in its essential mode of thought, is but the more insidious."[27] The philosopher who had claimed to strip off all masks had morphed into the paradigmatic masked philosopher. In the 1950s, trust that a mask *could* be thrown aside became derided as a trademark of insufficient analysis that had failed to see another mask lying just beneath it. Taken as a claim that what appears empirically masks the proper structure of things, the *larvatus prodeo* sentence came to characterize structuralism's lack of interest in the empirical. Thus Foucault writes, for example: "[D]oesn't the text concerning the revealed secret [of Raymond Roussel's writing] have a secret of its own . . . masked by the very light it brings to bear on others?"[28]

No less concerned with the masks of sincerity was Merleau-Ponty, who in several elegiac pages on Descartes in his posthumously published 1952 text *La Prose du monde* (1969; *The Prose of the World*) described "our" difficulty of distinguishing his thought from his influence, his life from the reception of his writings.[29] For Merleau-Ponty, *larvatus prodeo* was nothing short of Descartes's "motto"; and it presented Descartes, not as a philosopher of pronounced sincerity committed to overcoming doubt,[30] but as one hidden behind his own masks, and even more so behind those of his posthumous persona, not least because of the awkward mediation effected by his relentless self-presentation.

And thus the philosopher of the *lumen naturale* became a figure crucial to "our" understanding of the problem of philosophy *because* he could not be understood solely as an author, a thinker, a living person, an institution, even an influence. His effort to balance sincerely the different elements of reason and "our" effort to understand him as a key inspiration of modern thought left "us" with a theater of masks, each of which overwrites the other in our hermeneutics of the prose of the world. From certainty to enigma, then: the cogito dissipates in the actor's makeup. Well into the 1970s, this idea of an "illustrious mask" that had ostensibly felled many a commentator in their attempts to find the "true Descartes" behind it was a staple in the deconstruction of Cartesian thought.[31] Rather than a world of sincere faces, philosophy was once again, in Foucault's formula, a *theatrum philosophicum*.[32] An author unmasking herself was an actor who wore a new mask—a stratagem that Foucault was content to apply to himself as well.[33]

There was yet another strategy for undoing the visage. No less famous than Beauvoir's *Mandarins* was *Three Studies for Figures at the Base of a Crucifixion*, a haunting triptych by the Irish-born painter Francis Bacon. First exhibited in 1944, it launched the artist's career in France: Bacon's figures at the foot of the cross retain sufficiently many elements from human figures to confer the title a certain plausibility. They relate it to inordinately disfigured humans who experience the passion in the absence of a cross, or they situate the viewer herself on the cross, staring down. At the same time they foreground facial characteristics that denote threat and violence (teeth, distorted lip), which are corroborated by the formlessness and de-characterization of the figures themselves.[34] The face, like the body, is broken; it testifies to violence done *to it* and to violence *it* can bring about. By being defaced, these figures *both* suffer disfiguration *and* threaten to impose their "order." Writing about Bacon in 1980, Gilles Deleuze would interpret his strategies in terms of *the* face giving way to *a* head:

Bacon is a painter of heads, not faces, and there is a great difference between the two. For the face is a structured, spatial organization that conceals the head whereas the head is dependent upon the body, even if it is the point of the body, its culmination. . . . Bacon thus pursues a very peculiar project as a portrait painter: to dismantle the face, to rediscover the head or make it emerge from beneath the face. . . . In place of formal correspondences, what Bacon's painting constitutes is a *zone of indiscernability* or *undecidability* between man and animal. Man becomes animal, but without the animal becoming spirit at the same time . . . the physical spirit of man presented in the mirror as Eumenides or Fate."[35]

Through his use of smudge, blurring, and defacement, Bacon became important to postwar existentialism, mainly because he offered, not a distinct expressive alternative to the face, but rather an opaque play of animal and man, face and head, subhuman and "Eumenid or Fate."

Loss of the face and descent into the subhuman—Fury, Eumenid, or fate—became a major cinematic preoccupation. In his 1960 *Theory of Film*, Siegfried Kracauer famously used Medusa's head to argue that humans could not experience the world at its most brute. "Now of all the existing media, the cinema alone holds up a mirror to nature . . . we do not, and cannot, see actual horrors because they paralyze us with blinding fear . . . [but] only by watching images of them which reproduce their true appearance."[36] To identify cinema with a mirror of nature, Kracauer cited a single film: Georges Franju's *Le Sang des Bêtes* (1949; *The Blood of Beasts*), a documentary about Paris abattoirs whose images, like "the litter of tortured human bodies in the films made of the Nazi concentration camps,"[37] "beckon the spectator to take them in and thus incorporate into his memory the real face of things too dreadful to be beheld in reality."[38] The French New Wave, too, adopted Franju's film as the carrier of an unbridled realism; but Kracauer went one step further, identifying it with cinema's entire realist purpose—to "redeem horror from its invisibility behind the veils of panic and imagination."[39] Franju himself, however, stepped back from this aesthetics in his 1959 narrative film *Les Yeux sans visage* (*Eyes without a Face*). There the protagonist is a young woman whose face has been mutilated in a car accident. While her surgeon father kidnaps girls to peel off their faces and graft their skin onto hers, Christiane—the film's Eumenid—hides constantly beneath a mask. She shows her face to a victim whose face she is about to receive, but only in two very quick shots, during which the camera is out of focus[40] (fig. 11.1).

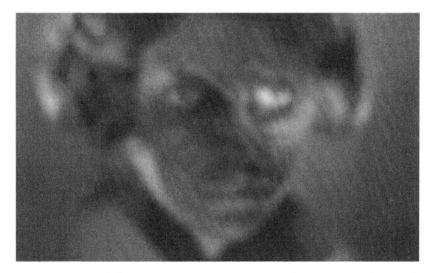

FIGURE 11.1 Still from *Les Yeux sans visage* (*Eyes without a Face*): Christiane's bare head without a face, seen only out of focus.
SOURCE: *Les Yeux sans visage* (Georges Franju, 1959), Criterion Collection DVD.

Franju, in other words, regaled viewers with the unviewable head of Medusa in the two blurred shots of Christiane's bare head.[41] Cinema could not reveal horror at its purest, for it would "paralyze us with blinding fear." Unlike *Blood of Beasts*, where the image of horror is put on display, *Eyes without a Face* keeps it blurry, the promise of a revelation quickly denied. *Pace* Kracauer, the film screen is *not* Athena's polished shield; *pace* the New Wave, reality has not been rendered accessible, nor has it been redeemed.[42] We can't really look into the depths of horror, right at the face of Medusa: representation discloses yet remasks the horror.

Believing oneself to have vanquished the world of masks and representation—to have acceded to transparent interpersonal relations—was self-deceit of the kind practiced by Rousseau and the Rorschach-test psychotics Starobinski wrote about. Levinas insisted that the distance from the other is absolute, and Lacan mocked presumptions of access to a pure truth: "'I, truth, speak . . . ' and the prosopopoeia continues," he wrote in 1966.[43] The experience of pure sublimity or pure horror is historically impossible: ours is a world of opacity, masks, and disguise.

This same sense of a constant masking and remasking inspired Fanon; for him, however, it was consistent with a hard demand for liberation. If black inferiority was in the first place a matter of economic oppression and alienation, it was also a matter of interiorization of that inferiority.[44] To undo it, one had to obsess over the masks of white and black people and the economic structures printed on them thanks to centuries of oppression, in the hope that real faces might emerge.

The Other

In the *Vocabulaire technique et critique de la philosophie*, André Lalande offered the following definition of *autre* ("other"):

One of the fundamental concepts of thought; as a result, impossible to define. It is opposed to Same [*Même*], and expressed also by the words *divers*, *different*, or *distinct* . . . [it] is specifically applied to the objective existence of alterity. See Identical [*Identique*] and Same [*Même*].[45]

Astonishingly, *the other* was a concept so fundamental to thought as to stump the philosopher authorized to offer the standard technical definition that should ground thought's transparency to itself: all Lalande could do apart from listing synonyms and antonyms was to throw up his hands at the task and note that *autre* concerns the "objective existence of alterity." Anyone turning to the entries recommended for clarification purposes— *même* ("same") and *identique* ("identical") would be just as underwhelmed: the entry for *même* merely redirects readers to *autre* and *identique,* and *identique* in turn redirects to *même* and *autre.* Noting that *identique* derives from the Latin pronoun "*idem,* the same," the entry then continues with the same sentence: "one of the fundamental concepts of thought: as a result, impossible to define." The dictionary at least references some uses of "the identical," but the point is pretty clear: "identical" and "other" were too basic for direct philosophical explanation.

Edmond Goblot's 1901 *Vocabulaire philosophique* also referred *autre* to *identique,* but was at least somewhat more explicit in its account of the latter. After a formal definition of the relation of identity, Goblot wrote:

Identical is also used in a more rigorously etymological sense (idem, the same) to designate what is one and the same thing, what remains substantially one whatever the variance of its attributes, accidents, modes. *The I is identical.*[46]

The last point comes in almost on the sly. Today some imagine too easily that the "structuralist" critique of identity and selfhood attacked a straw man. But, in 1900 as in 1922, the self, the same, and the identical shared a broad territory, which encompassed, if simply as their limit, the concept of the other.

After 1945, when "the other" came into wide use, it became even more "fundamental," in the sense that it spread across very different intellectual movements. Its uses were more precise and quite impossible to map onto one another. The symmetry between self and other was broken, the priority of the self dissipated. Christian, especially personalist arguments on the duty of care for others spoke of the insufficiency of any concept of the self that untethered the human being from God, dislodging society from its place as a community under God. Phenomenology and existentialism, precisely because of their subjectivism and reliance on the irreducibility of consciousness, treated the other as impossible for this consciousness to capture or assimilate. Camus's *L'Étranger* similarly turned the asymmetric relation between self and other against the self, which it represented as violent, and made famous this feeling of not conforming to social and cultural norms—a feeling previously attached to the political Right—as a generalized estrangement from society that extended to human existence itself. Sartre and Levinas generally agreed on this matter: no philosophy before theirs had adequately theorized the other and the responsibility one bears toward another. Hegelian dialectics, which was woven into existentialism and Marxism, regarded alterity as something produced by the dialectical unfolding of history, thought, and life. Marxism focused on alienation—the worker's alienation from the product of his or her labor. This allowed Marxist thinkers to expand their scope and consider the consumer's dependence on goods in terms of alienation too. Psychoanalysis, especially Lacan's, focused relentlessly on the ego's invasion of territories of the unconscious, construed as "other." Anthropologists began to present colonized and indigenous others as the "real" other.[47] Compounding their critique of the self, these approaches pointed to sites of non-identity and heterogeneity; threatened as it was by the self, the unassimilable, ineradicable other was worth defending.

A philosophical lexicographer working in the 1950s would thus have been flummoxed by an even more nettlesome other, but for different reasons from those of his or her predecessors. Any attempt to chart these varieties of otherness into a single account would have required either a specious or a highly creative effort. The other was key to the intellectual language, yet the roles it played in competing conceptual systems were often quite different. This meant several things. First, emphasis on the heterogeneous reflected a series of widely shared mistrusts: of celebrations of community, of claims to unmediated "communication" between speaker and listener, of theories of a singular, undivided self. Second, the other served the blending, conjoining, or translation of conceptual systems: it helped philosophers in particular to adapt *parts* of a philosophy without subscribing to the whole thing. This contributed to the prioritization of the other across different domains: practices of social homogenization would generate much the same critique as an oppressive concept of selfhood. What was "other" in each case survived translation.

By 1979, it was possible to write a history of the past half-century of French thought and title it *Le Même et l'autre* (trans. as *Modern French Philosophy*).[48] It is not my purpose in this chapter to compete with Vincent Descombes's book or with Samuel Moyn's account of the interwar and Christian origins of the other.[49] Moyn's subject, Emmanuel Levinas—

who from the later 1950s on foregrounded the self's separation from the other and offered the classic ethical argument for the other's irreducibility to the wishes of the ego—is the paradigm of the preoccupation with defending alterity as the only possible source of ethics. Similarly, Peter Hallward, Knox Peden, and others have examined the place of the other in the mid-1960s journal *Cahiers pour l'analyse* prepared by Louis Althusser's students.[50] My objective is rather different: to chart some of the allied pathways that were available for the use of alterity in the critique of any self-identical subject and of any ethics that did not assume separation, opposition, and the bruising of a limited self. To tell the story of the other in the postwar period is also to explain how it was involved in a thinking of ethical and political transparency. By 1961, when Levinas published *Totality and Infinity*, this argument had been stenciled fairly carefully—if not always in the explicit, unyielding form Levinas gave it.

Ethical Transparency and the Problem of Heterogeneity

Descartes's conception of the philosopher as *honnête homme* provided the moderns with a forceful and efficient language that blended the ethical dimension of transparency with visual and social ones, above all in constructing the philosopher's persona. Post-Cartesian developments—notably Locke's *tabula rasa*, Rousseau's aim at purity, Kant's understanding of finitude, Victor Cousin's production of an autarchic, internally unified, fully independent self[51]—guided several styles of interpersonal transparency, community, fusion, and love, which grounded all engagement of the other. In the twentieth century, ethical transparency found in these pasts a series of *points d'appui* for the social and ethical commitment of philosophical labor in the defense of the clear, transparent self. Like Descartes's *honnête homme* and, at the other end of this history, Sartre's argument on responsibility (and his persona as an existentialist public intellectual), the approach to philosophy that foregrounded theories of ethical transparency relied on long-standing conceptions of the philosopher's self and his ethical commitments.

In the postwar period, these *points d'appui* added up to the history of a particular kind of subjectivity, which had blended pure consciousness with clarity of intentions, individual autonomy, true self-knowledge, and ethical purity. The concept of "the other" fit snugly within this system of ideas, although it lacked the symmetry imagined by Lalande. Against that tradition, Sartre's account of the other—with its attention to the self's incapacity to grasp this other, its tendency to objectify it, and its fundamental responsibility for it—fired the opening salvo. Partly because of its famous passage on shame, the account in *Being and Nothingness* became the best known, though by no means the only or the most easily accepted one. "The other," no longer a derivative of "the same," "the identical," or "the self," could be contrasted with them far more affirmatively, because it was now backed by a set of often very different notions—ambiguity, dialectics, heterogeneity. It disrupted the belief that a pure, ethical relation to fellow human beings was possible; the *honnête homme* would not guarantee ethics or harmony. By emphasizing that the relation of self to other was imperious and mired in violence, "the other" called for the retheorization of this asymmetry and the recognition of violence as an essential component of interpersonal relations. In this way the critique of subjective and ethical transparency slipped easily into a critique of political morality and political transparency in general. "The self" was expansive and dominant at the level of the subject, just as "the same" threatened to neutralize difference and heterogeneity at the social level.

From Ambiguity in Political Morality to the Existentialization of Alienation

As long-standing a concern as any in French thought, political morality after World War II was steeped in ambiguity to the extent of transforming it into a positive concept. We have seen this in Merleau-Ponty, who used the ubiquity of violence to argue against certainty in history and turned ambiguity into a structural component of existential thrownness. Simone de Beauvoir, who forcefully articulated the status of woman as "other" in *The Second Sex* and then pursued an ethics of ambiguity, was, however, far more influential.[52] "As long as there have been men and they have lived, they have all felt this tragic ambiguity of their condition, but as long as there have been philosophers and they have thought, most of them have tried to mask it."[53] For Beauvoir, the discord between our subjective conscious experience and our condition as objects in the experience of others is constitutive of ethical life, mainly because it generates essentially ambiguous relations of alterity. "Let us try to assume our fundamental ambiguity," she continued. Claudia Card has contrasted Anglo-American conceptions of ambiguity as a flaw with Beauvoir's interest in

a being who is, on one hand, conscious, a choosing subject, an agent, and on the other hand (at the same time), an object of perception (both others' perceptions and one's own), at the mercy of forces beyond its control. . . . As situated beings, all humans share this fundamental ambiguity of being at once subject and object. Beauvoir's attitude toward this condition is not to regard it or the tension it produces as undesirable, a flaw to be eliminated if possible. For Beauvoir, ideally we embrace and live our ambiguity. This belief lies at the heart of her humanism.[54]

Beauvoir took ambiguity to be a basic ethical problem for the subject: "tragic" as it may be, it is also the mark of freedom and the force of our temporal existence. In such conceptions, *ambiguity* emerged so to speak "from without" and then was—had to be—assumed within, straining the self internally, indicating the self's dual capacity for violent excess and tense fragility thanks to an othering that could not be avoided. But it was two other concepts in this conceptual web, namely *dialectics* and *alienation*—the signature concepts of the Hegelian and Marxist traditions—that, together with a concomitant concept of the *heterogeneous*, helped conceptualize a broader opposition to a homogenized, neutered society supposedly bereft of difference and dialectic.

Dialectics and alienation were perhaps the two concepts that made possible and organized the figure of "the other." For intellectuals drawn to the "Hegel renaissance" that began in the 1930s, conflictual intersubjectivity was as essential as the internal division of the self. The dialectic of recognition presented by Alexandre Kojève as the definitive historical conflict of masters against slaves seeking to become citizens was paralleled by the understanding of the "unhappy consciousness" as an internalization of this dialectic into the human self.[55] These trends contributed to the perception of an individuality imperiled by sociability, threatened by and threatening to others. Turned into a me–you confrontation, dialectics complicated any ostensibly subjectivist phenomenology such as Husserl's: the self was now in constant flow, its harmony pained by all kinds of social, political, metapolitical, and subjective breaks. For Sartre, dialectics distinguished Hegel from philosophers like Husserl and Heidegger, who could not think intersubjectivity because they allowed no room for disjunction and communication between two existents.[56] Dialectics' ever renewed deployment of contrasts and use of negation to render self-identity impossible were telescoped into an imbalanced intersubjectivity, which equated transparent communication with mysticism or communitarianism.[57]

The Hegelian self strengthened the Marxist notion of alienation, in which the worker is internally divided — at once held firm yet torn asunder — by her or his labor. According to Georges Friedmann, for example, the technological domination of the worker destroyed all hopes of progress. The entire dream of ending alienation and restoring purity to human relations—the revolutionary promise of communism—then yielded a core conceptual axis shared between postwar critiques of modernity. Dialectics and alienation did not institute a settled conception of otherness, but they did transpose social relations into the self. If, as Sartre quipped, "hell is other people," this was so not least because languages of dialectics and alienation could absorb alterity from the social level and inject it into the divided self. For an afflicted existentialist, "estrangement"—this sense of being overwhelmed and pushed away—amounted both to a closing into oneself and a recognition that this self could and should be celebrated in terms of freedom. Sartre and Beauvoir rephrased and redirected the Hegelian–Marxist pressure. Capitalist modernity denatured the self and destroyed any possibility of genuine relations with others. Sartre's solution, which reimposed transparency through action, seemed at once satisfactory—to him—and deeply flawed—to most others—if the spiral of self and other were to be seen for its decentering of both.

Against Homogeneity: Georges Bataille
beyond Capitalism and Romanticism

A third point on the web, a concept concomitant with dialectics and ambiguous political morality, was the concept of the *heterogeneous*, construed in opposition to a homogenized, neutral society bereft of difference and dialectic. Indeed, a quite different opening for thinking otherness emerged with the blend of literary and sociological philosophy that characterized Georges Bataille's late interwar and wartime writings; and it persisted, somewhat transformed, into his writings of the postwar period. Like Sartre, Bataille found inspiration in Marxism and dialectics; but, even as he *agreed* that the distance to the other was impossible to traverse and he treated it as a mystical experience, Bataille approached alterity very differently. Confronted by the "end of history" that Alexandre Kojève propagated in his course on Hegel, Bataille reacted by fusing this notion of history, decelerated to a painful standstill, with Durkheimian anxiety over the loss of symbolic power and with a Schmittian narrative in which the advent of liberalism in the nineteenth and twentieth centuries "neutralized" differences and overran genuine sovereignty.[58] His critique of fascism in the 1930s reflects this fusion in a conceptualization of homogeneity. "As a rule, *homogeneous* society excludes every *heterogeneous* element, whether filthy or noble."[59] Unlike capitalist societies or the Soviet Union, fascism produced a new heterogeneity: a new ecstatic union with the chief–leader that "is not simply a uniting of powers from different origins and a symbolic uniting of classes: it is also the accomplished uniting of the *heterogeneous* elements with the *homogeneous* elements, of sovereignty in the strictest sense with the state."[60] Yet this was an illusion: fascism's (re)heterogeneization of modernity did not emancipate human beings from the power of the leaders or of the mass and did not allow for the creation of any *self*-sovereignty. Its imposition of sovereignty was repressive *tout court*.

By the late 1930s, Bataille felt that he could not sustain the antifascist, socialist romanticism that underlay this argument. Disappointed by the war, whose destructive "challenge" to "everything" did not satisfy his antibourgeois liberatory fantasy,[61] Bataille experienced a "mystical" interiorization.[62] "Once war broke out, there was no way I could wait any more—wait, that is, for the liberation which this book is for me."[63] Interiority swallowed heterogeneity. In *L'Expérience intérieure* (1943; *Inner Experience*), Bataille pressed the self to reach beyond itself, to a "summit" where it would overcome its homogeneous tie to external objects and form a radically *other* relation to them—one that made true communication possible.[64] Sovereignty rested in escaping all determinations, moving away from everyday life and politics toward an authentic internal other. Social transparency, even in heterogeneous circumstances, was an illusion; selfhood could not have moral credentials if it lacked depth—or if, following Durkheim, it emptied itself out for the sake of a transparent social ecstasy. Only individual *subjects* who rejected the homogeneity of modern bourgeois subjectivity could conquer their subjection and become self-sovereign, but only internally and almost without experiencing it "themselves." Heterogeneity was a fleeting experience—extravagant moments of excess or ecstasy—like sovereignty, the exception in a homogeneous life.[65]

After World War II, Bataille approached heterogeneity again, but this time in an explicit effort to dislocate sovereignty from political hegemony.

In *La Part maudite* (1949; *The Accursed Share*), he refused bourgeois and communist economic rationalism as fundamentally homogenizing. Otherness had to be reinjected into the homogeneous relations enforced by economistic rationality. The desiccated self was one with "the same," except when it was confronted with an "economy of the self" enforced by bourgeois capitalism and Soviet accumulation. In such moments, the self recognized itself as struggling against reduction, and it moved—or was moved—to practices of excess, waste, or supreme giving. These became acts of true sovereignty: masterful negations of economic rationalization and political uniformity. Harmony with the world had not been possible since the earliest moments of humanity, when it was memorialized in the paintings on the walls of Lascaux and other Paleolithic caves, which marked the birth of representation and the recognition that this harmony had been forever breached.[66] Rather than tolerating promises of harmony, one needed to direct such practices of anti-economical self-sovereignty against oppression and political powers of Left, Right, and Center.

Thus Bataille's interwar romanticism gave way to a theory of social forces that demanded that the self seek and even momentarily reach the heterogeneous. For a thinker who had long derided purities of this sort as anything but good, the production of otherness in relations with others became the only romanticism or mysticism worth pursuing, one that preempted communist and capitalist binaries, and could only be satisfied by a sovereignty opposed to any and all subjection to sameness and neutrality.

Bataille's idiosyncrasies should not make us forget that watered-down versions of the humanism he espoused enjoyed popularity. The idea that the human is constitutively self-surpassing, involved in becoming other, in moving toward the introjection of the heterogeneous and toward a truer form of communication shaped efforts in critical thought (including unorthodox Marxism), in theologically inflected philosophy, as well as in more popular answers to the question "What is the human?" It had nonconformist political ramifications as well: already in 1946 Dionys Mascolo praised Saint-Just and claimed that "culture ceaselessly works to pull back to the norm anything that seems to promise any development, anything that, in man, surpasses the limits of man as he is known. . . . What surpasses man—excess, incensed desires, dreams, madness—surpasses him toward a human that we can only presage, and to whom we know we will one day appear completely obsolete."[67]

In the 1950s Bataille and Mascolo belonged to a more or less informal group—the Group of the Rue Saint-Benoît—around Mascolo himself, Marguerite Duras, Robert Antelme, and Maurice Blanchot. The group's protagonists took center stage in political debates when they wrote and circulated the *Manifesto of the 121*, which called upon French soldiers in Algeria to disobey orders in the name of Algeria's freedom. The association of insubordination and self-sovereignty in the name of self-surpassing, and indeed of reaching the other, was strongly Bataillean. Bataille himself did not sign the manifesto, but, as Stuart Kendall has argued, leaders of the group "shared the experience of this hopeless search, this openness to the impossible," which guided the manifesto's appeal to freedom through a use of expressions like "spontaneous conscience."[68]

Emmanuel Levinas's own celebration of the other needs to be understood in this context too. The other transcends me, inasmuch as transcendence belongs, as in Bataille, to exteriority, to an infinity that I can never arrest, not even through violence. This transcendence connects me to others even as it separates me from them:

Transcendence designates a relation with a reality infinitely distant from my own reality, yet without this distance destroying this relation and without this relation destroying this distance, as would happen with relations with the same; this relation does not become an implantation in the other and a confusion with him, does not affect the very identity of the same, its ipseity, does not silence the *apology*, does not become apostasy and ecstasy.[69]

This "reality infinitely distant from my own reality" buries any hopes of transparency. Separation is essential to a concept of humanity as open and promoting a strict ethical relation to the absolute others with whom I experience life and society.

The real must not only be determined in its historical objectivity, but also from interior intentions, from the *secrecy* that interrupts the continuity of historical time. Only in the basis of this secrecy is the pluralism of society possible. It attests this secrecy. We have always known that it is impossible to form an idea of the human totality, for men have an inner life closed to him who does, however, grasp the comprehensive movements of human groups. The way of access to social reality starting with the separation of the I is not engulfed in "universal history" in which only totalities appear.[70]

The message offered by these authors was clear: transparency generates a form of social homogeneity that erases alterities and encourages submis-

sion and conformism even in the name of purity and "revolutionary virtue." Wouldn't then a demand for social and ethical transparency amount
to an institutionalization of violence? The figure who would formalize these
questions, bring them to the center of philosophical discussion, and perfect
Bataille's language of homogeneity was Michel Foucault. Already in his first
book—published in 1961, shortly before Bataille's death—and down to his
later work, madness, the heterogeneous, and the other belonged together:

> What happened in the eighteenth century was a slippage . . . thanks to which the
> structures of the reasonable and the rational became interwoven. . . . The mad-
> man, who was the outsider par excellence, pure difference, "other" to the power
> of two, became in this very distance the object of rational analysis, fullness of-
> fered to knowledge and evident perception, the one precisely to the extent that
> he was the other.[71]

And it was Jacques Lacan who, partly on the basis of his understanding of
the other, would offer an argument for undoing this modern norm.

Jacques Lacan and the Unconscious as Other

Perhaps the definitive ethical structuring of "the other" can be found
in the early work of Jacques Lacan. A redefinition of the other that would
not have even a glimmer of unity with the self was necessary, if the concept was to have any usefulness for a system that worked with the notion
of an unconscious as "other" and aspired to treat intersubjectivity, internal division, alienation, the ethical imperative, and the call of heterogeneity rigorously. Lacan declared: "It is often what appears to be harmonious
and comprehensible which harbors some opacity. And inversely it is in the
antinomy, in the gap, in the difficulty, that we happen upon opportunities for transparency."[72] Lacan's teaching and writing in the early postwar
period signals the spread of "the other" beyond existentialism and Hegelianism, into disciplines like psychoanalysis: Lacan deployed selfhood and
otherness in his famous 1949 essay on the "mirror stage," in his early seminars, and in his subsequent treatment of "other" versus "Other."

Lacan began his treatment of the other with a critique of existentialism both for its lackadaisical account of concept formation and for the generic quality of its ethics. In his 1954–55 seminar he ad-libbed:

> One of our colleagues, our ex-colleagues, who used to hobnob a bit with *Les Temps*
> *modernes*, the journal of existentialism, as it's called, told us as if it were news that

in order for someone to be analyzed he had to be able to conceive of the other as such. A real smart alec, that one. We should have asked him: What do you mean by the other?—his fellow man, his neighbor, his ideal I, a washbowl? These are all others.[73]

Fastening on phenomenology's presumed ownership of intersubjectivity and its understanding of selfhood, Lacan exploited the ambiguity of Rimbaud's line *Je est un autre* ("I is an other")[74] to ask whether one might not seek alterity within that very self. His already famous 1949 essay "The Mirror Stage as Formative of the *I* Function as Revealed in Psychoanalytic Experience" had laid out these problems of the other by placing existentialism—and its utilitarian representation of society as a "concentration-camp form of the social bond"—squarely in Lacan's crosshairs:

existentialism can be judged on the basis of the justifications it provides for the subjective impasses that . . . result therefrom: a freedom that is never so authentically affirmed as when it is within the walls of a prison; a demand for commitment that expresses the inability of pure consciousness to overcome any situation; a voyeuristic-sadistic idealization of sexual relationships; a personality that achieves self-realization only in suicide; and *a consciousness of the other that can only be satisfied by Hegelian murder*. These notions are opposed by the whole of analytic experience.[75]

Why was such a full-throated attack so critical for a short essay intent on showing that the I is formed out of a relationship with its mirror image? Because Lacan was developing a genetically and structurally complex theory of self and other. His contempt for existentialism was matched only by that toward theories promoted by psychological schools that began from the cogito to rebuild the unity of the *I* at the expense of the unconscious. The picture of the self that Lacan countered with was, if anything, even bleaker than theirs: the genesis of the ego was coextensive with the deformation resulting from its apprehension of others and its confrontation with its reflected self. The self was internally divided and in constant struggle with the world.

In "The Mirror Stage" Lacan placed the formation of the ego in the first six to eighteen months of life and associated it with the child's identification with its mirror image. This process happens "prior to its social determination"[76] and is more fundamental to human experience than any "homeomorphic" or "heteromorphic" identification. The encounter with one's own form also precedes any genuine experience of an ego–other contrast; in fact it produces the ego through a visually mediated amalgamation of that mirror image which is neither quite oneself nor quite another. The child is abruptly pulled onto this stage, and staggers to make it its own. It undergoes complex, internal, and uncontrollable transformations guided by the unconscious's distorted interaction with the "clean" external image in the mirror. There follows a misrecognition of one's mirror image as one's real self—a recognition that generates at once *internal* and *external* alienation.

This emphasis on misrecognition and alienation marks an important maneuver in Lacan's thought. In an abbreviated 1938 encyclopedia article version of the seemingly lost 1936 original,[77] the mirror stage enables the "adaptation" of the partly formed self to the environment. While acknowledging that internal alienation occurred as a result of identification, in that text Lacan treats adaptation to the external world as a prerequisite to the organism's social functioning. By 1949, he had dropped the rhetoric of adaptation. Setting up the ego and propping oneself up are *imaginary* processes: they occur through the absorption and redeployment of the environment or outside world,[78] understood as a theater or spectacle of images and imagos. The process of self-construction and maturation is one of profound deformation. It is a fundamentally alienating experience, because it is based on enforcing a fusion:

the mirror stage is a drama whose internal pressure pushes precipitously from insufficiency to anticipation—and, for the subject caught up in the lure of spatial identification, turns out fantasies that proceed from a fragmented image of the body to what I will call an "orthopedic" form of its totality—and to the finally donned armor of an alienating identity that will mark his entire mental development with its rigid structure.[79]

The claim that the self cannot arise without a prior process of internalizing the image of the object makes that image, the corresponding imago— that is, its idealized version or deformation—and the corresponding process of deformation that gives rise to the separated ego "the true object of psychology."[80] The mirror stage thus inscribes alienation into the self via the imaginary self-construction of the ego, through a process of self-identification that buttresses narcissism while aggressively fissuring this self. If the self started by being thoroughly "unformed" vis-à-vis social and interpersonal matters, by the end of this process it is more than "formed"—it is deformed in the sense of being mediated, "adapted" in a pejorative sense, and hence capable of "proper" social behavior:

It is this moment [when the mirror stage comes to an end] that decisively tips the whole of human knowledge into being mediated by the other's desire, constitutes its objects in an abstract equivalence due to competition from other people, and turns the *I* into an apparatus to which every instinctual pressure constitutes a danger, even if it corresponds to a natural maturation process.[81]

The newly formed "I" has become the guardian of the self's participation in the social realm and represses, blocks off in the unconscious alone, the very instincts that compete in the inner world. And the proto-intersubjectivity of encounters with the self and the other across the mirror constitutes that inner world, together with the dialectic of recognition generated at this stage.

This idea—that the creation of the ego also generates internal otherness by forcing an alienating rupture between the ego (or the "I") and the unconscious—began here as a *genetic* proposition and shifted in the early 1950s to one that is both genetic and *structural*. In other words a hypothesis that considers the mature "I" to be structurally underwritten by the unconscious which is now other to it. At the post-mirror stage otherness occurs not only in the experience of other people and objects via their imagos, but also "internally." Language in particular plays a crucial role here, as it is internalized with the advent of intersubjectivity. It functions at an unconscious level that the "I" does not control: it occupies a slot that can only be examined thanks to Freud's "discovery" of the unconscious.

During the early 1950s, Lacan connected these two processes: *the othering of unconscious instincts by the ego* (which becomes dominant with the conclusion of the Oedipus complex); and *the introduction of language*. He adopted a terminology in which "the other" (lowercase "o") still referred to others within one's field of experience and refracted through the constant reconstruction of imagos. But then he added "the Other" (capital "O"), which designated the unconscious and its symbolic order. Alienated through the formation of the ego, the unconscious assimilates the language in whose universe the subject enters—the language that now lies beneath the ego—and, in doing so, it also transforms it. Lacan famously noted that "the unconscious is structured like a language." In this manner the unconscious completes its transformation into the Other—an other that is more alien to the "I" than any others that this "I" will ever experience in the world through the mediation of the imaginary.[82] Lacan thus dichotomized the self by introducing an altogether new metapsychological language into Freud's universe. In the second year of his seminar, 1954–55 (and also in contemporary essays, especially "The Function and Field of Speech and Language in Psychoanalysis," originally published in 1953), he identified the Other—that "absolute other"—with the unconscious experienced by the falsely hegemonic "I." This move was accompanied by a broader complexification of Lacan's system: he hypothesized a triad of "Imaginary," "Symbolic," and "Real"; and he declared "the subject" of psychoanalysis to be the subject (or agent) of unconscious activity, as opposed to the classic subject—the thinking, speaking conscious subject since Descartes's *ego cogito*. This was a recurrent theme of the period: Lacan wrote, for example, that the particularity of psychoanalysis in psychiatric practice resides in the *specific* function it grants to speech, which rearticulates Freud's argument that "the axial reality of the subject isn't in his ego," and that "the unconscious is the unknown subject of the ego . . . it is misrecognized by the ego."[83] The unconscious, the constantly misrecognized and misunderstood "core of our being,"[84] was an absolute Other that mediated a structural understanding of the fact and action of otherness within the self. The homonymy between "other" and "Other" only strengthened this point, emphasizing internal as well as social alienation, the language around the "I" that traversed into and beneath it. Lacan repeatedly noted, for example, that "the unconscious is the Other's discourse," or that "desire is the Other's desire"—a formulation for which he used both "other" and "Other" on different occasions.[85]

Lacan began the aforecited 1954–55 seminar by noting that the "unconscious completely eludes that circle of certainties by which man recognizes himself as ego."[86] Beyond and below intersubjectivity, it serves as a structural precondition of identity and alterity. It is

an absolute other, I mean an other beyond all intersubjectivity. This beyond of the intersubjective relation is attained most especially on the imaginary level. What's at issue is an essential alien [*dissemblable*], who is neither the supplement nor the complement of the fellow being [*semblable*], who is the very image of dislocation, of the essential tearing apart of the subject. The subject passes beyond this glass in which he always sees, entangled, his own image. All interposition between the subject and the world ceases. One gets the feeling that a passage into a kind of a-logic occurs, and that's where the problem in fact begins, for we see that we are not in it. And yet the logos doesn't forego all its rights here.[87]

No longer is transparent glass a figure of immediacy: like the mirror, it is a mediator of the self to itself. "An other beyond all intersubjectivity" retains intersubjectivity, but only as reconstructed from within;[88] and the entire point of psychoanalysis is to recover something from this absolute Other, this unconscious, that constitutes its subject.[89] The relationship of the Other both with the ego and with the particular "other" who is the analyst undersigned a profound lack of self-transparency and interpersonal transparency—especially in the analytic relationship, which aimed to "raise" the unconscious to spoken discourse.

The primordial condition for [the analyst's concrete intervention] is that the analyst should be thoroughly convinced of the radical difference between the Other to whom his speech should be addressed, and the second other who is the One he sees before him, about whom and by means of whom the first speaks to him in the discourse it pursues before him.[90]

As intersubjectivity is underwritten genetically at the mirror stage and structurally through the introjection of language into the unconscious, the deforming ("orthopedic") and even violent character with which it had been associated in "The Mirror Stage" becomes, through the ego, part and parcel of the repression of "the core of our Being." The transferential relationship of analyst and analysand aims to counteract that violence and to offer an ethical space in which one's authentic desire can be recognized and a sustained undoing of this violence is possible—but only "at the cost" of accepting irreducible alienation and of refusing any possible transparency. Psychoanalysis becomes a science of internal and external separation, a guard against community and against the ego-based oppression of the heterogeneous, which survives within and between "individuals."

Throughout the remainder of his career Lacan did not tire of saying that the key ethics of psychoanalysis was expressed in Freud's *Wo Es war, soll Ich werden* ("Where the 'it' [*id*] was, there shall the 'I' [*ego*] be"). Translating and rephrasing the dictum a number of times,[91] he emphasized the ego's dialectical recognition that it must grow to comprise unconscious desire in its subjectivity; he also described a sense of reconciliation through the recognition of this alterity—a "reintegration and harmony, I might even say . . . reconciliation" between ego and id.[92] The goal was not to erase the other within and announce a new transparent self, but rather to manage the relationship between "I" and "Other" in such a way as to facilitate each patient's idiosyncratic subjectivity. Thus the term "other" negotiated, on new grounds, impulses originally granted it by phenomenology and dialectics, which Lacan "liberated" from them. The heterogeneous was formalized as systematically disrupting a domain formerly conceived of as closed. It marked the human being as defined by a systematic violence in the misrecognition and repression of unconscious desire. It offered internal otherness as a mirror of social fragmentation and of attempts to heal them with an ethical imperative that had thus far been ignored or undermined. As Michel de Certeau would emphasize in an admiring essay, Lacan's speech and teaching became a discourse *for* the other, a constant effort to emphasize how the unconscious broke up into the meanings generated by language within the self. Lacan's entire performance in his seminar was an effort to allow the Other its day in the sun, in full knowledge that this could not be sustained:

> Like his "patient," the analyst lets his [speech] recount that part of his story which "escapes" him and which "flushes" (like a hare is flushed) the Other represented by all those anonymous and scattered listeners. But he also knows that the swarming of interpretations engendered in the crowd [of his listeners] will never confer a meaning or an acceptable image upon the wordgames or ramblings received from the Other whom he does not know. . . . He is speaking for the Other, as one would speak in one's hat, fruitlessly.[93]

Not only was it impossible in philosophy and the human sciences to maintain claims to self-identity after this psychoanalysis: even the notion of a homogeneity of the self could be refuted as a distinctly hegemonic and oppressive enterprise. Ethically, Lacan's restoration of the unconscious to its supposedly rightful battle with the ego became a site of refusing just this hegemony of an ego imposed by outside powers. If, for Sartre and Levinas, halting the power and self-assertion of a self-identical subject was the foundation of ethics, in Lacan's view, their concept of the self still retained a fundamental self-identity and genuinely threatened the chance of undoing repressive homogeneity and transparency. In his argument, otherness covered not only the subjective and historical repression of the unconscious, but also its primary relation with the ego and intersubjectivity. The other and the Other were guarantors of the failure of wholeness, homogeneity, homogenization.[94]

The ideal of transparency—of the self, of interpersonal relations, of a pure society—was decisively undermined at this point. Transparency served Lacan and Bataille as the symbol of a subtle, pervasive violence characteristic of the entire history of the modern West. In the pejorative representation of self-identity offered by Lévi-Strauss and his fellow anthropologists, this transparent and homogenous self became the carrier of an oppressive homogenization and the false dream of a society without others. In the 1980s, the Antillean poet Édouard Glissant would fight this falsely eirenic harbor of homogeneity, selfhood, and transparency: for him, too, Western transparency encased and destroyed cultural particularity. But opacity—transparency's unintelligible "other"—could give a reliable anti- and postcolonial account of how the West had bowdlerized other cultures through enforced homogenization.[95] Lacan outlined the "internal" psychoanalytic ground in which the power of this Western self dominated and repressed desire—in the self, but, by extension, also in the sociopolitical realm.

12

The Norm and the Same

Here it is a wall of language that blocks speech, and the precautions against verbalism that are a theme of the discourse of "normal" men in our culture merely serve to increase its thickness.

Jacques Lacan, "The Function and Field of Speech and Language in Psychoanalysis" (SLP 282/233)

The language of *the other* irrupted in the 1950s in parallel with that of *the norm* and *the normal*. The two had similar ethical and political implications in that, in different ways but using quite similar arguments, they upended the established meanings and conceptual alliance of the terms "self," "normal," and "same." This turn is conventionally situated in the 1960s and associated with Michel Foucault's *History of Madness*; with the (belated) reception of Georges Canguilhem's *The Normal and the Pathological* among the students of Louis Althusser; with the antipsychiatry of Félix Guattari and others; and with the newfound prominence of a quasi-surrealist literary tradition that celebrated abnormality, excess, and ecstasy and embraced authors like Friedrich Nietzsche, Georges Bataille, Antonin Artaud, Michel Leiris, and Raymond Roussel. The countervailing of norms led in the 1960s and 1970s to a liberation ethic around sexuality, the marginal, and the oppressed and to the problematization of the equivalence between the normal, the healthy, and the right, taken for granted until then. Intellectuals ceased to think of norms and normality as ideals, rules, or goals; they began to see them as forces that generate, homogenize, and impose value judgments.

Still, it is a mistake to date this shift to the 1960s and to rummage for its trigger in literature or philosophy. It was medicine, sociology, and psychiatry that unleashed the theoretical renegotiation of the normal or healthy body, of the psychiatric patient, of societies domestic and foreign. Offering a critique of norms, these disciplines imposed a move away from the traditional conception that *theoretical* sciences are superior to *applied* or technical ones (e.g., psychology over psychiatry; biology over medicine and pathology; philosophy over the human sciences). Since the mid-nineteenth century "the normal" had served as a means of establishing an idealist perspective, of legitimizing abstract theoretical disciplines, and then of applying their results through empirical methods. But, from the 1920s, the scientific and philosophical observer was quite abruptly reconstrued as an active participant. In parallel, the earlier position, in philosophy and biology, that the norm was a transparent rule, an ideal, and an applicable model fell prey to demonstrations of its artificiality; it was the twilight of idealism. As part of this process, values called "natural" were reinterpreted as political and metapolitical judgments, and thus contributed to the terms in which the 1960s were articulated—such as the assault by alternative, lived truths on established, supposedly transparent and objective rules. French thinkers, without simply refusing all norms (though in the 1970s such positions were advocated as well),[1] treated normality in human affairs as derivative of politically and scientifically imposed norms. On this view, normative practices and ideas of normality in science depend on a false connection between objectivity and naturalism, thanks to which they play a formative role in human beings' experience of the world. They enforce homogeneity by naturalizing particular cultural values as rules; and they damage those who do not fall under the rubric or classification of "normal."

How did classic conceptions of the norm and the normal become an object of epistemological and political mistrust? How did the new biomedical and psychological understanding oppose scientific and policy-oriented epistemologies that relied on the reduction of social complexity to normality-oriented and adaptive norms? In what follows I first discuss interwar debates about norms and the normal, then attend to the replacement of that style of approach by nascent concepts in anthropology, philosophy of medicine, and psychoanalysis.

The disaggregation of the norms–normal unit is correlated to the critique of transparency in several ways. First, it reinforced the effect of the language of *the other* by introducing *the same* into the equation. If the former turned outward, the latter turned inward, fracturing the possibility of a "normal" same or self. For Canguilhem, Lacan, and Foucault, this signaled the structural instability of subjectivity and observation. Second, once the "normal" became questionable, transparent naturalism looked just like the sort of framework that permitted organizing human life on violent top-down principles. Leroi-Gourhan attacked the naturalization of biological and physical norms; Canguilhem targeted idealism's and Comtean positivism's assumption of a neutral and transparent correspondence between mind and world; and Lacan tied traditional concepts of "the normal" to psychosis and to a hegemonic, destructive normality.

Thus postwar antihumanism was tied to the view that classic notions of individuality and society were homogenizing and exclusivist. By definition, a norm indicates that whatever falls under its hermeneutic scope is transparent, whereas now the question was to show how what appeared fundamentally heterogeneous was simply not ruled, and hence was oppressed on account of being anomic and abnormal. Norms were inherently marginalizing and thus potentially destructive, although they were also generative and productive—as claimed Canguilhem and the later Foucault. If humanism had assumed a shared nature or a fundamental identity of humans, this hypothesis gave way to a search, both *within* and *beyond* the purview of humanist norms, for individuality and differences that were opposed to them and that could disclose the opaque and burdened character of philosophy and society. When we look at transparency as the presupposition that makes norms and their imposition on others possible, the anxiety around it is evident even if concern with it is merely implicit.

The Traditional Landscape
The Norm and the Normal According to Lalande's Vocabulaire

The need for a formal definition of "the normal" was clear to philosophers at start of the twentieth century. In 1901, Edmond Goblot's *Vocabulaire philosophique* restricted it to biology and pathology. The definition of "the normal type" being "quite difficult," Goblot half-heartedly offered the common but insufficient contrast with "the pathological."[2] Twenty-two years later, André Lalande's *Vocabulaire technique et critique de la philoso-*

phie offered a clear idea of the accepted meanings of "the normal" and "the norm" in philosophy from the *belle époque* through to the interwar period.

Lalande crafts the following definition of "norm":

Norm (from the Latin *norma*, γνώμων, a right angle formed by two perpendicular lines. . . . Concrete type or abstract formula of what must be, in everything that admits of a judgment of value—ideal, rule, goal, model.[3]

He explains that this was a term that had entered widespread use only recently, on account of its "great advantage of furnishing a generic name for the diverse ideas enumerated above, which it is often useful to consider as a whole." Norms render the "must be" of ideals, rules, goals, and models. Lalande then defines three senses of "normal," two of which would derive from "norm":

(1) "perpendicular (see *Norm*): what bends neither to the right nor to the left, by extension, what keeps to a correct mean";

(2) "what is as it must be. The word in this sense is an attenuated synonym of *good* and *just*";

(3) "in the most usual sense of the term, what is encountered in the majority of the cases of a determined species, or what constitutes either the mean or the module of a measurable character."[4]

The instability of "normal" presents a series of potential contradictions, which the ensuing discussion both unpacks and performs. Lalande notes that slippage from one sense to the other is possible, even frequent, due to the word's alliance with concepts such as "norm and normative" and with "the realist tradition, for which observable generality is the sign of an essence or an Idea."[5] Lalande then lays out appraisals of the term's "equivocal" and "confusing" character: sometimes "it designates a fact, possible to confirm scientifically, and sometimes a value attributed to this fact by him who speaks, by virtue of an appreciative judgment." He associates the third meaning with Durkheim, from whom he quotes on "normal" social facts;[6] he also adds a long footnote that complicates matters by introducing a "common confusion" between *normal* and *ideal,* for example in Auguste Comte's reliance on normal—"which he ordinarily understands in the second sense: 'France, the normal center of the West'" (or in the sense of the *Écoles normales* established during the Revolution). The entry closes with three objections to definition (3)—one of them from Jules Lachelier, one of the founders of neocriticism—which Lalande apologetically admits on grounds of its frequent use (and for this he blames sociology).

For idealists like Lachelier and Lalande, only the aprioristic and formal definitions captured the proper sense of "normal." This view went hand in hand with a disparaging attitude toward any use that might seem to convey a value judgment or an empirical or sociological normativity. The pointed effort to defend a properly philosophical meaning, restricted to definitions (1) and (2), makes obvious the belief that anything but a rule-grounded criterion would threaten the idea of normality: on this idealist approach, norms and normality are mutually constitutive. They are singular and absolute: they operate with rigor only when they exclude all that threatens the singularity of the norm and its co-identity with the normal. This explains the downgrading association of the third definition with Durkheim's sociology. There is no room for parallel competing norms in philosophy, and any dependence of norms on values signals *not* multivalence but confusion and opacity.

The definition of "normative," which comes next in Lalande's *Vocabulaire*, also played into this institutional view of "philosophy versus sociology." Here again, two properly philosophical definitions—(1) "what constitutes or enunciates a norm"; and (2) "what concerns norms: 'normative sciences' are those whose object is constituted by judgments of value"[7]—are followed by a problematic third: "what creates or imposes norms." As if backed into a corner, Lucien Lévy-Bruhl, a philosopher supportive of Durkheim's sociology, bristled at the implication that "normative sciences" generate norms rather than studying them. Even he could go no further than admit that, if sciences like sociology did not rely on rules and normative ideals, but invented them, then they would be merely empirical domains without a proper philosophical base.

The Sociological Conception of Normality from Halbwachs to Leroi-Gourhan

To understand Lévy-Bruhl's defense of normative sciences, we need to retrace their challenge to the norms and normality inbuilt in idealist philosophy. The term *normative sciences* was first used by the psychologist Wilhelm Wundt and designated logic and ethics as sciences that require "the inquirer to *estimate* the relative values of facts." The "normative point of view," Wundt wrote in 1871, contrasting it to the "explicative" sciences, "considers objects with reference to definite rules which find expression in them."[8] Lalande's definition largely rehearsed Wundt's ideas, but to different ends. Lévy-Bruhl recalled that he had criticized philosophies of morality that called themselves "normative," on the grounds that this name invited a clash between descriptions and prescriptive practices. Philosophy having failed to construct a science of morality, Lévy-Bruhl turned to sociology.[9] In Durkheim's sociology, with its organicism and prioritization of society over the individual, "the normal" was tethered to each particular society, and sociology itself could claim to be a normative science thanks to the dichotomy normative–explicative. Lévy-Bruhl's refusal to grant that "normative" could be taken to mean "creating or imposing norms" aided sociology's claim that normality is socially specific, against philosophers' accusations of a willy-nilly relativism reliant on invented categories. For this reason, his attitude was at the heart of debates with neocriticists like Lachelier, for whom norms were universal synthetic a priori judgments. As "the normal" was pulled in different directions, both philosophers and sociologists attempted to restructure it to their advantage.[10]

In *Les Règles de la méthode sociologique* (1895; *The Rules of the Sociological Method*), Durkheim had specifically sought to address "the normal type" as a *sociological* category, which derived from the character, priorities, and adaptive qualities of particular social value systems.[11] This theory was elaborated by Maurice Halbwachs in 1912, in a thesis about *l'homme moyen* (the "average man"), a concept that Adolphe Quetelet had introduced into statistics half a century earlier.[12] Halbwachs (who would later author well-known studies of suicide and collective memory) analyzed Quetelet's explanation of the regularity of social phenomena behind the perception that "norm" was an "average" and summarized Quetelet's position like this: "the qualities of the average man "develop in a correct equilibrium, a perfect harmony, distanced equally from the excesses and defects of every species." This perfection consists in "the harmony and convenience of all parts among themselves." The average man would thus be 'the absolute type of the beautiful and the good in the most general sense."[13]

Halbwachs targeted precisely this deliberate confounding of *statistical average* and *ontological normal*, the impression that one confirmed the other.[14] "[Quetelet] believes that, in society, as in the world of living beings, the most frequent average is the best, the ideal. The foundation of this conviction is, in all, a teleological conception of the universe."[15] Halbwachs's squarely Durkheimian perspective worked to undermine Quetelet's sense that, through statistics, he was reaching *directly at facts*. This allowed him to contrast Quetelet's "normal man" with Durkheim's "normal type": despite certain similarities, they diverged because sociology treated the normal as a product of relations with the environment.[16] For Durkheim, "what makes a characteristic normal is that it is 'a mechanically necessary effect' of the conditions of organisms' existence or a 'means that allows organisms to adapt.'"[17] Statistics is an explanation that disregards its explanatory function, whereas sociology deems "normal" a type particular to a group that is best determined by the group itself in its internal and external relations.

Quetelet willingly considers men as many copies of a single model, which only some of them approximate and they represent the average: but the model is conceived as an individual, and the copies that approximate it are individuals. We believe that between individual types thus defined and elementary physical or organic forces, there exist social species whose nature, far from ever being able to express itself in its entirety in the nature and movements of an individual (however "average" we may suppose him to be), only appears in his consciousness truncated and deformed, since, rather than emanating from individuals, these social species dominate and determine them.[18]

Halbwachs's position may have raised questions about statistical formalism but did little to resolve the debate: superimposing an adaptation-based model on the identification of the normal with the social norm did not decisively undermine the association between average and norm; nor did it assuage the idealists who worried about the reduction of norms to social values.

The Glass Man, 1937

The link between the idea of a normal, normative human and transparency is best illustrated with the help of a tool designed in the 1930s for exactly that purpose: the Glass Man from the 1937 Universal Exhibition in Paris (fig. 12.1).

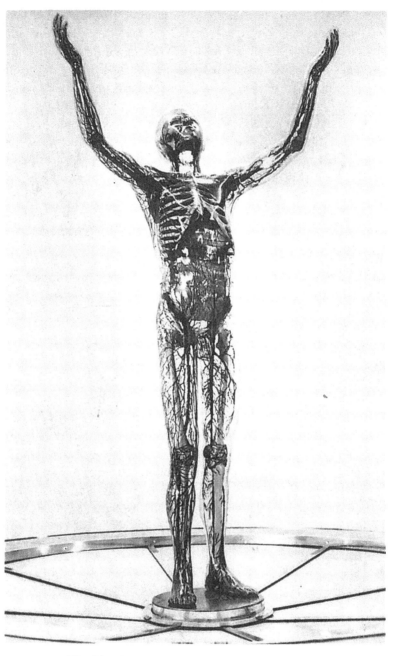

FIGURE 12.1 The Glass Man, 1937.
Photo by the author.

Designed by the Hygiene Museum in Dresden and first shown at the International Hygiene Exhibition of 1930, the Glass Man was a life-size transparent male figure mounted on a pedestal. It consisted of models of the human skeleton, organs, the nervous system, and the circulation system, wrapped in a "transparent synthetic" shell[19] and, like the Glass Woman that accompanied it, became a popular tool in public illustrations of anatomy and in representations of the body. Its arms extended symmetrically up, palms facing inward, in a gesture of receptivity, prayer, and grandeur, as if it signaled beyond itself but did not receive a divine response. It portrayed a certain idealized humanity. Its transparency conferred the viewer the ability to see through the skin, "inside" a person; it also made the figure into a paradigmatic specimen, a carrier of sameness and normality. At the Chicago World Fair of 1933, the Glass Man was placed in such a position as to suggest that, in Robert Rydell's words, visitors were "exposed before a powerful deity—the modern god of science."[20] The Nazis used the Glass Man as a model of Germany's scientific achievements. At the 1937 Universal Exhibition in Paris it was one the most highly attended exhibits.[21]

In the French context the Glass Man was more than a model of research: it embodied a conception of the normal. The sixth volume of the *Encyclopédie française*—which appeared that same year under the editorship of the surgeon René Leriche—portrayed this same conception of the normal in its frontispiece, to facilitate an analogy between the pair normal–pathological (which structured the volume) and the pair theoretical–applied in the realm of science (fig. 12.2).[22]

Divided into two parts, "L'Homme normal" and "L'Homme malade," the encyclopedia took the view that physiology, theoretical biology, and psychology dealt with the normal, while pathology and psychiatry pursued the pathological. The normal and the pathological were foundational terms when it came to the hierarchy of the sciences, the frames of knowledge, and the relation between "science" and "technique." The Glass Man was a model of internal health that affirmed the reach of science into the humanity that it celebrated. It reconfirmed pretenses to human perfection and to the priority of the sciences of the "normal" over sciences that dealt with the "pathological."

6'04 - 3

FIGURE 12.2 "La Santé." Frontispiece of *L'Être humain*, volume 6 of *L'Encyclopédie française*.
SOURCE: Leriche 1936. No photo credit available

The Reversal

The pivot in the conception of norms began around World War II and targeted precisely this set of associations. Three cases are particularly valuable here: André Leroi-Gourhan's ethnology, Georges Canguilhem's theorization of medicine and biology, and Jacques Lacan's treatment of psychoses in psychoanalysis. As a result of these contributions, pathology would redefine individuality and displace the idealism of progressivist and transparentist hopes.

A New Sociology: André Leroi-Gourhan

One radicalization of Halbwachs's position was offered by André Leroi-Gourhan in his 1945 book *Milieu et techniques*. Leroi-Gourhan articulated afresh the sociological school's critique of natural norms, specifically by rejecting the claims of physical anthropology regarding the utility of average physical characteristics for understanding ethnic or species-wide norms. Attempts to take the "racial mean" of cranial volume as meaningful were deeply flawed:

The same index 76.8 [that is racially identified with dolichocephaly in a number of populations] appears not as a "mean" but as individual variation of the skulls of millions of individuals of all times and almost all countries. Given that (except for extreme cases . . .) any such index carries the same capacity for designating, by a certain type or by several types that are not apparent to it, innumerable individuals all over the globe, the method of cephalic indices [skull volume], after having raised great hopes in the last third of the nineteenth century, suffers today from a quite serious eclipse. Such is the case with all isolated processes of exact measure applied to ethnology.[23]

Leroi-Gourhan did more than advocate for an ethnological hermeneutics that refused monocausal and reductionist explanations. Complex factors from the outer and inner environment towered over mathematically and statistically determinable elements of biological constitution. While paying heed to Marcel Mauss's reworking of sociology into a new ethnology, Leroi-Gourhan gave new significance to Durkheim's organicism by arguing for an isomorphism between the individual organism and society.[24] He combined the distinct registers of physical anthropology, organicist sociology, and ethnology into a theory of dynamic biocultural transformation that could be applied in the *longue durée*, to populations and even to the entire human species. Such a holism had no use for the attempt to found norms on *physical* characteristics alone, as if those had appeared independently. Causal factors at the social level *could* be discovered and articulated with as much precision as mathematically or statistically determined physical facts.[25] But norms were dependent on *milieux*, traditions, histories of borrowing, and responses to social pressure: for Leroi-Gourhan, human history was a process of transformation through particularization, adaptation, conquest, and so on that generated considerable differences among different societies, groups, subgroups, and individuals.[26] In all these formations, relations between the group and its members were such that individualization continued to operate at every level while the group retained its "organic unity." In Leroi-Gourhan's terms, "masses," "groups," and "individuals" are subject to parallel processes of individualization. Thus normative idealizations and fulcra of apparent normality are false methodologically as well as ontologically. Halbwachs's attack on the statistical normal or average now acquired ontological and heuristic force over *all* norms and normalities. "Facts" could be scientifically determined at various levels, in different fashions, and in relation to different types of object: "there is . . . at the base of human evolution, a geometric cause of particularization."[27] Norms offered no more than local, tentative, self-descriptive values by which populations, societies, and individuals could be compared. Society was at once more organic and more normative than bodily artifacts could ever be, but only because it was individualized at all levels.

From Universals to Norms: Georges Canguilhem

A second shift came in 1943, with the publication of Georges Canguilhem's *The Normal and the Pathological*, which formulated a concern that was felt across medical thought: that medicine, biology, and psychology "create and impose" norms that determine and hamper rather than aid diagnosis, treatment, and the understanding of the individual patient.[28] In Canguilhem's version of this critique, scientific thought relied on a reductionism that was often epistemically necessary yet always problematic. The operations of knowledge had to be made sensible and available to the very act of knowing: that is, one had to know not only *how* it is that one knows something but *how this knowing defines what* one knows. By this move knowledge ceases being a transparent process—knowledge of "pure" data.[29]

Canguilhem sought to dismantle a thesis that dated to the 1830s, when it was first proposed by the physiologist V.-A.-F. Broussais. According to him, any disease or pathological condition was no more than a quantitative modification of the normal condition. In his approach "the norm" coincided with the normal and was the one and only right norm (much as in Lalande's definition). The normal was identifiable with health, conceived of as a statistical or formal norm, and there could be no norms specific to disease—only aberrations from the normal. These conceptual identities in turn established homogeneity between patients in the frame of clinical observation. Pathological conditions and their carriers—the ill— were *available* to physicians and biologists through their aberrations from the normal; they were essentially undifferentiated from one another and could be compared and underrated in the same way, if to different degrees. Further, this meant that disease had no ontological import: a patient was basically deficient vis-à-vis the norm, while the term "normal" acquired a "properly absolute or essential meaning."[30] This, Canguilhem showed, was then institutionalized in philosophy and sociology by Auguste Comte, who openly cited Broussais, and in experimental medicine and pathology by Claude Bernard.

Comte transformed this identification of normality with health into a political and metapolitical concept and tied it to order and progress; thus progress toward positive order confirmed particular norms as normal, and disease was associated with aberrations from reason and history.[31] With the rise of scientific positivism, the view that health stood for a normality deemed politically progressive, rational, unmetaphysical, and orderly became as significant in politics as in human subjectivity.

For Canguilhem, this approach to pathology locked the place of medicine in modernity as a privileged kind of applied knowledge, which de-differentiated individual experiences of disease and suffering and attached them to a system of study, diagnosis, and recuperation. An elaborate language emerged to help physicians identify types across spectra of similar cases, effectively bypassing the individual patient, for whom illness is a specific and qualitatively heterogeneous experience.[32] The individual had become a medical subject, both in the sense of being structured into medical thought and in the sense of being structured vis-à-vis the standard of health. Her experience, the difference between her life and others' lives—or even just her life at different moments in time, following different paths of suffering and recovery—was erased; when sick, she was simply depreciated vis-à-vis the cult of health.

The work of recent medical thinkers sanctioned Canguilhem's observation that disease presented the philosopher as well as the physician with a problem of experience. Reconsiderations of the normal offered by the French surgeon René Leriche and by the German-Jewish neuropsychiatrist Kurt Goldstein were conspicuously at odds with the conception derived from Comte and Bernard, as well as with idealist and sociological definitions. In 1940, Leriche was perhaps the best-known French surgeon and medical thinker: his fame, after World War I, was earned especially thanks to his *chirurgie de la douleur*, a kind of surgery designed to engage and alleviate a patient's pain.[33] Canguilhem would never tire of repeating Leriche's motto: "Health is life lived in the silence of the organs, while disease is what irritates men in the normal course of their lives and work, and above all what makes them suffer."[34] He considered Leriche's position to be symptomatic of a new tendency, attentive to the singularity of the patient's suffering.[35] Leriche's angle on the order of health as silence, which was then confronted with suffering, led to a "new vital order," ready to supplant the tired model of disease sliding away from norms.[36] Canguilhem did not, however, treat Leriche altogether uncritically; in his view, the latter did not quite recognize the consequences of his own position for vital subjectivity.[37]

Leriche pointed the way but Goldstein had already traveled it. Studying brain-injured soldiers, Goldstein was startled by the distinctiveness of each patient's suffering and by the different ways they sought to compensate for physical and other losses. He thought that, except in "catastrophic" situations, the diseased body is *not* normless; it just tends to obey *different norms* from those of the normal body.[38] For the individual patient, disease involves a new life, characterized by new physiological constants and new mechanisms. The physician has to attend to the particularity of these mechanisms, not dream of a unifying norm of health.[39]

Canguilhem first encountered Goldstein's thought during a course on "pathological psychology" taught by the psychoanalyst Daniel Lagache in 1941–42 in Clermond-Ferrand.[40] For Goldstein, as Canguilhem would stress, the healthy needed to be rethought as "more than normal," health and normality needed to be rethought as what *constructs* norms, and disease was a situation in which the patient was suspended from, and lived with, new, deficient norms.[41] Canguilhem translated his reasoning as follows. The normal, healthy body is not an ontological average for all bodies. Health is vital creativity, the capacity to play with forms of life, create, and transform them; it means freedom from physiological and environmental constraints. "Health, taken absolutely, is a normative concept defining an ideal type of organic structure and behavior; in this sense it is a pleonasm to speak of good health because health is organic well-being."[42] This is what it means to say, with Goldstein, that good health is "more than normal" and *creates* norms.[43] The medical observer's involvement in the subject's norm-constructing process or in the patient's suffering was itself a fundamental normativity of *vital* origin, that is, in excess of simple knowledge. Canguilhem's concept of *vital norms* represented norms as a nontransparent mediators, at once creative and reductive, between thought and knowledge on the one hand, social and biological life on the other.

It would be wrong to see the physiological and pathological focus of Canguilhem's work as anything short of profoundly philosophical. Giuseppe Bianco and Dominique Lecourt have shown his commitment, ever since his 1926 thesis, to puncturing Comte's theory of order and progress, which he interpreted as a system that introduced homogeneity and normalization as prerequisites for progress toward universal normality.[44] Canguilhem's attention to norms and the philosophical problems they pose matured in a work titled *Traité de logique et de morale* (Treatise on Logic and Morals) that he co-authored in 1939. Discussing the "value of science," Canguilhem and Camille Planet asked whether "Science can, without being unfaithful to its proposals, effectively 'comprehend' . . . all of Experience by referencing a unique Norm."[45] By way of response, he offered a survey of the skeptical reception, in science and philosophy, of the thesis that the value of science lay in its claim to possess a unitary norm that carried the "truth." His conclusion all but embraced this skepticism.[46]

Canguilhem made norms and normality central to his philosophical teaching during the Occupation. At the invitation of the philosopher Jean Cavaillès, he began teaching at the Université de Strasbourg, which had moved to Clermont-Ferrand, in the Vichy zone. In 1942–43, while participating in the resistance and completing his medical studies, Canguilhem taught a course titled "Norms and the Normal" that offers a clear picture of his philosophical priorities in the engagement with normality and pathology. Norms, even if considered rules, could not be treated as ideals or goals. They emerged (as they had in the 1939 *Traité de logique et de morale*) as corrective or organizational efforts in a chaotic world:

A rule of evaluation only acquires meaning if through it we assume we obtain something we otherwise did not possess. A logical rule must guide us to truth, a juridical rule to justice. The normal is thus the fruit of a normative intention and a norm-setting decision which is implicitly a recognition of an unacceptable situation of basic indetermination. What comes first is thus not the Golden Age, that is, a form of universal experience where everything immediately conforms to the norm. Rather, what comes first is chaos, that is, an undetermined complex of all qualitative possibilities. Even better, what comes first is the ambivalent relation between chaos and the Golden Age.[47]

Canguilhem then upended the entire argument offered by Lalande, distancing the normal from the norm:

The normal is what is normative *in a given situation*. In effect, "normal" can have two meanings: either the normal is the norm itself as it is seen to represent all the facts or aspects that we have already linked in a positive result; or the normal is any fact or object that has been referred to the norm and positively appreciated, and may from there and in turn serve the norm. The normal is then always some object or activity which it is possible to experience and in this regard, the normal emerges from the affirmation of existence but is always a standard [*exigence*] that is legitimate, and in this the normal arises out of affirmations of value.[48]

A few philosophical consequences can be drawn from Canguilhem's revision of the notion of norm. First, following Goldstein, he pointed out that idealism and intellectualism were "transparent and inert" in that they nullified the distinctiveness of living organisms. Idealism assumed that the living beings it dealt with were physiologically isomorphic and hence ontologically homogeneous—their own histories and experiences were not qualitatively individualized.

Second, Canguilhem targeted positivist conceptions of the dependence of medicine on biology, which identified progress with biological research and, again, subordinated the individual character of a patient's experience. By working en bloc with non-case-specific representations of disease, positivist medicine eliminated from its radar both individual reactions to a nosological entity and the experience of suffering. This (to repeat) was to see norms as universals and pathologies as simple, perhaps reversible, deviations from them. As a corollary, health was then extrapolated from the individual to society, as an achievable condition in which a single formal ideal was revealed by historical progress. Through the homogeneity of the normal and the pathological and the identification of the normal with the norm, positivism created an incalculably pervasive conceptual scheme: an imaginary of society in terms of health, order and disease. But, as Maurice Blanchot also objected, disease still "infests" this history and this law.[49] "Until now," in Canguilhem's words, "pathology has retained so little of that character which disease has for the sick man—of being really another kind of life"—a life not simply naked to the physician's notions and system of thought but profoundly other.[50]

Third, Canguilhem put considerable effort into directing his interpretation of medical–physiological problems specifically against a *philosophical* history of the concept of the normal and simply dismissed the sociological approach.[51] Although he explored Halbwachs's "very rigorous examination" of Quetelet alongside Lalande's *Vocabulaire* entry,[52] he never so much as mentioned Durkheim, whose *Rules of the Sociological Method* devoted an entire chapter to "the normal and the pathological," and he carefully avoided discussing both Durkheim's critique (with which Halbwachs concluded) and Lalande's third (sociological) definition of the normal. Canguilhem made explicit his distance from Durkheim in his 1942–43 lectures on "Norms and the Normal" and in a course on Durkheim in 1947:

For Durkheim, who identifies the normal and the mean, any attempt toward the realization of a state superior to the normal is utopian. Durkheim seems to believe that the conservation of social structures is *in itself* an ideal. As if it had not been always true that one does not conserve except by reforming. Durkheim, who reproaches Comte for having edified a social statics before any social dynamic, did not, all told, grasp better than him the authentically dynamic character of human evolution.[53]

Regardless of whether this antipathy originated in Canguilhem's strict neo-Kantian education or in mistrust of the scientificity of the *Année sociologique*, it afforded him a space in which he could disown any influence from Durkheim and yet appropriate the core of his critique of the idealism espoused by Lalande, Lachelier, and Brunschvicg, absorb it into philosophical and biomedical thought, and present it as *his own*. In other words, Canguilhem broke the philosophy–sociology opposition from within philosophy, using, without acknowledgment, a tradition that had been fighting philosophy's rigidity from the outside.

Finally, Canguilhem wrote his *The Normal and the Pathological* while participating in the resistance to Vichy. Although historians have determined that disappointment with the pacifism of the early 1930s and engagement in a more combative antifascism prompted Canguilhem to turn to the study of medicine,[54] a properly political reading of *The Normal and the Pathological* has not, to my knowledge, been proposed.[55] And yet the political intent of the book is hard to miss: in the context of Nazism's "purification of the national body"—which swept away Jews, Roma, the hereditarily ill, homosexuals, and "asocials" as biologically inferior[56]—Canguilhem forcefully rejected the equivalences between norm, the normal, and the healthy and any sense of a given type or norm, national or universal. Considering them to be inherently dismissive of human experience and life and depreciative of those placed in or beyond the margins of the normal, Canguilhem proposed the existence of multiple and complex norms in health and offered a notion of individuality that would remain unbound by the "single norm" model, free from the coercion and exclusiveness in the normal–pathological dichotomy.

Canguilhem's critique of Durkheim expanded, however, beyond Nazi and Soviet "equalization," into a critique of progressivist liberalism as a whole. In language bordering on Marxism, Canguilhem argued that liberalism normalizes the bourgeois viewpoint and promotes an objectification of the working class.

The liberal type only appeared *normal* because it dissimulated the powerlessness of the working class to develop a consciousness of its own norms of life, and certainly not because all of society had become adapted to liberal norms. If the liberal system has ceased to appear normal, this is because it was not adequately normative at the moment when it appeared to be settled in the given conditions of economic existence.[57]

On another register, Canguilhem effectively demonstrated Sartre's 1946 claim that "the cult of humanity ends in Comtean humanism, shut in upon itself, and . . . in fascism."[58] Canguilhem's was not the liberal self but the individual as a deeply threatened figure who, simply by virtue of persisting, contributed to the creation of new norms, even constituted a resistance force to the politics of exclusion and annihilation and to a liberal humanist naturalization that treated norms as transparently true. Speaking before the Alliance israélite universelle in 1955, Canguilhem argued that the analogy between organism and society, which at the time was returning to the fore thanks to cybernetic arguments on self-regulation, was highly problematic if it was taken to indicate *social* and *subjective* harmony. Instead, it had to be mobilized to disclose the political violence implicit in transposing biological registers onto social ones or reducing the social to biology.[59] Canguilhem's individual was at once deeply threatened and excessive. The call to think of what *exceeds* the singular classic norm—the norm organized by the "normal"—as something more than just defective, adaptable, or homogenizable, in other words, advocacy of an "anomic" individuality not bound by specific manmade laws, was a forceful opening for a new way of imagining politics and society.

Psychopathology and Lacan

Canguilhem is often credited with shifting the discourse around the problem of the normal and the norm in biology and medicine; but, as we have seen in discussing Leroi-Gourhan, he was not alone in taking this course or in rethinking the relationship between theoretical and applied sciences around these values. In psychopathology, the psychiatric patient was examined with a new interest in the relationship between normality and pathology. Psychopathology was also invested in destabilizing psychology. By 1945, Piaget's work was becoming foundational in theoretical and developmental psychology and contributed to a reassertion of traditional concepts of the normal in the field. The 1951 *Vocabulaire de psychologie*, edited by Henri Pieron—a key figure in theoretical psychology already before World War II—also redefined *norme* in a highly traditional manner, as "what must be taken as a model or as a rule," and proposed four definitions of *normal* that treated the normal individual as one whose "characteristics are situated inside the 'margin of variation' and 'normal distribution' of the population to which he belongs"—and also as "average" and "ideal."[60] Psychiatrists found these definitions highly problematic. As Canguilhem reported, they "have reflected on the problem of the normal better than physicians. . . . Many have recognized *that a mentally ill person is an 'other' person*, not merely a person whose disturbance is an extension or enlargement of the normal psyche. In this domain, the abnormal is truly in possession of other norms."[61]

Footnoting this observation, Canguilhem—who was viscerally opposed to psychology, especially behaviorism, on account of its mechanistic conception of the individual—pointed out three such psychiatrists:

Eugène Minkowski, Daniel Lagache, and Jacques Lacan. Lagache was aware that Canguilhem's reliance on Goldstein was inspired by his own teaching. In a 1946 review of Canguilhem's *The Normal and the Pathological*, he contended that psychopathology and psychoanalysis underlay Canguilhem's reconceptualization. He also connected Canguilhem's and Goldstein's emphasis on "anxiety, conflict, and lived experience" to Freud and William Stern.[62]

Minkowski, Lagache, and Lacan entered the psychoanalytic revolution of the 1930s from different, conceptually unstable psychopathological traditions, and all began studying psychological phenomena inimical to the psychological identification of the normal with the norm. Lacan completed and published his thesis on paranoid psychosis in 1932;[63] Lagache his, on verbal hallucinations, in 1934.[64] Minkowski, who had first worked under Eugen Bleuler and was strongly influenced by Henri Bergson and phenomenology, defended a dissertation on the "loss of vital contact" with reality in 1926 and published a study titled *La Schizophrénie* the next year.[65] All four works belonged in an intellectual climate of considerable methodological openness: this was a period that saw pioneering reformers like Piaget, the organo-dynamist Henri Ey, the psychoanalyst and homeopathic physician René Allendy (best remembered for having treated Anaïs Nin and Antonin Artaud) and, of course, Freudian psychoanalysts.[66] The pathological raised the question of alternative norms to be sought for patients who could not be simply "restored" to "normality."

After World War II, no thinker wrote more broadly or with greater originality on this subject than Jacques Lacan. His seminar of 1955–56 was devoted to psychosis and aggressively reworked the abnormal or pathological subject's relations to the normal. Targeting Freud, Emil Kraepelin, and Karl Abraham, along with a whole way of writing about paranoia, Lacan argued that their interpretations profoundly misunderstand the problem of normality by assuming that all apparent divergences amount to pathologies.

the whole discourse on paranoia . . . bears the mark of that misrecognition. You can test this while reading Freud, or almost any author—you will find pages, sometimes entire chapters, on paranoia. Take them out of their context, read them out loud, and you will see the most wonderful descriptions of the behavior of everyone. It was touch and go whether what I read out loud before, from Kraepelin's definition of paranoia, defined normal behavior.[67]

Focusing on a case that Abraham "misattributed" as exemplary of *dementia praecox*, Lacan continues:

These supposedly *conclusive* cases are so completely ambiguous that one wonders how it's possible to maintain the illusion for one second, unless through a sort of eclipse of the critical sense that seems to seize all readers as soon as they open a technical work, specially where our experience and profession are concerned.[68]

Once he has established the fundamental difficulty of distinguishing symptoms, Lacan proposes that the list of behaviors be replaced by a hermeneutics of the perception of reality and of the psychological defense against it—in both the "normal" and the psychotic subject.[69]

Lacan's main postulate about normality in the seminar is that the structure of delusion is not on its own different from the structure of healthy perception. Instead of considering delusion and pathology to be aberrations, one should treat normality as the result of a particular *homogenization and normalization*, which represents an essential process in the development of the subject. Having already emphasized the relationship between paranoiac knowledge and "normal" knowledge in his early work,[70] Lacan reiterates the point that the "normal" subject exhibits delusional and pathological characteristics:

What characterizes a normal subject is precisely that he never takes seriously certain realities that he recognizes exist. You are surrounded by all sorts of realities about which you are in no doubt, some of which are particularly threatening, but you don't take them fully seriously, for you think, along with Paul Claudel's subtitle, that the worst is not always certain, and maintain yourselves in an average, basic—in the sense of relating to the base—state of blissful uncertainty, which makes possible for you a sufficiently relaxed existence. Surely, certainty is the rarest of things for the normal subject.[71]

At stake in delusion and certainty is, of course, the experience of the external world, more specifically the sense that this experience is fragmentary and untotalizable. Psychosis is in this respect a particular *enforcement* of transparency, a loss of reality or imposition of oneself onto reality without regard for alternative scenarios.

Lacan takes pains to attack the commitment to clarity and certainty of thought, which he considered a pillar of philosophy since Descartes's cogito. Certainty is not a desideratum; on the contrary, it is the province of the psychotic's fantasy of unity and uniqueness. The dream of certainty as self-transparency of thought is the false Ariadne's thread that has entangled the course of philosophy itself:

> consciousness has been emphasized as the foundation of certainty—must a thought, to be a thought, necessarily think of itself thinking? Must all thought necessarily perceive that it's thinking of what it is thinking? This is so far from being straightforward that it immediately leads into an endless play of mirrors—if it's the nature of thought to think of itself thinking, there will be a third thought that will think of itself thinking thought, and so on. This small problem, which has never been resolved, suffices on its own to demonstrate the insufficiency of the subject's foundation *in the phenomenon of thought as transparent to itself.*[72]

The subject cannot function in the transparency and certainty of thought. Unlike the psychotic in his imagined wholeness and self-multiplication, the normal subject experiences the world, her body, and their relation as fragmented. This calls for neither solace nor anguish.[73] With reference to Freud's famous essay on Daniel Paul Schreber, Lacan writes:

> The subject's relationship to the world is a mirror relation. The subject's world will essentially consist of the relationship with that being who is the other for him, namely God himself . . . these two characters, that is, God, with all that he implies, the universe, the celestial sphere, and on the other hand Schreber himself, literally decomposed into a multitude of imaginary beings with their toing-and-froing and their various transfixions, are two strictly alternating structures. They develop in a way that is . . . *permanently elided, veiled, domesticated* in the life of a normal man—namely, the dialectic of the fragmented body in relation to the imaginary universe, which is subjacent to a normal structure.[74]

Schreber's disorder is not structurally a pathological *deformation* of normal subjectivity: it engages characteristics that exist within this subjectivity but under normal circumstances are "elided, veiled, domesticated." Thus the normal state does not simply encompass the pathological; it attempts to override it. This brings us to the second element of Lacan's analysis of normality: crucially, this process of imposing order on one's psychological chaos is a *process of normalization*, which accompanies both the child's development and the implementation of practices (medical, psychiatric, training) that later guide the subject in society. Normalization has very different meanings in Lacan and in Pieron's *Vocabulaire*—where it had a specifically statistical and uncritical function. As we have seen, Lacan had made this argument as early as 1949, in his revised "Mirror Stage" essay, where the toddler moves "from a fragmented image of the body" through to "the finally donned armor of an alienating identity." This pathway into alienation and constrictive normalization is crucial for Lacan's account of subjectivation, of how the self enters society. This pathway also indicates that the normal adult subject and the norms she represents are not natural products but carry the residues of the creation of an alienated identity.

Lacan's ensuing contention that the Oedipus complex is Freud's name for a process of socialization, normalization, self-alienation, and hence identity formation returns decisively in the seminar on psychoses. By then Lacan has developed a properly structuralist terminology and couches the theme of normality and normalization in the language of the subject's entry into the symbolic order.

If the Oedipus complex isn't the introduction of the signifier then I ask to be shown any conception of it whatever. The level of its elaboration is so essential to sexual normalization uniquely because it introduces the functioning of the signifier as such into the conquest of the said man or woman. It's not because the Oedipus complex is contemporary with the genital dimension or tendency that it's possible to imagine even for a single instant that it's essential to an actual human world, to a world that has its structure of human reality.[75]

At stake in the "Oedipus complex" was not so much the social organization of the genital phase as the introduction of the "I," the ego, into a world structured by signifiers with different meanings, a world to be "conquered" even as it remains forever foreign and other.

With this, Lacan has departed fundamentally from the traditional strict contrast between the normal and the pathological, which Canguilhem, too, had rejected as destructive. The normal is not the natural; it is a social norm, necessary yet profoundly denaturing. In his iconoclastic style, Lacan inverts the language of "adaptation" current in psychology, arguing that maturation achieves the deformation of the self into a "normalized" individual. Rather than accept a behaviorism that "castrates" "human reality,"[76] and rather than look at the norm as a median to which the "maladapted" need to be brought back, Lacan pictures normality as a straightened-out form of human existence that has managed to subvert the fragmented, diffuse, uncertain, and too natural existence of the infant. In his previous seminar, on the ego (1954–55), Lacan had made clear his position on "normality." Psychiatrists needed to accept that, because speech and language always operated beneath the "I," no therapeutics based on normality and the ego could reach it—the sequela being that normaliza-tion only deformed the subject further.

Speech is mother to the misrecognised part of the subject. And that is the level pe-culiar to the analytic symptom—a level decentered in relation to individual expe-rience, since it is that of the historical text which integrates it. From then on, what is certain is that the symptom will only give in to an intervention interceding at this decentered level. *What will fail is any intervention inspired by a prefabricated reconstruction, one forged out of our notion of the normal development of the individ-ual, and aiming at his normalisation—here is what he was lacking—here is what he must learn to submit to by way of frustration, for instance.*[77]

Here the norm and the normal are (decidedly) unnatural formations es-sential to the human being's entry into the symbolic order, structures that transform an amorphous, anomic, abnormal being into a social subject and a psychological individual. If Canguilhem aimed to defend the threat-ened individual, Lacan instead targeted this same "individual."[78]

This is not to say that, for Lacan, norms are altogether false or un-necessary,[79] or that psychoanalysis did not itself reveal, establish, or engage norms and the normativity of certain active, productive elements of the psyche (notably the superego).[80] On the contrary: managing these norms and the possibility of maintaining psychoanalysis as a normative but not formalizing process was a central promise in Lacan's publications, seminar, and psychoanalytic training. Throughout his writings on technique and on the training of analysts, he frequently reiterates that analysis is a subject-forming process, not only a corrective technique, and certainly not a means of retrofitting individuals to social norms.[81] This desire to imagine a psycho-analysis that makes room for non-adapted selves is one of the principal rea-sons why Lacan's teaching and writings became so attractive and influential at a time frequently described as a revolt of sons against their fathers. Lacan also expresses doubts about the normative self-assurance of psychoanalysis: "Who will sweep this enormous pile of dung out of the Augean Stables of analytic literature?"[82] He endorses Freud's bouts of skepticism about the for-mat of psychoanalytic practice that he himself had instituted and that had "become the norm."[83] And he repeatedly seeks to field "opacity" right in the heart of psychoanalytic technique,[84] against contemporary pressures to turn the latter into a standard practice like those of ego psychology—a move-ment that he reviled as "infatuated" with normalizing patients.[85] Finally, Lacan asks time and again how "normal," off-center, or neurotic the psycho-

covery and recognition of a third order, a third regime: that of the symbolic."[2] I will refer to it as the *third order*: an intermediary between the universal (the ideal, the formal, the natural, the absolute) and the particular (the empirical, the relative, the merely cultural).[3] As has been often recognized,[4] this third order rendered altogether impossible any transparent (or even direct) relationship between humans and their world, consciousness and reality, ideals and practices. It denied the famous scholastic requirement of truth: that there be correspondence between mind and reality (*adequatio intellectus et rei*) as if the mind's door to the world were made of glass. Thus understood, "structuralism" not only rejected traditional idealism but competed against the subjectivism of phenomenological and existentialist forms of antifoundational realism. It had much in common with the historical and epistemological pursuit of intellectuals like Koyré and Canguilhem, except that, in its formalization of the third order, it discounted their historical and conceptual causalities as undertheorized.

The third order provided the formal basis necessary for systematizing non-transparency and complexity; inquiry needed to be mediated by it or remain merely empirical. To the extent that structuralism "decentered the subject," it did so by setting it among relations between potentially meaningful elements, and by postulating that it was incapable of offering a sufficient account of these relations and elements. Hence the subject lacked sufficient access to understanding what conditioned its own speech and meaning. By figuring language as *the* paradigm of this "third order" and by deriving other "tertiary" orders from its example, thinkers from Lévi-Strauss and Lacan on came to depict a wide array of problems—communication, intersubjectivity, society, kinship, normativity, truth, power, knowledge, the self—as mediated by a system that exceeded all actors and remained opaque to them. They seemed to knock down epistemological assumptions that philosophers had taken for granted in the past.

After reviewing a series of instantiations of this third order, the chapter will conclude by reconsidering two classic themes related to the place of language: its capacity to clarify the relationship between the human subject and the world; and the thesis about the status of French as an exceptionally "clear" language. Structuralism freed language from two classic associations: Cartesianism, which had tied it to *clear* thinking, and nationalism, according to which transparency was a specific characteristic of the superior French language.

Lévi-Strauss: The Scandal of Incest and the New Order of Knowledge

Claude Lévi-Strauss's *Les Structures élémentaires de la parenté* (1949; *The Elementary Structures of Kinship*), the product of his long period of comparative research at the New York Public Library, and perhaps the first book to appropriate structural linguistics for a non-linguistic science, staged the structural third order already in its opening pages, in a famous paragraph on nature, culture, and the prohibition of incest.[5] In order to distinguish "nature" from "culture," Lévi-Strauss argued that universality should be understood as a criterion of nature, while "everything subject to a norm" should be understood as a particular—a cultural phenomenon. The prohibition of incest, at once universal and particular, bridged the two: it was the one irreducible element of all marriage systems, yet it was established differently in each culture, subject always to different norms. It also failed to satisfy biological, psychological, or other non-social needs. In other words, although it was a universal, it could not be taken as a natural fact.[6] It was a hinge between these two orders, and also a "scandal" (i.e., a snare or stumbling block, as in the original meaning of the term).

Wherever there are [rules in patterns of behavior removed from instinctive determination,] we know for certain that the cultural stage has been reached. Likewise, it is easy to recognize universality as the criterion of nature, for what is constant in man falls necessarily beyond the scope of customs, techniques, and institutions whereby his groups are differentiated and contrasted. . . . The double criterion of norm and universality provides the principle for an ideal analysis which, at least in certain cases and within certain limits, may allow the natural to be isolated from the cultural elements which are involved in more complex syntheses. Let us suppose then that everything universal in man relates to the natural order, and is characterized by spontaneity, and that everything subject to a norm is cultural and is both relative and particular. We are then confronted with a fact, or rather, a group of facts, which in the light of previous definitions, are not far removed from a scandal: we refer to the complex group of beliefs, customs, conditions and institutions described succinctly as the prohibition of incest, which presents, without the slightest ambiguity, and inseparably combines, the two characteristics in which we recognize the conflicting features of two mutually exclusive orders. It constitutes a rule, but a rule which, alone among all the social rules, possesses at the same time a universal character.[7]

Lévi-Strauss grounded his study at this intermediate level, proposing to avoid both the problematic empiricist approach and any naturalist one. He denied empirical research any power to reveal more than the normative foundations it is based on. He also enlisted to his cause this failure of a priori formalist analyses: he was not merely syncopating a "composite mixture of elements from both nature and culture."[8] The incest prohibition

is the fundamental step because of which, by which, but above all in which, the transition from nature to culture is accomplished. . . . Before it, culture is still nonexistent; with it, nature's sovereignty over man is ended. The prohibition of incest is where nature transcends itself. It sparks the formation of a new and more complex type of structure and is superimposed upon the simpler structures of physical life through integration, just as these themselves are superimposed upon the simpler structures of animal life. It brings about and is in itself the advent of a new order.[9]

Notice the passage from the "scandal" of the incest prohibition to a "new order," a "new and more complex type of structure."[10] By conceiving of this prohibition as the most basic expression of the status of marriage as a system of exchange, Lévi-Strauss was able to relay it as a specific form fundamental to every culture, one that has laws and an economy of its own. The hinge laid out a separate order: cultural practices agglomerated around a local resolution of the incest problem without a foundation external to the culture. The rules of marriage and kinship, just like the economics of language, were experienced unconsciously: they allowed the anthropologist to build models that would not be limited or incidental.[11] As Lévi-Strauss made explicit in a paper of the same period, titled "Language and the Analysis of Social Laws,"

Language is a social phenomenon; and, of all social phenomena, it is the one which manifests to the greatest degree two fundamental characteristics which make it susceptible of scientific study. . . . Much of linguistic behavior lies on the level of unconscious thought. When we speak, we are not conscious of the syntactic and morphological laws of our language. Moreover, we are not ordinarily conscious of the phonemes that we employ to convey different meanings; and we are rarely, if ever, conscious of the phonological oppositions which reduce each phoneme to a bundle of distinctive features.[12]

Studying kinship systems allowed this unconscious level to become the focus of comparative work. This move generated a veritable analytic utopia: one could posit *laws*, evade the limitations of the observer-scientist's normative thought, and resolve a series of epistemological problems that emerged from all too easy empirical similarities and subjective interpretations—in other words from approaches that imposed transparency on the observer or, worse still, on individual participants:

> The road will then be open for a comparative structural analysis of customs, institutions, and accepted patterns of behavior. We shall be in a position to understand basic similarities between forms of social life, such as language, art, law, and religion that on the surface seem to differ greatly. At the same time, we shall have the hope of overcoming the opposition between the collective nature of culture and its manifestations in the individual, since the so-called "collective consciousness" would, in the final analysis, be no more than the expression, on the level of individual thought and behavior, of certain time and space modalities of the universal laws which make up the unconscious activity of the mind.[13]

Attempting to construct models was hardly new, of course, but Lévi-Strauss's deployment of the newfound hinge as the proper order of analysis could claim novelty in that it facilitated *systematicity at that level*, while both *including* the particular cultural–empirical data it looked at and *asserting that this order was expressed in* them. This systematization of language and kinship as a third order reduced past systems (notably Durkheimian sociology) to attempts rather than achievements. It denied that nature and culture were wholes that could be studied without mediation.[14] Even more, it dismantled the intellectual guile of "total" anthropological observation and ethnographic study (e.g., Marcel Mauss's "total man"), all the while absorbing their aspiration to totalization and symbolization; it drew data into a system that recognized that social life is lived unconsciously more than transparently.[15] Its laws, like the codes of linguistic communication, exceeded individual experience and also aprioristic formulations, yet offered themselves to theoretical study and to the construction of a hitherto untouched domain of knowledge.

Lacan's Introduction of the Symbolic

Jacques Lacan, at the time a personal friend of Lévi-Strauss's and Jakobson's, followed the former's conceptual moves closely.[16] In 1949, when he rearticulated his prewar essay on "The Mirror Stage" (and now echoed Lévi-Strauss's rejection of empiricism), Lacan devised a conceptual technology that he called "symbolic reduction." Symbolic reduction abstracted from experience an intermediate "grid" that would exceed it without abandoning its data for the sake of an abstract, voluntaristic alternative.

> were I to build on . . . subjective data alone—were I to so much as free them from the experiential condition that makes me view them as based on a language technique—my theoretical efforts would remain exposed to the charge of lapsing into the unthinkable, that of an absolute subject. This is why I have sought, in the present hypothesis grounded in a confluence of objective data, a *method of symbolic reduction* as my guiding grid.[17]

Both empiricism and naturalist, phenomenological, or traditionally universalist alternatives posit an absolute subject; a "symbolic reduction" avoids their pitfalls. This argument cannot yet secure the universality of this intermediate order, and only with Lacan's shift, in the early 1950s, from a "symbolic reduction as guiding grid" to a "symbolic order" would his own version of the "third" emerge in earnest.[18] "The Mirror Stage" is Lacan's precipice: it remains a discussion of the subject's entry into social life and intersubjectivity, carried out in terms of an inner–outer relationship mediated by the imaginary.

In "Au-delà du 'principe de réalité'" (1936; "Beyond the 'Reality Principle'"), an essay contemporary with the original formulation of the mirror stage, Lacan had criticized Freud's reality principle on the phenomenological grounds that objective reality is unavailable to the psyche. He qualified the central components of the personality (the ego–id–superego triad among them) as "imaginary."[19] Abandoning classic psychology's tendency to objectivity and hence to the relativization of subjective experience, Lacan participated in what I have earlier described as "antifoundational realism": a co-implication of subject and world that leaves the subject bound to the world and limited by a specific immanent perspective. For Lacan, the imaginary refracted the experience of reality and molded the total subject at the same time; such was the "function of imagos."[20] This warping, which affected the totality of the psyche, was still at stake in the 1949 version of "The Mirror Stage."[21] But the introduction of the symbolic, far more explicitly in "Fonction et champ de la parole et du langage en psychanalyse" (1953–56; "The Function and Field of Speech and Language in Psychoanalysis"), broke the subject–world bifurcation by offering a structure, a symbolic "field," that was separate from that of the imaginary. This field also pushed against the "Real"—which became Lacan's term for what lay beyond the reach of the imaginary and the symbolic, what destabilized their conquest of the world, what prevented the complete collapse of Lacan's theoretical system into solipsistic subjectivism.[22]

The symbolic decisively undermined the antifoundational realism of the imaginary by complementing it with a new order. If the specular "imaginary" forged a relationship between the self and something that could be understood as external "reality," the "symbolic" intervened to dislodge the sufficiency—even the possibility—of an imaginary–real binary. Lacan's adoption of a structural approach to the role of the unconscious opened a number of conceptual moves that facilitated his "return to Freud," or properly speaking his makeover of Freud's metapsychology. Best known among these innovations are his new, Saussurean emphasis on the total field of signification rather than on individual symbols linked via the patient's psychological history; the prioritization of the signifier, with its multiplicity of possible meanings, over the signified; the adoption of metaphor and metonymy from Roman Jakobson; and especially the identification of "the symbolic" with the unconscious itself. Lacan's claim that the Freudian "unconscious is structured like a language," perhaps the central impetus of his thought during the period, relayed a specific understanding of how language, in its elusiveness, structures subjectivity—how the symbolic sets up the underlying presuppositions of all experience *without* being a pre-given universal. This is especially evident in Lacan's citations of Lévi-Strauss.[23] In the famous "Rome Discourse" of 1953 (published as "Function and Field") as well as in his seminars of 1953–56, Lacan argued that priority should be given, not to Lévi-Strauss's nature–culture distinction, but to his placing of structure—language, the incest prohibition, kinship—*between* the two.[24] This in-between was the locus of the symbolic, the space where language originally crossed from "outside" (the symbolic in "social life," for lack of a better term), so that it could be redeployed "within" (the unconscious, as developed and then structured by language and the symbolic). Lacan argued for a relation of *identity* between the language–unconscious nexus in his thought and the "elementary structures" proposed by Lévi-Strauss, which were "conquering the very terrain in which Freud situates the unconscious."[25]

A general theory of the symbol could thus serve as the axis of a new classification of the human sciences. Freud's unconscious was coextensive with the new "symbolic" order, and Lacan made their assemblage into the central subject of "Function and Field":

Freud's discovery was that of the field of the effects, in man's nature, of his relations to the symbolic order and the fact that the meaning goes all the way back to the most radical instances of symbolization in being. To ignore the symbolic order is to condemn Freud's discovery and analytic experience to ruin.[26]

A field of symbols: identifying the ethnological study of elementary social structures with psychoanalytic inquiry into the terrain where interpersonal interaction joins the unconscious promised to revise even the natural sciences, whose relation to nature had a key symbolic component which remained "unstudied" and "problematic."[27] Symbols and symbolization shroud humans completely; they have an all but universal character and their "law" underwrites all human life and meaning formation within it.

Symbols in fact envelop the life of man with a network so total that they join together those who are going to engender him "by bone and flesh" before he comes into the world; so total that they bring to his birth, along with the gifts of the stars, if not with the gifts of the fairies, the shape of his destiny; so total that they provide the words that will make him faithful or renegade, the law of the acts that will follow him right to the very place where he is not yet and [also] beyond his very death.[28]

The key, for Lacan—as for Lévi-Strauss—is not so much the overpowering character of the symbolic order over the human enunciators of symbols. It is, rather, the location of structure and its capacity to enforce this kind of universalism.[29] Implicitly referencing Lévi-Strauss, Lacan suggests that what makes kinship structures possible and universal is "the richness of the forms," the number of possible combinations.[30] He transplants the incest taboo into his engagement with the Oedipus complex,[31] which he presents as the hinge for this structure, and he refers to the spread of marriage ties and kinship possibilities—and hence the multiple possible results of the Oedipus complex in the formation of personality—as "the Law": not a universal and a priori law, but one that emerges from biological development and culture and structures human experience. "In regulating marriage ties, [the Law] superimposes the reign of culture over the reign of nature, the latter being subject to the law of mating."[32] Lévi-Strauss did for Lacan what Fraser and Robertson-Smith had done for Freud when he offered a phylogenetic logic in *Totem and Taboo* to justify the Oedipus complex as an evolutionary and universal structure. We come full circle when Lacan proceeds to identify the Law with the language order: its totality and its rules operate unconsciously but overwhelmingly. Psychoanalysis manages its role in the transformation of modern subjectivity by "aligning it with the movement in modern science [i.e., structural linguistics and anthropology] that elucidates it."[33]

Lacan's parallelism between the symbolic and elementary structures was on full display in the third session of his 1954–55 seminar on the role of the ego in Freud's theory. On November 30, 1954, Lévi-Strauss delivered a lecture titled "Kinship and the Family" at the Société française de psychoanalyse. When the seminar met the next day, Lacan found himself confronted with frustrations concerning Lévi-Strauss's notion of the "elementary structure" and the status of society in his thought. The questions directed at Lacan by his trainees and by the philosopher Jean Hyppolite principally involved the formation of the symbolic and its totality, as well as the danger that a certain biologism might creep up in these most "elementary" of structures. Had Lévi-Strauss adequately demonstrated that the independence and intermediary character of structure were features relevant to all societies?

In response, Lacan repeatedly identified with Lévi-Strauss, equating the "elementary structure" and the symbolic and treating them as paradigms of the unconscious. Lévi-Strauss was targeting naturalism; in its place "a new function, encompassing the whole [human] order in its entirety" was dominant, and it preceded any cultural particularity: "the symbolic function intervenes at every moment and at every stage of [the human order's] existence."[34] The symbolic function was "universal" neither as a transcendental entity nor as a classic mechanistic form that pre-orders the world. It was coextensive with universality by being constitutive and not merely "generic" (in the sense of "two arms, two legs, and a pair of eyes").[35] It accrued totalities that sculpted *this* human being *here* even before she or he has made the smallest effort: "everything that has constituted him, his parents, his neighbors, the whole structure of the community, and not only constituted him as symbol, but constituted him in his being."[36]

Lacan then commented on the superimposition of Lévi-Strauss's incest prohibition on to the Oedipus complex. The Oedipus complex "must be conceived of as a recent, terminal and not original, phenomenon," but, crucially, it was "both universal and contingent, because it is uniquely and purely symbolic."[37] Psychoanalysis had regained its place as a science within the semiotic and cultural universe deployed by Lévi-Strauss; against Bronisław Malinowski's famous rejection of the universality of the Oedipus complex, Lacan could bring it back as a decisive developmental form. "Both universal and contingent," it represented the stage at which language emerged in the subject, operating beyond its control—an agent of unconscious interiority, the otherness within.

Many of Lacan's principal themes would develop out of this Jakobsonian–Lévi-Straussian organization of the symbolic and its competitive cohabitation with the imaginary register as this last worked its way in the individual subject. For example, the "Name of the Father" motif that Lacan would pursue over the years belonged to the deployment of this symbolic, neither a priori nor empirical structure: it articulated both the subject's belonging to a social grid and that subject's entrapment within an encasing, prohibitive quasi-Oedipal structure. For that reason, the motif "sustains the structure of desire with the structure of the law—but the inheritance of the father is what Kierkegaard designates for us, namely, his sin."[38]

As Deleuze would recall, positing the symbolic at a level "deeper" than that of binaries like imagination–reality or inner–outer displaced them: "not just the real and the imaginary, but their relations, and the disturbances of these relations, must be thought as the limit of a process in which they constitute themselves in relation to the symbolic."[39] Even Lacan's "Real"—the complement to his "Imaginary" and "Symbolic," the counterpoint that exceeded both—was merely a disruption of the symbolic. It marked the inability of the splintered, morphed, semiotically constituted and constituting subject to render the world transparent even across these two highly complex systems. A disruptive, perhaps incomprehensible other would always exist beyond them.

The Symbolic in the 1960s: Michel Foucault

Lacan's appropriation of Lévi-Strauss's achievement was useful to philosophy students in the 1960s, particularly at the École normale supérieure, where Lacan continued his seminar after 1963, when the International Psychoanalytic Association barred him from training analysts.

Philosophers and historians have recently returned to the routes of structuralism's influence in the 1960s and have emphasized that the sym-

bolic third resonated strongly with concerns about form and the meaning of "science." Peter Hallward has done this for the students of Louis
Althusser, who developed the framework for a "philosophy of the concept."[40] In Hallward's words, they took for granted the Bachelardian dictum that "science can only begin with a principled break with experience
and 'sensory knowledge,' an epistemological *rupture* that enables a rational, self-rectifying explanation of problems that are not given in or even
accessible to lived experience."[41] For them, "the totality of social structuring is opaque to individual understanding," as Alain Badiou would
put it in a television broadcast in January 1966.[42] In Althusser's own language, subjectivity is not subjection in general but subjection to particular
political–ideological apparatuses. Scientific critique and the recognition of
ideological apparatuses as underlying structures required the structuralist
third, the symbolic realm; subjection to a *particular* political–ideological
apparatus (rather than subjection *tout court*) connoted the need to work
on, think, and even daunt subjection by taking on the totality formed by
this apparatus. For formalist and political purposes, the students associated
with the *Cahiers pour l'analyse* recuperated the symbolic third from Lacan
and Lévi-Strauss for uses of their own.

This position became ubiquitous, even axiomatic in the 1960s.
Whenever models were identified as structuring some aspect of scientific
research or human experience, they tugged at the terms established by this
third. A model that "we" construct, the non-structuralist Michel Serres
said, is "a μεταξύ, that is to say, an intermediate between a theoretical field
belonging to some scientific inquiry and a phenomenon from that field."[43]
This position also marked a definite development, beyond the antifoundational realist model of experience and knowledge that had structured so
many of the phenomenological and epistemological questions in the 1930s
and 1940s.

The novelty of the symbolic realm resided in the fact that it produced
a hinge, grid, or terrain on which philosophical truth could emerge. It undercut phenomenologies, like Sartre's or Husserl's, that could not adequately
respond to the demand for this third order; it made claims about the irreducible alienation of the subject—its non-self-coincidence—commonplace; it
parleyed multiple possible sites for alterity, thereby denying its erasure. Language and representation harbored a wild distortion of any supposed immediacy of experience and speech, and this distortion eschewed social and

ontological theories. The structuralist third order thus inflected some of the central problematics and dynamics of contemporary thought while shaking, grinding, even shocking the ground on which these stood.

Nowhere was this clearer during the 1960s than in Michel Foucault's work, and particularly in his notions of discourse and order in *The Order of Things* (1966). Foucault had already used semiotics to recast the problem of norms in *Folie et déraison* (*History of Madness*), where he reoriented his Canguilhemian examination of psychiatric normality and pathology, evident in his earliest writings,[44] toward a logic of the sign and the exclusion of the mad from the symbolic order.[45] But Foucault showed a particular talent for staging the permutations of the neither aprioristic nor empirical locus of the "*order*" of Western thought, which he set out to study in *The Order of Things*. Despite his vigorous objections to being called a structuralist, here he studied the conceptual foundations of biological, linguistic, and economic thought as an order, in a manner that replicated the structuralist site of language, structure, and the symbolic. Loath to admit Lévi-Strauss's synchronicity and antihistoricism, Foucault spoke of the historical emergence of modern and contemporary thought, but this should not imply that he abandoned the "in-between" order—on the contrary.[46] In his preface Foucault announced his project as a study of the "history of the Same," a history of "how a culture experiences the propinquity of things, how it establishes the tabula of their relationships and the order by which they must be considered. Within this history of resemblance," of what it is "to be distinguished by kinds and to be collected together into identities,"[47] his aim was neither to offer a description of the recursivity of empirical cultural codes nor to operate at the level of general philosophical interpretations. Instead, he argued, the work aimed to establish an intermediary dominion

which, even though its role is mainly an intermediary one, is nonetheless fundamental: it is *more confused, more obscure*, and probably less easy to analyze. It is here that a culture, imperceptibly deviating from the empirical orders prescribed for it by its primary codes, instituting an initial separation from them, causes them *to lose their original transparency*, relinquishes its immediate and invisible powers, frees itself sufficiently to discover that these orders are perhaps not the only possible ones or the best ones.[48]

This "intermediary," "confused," "obscure" domain is about "what made [knowledge] possible"; hence it fundamentally affects order and efforts at ordering, coherence, and resemblance. Foucault speaks of the epistemolog-ical effort to find an intermediary site, the level of the "conditions of pos-sibility," of the order of order itself.

Such an analysis does not belong to the history of ideas or of science: it is rather an inquiry whose aim is to rediscover on what basis knowledge and theory be-came possible; within what space of order knowledge was constituted; on the basis of what historical a priori, and in the element of what positivity, ideas could appear, sciences be established, experience be reflected in philosophies, rationali-ties be formed, only, perhaps, to dissolve and vanish soon afterwards. . . . What I am attempting to bring to light is the epistemological field, the episteme in which knowledge, envisaged apart from all criteria having reference to its ratio-nal value or to its objective forms, grounds its positivity and thereby manifests a history which is not that of its growing perfection, but rather that of its condi-tions of possibility; in this account, what should appear are those configurations within the space of knowledge which have given rise to the diverse forms of em-pirical science.[49]

What Foucault's attacks in his "archaeology" of the "classical age" tar-geted was scientific claims at times treated as true or transparently avail-able, whereas the "epistemological field" would lie at once within and beneath empirical knowledge. As he elaborated the problem of discourse in the late 1960s, Foucault linked the institution of this order to the dis-missal of a Cartesian transcendental subject as well as of psychologisms. In *L'Archéologie du savoir* (1969; *The Archaeology of Knowledge*), he approached this third order almost formally and pointed to it as the site of the episte-mological historian's work:

Discourse is not the majestically unfolding manifestation of a thinking, knowing, speaking subject, but, on the contrary, a totality, in which the dispersion of the subject and his discontinuity with himself may be determined. It is a space of ex-teriority in which a network of distinct sites is deployed. I showed earlier that it was neither by "words" nor by "things" that the regulation of the objects proper to a discursive formation should be defined; similarly, it must now be recognized that it is neither by recourse to a transcendental subject nor by recourse to a psy-chological subjectivity that the regulation of its enunciations should be defined.[50]

The third here is *active*, self-organizing, self-regulating, a network preg-nant in meaning and within which conscious or linguistic activity may be inscribed, affecting both words and things, and above all playing the very subjects by which it is usually supposed to have been created. To study within discourse but fail to rethink it as the organizer of knowledge and as the historical a priori was to accept a classic understanding of culture and to let oneself be cornered from two sides, by empirical analyses and transcendental philosophies. Instead, in this "intermediary," "confused," or "obscure" domain, it was possible for an analysis to be devised that would manage forms of power and statehood, technological schemata, and creation so that governance, articulation, and politico-theoretical enthusiasm would design the menu of future philosophical pursuits.[51]

Postscript: Language, Nationalism, and Clarity

If structures like language, the symbolic, or order provided a new framework for the study of major facets of human experience, the success of the structuralist gesture also affected the way in which the corresponding terms—"language" or "symbolic"—were understood in the postwar period. The question of what happened specifically to the *concept* of language when language itself became the paradigmatic form of structural analysis has not been addressed. The remainder of this chapter deals with the general implications of the structuralist treatment of language in the context of historical and contemporary depictions of the work and meaning of language. Two particular changes deserve attention. One was a departure from theories that related language to clarity of knowledge and ideas and to the quest for a universal and rational language at the foundation of true philosophy—a quest initiated by René Descartes and Gottfried Wilhelm Leibniz. The other was a departure from nineteenth- and twentieth-century celebrations of *French* as a language superior to others, notably in clarity.

Clarity in language has been a major concern for a full three centuries, from Descartes to Esperanto to Wittgenstein, and it continues to this day. The hopes pinned on a universal logic and the fantasy of a universal or natural language, at least from Descartes onward, depended on this philosophical ethics of clarity. Descartes, who made the quest for certainty a cornerstone of his thought, famously wrote:

If someone were to explain correctly what are the simple ideas in the human imagination out of which all human thoughts are compounded, and if his explanation were generally received, I would dare to hope for a universal language very easy to learn, to speak and to write. The greatest advantage of such a language would be the assistance it would give to men's judgment, representing matters so clearly that it would be almost impossible to go wrong . . . I think it is possible to invent such a language.[52]

Descartes was hardly alone in this dream; Leibniz's emphasis on the simple absolute and on the universal characteristic extended the search for a universal language of representation, and judgment into new areas.[53] It also promised an eirenic regime of shared understanding.

The Cartesian aspiration to clarity in ideas, knowledge, and communication—and also to clarity of style—was a recurrent dream in Western thought. John Stuart Mill called language "the atmosphere of philosophical investigation" and asked that both be "made transparent" in order to avoid ambiguity or confusion.[54] Léon Brunschvicg exemplified his contemporaries' anxiety over language's role when he wrote that language has always seemed to threaten idealism and the transparency of consciousness and reason: "This idealism of consciousness and reason, for which the spirit becomes transparent to the mind thanks to the deepening of its radical principle, has not ceased to appear to us threatened, across history, by the opacity of language that it calls to its aid to express itself outwards."[55] Language could not be trusted to deliver transparency and often had to be forced, massaged, jerry-rigged into clarity; yet it *could* and *should* create exactly this transparency of thought and action, with potentially far-reaching consequences.

The second change discussed here concerns the view that the French language was itself inherently "clearer" and capable of capturing the spirit of those who spoke it. Antoine de Rivarol's 1784 *Discours sur l'universalité de la langue française* was one of the first to claim that French had these two properties and was hence fundamentally superior to other languages and generated a superior national community. On the criterion of clarity, Rivarol produced an incipient hierarchy of languages and nations: "What is not clear is not French; what is not clear is still English, Italian, Greek, or Latin." Linguistic nationalism became a staple in the writings of Madame de Staël, Jules Michelet, and Ernest Renan, establishing a purism in language politics that persists to this day.[56]

The two lines of argument are, of course, not entirely distinguishable, since the French language has enjoyed several periods of scientific and intellectual dominance. But the second view, about its superiority, was particularly salient, given the ascendance of English and the wartime power of

German. Reviewing a work by the respected linguist Albert Dauzat titled *Le Génie de la langue française* (1942; *The Genius of the French Language*), Lucien Febvre concurred that clarity was the first essential characteristic of French. He even proceeded to offer his own account of how this came about: the development of French from Latin, Celtic, and German endowed it with qualities that none these languages nor any modern competitor (e.g., English) possessed.[57] Among philosophers, this was a touchy issue: the reception of Martin Heidegger in the later 1940s and 1950s had to deal with his own elegy to German and denigration of French as a poor language for philosophy[58]—a language insufficiently capable of recuperating an originary and authentic relation to being itself. For some of Heidegger's readers, for example, Alexandre Koyré, his understanding of language was part and parcel of his shift toward a mystical and politically suspect theory of truth; others, such as Jean Beaufret, his apostle in the later 1940s and 1950s, purported that Heidegger was on to something protean in his twin theories of language and truth.[59]

These concerns were obviously highly political. In the context of decolonization—and especially in the 1960s, when de Gaulle was president again—the argument that all languages are structurally equal struck against the cultural nationalism of conservatives who clamored for French cultural and political strength. The structuralist focus on the irreducibility of a complex and ultimately elusive structure of representation ran against the traditional French line on "clarity"; it had no place for the belief that an artificial language could be universal, either. The idea that language delimits a "third order" between experience and an a priori space was essential to its denationalization. It is hard not to see the broad adoption of the structuralist theory of language as symptomatic of an egalitarian incentive—not in the sense that some forms of human communication cannot be more complex than others, but in the sense that, as subjects are always situated within this third order, claims and concepts are always understood relationally and cannot easily be accorded greater, national-transparent authority.

This new attitude to linguistic clarity—the objection to "the Cartesian handling of the French language with its emphasis on analytic and scientific clarity at the expense of complexity of perception"[60]—has fueled a standard complaint about structuralism and the difficulty of French theory; but this complaint is at times turned on its head.[61]

The refusal of linguistic clarity should then be seen as an act that joined the scientific imperative of retrieving a place for language with a political imperative. The sense that language, desire, and culture were quasi-universal forms that refracted not only subjectivity and speech but knowledge and science facilitated what one may call the institutionalization of the rejection of transparency. Through the foregrounding of language, *representation* was established, in its perpetual non-correspondence, as a new point of departure that defined the chances of philosophy and literary–cultural studies, from Jacques Derrida and Louis Marin to Jean-François Lyotard. Language's becoming a "third," a form for the study of representation, was a major development, which definitively cast transparency as the illusory fantasy of overcoming the wall that was the order of representation itself.

Lévi-Strauss's World Out of Sync

In 1959, Claude Lévi-Strauss concluded an essay on the state of contemporary anthropology with this analogy:

Let us suppose, for a moment, that astronomers should warn us that an unknown planet is nearing the earth and will remain at close range for twenty or thirty years, thereafter receding and disappearing forever. In order to avail ourselves of this unique opportunity, neither effort nor money would be spared to build specially designed telescopes and satellites. Should not similar study be made of one half of mankind—only recently acknowledged as such—still so close to the other half that, except for the lack of money, its study raises no problem, although it will soon become impossible forever? If the future of anthropology could be seen in this light, no study would appear more urgent and more important. Native cultures are disintegrating faster than radioactive bodies. The moon, Mars, and Venus will still be at the same distance from the earth when that mirror which other civilizations still hold up to us will have so receded from our eyes that . . . we will never again be able to recognize and study this image of ourselves, which will be lost and gone forever.[1]

That "Western Man" should have come to be so out of sync with "his" world as to make his immediate representation of it—and of the human itself—a monstrous anamorphosis, promoting the gravest of injustices, was a central assumption of Lévi-Strauss's anthropological and philosophical project. It also defined the persona that he so strategically deployed in the 1950s.[2] It permeated his sense of the role of thought in the present world as much as his depiction of world history and of the place of human diversity in it. At the same time, this attempt made Lévi-Strauss stand out among the intellectuals of the postwar period. His refusal of humanism equaled his compassion for the suffering of others and as a result founded his entire project on a dual demand: to provide a formal theory of human societies; and also to turn the disappearing divergence of these societies into a moral cause.

Many of the intellectual priorities of Lévi-Strauss's argument are recognizable in the passage quoted above. Humanity, imagining its future, unites itself by gazing at the heavens and conceives itself to be a singular, future-oriented enterprise of scientific observation. Yet this unification is false, indeed blind to the violent homogenizing tendencies that underlie it. Homogeneity also enforces inertia—a slowing down of what Lévi-Strauss elsewhere called "hot societies." This is the real end of the promises of progress.[3] Hence an unnoticed process of distortion, which began long ago, is now coming to its inexorable conclusion and leaves this "Man" opaque to himself, unable even to see himself in the ever-receding reflection.

The argument about homogenization motivates Lévi-Strauss's commitments in his work from *Tristes tropiques* to the mid-1960s, in particular his social thought, his stance on the purpose and scope of anthropology, and his settling on Rousseau as the paragon of ethical–political truth and human harmony. Until the publication of *Tristes tropiques* in 1955, Lévi-Strauss was known for his well-received *The Elementary Structures of Kinship* and for the quarrel over his 1953 UNESCO text "Race et histoire" with Roger Caillois.[4] As we have seen, Lévi-Strauss's earlier work advanced structural anthropology as a discipline capable of comparing different societies by using a third order between nature and culture or between experience and transcendence. And *Tristes tropiques* was not a voice crying in the wilderness: it was a vivid, forceful expression of a set of concerns shared among French ethnologists after World War II, written in the genre of an Odyssey whose traveler-protagonist found increasing devastation across the traveled globe and back in his Ithaca above all. The rethinking of human diversity would dominate *Tristes tropiques*, where Lévi-Strauss now deploys *l'humanité* and *l'homme* so as to accentuate *difference* and *unity* respectively, prioritizing difference as a structural precondition of humanity, while expressing his dread at the contemporary standardization of "Man": "men can coexist on condition that they recognize each other as being *equally*, though *differently*, human, but they can also coexist by denying each other a comparable degree of humanity, thus establishing a system of subordination."[5] Equality does not suffice: difference and the granting of a "comparable degree of humanity" are just as important if equality is not to disintegrate into mere self-centered ignorance of other societies' norms. A society or culture cannot be taken to be inherently superior to others—and, en passant, Lévi-Strauss rejected the value of moral and social transparency for social comparison:

No society is perfect. It is in the nature of all societies to include a degree of impurity incompatible with the norms they proclaim and which finds concrete expression in a certain dosage of injustice, insensitiveness and cruelty. . . . No society is fundamentally good but none is absolutely bad; they all offer their members certain advantages, with the proviso that there is invariably a residue of evil, the amount of which seems to remain more or less constant.[6]

In *Tristes tropiques* Lévi-Strauss accentuated the need for difference in a famous pessimistic and antihumanist depiction of the uniformization under way:

Now that the Polynesian islands have been smothered in concrete and turned into aircraft carriers solidly anchored in the southern seas, when the whole of Asia is beginning to look like a dingy suburb, when shanty towns are spreading across Africa, when civil and military aircraft blight the primeval innocence of the American or Melanesian forests even before destroying their virginity, what else can the so-called escapism of traveling do than confront us with the more unfortunate aspects of our history? Our great Western Civilization, which has created the marvels we now enjoy, has only succeeded in producing them at the cost of corresponding ills. The order and harmony of the Western World, its most famous achievement, and a laboratory in which structures of a complexity as yet unknown are being fashioned, demand the elimination of a prodigious mass of noxious byproducts which now contaminate the globe. The first thing we see as we travel round the world is our own filth, thrown into the face of mankind.[7]

Radicalizing the analysis presented in "Race and History,"[8] Lévi-Strauss specifically targets homogeneity: "mankind has opted for monoculture: it is in the process of creating a mass civilization, as beetroot is grown in the mass."[9] And, in a passage worthy of Adorno, he contrasts a "primitive" mentality, which "cushioned" human beings by rendering nature awe-inspiring and indomitable, with Man's growing power, which is "surely little more than our subjective awareness of a progressive welding together of humanity and the physical universe, whose great deterministic laws, instead of remaining remote and awe-inspiring, *now use thought itself as an intermediary medium* and are colonizing us on behalf of a silent world whose agents we have become."[10]

These passages depict a humanity that has reached the end of history. Singularization, homogenization, and inertia render impossible any major difference or new change.[11] Attempts to render reality transparent to ourselves redouble the danger: we think that the universe rationalized by our theories is governed by objective, known laws, but our normative gaze enforces those laws to the detriment of alternative ways of life. Lévi-Strauss channeled the arguments of contemporaries who refused the character of unbiased, unmotivated, or objective analysis to scientific observation when he said that "planetary thought" entraps precisely those it pretends to set free in its "perfection" of knowledge.

This perspective on the devastation of societal difference is central to the book's claim to offer something different from the conventional travel narrative, whose growing industry of illusion and false authenticity preys on audience credulousness and the wish for human unity.[12] *Tristes tropiques* counteroffers an anthropology that, through

the study of these savages leads to something other than the revelation of a Utopian state of nature or the discovery of the perfect society in the depths of the forest; it helps us to build a theoretical model of human society, which does not correspond to any observable reality, but with the aid of which we may succeed in distinguishing between "what is primordial and what is artificial in man's present nature and in obtaining a good knowledge of a state which no longer exists, which has probably never existed, and which will probably never exist in the future, but of which it is nevertheless essential to have a sound conception in order to pass valid judgment on our present state."[13]

Rousseau, whom Lévi-Strauss quotes in this passage, offers an ethical and intellectual model for how anthropology should decline to represent "any society in particular."[14] How can the anthropologist succeed in the arduous task of undermining false narratives about the unity of "man" (*l'homme*) while devising systems adequate for the articulation and systematization of human difference? The answer is: through a profound displacement, a *technique de dépaysement*,[15] a practice of being actively out of sync with one's world in order to demonstrate the falsehood of its pretense of being itself in sync.

This figure—Lévi-Strauss's anthropologist—is deployed across three registers. On the first register, the anthropologist appears, not as a "normal" social being tied to his culture in the way others are, but as a solitary nomad whose station vacillates between two roles: godlike observer-analyst and sufferer from a "mental disorder" resulting from the protracted experience of self-imposed exile. He is human only in name:

> while remaining human himself, the anthropologist tries to study and judge mankind from a point of view sufficiently lofty and remote to allow him to disregard the particular circumstances of a given society . . . the conditions in which he lives and works cut him off physically from his group for long periods . . . he acquires a kind of chronic rootlessness; eventually he comes to feel at home nowhere, and he remains psychologically maimed.[16]

These dramatized doubts often intensify to paranoia over his super- and subhuman status, and leave Lévi-Strauss feeling used as an alibi for the West's cannibalization of humanity.

> Appreciating judiciously the immense conquests of the West does not prevent me from perceiving the strange paradox that allowed it to create ethnographers at the very moment when it undertook to destroy the object it accorded to their study; nor does it hold me back from being conscious of the role of alibi that we are forced to play. Only an alibi? Perhaps also a precaution—by a civilization that lends us guinea pigs for a moment before it eats them all the while hoping that our methods might one day help it understand the pains it now discovers in its belly.[17]

The anthropologist's humanism emerges only at the moment of homogeneity's triumph, when his own function and power has become obsolete.

The second register, dependent on structural analysis as much as on the anthropologist's fragile estate, concerns the conceptual grounding of "social" anthropology. Lévi-Strauss construed it at the expense of *philosophical* anthropology, whose demise he would relish in his famous 1962 critique of Sartre.[18] In keeping with his rejection of a "monocultural" humanism, Lévi-Strauss attributed the anthropologist a model of analysis that would reconstruct and organize societal difference, as he had done in *The Elementary Structures of Kinship*. In a short essay titled "The Three Humanisms," Lévi-Strauss tracked the origin of ethnology to the humanisms of the Renaissance and the Enlightenment. However, while he celebrated ethnology's new "universal humanism," he disparaged older humanisms as profoundly tainted by their persistent support for privileged classes and commercial–industrial interests.[19] "The Scope of Anthropology"—Lévi-Strauss's 1959 inaugural address at the Collège de France—further claimed for his science the status of guardian over humanity:

In this perspective, utopian as it may be, social anthropology finds its highest justification, since the forms of life and thought which it studies do not simply have a historical and comparative interest but correspond to a permanent hope for mankind over which social anthropology has mission to keep watch, especially in the most troubled times. . . .

Our science reached its maturity the day that Western man began to understand that he would never understand himself so long as, all over the surface of the earth, he took as his object only one single race or only one single people. Only then was anthropology able to affirm itself as what it is: an enterprise renewing and expiating the Renaissance in order to extend humanism to the measure of humanity.[20]

Lévi-Strauss's social anthropology took center stage just as philosophical anthropology was becoming exhausted and the unitary notion of "the human" seemed a poor basis on which to ground an ethics. (The term "social anthropology" was not even in use before 1938.[21]) In this climate, Lévi-Strauss's new enterprise deprived philosophy of any rights over a definition of the human.

For Lévi-Strauss himself, the idea that anthropology was the only human science capable of models of difference and humanity was not altogether new, though its target had changed. In the late 1930s, after his now famous expedition in the Amazon, where he encountered the Nambikwara and Tupi-Kabawib, Lévi-Strauss gave a lecture in Paris before the Centre confédéral d'Éducation ouvrière, titled "A Revolutionary Science: Ethnography."[22] Many sociologists (especially the Maussians) were socialists, and Lévi-Strauss's socialist commitment was profound: the title of his doctoral dissertation, written under Célestin Bouglé's direction, was "Les Postulats de la théorie du matérialisme historique principalement chez Karl Marx" (The Postulates of the Theory of Historical Materialism, Principally in Karl Marx),[23] and he published extensively in journals such as *L'Étudiant socialiste*. At the Centre confédéral, foregrounding the "minute" studies ethnographers carry out in "primitive" societies, Lévi-Strauss relayed that "every progress that we have made thus far in the knowledge of savage societies or primitive peoples . . . has always corresponded to a development of revolutionary critique."[24] Such "developments" included Alexander the

Great's conquests in western Asia, which for Lévi-Strauss paralleled the rise of Greek skepticism; the conquest of the Americas, supposedly contemporary with Montaigne's critique of institutions; the penetration of North America, essential to the prerevolutionary critique of the eighteenth century; and the Russian Revolution, which made possible the study of "primitive peoples" in Siberia and the Arctic Ocean. Vagueness over causation did not trouble Lévi-Strauss: ethnography demonstrated that "primitive" peoples were not simply left behind, only partially evolved in the supposedly "unilinear evolution of humanity"[25] that served to assert the superiority of European civilizations. The diffusion of evolutionary theory "to all domains of human knowledge" in the nineteenth century had spread the "absurd idea" that "by noting all the different forms that come from social institutions on the surface of the earth, across tribes and peoples, we can reconstitute *the* chain of evolution on the social sphere." Attributions of backwardness in conformity with a linear development "vitiated" the "knowledge of Man" and the revolutionary import of ethnography.[26] Ethnographic studies indicated that the spread of techniques, institutions, and philosophies was the result of borrowings from one society to another, which legitimized ethnography as the best study of *l'homme*, human difference, and the distribution of social institutions and had political potential for socialist internationalism: "our studies can complete the intelligibility of man."[27]

After the war and with the political collapse of evolutionist explanations of human society and history, ethnography's target shifted and its scope broadened for Lévi-Strauss. "Race et histoire," his 1953 essay for UNESCO, used ethnology to mount an attack on historical and philosophical fantasies of human social and biological development. As Lévi-Strauss's structuralism developed into a theory of experience, behavior, and belief—a theory that explicitly denied the human subject the capacity to individually understand their codes—nothing short of a refusal of philosophical determinations of "the human" would do. The universalism of humanist anthropology, tethered to modern imperialism and to lofty ideas about the unity of humanity, allowed Europeans to identify with the subjects of their study and exploitation; and so the reduction of humans to Europeans had been inescapable:

Whether in their case or our own, a good deal of egocentricity and naivety is necessary to believe that man has taken refuge in a single one of the historical or geographical modes of his existence, when the truth about man resides in the system of their differences and common properties.[28]

A specific ethnological argument accompanies this emphasis on European "egocentrism," namely the conviction that the world of American peoples was a profoundly unified culture. Mauss had already articulated it in a letter to Lévi-Strauss in 1937: "The more I think of what you write me [about the Ge], the more the unity of the South American world, even that of the North, and with even more reason that of Central America, seems to me certain, and the more this unity seems to branch out at an already very elevated point of civilization."[29] Lévi-Strauss would turn this into an explicit principle in *Mythologiques* (1964); but there his point was that such fundamental unities could allow for profound diversity, whereas European egocentricity leveled everything into the homogeneous world that Lévi-Strauss deplored.

On the third register, the anthropologist is born of the violent history of European empire, and in particular of a guilty conscience about it among Europeans. As we have noted, "his very existence is incomprehensible except as an attempt at redemption: he is the symbol of atonement."[30] In this regard, the anthropologist intentionally rejects his civilization so as to attend to those of others. Lévi-Strauss had offered the principal lines of this argument in the 1938 lecture, declaring the ethnographer to be a figure not of atonement and *apokatastasis* but one of revolution. The ethnographer's studies, his minute catalogues of artifacts, his descriptions of daily life facilitated a "knowledge of Man" that legitimized and clarified revolutionary concerns, although they left him uncomfortably in the unenviable position of conserving "primitive" societies.

The ethnographer is in effect someone singular when he belongs to the Left (which he almost always does, as you can see): he is on the one hand a man who strives to criticize the society in which he lives, to modify it, to destroy its organization and substitute something else for it; and on the other hand, from the moment when, no longer in his own society, he is instead in some tribe of savages, he becomes the worst conservative, the worst reactionary, in trying to protect these little tribes from civilization's infringement of it. Revolutionary in his own society, he becomes a conservator for the primitives.[31]

In 1938, Lévi-Strauss's ethnographer sees all, is always in the right: his revolutionary critique promises to make his society more transparent, just as his anthropology grasps and makes available the qualities of the "primitive tribes" that are to be protected. But by 1955, Lévi-Strauss was depicting his estrangement from French society as a cause of grave personal torment.

His commitment to humanist ideals had been tempered by the *dépayse-ment* he suffered in his forced 1941 emigration to the United States, which opens *Tristes tropiques*.

As he practices his profession, the anthropologist is consumed by doubts: has he really abandoned his native setting, his friends, and his way of life, spent such considerable amounts of money and energy, and endangered his health, for the sole purpose of making his presence acceptable to a score or two of miserable creatures doomed to early extinction . . . and on whose whims the success or failure of his mission depends? . . . does [anthropology as an occupation] result from a more radical choice, which implies that *the anthropologist is calling into question the system in which he was born and brought up?*[32]

Deprived of a proper world—the world he studies and the world from which he has been estranged, which nevertheless dominates his inner life[33]—the anthropologist translates the different registers, inner doubt, structural humanism, and displacement into an act of "calling into question the system in which he was born and brought up." This imbalance directly affects his temporal orientation in these worlds, and thus "the tropics are . . . out of date."[34] The anthropologist arriving in Brazil has moved back "imperceptibly in time," and the new world appears to be bound to temporal vectors that are different, even multiple, in any case alien.[35] Plagued by doubts and by civilizational guilt yet tied to a "refuge and a mission"[36] that leave him displaced and "maimed," the anthropologist assumes destabilization as the purpose that no one else can fulfill. Temporally, vocationally, geopolitically, it is through this mission of disjointedness that he can taint the supposed epistemological and ethical transparency of optimistic humanism. Beneath the ideology of continuous and undifferentiated human nature resides the fragmentation of this expansive, concretizing modernity. Only because the anthropologist is himself sufficiently distanced, forced into loneliness, distorted in his relations with others, out of sync with his world and that of his subjects does he have a chance to toy with the difference between societies and produce an abstract, formal model.

Because it was not bound either to a specific empirical reality or to a generic definition of "Man," structural analysis offered the "sufficiently lofty and remote" position that Lévi-Strauss wanted to occupy.[37] Lévi-Strauss is, of course, self-serving when he privileges displacement as a superior position from which he could gauge both the structural foundations of each society and the possibility of ethical relations with others. Yet it is more interesting that he decries the *unity of perspectives* and that he does so on the grounds that its "humanism" has resulted from a profoundly distorting and violent simplification of human experience. Anthropology can become a proper "science of Man" at the moment when it commits itself to undermining this "unity of perspectives." This task brings together the three registers at which the anthropologist operates and their attendant dilemmas: the question of understanding reality; the place of the human subject; and the structural approach to which Lévi-Strauss affixes his own sensibilities.

Lévi-Strauss's attention to the pre-subjective, pre-conscious codes and non-humanist structures of human life forced a transformation of the major epistemological movement that had emerged in the interwar period. This was the antifoundational realism that prioritized neither "consciousness" nor "reality" but the interwovenness and co-implication of the two and the obstacles blocking the access of consciousness to reality. Turning to structure instead of managing this realism, Lévi-Strauss denied that the experience of reality offers an acceptable standpoint for knowledge—*except* for the observer-anthropologist who embraces his "maimed" existence and sets about articulating the preconscious codes of human experience. By virtue of his "dislocatedness," this figure can:

(a) offer a systematic explanation of the sorts of human experience that falsify humanist homogenization and the sense of transparent relations with others;

(b) refuse a position that allows the subject to construe such a transparency, by demonstrating that every society is unified at a level unavailable to its members; and

(c) bring forth models of the structures that underlie social experience, but that are not themselves made explicit in that experience.[38]

The critique of epistemological transparency thus shifted: empirical interaction only presented consciously experienced reality; structure could reach beneath that. Lévi-Strauss insisted on models, codes, language because these arranged, *yet said little* of, particular lived situations and left intact the internal dynamics that generated the *image* of transparency for those who lived these situations. As he made clear in his early essays on linguistics and structuralism, no reality expresses the totality of meaning available to its participants—it expresses both more and less.[39] Because it is replete with meaning and too pliable from the observer's perspective, empirical reality is less than satisfactory for the anthropologist ("La réalité vraie n'est jamais la plus apparente," he notes in *Tristes tropiques*).[40] Addressed frontally, "reality" presents a false consistency; yet, studied as a particular permutation of a complex precultural whole, it displays formal elements that delimit and condition that whole. Like the participants, who are not aware of all the available meanings, the anthropologist, dependent as he is on the society of his origins and on his inner world, has to reconstruct the reduced conscious experience he observes. Kinship systems and myths are ciphers that are, each, particular enough yet unconsciously and only partially experienced. They sustain the anthropologist's sense of displacement and his pursuit of an abstract model that is neither a priori nor empirical and that aims to be universal without being transparently "real."

Difference—and not merely equality—between cultures and groups is essential to the very possibility of such a model: were conscious empirical reality sufficient, the anthropologist's dilemmas would dissolve and European humanism's intrusion into the worlds of others would triumph. The very foreignness of "the other" organizes the model for understanding it and for treating all cultures from an abstracted perspective. For this reason, difference offers a methodological premise that Lévi-Strauss found ontologically threatened and historically denied around him, as these civilizations were assimilated or driven to extinction. Against the false transparencies of humanism, he would turn to Rousseau to recover an alternative relation with the other—a solution that, as we shall see, would itself come to be criticized as a near mystical fantasy of interpersonal transparency.

The Ethnographer, *Cinéma-vérité*, and the Disruption of the Natural Order
Chronicle of a Summer

I learned with the Dogon that the essential character in all these adventures is not God, representing order, but the foe of God, the Pale Fox, representing disorder. So I have a tendency, when I'm filming, to consider the landscape . . . as precisely the work of God, and the presence of my camera as an intolerable disorder. It's this intolerable disorder that becomes a creative object. Marceline would never have walked alone, talking all by herself, if there hadn't been a camera there, if she wasn't wearing the microphone, if she didn't have a portable tape recorder. It was provocation; it was disorder.

Jean Rouch, Ciné-ethnography (2003: 154)

Thus the cinema can call itself *cinéma-vérité*, all the more because it will have destroyed every model of the true so as to become creator and producer of truth: this will not be a cinema of truth but the truth of cinema. This is the sense intended by Jean Rouch when he spoke of "*cinéma-vérité*."

Gilles Deleuze, Cinema 2: The Time-Image (1989: 151)

From Leiris, Griaule, and Lévi-Strauss on, ethnography thematized the ethnographer's return to Paris as an uncomfortable return from other to self: the hero arrives in a changed Ithaca, but no conclusive reconciliation seems likely. In a letter to Paul Valéry dated May 2, 1939, Griaule described Paris as a rat-filled sewer and himself as a man boxed in it; he wished he could somehow bridge the distance to the Dogon people he was studying without having to endure travel or to stay.[1] Lévi-Strauss, as we have seen, portrayed himself as someone permanently out of joint. The ethnographer who engaged with this thematic most interestingly was Jean Rouch, the director of the ethnographic films *Les Maîtres fous* (1956) and *Moi, un noir* (1959). Rouch marked his own return by teaming up with a leading revisionist Marxist, Edgar Morin, director of the journal *Arguments*, to make *Chronique d'un été* (*Chronicle of a Summer*).

Morin said to me, "Jean, you have made all your films abroad; do you know anything about contemporary France?" He said that I should turn my gaze onto the Parisians and do anthropological research about my own tribe. In fact I really didn't.[2]

Deeply committed to the *kino-pravda* (cine-truth) that Dziga Vertov had made famous in 1929 with *Man with a Movie Camera*,[3] Rouch and Morin embarked on their project with the explicit intention of asking Parisians, "How do you live?" This question was the original title of the film. *Chronicle* centered on workers' and professionals' ordinary life and work and instituted *cinéma-vérité* as the medium of a putatively transparent representation of the everyday. Yet this transparency was ambiguous and profoundly troubling, even to the directors and to the film's protagonists. A short examination of *Chronicle* allows us to unfold the layers of its two authors' intentions and understand how anxieties over transparency were ascertained, established, and covered over in the film.

Morin's *Cinéma-vérité* and Rouch's Situations

"We shoot the final encounter. I had dreamt of a sort of confrontation in a large room after projecting the film, with multiple cameras and microphones recording not only the reactions to the film but also the conversations that would start up spontaneously and according to the affinities among the different characters."[4] This was Morin's plan for the film's penultimate sequence, the screening of a near-final cut for the film's major characters—"not actors," claims the title sequence, "but men and women who have given moments of their existence to a new experience of *cinéma-vérité*" (see fig. 15.1). Morin anticipated it anxiously, as "a big final scene where the scales would fall and consciousness would be awakened, where we would take a new Tennis Court Oath to construct a new life."

It was not to be. The non-actors decried the film as incredibly tiresome, absolutely boring, full of generalities, unnatural, full of indecencies,

FIGURE 15.1 The New Tennis Court Oath: Screening of rushes from *Chronique d'un été* (*Chronicle of a Summer*). BnF, Fonds Jean Rouch, NAF-28464-C-bas.
Reproduced with permission of the Bibliothèque nationale de France and Jocelyne Rouch.

staged, artificial.[5] Each of its subjects complained that her or his co-participants acted at the moments when they were supposed to be sincere, talked to themselves rather than to the camera, and exhibited themselves unconvincingly. The film disappointed the dream of a revelation of truth; it would certainly not begin a revolution. For Morin, this was a shocking moment. He understood cinematic depiction as a mirror to reality; it surpassed fiction and documentary[6] by exposing *this* reality and its substructure. Having trusted cinematic truth and taken pride in the testimonies of Auschwitz, of factory work, and of the pains of workers' everyday life that it reported, Morin now witnessed the failure of the *vérité* he had so dreamt of—that complete overcoming of mediation that political revolution had failed to achieve and that he felt the film might instead manage. In conversation with Rouch at the end of the film, he persisted in the belief that the scenes were veridical and he resigned himself to the limitations.

Rouch was not nearly as naïve about the kind of reality that is represented on film. It is unclear whether *Chronicle* was the result of theoretical premises he would articulate soon, or whether its failure contributed to them; but Rouch already underlined intervention and aggressive camera work as the filmmaker's tool for *creating* truth—indeed for *extracting* it from the participants.[7] Two sets of reasons, ethnographic and political, account for his sense that the camera was *constructing* situations rather than passively *representing* them.

The cinematic representation of ethnographic reality had been an imperative ever since Mauss had taught, in the 1920s, that "cinema allows us to photograph life itself."[8] During the Dakar–Djibouti expedition, Griaule and his collaborators filmed and photographed processions from multiple vantage points in order to satisfy Mauss's demand that they comprehend events from every possible angle (see fig. 6.1). Griaule, who became a pilot and air force officer during the 1930s, broadened the use of cinema and photography, especially aerial, for purposes of mapping the organization of particular groups under study.[9]

Rouch became a student of Griaule's in the late 1940s, and he was strongly influenced by Griaule's research on masks and ritual. These studies date from the same period—the 1930s, when Griaule was working with Leiris[10]—and present the ethnographic encounter as steeped in role-play, power dynamics, elisions, secrets, and lies. James Clifford commented that Griaule's "accounts assumed a recurring conflict of interests, an agonistic drama resulting in mutual respect, complicity in a productive balance of power . . . [He] harbors no qualms about his own theatricality."[11] Indeed, in his crowning years at the Sorbonne and until his death in 1956, Griaule dramatized the ethnographer as strategist: a detective who had to conduct an inquest and wrest secrets that were kept from him.[12] Commenting on work with his informants—a process that Mauss had disregarded as a last resort[13]—Griaule famously wrote:

The role of the sleuth of social facts is often comparable to that of the detective or examining magistrate. The crime is the fact, the guilty party the interlocutor, and accomplices are all the members of this society. This multiplicity of responsible parties, the extent of the areas where they act, the abundance of pieces of evidence serving to convict appear to facilitate the inquest, but in reality they guide it into labyrinths—labyrinths that are often organized. . . . Not to guide the inquest is to allow the instinctive need that the informer has to dissimulate the most delicate points. . . . The inquest must be conceived as a strategic operation.[14]

Griaule's prosecutorial dramaturgy of the ethnographic encounter was central to Rouch's design of situations that would bring forth a measure of ethnographic truth.[15] Rouch redeployed it,[16] especially in his films, using not so much his on-screen persona as his intrusive directorial and camera perspective. He made this technique explicit in interviews and theoretical writings.[17] The film historian Georges Sadoul noted that "for Rouch the camera was essentially active. It was, in *Chronicle of a Summer* . . . not an obstacle to expression but on the contrary *the indispensable witness that motivates this expression.*"[18]

Rouch was equally invested in political and colonial questions. "The first time I heard a worker speak in the cinema," Jean-Luc Godard reminisced, "was in *Chronique d'un été*. Rouch apart, none of the people who have done films about workers have had any talent."[19] Rouch later described his stance as "anarchy without militancy," a description appropriate for his conviction that through his camera work he was disordering a well-established divine or natural order and staging something else in its stead.[20] In 1950, he was in the audience when Leiris delivered the talk "Ethnography Faced with Colonialism." Like Leiris and Lévi-Strauss, he was deeply uncomfortable about colonial power and wanted his science, which he felt was shackled by colonialism, to work toward a partial cure.[21] In his personal diaries, he attacked *des vieux coloniaux* who blocked the alleviation of conditions in Africa.[22] Rouch concluded the diaries with an imagined encounter in which *le Blanc* and *le Noir* finally approach each other, after having been standoffish for long. "The White man" will begin (in future tense) to tell of his world, and gradually "the Black man" will join in. The capital letters vanish along this process:

And the white man will perhaps understand that the black whom he believed so ignorant and so primitive, has his own techniques, his own coherent ways of thinking, an extraordinary philosophy of the world and of life, a civilization that nothing allows us to classify as lower than our own, certainly a very different civilization but also a very rich and just as valuable one. And then the white man and black man will be friends.[23]

Note the formulation: the white man begins to tell his story, then the black man responds. Where is the ethnographer in this exchange? Is he the white man? Rouch closes his "diary" at this point: as the white man of the encounter, he is also the writer who records it, staying silent on the margins. (Had it been published half a decade later, the passage would have made Fanon cringe; but, by the time Rouch returned to the problem, he might have seen it differently too.)

The politics of Rouch's position as participant-director was evident to contemporaries. As was recognized at the time, especially in the magazine *Cahiers du cinéma*, what made Rouch's films so remarkable—even exemplary[24] in their "openness"[25]—was their capacity to produce a space for identification with the subjects: "For Rouch, cinema is a means of communication— . . . what matters is to open as many eyes as possible to a reality which is hidden from us by prejudice, habit, the social conventions of the moment."[26] Godard pushed further: *Moi, un noir* was not only an account of black men's lives or urban impoverishment in African cities (specifically, the Treichville suburb of Abidjan, Côte d'Ivoire), it was a direct attempt to identify with them: "In calling his film *Moi, un noir*, Rouch, white just like Rimbaud, declares *I is another*."[27] The exchange of identity recalls Lévi-Strauss's own scenes in Brazil. Gilles Deleuze enjoyed radicalizing Godard's description:

The Ego = Ego form of identity (or its degenerate form, them = them) ceases to be valid for the characters and for the film-maker, in the real as well as in the fiction. What allows itself to be glimpsed instead, by profound degrees, is Rimbaud's "I is another" [*Je est un autre*]: Godard said this in relation to Rouch; not only for the characters themselves, but for the film-maker who "white just like Rimbaud, himself declares that *I is another*," that is, *me a black* [*Moi, un noir*]. . . . This is no longer *Birth of a Nation* but the constitution or reconstitution of a people, where the film-maker and his characters become others together and the one through the other, a collectivity which gradually wins from place to place, from person to person, from intercessor to intercessor. I am a caribou, an original . . . "I is another" is the formation of a story which simulates, of a simulation of a story or of a story of simulation which deposes the form of the truthful story.[28]

Undoing the traditional form of fiction and documentary contributed to *staging* the reality of these subjects in a truthful and seemingly immediate fashion. The *maîtres fous* who, in their spectacular mouth-foaming trance, appropriate or attack French colonial officials are figures not just to watch but to identify with: they bring out a drama that is truthful less because it is their mystical state than because, *thanks to the film*, it becomes a reality for observers. What Rouch would call a disruption that took place through his camera also made possible the mystical exchange of identity imagined by Godard and Deleuze, which Rouch set up for viewers to take up as well. The capacity to become another by baring oneself to this other's truth and difference was vital to the achievement of these ethnographic films.

Chronicle and the Return to Paris

In "L'Ethnographie devant le colonialisme" (1950; "Ethnography Faced with Colonialism"), Leiris argued that a counterethnography of western Europe by those who were still mere subjects of the ethnographer's gaze was scientifically and politically essential.[29] From this perspective, Rouch *un Noir* had a very different standing from Morin the Parisian, and this was reflected in the formal dimensions of the work. Morin preferred to sublate fiction and documentary, whereas for Rouch, the return to Paris colored questions of mediation, creation, and possibility. Discussing the project with Morin and Marcelline in the film's opening scene, Rouch remarks: "You see Morin, it is an excellent idea to bring men together around a table—it's just that I don't know if we'll manage to record as normal a conversation as if there were no camera." A palpable anxiety persists: Were the strategies that had worked for creating situations in Africa still available in Paris? Or did camera awareness muddy the waters? Morin concentrated on the question "Are you happy?" Once viewers are introduced to Angelo, a Renault factory worker, however, this quietly shifts to "Are you satisfied with your living conditions?" While Morin began to examine living conditions and underlying structures, Rouch was intensely occupied with staging clashes (or rather staging Morin, so he could stage clashes) and, later, with editing them in a style more appropriate to fiction film. Some scenes deserve particular attention in this respect.

First, the film contains a scene directly reminiscent of the "black man–white man" episode in Rouch's 1950 diary, but it adjusts it considerably (see fig. 15.2). Rouch creates a tense, confrontational exchange by having the white Jewish Marceline explain the number tattooed on her arm to the black African student Modeste Landry.[30] While in the diary the encounter began with the white man's telling his story and ended in

FIGURE 15.2 *Chronique d'un été* (*Chronicle of a Summer*) (1961): joyful beginning of the white man–black man scene atop the Musée de l'homme in Paris. Rouch on the far left, Morin second from right, Marceline third from right.
SOURCE: *Chronique d'un été* (Edgar Morin and Jean Rouch, 1961), Criterion Collection DVD.

friendship, here the attempt to give an impression of shared suffering and sympathy between the camp survivor and the African student is abruptly interrupted by a discussion of violence in the Congo, which leads participants to a polite standoff. The scene is then interrupted by another, in which Marcelline, now alone with the camera, tells her story as she walks. It is as if Rouch and Morin were establishing a competition between the trajectories of the two characters; but, despite their express desire for political resistance to European power, reconciliation and friendship do not follow.[31] The pastoral fantasy has given way to competition in suffering.

Were we to suppose, then, that Rouch was returning to the darkness of Europe—from anticolonialism to the Holocaust—we would have to treat Marcelline as a gauge for the success of Rouch's attempt to reimport his technique back from Africa. Yet this supposition is wrong too. In the next, quite famous scene, filmed at the Place de la Concorde, she speaks movingly of her father's death at Auschwitz; she seems very absorbed in her words. Yet later she tells Rouch that she was simply acting: not to be up-staged by another character's theatricality, she took it up for herself as well:

After being intimidated the first time I was filmed, I controlled myself, completely dominating my personality, dramatizing with words, with my face, my tone, with gestures. Being particularly aware that the camera was there . . . there was a certain directing of me by me, since there was no other direction for the actors. . . . I chose a character that I then interpreted within the limits of the film, a character who is both an aspect of the reality of Marceline and also a dramatized character created by Marceline.[32]

At the end of the film, having just been challenged by their own characters, Rouch and Morin are particularly troubled about this scene. Rouch, who trusts his capacity to disrupt the natural order and pull something out of any participant, simply refuses to accept that acting was an option. Morin, even more insistent, moves to a language of authenticity.

MORIN So that's the fundamental problem, because us, what we wanted . . . if people think that these are actors or exhibitionists, then our film is a failure. And at the same time, I can say that I know, that I feel that they are neither actors nor exhibitionists.
ROUCH Only one can't be sure of that.
MORIN For whom? [Who do you mean?]
ROUCH They themselves can't know. You understand when, for example, Marceline says she was acting on the Place de la Concorde . . . we were witnesses!
MORIN Yes.
ROUCH She wasn't acting!
MORIN If she was acting, you could say it was the most authentic part of herself when she was talking about her father. . . . It's not an act, you know, you can't call that an act.[33]

How are we to understand the viability of a *cinéma-vérité* that held aware-ness of "staging" to be essential to a performance yet was troubled if that performance failed the test of genuineness? Sam DiIorio has very usefully situated the film on a precipice between two film theories: André Bazin's phenomenological realism, which around 1960 was fading from the scene; and the 1960s–1970s approach to the self-referential film in *Cahiers du cinéma*.[34] Morin's and Rouch's question deserves attention in its own right: How can we represent life truthfully to a point where the form of repre-sentation disappears in the record of everydayness, where substructure and living conditions become sound and image (as for Morin), or where the camera has made it possible for entirely truthful exchanges to be staged (as for Rouch)? It is precisely the hope for a transparent, self-effacing representation that is set up *to fail.* The success of the film rests on the back of this failure, itself admitted and theatricalized in the film, along with Rouch's "Only one can't be sure [that they are 'neither actors nor exhibitionists']."

Michael Fried's language of absorption and theatricality is particularly useful for clarifying the ambiguities of Morin and Rouch's divergent intentions and interpretations.[35] Theatricality was a fundamental threat for Morin ("I can say that I know, that I feel, that they are neither actors nor exhibitionists"): it demonstrated the failure of the project, insofar as it burst the fiction of a transparency effected in and through the film. *Cinéma-vérité,* in the simple form offered by Vertov, was not possible. At times Rouch too finds this puzzling ("She wasn't acting!"). In his return from "black" to white, from othered to self, and acknowledging the failure of the pastoral fantasy, he doesn't quite understand how characters might actually dissimulate while they look and sound perfectly absorbed. But he also has a more complex view, in which the Griaulian ethnographer's prosecutorial approach trumps Bazin's phenomenological realism. The camera guarantees sincerity if and only if the participants remained as absorbed as his African subjects (or his entranced *maîtres fous*) had been.[36] Marcelline could not have been acting, because she was so absorbed that no theatricality actually affected her performance. Confronted with the problem of theatricality and falsehood, Rouch deals with them by embracing them, by airing the characters' disappointments and having with Morin a discussion about the film's failure where he can emphasize the dangers of acting and exhibitionism. Replicating the technologization of Griaule's ethnographic method, which he had developed in and through the camera, he transforms the discussion in which the characters themselves disown sincerity and absorption into a testimony of sincerity and absorption, so that acting is no longer a threat. (In his 1963 film *Le joli mai,* Chris Marker followed in Rouch's footsteps by using interviews that favored absorption, then cutting in order to impose his interpretation—a technique he called *ciné, ma vérité.*)

It is worth recalling that, if the directors pretend to fold their cards at the end of the film, the ostensible collapse of a dreamt-of transparency matters just as much for its subsequent *success*; for it did institute *cinéma-vérité.* The film thus doubled Rouch's gesture of creating absorption and situations, and it did so through its capacity to show its own constructedness. That allowed filmmaking to bring forth a reality that would otherwise remain hidden and could not be experienced anywhere except in this space of *vérité* that went beyond fiction and documentary.

Rouch, *un Noir* upon his return to Paris, remained ambivalent between absorption and theatricality, unable to experience an unmediated truth, ready to deny its existence for others. He also opened an ongoing debate on filmed truth and the representation of reality for a public that had little interest in theories. As for *cinéma-vérité*, since its instauration, it has depended, not on transparency, but on the failure and renegotiation of transparency, on the non-erasure of representation. It showed how film could be a medium that might only *pretend* to efface itself. In the failure of this effacement—in the collapse of naïve transparency—lay the fiction of *cinéma-vérité* as the degree zero of representation.

PART IV

THE ROAD TO 1967 AND
THE RETHINKING OF MODERNITY

Return to Rousseau

Lévi-Strauss, Starobinski, Derrida

"We are never done with Rousseau," declared Jean Starobinski in a 1962 article. "Every generation discovers a new Rousseau, in whom it finds an example of what it desires to be, or of what it passionately rejects."[1] Lévi-Strauss's and Starobinski's were by no means the only Rousseaus in postwar Paris: between 1945 and 1957, no fewer than 230 books on Rousseau and republications of his works fulfilled the copyright registration (*dépôt légal*) and were entered into the Bibliothèque nationale catalogues. Around 1960, a Pléiade edition of his complete works became a major collaborative undertaking. In a footnote explaining his limited engagement with Rousseau's interpreters in *Of Grammatology*, Jacques Derrida expressed admiration for no fewer than fifteen authors.[2] Amid these engagements, those that Starobinski and Lévi-Strauss proposed in their respective studies *Jean-Jacques Rousseau: Transparency and Obstruction* (1957) and *Tristes tropiques* (1955) and furthered in essays during the early 1960s stand out. Both demonstrate that Rousseau is central to modern subjectivity, and hence to our understanding of the highly problematic logic of transparency underlying it. For Starobinski, this logic was based on "auto-affection," the self's preconscious sense of itself, which produced Rousseau's paranoid self-enclosure. For Lévi-Strauss, it was tied to a homogenizing, imperialist culture of the self that Rousseau and contemporary anthropology worked to undermine. This chapter presents Lévi-Strauss's use of Rousseau, which was designed to complete and historicize his account of the anthropologist's task, compares his Rousseau with that of Starobinski (for which see the Introduction), and concludes with Derrida's effort to rethink the place of Rousseau and of Starobinski's and Lévi-Strauss's representations of Rousseau in contemporary engagements with interpersonal relations, transparency, and the politics of philosophy.

Starobinski and Lévi-Strauss

Lévi-Strauss's self-identification with Rousseau quickly became legendary. In *Tristes tropiques* he exults:

Rousseau, our master, Rousseau, our brother, toward whom we have shown so much ingratitude, but to whom each and every page of this book could have been dedicated, were such an homage not unworthy of his great memory.[3]

Across the pages of *Tristes tropiques*, Rousseau comes out as the author who offers the anthropologist *both* a means of showing the fragility and violence of the humanist self and an absolute imperative to treat the most alien of others as an ethical source of scholarly commitment. Rousseau was, first and foremost, the philosopher of a way out of the violence, homogenization, and opaqueness of "Western Man."

In 1962, seven years after the *grand succès* of *Tristes tropiques*, Lévi-Strauss and Starobinski participated in a conference in Geneva that marked the two hundred and fiftieth anniversary of Rousseau's birth. Lévi-Strauss's Geneva lecture reached a broad audience, since it was published in English, French, and Spanish under the title "Rousseau, the Father of Anthropology," in two issues of the *UNESCO Courier*.[4] Through a complex genealogical operation, Lévi-Strauss devised his hero—"Jean-Jacques Rousseau, Founder of the Sciences of Man" (to use the title under which he republished the lecture)—as the forefather of structuralism, and hence as the thinker who legitimized Lévi-Strauss's own fusion of abstract models with a confessional ethnography and the warrior who had assaulted the Cartesian and humanist ego. Rousseau had invented a counterscience that had to wait for the advent of structuralism and the decline of the Western ego before it could see the light of day. It was possible to "reclaim" him now, when humanism had shown its true, violent face and had produced its own moment of doubt and guilt in the rise of anthropology.[5]

This concurrent reclamation of Rousseau, rejection of the unification and homogenization of human experience, and recognition of the
violence inherent in our Cartesian modernity formed the task of contemporary anthropology:

It is today . . . that his thought takes on a supreme magnitude and acquires all
its significance. In this world, more cruel to man than it perhaps ever was, all the
means of extermination, massacre, and torture are raging. We never disavowed
these atrocities, it is true, but we liked to think that they did not matter just because we reserved them for distant populations which underwent them (we maintained) for our benefit and, in any case, in our name. Now, brought together in
a denser population which makes the universe smaller and shelters no portion of
humanity from abject violence, we feel the anguish of living together weighing on
each of us. It is now, I repeat, by exposing the flaws of a humanism decidedly unable to establish the exercise of virtue among men, that Rousseau's thinking can
help us to reject an illusion whose lethal effects we can observe in ourselves and
on ourselves.[6]

Lévi-Strauss presented the Rousseau of the *Discourse on the Origin of Inequality* and of the *Reveries of a Solitary Walker* as a philosopher responding specifically to Cartesian subjectivism. Against Descartes's *Cogito ergo
sum*, he asked: "'What am I? . . . ' 'Am I?'"[7] This gesture was essential for
Lévi-Strauss, because it made Rousseau (and Rousseau alone) a critic who
rationalized the study of other people and explained its benefits for a conception of the human being: "to study man, one must first learn to look
into the distance; one must first see differences in order to discover characteristics."[8] Rousseau fulfilled the conditions necessary for Lévi-Strauss's
work to become possible. By rejecting the majesty of the Western self, he
rendered historically comprehensible a science that would finally "reject an
illusion whose lethal effects we can observe in ourselves and on ourselves."

Rousseau also legitimized Lévi-Strauss's dismissal of the politics
and racism of earlier generations. Insofar as these attitudes had serviced a
Cartesian logic and could not think difference, they would never launch
models like Lévi-Strauss's own structural anthropology. On the contrary,
Rousseau's refusal of "the forced identifications" of the ego[9] heralded precisely that recuperation of the human bond to nature, animals, and one
another dreamt of by Lévi-Strauss—which included genuine relationships
and quasi-mystical identifications between "the anthropologist" and indigenous "others." Lévi-Strauss's unpublished drafts for the Geneva lecture

make clear the "key role" of identifying *not* with one's own but with the humblest and the weakest, those who are farthest from oneself. Identification, he wrote in one sketch, "is the key to Rousseau's thought and to any possible morality."[10] In another he emphasized the "two complementary aspects" of Rousseau's thought that he, Lévi-Strauss, would develop: the identification with the other—"the other that is most 'other,' weakest, humblest"—and the "refusal of identifying with oneself, that is to say the refusal of anything that renders *us* 'acceptable.'" It was through these positions that he could claim: "the I is the weakest and humblest of others."[11]

Lévi-Strauss's hostility toward violent, illusory identifications with one's own kind relied on a particular reading of Rousseau's views on Man's relationship with Nature. He attended in detail to Rousseau's understanding of pity, compassion, and tenderness, which he interpreted as devotion to *living beings* regardless of their difference from "me"; and in this context he rehearsed many of the features of his "anthropologist": her lack of place and home, her capacity to find the "fissures" of human society.[12] Compassion chaperoned a preconscious and "natural" relationship with others, a continuity between *all* living beings and opposed to any ethics that presumes identification specifically with one's own kind.[13] One has a chance of forming ethical relationships, not by connecting to the human element, but by being close to "nature" and hence refusing to make oneself the source of identifications.

Rousseau's revolution, pre-shaping and initiating the ethnological revolution, consists of refusing forced identifications, whether of a culture with that culture, or of an individual member of a culture with a character or social function that this same culture tries to impose on him. In both cases, the culture or the individual claims the right to free identification, which can only realize itself *beyond* man with all that is alive and, consequently, suffers, an identification also before the function or the character, with a being not yet shaped but given.[14]

In his attack on philosophical anthropology, Lévi-Strauss found in the ethnologist an anti-epistemological naturalist. This was, again, based on *differences*. Rather than a Rousseau who insisted on *models* and was "preposterously accused of having glorified a state of nature,"[15] here emerged one who made anthropology work by placing it in society with nature:

Freed from an antagonism which philosophy alone sought to stimulate, the self and the other recover their unity. A primordial alliance, revived at last, enables them together to found the *we* against the *him*. It is an alliance against a society hostile to man, and which man feels all the more prepared to challenge since Rousseau, by his example, teaches him how to elude the unbearable contradictions of civilized life. For if it is true that nature has rejected man and that society persists in oppressing him, man can at least reverse the poles of the dilemma to his benefit and *seek the society of nature to meditate there on the nature of society.*[16]

Though still in line with his glorification of societies without writing in *Tristes tropiques*, here Lévi-Strauss's vilification of the self in favor of community and unity and his primitive empathy with forms of life came close to a call to action. Indeed, he wrote, such a unity with all living beings offers "through Rousseau's voice[,] the principle for all collective wisdom and action . . . the only principle which, in a world so encumbered that reciprocal consideration is rendered more difficult but all the more necessary, can enable men to live together and to build a harmonious future."[17]

This proposal may appear at odds with Lévi-Strauss's professed antihumanism, his sense that the contemporary world is falsely amalgamated in a particular Western fashion. Lévi-Strauss proposed this alternative unity by "jumping" three centuries back to Rousseau and three centuries forward again to his time, so as to dislodge the continuity of the present time and its imposing character. It was an impossible counterutopia, which followed from and complemented the theoretical matrix on the near-absolute separation from the Nambikwara, on the preconscious structural basis of kinship and myth, and on the anthropologist's guilt-ridden yet redemptive persona. Put another way, he decried a world where humanistic impulses do no more than coat the violence of a Westernizing cohesion, a society that denies man "the opportunity of this primitive feeling of identification," and offered in its place a transparency between beings, articulated by way of his identification with Rousseau. The ethics that Lévi-Strauss proposed, with Rousseau as his witness, was as necessary as it was impossible: without it the rejection of modernity would lose its force, be nothing but the guilt left behind by Western consciousness.[18]

A number of conversations can be glimpsed from this reading of Rousseau. First, for Lévi-Strauss, Rousseau played a role remarkably similar to that of Freud for Lacan. Just as Lacan considered Freud to have carried out the Copernican revolution that decentered the ego (a revolution that was repressed and rejected), Lévi-Strauss pointed to Rousseau as the philosopher who inaugurated proper observation and split this new observer and subject, suggesting that "there exists a 'he' who 'thinks' through me and who first causes me to doubt whether it is I who am thinking."[19] Further, Lacan had proclaimed that humanism and modern science would fall to the stroke of psychoanalysis, whose concept of the split subject gave priority, against them, to thoroughly desubjectivising structural approaches to being and its supposed singularity. Lévi-Strauss credited Rousseau with having "founded" the human sciences *against* the rising humanistic trend and with having tilled the ground for the development of anti-subjectivist, scientific models premised on care for the other. For both Lacan and Lévi-Strauss, the existence of a precursor made genuine care for an "other" possible and proved the demise of the self-transparent modern self.

Second, Lévi-Strauss's Rousseau contrasted Starobinski's in significant respects. Both thinkers turned to Rousseau to spotlight the profound difficulties and problems of subjectivism: Starobinski interpreted Rousseau as radicalizing subjectivism to an absurd, self-destructive extreme; Lévi-Strauss used Rousseau against this subjectivism, indeed discovered in him a social ethics concerning the insufficiency of self-identity and the primacy of compassion for the other. Whereas for Starobinski the pull toward purity produced only a temporary displacement of masks bound to resurge later, Lévi-Strauss found in a different Rousseauean purity a countermodel that allowed him to explore methodologically what he denied ontologically: the possibility of a transparent relationship between human beings.

Two points of contrast bear further discussion, because they give a sense of this generation's rediscovery of Rousseau. First, early on in *Jean-Jacques Rousseau*, Starobinski superimposed Rousseau's premise of a state of nature uncontaminated by society onto the hypothesis of a pure childhood in which appearance and reality have not yet come into conflict.[20] He telescoped Rousseau's theory of human nature and history by means of personal autobiography. Lévi-Strauss, on the other hand, treated the state of nature as a heuristic device, a structural premise for the argument that modern society is in a fallen and profoundly opaque state. For him, crucially, Rousseau's state of nature is a *structure*: not a purer, historically prior state from which humans have fallen, but a structure that every society develops further and that makes comparison and critique possible. Second, where Lévi-Strauss saw the possibility of a new ethical–political purity in one's relations to another because Rousseau's *positive* model of recovery stood guarantor to it, Starobinski identified Rousseau's political commitment with a liberation project of a different kind, namely, from the "masks" that organized aristocratic and bourgeois society. Far from seeking, like Lévi-Strauss, a communion with the other that preceded consciousness, Starobinski focused on Rousseau's investment in the rebirth, through the festival, of "Man" in his purity, unencumbered by representation. People at a festival "would celebrate a new transparency: hearts would hide no more secrets, communication would be completely free of obstacles. Since everyone present would be simultaneously audience and actors, they would have done away with the distance which, in the theater, separated the stage and the auditorium."[21]

This Rousseau commits himself to an ethics of rejuvenation through the breakdown of obstacles to communication and representation and through the restoration of one's community as spectacle. Lévi-Strauss's Rousseau, by contrast, dislodges the self in order to retrieve it in the most other of others, *the subject of his anthropological and also autobiographical concern.*

Nevertheless, the differences between these two readings are less significant than the common space they delimited, the myth of Rousseau that they made current. In different ways and with different consequences, both Starobinski and Lévi-Strauss found in the self the supreme mask of Western civilization. For Starobinski, this self was Rousseau's "soul transparent as crystal"; for Lévi-Strauss, it was the overwhelming, transparent, Cartesian self against which Rousseau strategized. Most significantly, the two authors set the agenda around a fresh dissection of the interplay between purity and mask. They asked for a profound modification of the mystifying commitment to purity, purification, and self-perfection that had dominated modern thought and society and had produced a civilization that destroyed the world, all with good intentions and impunity. Rousseau offered at least the possibility of a certain redemption: "I am not 'I' but the feeblest and humblest of others."[22]

Derrida

Jacques Derrida's critiques of Starobinski and Lévi-Strauss in his 1967 *Of Grammatology* play precisely on the claims around transparency.[23] The objections to Starobinski, to whom Derrida was quite indebted, came mostly in a long footnote: framing the totality of Rousseau's work as Starobinski did would reinstate, at the methodological and critical level, the very transparency he critiqued in Rousseau's literary–philosophical work.

I wonder if, too concerned with reacting against a reductionist, causalist, dissociative psychology, Starobinski does not in general give too much credit to a totalitarian psychoanalysis of the phenomenological or existentialist style. Such a psychoanalysis, diffusing sexuality in the totality of behavior, *perhaps risks blurring the cleavages, the differences, the displacements, the fixations of all sorts that structure that totality.* Do the place or the places of sexuality not disappear in the analysis of global behavior, as Starobinski recommends? "Erotic behavior is not a fragmentary given; it is the manifestation of a total individual, and it is as such that it ought to be analyzed. Whether it is to neglect it or to make it a privileged subject of study, one cannot limit exhibitionism to the sexual 'sphere': the entire personality is revealed there, with some of its fundamental 'existential choices.'" . . . And does one not, in this way, risk determining the pathological in a very classic manner, as "excess" thought within "existential" categories . . . ?[24]

For all its apostrophizing character, this is an attentive, complex critique. Consider, first, the statement about "blurring the cleavages, the differences, the displacements": the approach favored by Starobinski appeared to Derrida to reinstate, perhaps despite itself, the transparency that it finds Rousseau to be troublingly obsessed with. Derrida's critique of Starobinski's appeal to a "phenomenological or existentialist" psychology in interpreting Rousseau focuses on its totalizing character (Derrida strikingly calls it "totalitarian"). To assume that Rousseau's motivations and psychology should be understood at this global yet singular level, Derrida suggests, is to grant Rousseau too much—to admit his claim to transparency as a satisfactory organizer of his person and the persona in his texts. As a result, different psychological angles that might heighten tensions have been lost in a single formula. Fastening on tensions in Rousseau's life and writing might have evaded replaying the problem of transparency at the methodological level—and would certainly undermine the sufficiency of a phenomenological reading as the basis for genetic criticism.[25]

Second, Derrida suggests that Starobinski stays within a "classic" mode of thinking the normal and the pathological that represents Rousseau's later work as taking the obsession with being "transparent as crystal" to pathological levels. The implication is that Starobinski retains a normativity that reinforces continuity between Rousseau's early and later work, between the movement toward transparency and the reinstatement of obstacles, so that one appears to him the cause of the other.[26] In his effort to take to pieces Rousseau's obsession with his own purity, Starobinski had stuck to a method that totalized it, replicated it, and ignored all the strains, differences, and tensions that Derrida considered crucial to Rousseau's theory of language. At stake here was the possibility of a method that would not only present the self-destructive spiral of transparency but also avoid it.

Derrida exercised a similar censure on Lévi-Strauss's *Tristes tropiques* and Geneva lecture. Central to his criticism were both the methodological transparency that Lévi-Strauss acquired through his commitment to Rousseau and Lévi-Strauss's thesis that peoples "without writing" are more authentic than those "with" writing. The Nambikwara were Lévi-Strauss's noble savages—the most humble, most basic, and most miserable of human societies. Commenting on Lévi-Strauss's glorification of Rousseau, Derrida interpreted the latter's anthropological mission as enmeshed in "the dream of a full and immediate presence closing history, the transparency and indivision of a *parousia*, the suppression of contradiction and difference."[27] This transparency of complete self-presence is what Rousseau sought for the self and for the community in order to rid them both of mediation.[28] For Derrida, Lévi-Strauss's identification with *this* Rousseau motivated the commitment to a community that is pure of violence and cunning, and pure of writing, too—a *transparent* community.[29] After emphasizing Lévi-Strauss's insistence on the goodness of the Nambikwara in *Tristes tropiques*, Derrida added:

Only an innocent community and a community of reduced dimensions . . . *only a micro-society of non-violence and freedom, all the members of which can by rights remain within range of an immediate and transparent, a "crystalline" address, fully self-present in its living speech*, only such a community can suffer, as the surprise of an aggression coming *from without*, the insinuation of writing, the infiltration of its "ruse" and of its "perfidy."[30]

Derrida recounted the Geneva lecture in much the same terms: Lévi-Strauss's "model of a small community with a 'crystalline' structure, completely self-present, assembled in its own neighborhood, is undoubtedly Rousseauistic."[31] He then highlighted Lévi-Strauss's substantial reuse of passages from his thesis—published under the title "La Vie familiale et sociale des Indiens Nambikwara" (1948; The Familial and Social Life of the Nambikwara Indians)—transformed so as to accentuate Rousseauistic purity.[32] Derrida was right: from his very first report to Marcel Mauss,

Lévi-Strauss had expressed some ambivalence about violence and the social life of the Nambikwara, nonetheless emphasizing its "extremely supple" collective nature.[33] In the thesis, Lévi-Strauss articulated both these aspects, but in *Tristes tropiques* he veered decidedly toward the "extremely supple" side and reduced or eliminated the violence. Lévi-Strauss's surviving typescript of *Tristes tropiques* contains a large number of pages from his published thesis, all cut up, pasted, and corrected (see fig. 16.1 and 16.2).

Many descriptive passages are not retouched, but passages dealing with violence are significantly amended and phrases that point to tenderness or purity in the Nambikwara are highlighted.[34] Here is, for example, a passage from the thesis pasted on page 327 of the typescript:

All hostile manifestations are stylized and reducible to gestures that use the sexual parts. The threat, or the hostile gesture of the Nambikwara consists in the aggressor holding his penis and with both hands and pointing it at the adversary, inflating his belly and pushing it forward, while bending the knees.

Lévi-Strauss altered it as follows:

All threats are reduced to gestures that use the sexual parts. A Nambikwara attests his antipathy in holding his penis with two hands and pointing it toward his adversary.[35]

By comparison to the stylized, whole-body motion described in the original, the second version presents an all but ridiculous gesture. It is no surprise that Lévi-Strauss would modify his text as his conviction that European culture homogenized indigenous groups grew. But, from Derrida's perspective, this paled by comparison to the near-mystical Rousseauistic attachment to the crystalline community.

Once he had pointed out the Rousseauism of that "completely self-present" community, Derrida proposed a history of this dream of self-presence, community, and transparency:

Self-presence, transparent proximity in the face-to-face of countenances and the immediate range of the voice, this determination of social authenticity is therefore classical: Rousseauistic but already the inheritor of Platonism, it relates, we recall, to the anarchistic and libertarian protestations against Law, the Powers, and the State in general, and also with the dream of the nineteenth-century utopian socialisms, most specifically with the dream of Fourierism. In his laboratory, or rather in his studio, the anthropologist too uses this dream, as one weapon or instrument among others.[36]

Derrida would go on to counter Lévi-Strauss's reading of Rousseau by deconstructing the latter's doubts about a community characterized by the plenitude of speech.[37] Still, the first offense of Lévi-Strauss's definition was its assertion that this community lived in the plenitude of a natural transparency *and was foreign to any violence*: these two features conditioned each other.[38] Lévi-Strauss's construct of a "crystalline structure" and "complete self-presence" excised the basic forms of mediation and violence that characterize all societies. Across numerous examples,[39] transparency turned out to be a carrier of the illusion that a community could survive without violence. In Lévi-Strauss's Rousseau-influenced reading, the Nambikwara lacked writing, hence they lived in a particular kind of authenticity and purity; it was possible to introduce violence in that society, but that would be an accidental occurrence.[40]

As for Lévi-Strauss's rejection of ethnocentrism, Derrida found it dependent on a "cleaning" operation that, in its zeal to end colonialism, produces the illusion of transparency between ethnographer and subject and ignores the pervasiveness of techniques that undermine it. If Lévi-Strauss thought he had overcome racism and the Western homogenization of the world, Derrida countered that his solution relied on a mystical, heterotopic reversion to transparency that brought the problem back in. His offer of a Rousseau-style alternative to the Western Cartesian ego would not suffice. Derrida called this structure "classic": it was marked by a purity that allowed the impurity of the world to become visible without the subject's sharing in it at all, or even being aware of it. The Nambikwara were supposedly contaminated by impurity only thanks to Lévi-Strauss's own intervention—his introduction of writing. This "classic" structure also gave Lévi-Strauss a sense of justification and legitimacy, because it permitted him not to ask whether the absence of violence does not presuppose a different, more basic kind of violence.

According to Derrida, on the contrary, violence permeates every relationship marked by writing.

Rousseau and Lévi-Strauss are not for a moment to be challenged when they relate the power of writing to the exercise of violence. But radicalizing this theme, no longer considering this violence as *derivative* with respect to a naturally innocent speech, one reverses the entire sense of a proposition—the unity of violence and writing—which one must therefore be careful not to abstract and isolate.[41]

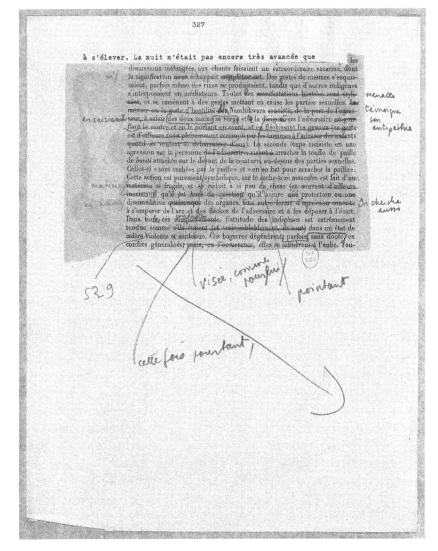

FIGURE 16.1 AND 16.2 Pages 327 and 328a of Lévi-Strauss's typescript for *Tristes tropiques*, with pages from *The Familial and Social Life of the Nambikwara*, collated and edited.

SOURCE: BnF, Fonds Claude Lévi-Strauss. Reproduced with permission of the Bibliothèque nationale de France and Mme. Monique Lévi-Strauss.

l'avons plus revu. Nous en fûmes réduits à remettre le présent à un autre indigène. Dans ces conditions, il n'est pas surprenant que, les échanges terminés,
l'un des groupes reparte mécontent de son lot et accumule pendant des
semaines ou des mois, en faisant l'inventaire de ses acquisitions et se rappe-
lant ses propres présents, une amertume qui deviendra de plus en plus agres-
sive. Bien souvent, semble-t-il, les guerres n'ont pas d'autre origine; il existe
naturellement d'autres causes, telles qu'un assassinat, ou un rapt de femmes,
soit qu'on désire en prendre l'initiative, soit que l'on veuille venger une précé-
dente attaque; mais il ne semble pas qu'une bande se sente collectivement
tenue à des représailles pour un dommage fait à l'un de ses membres. Bien
plus souvent, étant donné la très vive et permanente animosité qui règne
entre les groupes, ces prétextes bons à exciter les esprits sont volontiers
accueillis, surtout si l'on se sent en force, soit par l'importance de l'effectif
du groupe, soit par une alliance avec des bandes voisines contre un ennemi
commun, conclue par l'intermédiaire de messagers agissant comme ambassa-
deurs. La proposition de guerre est présentée par un individu exalté, ou qui
expose devant ses compagnons ses griefs particuliers, sur le même ton et dans
le même style où se font les discours de rencontre :

39. ï akïnaé jednaé yôdegaï kakonïé ardnïé yalauvisenïé (bï)

dont le sens, très approximatif, est : «Holà ! Venez ici ! Allons ! je suis
irrité ! très irrité ! des flèches ! des grandes flèches !» Les indigènes s'exci-
tent tellement à l'occasion de ces discours épiques, qu'il n'est possible
d'obtenir le commentaire des formules que bien après qu'elles ont été citées,
et sans doute de façon très infidèle. Mais la guerre n'est pas une matière à
décision purement profane; elle réclame une cérémonie préliminaire qui
déterminera si les présages sont ou non favorables. Revêtus de parures
spéciales : touffes de paille de *buriti* bariolées de rouge, casques de peau
de jaguar, les hommes s'assemblent sous la conduite du chef et exécutent
un danse et le chant spécial de la guerre. Un rite divinatoire est ensuite
accompli; le chef, ou le sorcier dans les groupes où il existe, va solennelle-
ment cacher une flèche dans un coin de brousse. La flèche est recherchée le
lendemain, si elle est maculée de sang, l'expédition est décidée, sinon on y
renonce. Beaucoup d'expéditions guerrières ainsi commencées se terminent
après quelques kilomètres de marche. L'excitation et l'enthousiasme tombent,
et la troupe rentre au logis. Mais certaines sont poussées jusqu'à la réalisation,

et peuvent être très meurtrières. Les Nambikwara attaquent habituellement
à l'aube et tendent leur embuscade en se dispersant à travers la brousse.
Le signal d'attaque est donné de proche en proche grâce au sifflet que les
indigènes portent pendu au cou. Ce petit sifflet, composé de deux tubes
de bambou liés avec du fil de coton, reproduit approximativement le cri du
grillon, et pour cette raison sans doute, porte le même nom que
cet insecte. Les flèches
de guerre sont les mêmes qu'on utilise normalement pour la chasse
aux grands animaux; mais avant de les employer contre l'homme, on
découpe en dents de scie les rebords de leur large pointe lancéolée. Les
flèches empoisonnées au curare, qui sont d'un usage courant pour la
chasse, ne sont jamais employées.

Unlike Lévi-Strauss, who insisted that an authentic, transparent community could exist so long as "permanent inscription" was not introduced, Derrida deemed speech and every other system of temporal, repeatable inscription, every kind of "*archē*-writing" (*archi-écriture*, "proto"-writing, virtually any form of inscription) and hence every interpersonal relationship as marked by the same structural violence. The violence of "what is commonly called evil, war, indiscretion, rape" *may* or *may not* take place, it may be accidental or constitutive—but it derives always from a more profound and hidden violence implicit in the institution of interpersonal relationships through naming and speech, indeed through *archē*-writing.

Recalling . . . that violence did not wait for the appearance of writing in the narrow sense, that writing has always begun in language, we, like Lévi-Strauss, conclude that violence is writing. But, coming at it another way, this proposition has a radically different meaning. It ceases to be supported by the myth of myth, by the myth of a speech originally good, and of a violence which would come to pounce upon it as a fatal accident. A fatal accident which is nothing but history itself.[42]

And, again, thinking about the "uniqueness" of proper names, Derrida comments:

To think the unique *within* the system, to inscribe it there, such is the gesture of *archē*-writing: *archē*-violence, loss of the proper, of absolute proximity, of self-presence, in truth the loss of what has never taken place, of a self-presence which has never been given but only dreamed of and always already split, repeated, incapable of appearing to itself except in its own disappearance. Out of this *archē*-violence, forbidden and therefore confirmed by a second violence that is reparatory, protective, instituting the "moral," prescribing the concealment of writing and the effacement and obliteration of the so-called proper name which was already dividing the proper, a third violence can *possibly* emerge or not (an empirical possibility) within what is commonly called evil, war, indiscretion, rape.[43]

The idea of a transparent community or a transparent and complete self-presence utterly fails to think the violence that underwrites all society and all interpersonal relations—the violence that inscribes subjects within a community and grants them status and presence within it, in other words makes them subjects. All society is premised on violence, as this *archē*-violence generates a second-order violence at the level of law, which only then gives it particular formulations.

Derrida's critique of Lévi-Strauss's anti-ethnocentrism is mixed with that of Levi-Strauss's confessional mode in speaking of the anthropologist.[44] When he vituperates ethnocentrism, Lévi-Strauss upholds the eighteenth-century fantasy of the natural goodness of the people he studies, their sincerity and transparency—which replicates his own self-portrait as sincere and transparent.[45] One point Derrida objects to is the postphilosophical claim that pre-philosophical (and only human) compassion for the other, attached to a (not really) non-philosophical negative anthropology, suffices to overcome humanism and to secure this alternative, nonviolent transparency as a base of human care. As we have seen in the previous chapter, Lévi-Strauss construes from paradoxes an anthropologist who could engage in a different relationship with the subjects of his study and, through them, with an "I" who is not oneself but "the feeblest and humblest of others."[46] However promising after the independence of Algeria in 1962 and the decline of French colonialism, this construction appeared fragile (if not self-deluding) to Derrida.[47]

Thus transparency reemerged for Derrida precisely when and where it had been deemed banished. The engagements with Rousseau promised to overcome the transparency that dominated the metaphysical tradition and the identifications between the hegemonic self and a hegemonic society. Yet Starobinski and Lévi-Strauss had only gone so far; in the end they reconstructed the self–society isomorphism and, with it, the rule of the subject over the world. This subject still nourished the belief that it had overcome its hegemony.

Return to Descartes

"The Last Tribunal of the Cogito"

I am thinking where I am not, there for I am where I am not thinking. . . . I am not where I am the plaything of my thoughts; I think about what I am where I do not think I am thinking.

Jacques Lacan, *Écrits* (2006 [1966]: 517/430)

French philosophers in the 1960s were convinced that theirs was a time for the recalibration of thought, that the history of philosophy had to be illuminated through the new philosophical developments alone, and that their work was bringing forth a radical rethinking of modernity, away from the hyperrationalist, colonial, and violent past and present—so much so that the elaborate rethinking of the modern philosophical tradition they proposed can be read today as a shared attempt to stop it and start afresh. No figure illustrates better than René Descartes the importance of modernity and its history for postwar thinkers. If Rousseau served as a crucial reference point for their understanding of the self's transparency and of intersubjectivity, it was Descartes who gave them the set-piece villain necessary for articulating and rejecting the modern thesis of the transparency of consciousness and of knowledge. Descartes was used for the purpose of advancing two related claims: that a self-transparent cogito had been formative for modernity; and that this was today a grand illusion, historically obsolete and philosophically destructive. Critical readings of Descartes were not incidental or local; together they delimited a systematic position of great significance for the structuralist generation. Consider the following three passages:

"I think therefore I am" (*cogito ergo sum*), is not simply a formula in which, at the historical apogee of a reflection on the conditions of science, the transcendental subject's existential affirmation is constituted together with its connection to transparency.[1]

If man is indeed, in the world, the locus of an empirico-transcendental doublet, if he is that paradoxical figure in which the empirical contents of knowledge necessarily release, of themselves, the conditions that have made them possible, then *man cannot posit himself in the immediate and sovereign transparency of a cogito*; nor, on the other hand, can he inhabit the objective inertia of something that, by rights, does not and never can lead to self-consciousness. Man is a mode of being which accommodates that dimension—always open, never finally delimited, yet constantly traversed—which extends from a part of himself not reflected in a *cogito* to the act of thought by which he apprehends that part; and which, in the inverse direction, extends from that pure apprehension to the empirical clutter, the chaotic accumulation of contents, the weight of experiences constantly eluding themselves, the whole silent horizon of what is posited in the sandy stretches of nonthought.[2]

Between the overture and the philosophical accomplishment of phonologism (or logocentrism), the motif of presence was decisively articulated. It underwent an internal modification whose most conspicuous index was the moment of certitude in the Cartesian cogito. Before that, the identity of presence offered to the mastery of repetition was constituted under the "objective" form of the ideality of the *eidos* or the substantiality of *ousia*. Thereafter, this objectivity takes the form of *representation*, of the *idea* as the modification of a self-present substance, conscious and certain of itself at the moment of its relationship to itself. Within its most general form, the mastery of presence acquires a sort of infinite assurance. The power of repetition . . . seems to acquire an absolute independence. Ideality and substantiality relate to themselves, in the element of the *res cogitans*, by a movement of pure auto-affection. Consciousness is the experience of pure auto-affection. It calls itself infallible and if the axioms of *natural reason* give it this certitude . . . it is because they constitute the very element of thought and of self-presence.[3]

All three passages identify the same problem in Descartes's cogito: its self-transparency and its figuration of the physical world as transparent, actually or potentially. All place Descartes at the origin of an objectionable modernity; and they do so with explicit reference to the cogito.

The first passage comes from Jacques Lacan's "L'instance de la lettre dans l'inconscient" (1957;"The Instance of the Letter in the Unconscious"). The second is from the chapter "Man and His Doubles" in Michel Foucault's 1966 *The Order of Things*—where Foucault develops his argument on the emergence of "Man" in the era of the human sciences. The third is from Jacques Derrida's *Of Grammatology* (1967)—like the other two works, a reputation-defining publication.

This node of engagements with Descartes was not restricted to structuralism.[4] Before moving to examine them in greater detail, I would like to locate them amid treatments of Descartes in France in and around the decade 1957–67. It is in these works that, as Canguilhem would phrase it, we glimpse the "exhaustion of the cogito."[5]

The Descartes of the 1950s and 1960s in French culture differed quite dramatically from the ones at both ends of this era: the pre–World War II Descartes and the Descartes of the 1980s, when some reclaimed his Frenchness against the supposedly Americanized or Germanophile philosophical priorities of their colleagues. André Glucksmann, who in the 1970s had lambasted his contemporaries for submissively shackling their thought to that of "master thinkers" (*maîtres penseurs*) could in 1987, without a hint of irony, title a book *Descartes, c'est la France*, as if philosophy could become genuinely French again by the sheer force of this identity statement.[6] Glucksmann's Descartes was not the generally accepted one; his gesture had a political value.[7] As for the pre-1945 Descartes, he had been placed at origin of clear and rational thinking and regarded as a role model, the philosopher who instituted modernity and critical reflection.

The Interwar Descartes Assemblage and Its Dismantling

That Descartes should be seen as the inaugurator of an era was not a new claim in the 1960s. The theoretical link that led from Descartes's *Discourse on Method* and *Meditations* to transparency and the historically constructive role of the cogito had existed since the interwar period. Two examples (besides, on occasion, Sartre) showcase this link: the poet Paul Valéry and the philosopher Léon Brunschvicg. Valéry—a self-pronounced devotee of Descartes—had enough clout as a poet among philosophers to be handpicked to inaugurate the 1937 International Congress of Philosophy, the Congrès Descartes, which was held in Paris in celebration of

the tricentennial of the *Discourse on Method*.[8] Four years later, in an introduction to fragments of Descartes's work, Valéry wrote of Descartes's famous illumination on November 10, 1619, as "an extraordinary intellectual
drama":

All of a sudden, someone's truth matures and radiates in him. . . . The term "illumination" is appropriate—nothing gives a more just image of this intimate phenomenon than the intervention of light into an obscure domain where until then
one only groped around in the darkness. With the light it becomes possible to walk
straight, and this path becomes coordinated with one's desire and goals. A whole
life is clarified, all of its acts become ordered with the work that becomes their
goal. An intellect forms, once and for all, the model of all its future endeavors.[9]

Valéry's sanctification of this conversionary Descartes is absolute, his identification with him precious. His words are a far cry from the irony with
which he speaks about the "Glass Man." Brunschvicg, too, emphasized the
correspondence between Descartes and the dawn of modernity.

Before Descartes, when people asked themselves *what do we know? what do we believe? what do we do?* they looked behind themselves. All responses were already
inscribed in books, whether sacred or profane ones. Since Descartes we have been
looking ahead of ourselves. Surely not everything, certainly, is yet to be found, but
everything must be examined anew, must be seen through our own eyes, to be
judged with our own mind.[10]

Brunschvicg read Descartes's contribution through the lens of a simplified
and anachronistic version of the famous three questions of Kant's critical
project; he made him break decisively with the historical and textual tradition and look toward the future. Doubt, examination, and judgment were
guaranteed to all of "us" who were born after Descartes, and they brought
truth and individuality ("our own eyes," "our own mind," as opposed to
"the people" before). In one stroke, Descartes set in motion the modern attitude, marked by reason, novelty, progress, and individuality.

From the 1930s on, this portrait of Descartes was relentlessly chipped
away at; by 1960, he was a foil for the philosopher. Descartes scholarship
persisted, notably in the work of Martial Gueroult and Ferdinand Alquié,
who feuded over the correct way to read Descartes and philosophical systems in general, or in that of phenomenologists like Paul Ricœur and
Maurice Merleau-Ponty. However, Descartes's pedestal as principal originator of the modes of experience and knowledge particular to modernity,

its hopes, and even its illusions, had cracked. Part of this took place thanks to the revalorization of the cogito brought about by the introduction of phenomenology around 1930.[11] Edmund Husserl's Paris lectures of 1929, which became his *Cartesian Meditations*, arranged a reconstruction of his conception of transcendental subjectivity such that the cogito now suddenly guaranteed reason and individuality.[12] This controversial shift had the immediate effect of linking Husserl's thought to Cartesianism.[13] For critics after 1950, speaking of Descartes meant speaking of the tradition and purpose of phenomenology as well, especially in order to criticize Sartre's emphasis on consciousness, which Marxists, structuralists, and epistemologists thought was restoring the hegemony of the cogito over other sources of experience, meaning, and power. When Ferdinand Alquié (who taught at the Lycée Louis-le-Grand and from 1952 at the Sorbonne) proposed that Descartes's pivotal achievement was the "metaphysical discovery of man," he postulated that this discovery had led Descartes to a "derealization"[14] of science, which was only grounded in the ontology of the cogito. With Descartes, science, technology, and man had been conceived anew—but Alquié's focus on the cogito led commentators to suggest that he served, alongside Sartre, as an intermediary in the identification of Cartesianism with phenomenology and in their mutual delegitimation.[15]

One direction for this critique was therefore to complain that the proposed self-transparency of the cogito was not an adequate recipient of meaningfulness. Maurice Merleau-Ponty objected that Descartes sometimes presented the cogito in a fashion that rendered it self-transparent: "for example, in the *Regulae* when he placed one's own existence among the simplest evidences . . . [which] supposes that the subject is perfectly transparent for itself, like an essence, and is incompatible with the idea of the hyperbolic doubt which even reaches to essences."[16] A second direction, exemplified by Bachelard's and, later, by Canguilhem's and Levi-Strauss's critiques of knowledge transparency, was to associate the cogito with technological modernity and problematize the two together. At the turn into the century, Émile Boutroux had claimed that Cartesian ethics distinguished itself from others through its "intimate union with science."[17] But now that unity between the cogito and technological science was no longer sustainable, and it appeared that the two did not work to further each other's progress. Yet they could not simply be decoupled. We have examined Canguilhem's view that tension between science–technique and subjectivity had riddled concepts of the body with terrible internal conflicts. The point was also made, and in no less dramatic terms, by Alexandre Koyré. In 1948 Koyré traced the modern hope that machines would liberate humanity to Descartes. This hope, he countered, has proved to be an illusion:

the machine [has] betrayed the hopes placed in it: intended to ease the pain of men, it appeared, on the contrary, to only aggravate it. The age of the machine, instead of being the golden age of mankind, proved to be the iron age. The shuttle and plectra did move by themselves, but the weaver remained more chained than ever to the loom. Instead of freeing man and making him 'the master and possessor of nature," the machine transformed man into a slave of its own making. In addition . . . by increasing the productive capacity of men, the machine, undoubtedly, created wealth, but spread misery at the same time . . . destroyed beauty and created ugliness.[18]

According to Koyré, machines had been a source of misery and violence during the entire past century. Machines had betrayed Descartes's dream of emancipation by fulfilling it. The present time could only be understood through stark contrast to that dream: technology dominated rather than eased human life. Like Canguilhem in his disparaging account of mechanism and Lévi-Strauss in his dream of a Rousseau who, to Descartes's "I know that I am, since I think," retorts "'What am I?' without any definite solution," Koyré proposes a way out of the "monocultural" technoscientific imperialism of the Cartesian West. These different Descarteses had similar intentions and proposed a similar history of modernity.

Thus one did not need to turn to Heidegger's "The Age of the World Picture" or to his "Letter on Humanism" (though many did) to learn about for the violence of a mechanistic modernity or to charge Descartes with having started it.[19] Thanks to the inspiration of Canguilhem, Marcel Mauss, and Lucien Febvre, technique remained a positively valued descriptor of how human beings handle their natural environment across different societies,[20] but the Cartesian hymn to the cogito was disparaged. Marxists such as Georges Friedmann and Kostas Axelos could privilege Descartes, but only among philosophers for whom the cogito had the power to "measure the reality of anything that is," and on the explicit assumption that the cogito was coextensive with bourgeois domination and alienation.[21]

Masks and Madness as Paths beyond
the Cartesian Subject

The suspicion was formed after World War II that, as an operator (and even as a mere particle) in philosophy, the *cogito* was complicit in a deeply misguided ethical, technological, and political project. Its correlate—that Descartes's era had come to its conclusion (or was about to)—was a new claim, which inverted Descartes's position without dethroning it. The cogito was not "first philosophy" any more and could not remain the generator of reason. Critically pursuing—or simply decoupling—the cogito–technology unit had the auxiliary effect of rendering Descartes obscure and enigmatic. The renewed attention to the *larvatus prodeo* passage contributed to this shift, completing the sense that Descartes had changed from a paragon of sincerity and clarity into a mask or an enigma. Academic squabbles had a similar effect; by 1956, Descartes and his place in contemporary thought were confusing. Twenty years after the celebratory 1937 Descartes Congrès, the Colloque de Royaumont dedicated to Descartes in 1956 is remembered mostly for the dispute between Ferdinand Alquié and Martial Gueroult over proper philosophical hermeneutics.[22] While Alquié supported the view that life and biography were relevant to understanding a work and Gueroult attempted to reduce history to the unity of a philosophical system, others, notably Jean Hyppolite, recoiled: there was something "enigmatic" about Descartes's lived experience that eschewed both approaches.[23] "Enigmatic" would have been an unthinkable qualifier back in Valéry's days. Now, however, Merleau-Ponty used it too, in *The Prose of the World*, where he also called Descartes "obscure":

No less obscure in his own eyes than ours, Descartes could act as though he did not have the key to his own life . . . perhaps there is no single key to Descartes's life. It may seem enigmatic only in the same way as do the irrational, the pure fact, the inherence of a mind into a particular time—in other words, enigmatic in itself, without any solution existing.[24]

But this was hardly about Descartes's biography: indeed the relationship between a philosophical system and history was in question. Given both the difficulty of recovering the historical Descartes from under the weight of interpretations and the entwinement of subsequent philosophies with his, how would one approach his system? For Merleau-Ponty, even if a mid-twentieth-century philosopher were to banish from view a massive history of interpretations, she would still not alight on a genuine Descartes.

Canguilhem

The complications of Georges Canguilhem's earlier approach, which undermined the identification of the cogito with science and progress, activated an interesting attempt to square the circle that also splintered into masks. In his 1959–60 seminar at the Sorbonne, Canguilhem returned to the question of Cartesian mechanism and to the opening quotation in the *Treatise of Man*, which had motivated his earlier analysis of Descartes. Rather than rework the machine–organism contrast, he stated that, for Descartes, "organization and life have two contradictory roles: they are at once *models* and *masks.*" Canguilhem restructured questions concerning the cogito and technology so they would encompass nature as it appears from the perspective of human and divine constructions of the world:

As a model for the human engineer—the builder of machines and automata—the organism is not entirely supplanted by its substitute. It is only for God—and for Descartes—that the automata created by God equal their models. Other humans can only distinguish between animals and the speaking, hence thinking, man, but they can only remain deceived by the perfection of imitation. Thus [for them], the organism appears as the mask of the machine. But the recognition of a mask as mask presupposes the consciousness of a power to lift the mask. As a result, the organism is a mask, a deceiving appearance, *even* for God (and for Descartes). We are thus reduced to asking ourselves: why did God create masks playing the role of models? This is a contradiction: it results in a claim that God imitates a nothingness [*rien*], a negation, a deception. Differently put, this results in a claim that God, in creating man as a soul *joined* to the body, created man as a natural power of initial illusion concerning the nature of the body. God could have created a man-machine, the machine human, *and* the thinking-human. Why did he create the *living*, that is, sentient, human being? If man were not *living*, he would not need to build a general theory of living beings without life. The scientist would not then have to deny the reality of the living human being.[25]

This is an astonishing and labored passage, and I can only scratch its surface here. That organisms would be at once machines, models, and masks was perhaps the perfect conclusion for Canguilhem's long-term anguish over Descartes. Descartes had denied the reality of the living being, of life itself. To arrange his thought around masks and models was to watch "life" squirm within his system: if Descartes had helped launch a modernity that denigrated and subjugated life to the imperatives of abstract knowledge and to the rule of the machine, these masks and models pointed to what exceeded Descartes's philosophy: a life unsuccessfully regulated through mechanical reduction and an ever-expanding set of masks, on one's own face and on everything one encountered.

Lacan

The strategy of discovering masks in claims to knowledge was perfected by Lacan, who in his famous 1963–64 seminar stated that the *larvatus prodeo* passage expressed Descartes's "secret ambition."[26] The enigma that Hyppolite had mentioned, this source of the Alquié–Gueroult debate, was an invitation for Alquié's friend Lacan: *larvatus prodeo* and Descartes's "biography, his approach, [are] essential to the communication of his method, of the way he has found to truth." It was an invitation to theorize what Lacan called the *aphanisis* ("disappearance, effacement, removal" in Greek) of the subject, expressed in part through the problem of self-knowledge. Time and again, indeed in some of his most significant texts, Lacan engaged self-knowledge as a vicious circle and retorted to claims of self-unmasking that any mask thrown aside leaves behind a new and perhaps even more deceptive mask. In his "Seminar on 'The Purloined Letter'" he notes:

What could be more convincing . . . than the gesture of turning one's cards face up on the table? It is so convincing that we are momentarily persuaded that the prestidigitator has in fact demonstrated, as he promised he would, how his trick was performed, whereas he has only performed it anew in a purer form; this moment makes us appreciate the supremacy of the signifier in the subject.[27]

The same theme had appeared a few years earlier, in 1953, "The Function and Field of Speech and Language in Psychoanalysis," where Lacan wrote about Freud on jokes. As the joke strikes at something the unconscious knows to be true but that remains disturbing to the (conscious) subject, a masked play is suddenly staged that tames the joke's lure and force:

"He who lets the truth escape like that," comments Freud, "is in reality happy to throw off the mask." It is truth, in fact, that throws off the mask in coming out of his mouth, but only so that the joke might take on another and more deceptive mask: the sophistry that is merely a stratagem, the logic that is merely a lure, even comedy that tends merely to dazzle.[28]

And in "Science and Truth" (1966), in a formulation that refines earlier ones, Lacan described philosophy as a particularly insufficient way of approaching oneself: "'I, truth, speak . . .' and the prosopopoeia continues. . . . One does not see oneself as one is, and even less so when one approaches oneself wearing philosophical masks."[29] Masked I advance toward myself.

These passages are by no means the only instances of the trope of masks in Lacan.[30] Within his conceptual apparatus, it played a role in descriptions of the masking function of truth; of the veils worn by the language through which the self accounts for itself; and of in the ways in which the unconscious suddenly punctures this veil. The masks of the self served to caution the psychoanalyst who may imagine that she had halted the patient's fall into the abyss of the unconscious; masks also emerged time and again within the analytic session, in a fashion that amplified the instabilities of transference.[31] At stake here was the fall of Cartesian certainty and sincerity to the analytical force of the observer-scientist-analyst, who must sustain more than a technical analysis: the possibility of healing for a perpetually split subject, controlled in part by its Other, its unconscious, the language that tricks and exceeds it both from without and from within.

Foucault and Derrida

The second mode of critique of the cogito, as undermined by mechanism on one hand and by madness on the other, is best captured by the debate between Michel Foucault and Jacques Derrida over Foucault's analysis, in *History of Madness*, of Descartes's treatment of madness in the First Meditation. Rather than replay the debate,[32] I am interested in foregrounding two main aspects of it that were symptomatic of a change in the understanding of Descartes: Foucault's positioning of Descartes; and Derrida's argument about the proper way of historicizing the Cartesian cogito, of evaluating its relations to others, and of understanding the modernity of Descartes's conception of madness.

In the second chapter of *History of Madness*, Foucault famously correlated Descartes's institution of certainty in the *Meditations* with his exclusion of madness from the sphere of reason. This institution thus became foundational to the history of banning unreason in modernity, and hence to the history of reason and of modernity themselves. Foucault began with Descartes's doubt and, listing the reasons why Descartes thought that the truth could slip away from his rational interpretation, wrote:

Madness is an altogether different affair [from error or dreams]. If its dangers compromise neither the enterprise nor the essential truth that is found, this is not because *this thing*, even in the thoughts of a madman, cannot be untrue, but rather because I, when I think, cannot be considered insane. When I think I have a body, can I be certain that my grasp on the truth is stronger than that of the man who believes his body to be made of glass? Assuredly, says Descartes, "such people are insane, and I would be thought equally mad if I took anything from them as a model for myself." It is not the permanence of truth that ensures that thought is not madness, in the way that it freed it from an error of perception or a dream; it is an impossibility of being mad which is inherent in the thinking subject rather than the object of his thoughts. . . . The perils of madness have been quashed by the exercise of Reason, and this new sovereign rules a domain where the only possible enemies are errors and illusions. . . . Madness is banished in the name of the man who doubts, and who is no more capable of opening himself to unreason than he is of not thinking or not being.[33]

Foucault returned time and again to this dismissal:[34] among its central components is the sense that rational hegemony began with Descartes's cogito as sovereign purveyor and ruler of the world. The doubting subject is the guarantor of a newfound and transparent rule of reason over shadows, doubt, and unreason:

Men of the seventeenth century discovered in *the immediacy of thought present to itself* the certainty in which reason expresses itself in its primordial form. . . . It is true to say that the Cogito, 'I think therefore I am," is an absolute beginning, but it should not be forgotten that the evil genius has preceded it. And the evil genius is not just the symbol that sums up in a systematic way the dangers of psychological events such as images from dreams and errors of the senses. Half-way between man and God, the evil genius has an absolute meaning: he is both the possibility of unreason and the sum of all its powers. More than the refraction of human finitude, it designates the peril that beyond man might prevent him in a definitive manner from reaching the truth, *a major obstacle threatening not so much the individual mind as reason itself.* The *brilliant light of the truth of the Cogito* should not be allowed *to obscure the shadow of the evil genius*, nor to obfuscate its perpetually threatening power; until the existence and the truth of the outside world have been secured, he haunts the whole movement of Descartes's *Meditations*.[35]

In the seventeenth and eighteenth centuries madness was considered the "empirical form" of the "endless night" of unreason, which "lay beneath it, or rather defined the space of its possibility."[36] But in this paragraph Foucault switches Descartes's registers: he identifies the evil genius *both* with unreason *and* with what underlies reason. In other words, reason is shadowed by an unreason that is identical with the reign of the evil genius and with the shadow of that reign as well. The "brilliant light of the truth of the Cogito" today "should not be allowed" to "obscure" the shadow; unreason, too, served as an "other" that reason could not expunge and by which it continued to be haunted. In negotiating the "then" and the "now," Foucault insists that "now" (i.e., "after Nietzsche and Freud") we know of the threat of unreason and madness that exists both *beneath* and *within* the rational order. "Then" it was an ever-present shadow and the force of the light of reason promised its expulsion: the "immediacy of thought present to itself" (a perfectly adequate description of the self-transparent cogito) became the "primordial form" of reason, the "absolute beginning." Foucault's ambiguous phrasing asks us not to think that the "shadow" of the evil genius has been altogether bathed away by Light. To see the cogito as still guiding and organizing is to accept the violence it inflicts on the mad and to assume its false self-transparency as a right path through life and thought.

Derrida's critique of Foucault's treatment of Descartes makes a series of points eminently relevant to the contemporary status of the cogito.[37] First, in his judgment, Foucault seems to argue that madness and history are intertwined—more precisely, that the Cartesian exclusion of madness coincides with the emergence and the possibility of history.[38] By having history and subjectivity begin with and become possible through the exclusion of madness, Foucault was only echoing the view that Descartes stood at the fount of modernity.[39] Second, Derrida argues that Foucault could propose this view for two reasons: because he distinguished excessively between the First Meditation's arguments on madness and dreams; and because he fast-forwarded the movement from the rejection of madness to the institution of the cogito, avoiding all other sources of doubt (e.g., dreams). In other words, while Foucault thought that he was criticizing the notion of Descartes as originator of the *light* of modernity, in reality he replicated it. The existing structure located the Cartesian cogito at the "absolute beginning"; Foucault's omission of other reasons for Descartes's doubt, on the other hand, equated this beginning with a single and straightforward exclusion—that of madness. The fusion of this exclusion with the triumph of the cogito produced a misreading of the First Meditation that was still too indebted to the philosophical history of modernity.

Derrida proceeds with two interdependent rebukes, the first of which approximates the masked Descartes thesis. He casts doubt on the conviction with which Descartes raised the question of madness, interpreting it as intentionally hyperbolic.[40] For Derrida, the cogito in doubt is not Descartes's own; the specter of madness serves Descartes as a mask or a mediator in establishing other, more serious forms of doubt.[41] Second, Derrida claims that, rather than simply exclude madness, Descartes has the cogito triumph over it in a manner that allows its specter to persist, because madness survives *inside* reason: "Whether I am mad or not, *cogito sum*."[42] Instead of a Descartes for whom the cogito papers over this specter, Derrida recognizes a Descartes for whom madness resided within the self without displacing the cogito; instead of a Descartes who broke with what preceded him, Derrida sees a Descartes who coded an ostensible novelty *into* the premodern: "the transparence of self-relationship and the purity of auto-affection," which would define the subsequent era.[43] Blaming Foucault's reading fits Derrida's understanding of history much better: for him, texts *do not propel* shifts but rather bear their symptoms. No longer "the founder," Descartes becomes but "the most conspicuous index." Derrida refuses, in a more aggressive fashion than Foucault at this point, to consider Descartes *himself* and gestures against the whole trope of treating Descartes as instituting modernity. Nevertheless, he targets the cogito for pretending to do exactly this.

The "Last Tribunal of the Cogito"

Let us now return to the three passages which opened the chapter. The critical invocation of the cogito by Lacan, Derrida, and Foucault should be read against this contemporary figuration of Descartes as offering a mask of sincerity, a series of mechanist reductions, an array of exclusions, a purity of consciousness. Each passage involves not only a set of philosophical premises but subjectivity, its historicity, and a worldview that includes the place of humans in the world and the place of science in human consciousness. Reading their Descarteses as commensurate with a conception of modernity and the present raises a key issue, namely, the creeping sense of the present as a new time of rupture or shift.

Foucault

When Foucault asserted that "man cannot posit himself in the immediate and sovereign transparency of a cogito,"[44] he quietly tied Descartes to Husserl and Sartre. The conditions of possibility of knowledge render the cogito's transparency impossible, even though the Cartesian cogito is the fount of what happened in subsequent centuries. No appeal for a cogito or consciousness to remain transparent to itself, so as to displace life and knowledge, can override the way in which knowledge situates the human being on a hinge between immanence and transcendence. Prioritizing the structuralist third, Foucault refused the cogito's "sovereignty" over the world in a style reminiscent of Canguilhem's "Machine and Organism" and of his own *History of Madness*, both of which anguished over the violence of this sovereignty, and he emphasized the whole field of "non-thought," "empirical clutter," and "chaotic accumulation" that the cogito would violently ignore. Reviewing *The Order of Things*, Canguilhem too described this argument as the "exhaustion of the cogito," stressing how it rendered obsolete the attacks directed at Foucault by Marxists and existentialists.[45]

The modern cogito is no longer the intuitive grasp of the identity, in the activity of thinking, of thinking thought with its being; it is "the constantly renewed interrogation as to how thought can reside elsewhere than here, and yet so very close to itself, how it can *be* in the forms of non-thought."[46]

Foucault's rejection of transparency is a fundamentally epistemological commitment to the idea that concepts like "Man," "transcendence," and "experience" are mutual and coextensive. Like Bachelard or Canguilhem, whom he made his precursors, Foucault thought that epistemology was fundamentally political, and that looking to non-thought meant undoing transparency so that a new era might begin.

Derrida

Derrida's own refusal of the transparent cogito subverted claims that epistemology, ontology, and politics can be conceived of as independent or foundational fields.[47] Central here was his critique of self-presence, which Derrida understood as a crux of the "logocentric" metaphysics to be pushed against: the long-standing belief that being can exist *and* be articulated as undivided, marked by no split, always present and transparent to itself. What happens with Descartes is this: the locus of presence is no longer being (for which Derrida uses *eidos* and *ousia*, "form" and "essence/ being," standard in the Platonic–Aristotelian tradition) or matter, but rather *representation*. The Cartesian cogito participates in an absolute self-certainty that reduces the whole world to its affirmation and description of it: "the mastery of presence acquires a sort of infinite assurance." This is Derrida's charge: through auto-affection, representation captures existence and claims it to be complete, untroubled by intrusion or contamination or deformation. "Being aware of oneself" affirmed and foreclosed all possible interruptions. The self-assertion of the cogito amounted to a statement that one can affirm into existence, indeed that *one has done so*, and has accorded certainty and truth through the experience of self-transparency. Before the "internal modification" that was Descartes, truth was allocated to being; with him, it was allocated to the subject. After the Cartesian cogito, everything was conditioned, reduced, and mastered by a consciousness that affirmed itself as complete.[48] As in the critique of Lévi-Strauss, where Derrida observed that transparency masked a profound violence, here he finds it masking a no less violent erasure of complexity.

Lacan

It is fitting to close this account of the postwar Descartes by looking at Lacan's repeated call for a "return to Descartes," which, as Alain Badiou has noted, was systematic and fully entwined with Lacan's advocacy of a "return to Freud."[49] More than a return, this was also a response: perhaps more explicitly for Lacan than for any other thinker, Descartes offered a counterpoint for his idea of a split subject, fundamentally non-transparent to itself, stuck in its inability to ever master the unconscious. Taking it for granted that in the cogito "the transcendental subject's existential affirmation is constituted together with its connection to transparency,"[50] Lacan developed this statement in two directions. One was the advocacy of a split subject, along with all the hallmarks we have examined: the other, madness as forcibly masked and "normalized" by the "I," the status of the symbolic as a third order between transcendence and immanence. The other direction was the status of science, conceived of through contrast between the present and "the historical apogee of a reflection on the conditions of science."[51] By "science" Lacan meant here much more than his critique of ego psychology, criminology, and adaptation psychology; he meant the capacity for a knowledge that encompassed this split, opaque, self-masking self. Lacan routinely identified Descartes's *cogito ergo sum* with transparency of self-knowledge, in order to couch in a rhetoric of self-evidence the claim that the cogito is secured by a "transparency" of the mind to the ontological affirmation of the "I." While Descartes would construct knowledge and self-knowledge out of this affirmation, Lacan would use it to poke holes in them and to divide the subject between a *subject of the signifier* and a *subject of the signified.*

In his 1954–55 seminar, Lacan allocated "I think, therefore, I am" to the new subjectivity of ego psychology and existentialism, to which it was "so essential." But,

> if it is in fact true that consciousness is transparent to itself, and grasps itself as such, it does seem that the *I* is not on that account transparent to it. . . . The apprehension of an object by consciousness does not by the same token reveal to it its properties. The same is true for the *I*. If this *I* is in fact presented to us as a kind of immediate given in the act of reflection by which consciousness grasps itself as transparent to itself, for all that, nothing indicates that the whole of this reality . . . would be exhausted by this.[52]

Here Lacan attacks one consequence of the self-affirmation of the "I," namely, its conceptual unity, arguing instead for a thorough dissociation of consciousness from the I and against the capacity of consciousness for proper self-apprehension.[53] The operation of finding ways to pry apart the subject so as to let through the speech of the other, of the symbolic, of the unconscious structured like a language carried into the subject the unmasterability that begins with this subject's entrance into the symbolic interpersonal domain. *Cogito ergo sum* seemed sufficient for "the subject of the signifier"—the consciousness that speaks, inquires about itself, believes itself indivisible. But there was also "the subject of the signified": this was the subject living in the polyvalence that reigns over signs and symptoms, both in the outside world and in the unconscious. The subject of the signified necessarily remained outside the scope of the ego's operations: meaning for it was never singular, never assured. The possessive form in "the subject of the signified" allowed this subject to be owned by the play of signification. The two subjects thus could not be understood as identical with or transparent to each other. As in Foucault, the cogito was demoted to the status of a placeholder tasked with the peculiar function of telescoping Descartes, Husserl, and Sartre into an overarching and historically consistent foil for the new. Lacan's new "subject of science," like the subject of the signified, began in a non-thought that was nevertheless a science, a speech, an otherness to be recuperated and (to a degree) known again.[54]

Conclusion

The problem of knowledge, together with the reactions to its fundamental incompleteness in postwar epistemology, has been a near constant concern in this book so far. No less significant has been the problem of self-knowledge, and Descartes and Rousseau serve as cardinal forces and figures resurrected in postwar history to cause mutations and reevaluations. If Jean Starobinski's Rousseau book demonstrated the pitfalls of trust in self-transparency, and if Canguilhem showed the mechanistic violence involved in Cartesian knowledge, Lacan's long-standing engagement with Descartes and transparency constituted perhaps the last nail in the coffin of French belief in self-knowledge. While Canguilhem and Foucault reorganized self-knowledge with the help of knowledge in general, Lacan attempted the reverse operation: to wedge the unconscious and language into a split subject, so as to press for a new and satisfactory language and science to develop.

Little in the emergence of structuralism, in its obsession with subjectivity, science, and history, and in its consolidation on the French postwar intellectual scene matches in importance its reconstruction of the past and its apparent resolution of the question of how to understand the origins of modernity and their relation to the contemporary moment. Having presented Kantian reason, in the 1930s–40s, as the expression of a kind of idealism incapable of engaging reality, philosophers could then, in the 1950s–60s, look at the violence of World War II as a kind of *Menschendämmerung* that witnessed the incapacity of liberalism, democracy, and the entire theologico-political apparatus of modernity to offer solutions. And here lies, in many respects, one major value of studying the place of transparency in the historical–philosophical reflections on Descartes and Rousseau offered by Lévi-Strauss, Lacan, Foucault, Derrida, and non-"structuralists" like Canguilhem and Starobinski. Across these readings the same picture emerges: Descartes's monumental achievement inaugurated, or at least announced, the modern era. This was an era dominated by a self-sufficient and self-transparent cogito, which brought with it violence and a profound distortion of knowledge and intersubjectivity, as well as a notion of progress and a reduction of human beings to machines that was as unwarranted epistemologically as it was exclusivist and destructive politically. It was not just by sleight of hand or for show that philosophers treated these ideals as spoilt, or Cartesian modernity as obsolete, hopeless, and destructive. Against such values stood the potential of a philosophical apparatus that offered to diagnose the violence of this transparency and to reveal opaque, even obscure spaces through which alternatives to the exclusionary "machine" of normativization and technological domination could emerge.

Canguilhem and Lacan, and Derrida too, worked on exactly this set of problems: they demonstrated that the failure of self-knowledge *must mean* the failure of science to account for the self; it *must mean* the failure of humanism to promote the right kind of human being. Before Foucault looked at madness as a form of otherness instituted by psychiatry and philosophy, Lacan had grappled with the elusive question of how to make the "other" speak through language without being reduced to it. Overcoming a modernity founded by Descartes was not a facile advocacy of an "end of history," nor a dangerous "anti-Enlightenment" ideology. Historians have enjoyed using these terms in accusatory form. But to show even the least bit of sympathy to Canguilhem, Lacan, and the generation that surrounded them and proposed to pick apart Cartesian modernity is to recognize that, for better or worse, his and theirs was an effort to recognize that the world was not as the moderns had promised, that "Man" did not see his own face in the mirror, that communication could not be trusted to carry one meaning, that curing patients was no given, and that the skepticism that emerged in the early postwar period was morphing into a huge effort to rethink the modern tradition and perhaps heal it without repeating its violence.

"Speak Not of Darkness, but of a Somewhat Blurred Light"

Michel Foucault, Modernity, and the Distortion of Knowledge

Few thinkers have used the term "transparency" as much or as rigorously as Michel Foucault does in *Les Mots et les choses: Une Archéologie des sciences humaines* (1966; *The Order of Things: An Archaeology of the Human Sciences*).[1] I have circled around this book and its role in other dialogues: first, in the postwar preoccupation with the idea that modernity has enforced homogenization at the cost of estrangement and deprecation of the other;[2] second, in structuralism's study of a "third," symbolic register; third, the recalibration of Cartesian thematics. The work bears closer examination: Foucault handled the term "transparency" as a key to the arc of modernity, and as a profound illusion of his time.

The Order of Things offered an account of the rupture of modernity with the early modern period—especially the period 1650–1800, conventionally known in France as the "Classical Age"—and of the consequences of that rupture for the century and a half that followed. Foucault judged that the beginning of the nineteenth century constituted a hard epistemological break from the preceding period, but not as a result of political events (e.g., the French Revolution) or of developments in philosophy (e.g., German idealism). It was instead concomitant with the "seismic shift" in the foundations of thought that reshaped the very meaning of life, labor, and language, turning them into new foundations for knowledge and producing comparative linguistics, political economy, and biology. Representation and its instantiations in language, the control of wealth and labor in economic analysis, and the conceptual and practical management of biological nature and life now tethered *knowledge* to a conception of *man* that served as its source and ultimate referent. Human sciences such as psychology, sociology, and ethnology were also born of this process. Modernity was fundamentally about man: insofar as man was both the knowing subject and the object that knowledge sought to determine, man inflected all knowledge of society, language, and history, of the psyche, of nature, indeed of all representation and exchange. Man gave representation a shape and installed himself as that shape.

The first part of this chapter shadows Foucault's use of the word *transparency*. Foucault equated transparency with representation in the classical age. In modernity, this equivalence ended; transparency became a misguided expectation. If human finitude—established alongside the transformation of labor, life, and language around 1800—imposes a "screen" on knowledge, the hope for transparency veils and distorts even that screen. The second part concerns the engagement of *The Order of Things* in the 1960s debate regarding the human sciences, which were believed to be proceeding blindly, without support from philosophy and in the absence of a guiding concept of the human. The final part rereads the conclusion of *The Order of Things* in order to argue that Foucault devised a far more ambiguous present than is usually recognized. In the long endgame of the book's last two chapters, he outlines a potential movement of knowledge toward a kind of transparency that we cannot capture, one that, while in line with knowledge, escapes the human, not only as the construct of the human sciences, but even as a subject or object of knowledge.

Transparency and Representation in the Classical and Modern Periods

Transparency is a fundamental basis, term, and goal of Foucault's classical age. His principal use of "transparency" and associated terms concerns the functioning of representation and knowledge in the classical age (which he contrasts to the Renaissance that preceded it), and especially the relation between language and the world. In the Renaissance, he notes, lack of transparency in the book of the world was explained by appeal to the Babel story in Genesis 11.[3] Language, having lost its original transparency by God's decree in the Tower of Babel, was an object *within* discourse, not one premised on or exhausted by its representative value;[4] it lacked universality and was "not a totality of independent signs, a uniform and unbroken entity in which things could be reflected one by one, as in a mirror, and so express their particular truths . . . but an *opaque*, mysterious thing."[5] This formulation allows Foucault to chart language not as a glossy boundary between man and nature (between "words" and "things," as in the French title) but as an object of study for hermeneuts, alongside other systems of signs. Semiology and hermeneutics do not pass through it, as it were; but, "like animals, plants, or stars, its elements have their laws of affinity and convenience, their necessary analogies."[6] According to Foucault, what set up ordering practices in the Renaissance was the *resemblance* between things (and words were just such things) rather than the *representation* of one by the other. Language merely offered support for *particular* similitudes, identities, and differences; it "combines here and there with the forms of the world and becomes interwoven with them: so much so that all these elements, taken together, form a network of marks in which each of them may play, and does in fact play, in relation to all the others, the role of content or of sign, that of secret or of indicator."[7]

Nothing describes Foucault's contrast between the Renaissance and the classical age better than language's shift to a transparent system of signs for the representation of things. What the Renaissance saw as lost in Babel, the classical age retrieved: language was now "*deployed within representation and in that duplication of itself which hollows itself out.*"[8] Foucault starkly pronounces transparency the central characteristic of representation in the seventeenth and eighteenth centuries.

Put differently, in the sixteenth century the transparency of nature was "clouded" from the very beginning, and this set the hermeneut on a path of trying to make it more transparent.[9] The dissociation of similitudes in favor of an analysis based on identity and difference heralds the end of the Renaissance. In the classical age, language "has withdrawn from the midst of beings themselves and has entered a period of transparency and neutrality" to the point that it "does not exist [but] it functions."[10] Representations generated by systems of signs are now premised on an essential transparency between them and nature, a transparency whose reign must now itself be made transparent. "In its perfect state, the system of signs is that simple, absolutely transparent language which is capable of naming what is elementary; it is also that complex of operations which defines all possible conjunctions."[11]

This change, Foucault specifies, is not limited to an abstract understanding of representation; it is the foundation of language. Now, "language is deployed within representation";[12] its transparency is essential in that language lies *with* what it expresses *in* the movement of expression and does not create a duplicate, a crust of thought, as was previously imagined. It seeps into thought and vanishes in its deployment. Examining thought equals examining language. As language becomes "so transparent" to representation and discourse, Foucault proceeds to multiply the sites of transparency:[13]

In the Classical age, discourse is that translucent necessity through which representation and beings must pass—as beings are represented to the mind's eye, and as representation renders beings visible in their truth. The possibility of knowing things and their order passes, in the Classical experience, through the sovereignty of words: words are, in fact, neither marks to be deciphered (as in the Renaissance period) nor more or less faithful and masterable instruments (as in the positivist period); they form rather a colorless network on the basis of which beings manifest themselves and representations are ordered.[14]

This transparency functions both as an algorithm and as a utopia of linguistic representation.[15]

Foucault understands transparency as the motor of classical representation, its program and its end, the language of its language, a "colorless network" that is replicated in ontology.[16] Its contrary can receive various names such as "opacity," "obstruction," "residuum." Finally, Foucault gives no disparaging judgment on classical transparency: it was crucial to the structure of knowledge and representation and therefore served as a particular, self-effacing epistemological veil.[17]

Things changed dramatically at the end of the eighteenth century. In a chapter appropriately titled "The Limits of Representation," Foucault describes how limits emerged during the formation of the very systems of knowledge that underpinned representation: biology, political economy, linguistics.[18] These sciences turned to history and to "man": the schemata of classification that transparent representation had introduced came undone. In language, the study of inflections broke ground for comparative linguistics,[19] and the historical comparisons that followed allow Foucault to use the term "transparency" critically: he emphasizes elements of language whose analysis requires history, comparison, and depth and grants them an "enigmatic density."[20]

The material unity constituted by the arrangement of sounds, syllables, and words is not governed by the mere combination of the elements of representation. It has its own principles, which differ from language to language: grammatical composition has regularities which are not transparent to the signification of the discourse.[21]

A similar limit was reached in literature thanks to Sade, whom Foucault treats as "attain[ing] the end of Classical discourse and thought." As Cervantes had ended the Renaissance, so Sade captures "the fresh violence of desire in the deployment of a representation that is transparent and without flaw."[22] The Classical age "collapses" and knowledge loses its definitive attributes:

At the time of Descartes or Leibniz, the reciprocal transparency of knowledge and philosophy was total, to the point that the universalization of knowledge in a philosophical system of thought did not require a specific mode of reflection. From Kant onward, the problem is quite different; knowledge can no longer be deployed against the background of a unified and unifying *mathēsis*.[23]

Now the order of language has "has lost its transparency and its major function in the domain of knowledge."[24] This loss was noted by contemporaries: reviewing the book, Gilles Deleuze identified the classical period with representation itself, to argue that with modernity, representation folds upon itself and "the upsurge of the obscure" takes place.[25] Foucault's use of metaphors on the fate of classical discourse again indicates that "transparency" was a technical term: "the order of Classical thought can now be eclipsed . . . it enters a region of shade. Even so, we should speak not of darkness but of a somewhat blurred light, deceptive in its apparent clarity, and hiding more than it reveals."[26]

The structural shift in knowledge and representation generated the new matrix of labor, life, and language out of which the human sciences developed. With their emergence, and thanks to their awareness and study of human limitations—or "analytic of finitude"—transparency becomes inoperative. The introduction of man into the structural foundations of knowledge generates a new order that has a distinct use for transparency.

Insofar as knowledge is now structurally displaced, internally deformed by man, "transparency" becomes a device for pretending that the erstwhile continuity between speaker, language, representation, and world continues undistorted—which is false. When, in constructing their specific rationality and anthropology, the human sciences appeal to transparency or indicate that their product is transparent, they are participating in a decidedly illusory practice. Philosophical claims to transparency proved not just epistemologically and ethically meaningless, but profoundly flawed.

The Human Sciences and Philosophy in Postwar France

Outside France, Foucault's subsequent focus on the "human sciences" and their relation to "anthropology," like his insistence on a transformation in the structure of knowledge itself during the nineteenth century, may have appeared quite foreign, but he was by no means original in using this rhetoric in his epistemology. Philosophical anthropology was an important subject of study *because* it had been called into question by the existentialist and antihumanist displacement of man in the early postwar period. Moreover, the claim that the human sciences unsuccessfully sought or produced a conception of man and competed with philosophy became a matter of broad concern, if not excitement. The redescription of ethnology as "anthropology" undermined purely philosophical anthropology and contributed to the humanization of knowledge.

The rather conventional philosopher Georges Gusdorf, who taught in Strasbourg, was an excellent foil for Foucault's *The Order of Things*. In 1960 Gusdorf had published an *Introduction aux sciences humaines*, and in 1966–67, right after Foucault's book, he brought out a two-volume history titled *Les Sciences humaines et la pensée occidentale* (*Human Sciences and Western Thought*).[27] Gusdorf argued that only through philosophy could the human sciences provide a "fundamental," "first," or "true" anthropology, of the philosophical rather than empirical variety, yet philosophy had parted ways with the human sciences in the twentieth century. At present, "the human sciences, unaware of their proper meaning, are deployed in an epistemological void. Abandoned to themselves, specialists are content to blindly obey their technical imperatives, they accumulate information in its raw state, without questioning their own questions."[28] It is hard not to read this passage as an attack on Lévi-Strauss and the anthropologists,

Piaget and the psychologists; but Gusdorf was also targeting French subservience to German thought, especially that of Hegel, Husserl, and Heidegger, which, he thought, foreclosed "meaningful" anthropological writing. The human sciences, he believed, had to be reconciled with a specifically French trajectory of philosophy that went back to the nineteenth century. This would give philosophy the room necessary to build an understanding of the human, and the human sciences the room to co-determine it from mostly empirical points of view.[29]

Gusdorf may not have been a major intellectual voice, but his writing exemplified the particular anxiety about what kind of knowledge of human existence followed from the sciences and their interaction with "philosophy."[30] His concerns passed from individuals to institutions. "If philosophical anthropology has become an urgent task in contemporary thought, this is because all the major problems of this thought converge on [anthropology] and make us cruelly aware of its absence," Paul Ricœur noted, also in 1960.[31] Ontology, modernity, and the human sciences—which "disperse in disparate disciplines and literally do not know what they are talking about"—all suffered from not knowing of what man is. Lévi-Strauss's debate with Ricœur and his critique of Sartre's *Critique of Dialectical Reason*, in which he famously argued that the point of the human sciences was *to dissolve man*, raised similar questions. *Sciences humaines* became a major disciplinary and organizing concept in the late 1950s: conferences, even entire institutions were devoted to what they meant.[32] In 1964, the Colloques de Royaumont, a center for international colloquia on themes of contemporary philosophical and humanist concern, was renamed the Fondation Royaumont pour le Progrès des Sciences de l'Homme. The leading French publisher Gallimard began a new book series, the Bibliothèque des sciences humaines; Émile Benveniste's *Problèmes de linguistique générale* (1966; *Problems of General Linguistics*) was the first to appear in that series; Foucault's *The Order of Things* followed a few months later.[33] Marxist engagements with the status of "the human" in capitalist societies—especially in the journal *Arguments*, which dedicated five issues to the subject in six years—similarly sought a rapprochement with anthropology and psychology that would undo "capitalist man" and the ways of knowing "him."[34] Finally, antihumanist critiques of philosophical anthropology had changed their terms altogether. Asking about science, knowledge, and the human gave them a new start.[35]

Jean Hyppolite's paramount influence on Foucault (and others) in these matters is well known.[36] In his book *Logique et existence* (1952; *Logic and Existence*), which marked the generation of Foucault, Derrida, and Deleuze, Hyppolite strove, by prioritizing being and logic, to find a new place for the human: "Man does not possess the freedom that allows him to wander from one determination to another or to be dissolved in abstract nothingness; rather freedom possesses him," he wrote. "Through this freedom . . . man does not conquer himself as man but becomes the home of the universal, of the logos of being, and capable of truth."[37] This definition strove for an ontological and logical way for the human to remain conceptually in suspension.

Jules Vuillemin has not received the same amount of attention, although he was equally influential in the recasting of the human sciences. In his *L'Héritage kantien et la révolution copernicienne: Fichte, Cohen, Heidegger* (1954; The Kantian Legacy and the Copernican Revolution: Fichte, Cohen, Heidegger), Vuillemin articulated a Heideggerian existentialism that he clearly intended in contradistinction to Sartre's, and ended his work by asking whether this was not the time for a new "Ptolemaic" revolution against the "Copernican" one that had occurred with Kant. Against a Kantian reason "more proximate to gods than men, to eternity than time," Vuillemin sought to recapture the "originary finitude" of individual, subjective time.[38] Existentialism had only gone so far, failing to unburden the human of the confusion resulting from its co-determination with "science." Returning to a "Ptolemaic" human subject would allow a properly existential anthropology to resituate its subject.

How are we to understand such a claim? Vuilemin's engagement with humanism in his *Essai sur la signification de la mort* (1948; Essay on the Meaning of Death) offers some clues. By his account, modern humanism's metaphysical and scientific claims could be rejected as confused and overreaching; but the methodological force of humanism, its articulation of a phenomenological "I" that could validate it, needed to be reasserted.[39] A return to the human self was essential, especially since the meaning of life and death would otherwise remain laden with heroic delusions and confused concepts. Using Heidegger and Kantian thinkers from outside the French context,[40] *L'Héritage kantien et la révolution copernicienne* advanced from this existentialism to offer the philosophy of history a new structure. Echoing Brunschvicg, Vuillemin identified Kant's transcendental philosophy with the birth of a properly "modern" science, but also believed that this break with a premodern past needed to be followed by a second break. After 150 years of Kantian modernity, Vuillemin distinguished Kantian "time of reason and truth" from an originary temporality of human beings. He claimed that Kant's "Copernican revolution" never "attained the true time of finitude" but colluded with a science that adapted human finitude to the transcendence of scientific truth. This distorted human time and experience to the benefit of non-human, scientific, ultimately transcendental time, and it also distorted anthropology by attaching it not to *man* but to abstract sciences. Vuillemin advocated a temporality folded by human finitude that needed to complete the Heideggerian and existentialist gesture toward "originary time." This purely human temporality could outpace a modern, scientifically inflected anthropology and the "anthropomorphism" of science caused by Kant's theory of time, for a more properly human time to be rescued from the sciences for the benefit of the future.

The Kantian problem was central to Foucault as well. In a course he taught at the École normale supérieure that same year, 1954, on "Problèmes de l'anthropologie," he foregrounded a passage in Kant's *Logic* where Kant argued that his three critical questions—What do I know? What may I hope for? What ought I do?—were always underwritten by a fourth one: What is Man?[41] Exactly like Heidegger and Vuillemin, Foucault evaluated Kant's fourth question as his central contribution and as the basic question of nineteenth-century thought.[42] "In the course of the nineteenth century, responses to the fourth Kantian question proliferated, while the other three questions were neglected. Anthropology became a naturalist philosophy of man in which the critical dimension [of Kant's project] was abolished."[43] The fourth Kantian question retained its priority until Nietzsche reopened the entire problematic by denying the foundational status of man.[44]

The Bifurcation of Antihumanism

Foucault's conclusion to *The Order of Things* is notorious for its assertive antihumanism. Foucault transposed Kant's four questions (whose arrangement in his *Logic* dated from 1800) onto his schema for the genesis and structure of modern knowledge.[45] Yet, despite his interest in Kant and even his alliance with Nietzsche, Foucault thought that philosophy was an insufficient guide to the meaning of the human in the preceding two centuries.[46] It had not founded modern representation or the human sciences and could not of its own overcome either them or the force of humanism.[47] Thus, although Foucault's vision of modern history largely converged with that of Vuillemin (who was a close friend),[48] Foucault argued something quite different. Rather than say that philosophy needed to return to human finitude (as Vuillemin had postulated), he pressed epistemology to track the rise and goals of the sciences, and perhaps bring news of their end. He scorned the Marxist revolutionary promise as a fish in nineteenth-century water, unable to breathe in the current regime of knowledge and power.[49] He laughed at the more hopeful or utopian discussion around the human sciences, which expected them (as Gusdorf did) to co-produce the new anthropology.[50] In his judgment, the determination of knowledge by the human sciences had run its course and was now a distinct threat:

"Anthropologization" is the great internal threat to knowledge in our day. We are inclined to believe that man has emancipated himself from himself since his discovery that he is not at the center of creation, nor in the middle of space, nor even, perhaps, the summit and culmination of life; but though man is no longer sovereign in the kingdom of the world, though he no longer reigns at the center of being, the "human sciences" are dangerous intermediaries in the space of knowledge.[51]

No negotiation was possible: having turned "man," this modern abbreviation of the human, into both the subject and the object of knowledge, the human sciences could not, in the middle of their own decline, hail any new anthropology. Abolishing man in this scenario would make it possible to reopen the "space" of knowledge, to tear apart the structures of anthropomorphism in order to retrieve that space:

all efforts to think afresh are in fact directed at that obstacle: whether it is a matter of crossing the anthropological field, tearing ourselves free from it with the help of what it expresses, and rediscovering a purified ontology or a radical thought of being; or whether, rejecting not only psychologism and historicism, but all concrete forms of the anthropological prejudice, we attempt to question afresh the limits of thought, and to renew contact in this way with the project for a general critique of reason.[52]

These "efforts to think afresh" thus resulted in the adjudication of *a new* displacement of thought, akin to those that had inaugurated and ended classical thought. Should this displacement occur, "man would be erased, like a face drawn in sand at the edge of the sea."[53]

But *how* the direction of this present was to be conceived is less clear than this famous slogan allows us to appreciate. Foucault articulates the coming to an end of the human sciences by looking at how ethnology (note his retention of the term over Lévi-Strauss's "anthropology") and psychoanalysis emerge from the human sciences to span "the entire domain of the human sciences" while liberating themselves from concepts of man.[54] They work, as "Levi-Strauss said . . . to dissolve man."[55] In this regard, psychoanalysis and ethnology converge and innovate: they restore a theory of language that is neither subservient to man and historicity nor stressed to their limits. Psychoanalysis structures a system of desire, law, and death, thereby undermining the self-evidence accorded to anthropological finitude; ethnology confronts instead historicity and the singularity of a humanist anthropology. They combine in a linguistic theory—structural linguistics—and, "to a gaze forearmed by linguistics, things attain to existence only in so far as they are able to form the elements of a signifying system." This is a "naked" or pure language, safe from the anthropologism that has haunted modernity, indeed, a language that perhaps restores the long-lost purity of representation in order "to articulate itself on the pure forms of knowledge."[56] Such expressions of purity and unity structure the ambiguity of "the present, and perhaps the future" that "contemporary culture is struggling to create."[57] They are the products of this culture, yet they are utterly external to it.

Here the army of figures of transparency that Foucault has developed throughout the book comes to play an important role in the imagery he offers for *two* understandings of knowledge and "our" relationship to it.

First, we find Foucault foregrounding, as in the passages above, figures that manage the exit from the "anthropological sleep."[58] He pushes against the anthropological dominance of the Modern Age, listing options before casting his pursuit as a countergesture to this dominance:

whether it is a matter of crossing the anthropological field, tearing ourselves free from it with the help of what it expresses, and rediscovering a purified ontology or a radical thought of being; or whether, rejecting not only psychologism and historicism, but all concrete forms of the anthropological prejudice, we attempt to question afresh the limits of thought, and to renew contact in this way with the project for a general critique of reason.[59]

In either direction, the figures that Foucault marshals work toward this image of a mastery of the exit from anthropology. With them, the idea that transparency is an *illusory self-sufficiency* of this anthropology comes front and center. Nowhere is this clearer than when Foucault raises the specter of transparency as an axis linking man and the cogito, *both* of which he now wishes to discard: "Man cannot posit himself in the immediate and sovereign transparency of a *cogito*."[60] This emphatically negative statement obviously targets Descartes, Husserl, and Sartre as philosophers who retained a self, and to this extent it is a critique of the philosophical endeavor itself. More important, as since Canguilhem the transparency of the Cartesian cogito was often the target of criticism, Foucault was now able to go a step further and target not only the cogito but Man.[61] (Canguilhem recognized the difference between his earlier position and Foucault's, and captured it in the title of his review of the book: "The Death of Man, or Exhaustion of the Cogito?")[62] Getting rid of both man and the cogito could restructure the anthropological field, and perhaps posit of knowledge and experience very differently. Antihumanism thus pushes at doors that are already ajar, but the exit they lead to promises an end to the transparentist anthropology; and at times Foucault presents this process in nearly liberatory or voluntarist colors. The great, tense promise of our times is that we may actively overcome the distortion that hides in the conglomerate of knowledge amassed by the human sciences.

Along with this set of figures, which present transparency and anthropologism as a modern illusion, there is a second set. To read Foucault carefully is to parse the different strands of his account, and hence to consider his strong ambivalence toward the passage out of modernity. In this second set, *a certain* transparency is precisely what can be expected in the future, yet it cannot be captured by Man, by the subject, or by "our contemporary culture": it is unthinkable, perilous, self-contained and detached, truly other. This perhaps pure otherness is achieved in two poles of "our culture": literature à la Antonin Artaud and Raymond Roussel, which is "language stripped naked"; and formal languages, especially mathematics and logic.[63] The latter, newly evolved, "open up the possibility, and the task, of purifying the old empirical reason by constituting formal languages." It is this purity, this form (which is not, he insists, a formalism) that, being so different from modern *epistēmē*, guarantee what Foucault envisions as a truly new order of knowledge. It does so by virtue of arising from the current order of knowledge, which "still serves as the positive ground of our knowledge,"[64] and of showing "our" inability to think outside of the modern *epistēmē*: "we" remain to wallow within the space of the "Last Man," while this new order develops as a very nearly absolute other.

What occurred at the time of Ricardo, Cuvier, and Bopp, the form of knowledge that was established with the appearance of economics, biology, and philology, the thought of finitude laid down by the Kantian critique as philosophy's task—all that still forms the immediate space of our reflection. We think in that area.[65]

Sans man, knowledge can acquire a new purity. Yet "we" *only* "think in that area," and "our reflection" remains within the distortive immanence of the human sciences. Or, as in a difficult passage that equates the Nietzschean death of God with this new death of man:

Rather than the death of God—or, rather, in the wake of that death and in a pro-found correlation with it—what Nietzsche's thought heralds is the end of his mur-derer; it is the explosion of man's face in laughter, and the return of masks; it is the scattering of the profound stream of time by which he felt himself carried along and whose pressure he suspected in the very being of things; it is the identity of the Return of the Same with the absolute dispersion of man.[66]

Two features of this passage startle: "the return of masks"; and "the iden-tity of the Return of the Same with the absolute dispersion of man." In both cases, transparency of representation remains unavailable; "this peril-ous imminence whose promise we fear today, whose danger we welcome"[67] is experienced as our folding back into the immanence of the human sci-ences in a "return of masks" and in the "Return of the Same," which will not go away while the new, perhaps transparent order of things lurks be-yond the horizon of human thought.

Thus, whereas in the earlier strand of figures of transparency it was possible to seize this shift and to shed both transparency and Man, in the second strand transparency belongs to the future order of knowledge and transparency is precisely what is unthinkable, what we fail to approximate as we find ourselves amid the masks and the Same. Thus the future order opening out of formal languages is not a return to the classical period; "it is not the irruptive discovery of some long-buried evidence; it does not in-dicate a folding back of thought upon itself," in which the transparency of language and representation were a given.[68]

From this perspective we might sample the concluding questions of Foucault's argument less as announcements of the dispersion of the human (which is the obvious stylistic thrust of the passage) than as ambiguities imposed by the new "unity" of language. This language mirrors that of classical, transparent representation, except that it is utterly unavailable to "us":

> If *this same language is now emerging with greater and greater insistence in a unity that we ought to think but cannot as yet do so,* is this not the sign that the whole of this configuration is now about to topple, and that man is in the process of perishing *as the being of language continues to shine ever brighter upon our horizon?* Since man was constituted at a time when language was doomed to dispersion, will he not be dispersed when language regains its unity? And if that were true, *would it not be an error—a profound error, since it could hide from us what should now be thought—to interpret our actual experience as an application of the forms of language to the human order?*[69]

The last question in this passage marks an absolute break: the "death of man" is not an overcoming but a decisive loss of the human—and of "us"— in a bifurcated present that stares in fear at the near future.

We might then conclude by emphasizing the profound ambiguity that cuts across the book's famous conclusion. On one possible interpretation, the "modern" age is over, human sciences have run their course, and it only remains to understand the present as nothing but a break with modernity. *The Order of Things* aims to effect (or complete) this break. But there is also a second interpretation, in which the present is locked within modernity and participates in its movement of self-critique while prophesying its undoing. Here *The Order of Things* plays a diagnostic role, not a performative one: it facilitates the transformation but declines to envisage the shape of the new order of things. In *The Philosophical Discourse of Modernity*, Jürgen Habermas scoffs at the fact that Foucault accorded his method and his conception of discourse a "unique transparency";[70] here, on the contrary, this discourse seems striated by the very concepts that participate in its mutation. Thus interpreting the place of the present moment in Foucault depends on this ambiguity, this tension, this bifurcation. According to the first thrust, the death of Man can be celebrated, the future is almost within grasp, distortion and transparency are being overcome. According to the second, this future knowledge has no exterior and no substratum, it captures everything, not merely what it itself makes possible; and yet this can only be experienced in terms of a threat from the perspective of the present time. "We"—this almost sovereign "we" that Foucault so obsessively contrasts with Man—stand paradoxically as both the herald of the new impossible age and the residuum that cannot find itself in its dangerous future transparency.

The next chapter will engage a similar concern with the status of knowledge and language: one that comes from Jacques Derrida and questions the place of cybernetics. This thread continues in the late 1970s with Jean-François Lyotard, who will question the status of information. Despite substantial differences, all these accounts converge and delimit a common problematic.

Cybernetic Complexity

Prehistory, Biology, and Derrida's Program for Liberation

In earlier chapters I discuss Derrida's critique of transparency as he teased it out of the work of Lévi-Strauss and Foucault. To show the consequences of this critique, the current chapter bridges two of the central themes of Derrida's *De la grammatologie* (1967; *Of Grammatology*): its promise of a "liberation" of the *trace*, and its treatment of then recent languages of communication (i.e., cybernetics and information theory) that claimed fundamental, even universal language status. Cybernetics, both directly and through its influence on biology and paleontology, posed a series of problems for the grammar of philosophy in the 1960s, notably for the grain of history, the relationship between philosophy and the sciences, and the shift from transparency to complexity. By positioning philosophy vis-à-vis biology and cybernetics, indeed, by taking up cybernetics and seeking to "liberate" its program, *Of Grammatology* radicalized the broad histories and languages for the human proposed by biological and paleontological theories based on cybernetics and thereby superseded the often technophobic reaction to scientific determinism exhibited since Friedmann and Canguilhem. It also displaced Hegelian and Heideggerian formulations of history, Derrida tending instead to rearticulate the form of history by proposing a dynamic and hyperdeterminist complexity that cybernetics had not "yet" achieved.

To give a sense of these developments, I trace part of the emergence of cybernetics in France in the 1950s and situate Derrida's reading of André

Leroi-Gourhan's *Le Geste et la parole* (1964–65; *Gesture and Speech*) amid the main claims of *Of Grammatology*.[1] Derrida's highly critical interpretation of François Jacob's *La Logique du vivant: Une histoire de l'hérédité* (1970; *The Logic of Life: A History of Heredity*) in his 1975 seminar at the École normale supérieure similarly serves to highlight how he reworked concepts common in the world of cybernetics, information, and DNA. For Leroi-Gourhan, *Gesture and Speech* involved a significant turn away from his earlier conception of techniques and norms toward a cybernetically inflected approach to the emergence of tools and language in the development of the entire genus *Homo*. François Jacob's towering place in biology and in its history in France helped establish the import of information, communication, and cybernetics in ushering in the DNA paradigm (on whose basis Jacob himself built his model of the operon). Meanwhile cybernetic models proved valuable to structuralism, from Lévi-Strauss and Lacan to the *Cahiers pour l'analyse*, because they occupied a place analogous to that of language or structure—to what Foucault had invested in as "formal languages." Nevertheless in Leroi-Gourhan, and especially in Jacob, such models meant far more. They were the ciphers of all possible meaning in the life and history of the species and they structured the interaction of human beings with information at every level. Vis-à-vis the language of "program," "code," "flow," "feedback" and so on, Derrida's *différance* enacted a conceptual reworking that did not hold back from the deterministic character of cybernetics but integrated and intensified it for the benefit of a philosophy of history and a "history of life."[2]

The Birth of the Cybernetic Idiom and Its Value in French Biology

Cybernetics and information theory were largely imported into France in the early 1950s; because of their shared language and their relevance to the electronic revolution, the two were perceived as joint American imports and not often distinguished.[3] Norbert Wiener's *Cybernetics, or Control and Communication in the Animal and the Machine* (1948) was actually first published in English in Paris by Hermann & Cie just prior to its more famous publication by John Wiley in New York (see fig. 19.1). His 1950 *The Human Use of Human Beings* was also quickly translated, as *Cybernétique et société*, in 1952.[4]

ACTUALITÉS SCIENTIFIQUES ET INDUSTRIELLES

1053

CYBERNETICS

OR

CONTROL AND COMMUNICATION

IN THE ANIMAL AND THE MACHINE

BY

NORBERT WIENER

Professor of Mathematics at the Massachusetts Institute
of Technology
Guest Investigator at the Instituto Nacional de Cardiología
de México.

PARIS

HERMANN & Cie, ÉDITEURS

6, Rue de la Sorbonne, 6

THE TECHNOLOGY PRESS   JOHN WILEY & Sons. Inc.

Cambridge, Mass.   440 Fourth Av., New York

1948

FIGURE 19.1 Cover of the first edition of Norbert Wiener's *Cybernetics* (Paris: Hermann & Cie, 1948).
Photo by the author.

Wiener's reception in France was quite enthusiastic. He was ranked above Claude E. Shannon, Ross Ashby, Heinz von Foerster, or Warren McCulloch, and information theory and cybernetics entered the French lexicon more or less under his aegis. They transformed the understanding of communication in the relevant sciences and beyond.[5] As early as 1951, Louis de Broglie, in his capacity as permanent secretary of the Académie des sciences, introduced a 1950 conference on cybernetics by defining it as:

the science of the relations, regulations, and transmission of information. Precisely because this definition is a bit vague, the domain of its application appears today to be very extensive: cybernetics is of great importance not only for all questions concerning telecommunications, nor only for all the problems concerning regulatory apparatuses and the servomechanisms that arise more or less directly from them. Sciences as diverse as biology, psychology, psychopathology, and even sociology and political economy can use its conceptions and its methods.[6]

In the mid-1950s, cybernetics was a subject of broad discussion in philosophy and social science. As has been argued, it contributed fundamentally to structuralist thought, particularly in the case of Lévi-Strauss, but also those of Lacan, Jakobson, Barthes, and others.[7] Raymond Ruyer, in his 1954 *La Cybernétique et l'origine de l'information*, felt comfortable enough to begin with a definition of cybernetics ("from the Greek word for 'governing,' a science of information machines, whether natural or artificial")— and to outline a transnational history with parallels between American interdisciplinary work and "analogous" encounters in France.[8] A year later, Canguilhem issued an aggressive, somewhat rushed critique of the expansion of cybernetics into social and political philosophy.[9] By the early 1960s, one could expect solid knowledge of the major concepts of cybernetics and information theory among scientifically minded philosophers. Terms such as feedback loop, closed system, flow, operational sequence, and *dispositif* entered the lexicon of philosophy alongside those of computing and biology. In 1962, the *Revue philosophique de la France et de l'étranger* featured work on the new discipline; two years later, the Colloques de Royaumont organized a conference devoted to cybernetics, then published its proceedings. The conference featured Wiener himself as keynote speaker, shortly before his death. Introducing him was the philosopher Gilbert Simondon, whose two theses on individuation and technics were profoundly affected by cybernetic thought.[10] In the late 1960s, when Wiener was effectively canonized among twentieth-century thinkers,[11] cybernetic models permeated the work of some of Althusser's students in the *Cahiers pour l'analyse*. Jean-François Lyotard's *La Condition postmoderne: Rapport sur le savoir* (1979; *The Postmodern Condition: A Report on Knowledge*) found cybernetics and information theory to be vital to the emergence of the postmodern dynamic. But in what follows I will look at Leroi-Gourhan and Jacob first, and then move on to Derrida.

André Leroi-Gourhan

Shortly after World War II, André Leroi-Gourhan moved from ethnology to prehistory and paleontology and became profoundly invested in rethinking the purpose of anthropology. In *L'Homme et la matière* and *Milieu et techniques*, the two volumes he published in 1943–45, he had set out to demonstrate that technical objects are the fundamental medium of human ethnic groups and their world, and hence an exemplary index of ethnic particularities and criterion for comparisons.[12] Because the body itself is technically mediated,[13] because different ethnic groups handle different (or even highly similar) objects in different ways, because, finally, such groups manage their natural and social environments only through their tools and the ways they handle these tools, technical activity was the fount of all social activity and individuation. By 1962, when Leroi-Gourhan joined the chorus pronouncing ethnology the only true source of humanism, he further proclaimed that prehistoric ethnography had demonstrated that the only major transformation of humanity since the appearance of *Homo sapiens* concerned the experience of distance, the complication of "technique" and technology, and the use of the human body, all of which had happened over the preceding century.[14] The present time was characterized by the technological exteriorization of the nervous system, the elimination of distances, and an increasingly complex entanglement of individuals within societies.[15] However, "the creation of ethnic values is an attainment particular to *Homo sapiens*, [and] one that we are in the process of losing"; and the following two centuries, he prophesied, would be experienced as very difficult.[16] After that, the path of "conscious humanization" would ease, provided that a "vital space" was preserved that would be the province of ethnological historization.[17]

Le Geste et la parole (*Gesture and Speech*), which appeared in two volumes in 1964–66, embedded this sensitivity to the contemporary disappearance of human complexity in a cybernetic account of the origin of humanity. Leroi-Gourhan again began by situating prehistory and paleontology, which he contrasted with evolutionary biology. In his view, rather than inaugurating the twentieth century, Darwinism had completed Buffon's eighteenth-century project.[18] The thread "from ape to man" that Darwinism had popularized was highly problematic, and paleontology had finally bypassed the pithecanthropoid paradigm—"the monkey problem," which had handcuffed it to racist theories and a "hard," undifferentiated concept of "man."[19] Thanks to discoveries that were recent in the mid-1960s, the criteria for humanity adopted in paleontology and ethnology were distinctly postevolutionary.[20] These disciplines still assumed evolution but placed humans on a very different footing. Definitive among the new criteria was early humans' attainment of erect posture, which accounted for two more achievements: a new relationship between the cranial cavity and the neck, which shortened the face and allowed certain parts of the brain to grow; and the structural transformation of the hands from instruments of movement into instruments for the use of tools. Leroi-Gourhan called these two developments "liberations" on which hominization depended. The liberation of the hands caused technical innovations that, step by step, made possible non-motor and non-goal-based movements and actions; the liberation of the brain had totally overriden *Homo sapiens*'s mammalian heritage and produced language, new kinds of social organisms, ethnic communities and values, and a singular level of activity and complexity.

Two moments in the hominization process are particularly relevant to our theme: the emergence of writing and the development of complex tools. The two are coextensive, perhaps they even constitute a unit. Language appeared around the same time as complex tools (as opposed to the basic ones gradually "exuded" by "human brains and their bodies").[21] "Before writing, the hand was used principally for making things and the face for language,"[22] but complex tools were intimately related to language and demonstrated the formation of a "reflective intelligence," that is, the brain's initiation of a social rather than merely biological program.[23] Like tools, language was in hominids a matter of "neuromotor organization and the quality of cerebral projections" and, already with Neanderthals, symbolization was identified with "thought . . . being applied to areas beyond that of purely vital technical motor function."[24] In the beginning, language "would have been composed of already available and not totally determined symbols"[25]—the crucial point being that these symbols were "not totally determined." In structuralist terminology, this meant they were still fully biologically conditioned rather than arbitrary. The decisive break with the biological world came about[26] once linguistic signs were found to be arbitrary and "determined" in this social world and as particular tools mediating bodily engagement with the environment also became less biologically conditioned. Tools and language came to condition the suprabiological, social world that regulated human groups and their relation to nature, especially after the invention of writing.

As Leroi-Gourhan moved into a closer study of language, technics, and human economy, his own terminology became decisively cybernetic. He had already urged that the relation between society and technics be thought of, not in terms of one-directional causation from the former to the latter, but "as a *two-way flow* springing initially from the world of matter";[27] and for this he had proposed a "concept of operating sequences."[28] Now, discussing the different forms of individual and social memory that underpin the establishment of society, he used terms such as "human operational behavior,"[29] "operational memory,"[30] "human technical behavior,"[31] and "the mechanical operational sequences"[32] that "form the basis of individual behavior."[33] As tools grew in complexity, they became "operating programs,"[34] and the liberation of the hand from direct motor function facilitated a "program" in which particular gestures could be understood.[35] In tracing the development from early human history to the present, Leroi-Gourhan emphasized the exteriorization of memory, which he characterized as a program that defines humanity's spread over the natural world. Crucially for the cybernetic prioritization of technics and writing, this program, which is coextensive with the expansion of society, "consumes" the human.

The human internal economy, however, was still that of a highly predatory mammal even after the transition to farming and stockbreeding. From that point on the collective organism's preponderance became more and more imperative, and human beings became the instrument of a technical and economic ascent to which they lent their brains and hands. In this way human society became the chief consumer of humans, through violence or through work, with the result that the human gradually gained complete possession of the natural world. If we project the technical and economic terms of today into the future, we see the process ending in total victory, with the last small oil deposit being emptied for the purpose of cooking the last handful of grass to accompany the last rat. The prospect is not so much a utopia as the acknowledgment of the singular properties of the human economy, an economy of which nothing as yet suggests that it may one day be properly controllable by the zoological (i.e., intelligent) human.[36]

The arrangement that Leroi-Gourhan diagnosed here—that society and human economy in principle eliminate individuality for their own benefit—made problematic the possibility of changes in the human, unless the biological–technical factors that determined it (posture, use of hands and teeth, etc.) were to be controlled.[37] Thanks to contemporary transformations, humanity was in the process of losing some of its particularities, notably ethnic ones.[38] The homogenization effected by the West threatened to destroy the entire brain-based edifice that replaced the biological and thus to reduce to a technologically mediated neo-biology differences in the social sphere. Humanity was in the process of dehumanizing itself through "rebiologization."[39]

The reason for Leroi-Gourhan's interest in cybernetics should be fairly clear. As he turned the project of comparing technical and social behavior in his 1943–45 works *L'Homme et la matière* and *Milieu et techniques* into a program that accounted for hominization, technics, writing, and human history, cybernetics gave him an opportunity to upgrade the claim that technical activity was the source of all social activity and individuation. Mauss's approach to techniques of the body did not offer a suitable language for the human–environmental interactions Leroi-Gourhan was analyzing, and especially not for his effort to present technical objects as regulatory feedback devices in the human economy. Cybernetics also allowed for human "history" to be understood beyond the limitations of Darwinism and to be placed under a dynamic model. It helped Leroi-Gourhan theorize tools as a kind of symbolic third, similar to language in Lévi-Strauss's schema: as a hinge between the natural and the empirical that would ground both biological universality and the particularism of social activity. The cybernetic idiom permitted him to slide from speaking of techniques of the body to speaking of programs, codes, and "technical behavior" that affected not only tools and techniques but indeed the regulation of all processes, even at the physiological level, by societies. And in this "language" he could show, for example, how cultural differences of the ethnic variety structured human societies, how their loss hardened and rigidified the entire system.[40]

Dance of the Chromosomes:
François Jacob's History and Theory of Life

The fact that Leroi-Gourhan accentuated the separation of the genus *Homo* from evolution in general can be partly explained by suspicion about the hermeneutic value of Darwinian evolution—an attitude that persisted in postwar France. It was not that non-evolutionary biological models were preferred, or that natural selection was rejected.[41] Rather, evolutionary models were deemed insufficient for a proper account of the genesis of the complex body, let alone consciousness or individuality. Given its close proximity to racism, the scientism of evolutionary theory was also especially threatening to ethnologists like Lévi-Strauss.

Things changed rapidly in the 1960s. By 1962, information theory and cybernetics had prompted a *philosophical* justification for, and a return to, genetic biology, evolutionary biology, and neurophysiology, and the language of cybernetics was quickly naturalized across these fields.[42] In 1965, François Jacob, Jacques Monod, and André Lwoff won the Nobel Prize for their work on protein synthesis and viral contagion and became intellectual stars overnight. Other French scientists, such as the population geneticist Philippe L'Héritier and the neurophysiologist Alfred Fessard, were also achieving international renown.

This spearheaded the shift back to an evolutionary scheme based on the neo-Darwinian modern synthesis, along with a new ordering of the sciences and a new history of humanity and knowledge. Not only did the "central dogma" of molecular biology—one gene, one enzyme—thrive in the domestic intellectual landscape and provide a concrete explanation for the origin and development of life; it also forcefully undermined the antideterminist animus of philosophies like Canguilhem's[43] and posed a significant threat to Hegelian thought, much more emphatically than paleontology was doing. By 1966, Canguilhem, too, would write about DNA as causing a definitive shift both in the structure and in the language of knowledge: "message, information, program, code, instruction, decoding, such are the new concepts of the knowledge of life," he proclaimed.[44] Throughout the later 1960s, Jacob was particularly visible on the intellectual scene.[45] The history of biology he produced in 1970 under the title *The Logic of Life* established the DNA paradigm as a "book of life"; he used there concepts generated in the course of his work on the lac operon model and presented them as foundational for the syntax of biology—and for its history as well.

> Heredity is described today in terms of information, messages, and code. The reproduction of an organism has become that of its constituent molecules . . . what are transmitted from generation to generation are the "instructions" specifying the molecular structures: the architectural plans of the future organism. . . . The organism thus becomes the realization of a program prescribed by its heredity. The intention of a psyche has been replaced by the translation of a message. . . . With the application to heredity of the concept of program, certain biological contradictions formerly summed up in a series of antitheses at last disappear: finality and mechanism, necessity and contingency, stability and variation. The concept of program blends two notions which had always been intuitively associated with living beings: memory and design.[46]

Jacob's *The Logic of Life* thus employs a cybernetic lexicon to reinterpret biological and human history—including the history of modern knowledge, which had wandered from synthesis to synthesis until protein synthesis completed and integrated past ones.[47] "Biologists no longer study life," Jacob writes, but rather "the algorithms of the living world."[48] The objects of biology, "living systems, their function, their history,"[49] are "systems of systems"[50] modeled on the requirements of war and industry, which "drive physics and technology."[51] Moreover, as "the genetic code is almost completely known today,"[52] it still remains to study the interaction among different programs and between them and their milieux.[53] If nature is a matter of complexity, organization, and integration,[54] it is perhaps not surprising that the central metaphor to which Jacob arrives is one of crystallization:

> Many of the forms we admire in cells exhibit the same properties as crystals. Crystallization implies a union of like units, a geometry strictly ordered by the forces which arrange and unite identical molecules. Whether particles, layers, fibers or tubules, most structures seen under the microscope show these characteristics . . . the construction of these organelles does not require any mysterious principle, any force unknown to physics, any factor not contained in the structure of the constituents themselves . . . between the living and the inorganic world there is a difference not in nature, but in complexity.[55]

To put things in a Hegelian perspective: a triumphalist work that concludes with its author's achievement of absolute knowledge, *The Logic of Life* was both a theory of life and a history of organization, integration, and knowledge. It was the *Phenomenology of Spirit* of the DNA age.

Jacques Derrida

As already suggested, mistrust in transparency was central to Derrida's deconstruction, his refusal of self-identity and his signal concepts, from *différance* through spacing to auto-immunity. That Derrida found transparency highly problematic is evident from his extensive critique of the transparent community "imagined" by Lévi-Strauss among the Nambikwara and, just as significantly, from his identification of transparency with logocentric beliefs in a transcendental signified—a pure truth residing in unmediated speech. Derrida used the term "transparency" when referring to the (false) hopes of transparent relations *before* or *outside* language that have been or must now be abandoned.[56] Just as philosophically unsustainable, for Derrida, were Cartesian and Rousseauean erasures of mediation and conceptions of the self as pure and transparent. In the opening of the "Introduction to the Age of Rousseau," while discussing the transparent cogito, Derrida decried it along with trust in "the transparence of self-relationship and the purity of auto-affection."[57] Further references to transparency appeared at crucial points of the argument—for example, where Derrida presents the trace as an "absolute origin of sense" in order to show that no ontological, anthropological, or other logocentric claim can be established that would be prior or external to the general sense of writing he promotes:

The trace is the *différance* which opens appearance and signification. Articulating the living upon the nonliving in general, origin of all repetition, origin of ideality, the trace is not more ideal than real, not more intelligible than sensible, *not more a transparent signification than an opaque energy* and no concept of metaphysics can describe it.[58]

Transparency reappears in a heading ("Algebra: Arcanum and Transparence") in Derrida's critical discussion of the dream of a universal, perfectly clear language proposed by Descartes and pursued by Leibniz.

Of course, in 1967, when *Of Grammatology* appeared, the dismissal of transparent signification came as no surprise to readers of Saussure and of the structuralists, nor of Hegel and of Hegelians of the 1950s. Putting trace and *différance* before all sense, all time, and all metaphysical systems had the effect of ruining epistemological, ethical, and political fantasies of transparency. But *how* this alternative to transparency was to be understood was a more complex question, and Derrida's use and critique of cybernetics (which he thought did not go far enough) are essential to understanding the dynamic complexity that he counterproposes, the meaning and force of the claim that the trace is not a mere intermediary, that it precedes and founds the very possibility of mediation. Alongside the usual suspects who influenced Derrida's invention of *différance*, cybernetics and Leroi-Gourhan clearly inspired its "liberation."

Derrida's support for cybernetics' dominion over communication is affirmative, even fervent. Early on in *Of Grammatology*, in an oft-cited but rarely contextualized passage, he wrote:

If the theory of cybernetics is by itself to oust all metaphysical concepts—including the concepts of soul, of life, of value, of choice, of memory—which until recently served to separate the machine from man, it must conserve the notion of writing, trace, *grammē*, or grapheme, until its own historico-metaphysical character is also exposed. Even before being determined as human . . . or nonhuman, the *grammē*—or the *grapheme*—would thus name the element.[59]

Similarly, when expanding the notion of writing beyond "linear" and phonetic writing systems to "all that gives rise to an inscription in general," Derrida notes:

It is also in this sense that the contemporary biologist speaks of writing and program in relation to the most elementary processes of information within the living cell. And, finally, whether it has essential limits or not, the entire field covered by the cybernetic program will be the field of writing.[60]

Cybernetics thus appears allied to the grammatological endeavor; it poses none of the usual problems of logocentrism and promises to go much further than Husserlian phenomenology could—"far beyond the possibilities of the 'intentional consciousness.'"[61] Moreover, the program ("pro-gram") it carries is prior to any humanist conception of life, soul, or difference between animal, human, and machine:

the development of the practical methods of information retrieval extends the possibilities of the "message" vastly, to the point where it is no longer the "written" translation of a language. . . . This development, coupled with that of anthropology and of the history of writing, teaches us that phonetic writing, the medium of the great metaphysical, scientific, technical, and economic adventure of the West, is limited in space and time and limits itself even as it is in the process of imposing its laws upon the cultural areas that had escaped it. But this nonfortuitous conjunction of cybernetics and the "human sciences" of writing leads to a more profound reversal.[62]

As Edward Baring notes apropos the dash in "pro-gram": "*Différance* preceded and constituted Man, and a genetic 'pro-gram' was more fundamental than any distinction between Man and beast, uniting all forms of 'life' from the amoeba to the new electronic programs of a cybernetic world."[63] The biological reference is no throwaway: Derrida noted that the notion of the trace "seems currently to be dominant and irreducible"—"in Nietzschean or Freudian discourse . . . [as] in all scientific fields, notably in biology."[64] What's to gain from attaching cybernetics to grammatology? A first hint appears in the book's "Exergue" where Derrida claims that "[b]y alluding to a science of writing reined in by metaphor, metaphysics, and theology, this exergue must ... announce that the science of writing—*grammatology*—shows signs of liberation all over the world, as a result of decisive efforts."[65]

This liberation of the science of writing—an "intrascientific and epistemological" liberation[66]—is directed against metaphysics and theology. We might recall Heidegger complaining, in "The End of Philosophy and the Task of Thinking," that cybernetics was ontologically and politically suspect.[67] By contrast, Derrida's phrasing of "signs of liberation" owes an underappreciated debt to cybernetics, whose blows to metaphysics he praised and which could be said, much more justifiably than structuralism (which remained a logocentrism), to show grammatology's signs of "worldwide liberation." The word "liberation" itself refers specifically to Leroi-Gourhan, for whom the liberation of hand and brain were essential to humanization, albeit not without a profound deformation of the human. When Derrida proposed a liberation of the science of writing—that is, of the trace and of *différance*—he was well aware of Leroi-Gourhan's doubt, because he repeats Leroi-Gourhan's passage, in all its contentiousness but without criticizing it, in an endnote.[68] He was equally aware of the importance that "liberation" had for Leroi-Gourhan in the context of the emergence of writing; for he credits Leroi-Gourhan with a theory of the "liberation"—or exteriorization—of memory, which he clearly contrasted, and preferred, to Lévi-Strauss's view that the invention of writing was a form of enslavement: "What is going to be called *enslavement* [by Lévi-Strauss] can equally legitimately be called *liberation*."[69] Leroi-Gourhan had proposed both the "linearization" of writing—its rise as a derivative of speech—and the notion that writing, naming, and an ethnic group's self-definition were a precondition to any mode of designating the human.[70] Derrida objected to Leroi-Gourhan's belief that written language represented the triumph of linear and phonetic writing and to his worry that a technicist and teleological language (such as that of cybernetics) becomes "difficult . . . essentially impossible" to avoid.[71] But this was not at all a rejection of cybernetics: insofar as, for Derrida, cybernetics has not yet seen "its historico-metaphysical character exposed,"[72] Leroi-Gourhan's unwillingness to find any openings apart from that occasioned by linear writing left room to pursue a "liberation" premised on cybernetic thought and its overcoming of linearity.

"The end of linear writing is indeed the end of the book," Derrida commented on Leroi-Gourhan,[73] echoing his own "program" for the end of the book.[74] Here the radicalism of the grammatological endeavor becomes clearest. The limits that worried Leroi-Gourhan open instead a new "liberation," akin to those of hand and brain: that of nonlinear writing and, with it, the overcoming of the human and science into "pluridimensionality" and into "a delinearized temporality" that will benefit "human" life as well.[75]

Cybernetics—like dialectics and structural linguistics—ended up being partly displaced and subordinated to the argument. But my principal concern is that Derrida granted himself sufficient leeway to propose in *Of Grammatology* that *différance*, which one year later he would subsume "under the privileged heading of Hegelianism,"[76] be understood as a kind of regulatory device that produced dynamic complexity. The problem with the (still metaphysical) cybernetic theory and its anthropological applications was that it was too rigid and fell back on a static, self-enclosed, circuit-like system; it retained a humanist element that forbade the self-deployment of the program in an "exorbitant" fashion. *Différance* stands against the denaturing of humans predicted by Leroi-Gourhan insofar as it is inscribed before and into life—including individual life, spacing, temporality, but it also makes possible the pluridimensionality and delinearized temporality that the era of phonetic writing has long suppressed. Cybernetics had found an opening beyond phonetic writing by providing a language devoid of logos and aspirations to transparent human communication. But only once it was liberated into an exorbitant dynamic could it fulfill the creative differential movement it promised.

Derrida and the Text of Biology

Derrida's 1975 seminar *La Vie la mort* (Life Death), better known for its long interpretation of Freud's *Beyond the Pleasure Principle* (subsequently published in *The Post-Card*),[77] includes two lectures, the fourth and the fifth, that propose a detailed reading of Jacob's *The Logic of Life*, beginning with Jacob's understanding of heredity in cybernetic terms.

Derrida's interpretation of genetics hinges on Jacob's description of the DNA and of life *as a text*.[78] Focusing on Jacob's refusal to see life as independent of the language of communication and cybernetics, Derrida turns the primacy of the text into a basis for understanding the relationship of the models of biology to life.[79] On this basis, he proposes a series of interpretations: of the structure of Jacob's "very dialectical, Hegelian" text;[80] of the purpose and limits of biology; and of the concepts central to Jacob's articulation of life as *self*-reproducibility. Three gestures in particular matter in the present context.

First gesture: just as, in *Of Grammatology*, he refused to see information, message, and text in terms of mere mediation or model, here too Derrida objects to Jacob's understanding of information, programs, and regulation in these terms. The priority and complexity of the text precludes its reduction to a model, and Derrida, again radicalizing the symbolic third that hinges and unhinges nature and culture, universal and particular, presents the idea of a model of life as highly problematic.

If the object, the referent of a scientific text (and science itself is a text); if the object of a scientific discourse (and science itself is a discourse); if such an object and such a referent are no longer meta-textual or meta-discursive realities; if their very reality has an analogous structure or a basically homogeneous structure to the structure of scientific textuality; if the object (the living being i.e. reproducibility), the model and the scientific subjectivity (the knowing subject, etc.) have an analogous structure, namely that of the text, one can no longer speak of [knowing] subject, of [known] object and of analogical model. . . . The text is not a third term in the relationship between the biologist and the living being: it is the structure itself of the living being qua common structure between the biologist—qua living being—the science qua production of life, and the living being itself.[81]

By deprioritizing the self-sufficiency of models, Derrida gives himself room to attend to what Jacob calls accidents, mutations, and supplements—which correlate with his own "logic of the supplement" ("I do not impose this

word ['supplement'] on Jacob, he returned to it himself several times")[82]—
proposing that they be interpreted less as distortions and more as elements
that build on one another and transform the place and form of life through
supplementation. In an effort to stand against the new determinism of molecular biology, to refuse the mechanistic singularity of a genetic model that
would be the simple, direct, only cause for *every* biological effect, Derrida
suggests that this determinism *does not go far enough*; and he reasserts the
hyperdeterminist force of the grammatological endeavor. The genetic logic
of life fails insofar as it fails to think through the supplement that also determines, the model that *also* structures, the living being who *always* falls under
differential determinations.

Second gesture: Derrida refuses to read *The Logic of Life* as extra-
philosophical,[83] both because of the place of biology among the life sciences and human sciences[84] and because of the philosophical character of
terms like model, sexuality, death, reproduction, and so on. In particular,
Derrida integrates Jacob's theory of self-reproduction in the context of the
Marxist discourse of production and, crucially, associates Jacob with none
other than Hegel.[85] Once again, a cybernetic historical form overwrites the
Hegelian one in order to obviate it.

This is central for a third gesture: Derrida's focus on Jacob's conception of integration, both at the level of cell biology and at the level of the
place of biology in the history of modern knowledge. The reference to
Hegel matters to the extent that it helps Derrida admonish Jacob for practicing a particular kind of essentialism when he uses concepts of integration and reproduction: according to Jacob, biological reproduction results
in "no change of essence."[86] In Derrida's view, Jacob did not reveal an essence behind appearances but rather an essence generated through integration and maintained through reproduction over generations, in spite of
the accumulation of mutations and slight transformations. Derrida's insistence on these themes as *supplements* is relevant to his effort to disrupt the
impression that "integration" would provide an altogether new language
for this biology. No less significantly, Jacob's interpretation of these "supplements" as accidents with no bearing on "the essence" results in a reduction of sexuality and death to errata—accidents not integral to the living
being.[87] In a way, the very mechanism of self-reproduction lost the system-
disturbing quality, the feedback, that is supposed to help it construct novelty: what is necessary for thinking this novelty is *différance* rather than a

(quasi-)Hegelian dialectics. The history that biology constructed, both for its knowledge and for its object—life—is too tied to a metaphysical conception of cybernetics.

Philosophy thus presented itself as a destabilization of integration: it is not that integration should be refused, but rather that it should be exposed in its insufficiency, with the help of the *différant* that already lay within it. Integration (whose political implications, dating from French policies in Algeria, was hardly lost on Derrida) tended to close off a system, to render it static and transparent. To outdo this limitation—especially in the framework of thirty years of obsessive "encoding" of life as genetics—Derrida proposed a hyperdeterministic complexity, which attempted to master and liberate the dynamism of those forces that short-circuit, undo, or change a system from the inside.

PART V

AFTER 1968

The Present Time and the Agent
of History before and after May 1968

Gilles Deleuze emphasized structuralism's moment through typography: "*This is 1967.*"[1] Once May 1968 had hit, the horizons of philosophy changed dramatically, and from where he stood in 1972, structuralism's "work in progress" had been interrupted. Indeed, for the philosophers I have engaged in recent chapters—Canguilhem, Foucault, Derrida, Lacan—their moment in 1967 seemed very different then from what it later would.

A fork, a relay, or a fissure had appeared in the present—and perhaps in time itself—whereby two very different temporal and historical horizons seemed possible for modernity, for "the human," for philosophy, for knowledge, even for society. In 1965–67, the contrast between these horizons was repeatedly described as a conflict between the future on offer and an *other* temporality that was perilous and exciting. This fissure had everything to do with the collapse of the imaginary of transparency, because it turned the present away from its anticipated humanist course of progress and general social improvement and toward a future that seemed better able to remedy the scars of the century by conceptualizing the information, language, and computing innovations that were rapidly changing the present time. Even a revolution could not constitute a major rupture with the future anticipated in modernity and humanism: some figures, for instance, Philippe Sollers, asserted that the only true economic and social revolution would be predicated on a "symbolic" one.[2] Without that, the future remained the same. Humanism still warranted the continuation of a way of life and paraded a deceptive belief in some experiential transparency in the name of "the human" and "progress," but the new alternative left all that behind. Any transparency that might arise would be essentially independent of human individuals: it required such a "symbolic" revolution or a decisive shift in the foundations of knowledge. It was the province of language and information and fell outside experience and human consciousness. Structuralism in particular gave a sense that the work of rethinking the past two centuries, combined with recent philosophical–anthropological revolutions, revealed the structures that underlie history and a shift such as that predicted by Leroi-Gourhan, Lacan, Foucault, or Derrida was possible.

Philosophers took for granted the failure of transparency on all fronts: in empirical and transcendental approaches to knowledge, in phenomenology, in heart-to-heart ethics, in dreams of community. They wrote as if they were preparing a new Enlightenment and looking at the present through a new lens, which could pull thought out of the homogenizing, destructive, shortsighted humanism of past centuries. Their tools were many and powerful: language, the order of information, the critique of norms, the castles of knowledge under reconstruction through cybernetics or anthropology, the appeal of heterogeneity and alterity, the unconscious codes and grids that are vital to the deployment of knowledge. They assembled an imaginary that demanded an urgent retheorization of time and presentness and pointed beyond the temporal limitations of humanism.

Meanwhile, criticisms of everyday life and of the political situation strengthened the disaffection of the French Left. By 1968, they had steered anti-capitalism into a narrative of resistance to state power. The all-too-real revolt of May '68 consigned the "structuralist" 1967 to the dustbin of history and altered profoundly the direction of French thought by pointing out anew an agent for historical action. The student–worker movement was the first and most general incarnation of this agent; in the ensuing years, it was replaced time and again, perhaps most famously by the Chinese proletariat, which French Maoists treated as the clearest expression of a new, revolutionary general will, capable of changing the structure of modern society. From the perspective of state–society tensions, May '68 was the timely, explosive manifestation of a frustration that had built over time and maneuvered the radicalization of Marxist thought into revolution. For those thinkers who associated themselves with post-1956 anti-capitalism, May '68 certainly marked the fulfillment, however temporary, of long-standing hopes. But the events of May created severe complications for the contemporary philosophers we have examined so far, deforming or even breaking apart their generally structuralist logics. The movement toward desubjectivation and release of human control over language, information, and communication came face to face with a concrete revolutionary agent that pursued "real" social transformation. May '68 cut across the conceptual web and changed the register from epistemological–ontological to political, installing antistatism and the treatment of power and ideology at the threshold of philosophical and political engagements, including with transparency.

Temporal Bifurcation

Virtually every philosophical system since Sartre's in 1943 put "the present time" on the agenda. But, rather than addressing it directly, most philosophers detoured via language, existence, dialectics, structure, and history. Merleau-Ponty sought alternatives to Husserl's "living present" and to Heidegger's "authentic temporality."[3] Vuillemin spoke of the "philosophical moment" in terms of a "neo-Ptolemaic revolution" that could enable properly human finitude and temporality. (Lacan instead laid claim to a "Copernican revolution" through his "return to Freud.")[4] Proudly "out of date," Lévi-Strauss decoupled himself from the present while denying history's epistemological value. By 1965, with the radicalization of a skepticism begun in earnest with existentialism, with the loosening of Hegelianism, and with the rebuttal of progress, the "present moment" became an explicitly temporal problem: from Leroi-Gourhan to Foucault, from Canguilhem to Derrida, from Lacan to Jacob, the same sequence of conflict emerges, as though philosophies intersected like meridians at the conceptual pole of "the present time." During the decade leading up to 1967, structural knowledge was equated with liberation. Human beings could not, in their current temporality, know or control the direction of their time, but codes and languages could.

More exactly, for these thinkers, the present pitted two historical and temporal narratives against each other: modernity and an "other" future. A closed, unchanging establishment had inculcated the sense that humanism meant elitism, technocracy, the application of science to human guinea pigs, the exclusion of those deemed abnormal, and so on; and it controlled most processes of emancipation and all universalism, allowing just enough change to ensure its continuation. The "other" future extended instead from the ciphers of a different present, a different force. Thus Leroi-Gourhan dreamt that a technological liberation from current humanity would arise from the recent exteriorization of memory—this surpassing of humanity would correspond in magnitude to the anthropogenetic liberation of hand and face that had taken place millions of years ago. François Jacob used the language of protein synthesis to devise a biological ontology that cast life in the language of information and control. Such a language was a source of agency that human beings still ignored at their own peril.

One originality of Lacan's call for psychoanalysis to become a radical theory[5] lay in its even more explicit sense of contemporary bifurcation. Toward the end of the 1950s, Lacan's thought turned in the direction of placing increasingly more weight on the father. The most significant aspect of this change, and also its motor, was Lacan's realization that alienation was not to be overcome but to be pursued and mastered. Being itself was split and non-transparent, hence not restorable to an authentic wholeness, as in Heidegger. Language and the unconscious were sites of a transparency unavailable to the ego.[6] The "repugnant" human sciences imagined they had found a "human essence." Theirs was "the very call of servitude," whereby psychology "provid[ed] services to the technocracy."[7] Only psychoanalysis could be a science of the split subject, reveal "the structure in which this identity [of the particular and the universal] is . . . disjunctive of the subject" and "relegate" the complete individual and the totalized community "to the status of mirages."[8]

A particular temporality followed from this analysis of the split subject. While Lévi-Strauss proclaimed himself the last Odysseus, one whose science "dissolves Man" and completes the course of the West—Lacan was promising that a new knowledge of the fragmented subject *was* possible. In psychoanalysis, speech and language founded a new therapeutics, premised on split and suture, alienation, abnormality, and anomy. The metahistory that Lacan offered (at times explicitly, at times not) for this thesis—which derived from Koyré and Canguilhem among others[9]—featured it as his eureka, against the background of a present oppressed by efficient scientism and the objectification of the human as cogito, object, and feigned whole. Lacan undertook to show, *in this present*, how internal alienations and language can attend to new and repressed forms of meaning and articulate a different subjectivity and sociality.[10] Just like the self, the present (1966 for *Écrits*) was split between a modern humanist tradition that discarded the neurotic and her truth, and a psychoanalysis that restored that truth.

Foucault's ambivalent conclusion in *The Order of Things* (1966) belongs in the same category. Against the continuing hegemony of the human sciences, Foucault's prognosis of an effacement of "Man" translated as a "perilous imminence whose promise we fear today, whose danger we welcome." In this "perilous immanence" Foucault heralded the return of a transparency that would be unintelligible to us but immanent to knowledge itself."[11] The dispersal of the human left the throne empty for a discursive transparency that generated new ways of speaking and knowing. If, for Leroi-Gourhan, the present time marked the exhaustion of the human and the beginning of a transformation of the species, for Foucault, the *now* of the powerful modern age, dominated as it was by the human sciences, could only be overcome in the future by a non-human system of language and knowledge.

Derrida, too, attempted to destabilize the present, particularly through his concept of *différance*. Both difference and deferral were inscribed in every trace: every trace signaled difference from other traces, creating both space and time in its inscription. Thus *différance*—both as the creation of form and as its "temporization"—preceded all identity. Breaking apart the sufficiency of presence in his critique of ontology, Derrida denied the concurrence of presence and present time. Furthermore, despite arguing that, of the current epoch, "we merely glimpse the closure. I do not say the end,"[12] he was quite open to the liberatory and dangerous future he thought might follow: "the science of writing—grammatology—shows signs of liberation all over the world," he asserted.[13] Although not certain, this "liberation" was at least "globally" signaled. It belonged not to "Man" but to a grammatical science that could effect a new knowledge, a new culture, new values and meaning.

it is a peculiarity of our epoch that, at the moment when the phoneticization of writing—the historical origin and structural possibility of philosophy as of science, the condition of the *epistémé*—begins to lay hold on world culture, science, in its advancements, can no longer be satisfied with it. This inadequation had always already begun to make its presence felt. But today something lets it appear as such, allows it a kind of takeover, without our being able to translate this novelty into clear cut notions of mutation, explicitation, accumulation, revolution, or tradition.

These values belong no doubt to the system whose dislocation is today presented as such, they describe the styles of an historical movement which was meaningful — like the concept of history itself—only within a logocentric epoch. . . .

. . . For that future world and for that within it which will have put into question the values of sign, word, and writing, for that which guides our future anterior, there is as yet no exergue.[14]

The present time indicated an opening out of the heavy burden of modernity: difference was inscribed within it, and a future based on it was at least imaginable—even if no preface for it existed "as yet."

For all the divergence between their pursuits, these philosophers expressed a new skepticism and a new attitude to modern history. They actively emptied today's leading epistemological and political economies (and even revolutionary hopes) of their meaning, and just as actively dissolved the humanist present so as to begin to ask about the human and knowledge in the future. This is what I propose to call the *narrative of a bifurcation of the "now."* In this narrative, ending transparency did not mean succumbing to opacity; it meant endorsing complexity and irreducibility, taking up a chance at the liberation of difference and self-division. The dismantling of transparency finally acquired a positive meaning: it meant engagement with the multiplication of this difference; a reign of code, from DNA to Derrida's *trace*, confronted with a non-sovereign humanity; a new relation to one's milieu, in which each was perforated and also built up by these codes; and an attitude of inclusion of others, particularly the repressed, at the expense of the "normal." If "battlefield of temporalities" serves as one metaphor for a struggle between competing options, "forking" or "bifurcation" of time might be another. One tine of the fork was weighed down by modernity. The other thrust toward radical and unpredictable transformation: a loss of the self compelled by forces beyond human control. The impossibility of self-identity *in time*—not only as an abstract idea but in the formerly smooth fabric and logic of reality—channeled all these conflicts, conjuring complexity and the supersession of humanity.[15]

A 1968 Effect

This supersession of modernity that was on the horizon evaporated with May '68. The structuralist advocacy of non-agential forms—linguistic, computational, or symbolic—that broke apart the present lost credibility and currency in the face of social struggle. This loss was in part due to the events of May themselves: they were collective political acts of men and women with an agency that was decisively political and social.

The authors discussed in recent chapters did not simply abandon their earlier arguments; May '68 and its aftermath did not produce a simple caesura. Besides, ideals of revolutionary transformation existed before. By 1965, Althusser and his students had begun their Maoist experiment and annexed their epistemological engagements to a "scientific" *and* revolutionary brand of Marxism. The events of May '68 gave a "live" demonstration of the logic of revolution and of the Marxist approach to history; and, by demanding that everything be overturned, students in particular also exploded anxieties about transparency, including social transparency, and set them in a different direction. The "spirit of May" was characterized by utopian neo-proletarian calls to undo all power relations and by the fantasy of a festival destined to overpower the society of work, commodities, and spectacle. Exponents famously expressed utter disdain for any structured and hierarchized society and mistrust in its capacity to evolve into an open, enlightened body; and this sentiment was mainly directed at the state as the leading agent and weapon of capitalism.

With May '68, transparency quickly became a problem of political thought. Some interpreters highlighted an anarchist–anomic agency, others a class-struggle trajectory in awe of Mao's Cultural Revolution. Virtually everyone treated the state as a repressive machine and insisted on society's need to be properly mirrored in its own management. Self-management (*autogestion*) in factories, rejection of governmental repression, and an aspiration to new norms inherent in society characterized this antistatist tendency.

These trends mined another imaginary of transparency detailed above. In chapters 8, 9, 10, and 12, I discussed the emergence of figures of autonomy, normativity, and alienation that contributed to state–society antagonism, to the delegitimation of state control, and to beliefs in a certain independence from state-based and bourgeois–scientific norms. These figures—the *résistant*, the gangster, the *inadapté*, *the anomic individual*—appealed now as contrarian, autonomous ideals, socioeconomic but also *moral* reactions to the state's efforts at organizing a society that was only partially under its control. Their style of resistance propelled an imaginary that developed fully during the student revolts, feeding their anomic and anti-establishment tendencies.

Thus the arguments against norms imposed by the post-Vichy state, by capitalism and planning, and by political developments since the early postwar communist strikes had consequences beyond their proponents' immediate reach. The idea that the state, which sent police to deal with students and seemed committed to forcing society into submission and obedience, might be the source of an open, integral society seemed laughable. From this perspective, the gangster, the maladapted adolescent, and the communist student acquired moral, political, and symbolic strength. The generation born between 1938 and 1950 found around the mid-1960s a certain cultural expression in New Wave cinema—an inspiration for post-Soviet Marxists who operated with the notion of alienation.

Some of these figures reclaimed *clandestinity* against normative or political marginalization and oppression as a value morally superior to conformity. But the "rebels"—from antitax nativists in the Poujadist movement through Algerian demonstrators in the years before independence to students—also sought to come out of hiding and into the light and to become respected political claimants and thus proper political subjects. Algeria in particular contributed to an understanding of a controlled and oppressive public space, given the systematic repression exercised by police and the killing of Algerian demonstrators, especially on and around October 17, 1961. Infamously, these events remained mostly invisible in the French press and fed perceptions of a cover-up that would explode in the 1990s.[16] That month, Sartre returned to the imagery he had used in 1944 in "The Republic of Silence," where he asked who has the right to impose the day, who has justification for hiding in the night, what morality lies behind all this. Now, in the introduction to Franz Fanon's *The Wretched of the Earth*, which appeared a few weeks after the October demonstrations and police killings, Sartre decried the repression carried out against the Algerian National Liberation Front by associating state torture with sunlight: "the blinding glare of torture is high in the sky, flooding the entire country."[17] In the 1990s, the philosopher Jacques Rancière would also comment on the events of October 1961 in a language of visibility:

That day, with its twofold aspect (manifest and hidden), was a turning point, a moment when the ethical aporia of the relationship between "mine" and the other was transformed into the political subjectivation of an inclusive relationship with alterity. The crucial thing about the effect of that day was the way in which the questions of the visibility and invisibility of repression became interwoven into the three relationships that were in play . . . between Algerian militants and the French state; between the French State and "us"; and between the Algerian militants and "us." From the French State's point of view, the demonstration meant that Algerians in struggle had emerged within the French public space as political participants and, in a certain sense, as French subjects. The results of that intolerable event are well known: savage beatings and drownings. In a word, *the police cleared the public space* and, thanks to a news blackout, *made its own operations invisible.*[18]

Rancière may be overstating the importance of "that day" thanks to hindsight, but the point on visibility remains. From the perspective of social transparency, the 1960s saw a series of political agents in the shape of antagonists to centralized power who fought for visibility in the public space and claimed moral and economic agency and authenticity.

Even though May '68 was not about "governmental" transparency, it certainly involved fears regarding the transparency enforced on social space, the perception that the state was too much of a police state, and the recognition of capitalism as the driving force of an alienated and denatured present. Philosophical attempts to handle the broader state–society antagonism articulated it through concepts and images. The students who chanted "À bas l'état policier!" were not calling for open governance; they fused, with great success, the episodic image of this or that *flic* (cop) with the general image of a police state that enforced a planned capitalist logic on their lives and thus misshaped any genuine future; "À bas!" was the counteragent of this, at once impersonal and active.

At the heart of all this lies the history of French *gauchisme,* which is well known thanks to historians such as Julian Bourg, Michael Scott Christofferson, Warren Montag, and Camille Robcis.[19] Instead of retracing it, I should like to emphasize its tendency to portray a new, antinormative agent of history. In some of their most famous political texts, four very different intellectuals—Louis Althusser, Guy Debord, Pierre Clastres, and Michel Foucault—outlined, refused, and argued against the ostensible transparency enforced by state apparatuses, and in the process they provided a logic for political struggles. Even in the early stages of the 1966–68 Union des Jeunesses communistes Marxistes-Léninistes (UJC-ML), which preceded the Gauche prolétarienne (GP), Maoism pointed to a new kind of transparency in the Chinese proletariat: a universalizable general will à la Rousseau. The fourth point of the founding declaration of the UJC-ML proposed to form revolutionary intellectuals linked to "the workers and the working people" and to institute "new forms of organization" that would realize this "task."[20] The Cultural Revolution appealed to French intellectuals mainly on account of the ideologically active proletariat behind it: a huge force and a vast population that was identified with the classless communist state, with the world proletariat, with the anticolonial other. This was easily imported as a model of radical, universalist student activism opposed to state oppression. As Robcis puts it: "For Althusser's students, Maoism offered the possibility of being 'here and now,' of participating in the great historical revolution, of having 'China in our heads.'"[21] They would refuse mechanisms of state opression and authority while endorsing a transparency of the "general will" variety that deployed similar mechanisms. For example, the GP endorsed the use of violence after 1968 on the argument that, if the state acted on behalf of class interests, the intellectuals' and workers' response had to demonstrate exemplary violence; anything short of that would fail to signal real dissociation from the state and its repressive apparatus.

Paths against the State
Louis Althusser

A version of this logic came with Louis Althusser, whose "Ideology and Ideological State Apparatuses" in 1969 dismissed the notion that a pure, non-ideological position—a selfhood before subjectivity—was possible. As early as 1964 Althusser articulated his position thus:

[The Cultural Revolution's] ultimate goal is to transform the masses' ideology, to replace feudal ideology by a new ideology of the masses, proletarian, and socialist—thus, to give to the socialist economic infrastructure and political superstructure, a corresponding ideological superstructure.[22]

By 1969 he had refined this argument by demarcating the state—that is, the dominant "repressive state apparatus" in capitalism—and separating it clearly from ideological state apparatuses, which effect subjection. Concerning the state itself,

the Marxist tradition is strict: in the *Communist Manifesto* and the *Eighteenth Brumaire* . . . the State is explicitly conceived as a repressive apparatus. The State is a 'machine' of repression, which enables the ruling classes . . . to ensure their domination over the working class, thus enabling the former to subject the latter to the process of surplus-value extortion (i.e. to capitalist exploitation). The State is thus first of all what the Marxist classics have called *the State apparatus*.[23]

The "repressive state apparatus" functions through violence; by contrast, ideological state apparatuses function through quiet indoctrination.[24] Althusser specifically argued that repressive and ideological state apparatuses structure and then affect—that is, coax, enforce, distort, splinter, choke—the *private* realm. He mentioned "private" only in order to evacuate that space, which was, as Antonio Gramsci had claimed, merely a fiction of bourgeois law:

The State, which is the State of the ruling class, is neither public nor private; on the contrary, it is the precondition for any distinction between public and private. The same thing can be said from the starting-point of our State Ideological Apparatuses. It is unimportant whether the institutions in which they are realized are "public" or "private." What matters is how they function.[25]

The denial of privacy was hardly original. But to say that ideological state apparatuses "expropriate" privacy from all of society was a decisive novelty. Althusser famously observed that subjection began with interpellation, as in the "little theoretical theater" of someone's responding —to being hailed by a policeman—such that "what thus seems to take place outside ideology (to be precise, in the street), in reality takes place in ideology."[26] Ideology could not be simply discarded or identified with the views of one's opponents as opposed to one's pure truth; "the mastery of its 'practice'" was inculcated through the teaching of a "know-how."[27] In the ever-presence of ideology, class struggle had to take seriously the representations of social relations, because these were fundamentally *imaginary* (in Lacan's sense).[28] "Individuals are always-already interpellated by ideology as subjects, which necessarily leads us to one last proposition: *individuals are always-already subjects*."[29] To complete the argument, class struggle could satisfy the condition of being both a universal and a "scientific" claim through recognition that it was impossible to be outside ideology and fighting on behalf of that "outside." Ideology's pretense to transparency crashed here against the theoretical refraction of praxis as a "scientific," de-ideologizing class struggle. Science could be weaponized precisely against the social forms and "human sciences," which ignored their own class basis and force of subjection.

Guy Debord

No less emphatic than Althusser and his students was the Situationist International (SI) group around Guy Debord, with its attack on a contemporary "society of the spectacle." The parallel development of the critique of bureaucracy in *Socialisme ou Barbarie*—the journal of the eponymous group of radicals around Cornelius Castoriadis and Claude Lefort (see chapter 10)—had created a sense that, by the postwar period, an unmediated society was only a dream. The radicalism of the Situationist International since the late 1950s folded these social ideas about bureaucracy and consumer capitalism into a whole they labeled "spectacular capitalism." "Spectacle" in this usage was the loss of subjectivity into images imbued with false, quasi-religious value and structured by the abstraction of value. Debord's understanding of this spectacle as a "social relationship mediated by images" that attacked "directly lived reality" dated to his writings from the late 1950s[30] and returned voraciously in his book *La Société du spectacle* (1967; *Society of the Spectacle*), where the spectacle appeared as the fundamental socioeconomic form and medium of modernity. As a symbol of universal capitalist falsehood parading as truth, it dissimulated through an enforced transparency all real relations of production and consumption.[31] Debord, who obsessed with the theatricalization and visuality of abstract relations of production, wrote profusely of an "alienating totality and unity" that only his vanguard politics could overcome. Spectacular society was hopelessly broken, only kept together by the mystifying power of the spectacle. Representation in and through the spectacle involved acceptance of its masks, which covered relations between individuals that, outside capitalism, supposedly remained independent, largely unmediated, and transparent.[32] Debord's assessment of alienation as experienced brutally by every participant in the spectacle prompted his Rousseau-inspired argument that revolution against "spectacular" society would inaugurate an exuberant "festival." May '68 and the Commune were for him cases in point.[33] He set up the idea of the festival against the background of a tradition of apocalyptic writing and propagated it as the end of distorted representation.

The festival promised the lived experience of an exuberant transparency that could redeem from alienation. Its revolution had a society-wide target—spectacular capitalism—and an agent capable of overturning it. Only this revolutionary praxis could bring about redemption:

Self-emancipation in our time is emancipation from the material bases of an inverted truth. This "historic mission to establish truth in the world" can be carried out neither by the isolated individual nor by atomized and manipulated masses, but only and always by that class which is able to effect the dissolution of all classes, subjecting all power to the disalienating form of a realized democracy to councils in which practical theory exercises control over itself and surveys its own action. It cannot be carried out, in other words, until individuals are "directly bound to universal history"; until dialogue has taken up arms to impose its own conditions upon the world.[34]

"That class which is able to effect the dissolution of all classes" and "individuals directly bound to universal history": the transparency ideal returns in the festival precisely to index the agent of a transformative revolutionary praxis.

Pierre Clastres

At times anti-Marxist arguments carried an even more virulent antistatism: fears that the state may pry into society fueled the notion of a "spectral domination" supposed to have built social hierarchy and fragmentation, foreclosing any chance of community. Pierre Clastres is conspicuous for this argument, which he labeled "Society against the State" and presented in anti-Hegelian and anti-Marxist terms in his 1974 book *La Société contre l'État*.[35] Clastres targeted *political* rather than *social* alienation and expressly disavowed Marxist accounts of the latter; he also made "the other" into a moral and political criterion, continuing Lévi-Strauss's thought. In his opposition to any state claim to internal continuity and homogeneity—his radicalization of antistatism—Clastres, too, developed a peculiar brand of Rousseau-like primitivism without falling prey to the promise of historical agency. The state, he argued, triumphed by legitimizing its institutional violence and by imposing a command–obedience structure. It methodically overpowered alternative political logics, instituted a class system that had not preceded it, and negated natural law by producing its own justice and law. Once introduced, generally from the outside, the Hegelian state always won by co-opting or by crushing.[36]

A one-time student of Lévi-Strauss, Clastres developed his teacher's argument that hierarchy and inequality were products of state mechanisms: his essays on this theme go from the late 1960s until his death in 1977.[37] He made himself known for the view that the distinction between societies *with* a state and societies *without* was rigid: state mechanisms and sovereignty were absent from archaic or "primitive" societies, which actively resisted them.[38] Partly because he dismissed "simplicity" as an ethnocentric value, partly because of his proximity to Claude Lefort, Clastres did not argue that a stateless society was simply true, uncorrupted, nonviolent, "neat," or "transparent"; "a careful and prolonged observation of primitive societies would show that they are no more immediately transparent than our own."[39] Nevertheless he saw such societies as the only ones in which power was shared and exercised without hierarchical or sovereign activity, and in later years he tended to advocate a kind of primitivism born of such views.[40] Because "primitive" economic activity aimed at the maximization of leisure rather than accumulation and, in consequence, no leadership or planning was required, a subsistence economy was an affluent society—a formula that Clastres enthusiastically adopted from Marshall Sahlins.[41] The institution of the power to compel, which preceded economic and social alienation, caused the transition from a subsistence–leisure economy to a productive one.[42]

Thus the state decisively transformed social order; moreover, the development of power through political acts such as instituting rulers produced political alienation in the ruled.[43] In his crucial essay "The Bow and the Basket" (written in 1963, at the peak of Lévi-Strauss's influence), Clastres argued that the social structure subtending all collective life systematized latent arrangements of differences and their potential for open conflict. This was a space that preceded the state, and it needed to be understood *as such* if the construction of meaning was to be possible. Clastres's structuralist account of Guayaki life allowed him to articulate the song of the Guayaki as a universe of meaning with its own horizons, produced continually in the practice of singing and *not* regulated politically. It was, in a sense, pure speech:

There is no paradox . . . in the fact that what is most unconscious and collective in man—his language—can also be his most transparent consciousness and his most liberated dimension. *To the disjunction of speech and signs in the song corresponds the disjunction of man and the social world for the singer, and the conversion of meaning into value is the conversion of an individual into the subject of his solitude.*[44]

This meant several things. Society has been severed from the unconscious level at which the system that defines it linguistically and economically operates. There is no transparency at the social level, but there is a theater of operations that is fundamentally linguistic and social. In an archaic society, in the absence of political pressure, this theater was active on its own.

In subsequent years, especially in the early 1970s, Clastres radicalized and even turned on its head Lévi-Strauss's paradoxical argument about the complexity and "crystallinity" of the Nambikwara community, which Derrida had also criticized. First he pointed out occasions when chiefs *failed* to impose their authority.[45] For example, Lévi-Strauss wrote of a chief who tried unsuccessfully to usurp power by exploiting his newly learned knowledge of writing. In *Society Against the State*, Clastres multiplied examples of this sort in order to show that archaic societies actively refused kingly power. Second, Clastres politicized and expanded the "other" with which Lévi-Strauss had, Rousseau-style, identified himself. He projected closed, archaic societies of the contemporary world onto the deep past and argued that their otherness was in fact an internal factor of their dynamic stability. The self-regulating archaic society in which power was automatically shared by all members was not altogether unlike the "spectral" society he saw struggling against the state; but it reached much farther. Thus Clastres had no difficulty decrying the contemporary state as essentially fascist:

The machine of the state, in all Western societies, is becoming more and more statist, which is to say that it will become more authoritarian . . . with the deep support of the majority. . . . The statist machine is heading towards a kind of fascism, not the fascism of a party, but an interior fascism.[46]

Nevertheless, resistance would not come from within. Unlike the Chinese proletariat with its "general will" that so riveted the Maoists, the internally differentiated, non-transparent other did not claim that the political situation could simply be redeemed. These different moves created bridges from structuralism to Clastres's position after 1968 and his proximity to Claude Lefort. His intensifying antistatism amounted, in Samuel Moyn's words, to "a post-centralized, non-hierarchical, pluralistic, and above all participatory vision of politics" or, in Clifford Geertz's less charitable summation, a moralizing neo-Rousseauean primitivism.[47] Signs of a countertransparency did emerge—not at home, where the war against the state had to be fought, but at least in the disappearing societies that had disintegrated.

Michel Foucault

Lastly, let us turn again to Foucault, who in the 1970s produced one of most memorable post-1968 images of state power: the vision of Jeremy Bentham's Panopticon prison as the foundation of modern "carceral" society.[48] As we have seen, in *The Order of Things* transparency appeared as a major problem once the single order of "classical" discourse had broken down. When Foucault returned to the problem of transparency in *Surveiller et punir* (1975; *Discipline and Punish*), he tied it to the major themes of his later account of power. Arrayed in rows of cells equidistant from a central tower and clearly visible from it, prisoners in the panopticon could not see inside it in their turn; hence they would not know who observed them, when, and how. Each prisoner was entirely transparent to the observer but could not see back, thereby being forced to internalize that someone was always watching. The asymmetrical gaze in this model captures the power imbalance of a punitive society where spectatorship has an inbuilt mechanism for disciplining the seen.

Already in his earliest discussions of the Panopticon, for example a 1973 lecture at the Collège de France, Foucault described the Panopticon in terms of "transparency" and "permanent visibility."[49] The dependence of the power theme on an antistatist and "radically anti-institutional" perspective in his 1973–74 lectures gave way to a different argument in *Discipline and Punish* on the *productivity* of power, the way it molds its subjects, and on its twinned independence from state force and involvement with it. Rigorously avoiding the reduction of power to state power (partly in order to outgrow the image of a state that imposes itself directly on society), Foucault spoke of a surveillant society, a punitive society, a disciplinary society, a securitarian society, and so on, all superimposed upon one another. Of the apparatuses encoding vectors of power, Foucault thought the Panopticon the purest.[50] It relied on a number of operations: first, scopic asymmetry—the supervisor's capacity to see without being seen;[51] second, the prisoner's subsumption of an ethic of visibility and transparency that "assures the automatic functioning of power";[52] third, the "social moralization" of the prisoner and, by extension, of every surveilled subject;[53] and, finally, a more general process of homogenization and de-individuation.[54]

This had distinct consequences for Foucault's contemporaries, whom we have just considered. Writing clearly against Debord's account of the spectacle, Foucault stated:

Our society is one not of spectacle, but of surveillance; under the surface of images, one invests bodies in depth; behind the great abstraction of exchange, there continues the meticulous, concrete training of useful forces . . . it is not that the beautiful totality of the individual is amputated, repressed, altered by our social order, it is rather that the individual is carefully fabricated in it, according to a whole technique of forces and bodies.[55]

But, just as significantly, he would not admit that society itself could be the basis of a politics that functioned without and against the state; Foucault registered his distance from Clastres by eliding a centralized state and by relegating it to "traditional" sovereignty rather than "modern power." Nor was class struggle—which according to Althusser could be guided "scientifically"—much more than a fantasy. The term Foucault regularly used to denote the role and force of schools, prisons, and the army, much as Althusser had done, was, instead, "state apparatus."[56]

Foucault did find inspiration in a different contemporary when he aligned Bentham's Panopticon with Rousseau's transparency dream. This was Starobinski, whose Rousseau's dream of crystalline purity had reached from his heart to revolution itself:

Bentham is the complement to Rousseau. [Rousseau too had] the dream of a transparent society, visible and legible in each of its parts, the dream of there no longer existing any zones of darkness, zones established by the privileges of royal power or the prerogatives of some corporation, zones of disorder. It was the dream that each individual be able to see the whole of society from whatever position he occupied, that men's hearts communicate each with the other, that gazes not encounter obstacles, and that opinion of all reign over each. Starobinski has written some most interesting pages about this in *Jean-Jacques Rousseau: Transparency and Obstruction* and in *The Invention of Liberty*.[57]

In treating the later eighteenth century as the origin of a movement whereby transparency and bodily techniques created and displayed power relations at their purest, Foucault also used the Panopticon's exemplary value on the subject of transparency to effect an operation internal to his body of work. The moment around 1800 when transparency was being torn asunder as a principle structuring language and its operations was now also the moment when transparency became the degree zero of power relations. Foucault's anticipation of the "death of man" theme in the 1960s gave way to a hermeneutic history of the present that narrated, with obstinate recursiveness, the development of a machinery devised for disciplinary punishment since the late eighteenth century.

In the political domain, transparency was no longer concerned homogenization, as it had been in the 1950s, or with the possibility of a general will and new agent of the universal; it was shorthand for domination. In question was not the denigration of vision but rather the deployment of visually laden forces within the supreme apparatuses of power, illusion, and dissimulation. Transparency, in Foucault as in Althusser and Debord, was central and semantically clear: these authors' competing theoretical approaches closely operationalized the conflict between state and society to somewhat divergent and heavily critical ends but always with a claim (explicit or not) that transparency was but the hard, imposing labor of power. Across these intellectuals' work we see a repoliticization of the theme of transparency: the symbolic, representational, temporal horizon of philosophy in the 1960s gave way to the problem of state domination and to attention to a historical agent envisaged as undoing it. As antistatism became the order of the day in the years 1969–75, as the philosophical and symbolic priorities evaporated, a new, *political* articulation of transparency became standard.[58]

The Myth of the Self-Transparency of Society

Claude Lefort and His Circle

Throughout the postwar period, and especially from the 1970s on, European and American political thinkers came to prize an open civil society: transparent government, the public sphere, and clear communication were mainstays of liberal and democratic thought. In Anglo-American and German traditions of democratic theory, elements of transparency appeared to be directly constitutive of liberalism and democracy. Jürgen Habermas's thesis *Strukturwandel der Öffentlichkeit* (1961; *The Structural Transformation of the Public Sphere*), for example, attributed the eighteenth-century rise of the public sphere and the critical discourse involved in it to a social openness that made democracy viable. In a manner that tells us much about openness as a desideratum in early-1960s West Germany, Habermas emphasized the centrality of transparency in modernity and contrasted the public sphere to the rising strong states and the market, both of which unbalanced and limited it.[1] In his *Theorie des kommunikativen Handelns* (1981; *Theory of Communicative Action*), transparency and clarity were as much desiderata as requirements for true communication. In *Der philosophische Diskurs der Moderne* (1985; *The Philosophical Discourse of Modernity*), Habermas further deplored French thinkers' inability to pursue a certain transparency as a consequence of their "nihilistic despair and radical skepticism."[2] He was hardly a lonely voice. From John Rawls, who developed the notion of a "publicity condition" of good government in his *A Theory of Justice* (1971), to Soviet and Eastern-bloc dissidents, who went public with their *glasnost* (openness) demonstration for the first time on December 5, 1965, transparency was in. Charles Taylor, writing in a Hegelian vein, postulated self-transparency specifically within the scope of agency, explicitly pivoting away from a Cartesian perspective of the immediate self-transparency of thought and toward a sense of the self as achievement; en passant he refused Freud's "most notorious doctrine of the non-self-transparency of the human psyche.[3]

The rise to prominence in France of a new generation of democratic theorists in the 1970s might have signaled a similar repatriation or rehabilitation of transparency; one might expect that democracy and the famous antitotalitarian moment would align French thought with contemporary European and American trends. But this was far from being the case, as is evident in the work of the anthropologists, political theorists, and historians who surrounded the influential philosopher Claude Lefort.[4] If anything, Lefort and his associates in that "new" democratic theory—notably, Miguel Abensour, François Furet, Marc Richir, and Pierre Rosanvallon, but also Marcel Gauchet, Bronisław Baczko, and, to a degree, Cornelius Castoriadis—sharpened and institutionalized the critique of transparency and used the term *transparency* in a univocal, single-minded fashion, to reference one of the major fictions of totalitarian (especially contemporary communist) states: a society transparent to itself. More forcefully than in earlier critics, the "self-transparency of society" appeared in these authors as a dangerous fallacy against which democracy had to struggle. In a 1978 essay titled "Marx and Civil Society," the political theorist Pierre Rosanvallon, one of the main theorists of factory self-management (*autogestion*) in the 1970s, turned this argument into a formula: "totalitarianism is . . . the last word of the utopia of social transparency."[5]

At stake in what follows are less the origins of Lefort's concept of transparency than the goals toward which he and his circle mobilized it and at the way they turned it to the benefit of a metahistorical, philosophical, and political position. Transparency played a constitutive role in their broader account of the political ontology of individuals, states and societies, of the history of democracy and the place of the French Revolution in it, of the symbolism of power, and of the force and ostensibly ubiquitous threat of totalitarianism. I start by tracing Lefort's evolving use of the term *transparency* in the period 1965–80; then I consider the role of the historiography of the French Revolution in the elaboration of an equivalence between totalitarianism and transparency; and finally I look at Lefort's and Rosanvallon's sense of the broader implications of this political–historical theory.

Claude Lefort on the Fiction of
Social Transparency, 1965–80

For Lefort, the question of a "self-transparent society" was inseparable from the critique of communist bureaucracy that he and Castoriadis had advanced in *Socialisme ou barbarie*, the journal they had co-founded in 1949 and in which Lefort was intermittently active until 1958. Lefort was well aware of the theme's significance in the phenomenology and politics of his teacher Maurice Merleau-Ponty—not least in his argument on "ambiguity"—as well as of the contrast between transparency and the density of the symbolic in Jacques Lacan.[6] Nevertheless, the "self-transparency of society" does not seem to have been particularly significant for him until the mid-1960s. He first referred to it in 1965, in a talk before the Cercle Saint-Just that he published in the journal *Annales: Economies–Sociétés–Civilisations* the following year under the title "Pour une sociologie de la démocratie." In this piece Lefort treated openness between different sectors of society as essential to democracy—a continual and dynamic process that involved the public dimension of behavior and knowledge. This openness required the "fiction" of a society transparent to itself.[7] Lefort's tenor was affirmative, despite the ambiguity of the term "fiction" and his subsequent, expressly antitotalitarian argument that conflict (rather than transparency) is essential to democracy.[8]

By the early 1970s, as Warren Breckman has shown, Lefort, having moved away from socialism, no longer associated the self-transparent society with communication and socialization, but with an ideological, frequently totalitarian discourse that tended to erase conflict.[9] This fiction allowed those in power to pretend that a homogeneous "one" had replaced social divisions. In 1971, the editorial board of *Textures* (which Lefort had just joined and which already included his students Marcel Gauchet and Marc Richir) launched the journal's first engagement with political theory with an editorial that noted that, "if May '68 has taught us a single lesson," it was that "there is no privileged site where political discourse would miraculously change into a transparent expression of political truth."[10] It was imperative to reject all the fusions between the layers of intention, discourse, action, and truth that Maoists and structuralists supposedly adopted. This imperative would remain at the heart of the group's political arguments on utopia, ideology, political activity, and state force. Any flattening of these quasi-distinct realms created the misconception that the *imagination* of society and its *reality* were one and the same, that the gap between society and its symbolic representation (what Lefort called the *symbolic division* within society) could be erased.

A far more complex elaboration of the transparency problem appeared in Lefort's seminal 1974 essay "Esquisse d'une genèse de l'idéologie dans les sociétés modernes" ("Outline of the Genesis of Ideology in Modern Societies"), which engaged modern bureaucracy and Soviet totalitarianism as the leading forms of an antibourgeois, antidemocratic discourse. Totalitarianism's utopian fantasy painted the bourgeois present as irrational and the historical past as opaque to all but the totalitarian, self-transparent regime. Traditional "hegemonic" domination, the "other" that the regime had to eliminate, could only be overcome through a fusion and unification of the people, which amounted to the erasure of representation. Lefort returned to his view that both bourgeois and antibourgeois discourses were "haunted by the fiction of a society which is, in principle, transparent to itself."[11] Extending his earlier claims regarding bureaucracy, he proposed:

The bureaucratic fantasy is to abolish the historical in History; to restore the logic of a "society without history"; to identify the instituting moment with the instituted; to deny the unpredictable, the unknowable, the continual loss of the past, under the illusion of a social action, transparent to itself, which would monitor its effects in advance and which would maintain continuity with its origin.[12]

His passage articulates *ex negativo* a number of priorities in Lefort's democratic anthropology: as opposed to bureaucracy, democracy separates society's instituted existence and history from its origin—the moment of its institution. It does not enforce false continuity with this origin—a continuity that would deny history, ambiguity, and contingency—but preserves openness to "the unpredictable and the unknowable." It dismisses the illusion that hierarchy could simply be undone and representation made self-identical. But, if bureaucracy is an internal threat to democracy, totalitarian homogeneity constitutes both the radicalization of this bureaucracy and its othering, a threat that has become external. Totalitarian homogeneity is so permeated by transparency as to be defined by it.

The mass party is the instrument *par excellence* of totalitarianism, through which the consubstantiality of the state and civil society is manifested. In every forum, it embodies the principle of power; it diffuses the general norm which provides the assurance of a sort of reflection of the society on itself and, with the polarization of society towards a goal, delivers it from the silent threat of the inertia of the instituted, making it possible to grasp its identity under the imperative of activism. . . . It projects into its own internal relations the very unity which it guarantees for the whole of society. It is in itself a system of signs which allows a hierarchy to be formed, which enables a split to be produced between the apparatus and the base, between the leaders and the followers, which enables sectors of activity to be partitioned off; and these operations are carried out while simulating a self-transparency of the institution, a reciprocity of decisions and a homogeneity of the body politic.[13]

Lefort speaks here only of a "simulation" of the self-transparency of the mass party.[14] The implication that true transparency could be contrasted to this simulation is quickly inverted: the dissimulating institution has a precise interest in indicating that it has overcome social division and is fully coextensive with society, all the while retaining and reconstructing its bureaucratic, all-controlling form, which enforces transparency without ever acknowledging it. This lie and the homogenization of the body politic are accompanied by totalitarianism's creation of a new, oppressive hierarchy, which, it bears repeating, the logic of transparency covers up.

Lefort would invoke this formulation over and over again, and in the ensuing years the critique targeted Marx and contemporary Marxisms more explicitly. In his 1976 book *Un homme en trop* (*One Man Too Many*)—his meditation on Aleksandr Solzhenitsyn's *Gulag Archipelago*—Lefort unambiguously connected transparency with the Soviet homogenization of society.[15] His critique of totalitarianism and of its apparent coextensiveness with contemporary Marxism was based on this connection: here as elsewhere, Lefort scorned his Marxist contemporaries, for whom

the real is transparent by right: meaning can be read in facts themselves, and the theory which they reclaim for themselves is by the same token transparent, its meaning is given by right to whomever makes the effort to take it up. The passage from reality to theory, like that from theory to reality, is always evident; it is hardly a passage at all: they both exist in the same light.[16]

The flip side of transparency is its power of occultation—a feature that follows from the ascription of transparency to a positivist epistemology.[17] Lefort specifically blamed Marx for failing to recognize that the idea of a complete, structurally organized knowledge of the world would replicate the very power relations that he had aimed to overcome.[18]

This last argument—that all claims about the collapse of power participate in the development of a complete or absolute knowledge that recreates power, and makes it absolute—would become central to Lefort.[19] In Marx's particular formulation, Lefort recalled, the "transparency" of social relations under capitalism is analytically available to the student of these social relations.[20] It only becomes a real transparency, however, in the socialist world. But this posed a whole array of problems. The availability of social relations to the interpreter resulted in conceptual contradictions that Lefort claimed Marx had intentionally staged:

> The idea that social relations finally become transparent in the bourgeois world is contradicted by the description of the "enchanted world" of capitalism, by the description of large-scale industry as a "mechanical monster" which makes individuals its organs, and by the image of bourgeois revolutionaries as being haunted by ghosts which whisper their lines to them.[21]

Religious–ideological occultation then led to the revolutionaries' belief that the meaning of their actions was transparent. The actors' self-conviction bore within it the discursive and ideological refusal of self-division and committed these actors to the reconstruction of the same power relations and system of knowledge that they claimed to have overcome. The very claim to transparency led to a totalizing ideological transparency that destroyed the original impetus.

By the late 1970s, transparency and totalitarianism were not only co-implicated in Lefort's essays but mutually constitutive, annexed to each other as well as to the idea of an ideology of social, perceptual, and expressive fusion—Lefort's "the One." In 1979, republishing his 1950s–1960s writings on bureaucracy, Lefort added a preface in which, inscribing "transparency" back into his earlier work, he noted: "As to the idea of an achieved socialization . . . I acknowledged that it upheld the myth of social indivision, of social homogenization, of society's self-transparency; moreover, I came to see that the disastrous consequences of this myth were indeed revealed by the totalitarian attempt to inscribe it in reality."[22] The language and overall figure of totalitarianism was by this point established: sutured, syncopated, the social in totalitarianism became a One that could only conceive of external opposition and internal division as threats. The following passage, from "The Image of the Body and Totalitarianism" (published in 1979), is paradigmatic in style and argument:

> At the foundation of totalitarianism lies the representation of the People-as-One. It is denied that division is constitutive of society. In the so-called socialist world, there can be no other division than that between the people and its enemies: a division between inside and outside, no internal division. After the revolution, socialism is not only supposed to prepare the way for the emergence of a classless society, it must already manifest that society which bears within itself the principle of homogeneity and self-transparency. The paradox is the following: division is denied—I say denied, since a new dominant stratum is actively distinguishing itself from the rest of society, since a state apparatus is separating itself off from society—and, at the same time as this denial, a division is being affirmed, on the level of phantasy, between the People-as-One and the Other. This Other is the other of the outside. It is a term to be taken literally: the Other is the representative of the forces deriving from the old society (kulaks, bourgeoisie) and the emissary of the foreigner, the imperialist world.[23]

As an ideological mechanism and governmental practice, totalitarianism removes social division, credits itself with truth and purity, treats its power as immediate and undistorted, and enforces social homogeneity and transparency. We find here, in Lefort's attack on Soviet communism, all the major tropes discussed earlier in this book: the claim that normative and normalizing power effects a socially destructive homogeneity; the claim that this power, and transparency alongside it, represent every internal other as an enemy and then exclude it from the communal body; and the claim that an erasure of representation—indeed of the symbolic domain itself—amounts to organicism and reduces language to the transparent communication of orders that may not be disobeyed. By the time of Lefort's development of his most influential post-1968 ideas, non-transparent representation—or rather the notion that representation presupposes distortion and symbolic transformation—was a characteristic theme in linguistic and literary discussions, from Benveniste to Foucault and Derrida. It was perhaps Lefort who most explicitly rendered this non-transparency into a requirement of democratic politics, aesthetics, and morality. Lefort's identification of the "People as One" with totalitarian transparency was based on the same public discussion of norms, others, and language as that of his politically quite different contemporaries.[24]

Similarly tied to contemporary discussions was Lefort's manner of tracing the origin of these concepts to the eighteenth century. His meta-history of modern power presented the eighteenth century as the point of emergence of democratic thought and the origin of its contemporary iteration; but it also foregrounded that period's cooptation of the early democratic aim of openness by bureaucracy, and hence its being the direct ancestor, *through* and *because of* the call for transparency that originates in democratic thought, of the totalitarian logic that dominated so much of the twentieth century. The 1966 essay registered the fiction of transparency as an essential feature of democratic communication in the eighteenth century; and later on Lefort often highlighted these democratic roots in his account of transparency as a descriptor of totalitarianism.[25] The metahistorical account of political origins was as relevant to totalitarianism as to the new understanding of the French Revolution that spread in the 1970s—particularly in the interpretation of François Furet.

The French Revolution: Richir, Furet, Baczko, Lefort

The string that bound transparency to totalitarianism, established by Lefort and his circle, strengthened thanks in part to a series of new interpretations of the French Revolution proposed by figures close to Lefort, notably Miguel Abensour, Marc Richir, Bronisław Baczko, and François Furet.[26] Furet remains most closely identified with this "new," polemical, and influential reinterpretation of the French revolutionary and historiographical tradition, but the breath of revisionism was already warm. From Abensour's account of Saint-Just through Richir's study of transparency and revolution to Baczko's treatment of the eighteenth-century utopian imagination, the stage for Furet's approach was set, and with it a reinterpretation of the Soviet Union and its terroristic modernity.

Abensour's work in the late 1960s followed from his 1962 doctoral dissertation on Saint-Just and juxtaposed the latter's political and legal thought with accounts of the modern utopian imagination, which Abensour would continue to study over the next thirty years. In 1974, the Belgian phenomenologist Marc Richir published a book-length interpretation of Johann Gottlieb Fichte's 1793 *Contribution to the Correction of the Public's Judgments on the French Revolution* and titled it "Révolution et transparence sociale" ("Revolution and Social Transparency"). Referencing Lefort, Abensour, and Marcel Gauchet, Richir inserted the concept of transparency into virtually every aspect of his interpretation. Arguing, against Marxist historiography, that it was not the bourgeoisie that made the revolution but the revolution that created the bourgeoisie,[27] Richir held a mirror up to the Marxist positions of Daniel Guérin, Albert Soboul, and Georges Lefebvre, arguing point by point against their philosophy of history. According to him, the fundamental question for the revolutionaries had been *what kind* of transparency would be the most satisfactory and how a proto-communist transparency came into conflict with bourgeois and statist accounts.[28] Richir's was a Revolution haunted by its own divisions, by the competition between *sansculottic* terror and Jacobin terror, between the pressure imposed by Gracchus Babeuf and the Conspiracy of Equals, between attempts to provide a state capable of sustaining the revolutionary impetus and attempts to support the new regime. The horns of the revolutionary actors' dilemma appeared to have been the "despotism of bourgeois civil society through the intercession of the state apparatus that it has given itself" and the "'totalitarianism' of a State living off its dream of its own transparency to the benefit of a communist society."[29] The pursuit of the universal and of pure regeneration raised a "totalitarian specter" in the French Revolution, which was all the more significant since, as Richir saw, there was "an extraordinary *opacity* between sociopolitical theory and practice, as if the desire of transparency which must in principle strengthen and institute the new regime (the 'revolutionary' state) was doubled at the same time by a fantastic opacity of civil society, by the rising complexity of this last to the degree that it was seen to re-enter the principles of the Revolution."[30]

Opacity between theory and practice produced the subsequent conflicts over "real" democracy, over the state and its supposed ownership, over the desire to reconcile the revolutionary impulse with the present or the immediate future and install a plenitude of social purity. Here Richir took from Lefort as much as he gave back: an entire logic of revolutionary activity that accounted for modern divisions as well as for the fantasy of their undoing, in a fusion of the symbolic and the real dimensions of politics. The revolutionary faith in transparency had collapsed into a "mirage," a "spectacle."[31]

In 1964, Baczko, a Polish intellectual historian and philosopher who had been close to Leszek Kołakowski in Warsaw, published a study of alienation in Rousseau titled *Rousseau: Samotność i wspólnota* (*Rousseau: Solitude and Community*). He emigrated to Geneva in the early 1970s and forged links with Lefort's circle, publishing repeatedly in the lefortian journal *Libre* in 1977–80.[32] In his *Lumières de l'utopie* (1978; *Utopian Lights*), Baczko argued that the utopian city imagined in the later eighteenth century was fundamentally "a transparent whole."[33] The purpose of the invention of a notion of history as progress in the eighteenth century was to realize in this transparent city the rational utopia that now concluded this history.[34] In crossing the gulf into utopia, Baczko's eighteenth-century intellectuals were designing a society that would allow for genuine transparency, much as Starobinski had argued. Baczko's Revolution was suspended between the application of a Condorcet-style dream of progress and the *realization* of this utopia, in which the fantasy of transparency would make unnecessary all history or action that fell outside the scope of this progress.

The realization of utopia (Baczko), the gap between intention and action (Lefort, Richir), the opacity between theory and practice, and especially the contrast between an opaque imaginary attached to civil society and a terroristic or totalitarian transparency (Richir), the identification of Saint-Just and Robespierre with Rousseauean legacy of transparency and the Terror as its expression (Abensour, Baczko, Lefort): these are the central motifs in the application of the concept of transparency to both the French Revolution and the practice of totalitarianism in the 1970s, and they would all reemerge in François Furet's *Penser la Révolution française* (1978; *Interpreting the French Revolution*). Samuel Moyn describes how in the mid-1970s, inspired by the work of Lefort and other participants in the *Textures* and *Libre* groups, Furet dramatically revised the essays that would make up that book.[35] He, too, used the term *transparency* in an almost technical sense; like Richir, he denied that any "transparency" existed between the revolutionaries' intention and the effect of revolutionary action.[36] He unfavorably contrasted Michelet's attachment to a "transparency" of values, actions, and the people with Tocqueville's historiographical distance from that fantasy[37] and repeatedly dismissed any self-transparency of "the people."[38] He emphasized transparency's ideological appeal in the assault on enemies of the Revolution—especially to Jacobins, who considered revolutionary power to derive from one's self-effacing portrayal as transparent to "the people." Robespierre

> alone mythically reconciled direct democracy with the principle of representation, by installing himself at the summit of a pyramid of equivalences whose continued existence was guaranteed, day after day, by his word. He *is* the people to the *sections*, to the Jacobins, to the national representative body. And it is this transparency between the people and all these places that speak in his name—beginning with the Convention—that must be constantly instituted, controlled, reestablished, as the condition of the legitimacy of power, but also as its first duty: and that is the function of the Terror.[39]

For Furet, Rousseau was at the historical root of this perception: his argument on the general will, bolstered by Robespierre's self-portrayal, generated both the democratic impetus and its "undoing" through transparentist identification of the people with the general will.[40]

Lefort in turn picked up aspects of Furet's argument, particularly those related to the opacity of an ideology that pretended to be transparent. In an essay on Furet published in the aftermath of Furet's controversy with Albert Soboul, Lefort reproduced both Furet's and Richir's accounts, emphasizing their contrast between civil society and dictatorial terror, and pursuing the symbolic self-construction of civil society as the central problem of the Revolution. Contra Habermas, civil society stood *against* transparency, which in turn denied symbolic division as well as the dynamism of history, its non-self-coincidence. (Marxists, Lefort argued, persisted in schematizing the Revolution so as to make it transparent to political agency.)[41] The goal, for Lefort, was to imagine the symbolic division of society—especially a society that proclaimed its unity and homogeneity—and to restage the empty place of power in order for a democracy to take over, a democracy that would abandon its pretense to truth and authenticity. After May '68, one had to rescue the social imaginary from associations with the chain of revolutions from 1789 to 1917. Hence it was vital to reinstate a canon of modernity that respected symbolic division and recognized the violence concealed in notions of authenticity and transparency.

Particularly significant in this regard was the group's treatment of Rousseau, which largely completes the story of his post–World War II reception as I have followed it. In Lefort's and his colleagues' judgment, Rousseau's political radicalism deserved a place in a history of order and violence; his advocacy of personal and political transparency was both a promise of communication, individuality, and democracy and a utopia of the purity of self and of social homogenization. The Rousseauean and anti-Rousseauean end of the eighteenth century in the Terror is the moment of a fundamental division, out of which both modern democracy and modern terror emerge.

This conception of the eighteenth century remained in all essentials congruent with the forms proposed by, say, Foucault or Derrida, regardless of the Lefort group's persistent hostility to "poststructuralists."[42] Again in congruence with the structuralist hopes of the late 1960s, albeit in a more political and specifically democratic vein, the present moment came into focus in Lefort's circle as a time in which a real democracy could reemerge, not by reference to the eighteenth-century democratic ideal of communication and transparency so much as through an institutionalization (for want of a better word) of the uncertainty and ambiguity of society and social action and through constant testing of the relation of knowledge to reality:

> a society which would ensure the greatest intelligibility of social action would be one in which there would be, in each domain, a testing of reality, a knowledge of the possible and the impossible, a taking into account of the resistance of men and things and, consequently, a grasping of the particular conditions of the various forms of relationship and work. Such a society would in principle be resistant to the totalitarian project.[43]

Echoes

Transparency did not occupy the same place in the political thought of members of Lefort's group, including the anthropologist Pierre Clastres and the philosopher Marcel Gauchet.[44] Although Clastres specifically formulated the state–society problem in characteristically antistatist terms, he, like Gauchet, evaded the question of social transparency. Castoriadis's argument on "the imaginary institution of society" remained, for Lefort, attached to a potentially dangerous political voluntarism because of its endorsement of society's self-institution in democracy.[45] Lefort might even concur with Habermas's critique of Castoriadis: "Autonomy and heteronomy are ultimately supposed to be assessed in terms of the authenticity of the self-transparency of a society that does not hide its imaginary origin beneath extrasocietal projections and knows itself explicitly as a self-instituting society."[46]

Pierre Rosanvallon also moved from Castoriadis toward Lefort. Rosanvallon had been central to the theoretical efforts of the self-management (*autogestion*) movement, which advocated the exercise of spontaneous socialist practice in factories and opposition to managerial power. In the late 1970s, however, Rosanvallon stepped back from active political life and devoted himself to scholarship on democracy and liberalism, adopting several of Lefort's categories. An important goal of his 1979 *Le Capitalisme utopique: Critique de l'idéologie économique* (*Utopian Capitalism: Critique of Economic Ideology*), he argued in the introduction, was to respond "to the question concerning the origins and the formative movement of this utopia of the transparent society."[47] Offering up Marxism as a transparentist ideology, Rosanvallon considered Marx's work to be largely derivative of the philosophical anarchist William Godwin and to bundle together the philosophies of Rousseau and Adam Smith. On the intertwined histories of liberalism and capitalism, Rosanvallon developed a detailed schema of his own, which diverged essentially from Lefort's, especially as regards the rather easy meld of 1789 with contemporary "totalitarianism" and the meaning of transparency in politics.

On account of their elimination of any creative or open place in democracy, echoes of these critiques of transparency would persist into the 1990s; in some cases they were little more than echoes. Abensour pursued his study of modern utopianism and of the self-transparent subject's coming to self-consciousness (notably in Feuerbach and Marx) in terms closely reminiscent of Lefort and of Clastres, in whose memory he titled his account of modern democracy in *La démocratie contre l'État: Marx et le moment machiavélien* (1997; *Democracy against the State: Marx and the Machiavellian Moment*).[48] Rosanvallon diverged most from the others: the 1999 edition of his 1979 *Le Capitalisme utopique*, now subtitled *Histoire de l'idée de marché*, simply replaced the original preface (which included warnings about social transparency) with a new preface on the market and the history of liberal utopias.[49] This change demoted the analysis of Marx from its pivotal position in the critique of contemporary ideology to that of an aside in the history of liberalism. The political–economic context of the 1990s had obviated the need for a discussion of totalitarianism and transparency and the history of political and economic liberalism took priority. In his *La nouvelle question sociale: Repenser l'État-providence* (1995; *The New Social Question: Rethinking the Welfare State*), Rosanvallon was more measured: the reason for the aspiration to transparency was a modernist democratic ideology that aimed at the rationalization of "an irrational, opaque universe." Tracing this ideology to a desire, in the 1960s, for a "calmer" democracy, Rosanvallon insisted that transparency is inevitable in democracy: the creation of social solidarity requires the practice of transparency in order to overstep the distance between deliberative democracy and the order of nature, through an order of social and political rights.[50] Rosanvallon would henceforth pursue a somewhat questionable distinction between social and individual transparency, noting that the former is "inherent in the very logic of modern society," but calling for "opacity of individuals," and thus in a sense aligning freedom with privacy of information.

We might conclude this chapter with two outsiders to Lefort's group because, in retrospect, both are somewhat surprising. One is Bernard-Henri Lévy, who is remarkable here for his political biography and his concurrent attacks on Stalinism, Gilles Deleuze, and Jean-François Lyotard. In his book *La Barbarie à visage humain* (1977; *Barbarism with a Human Face*), Lévy dramatized Lefort's position—indeed alongside Sartre's "republic of shadows":

It is false, for example, that totalitarianism is, as is still said, a version of obscurantism. . . . [Rather, the State's appropriation of society] can tolerate no corner, no zone of shadows which would provide a haven for some possible dissidence. It is intent on abolishing the gap that has always been maintained between the civil and the political, it will not rest until it has cleared up every dark corner and blind spot on the social surface. It conceives this surface as entirely smooth and translucent, like a faithful mirror reflecting its own image . . . the fascist State is first of all a State that looks: Jean Moulin is the man of shadows, and his torturers were the ones who held the light. Totalitarian societies are transparent societies governed by insomniac Princes dreaming of glass houses.[51]

In this popularization of the democratic imagination, which incorporates discourse, visuality, and state power, the rejection of transparency reaches one of its most spectacular peaks—and also one of the last.

A second figure who somewhat surprisingly shows the reach of this argument's influence is Laurent Fabius, François Mitterand's second (and first "modernizing") prime minister (1984–88). Writing after that tenure, in his 1990 *C'est en allant vers la mer*, Fabius argued that the French Socialist Party should commit more permanently to a "modernized" rather than a radical socialism, and he rehearsed the critique of the myth of society's self-transparency to the point of banalization. Against his vision, he claimed, stood the traditional, outdated socialist dream: "After battles and tears, what would follow was the society without exploitation, oppression or alienation—'without classes, war, or State'—pacified, unified, transparent to itself."[52] Mitterand's governments, which were pursuing a policy of "information transparency," had sought to replace that old, "fantastical" socialism and the transparency "myth." This shift drove the left-wing republican universalism of the 1980s: the new democratic theory, a humanism of *nouveaux philosophes* like Lévy, and the "modernizing" new French Socialist Party. It could still conceive of itself as opposed to transparency, even while creating a new home for it.

Nineteen Eighty-Four

Information, the Scrambled Signs of the Ideal,
and The Postmodern Condition

Orwell's *Nineteen Eighty-Four* in 1984

The year 1984 was marked by a spate of intellectual events commemorating George Orwell's *Nineteen Eighty-Four* and attempting to compare the present moment to Orwell's prognosis. Among the French intellectuals who participated, two stand out: Claude Lefort and Jean-François Lyotard. Lefort argued that the literary quality of the novel undermined any facile "antitotalitarian" reading because it coded ways in which Winston, Orwell's protagonist, half-knows the truth about the regime and hence effectively colludes in his own destruction. Winston's inability to construct a full-fledged alternative to Oceania's scenario confirms Oceania's control and its unification of the symbolic. Whenever Winston attempts a "fierce defense of self-consciousness" against the state's distortive and expropriating discourse, his "self vacillates before the enigma of the body, of the past, of death; it is threatened from within by faith in the indestructibility of appearance as such and of the event."[1]

By "threatened from within," Lefort designates totalitarianism's singularization of discourse. Winston's very body betrays his attempt to defend himself from the state; it dooms him by revealing his inability to effect the symbolic division that the state had succeeded, even at the physiological level, in denying.

Lyotard, for his part, welcomed Lefort's attention to the book's style but reached diametrically opposite conclusions. Explicitly, against Lefort's contrast of totalitarianism and unachieved freedom, Lyotard wondered: Didn't the novel's obsession with writing point to something that "critique" could not reach?[2] Critique tended to run out of steam when confronted with totalitarianism, and Lefort was imposing his theory on the novel and seeing the two as relevant to the present moment. The novel offers transient yet important moments of resistance—even though Winston's body and writing, his love and consciousness are eventually crushed by Big Brother. Lyotard considered this frail, pathetic, eradicable resistance to be crucial. If such moments could be salvaged, they represented a signal confrontation—felt and written by Winston—with hegemonic power.

The prophesy of a regime that had to be resisted, yet from which no escape was possible, was now experienced differently. Lyotard did not think that Orwell's text, through its binary of oppression and freedom and its individual hero's struggle in the dark, had anticipated the current forms of political domination. He had no doubts as to the meaning of the real 1984, which he considered far too complex and pernicious for Orwell—much more sinister than the targets of monikers like "totalitarianism." In the 1980s, "mediatic democracies (the contraries of a republic)" armed with "technosciences working with and on language, [and] the general decline of modern ideals" constituted the threat:

Modernity, for at least two centuries, has taught us to desire the extension of political liberties, of sciences, arts and techniques. It has taught us to legitimize that desire because *this* progress, it claimed, was going to emancipate humanity from despotism, ignorance, barbarism, and misery. The republic is the citizens' humanity. This progress marches on today under the more shameful name of development. But it has become impossible to legitimize this development by way of a promise that it will emancipate all of humanity. This promise has not been fulfilled. Its betrayal is not due to a forgetting of the promise—it is the *promise* itself that forbids us from believing in its development. Neo-analphabetism, the impoverishment of the peoples of the [global] South and the Third World, unemployment, the despotism of opinion and thus of prejudice exercised by the media, the law that what is good is what performs well: none of this has been due to a lack of development, but to development itself. This is why we can no longer try to call it progress. The promise of emancipation was recalled, defended, detailed by great intellectuals, that category that was born with the Enlightenment, guardian of ideals and of the Republic. Those who seek to perpetuate this task today in any other form than through resistance of the *minima* to all totalitarianisms, those who have imprudently found the just cause in the conflict between ideas or the conflict between powers, the Chomskys and the Negris and the Sartres and the Foucaults, have been dramatically mistaken. The signs of the ideal are scrambled. A war of liberation does not announce that humanity continues to emancipate itself, nor does opening a new market predict that it will enrich itself; the school does not form citizens, at most it prepares professionals.[3]

This was the new 1984: "the signs of the ideal are scrambled," new forms of control left little room and no logic for resistance. A new celebration of transparency had also begun.

1983, the Seventies, and the Revival of Transparency

In his book *Tranzparenztraum* (2013; The Transparency Dream), the philosopher Manfred Schneider offers a broadly linear history of the rise of transparency as an ideal in Western thought. In the past two decades, he claims, what has long been a vague dream has now crystallized into a messianic illusion.[4] Momus, the Greek god of satire, had complained about the lack of windows into the human heart; for Schneider, we have applied the remedy by blasting open such windows without mercy or qualm.

But the current dominance of the transparency ideal cannot be thought of as final or politically unambiguous, and certainly not as a linear, *longue durée* advance of light (even false light) through darkness. If anything, for a good thirty or forty years, transparency met with no less fear than contempt in the French context. In the postwar web of concepts, this reaction involved an intellectual renegotiation of ideals that reached its apex in the mid-1960s and was overtaken and modulated by a parallel negotiation over the relations between state and society. In both cases, fear of and contempt for transparency triggered the effort to create something of a new Enlightenment as a way to respond to a vastly changed world, which had rendered old ideals pernicious.

This attitude began to change in the later 1970s, and in the mid-1980s transparency was consecrated as the object of a new worship. This process was piloted by the one political event capable of bridging the separation between state and society—François Mitterrand's ascent to the presidency. After May '68, the creative thrust of the antitransparentist positions was somewhat stunted; the more visible ones coalesced around antitotalitarianism. In the 1980s, the shifts in governmental policy and the need for their intellectual legitimation marginalized the critique of transparency.

During the 1970s, the French Left had been forced to confront the rise and utility of new information technologies. Until then, from Georges Friedmann to Guy Debord, the Left had depicted technology as a dehumanizing force that, for all its promise, worked mostly as "technoscience": it belonged with bureaucracy and contributed mostly to alienation—to the motorization and rigidification of labor and life. Jacques Ellul's postwar warning about the perils of technology, its illusion of progress, and its framing of human life became influential.[5] Lefort and Castoriadis worried about information in the context of bureaucratic power. In 1966, Lefort made the point that any democracy should examine the domain of information with great care; and he recoiled before concepts that belonged to information theory, whose sufficiency and scientificity he denied.[6] Self-management-style factory socialism debated the problem of technologization specifically under the rubric of transparency. In *CFDT Aujourd'hui*, the main journal of the Confédération française démocratique du travail, authors treated computers as central to the transformation of the workplace and society. They did so with considerable anxiety: in a paradigmatic 1974 article titled "Le Socialisme = autogestion + ordinateur?" ("Socialism = Self-Management + Computer ?") Philippe Lemoine, then a committed ecological activist (later the CEO of the supermarket chain Monoprix), emphasized that norms imposed by a computerized society would likely abandon universality and devise and enforce new forms of exploitation:

To always proclaim the technical efficiency of rationality has, in fact, a profoundly totalitarian character. . . . At stake is not only the possible police use of computers, but the totalitarian character of an information society. Everything would be transparent. No more shadows, no more ambiguities. In the name of this myth the most arbitrary models would be imposed. A transparency of social facts would make us believe that a discourse exists beneath society and conflicts, which would serve to protect [the current system] from every menace.[7]

We have already come across one kind of stress over totalitarianism—namely, that it washes away with light those shadows in which heterogeneity, privacy, and difference might survive. Here the idea is that information and computerization conceal a threat that is ideological as much as economic. The capacity of information *itself* to acquire normative status remained a major left-wing concern associated with social transparency in the 1970s.

Yet the 1970s also introduced theories of communication that contributed to a new identification of "transparency" with "institutional openness." The French translation of Jürgen Habermas's *Strukturwandel der Öffentlichkeit* (1961; *The Structural Transformation of the Public Sphere*) as *L'Espace public* in 1978 is a case in point: once *Öffentlichkeit* (referring to the "public sphere") was equated with public *space* and placed at the origin of bourgeois modernity, it offered an explanation that sidestepped Marxist or Rousseauean ones and championed it for the present as well.[8] Habermas's subsequent advocacy of transparency in communicative action clashed with French approaches to communication and language.[9] Some French philosophers who kept their distance from structuralism agreed. Michel Serres saw no reason to hunt transparency with the eagerness demonstrated by many of his contemporaries. Paul Ricœur refused the structuralist view of language as a priori opaque to the subject.[10] In his *Le Conflit des interprétations* (1969; *The Conflict of Interpretations*), only the symbol is opaque, *not* the sign.[11] Language could also be simple openness to the world. Ricœur did not go as far as Hans-Georg Gadamer, who held transparency to be essential for a multiplicity of interpretations to be even plausible;[12] he simply called the issue of transparency a false one.[13] To the extent that (to paraphrase François Dosse) a "humanization" of certain social sciences occurred in the 1970s, for example, in the work of Bruno Latour and Isabelle Stengers, this was partly because information was no longer treated as nontransparent and obstructive to human understanding.[14]

These introductions paralleled a profound revision of the relationship between administration and citizenry that began in the later 1970s. Echoing developments in the United States—the Freedom of Information Act and the controversies following the Watergate revelations—French governments gradually warmed to the rhetoric of governmental transparency and freedom of information. In 1976, Foucault could still claim that it was "self-evident" that power relies on its own dissimulation and "is tolerable *only on condition that it mask a substantial part of itself.* Its success is proportional to its ability to hide its own mechanisms. . . . For it, *secrecy is not in the nature of an abuse; it is indispensable to its operation.*"[15] What surprise was there if power covered up its dirt and violence? However, only a decade later, commentators recognized that a *new* relationship had developed between state and citizen, and now the state *owed* the individual not secrecy but *openness.* Supposedly, this had not been the case before.[16]

Valéry Giscard d'Estaing signed the French equivalent of the Freedom of Information Act on July 17, 1978. Even though, as Julian Bourg has argued, when "the far left contributed directly to a reinvigoration of civil society" it did so at times by demanding governmental transparency, nothing was afoot yet, and this was a gesture of limited significance.[17] Giscard's presidency, especially during the prime-ministership of Raymond Barre, used a rhetoric of private ownership, within which freedom of information was easily drowned. In the 1980s, a very different administration was faced with the political value of a "right to information."[18]

In 1981, the newly elected socialist President François Mitterrand began a program of economic nationalization; realistically, nothing more consequential could happen to leftist economic programs of the 1970s. Nationalization heralded the French Socialist Party's commitment to redressing economic inequality and to putting an end to social confrontations. The post-1968 conviction that society was straitjacketed and systematically violated by the state could be abandoned. But the program largely failed in its economic goals and was abruptly reversed in March 1983 by Mitterand's "austerity turn" (*tournant à la rigueur*). The modernizing wing of the Socialist Party took over and attached transparency to the information and computing revolution, which it saw as the main way forward for socialist ideas. Whereas until 1983, *autogestionnaires* agonized over a computerized society supposed to enforce totalitarian transparency, from then on the promise of modernization through computing and information transparency became a plausible ideal—a new utopia. A ministerial report signed that year by Laurent Fabius, then minister of industry, and Alain Savary, the minister of national education, proposed that "a system for research and the archiving of information in an office has no meaning unless it be accessible to all, that is to say, transparent and sufficiently readable."[19] In a few months, Fabius was prime minister. He recoiled from socialist transparency utopias, but he and his government committed heart and soul to an argument that welded information transparency and Mitterrand's project of industrial restructuring and modernization. Fabius's colleague Michel Rocard—a former Maoist sympathizer, famously suspicious of state power in the 1970s, then prime minister in 1988—acclaimed the transparency of the state's functions wholeheartedly in the 1980s.[20] In his 1987 book *Le Cœur à l'ouvrage*, Rocard welcomed transparency as the real pivot of "mediatized" information societies: a pivot for a free press, for public action, and for the democratic function of information.[21] Public administration and social democracy, had a new goal, and international institutions—especially those of the European Economic Community—were all too happy to oblige.[22] By 1990, sociologists as different as Jean-Louis Servan-Schreiber, Jean Baudrillard, and Jean-Pierre Le Goff agreed that transparency had abruptly become a catchword, a political interface, and the leading myth of "managerial ideology."[23] It was possible to draw a direct line back to Giscard's 1978 law and track the rise of a transparency dogma, whitewashing the state–society conflict, across the intervening decade.[24] Contrasting the moment to the half-century that had preceded it, Lyotard traced the birth of the critique of transparency to the intellectual shock of the 1929 crisis:

Starting with the great (international) crisis at the end of the 1920s, French thinkers took over those elements of the most radical critical tradition . . . to continue a reflection on the profound transformations affecting the nature of community and on the hidden aspects of the so-called "subject" of that community revealed by those transformations. . . . They subjected the philosophy of the subject (the legacy of Descartes and the "philosophes" of the eighteenth century) to a strong critique, along with the ideas of transparency, self-evidence, free will, communication, and the adequacy of reason.[25]

Half a decade into the turnaround in the public fare of transparency, this brief outline of intellectual history pinpointed the birth of an era that was coming to an end. Lyotard was writing in the past tense: information had become the code, embodiment, and economy of the new socialism.

Transparency, baptized "freedom of information," joined the crowd of human rights.[26] As part of the language of modernization and computerization, it would define the path of the socialists for at least a decade. Concluding the intellectual odyssey of the French Left since '68, the period 1983–85 also marked the closure of the systematic critique of transparency. Until then, liberal policies had been advocated by the Right. By 1985, a socialist government that only yesterday had used economic nationalization to overcome state–society frictions began to imagine the future in terms now often abbreviated to "neoliberal." Paradoxically, in order not to be co-opted by the powers and language of a society of management, information, and computerization, it began to co-opt them itself. Accessibility of information and governmental efficiency became mantras of the Left and, alongside them, a republican universalism of *laïcité*—the French variant of secularism—emerged as the consensus solution for delimiting a free, open "public space" and for dissolving barriers between France and the world.

Lyotard

In the late 1960s, intellectuals had been looking at a present future of post-cybernetic complexity, in which human beings would have little power. In the 1970s, while the political Left was changing, that present future quickly became yet another future past. Discourse, post-cybernetic deconstruction, the symbolic realm's erasure of "Man": all their prophecies had lost force by 1984. The harmonization between socialism and technology prompted a new universalism, committed to future technological liberation. In his 1984 text on *Nineteen Eighty-Four*, Lyotard argued that the signs of the ideal were now scrambled (*brouillés*), and that the ideals of modernity were lost not because they had failed but because they had mostly *succeeded*. They had become the language of politics, emancipation, freedom, individuality; this success had hollowed them out. What replaced totalitarianism as a threat was this faux pluralistic universalism which efficient "mediatic democracies" used at the expense of subjects and citizens.

For Lyotard, this threat was a matter of politics as much as one of aesthetics and desire. He had begun his intellectual career with articles in *Socialisme ou barbarie* against the occupation of Algeria. Later he buttressed the antibureaucracy argument in aesthetico-political terms, eventually falling out with the group behind the journal. Lyotard's specifically philosophical publications began in 1954, with his book *La Phénoménologie* (*Phenomenology*). He gradually assembled his own, literary–aesthetic rendition of phenomenology, laid down in *Discours, figure* (1971; *Discourse, Figure*), which formed the kernel of his later thought. Largely conceding the limitations of phenomenology, Lyotard opened by presenting the realm that the eye encounters—the figural—as a realm governed by opacity.[27] The visible involves a veil's being placed onto things, and it cannot be reduced to a readable text: the latter is by comparison *transparent*, except that it, too, is traversed by the figural. Everything perceived—images, artwork, voices, the speech of the other—is specifically *opaque*.[28] Endorsing ideas by Merleau-Ponty on the resistance of painting to reading and by Levinas on the irreducible alterity of the other's face, while holding back Derrida's famous claim that "there is no outside-the-text,"[29] Lyotard dubbed the figural realm "non-readable" or premised on a constitutive unreadability. The linguistic system that makes signification transparent operates only in the abstraction of the readable; by contrast, the given is *thick*. The subsequent years were the high point of Lyotard's "philosophies of desire." He argued in *Economie libidinale* (1974; *Libidinal Economy*)[30] that economies of desire always underlie both economic relations and our knowledge of them. His essay on Orwell's *Nineteen Eighty-Four* asked about the literary construction of Winston's experiences and desires—his frustrating inability to comprehend his world, his attempts at resistance—and the re-inscription of their alienating effect onto his own body and writing. Is not the love affair in *Nineteen Eighty-Four* a libidinal economy forced into submission and torture by a political economy threatened by its creation of narratives and alterities of life and love, however small? This libidinal economy, with its narratives and eradicable alterities, was quite different from the contemporary one, of which Lyotard declared that the signs of the ideal were scrambled. In the latter, phenomenological and psychic incomprehension paralleled international economic dislocation: the threat to life and love was there, albeit very different.

Lyotard's response to the transformation of French socialism around 1981 and 1983, his disdain for "progress," "development," and emancipatory programs, his invalidation of ideals new and old, his long list of failures of an "enlightened" modernity—all these molded new ways of responding and resisting the brave new world of the 1980s. First, in his opposition to socialist universalist humanism, Lyotard examined whether this humanism, amalgamated as it was with republican *laïcité*, was not an easygoing ideal designed to conceal the failure to suppress inequality.[31] His scornful statement that "the republic is the citizens' humanity"[32] assumed Marx's critique of rights and citizenship to treat republicanism's pretenses to universalist grandeur as mere dross. Second comes Lyotard's point about writing and mediatization, the norms of development, and the "law" that what performs well is good. For him, the power of mediatic–technological representation resided in its having taken the form of a "self-sufficient discourse" that imposes unity and clashed with evanescent moments. Lyotard held that only an ever-recurrent, fragile, transient otherness could exceed symbolic representation and its oppressiveness. Lyotard read *Nineteen*

Eighty-Four in such a way as to prioritize the *minima* of resistance—in Orwell's novel, the little confusions in language and turbulence in the world. These could still convey some of the conceptual hope of recent decades *against* the normalization of progress, which ignored disturbance and difference. Resistance was ultimately futile, inasmuch as it could easily be defeated, and yet it was both morally and politically necessary. Already in 1978, Lyotard expressly opposed Adorno's understanding of "critique" as too little too late; yet he mimicked Adorno's care for the *minima*—the little, even *least*, moments of alterity. To supersede critique, which missed the ways in which meaning was developed and politicized in an always aesthetic and libidinal universe, Lyotard turned to aesthetics.[33] In what was perhaps an appropriate response (given how Mitterand's ascent and austerity turn first redeemed, then betrayed the discontent and hopes of the 1970s), resistance would henceforth precede critique. In an approach later echoed by Derrida, Lyotard insisted on a minimal, ineffable resistance that, in its fragility, could help "others" withstand being swallowed by liberatory yet homogenizing ideals that ultimately fed the very regimes whose end they portended. Postmodernity had to focus on newly dominant economic and aesthetico-political regimes, in order to pursue narrative and philosophical mechanisms capable of at least momentarily dislodging them.

Information and Transparent Communication

Lyotard's position responded broadly to the new, progressivist, secular humanism of the 1980s and to the failures of critique and antitotalitarianism to deal with contemporary dangers. He had much to say against the new rhetoric of freedom of information and its advocacy of social and institutional transparency. As early as 1972, he had contrasted the text's propensity to achieve purity through abstract language with the subject's experience that textual information was mediated, represented, distended by the opaque figural realm. In the intervening years, the thickness of the figural was compounded by resistance and the *différend* (differend, meaning irreducible difference of opinion) and, through them, by Lyotard's adoption of earlier projects: epistemological obstacle, ethical alterity, political ambiguity and complexity, a persistent deconstruction of transparency and its metaphors. This thick given, economic as much as political, tended to pull in and erase the subject and its difference. Despite its worsening incomprehensibility, it found justification in recurrent narratives of light and progress that had led to "neo-analphabetism, the impoverishment of the peoples of the [global] South and the Third World, unemployment, the despotism of opinion and thus of prejudice exercised by the media, the law that what is good is what performs well."[34] At the center of all this were new forms of abstraction of information and knowledge. Lyotard granted as much in *La Condition postmoderne: Rapport sur le savoir* (1979; *The Postmodern Condition: A Report on Knowledge*), his most famous and badly misunderstood project, which must be read anew as a political epistemology of new economies of information and knowledge, articulated through a commitment to disrupting master narratives. In it, he raised the alarm about the economic and technological conditions that underlie the transformation of knowledge, their effect on state–subject relations, and the role of transparency in these structures. Communicational transparency was like liberalism, he argued:[35]

The ideology of communicational "transparency," which goes hand in hand with the commercialization of knowledge, will begin to perceive the State as a factor of opacity and "noise." It is from this point of view that the problem of the relationship between economic and State powers threatens to arise with a new urgency. Already in the last few decades, economic powers have reached the point of imperiling the stability of the State through new forms of the circulation of capital that go by the generic name of multinational corporations. These new forms of circulation imply that investment decisions have, at least in part, passed beyond the control of the nation-states. The question threatens to become even more thorny with the development of computer technology and telematics. . . . New legal issues will be raised, and with them the question: "who will know?" Transformation in the nature of knowledge, then, could well have repercussions on the existing public powers, forcing them to reconsider their relations (both de jure and de facto) with the large corporations and, more generally, with civil society. The reopening of the world market, a return to vigorous economic competition, the breakdown of the hegemony of American capitalism, the decline of the socialist alternative, a probable opening of the Chinese market—these and many other factors are already, at the end of the 1970s, preparing States for serious reappraisal of the role they have been accustomed to playing since the 1930s: that of guiding, or even directing investments. In this light, the new technologies can only increase the urgency of such a reexamination, since they make the information used in decision-making (and therefore the means of control) even more mobile and subject to piracy. It is not hard to visualize learning circulating along the same lines as money, instead of for its "educational" value or political (administrative, diplomatic, military) importance; the pertinent distinction would no longer be between knowledge and ignorance, but rather, as is the case with money, between "payment knowledge" and "investment knowledge"—in other words, between units of knowledge exchanged in a daily maintenance framework (the reconstitution of the workforce, "survival") versus funds of knowledge dedicated to optimizing the performance of a project. If this were the case, communicational transparency would be similar to liberalism. Liberalism does not preclude an organization of the flow of money in which some channels are used in decision-making while others are only good for the payment of debts. One could similarly imagine flows of knowledge traveling along identical channels of identical nature, some of which would be reserved for the "decision makers," while the others would be used to repay each person's perpetual debt with respect to the social bond.[36]

The state on the defensive; a new hierarchization of individuals, on the basis not of class but of information possession; an international system circumscribed by corporations that go beyond and escape national law, territory, and control; the legitimation crisis; financial and technological expropriation and abuse of information; the identification of money flows with knowledge flows: transparency would encompass it all—from the need for "free" information, through the principles necessary for communication to become more closely tied to economic power, to the mechanisms channeled by financial corporations into making the state a "factor of opacity."

Information, of course, has been central to this book—in Bachelard's obstacles; in structural theories of language; in Foucault's concern with the scaffolding of knowledge; in the cybernetic future imagined by Leroi-Gourhan and its liberating deconstruction by Derrida. It is difficult not to think that the interest in freedom of information that spread in the 1980s created a logic that has lasted to the present day, and has appropriated and deformed the more radical philosophical anticipations of the 1960s. If, in the 1980s, this logic promised a transformation of state–society relations, in the years to come the new freedom of information only fed the social homogenization that philosophers had so persistently fought against.

Because of the way in which Lyotard's trajectory contrasts with that of the French Left in the 1970s and 1980s on matters of transparent communication and progressivist universalism, this trajectory makes a perfect framework for the point with which I would like to conclude this book.

The turn into the 1980s oversaw the peak of the post-oil crisis, the decline into self-satisfaction of the antitotalitarian movement, a general withdrawal of structuralism, and the growing celebration of French modernity, culminating in the bicentennial of 1789. At that moment, the deconstruction of transparency traced in this book still offered an incisive means of resistance to economic policies, the state, homogenization, the flattening of information, injustice, and a cheap universality. In *Le postmoderne expliqué aux enfants* (1986; *The Postmodern Explained to Children*), Lyotard offered a picture of how his goal of a "politics of incommensurables," of "hardening differends into confrontations," was still available:

We have paid dearly our nostalgia for the all and the one, for a reconciliation of the concept and the sensible, for a transparent and communicable experience. Beneath the general demand for relaxation and appeasement we hear murmurings of the desire to reinstitute terror and fulfill the phantasm of taking possession of reality. The response is: let us make war on the whole, witness the unpresentable, activate the differends and save the honor of the name.[37]

A half-century after the 1929 crisis, to which he dated the earliest deconstructions of the transparency ideal, and a full generation after the Liberation, the means to contest a transparency paraded around as a solution to social problems, information-related problems, and ontological problems demanded a persistent if nomadic resistance. Resistance to totality, homogenization, normalization—on the whole, a rhetorical war, a witnessing turned into a mobilization of differends. Lyotard came relatively late to the deconstruction of transparency, but his war on it had a quality that could continue the opposition, the negativity, the antidogmatism. If, as I have argued, the state–society conflict that erupted in May '68 overtook the antisubjectivist and epistemological critique of transparency, the quasi-reconciliation of state and society achieved in the Mitterand era through freedom of information and the economics of modernization and austerity returned the contestation to the "new Enlightenment" in philosophy, which argued against its master narratives. But this new Enlightenment, too, had perhaps recuperated the promised liberation of the symbolic and, alongside it, the economy of knowledge. This was Lyotard's target. Hadn't the control of information, the new producer of a knowledge liberated from the subject, been coopted by a false reconciliation of state, economy, and society? Wasn't the disappearance of Man that Foucault had promised overtaken by the new inhuman architecture of economics and supposedly free information? Lyotard's plea for a reconceptualization of the economies of knowledge, his war through differends and minima, proposed a way to stop these recuperations, a way of arming and guiding anew the critique of transparency against the state, its power over information, and its dynamic of cooptation and violence, even of its loudest enemies.

This plea is one that still deserves its day, perhaps even more so now. For years the aestheticization of self-exposure has been legitimizing practices of data mining, and we have recently witnessed an abandonment of the dream of governmental openness that, after a three-decade ascendancy, had reached its apex in the early Obama years. With the election of Donald Trump and the return of nationalist authoritarianism in Europe, this abandonment is authorized, even pursued, by political leaderships that willfully neglect and embrace financial and technological power, cater to an opaque circulation of information, and pry apart society, particularly at its margins and at the expense of the weakest. Whether this renewed and damaging negotiation of transparency is short-lived or not, it has confronted our illusions about society and knowledge with the worst long-term dangers of technologically hegemonic regimes. In this environment, the dismantling of transparency that I have tracked in this book can serve as a differend, like Lyotard's, for thinking the subjective, social, and epistemological complexity and violence of the world now on offer. After all, justice cannot do its work without committed resistance to these spectacles of power, and sometimes it needs a shadow out of which to eventually arise.

Abbreviations

BN	Jean-Paul Sartre, *Being and Nothingness* (1992 [1943])
BnF	Bibliothèque nationale de France
CAPHÉS	Centre d'Archives de Philosophie et d'Édition des Sciences
CE	Jean Rouch, *Ciné-ethnography* (2003)
CHM	Jacques Derrida, "Cogito and the History of Madness" (1978 [1967])
DP	Michel Foucault, *Discipline and Punish* (1995 [1975])
EDC	Michel Leiris, "L'Ethnographie devant le colonialisme" (1988)
ESK	Claude Lévi-Strauss, *The Elementary Structures of Kinship* (1969)
F-*DE*	Michel Foucault, *Dits et écrits* (1994a)
FSM	Claude Lévi-Strauss, "Jean-Jacques Rousseau, Founder of the Sciences of Man" (1983)
GS	André Leroi-Gourhan, *Gesture and Speech* (1993)
HM	Michel Foucault, *History of Madness* (2006)
IFR	François Furet, *Interpreting the French Revolution* (1981 [1978])
ISA	Louis Althusser, "Ideology and Ideological State Apparatuses" (1971a)
J-*DE*	Martin Jay, *Downcast Eyes: The Denigration of Vision in Twentieth-Century French Thought* (1993)
KL	Georges Canguilhem, *Knowledge of Life* (2008b)
LL	François Jacob, *The Logic of Life* (1982)
L-*E*	Jacques Lacan, *Écrits* (2006 [1966])
L-*S1*	Jacques Lacan, *Seminar I: Freud's Papers on Technique* (1991)
L-*S2*	Jacques Lacan, *Seminar II: The Ego in Freud's Theory and in the Technique of Psychoanalysis, 1954–1955* (1988)
L-*S3*	Jacques Lacan, *Seminar III: The Psychoses, 1955–56* (1993)
MO	Georges Canguilhem, "Machine and Organism," in *KL*.
MT	André Leroi-Gourhan, *Milieu et techniques* (1975 [1943])

NP	Georges Canguilhem, *The Normal and the Pathological* (1991 [1943])
OG	Jacques Derrida, *Of Grammatology* (1997)
OT	Michel Foucault, *The Order of Things* (1994 [1966])
PC	Léon Brunschvicg, *Le Progrès de la conscience dans la philosophie occidentale* (1953)
PFM	Claude Lefort, *The Political Forms of Modern Society: Bureaucracy, Democracy, Totalitarianism* (1988)
PP	Maurice Merleau-Ponty, *Phenomenology of Perception* (1962)
PSF	Jean Wahl, "The Present Situation and Present Future of French Philosophy" (1950)
PWD	René Descartes, *The Philosophical Writings of Descartes* (1984–91)
RTS	Marc Richir, "Révolution et transparence sociale" (1974)
SAS	Pierre Clastres, *Society against the State* (1987 [1974])
SLP	Jacques Lacan, "The Function and Field of Speech and Language in Psychoanalysis," in L-*E*.
SSSU	Inspéction académique des Hautes-Pyrénées, Service de santé scolaire et universitaire
TM	Jean Starobinski, "Des taches et des masques" (1958)
TT	Claude Lévi-Strauss, *Tristes tropiques* (1992 [1955])
VM	Jacques Derrida, "La Vie la mort" (1975)
VTC	André Lalande, *Vocabulaire technique et critique de la philosophie* (1988)
WTP	Maurice Merleau-Ponty, "The War Has Taken Place" (1964c [1945])

Notes

INTRODUCTION

1. Starobinski 1988/1971 (subsequent citations are to both editions).
2. Ibid., 25–26/13–15.
3. Ibid., 26, 28/15, 18.
4. Ibid., 34/21.
5. Ibid., 218, 301/181, 254.
6. Starobinski explicitly diagnoses paranoia: ibid., 240–41/201–2.
7. Ibid., 283/239.
8. Ibid., 284–5/240. Starobinski's title for the subsection of his chapter 9 that examines the raising of walls trapping Rousseau as resulting from his quest for purity is *Intentions réalisées*.
9. Ibid., 116–21/92–97, noted by Jacques Derrida in *OG*, 353 n. 30.
10. Starobinski 1964: 101. On the influence of this argument, see, e.g., Michel Foucault's note on Starobinski, Rousseau, and the French Revolution in F-*DE*, 195.
11. Authorial transparency was a major concern of the Geneva School, with which Starobinski remains identified and whose focus was on highlighting the relationship of an author to his or her text. The secondary literature on Starobinski that references questions of authorial transparency includes Lawall 1968; Miller 1966; Colangelo 2004; and Vidal 2001.
12. TM, 792–804 (all quotations are from 796 and 797). The essay was republished as "L'Imagination projective" in Starobinski 1970: 238–54. On the mistrust of psychology among epistemologists and Marxists in the 1950s, see Bianco and Tho 2013, xxiii.
13. TM, 800. Starobinski was hardly alone in criticizing the Rorschach test. See Lévi-Strauss's citation of Margaret Mead's dismissal of the value of the test (Lévi-Strauss 1987, 12).
14. TM, 798.
15. Starobinski has recently written of Kuhn's influence on his own study of melancholia (2012: 10–12).
16. See Kuhn 1957: 17, 20.
17. Bachelard 1957: 9.

18. TM, 803.

19. Ibid., 804.

20. Poulet 1969: 63. Poulet followed this reading of Starobinski's "optimism, even . . . utopianism" with doubts as to whether "Starobinski's criticism, like Blanchot's, is doomed to end in a philosophy of separation" (ibid., 65).

21. Darnton 1988; Shklar 1988. Shklar does touch on the paranoid consequence of Rousseau's emphasizing his own transparency, but she neither considers it essential nor follows Starobinski's argument. Darnton 1984: 78 recognizes the significance of opacity for historico-anthropological study but treats it as something dissolved by proper analysis. See also Jay's account in J-*DE*, 80, 90–93.

22. Starobinski 1989: v–vi.

23. Starobinski 1946; on Rousseau, see 3: 219 there.

24. Starobinski 1946, 4: 375.

25. Ibid., 376.

26. Paul Valéry, "L'Homme de verre" (1903), in Valéry 1960: 44; translated as "The Man of Glass," in Valéry 1973: 44–45, translation modified. My claim is not that transparency had an exclusively positive hue before the war and that the situation changed afterward. Lucien Lévy-Bruhl, e.g., mocked non-Durkheimian sociology for its facile link between society and consciousness, saying: "The phenomena of our own consciousness are far from being 'transparent' to us" (Lévy-Bruhl 1927 [1903]: 119). Yet he also treated the primitive mind as irrational and praised rationality as aiming toward a kind of transparency. Marcel Proust's character Norpois disparaged a kindred notion of transparency when exclaiming, about a friend: "Who *wouldn't* know him, I ask you? The man's soul is as clear as crystal. Actually, that's the only fault one could find with him—it's not necessary for a diplomatist to have a heart as transparent as his" (Proust 2002 [1919]: 33; on Proust and transparency, see also the brilliant discussion in Cohn 1978, who began from the premise that narration in modernist literature, from *Tristram Shandy* up to Nathalie Sarraute's novels, made possible a transparency in literary character that the novels' authors specifically denied to actual humans). Here is a passage that captures Proust's notion of transparency as a literary ideal: "Impressions of the sort that I was trying to stabilize would simply evaporate if they came into contact with a direct pleasure which was powerless to bring them into being. The only way to continue to appreciate them was to try to understand them more completely just as they were, that is to say within myself, *to make them transparent enough* to see right down into their depths" (Proust 2003 [1927]: 185 emphasis added; see also 185, 187–88). Even though rejections of one kind of transparency before World War II routinely reverted to benefiting another, obviously the term had its critical uses. Similarly, I don't need to insist that transparency did have its occasional positive uses in the postwar era.

27. SLP, 270/224.

28. RTS, 10.

29. Barack Obama, "Transparency and Open Government: Memorandum for the Heads of Executive Departments and Agencies" (January 21, 2009), www.white house.gov/the_press_office/TransparencyandOpenGovernment (accessed January 10, 2017).

30. See critical works, especially in German, such as Han 2012 and Schneider 2013.

31. Adolf Hitler, "Speech at the Opening of the Great German Art Exhibition," in Anson Rabinbach and Sander Gilman, eds., *The Third Reich Sourcebook*, (Berkeley: University of California Press, 2013), 496.

32. Jaspers 2001: 11 (see also the chapter "Our Purification").

33. See Jaspers on a "life lived beneath a mask," cited in Michaud 2004: 43.

34. Vidler 1992: 220.

35. Barnstone 2005: 1–2.

36. Blumenberg 1987: 456.

37. Kotsonis 2014: 179–82 and ch. 6.

38. Fitzpatrick 2005: 3–5, 13.

39. Kotkin 1995: ch. 5; Halfin 2000; see also Hellbeck 2000 on diaries.

40. E.g., Herf 1997.

41. Goffman 1959; Trilling 1972.

42. Fried, "Art and Objecthood" (1967) in Fried 1998. For an often undialectical celebration of the twentieth century as a century of transparency in art, see Cohen 1995: 26.

43. Rabinow 1989: "Introduction to the Present."

44. Hartog 2003.

45. Veyne 1983: 38; 33–34.

46. Jacques Derrida coined the terms "New Enlightenment" in Derrida 1990, e.g., at p. 496, and "Enlightenment to come" in Derrida 2005; for a discussion, see Balibar 2012.

47. Bataille 1985: 31.

48. Reinhart Koselleck argues that "*Begriffsgeschichte* is always concerned with political or social events" and examines "prevailing" concepts (Koselleck 2004: 86). On the first count, I beg to disagree; on the second, I see no reason to treat what I here call a "minor" or "phantom" concept as mutually exclusive with "prevailing" ones, even as Koselleck focused on major and almost always famous concepts. That transparency should not be conceived of as a "major" concept (*Grundbegriff*) is suggested by its absence from Lalande's *Vocabulaire technique* (Lalande 1923) as well as from Cassin 2004 and Worms 2016.

49. On historical epistemology, see Rheinberger 2010; Daston 1991; Davidson 2002.

50. This group includes—to name just a few of the more important— Giuseppe Bianco (2015), Julian Bourg (2007), Ethan Kleinberg (2005), Samuel

Moyn (2004, 2005, 2012a, 2012b), Knox Peden (2014), Camille Robcis (2013), Judith Surkis (2012).

51. Jay 1993. I have been repeatedly and correctly advised to contend with Jay's book explicitly, but to do so I would have to contend with it at inordinate length; here I prefer to express my debt to it and indicate the broad difference of argument, theme, subject matter, and method.

52. Glissant 2006: 189.

53. A story similar to the one I offer here might be told from the perspective of other concepts, including some of those discussed in this book. But these concepts (e.g., norm and other) do not, of their own, imply each other, whereas the critique of transparency *does* tie them together. Perhaps this is because transparency was a relatively minor concept in relation to them and remained one of those notions that are *not* elaborated upon but are taken for granted, ligaments in the body of discourse without an always obvious role.

54. Geertz 1973: 5.

55. I should note at this point that I find Blumenberg's (2010: 1–5) mistrust of the self-sufficiency of concepts useful. At the same time the trickiness of distinguishing between concept and metaphor in the uses of transparency seems to me intellectually compelling: these uses bridged the gap between the two, and the ensuing ambiguity imposes the approach I'm following here.

56. This entire section is intended as a critique of Koselleck 2004: 75–92.

57. Besides Obama's memorandum cited in n. 29 above, see also David Cameron's pledge ("Open Government Partnership," www.opengovpartnership.org/country/united-kingdom (accessed January 10, 2017) to make the British government "the most open and transparent in the world."

58. See the discussion in Harcourt 2015, and also the essays in Levin et al. 2002.

59. On the notion of history of the present, see *DP* 23, 30, 31; Canguilhem 2012: 12–13; Leys 2010; Scott 2007b.

60. A case in point is Manfred Schneider's highly interesting *Transparenztraum* (2013), which is critical of the fantasy of transparency but is itself too linear and seems largely unaware of traditions (including the one described here) in which the refusal of transparency dominated.

61. E.g., Christie and Tansey 1998. Among more recent critical historical and conceptual studies of current positivistic fetishisms of the "openness" and "visibility" of data, thanks to which data "are not only taken to be unobstructed and accessible but are also conceptualized as discrete units that can be easily identifiable, are stable in their format and content, and can be moved across a range of contexts," see Leonelli, Rappert, and Davies 2017 (quotation from 191).

62. Vattimo 1992.

63. Han 2013.

64. Butler 2005: 42.

CHAPTER 1: WAS TRANSPARENCY AN OPTICAL PROBLEM?

1. Aristotle, *De anima* 2.7.418b26, trans. D. Hamlyn (Aristotle 1993a).

2. Ibid., 418b3 and 26.

3. On the history of *dia-* in *diaphanous*, see Alloa 2011: chs. 2–3.

4. Aristotle, *De anima*, 419a6 and 28.

5. Vasiliu 1997; Alloa 2011: ch. 2.

6. Descartes, "The World, or Treatise on Light," in *PWD*, 1: 85. See also his denial that air is a "mere nothing" in *Principles of Philosophy*, 1: 71, *PWD*, 1: 219.

7. Ibid., 30, *PWD*, 1: 203.

8. *VTC*, 586, s.v. "Lumière naturelle."

9. Descartes, *Principles of Philosophy*, 1: 43–45, *PWD*, 1: 207.

10. Ibid., 10, *PWD*, 1: 195–96.

11. Descartes, "The Search for Truth," *PWD*, 2: 399–420. As Charles Guignon has put it in referencing the role of Cartesian "natural light" for modern conceptions of knowledge, Cartesian transparency concerns "the attainment of complete clarity through the grounding of our beliefs in the intrinsic intelligibility of the *lumen naturale*" (Guignon 1993: 136).

12. Descartes, *Principles of Philosophy*, 2: 17, *PWD*, 1: 230.

13. Newton 1718: queries 18 and 23, pp. 324, 328.

14. *KL*, 99.

15. Diderot and D'Alembert 1751–65: s.v. "Transparence," 16: 558. Citing Newton's treatment of attraction, the article offered the (somewhat unsatisfactory) counterclaim that it is the unequal density of objects' parts, or the filling of their pores with "heterogeneous matter," or yet the absolute emptiness of these pores that allows for their reflection or refraction.

16. Diderot and d'Alembert 1751–65: s.v. "Lumière," 9: 717–22; also "Discours préliminaire," ibid., 1: vii–x.

17. Féraud 1787, s.v. "transparence." I am grateful to Peter Dreyer for this reference.

18. Levitt 2009: 4.

19. On light and utopia, see Baczko 1989.

20. Canguilhem 1987: 441.

21. See, e.g., Fuchs 1923.

22. Gadamer 1976: 205; Gadamer 2013: 216, 232.

23. In France, the use of Gestalt theory to criticize classic theories of perception was carried out only by a few phenomenologists, Aron Gurwitsch and Merleau-Ponty among them.

24. *J-DE*, ch. 2. Jay has argued that French thought after 1930 is marked by a rethinking of the category of vision, which lost the high status it had enjoyed in the West since the Enlightenment. Despite my enormous respect for Jay's *Downcast Eyes*, I describe a webbing of concepts and follow a path quite different from

what Jay does when he treats vision as a self-sufficient category and tracks a linear ascent to its "denigration" in twentieth-century France.

25. Wahl 1932: 3.

26. Marrati 2008: 34. On Bergson's influence around 1930, see Bianco 2015.

27. Bachelard 2002: 24; translation amended.

28. Mauss 2002; work protocols among Mauss's students already foregrounded these concerns around 1930.

29. On Merleau-Ponty, Gurwitsch, and Gestalt theory, see Geroulanos 2011b.

30. PSF, 49. See also Lacroix 1957: 19.04.4.

31. Baltrušaitis 1984: 8.

32. Charpentrat 1971: 161.

CHAPTER 2: FRANCE, YEAR ZERO

1. Deleuze 1989: xi; emphasis added.

2. Bazin 1958–62.

3. On the relation of perception to cinema in Deleuze, see Marrati 2008: ch. 2.

4. Sartre 1970: 661. Sartre credits Malraux with the idea that the chaos and joy of the Liberation involved an "exercise of the Apocalypse."

5. *Dieu Vivant*, 1 (1945): "Liminaire," 5; see also the two 1945 issues of the journal *Cahiers de la nouvelle époque*. For a discussion of the circle animating these journals, see Bianco 2012.

6. Alfred Métraux to Michel Leiris, August 8, 1945 (LAS/FML C.02.04.005).

7. Mascolo, "Si la lecture de Saint-Just est possible" [1946], in Mascolo 1993: 22.

8. Febvre 1946: 2.

9. Ibid., 1, 2–3.

10. Ibid., 1, 1–2.

11. Febvre 1945: 151.

12. Hartog 2003.

13. WTP, 139.

14. Ibid., 140.

15. Ibid., 148.

16. Ibid., 145.

17. Ibid., 144.

18. Ibid., 148, 151.

19. Ibid., 147.

20. Ibid., 145–46.

21. Ibid., 149.

22. Ibid., 152.

23. Ibid.

24. Levinas 2001 [1947]: 7.

25. Ibid., 9.

26. Ibid., 40.

27. Ibid., 41.

28. Ibid., 43.

29. Ibid., 52–53.

30. WTP, 147.

31. As is well known (and this passage corroborates it), Levinas frames his major concern with contemporary philosophy—his critique of ontology, particularly Heidegger's, whose influence was on the ascendant in France—in terms that suggest that Heidegger's Being offered neither a new "birth" for thought nor a "clearing" for existence.

32. Bataille 1981: 231, quoted in Kendall 2007: 195.

CHAPTER 3: THE WORLD'S OPACITY TO CONSCIOUSNESS

1. Wahl 1932.

2. Thus there was admiration for Sartre's accomplishment even among philosophers less than inclined to support him: Koyré 1998: 534; PSF; Lacroix 1957: 19.04.4.

3. *BN*, 11; emphasis added.

4. Ibid., 89, 246.

5. Ibid., 140. See also J-*DE* 282.

6. *BN*, 114. See also Sartre's contrast between "the intimacy and translucency of thought" and "the opacity and indifference of the in-itself," ibid., 737.

7. Ibid., 125. The context here concerns belief, but the argument extends to a psychoanalytical conception of the unconscious, which Sartre rejects for the same reason.

8. E.g., ibid., 438.

9. Ibid., 20.

10. Sartre 1957: 40; Sartre repeats this anxiety, again in terms of opacity, at p. 42.

11. Ibid., 93.

12. Sartre 2007: 56.

13. Sartre 2004: 72, also 6, 26, 116.

14. Ibid., 15, 27, 72.

15. Bianco 2009: 324. See also Sartre 1962: 39.

16. Sartre 1957: 98, 101.

17. I have highlighted the collapse of this distinction into an "anti-foundational realism" in Geroulanos 2010: ch. 1.

18. *PC*, §368, 2: 792.

19. Ibid., §76, 1: 135.

20. Ibid., §94, 1: 167.

21. Ibid., §147, 1: 302; §367–68, 2: 790–92.

22. Ibid., §369, 2: 795.

23. Jean-Louis Vieillard-Baron and Giuseppe Bianco in particular link Sartre's (joint) interests in transparency and solipsism to Brunschvicg. Vieillard-Baron 2000: 92; Bianco 2009: 324.

24. WTP, 144.

25. *BN*, 409–10.

26. Ibid., 428.

27. Ibid., 429. Canguilhem's framing of the relationship of a living being and its environment in *KL* is similar to Sartre's treatment of the interdependence between "me" and my environment. Without referencing phenomenology, Canguilhem echoed Sartre's arguments to the effect that the living being was at once central and eccentric to this milieu: the normal or healthy living being retained a measure of individuality and freedom from its environment.

28. *BN*, 411.

29. Ibid., 416.

30. Ibid., 428.

31. Ibid., 413.

32. Ibid., 90.

33. Ibid., 200.

34. Ibid., 82–83; translation modified. Sartre further insists on the transparency of consciousness in this context (*BN*, 89).

35. Ibid., 89.

36. Ibid., 101–3.

37. Ibid., 107, 108, 109.

38. Ibid., 106.

39. Ibid., 105.

40. Ibid., 107.

41. Ibid., 101.

42. Ibid., 109.

43. Ibid., 229. See Jay's comments on Sartre's "other" in J-*DE* 288.

44. *BN*, 343.

45. Ibid., 356.

46. Ibid., 559.

47. Ibid., 688.

48. Ibid.

49. Ibid., 707.

50. Châtelet and Pisier-Kouchner 1981: 879.

51. *BN*, 708.

52. It is perhaps possible to argue that, in *La Structure du comportement* (1942; written in 1938), Merleau-Ponty had been considerably less hostile to the term transparency; for example he considered the face as a "transparent" envelope of attitudes (Merleau-Ponty 1963: 167). By 1945, the term had lost all positive hue. See also J-*DE*, 308.

53. *PP*, 124, xii, 105.

54. Ibid., 353.

55. Ibid., 347.

56. Ibid., xi–xii. Merleau-Ponty (2007: 96) also praised Lachelier and Brunschvicg for criticizing positivism for its obsession with reducing facts to transparent laws.

57. *PP*, 241; see also 124.

58. See also the discussion of eye, mind, and transparency in Merleau-Ponty's "Eye and Mind," in Merleau-Ponty 1964a: 354.

59. *PP*, 350. On Merleau-Ponty's philosophical physiology, see Geroulanos 2011b.

60. *PP*, xi.

61. Ibid., 381.

62. Ibid., 424. On transparent consciousness as a Bergsonian retrospective illusion, see ibid., 380–81, and Bianco 2009: 381.

63. Merleau-Ponty 2001; Butler 2006: 193.

64. Merleau-Ponty, "Note on Machiavelli," in Merleau-Ponty 1964b: 223.

65. *PP*, 452.

CHAPTER 4: THE IMAGE OF SCIENCE AND THE LIMITS OF KNOWLEDGE

1. Canguilhem cited Sartre repeatedly in his teaching of the mid-1940s: see "La Notion de transcendance, juin 1945" and "Déterminisme et indéterminisme, février 1945," p. 10, in CAPHÉS, GC.11.3.13 and GC.11.3.7. Alexandre Koyré (1998: 534) resisted Sartre but wrote highly approvingly of his brilliance.

2. Foucault 1991: 7–24. Canguilhem's hostility to *Les Temps modernes* became especially forceful in the 1960s. In his homage to Jean Cavaillès, Canguilhem contrasted the latter (especially his heroism) with the existentialists; see, e.g., Canguilhem 2004: 36. See also Canguilhem's defense of Foucault's *The Order of Things* against "the naïve children of existentialism" (Canguilhem 2005: 77). On this cluster of problems, Peter Hallward's introduction in Hallward and Peden 2012 and Schrift 2006, esp. ch. 3, make excellent reading.

3. Chimisso 2008; McGrath 2014.

4. See the definitions s.v. "Science" in *VTC*, 2: 953–58 (especially definitions A, B, D); conversely, Lalande's section on contemporary "critiques" of the strong use of the term emphasizes this strong use.

5. See, e.g., Canales 2015.

6. I discuss the subject of "antifoundational realism" extensively in Geroulanos 2010: ch. 1.

7. Bachelard 2002: 18.

8. Rorty 1979.

9. Bachelard 2002: 24; translation amended.

10. Tiles 1994: 39.

11. Bachelard 1949: 11, 13.

12. Koyré, "Sur la pensée de Brunschvicg," Centre Alexandre Koyré, Fonds Koyré, pp. 2–3. I have not been able to find the passage that Koyré uses in Brunschvicg's voluminous writings; but see the exchange between Brunschvicg and Meyerson in Brunschvicg 1921: 61–64; also *PC* 2: §340.

13. See my discussion of Koyré in Geroulanos 2010: ch. 1; see also Zambelli 1998: 521–29 and the introduction in Redondi 1986. Koyré would later express regret over his earlier criticism of Brunschvicg's work (see Koyré 1963). See also the point that Kant (and, by implication, Brunschvicg) forced a transparent truth (Châtelet and Pisier-Kouchner 1981: 71).

14. Cavaillès 1976: 78. That this claim indicates Cavaillès's distance from Brunschvicg is an interpretation proposed by Canguilhem 2005: 91 and by Wahl in PSF, 36–37: "[Cavaillès] examines the presuppositions of intellectualistic thought in the light of phenomenology and of the last results of the logisticians; and he seems to come to abandon some of these presuppositions." For an excellent, detailed explanation of Cavaillès's relationship with Brunschvicg, and also of Cavaillès's reaction to Husserl's 1929 *Cartesian Meditations* lectures in Paris, see Peden 2014: ch. 1.

15. *KL*, xvii.

16. Ibid., xx.

17. See also the argument in Canguilhem 1963.

18. *KL*, xviii. In 1949, Wahl included Canguilhem among Brunschvicg's former students who had come to oppose intellectualism: "[Canguilhem] stresses the value of biological phenomena as giving us a richer idea of reality than the one which was given by pure intellectualism." Wahl credited intellectualism with the backlash it generated against its argument, but, as this passage makes clear, Brunschvicg and his generation were now being blamed for having advocated a form of thinking that considered the world merely transparent to thought; a new "richness" was now being sought (PSF, 37). Wahl's sense of Canguilhem's direction was based on a series of three lectures on "Biology and Philosophy" that Canguilhem had delivered at Wahl's Collège philosophique in the spring of 1947, which would make up the bulk of *Knowledge of Life*. The Collège philosophique, a somewhat ad hoc institution for philosophy lectures that Jean Wahl founded and coordinated from 1947 through the 1960s, was well attended (see the records at Institut mémoires de l'édition contemporaine, Fonds Jean Wahl, Dossier Collège philosophique; on the founding, see *Littéraire* of January 18, 1947 and *Aux Écoutes* of January 17, 1947: 9; and see also Faye 1985: 70–72). Canguilhem's manuscript notes for the talks are preserved in CAPHÉS GC.12.1.8; the critique of Descartes and the discussion of mechanism and finalism were very close to the published text.

19. Duhem 1954: 162.

20. Mauss 1950: 305.

21. *MT*, 436.

22. On Canguilhem's role as a protector of the generation of the 1960s, see Peeters 2013: 114, 129; Bianco and Tho 2013: xxii, translation amended; and Macherey 1996: 47–56.

23. Perhaps the clearest characteristic of this intellectual debt is the continued private expression of proximity and debt—e.g., the practice of sending autographed copies (in Derrida's case even offprints), which survive in Canguilhem's library.

24. *NP*, 239.

25. On the effect of relativity and Heisenberg's uncertainty, see Rheinberger 2010: ch. 2 and Geroulanos 2010: ch. 1.

26. Châtelet and Pisier-Kouchner 1981: 879. On Broglie and Kojève, see Geroulanos 2010: ch. 1.

27. Broglie 1929: thesis 8.

28. See the copy of Broglie 1929 in CAPHÉS GC.11.3.7 "Déterminisme et indéterminisme," 2–3. In his notes, Canguilhem objected to the mirroring of "the moral world" on "the material world," insisting, with reference to Comte, that there is only a material world interpreted by intelligence, which is an instrument of creation and freedom. Distinguishing moral interpretations from physical reality was a repeated concern of Canguilhem's: in another 1945 course, he insisted that individuality is not a phenomenon that belongs to the material world (e.g., the world of microparticles, physics, and determinism), but an aspect of living beings. See CAPHÉS GC.11.3.11 "L'Individualité, avril 1945," 9, 10–13, 17.

29. *KL*, 135.

30. CAPHÉS GC.11.3.7 "Déterminisme et indéterminisme," 8.

31. Ibid., 9.

32. Ibid., emphasis added.

33. Ibid., 11.

34. Ibid., GC.12.1.10 "Agrégation, sujets de leçons, 1947," "Le Progrès."

35. Ibid., "Les Limites de la connaissance," 16.

36. Ibid.

37. Canguilhem 1964–65: 13; in Bianco and Tho 2013: 21–22.

38. Canguilhem, "L'Objet de l'histoire des sciences" in Canguilhem 1983: 18.

39. *KL*, xviii.

40. S.v. "Progrès," in *VTC*, 2: 839.

41. Brunschvicg 1950: vii. Lalande saw the problem still more emphatically, as one about the unity of philosophy as a structuring mechanism for the organization of human thought: Lalande 1898: 566–67.

42. Febvre et al. 1930.

43. "La civilization . . . pour un Guillaume de Humboldt, s'annexait le domaine de l'ancienne police: la sécurité, le bon ordre, la paix établie et la douceur instituée dans le domaine des relations sociales" (Febvre, "La Civilisation," in Febvre 1930: 40).

44. Mauss, "Les Civilisations," republished in Mauss 1974: 476.
45. Friedmann 1936.
46. Ibid., chs. 3–4.
47. Febvre 2009 [1937]: 983.
48. Febvre 1945: 152.
49. Rheinberger 2005: 314.
50. Ibid., 326.
51. Bachelard 2002: 24; translation modified.
52. Ibid., 24.
53. Ibid., 19.
54. Ibid., 25; translation amended.
55. "The brain is the obstacle to scientific thought. It is an obstacle in the sense that it co-ordinates our movements and appetites. We have to think against the brain" (ibid., 248).
56. Ibid., 26; translation amended.
57. Canguilhem had already critiqued Comte on progress and order in 1927, in "La Théorie de l'ordre et du progrès chez Auguste Comte" (CAPHÉS GC.6.1). See also Canguilhem 1987.
58. Durkheim 1982 [1919]: 60.
59. Ibid., 61; emphasis added.

CHAPTER 5: MACHINES AND THE COGITO

An earlier version of parts of this chapter that appeared in 2015 as "Violence and Mechanism" in *Qui Parle* 24 (1): 125–46 is included here with the permission of the University of Nebraska Press.

1. See Canguilhem's aforementioned qualification of intellectualism as "transparent." His critique of Auguste Comte's theory of progress, already in Canguilhem's dissertation and especially in *The Normal and the Pathological*, runs parallel to the attack on reductionism.

2. In his accounts of tools and finalism, Canguilhem relied at length (and without citation) on Tétry 1948; see her analysis of the ambiguous relationship between tools and finalism, as well as her concern with the biologist's relationship to the living being (ibid., 13–16).

3. On technique in twentieth-century French thought, see Krell 2011.

4. *KL*, xvii; although that passage refers explicitly to neo-Kantianism, it applies equally to Descartes.

5. Recent political theory has cast vitalism as a progressive, posthumanist, and ecological form of romanticism. See Bennett 2010.

6. MO, 75–97.

7. This ambiguity is articulated very clearly in Charles Singer 1931: viii, who saw the divide between mechanism and vitalism as central to biological research.

8. See, e.g., the debates over internal regulation in British and American physiology, including in the work of Walter B. Cannon, John Scott Haldane, and others, who refused classical mechanism and wrestled with its possible alternatives.

9. Watson and Crick 1953: 737–38.

10. Schrödinger 1945.

11. Canguilhem's attitude to DNA as a genetic mechanism changed over time; later in his career he abandoned his earlier views on vitalism as dated (see Braunstein 2008: 79 n. 2).

12. Jacob 1982 treated life in an information theory–laden language of program and memory. See chapter 19.

13. See Merleau-Ponty 2007a [1951].

14. Siegfried 1949: 1, 9. On Taylorism, see the work of Georges Friedmann; also Rabinbach 1993: ch. 9.

15. Friedmann 1936, 1946.

16. Koyré 1990: 114.

17. CAPHÉS GC.11.3.4 "Technique et science, déc. 1944–janv. 1945, réutilisé et revu, novembre 1955," 7.

18. Ibid. 1, 9, where Canguilhem cites Marcel Mauss, Lucien Febvre's 1922 *La Terre et l'Evolution humaine* (at p. 9), and André Lalande. He repeats these references in MO where he also cites Leroi-Gourhan's *Milieu et techniques*, Friedmann's *Problèmes humains du machinisme industriel*, Julien Pacotte, and Pierre-Maxime Shuhl.

19. Boutroux 1927.

20. Koyré 1922: 199–200.

21. At this conference Martin Heidegger was also scheduled to present an essay, which he would soon revise into his famous 1938 lecture "Die Zeit des Weltbildes" ("The Age of the World Picture"), published in 1952, which accused Descartes of instituting a blend of subjectivity and technology that would define modernity. Heidegger sought (and failed) to become the leader of the German delegation, deeming the conference "a conscious attack coming from the dominant liberal–democratic concept of science." This picture of French thought relied on a rather dated and francophobic but not altogether inaccurate, indeed, quite prescient, understanding of what was taking place. See Safranski 1998: 324.

22. CAPHÉS GC 11.1, "Cours sur la finalité, 1941."

23. Canguilhem 1943a. Giuseppe Bianco dates Canguilhem's turn toward Bergson to the 1943 course; see his introduction in Deleuze and Canguilhem 2006.

24. CAPHÉS GC 11.1, "Cours sur la finalité," 10–11. Canguilhem's understanding of Aristotle is based on Pierre-Maxime Schuhl's *Machinisme et philosophie* (Schuhl 1938), at the time a highly regarded book, which Koyré 1990 [1948] also discussed. Canguilhem 2012: 67 refers to Schuhl as a friend.

25. Lecture "Organisme et totalité," in CAPHÉS GC 11.1, "Cours sur la finalité," 21–32, at p. 11. At this point Canguilhem did not suggest, as he would in

Knowledge of Life, that Descartes's attempted overcoming of finalism failed (see *KL*, 86–87).

26. CAPHÉS GC28.1.5, "Descartes Interrompu . . . 1948."

27. Ibid., GC28.1.3, "Notes de 1937 pour 'Descartes et la technique.'" I am grateful to Jacob Krell for pointing out the "Descartes et la technique" book project to me.

28. See Canguilhem's duplicate of a letter to the publisher from March 27, in GC28.1.5, "Descartes Interrompu . . . 1948," 5.

29. Chapters 1 and 3 of the typescript focus on Descartes's doubt (doubt as a foundation of the scientific method and general doubt respectively). See also Canguilhem's appreciation for Ferdinand Alquié, which he follows up with a critique of the mistrust of Cartesian metaphysics (CAPHÉS GC28.1.5, "Descartes Interrompu . . . 1948," 29).

30. Ibid., 29–30. On the impact of the atomic bombs on French culture, see Pace 1991.

31. IMEC Fonds Wahl: Dossier College philosophique, folder "3 chemises avec les programmes du collège."

32. MO, 83. On the novelty of Canguilhem's reading of the animal–machine, see Hacking 1998: 202–3.

33. MO, 84.

34. Ibid., 86; see also 89.

35. Ibid., 80.

36. Ibid., 82–83.

37. Ibid., 84; emphasis added.

38. Ibid., 83, 86.

39. Descartes, *Meditations*, *PWD* 2: 58.

40. Descartes 1972: 1–2.

41. MO, 85; emphasis added.

42. Ibid., 80; the reference is to Aristotle, *Politics* 1253b23–4b20 (see Aristotle 1993b).

43. MO, 79.

44. Koyré 1990 [1948]: 114.

45. Canguilhem discusses the relationships between thought and society at some length in MO, focusing on Aristotle's famous discussion of slavery and machines. In the passage cited above, Koyré emphasized the Cartesian dream as liberation from nature—a sense altogether absent in Canguilhem, whose reading of Descartes attributes many of the modern problems and cruelties against nature and others precisely to the establishment of the cogito as observer and manipulator.

46. MO, 96.

47. Ibid.

48. Ibid., 90.

49. Ibid., 95.

50. Ibid., 97.

51. CAPHÉS GC28.1.5, "Descartes Interrompu . . . 1948," 29–30.

52. *KL*, xvii.

53. Georges Canguilhem, "Qu'est-ce que la psychologie?" (1958), in Canguilhem 1983: 365–82. See also Braunstein, "Psychologie et milieu," in Braunstein 2007.

54. See Canguilhem 2008a, especially the description of psychology as a "permanent disaster" (p. 17) and the conclusion that a reduction of thought to the brain is the ultimate barbarism.

55. See Canguilhem 2012, "The Problem of Regulation."

CHAPTER 6: FROM THE TOTAL MAN TO THE OTHER

1. Stoczkowski 2008.

2. Alfred Métraux, "Un nouvel humanisme," in LAS/FML.B.S04.04.05.032. The text is marked as a new presentation of the book series L'Espèce humaine on the occasion of its twentieth volume.

3. At least since the 1930s (if not since the nineteenth century), anthropologists had urged the training of colonial officials in social anthropology, but the character and purpose of this training changed during decolonization. The training of bureaucrats and state agents was emphasized for example at the 1934 International Congress of Anthropological and Ethnological Sciences (July 30–August 4, 1934) in London. A copy of such an appeal can be found at the Muséum national d'histoire naturelle, Papiers Marcel Mauss, 2 AP 4 C 3 a ("Vœu émis par le Bureau").

4. See for example the letters from Griaule, Métraux, Lévi-Strauss, and also Dina Dreyfus (Lévi-Strauss) in Mauss's archives at the Bibliothèque du Collège de France and at the Bibliothèque du Muséum national d'histoire naturelle.

5. Mauss 2002 [1947]: 19, 34–35, 38. Technologies of observation, including photography and cinematography, were central to Mauss's project as early as the mid-1920s, and he presented a paper on this subject at an international meeting in Davos in 1928. See, in the same year, *Davoser Revue: Zeitschrift für Literatur, Wissenschaft, Kunst und Sport* 3 (7): 23.

6. Mauss 2002 [1947]: 34.

7. Rivet 1937.

8. The term *butin* is used already at the beginning of the expedition, e.g., in Leiris 1934: 69, 83; see also an article in *Minotaure* 2 of 1933 and Falasca-Zamponi 2011: 85 n. 78.

9. Griaule had thought of publishing a memoir and had anticipated Leiris's own memoirs (see his letter of August 24, 1933, in LAS/FML.B.S01.01.01.004), but had not expected Leiris's details on the tactics of threats, bribes, and the forceful removal of major sacred objects (*kono*). See Leiris 1934: 102–3; Jamin 1992; Clark-Taoua 2002.

10. Griaule wrote to Mauss to assure him that the collection of objects was

done under Mauss's own principles. See Griaule's letter to Mauss, June 29, 1931, at Muséum national d'histoire naturelle, Papiers Marcel Mauss, 2 AP4 2B 1G.

11. Henri Neuville, in Rivet 1937: 7.46.11. Neuville was against banning the term (7.64.14); but he insisted that communities of material interests, and not races, take priority (7.64.15). See also Neuville 1933: 469–70, and the discussion in Bocquet-Appel 1989: 25–26.

12. Meyran 2000: 72. According to Meyran, Rivet, e.g., seemed to accept the scientific character of the notion of race (ibid., 69).

13. On Griaule's institutional role, see Jolly 2001: 149–90.

14. Griaule 1957b: 14.

15. *MT*, 409–15, 418–20, 437–38.

16. Ibid., 309.

17. This is what I take Lévi-Strauss to mean when he wrote, in posthumous homage to Leroi-Gourhan, that while "counting on one hand" the occasions where the two had had a chance to exchange ideas would be to overestimate them, "we tried, he and I, to do more or less the same thing." See Bernot 1988: 201.

18. Marcel Mauss, "La Nation," in Mauss 1974, 3: 573–625.

19. Métraux to Leiris, August 8, 1945, in LAS/FML.C.02.04.006.

20. Leroi-Gourhan 1945: 25. See also Conklin 2007: 40; Jamin 1989: 108–9. For Jamin, the war amounted to a "theoretical liquidation" of the orientation and progressive values of Mauss's school. On Griaule, see Fiemeyer 2004: 61; Doquet 1999.

21. Métraux to Mauss, July 8, 1937 (Collège de France, Fonds Marcel Mauss, MAS 9.12).

22. Métraux to Leiris, August 8, 1945 (LAS/FML.C.02.04.005). See also Métraux 1978: 155. Métraux debated returning to France until mid-1946 (LAS/FML.C.02.04.009).

23. Métraux to Leiris, April 18, 1945, in LAS/FML.C.02.04.004.

24. LAS/FML.C.02.04.005.

25. Lévi-Strauss would offer a shorter but similar description of his return to France—which left him startled but feeling that he had come home: Eribon and Lévi-Strauss 1988: 259.

26. The language of restoration is not only an institutional one: Métraux repeatedly sent packages of goods to Leiris and other friends (see Métraux to Leiris, January 1, 1945, LAS/FML.C.02.04.003).

27. Lévi-Strauss 1953, esp. 114.

28. Métraux was pressing Leiris to persuade Gaston Gallimard to publish Ruth Benedict's work. See Métraux to Leiris, December 17, and December 29, 1948, in LAS/FML.D.S04.01.10.043–44, where Métraux emphasizes how much he values Ruth Benedict (clearly indicating that Leiris and Gallimard did not share that view). On Leiris taking over the series L'Espèce humaine (founded by Métraux, Rivet, and Georges-Henri Rivière) at Gallimard, see Armel 1997: 469–70. Métraux promoted a translation of Robert Lowie's *Primitive Society* (Lowie 1920).

29. Métraux 1950: 9.

30. See notably Brattain 2007; Shepard 2011: 273–97.

31. Maurel 2010: 49, 38.

32. Ibid., 49 etc.; Shepard, "Algeria, France, Mexico, UNESCO," 285.

33. See the discussion in Brattain 2007: 1393.

34. Ibid., 1388.

35. Lévi-Strauss 1987: 84–85; Lévi-Strauss 1975, 105, etc.

36. See the invitation from Robert C. Angell (May 15, 1950), in UNESCO SS/164.188 (also included in LAS/FML.B.S03.03.05.013) and the contract (UNESCO SS//174.027). Angell and Métraux had a close working relationship (see Métraux 1978: 289). Leiris's letter to Métraux of January 30, 1951 makes clear the latter's involvement (LAS/FML.B.S03.03.05.014).

37. Montagu participated in the writing of the UNESCO declaration and, together with Myrdal and Klineberg, was involved in its revision.

38. LAS/FML.D.S03, "Race et Civilisation": verso of page "3."

39. This was, of course, the overriding target of the antiracism campaign: Stoczkowski 2008: 72–4 (cited in Shepard 2011: 284) emphasizes that the Declaration on Race attempted "a point-by-point refutation of Hitler's *Mein Kampf.*"

40. Leiris 1975: 135; emphasis added. Henceforth referenced with page citations first in French, then in English.

41. Leiris's surviving notes (LAS/FML.D.S03, "Race et civilisation") give a clear sense of the references and citations underlying his actual text, as well as of his montage of them into an argument of his own. Some passages appear derivative of Linton and Benedict's respective work—see, e.g., the passage on the invention and transmission of cultural gains (Leiris 1975: 55/158, which derives in part from Benedict 1940: 12). Leiris copied Benedict's passage at length (see LAS/FML.D.S03, folder #3, page beginning with "[Plusieurs races pour faire . . .") and crossed it out after using it in his text. He proceeded the same way, e.g., with the passages on Japan (cf. Benedict 1940: 83 with Leiris 1975: 50–51/146). Montagu's and Metraux's works are treated like this too. Leiris did cite most of the authors he was using (and UNESCO's series of texts, which aimed at popularization, did not allow for footnotes). I insist on this montage procedure, not to suggest that the essay was derivative (the ideas in the repurposed passages were common knowledge among anthropologists), but to call attention to the interweaving of anthropological works as a method of dealing with the sociopolitical problem of race. On the use of montage in Leiris's literary work (especially early), see Hand 2002: 66, 87. See also the draft page (LAS/FML.D.S03, folder 3) beginning "Nos idées sur la culture sont . . . ," which is substantially modified at Leiris 1975: 70/166.

42. Leiris wrote on a copy of the declaration, crossing out its points as he integrated them in his text; see LAS/FML.D.S03, folder 3. See his very close reworking of paragraphs 1–2, 5, 7–8, 9 and 12 of the Declaration, in Leiris 1975: 27/144,

19/140, 16–17/139, 29/145 and 32,40,41–2/141,150,151 respectively. The paraphrase of §§7–8 is very nearly identical to the declaration's text, and §5 is repeated with exactly the same pejorative, *très lâche*, in Leiris's version ("very loose," modified in the English translation). See also Leiris to Métraux (January 30, 1951), LAS/FML.B.S03.03.05.014.

43. LAS/FML.D.S03, "Race et Civilisation." Leiris (1975: 25/143) cites Benedict.

44. See LAS/FAM.G.CS.01.02–06, divided into "biologists" "sociologists," "social anthropologists," "others," and "psychologists." The largest group is that of "social anthropologists" and includes references to Redfield 1943, 1944; Mekeel 1944; Kluckhohn 1949; Davis 1943; Benedict 1941, 1942.

45. Huxley and Haddon 1936. The book had recently been translated into French as *Nous, Européens* (1947).

46. The passage is from ibid., 114 (quotation and comment in LAS/FML.D.S03, unnumbered page).

47. Leiris 1975: 54/158; translation modified. This passage also reflects the evocation of cross-cultural borrowing in Lévi-Strauss.

48. See Griaule 1953: 7.

49. The fallout between Leiris and Griaule does not seem to have been as total as is sometimes suggested, although time and again Leiris clearly felt personally and professionally "humiliated" by Griaule. Nevertheless, Leiris did submit materials from the Dakar–Djibouti expedition to the Fonds Griaule at the Bibliothèque nationale and supported Griaule's views on the need for a more systematic training of colonial officials at meetings of the Office de la Recherche scientifique coloniale (see the minutes of meeting of June 4, 1947, in LAS/FML.B.S03.03.02.008). Leiris (1958: Introduction) also cited Griaule as an influence. In the 1930s, Leiris was considered nettlesome at best and a traitor to the cause of ethnology at worst, yet Mauss, Georges-Henri Rivière, and others continued to support him, as is attested by a letter from Rivière to Mauss of July 21, 1936 (Muséum national d'histoire naturelle, Papiers Marcel Mauss, 2 AP4 2B 2b R).

50. Mayoux to Leiris, June 15, 1949 (LAS/FML.B.S03.03.05.038).

51. Leiris 1949. The typescript bears a handwritten note that presents it as a response to Griaule's "Le Problème de la culture noire." Mayoux's expression of satisfaction that Leiris had written this "Note" (June 15, 1949) is preserved in LAS/FML.B.S03.03.05.038. Clifford 1988: 89 contrasts the two published texts, but apparently without knowledge that the contrast was intentional and pursued. Leiris's text appeared as "Les Nègres d'Afrique et les arts sculpturaux" (Leiris 1953), being printed immediately before Griaule's "Le Problème de la culture noire."

52. Leiris 1949, 1953.

53. Lévi-Strauss 1987 [1950]: 8–9; translation modified.

54. On Leiris's guilt, see Clark-Taoua 2002 and Armel 1997: 322. See also Clifford 1988; Falasca-Zamponi 2011: ch. 2.

55. First published in *Les Temps modernes* (August 1950), 357–74. See Armel 1997: 510.

56. EDC, 96.

57. Ibid., 102, 85.

58. Ibid., 109. The reference to the Union française is also a clear criticism of Griaule, who worked for its organizational bodies in France, including as president of the Commission on Cultural Affairs (président de la Commission des Affaires culturelles et des civilisations d'Outre-Mer à l'Assemblée de l'Union française) from 1948 to his death in 1956. See Griaule 1957a.

59. On these claims, see EDC, 95; 91, 101; 97, respectively.

60. Ibid., 88, 96. In this language of advocacy as well, Leiris was far from being original: it had, e.g., been standard fare in Bronislaw Malinowski's seminars. See London School of Economics Special Collections, Bronislaw Malinowski Archive 21.10 (1938), page beginning "Addenda et Corrigenda . . . ," where Malinowski writes flatly: "Duty of the ethnographer is to protect native interests." See also his colonial administration seminars in Malinowski Archive 6.7.

61. EDC, 99.

62. Ibid., 106.

63. Ibid., 111–12.

64. "Le Débat de l'UNESCO" 1951. See also Métraux's (1978: 307) notes on the trip to Limoges.

65. Leroi-Gourhan 1941: 31.

66. Ibid., 34.

67. See also Conklin 2007.

68. See Lévi-Strauss 2008 and Métraux, "Le Problème de la responsabilité de l'anthropologue qui met sa science au service de l'action" (May 1956), in LAS/FAM.G.AA.01.22. Such strategic use was not new; it was rather widely used among the Maussians: in presenting the series L'Espèce humaine at Gallimard in 1936, Métraux called it the oldest and youngest of the sciences (see Métraux, "Un nouvel humanisme," LAS/FML.B.S04.04.05.032; also Galletti 1989).

69. See Susan Sontag's reference to "the anthropologist as hero" in Sontag 1966: 69.

70. Leroi-Gourhan 1945; 1952; 1955; 1965; and 1968. That redefining ethnology had recently become a habit (*de tradition*) to its practitioners is noted by Leroi-Gourhan (1955: 90). See also *MT*, ch. 9, and the introduction to *L'Homme et la matière* (Leroi-Gourhan 1973 [1943]: 7, 12, 18; the revised 1973 edition expanded on the definition across the introduction).

71. Lévi-Strauss 1949: 1953; 1954; 1960; 1961b; 1961a; 1961–62; and of course "The Scope of Anthropology" (originally published in 1966), in Lévi-Strauss 1976 [1973].

72. On humanism, see also Lévi-Strauss 1953: 96.

73. Leroi-Gourhan 1955: 90.

74. Ibid., 91; *MT*, 406; Leroi-Gourhan 1952: 518.

75. *MT*, 405.

76. Leroi-Gourhan 1955: 94, 93.

77. Leroi-Gourhan 1952: 507–8.

78. Huisman 1962: 30.

79. Leroi-Gourhan 1962.

80. Ibid., 39–41.

81. Ibid., 44.

82. Ibid., 43.

83. See a 1950 issue of *Le Courrier de l'UNESCO* 3 (6/7): 1.

84. Métraux, "Le droit de vivre des peuples primitifs," in LAS/FAM.G.AA.01.23, 2. The text dates to Métraux's work for the Organisation internationale du travail.

85. LAS/FAM.G.AA.01.22, "Le Problème de la responsabilité de l'anthropologue qui met sa science au service de l'action" (May 1956).

86. Bertholet 2003: 205 suggests a similar spectrum.

87. Shepard 2011: 290–91.

88. From a September 1956 article quoted in Bertholet 2003: 229. Bertholet notes that Lévi-Strauss had signed the letter of the Comité d'action pour la paix en Algérie (guided by Mascolo, Antelme, des Forêts, Morin), which had also been signed by Roger Martin du Gard, François Mauriac, Sartre, Canguilhem, and others and published in *L'Express* on November 7, 1955.

89. Lévi-Strauss confirms his refusal to sign the Manifesto of 121 and cites in his defense others (notably Merleau-Ponty) who likewise demurred (Eribon and Lévi-Strauss, 1988: 259).

90. Lévi-Strauss 1975: 13 (translation amended).

91. Ibid., 124.

92. Lévi-Strauss, "Cultural Discontinuity, Economic and Social Development" (originally published in 1961), in Lévi-Strauss 1976 [1973]: 369–70, at 316 (translation amended).

93. Métraux, "Les Changements culturels et sociaux à travers l'action humanitaire" (typescript corrected in Métraux's handwriting), in LAS/FAM.G.AA.01.20, 2. On p. 14, Métraux insists that acceptance of innovations always involves a significant cultural battle.

94. Métraux 1957: 10.

95. Métraux, "Le Droit de vivre des peuples primitifs," in LAS/FAM.G.AA .01.23, 3.

96. Métraux 1958.

97. Brattain 2007: 1411–12.

98. Césaire 2001: 68. Césaire's principal target was Caillois's "Illusions à rebours" (Caillois 1954, 1955), in support of Lévi-Strauss's furious response to Caillois (Lévi-Strauss 1955). In his footnotes, Césaire further targeted a Belgian article

published in *Europe-Afrique*, January 6, 1955, that similarly attacked ethnologists committed to antiracism, notably Leiris and Lévi-Strauss.

99. Lévi-Strauss, "History and Dialectic," in Lévi-Strauss 1966: 245–69.

100. Ibid., 247.

CHAPTER 7: WHAT IS SOCIAL TRANSPARENCY?

1. Sartre 1947 [1944]: 499.

2. Ibid., 500; emphasis added.

3. Solzhenitsyn 1974–76.

4. Augustine 1992: 10.2; also 10.5, with its citation of 1 Cor. 13:12.

5. Ibid., e.g. 5.20.

6. One formulation of this visibility motif comes from Niklas Luhmann in "Contingency as Modern Society's Defining Attribute," in Luhmann 1998: 51–52.

7. J-*DE*, 91.

8. Bell 2003: 17, 28. Bell engages here with Marcel Gauchet's "hidden God" thesis (Van Kley 1999: 63). On the Jansenist "Kingdom of the Blessed" and the construction of community at a distance from absolutist power, see Marin 1989: 421–47.

9. J-*DE*, 91.

10. For the eighteenth-century origins of the problem of transparency in France, see, e.g., Michel Foucault's (2009: 71, 357) discussion of the *encyclopédiste* treatment of population as not simply transparent to the sovereign's action, and of the physiocrats' treatment of the same problem.

11. Baczko 1989, x; Vidler, 1990; Ozouf 1966; Revel 1975: 152.

12. Féraud 1787–88, s.v. "transparence." I am grateful to Peter Dreyer for this reference.

13. Regarding 1789, see Starobinski 1982; Friedland 2002: 250–53; Edelstein 2009: 186.

14. Maximilien Robespierre, "On the Principles of Political Morality (Speech of 18 Pluviôse Year II)," in Robespierre 2007: 113.

15. Baczko 1994; Edelstein 2017.

16. Schneider 2013: 161.

17. Guérin 1946.

18. Mascolo 1946.

19. Blanchot 1996: 18–19; emphasis added.

20. For a detailed treatment of Blanchot's engagement with transparency, see Geroulanos 2007.

21. Blanchot, "Literature and the Right to Death," in Blanchot 1995: 319.

22. See also the intellectual history of the place of paperwork and bureaucracy in political theory offered in Kafka 2012, which highlights the relevant paradox of bureaucracy's efficiency in the state's engagement with society.

23. Anderson 1983.

24. Bentham 1834: 101. On panoptic surveillance, see also Bentham's 1786 Panopticon and Foucault's discussion of it (addressed here in chapter 20).

25. *DP* 141.

26. Constant 1992: 86; quoted in Sheehan 2006: 9.

27. Marx 1988: 78.

28. See, e.g., Marx 1976 [1887]: 172–73.

29. Lefebvre 2002 [1961]: 36.

30. Ducoulombier 2013.

31. Walter Benjamin, "Surrealism: The Last Snapshot of the European Intelligentsia," in Benjamin 2005: 209.

32. "Fascism signified 'clarity, simplicity of method, linearity of application, rectitude, and honesty,' one supporter wrote in a typical paean to totalitarian 'transparency'" (Ben-Ghiat 2001: 33). See also Paxton 2005: 40, 117.

33. Châtelet and Pisier-Kouchner 1981: 318.

34. Michaud 2004: 74–101; Weindling, 1989: 9–10, 76–80, and ch. 8. That totalitarianism offered something of a transparent alternative to the social conflicts of the Weimar republic is a well-rehearsed theme: Peukert 1991: 241–43.

35. See the criticism of this position (which I have also held) in Peden 2014; and Worms 2009.

36. Hollier 1988; Richman 2002; Falasca-Zamponi 2011.

37. Groys 1992.

38. Quoted in Sophy Thompson, "Une Dimension invisible: La Transparence dans la peinture 1910–1930," in Cohen 1995: 59.

39. Balla and Depero 2009: 210. For Umberto Boccioni (2009: 117), too, transparency contributed to a "new reality."

40. Picabia 1978: 2: 218.

41. Cohen 1995; Vidler 1992: 217–27; Alloa 2008.

42. Scheerbart 1914: §111.

43. See Rabinow 1995: ch. 7.

44. Le Corbusier 1946 [1923], 220.

45. Ibid., 229.

46. Ibid., 237.

47. Ibid., 263.

48. Ibid., 289.

49. Le Corbusier 1971: 167, 96.

50. Ibid., 244.

51. Donaldson 2016b: 5, 9, 112, 381 et al. Donaldson writes: "In France, for example, 'secret diplomacy' [*diplomatie secrète*] was often used to mean not only negotiations kept secret from the public at large, but irregular and informal negotiations pursued by ministers and officials in violation of usual cabinet procedures. At stake in France was thus a particular nexus between secrecy and arbitrary or personal power, connected back in twentieth century argument to the *secret du*

roi of Louis XV. This feature of French debates actually made it easier to legitimize mere secrecy from the public, as long as internal executive hierarchy was respected" (5).

52. Article 3 of the 1958 constitution reads: "National sovereignty belongs to the people which exercises it through its representatives and by way of a referendum. No part of the people and no individual can appropriate its exercise." On the secret state, see Laurent 2009.

53. See Archives nationales, F/7/15323, clippings from *L'Humanité*'s publication *Les Trusts contre la France* (prefaced by Léon Jouhaux, Georges Politzer, and the biologist Marcel Prenant) on the ways in which "les oligarchies capitalistes, les dessous de l'activité d'une poignée d'hommes qui drainent l'épargne, rançonnent les consommateurs, ruinent les petites entreprises, exportent des capitaux, spéculent contre le franc et trahissent les intérêts de la nation" (67; also 68).

54 Rousso 1994.

55. Mornet 1949. Medical references were common; an article of January 1946 in the Confédération générale du Travail–directed journal *La Voix des policiers* spoke of "sweeping from the nation's soil" the Hitlerian and Vichyssois "miasmas." See also Ross 1995: 74. The sociopolitical use of *épuration* dates to the early nineteenth century; according to François Delaporte (1989: 52), to the cholera epidemic of 1832 in particular (Delaporte 1989: 52). Littré 1883 (1: 1473), s.v. *Épuré* uses medico-social references dating to the 1820s.

56. Virgili 2002: 252.

57. Cupers 2014: xx.

58. The famous cases of an antistatist psychiatry are the Jean Oury clinic, the work of Félix Guattari, and Fernand Deligny's research with autistic patients.

59. Pétonnet 1979.

60. "But what do you know about me, given that I believe in secrecy, that is, in the power of falsity, rather than in representing things in a way that manifests a lamentable faith in accuracy and truth? If I stick where I am, if I don't travel around, like anyone else I make my inner journeys that I can only measure by my emotions, and express very obliquely and circuitously in what I write" (Gilles Deleuze, "Letter to a Harsh Critic," in Deleuze 1995: 11). "I have a taste for the secret, it clearly has to do with not-belonging; I have an impulse of fear or terror in the face of a political space, for example, a public space that makes no room for the secret. For me, the demand that everything be paraded in the public square and that there be no internal forum is a glaring sign of the totalitarianization of democracy" (Derrida and Ferraris 2001: 59).

61. Conseil de l'Europe 1988.

62. Derrida 1992: 54–55.

63. Fernando 2014: 124.

64. Cavell 2003: 168n.

Parts of this and the following chapter were published in an earlier version as "An Army of Shadows," *Journal of Modern History* 88: 60–95, © 2016 by The Journal of Modern History.

1. Littré 1883, 3: 1198, discusses the etymology of *police*.

2. *DP* 213–14.

3. Ibid., 216.

4. Bergeron 1981: 10.

5. Locard 1918: 5. My thanks to Ken Alder for introducing me to Locard.

6. Locard 1923: 7–8; 1934: 6.

7. The complexity of the police was a subject of debate in the postwar years. See the front-page article "Trop de polices, pas de police!" in *Résistance* (September 5, 1945), which listed "the prefecture of police exclusive to the Département of the Seine, the Sûreté Nationale, which casts its rays on all of France, the gendarmerie, the Prévoté, the maritime gendarmerie, the gendarmerie of the sky, the financial police, the economic polices, of which there are at least a dozen, the police of the chemins de fer, military security, the sûreté publique, and all those that we are forgetting." The anonymous author went on to cry: "The authentic representatives of order are the first to deplore this state of affairs and order does not gain from it!" (1). Locard 1918: 59, too, had complained that the structure of the police undermined its efficiency and scientific potential.

8. Monet 1991–92: 54; quoted in Loubet del Bayle 2006: 209, 207–8.

9. Pinel 2004: 363.

10. Le Clère 1957: 128.

11. Ibid., 129. For a comprehensive account of the police resistance, see Baruch 1997.

12. Even relatively successful efforts at postwar reform (e.g., the Groupes mobiles de reserve, which were filled with resistance fighters, renamed Compagnies républicaines de sécurité, and mandated to preserve order) failed to remove the taint (Morin 2000: 221, 223; Pinel 2004: 367, 356–59; Koreman 1999: 48, 50).

13. See AN, F/7/15351, "Tract découvert à la Bastille le 6-4-1945." The author purports that policemen, "modest functionaries," were being sacked despite having played no role in "domestic and international politics" and blames compliance with communism.

14. Morin 2000: 231. See also "Le Mécontentement s'accroit à la Sûreté nationale," *France-Soir*, September 6, 1945; "Pas de grève de la police parisienne, mais un mécontentement," in *Le Pays* of the same date; and "Une Grève de la police est à craindre," *L'Époque*, September 5, 1945.

15. "En cas de guerre civile, voici les forces en présence," *France-Dimanche*, November 23, 1947. Rajsfus 1995 is an impassioned defense of police anticommunism (275–78).

16. *L'Époque*, September 21, 1948. See also the reproach, in *L'Aurore*, March 18, 1947, that policemen are not just functionaries but soldiers responsible for the security of the population of Paris.

17. "On va abolir le droit de grève . . . ," *L'Aurore*, August 26, 1948.

18. See "En violation de la constitution, le gouvernement veut priver la police du droit de grève," *L'Humanité*, August 26, 1948; "Ceux de la police n'ont que faire du droit de grève," *L'Aurore*, August 28, 1948.

19. Vichy's Law of September 18, 1943, which facilitated the use of firearms, was annulled by the law of March 31, 1945, which allowed only "legitimate self-defense." A subsequent ordinance signed by Minister of Interior E. Depreux further restricted the permission to use weapons in self-defense or in defense of others to cases of "actual" danger and unjust aggression. Direction generale de la Sûreté nationale, Ref. SN/Adm/Regl/8: 1535 (September 27, 1946).

20. On March 22, 1947, *Combat* estimated the reduction of police personnel at 28,052. Morin 2000: 227 calculates the reduction from 1945 to 1954 at 45%.

21. Loubet del Bayle 2006: 209, 207–8.

22. On the perception of ineffectiveness, combined with broad popular suspicion, as a threat to police work, see Koreman, 1999: 50.

23. "Trop de polices, pas de police!" *Résistance*, September 6, 1945.

24. AN, F/7/15351, H.C. XT/3 3/10, "Une opinion sur le malaise dans la police."

25. For articles expressing horror at the police, see Jean Ebstein, "La Police," Paroles, November 7, 1947, and Lucien Jacquet, "Pour ou contre la police?" *Le Libertaire* December 13, 1946. See also AN, F/7/15351, "Les Incidents de Tarbes."

26. See AN, F/7/15351, H.C. XT/3 3/10, "Une Opinion sur le malaise dans la police." "Les Raisons d'un malaise," *Police de France*, June–July 1954, speaks specifically of policemen's hopes of improving their situation at the end of the Vichy era and of the disappointment that followed. See also two articles in *L'Aurore* in December 1944: "Y a-t-il un malaise dans la police?" (December 12) and "Oui il y a un malaise dans la police" (December 20).

27. "Notre fédération est le bastion de l'indépendance," *Police de France* January–February 1954.

28. Berlière 2001: 352–53.

29. Louis Althusser's understanding of interpellation was based on this notion of an encounter between youth and police that was not characterized by affective, familial bonds but recalibrated a whole life. It also continued to be expressed in accounts of police strategies; see Dugléry 1996: 112.

30. See, e.g., the Ordinance of March 3, 1945, which replaced the Gounod Law of 1942 and maintained provisions promoting the participation of families in the development of family law.

31. It may help here to recall (without making causal claims) the turn to everyday life and its categories in the writings of Henri Lefebvre and Michel de Certeau, or Pierre Clastres's attack on statism.

32. Hoffmann 1956: 220, 223.

33. AN, F/23/404, Service du ravitaillement général, A.10 SAF (September 7, 1940).

34. Fogg 2008: ch. 1.

35. Mouré 2010: 263.

36. Ponge 1998: 11.

37. For the rhetoric of transparency in the literary Purge, see Watts 1998: 135. One might ask, with Blanchot, how much of this rhetoric addressed literature and moral philosophy rather than everyday life.

38. Mouré 2010: 281.

39. *Journal officiel*, October 19, 1944; Ordinance of October 18, 1944, on the confiscation of illicit profits.

40. The purging of the Ministry of Supply was ordered on October 26, 1944 (see that day's issue of the *Journal officiel*), yet most Vichy-era controllers were retained, given the difficulty of starting a new ministry from zero. See Grenard 2008: 266–67. For the ministry's continuing efforts in cases dating to the Occupation, see AN, F/23/409, Affaire Allard, and the Ordinance of October 18, 1944. For the use of trafficking as evidence of resistance activity, see F/23/409 Affaire Guibert. For claims about a "patriotic black market" during the Occupation, see Sanders 2001: 297; Grenard 2008: ch. 8; Jackson 2001: 487; Kedward 1999: ch. 2.

41. Mazower 2001: 53.

42. AN, F/23/404, Direction du contrôle du ravitaillement, "Rapport de renseignements (5 Août 1946)," 4.

43. Debû-Bridel 1947: 86.

44. Koreman 1999: 188.

45. AN, F/23/404, Organisations successives du ministère; the ordinance from the Secrétaire général du ravitaillement on illicit profits (1.ARC-1, January 6, 1945); and the letter of July 19, 1947, from the inspecteur général du ravitaillement on thefts of paper and the need to reorganize its distribution.

46. On the attractiveness of certain types of trafficking, see Grenard 2008: 260. On rural populations, food shortages, and exchanges of goods as involving a "habituation to illegality in everyday life," see Fogg 2008: 54.

47. AN, F/23/404, "Rapport de renseignement (5 Août 1946)," 9. "Gang" is in scare quotes and English in the original. The author includes descriptions of systems of collusion between agents and this "gang." Similar judgments were made by regional prefects (Koreman 1999: 178–79).

48. Fogg 2008: 25.

49. AN, F/23/404, Director of the Office for the Control and Repression of the Clandestine Market to minister of supply (August 1, 1946). See also the memo "État de repression en matière économique," p. 2, where the author claims that lack of specialization "disarmed" the gendarme.

50. Ibid., note 5–12 IG (May 6, 1947).

51. Delbo 1946.

52. "Un Trafic de tickets d'alimentation est découvert au Ravitaillement général de l'Isère," *Le Réveil*, July 23, 1948; "Il s'est produit des malversations au ravitaillement général," *Les Allobroges*, July 23, 1948. See also AN, F/23/409, Enquêtes betail et viandes, Affaire Brillet.

53. "Des hommes gagnant moins de 5000 francs par mois font la guerre aux rois du marché noir," *La Voix de Paris*, August 4, 1945.

54. Gouin sued Yves Farge over the latter's *Le Pain de la corruption* (Paris: Chêne, 1947). See Jankowski 2008: 85.

55. Delbo 1946.

56. AN, F/23/404, "Instructions générales à nos délégués," 4.

57. Ibid., director of the Office of Control and Repression of the Clandestine Market to the minister of supply, August 1, 1946.

58. On the specter of *poujadisme*, see Chapman 2008: 277–88.

59. "Les Anges gardiens de la police," *Le Libertaire*, August 2, 1946.

60. Berlière 2001: 352–53.

61. See Bommart 1951, turned into a film in 1953 by Jacques Daroy; Lambert 1950; and Lacroix 1954.

62. Gabin himself had fought with the Free French forces in North Africa and was a decorated war hero.

63. Jules Dassin's *Rififi* (1955) is perhaps the film that skirted the limits of these conventions most of all, by featuring an ageing gangster who quickly reneges on his own morality, yet remains sympathetic.

64. Nogueira 1996: 165.

65. The release of Melville's film (on the same month as Marcel Ophuls's first cut of *The Sorrow and the Pity*) fits with what Rousso sees as the end of the second phase of the Vichy syndrome: the widening of cracks in the repression of Vichy from collective memory and in the perception of the Fourth Republic as a new and relatively transparent public sphere.

66. The sociological notion of crime as innate to society and not as a pathological or morbid condition, as criminologists claimed, dates to Durkheim's early period (see Durkheim 1919: vi, 81–90).

67. Daniel Lagache, "Psychocriminogenèse" [1950], in Lagache 1979. This was Lagache's presentation at the 1950 International Congress of Criminology. He made a similar argument at the Société internationale de criminologie in Paris (September 15–24, 1952), and it promoted the influence of psychoanalysis in criminological circles. See Mucchielli 1994: 382; Heuyer and Pinatel 1953: 160.

68. Lagache 1979: 187, 189, 190–91, 202.

69. Lagache, "Un Gangster," in Laganche 1979: 222.

70. Lagache 1979: 200. Heroism's relation to rules is discussed by Freud in the early case of the Rat Man (see Freud 1955: 177).

71. Lagache, "Introduction à la criminologie," in Lagache 1979: 339.

72. Parrot and Gueneau 1959: 103–5.
73. Christian Debuyst, "Étienne de Greeff," in Mucchielli 1994: 339. Lagache helped introduce de Greeff to France (Mucchielli, "Sens du crime," in Mucchielli 1994: 383).
74. Lebovici, "La Psychologie de groupe," in Heuyer and Pinatel 1953: 169. Lebovici would become a critic of Lacan.
75. Lacan 2001: 123.
76. Bataille 1991: 9–10.
77. Lacan, "Prémisses à tout développement de la criminologie," in Lacan 2001: 121.

CHAPTER 9: BETWEEN STATE AND SOCIETY, II

1. Jobs 2007.
2. I render *inadapté* as "maladapted," rather than "maladjusted," because of the importance of adaptation as a biological as well as behaviorist concept in contemporary scientific and philosophical thought, where it was specifically identified with the failure to follow particular "healthy" norms (see *KL*, ch. 5). "Adjustment," the Anglo-American equivalent of adaptation at the time, does not quite carry the force identified today with "adaptation."
3. Fishman 2002: 152. Fishman's account correctly emphasizes the complexity of diagnostic categories, including inadaptation (which she dates from Georges Heuyer). Lagache presented "Les Techniques de psychologie humaine" to the Vichy Conseil technique de l'Enfance déficiente et en danger moral in 1944, but the term *inadaptation* was still specialized and infrequent. The mid-1950s were the crucial years when *inadaptation* became a medical–juridical obsession. On Heuyer and juvenile delinquency, see also Lefaucheur 1994, and Lagache 1977: 455, 460.
4. Rousselet 1956: 117–26. François-Unger 1957: 289; Favez-Boutonnier 1957: 13; Michaux and Duché 1957: 224. See also AN, F/17/17956, Inspéction académique des Hautes-Pyrénées, Service de santé scolaire et universitaire, "Contribution à l'étude des possibilités d'amélioration dans les méthodes du contrôle médical" (June 23, 1959), 2.
5. Georges Heuyer, director of the First International Course of Criminology, proposed a motto for this scientific ideology: "the human is not a whole; s/he is inseparable from the milieu" (Heuyer and Pinatel 1953: 21). Psychoanalysts also used the concept of environment.
6. Giraud1975: 187.
7. Sangline 1955: 91; Favez-Boutonnier 1957: 1–3. The influence of cinema was debated at length; claims that children repeat "exactly" what they see on screen were made in Michaux and Duché 1957: 223. On HLM housing, see Chombart de Lauwe 1959: 245.

8. AN, F/44/103, "Colloque sur l'équipement socio-éducatif" (9–10 December 1959); "Évolution de la délinquance juvénile (Période d'après-guerre)", 11.

9. AN, SSSU, 4/27-07 (March 23, 1959), "Rapport du médecin-inspecteur régional."

10. Centre national . . . de la protection judiciaire de la jeunesse 1963b: 72.

11. Centre national . . . de la protection judiciaire de la jeunesse 1963a: 25, 27. Psychologists asking young delinquents about their relationship with the environment announced that 78.29% of them were pleased with it or accepted it, while 10.74% rejected it and some 8.77% described it unfavorably (99). Still, some 40% were found not "normally adapted" to their school constraints (100).

12. Lebovici et al. 1951: 15; also 2.

13. The leading criminologist Étienne de Greeff declared in 1947 that divorce was a sure factor in child delinquency—since 80% of delinquent children were children of divorced parents—and a "probable" factor in adult criminality (Greeff 1947: 60).

14. Piaget and Inhelder 1955: 310–11; 1947. Piaget's influence is evident in Giraud 1975: 188.

15. Piaget 1971: 241.

16. Piaget and Inhelder 1955: 306.

17. In AN, F/44/103, "Enfants en danger moral et social," the author notes the urgency of juvenile criminality and counters by proposing efforts to "create complete persons."

18. On the novelty of criminology (*anthropologie criminelle*), see Heuyer and Pinatel 1953: 13–14, 29–30.

19. Greeff 1947: 111.

20. See AN, F/17/17956, C.SSU.3, "Instructions portant modification des modalités d'exécution du contrôle médical scolaire." Internal SSSU memos tell much the same story: a 1943 memo on the organization of medical control in Vichy schools aimed only "to surveil the psychic state of those concerned" (17957, "Circulaire sur l'organisation provisoire," November 11, 1943). Amid the major health concerns of the late 1940s, psychiatric concerns were not cited as an issue (INSEE 1947). They continued to be absent in 1951, but generic psychiatric evaluations had begun; by 1957 virtually all memos and *circulaires* contained discussions of *inadaptation*.

21. Chambost 1950: 161. The author was at the time an inspecting physician with the Contrôle de santé scolaire et universitaire (C.SSU).

22. On "behavioral" problems, see AN, F/17/17958, Dossier enfance inadaptée, "Projet de circulaire," 1.

23. Ibid., 17956, SSSU, "Contribution à l'étude des possibilités d'amélioration dans les méthodes de contrôle médical utilisées en médecine scolaire (23 juin 1959)," 2–3. 17958 discusses the treatment of variola, influenza, and polio epidemics in 1954–57.

24. Ibid., 17956, C.SSU. 3/636 (Paris, June 13, 1960).

25. Ibid., "Instructions portant modification."

26. Ibid., "Docteur Ouillon," 10: "We must screen not only for intellectual delays [*retards intellectuels*] but also troubles of affectivity, character, behavior, imagination, psycho-motor instabilities, perverse tendencies, etc."

27. Chambost 1950: 164.

28. AN, F/17/17958, Dossier Activités de l'HSU; Dossier enfance inadaptée, "Commission nationale de l'enfance inadaptée, 21 février 1956."

29. Ian Hacking, "Making Up People," in Hacking 2002: 91–14.

30. Gangsters appear in New Wave films in a negative or comedic light; Truffaut mocked the gangster genre in *Shoot the Piano Player*. Still, the genre continued to flourish in the 1960s.

31. Poster 1975.

32. Canguilhem, "Qu'est-ce que la psychologie?" in Canguilhem 1983: 378.

33. TM, 797. Starobinski cited Sartre, but not Lacan, and included many of the essentials of the structuralist critique of modern psychiatry.

34. L-*E*, 246/204.

35. Foucault 2006. On privacy in the Vichy era, see Jackson 2001: 281–82; Pollard 1998: 120.

CHAPTER 10: ALIENATION, UTOPIA, AND MARXISM AFTER 1956

1. I have discussed this theme in Geroulanos 2010: ch. 2.

2. Benjamin 2005: 209.

3. Consider the occasional ambivalence of Paul Nizan (1971: 270–71); see also Aucouturier 1998: 4; Pudal 2003: 77–96.

4. Judt 1992: 237, also 238.

5. Ulbricht, *Neues Deutschland*, August 22, 1948.

6. Merleau-Ponty 1964b: 361.

7. Mascolo 1953: 507.

8. Ibid., 509.

9. Camus 1948.

10. Mascolo 1953: 508.

11. Sartre, *Dirty Hands*, in Sartre 1989b: 218.

12. Merleau-Ponty 1973: 12.

13. WTP, 144.

14. Ibid., 152.

15. "Les Jours de notre vie" was reprinted as "L'URSS et les camps" (Merleau-Ponty 1960). See further Geroulanos 2010: 273–77.

16. Merleau-Ponty 1960: 332, 334.

17. Ibid., 340.

18. Ibid., 334.

19. Merleau-Ponty 1973 [1955]: 15.
20. Ibid., 67.
21. Ibid., 138 n. 78; see also the critique at 197 n. 137.
22. Ibid., 133.
23. Ibid., 144.
24. Castoriadis 1988: chs. 4, 5, 7.
25. *Arguments* 1 (December 1956), 1.
26. Axelos 1969: 161 lists these parallel journals as *Aletheia* (France), *Praxis* (Yugoslavia), *Études* (Belgium), *Passato e presente* (Italy), *Das Argument* (Germany), and *Dialoog* (Netherlands).
27. Weber was published in no. 17; Heidegger in 7, 13, 20, 24; Lukács in 11; Korsch in 16; Adorno in 14, 19; Marcuse in 18, 21.
28. *Arguments*, nos. 12–13, 18, 21, 22.
29. This was Axelos's main philosophical concern. *Arguments*, nos. 15, 16, 24, 27–28.
30. *Arguments*, nos. 6, 10, 17, 25–6.
31. For a journal whose popularizing tendencies were limited by contempt for simplistic theories of emancipation and that routinely published texts by authors as different as A.-J. Greimas, Octavio Paz, Leszlek Kołakowski, Martin Heidegger, Maurice Blanchot, and Daniel Bell, *Arguments* captured a fairly wide audience, printing 3,000 copies and selling "more than 400 only on the Boulevard St. Michel," as a 1962 editorial declared (*Arguments* 27–28, p. 124). By 1962, when it "sabotaged itself," all but seven of its twenty-five issues had ostensibly sold out (p. 129). The accompanying book collection at Éditions de Minuit (Axelos 1969) published titles by authors who combined the ontological and Western Marxist traditions with critiques of contemporary literature and culture.
32. Jay 1980: ch. 9.
33. Lefebvre 2002: 36.
34. Marx 1976 [1887]: 173.
35. Lefebvre 1995: 69.
36. Ibid., 16.
37. Lefebvre 1965.
38. Lefebvre 1992: 27.
39. Debord 1995: §12 p. 15; §219, p. 153; etc.
40. Debord 1966.
41. See *L'Internationale situationniste*, 11(October 1967): 52.
42. Debord 1967 [1994]: §2.
43. Althusser 1990: 144.
44. Ibid., 144–45.
45. On Althusser's antihumanism, see Robcis 2012: 51–69.
46. Althusser 1971b: 172.

47. Althusser, "From Capital to Marx's Philosophy," in Althusser and Balibar 2009 [1968]: 13.

48. Ibid., 36–37, also 39.

49. Althusser 1990: 39. See also the discussion of Feuerbach and Marx, which again uses "transparency" thoroughly in the negative, on 186–87.

50. In light of October 17, 1961 (on which day police killed over two hundred Algerian demonstrators in Paris), Rancière considered the recognition of the social as "no longer" a space of "the manifest" to be more recent than I suggest here. The historical and dialectical pursuit of truth was finished, he writes, "whereas history was once a process that turned alienation into truth, local communities based upon belief are all that remain. The social is no longer the instance of the "manifest," or the site where the truth becomes a meaningful political movement. It is the instance of obscurity once more. But the obscurity of the belief that can establish bonds is now seen as the only thing that can confer meaning" (Rancière 1998: 26–27). Social transparency was the focus of Lyotard's treatment in his book *Economie libidinale* (1974) of Marx's theorization of "the mystery of labor" and its "erasure" in Capital (Lyotard 1993a: 134).

CHAPTER 11: FACE, MASK, AND OTHER AS AVATARS OF SELFHOOD

Part of this chapter was originally published in *French Politics, Culture, and Society*, 31 (2): 15–33 in 2013 as "Postwar Facial Reconstruction."

1. Fanon 2008 [1952]: 1.

2. *Encyclopédie* 17: 355.

3. Littré 1883: s.v. *visage*.

4. Delaporte 2008: chs. 2–3.

5. Merleau-Ponty 1963: 167; emphasis added.

6. Sartre 1970 [1939]: 560–64, 560, 562.

7. Ibid., 564.

8. Moyn 2005: 223 n. 58. Moyn notes that Picard may well have influenced Levinas.

9. Lubac 1950 [1945]: 67; emphasis added.

10. Mauriac 1951, quoted in Affron 1998: 172.

11. Bazin 1971: 133, translation amended. More recent film-theoretical accounts of the face have generally avoided Bresson's (and Georges Franju's) engagements: Aumont 1992; Blümlinger and Sierek 2002.

12. Levinas 1969: 81.

13. Ibid., 79. At this point in *Totality and Infinity*, thanks in part to the irreducible nature of the face and the contrast it engineers between me and another, Levinas most explicitly contrasts the two central terms of his title: "If totality cannot be constituted, it is because Infinity does not permit itself to be integrated" (80).

14. Levinas, "Max Picard and the Face," in Levinas 1996: 95.

15. Levinas 1969: 197, 202–3.

16. Barthes, "The Face of Garbo," in Barthes 1972: 57.

17. Delaporte, Devauchelle, and Fournier 2010: esp. 199–226. Devauchelle, the lead surgeon of the operation, further discussed the status of the surgeon in relation to such a graft at 257–68.

18. Franju's debt to surrealism has been examined by Lowenstein 2005: 18–25.

19. Beauvoir 1999: 43. This was by no means the only occasion where Beauvoir thematized a situation or act of "not having" or "losing a face. See, e.g., Beauvoir 2006: 173.

20. *BN*, 340–65.

21. Ibid., 350.

22. Buraud 1948: 11–12.

23. Descartes 1903: 213.

24. In doing this, Canguilhem cited Leroy 1929.

25. Canguilhem in CAPHÉS GC28.1.5, "Descartes Interrompu . . . 1948," folder "Introduction," 26.

26. Ibid., folder "Troisième chapitre: Le Doute," 27.

27. Maritain 1946: 31, 33–34.

28. Foucault, "Dire et voir chez Raymond Roussel" (1962), F-*DE*, 1: 208.

29. Merleau-Ponty 1973.

30. Ibid., 92.

31. See Jean-Luc Nancy's mockery of this tradition of interpretation in Nancy 1979: 63.

32. Foucault 1970: 885–908.

33. Foucault 1980.

34. Noted in the Tate Modern's earlier caption to the image, www.tate.org.uk/servlet/ViewWork?workid=674 (last accessed January 20, 2011), which has since been rewritten.

35. Deleuze 2003: 20–21.

36. Kracauer 1997: 305.

37. Ibid., 306.

38. Ibid.

39. Ibid.; emphasis added.

40. I have discussed this film in detail in Geroulanos 2013.

41. Caillois 1964: 99, 101–2, will take an intermediate position: "The Gorgon's head" is not the purest of horrors, but "nothing more than a mask" and a ruse.

42. Kracauer 1997: 305.

43. L-*E*, 736.

44. Fanon 2008: 4.

45. *VTC*, 1: 104.

46. Goblot 1901: s.v. *identique*; emphasis added.

47. One should mention here Ann Stoler, Joan W. Scott, Frederick Cooper,

Gary Wilder, Alice Conklin, Judith Surkis, Todd Shepard, Jacques Le Sueur, Carolyn Dean, and John Monroe. This is discussed in chapter 14.

48. Descombes 1979.

49. Moyn 2005.

50. Hallward and Peden 2012: vol. 1.

51. On Cousin, see Goldstein 2005. Canguilhem (1930) took the side of Comte against Cousin because the latter postulated not only the self's self-identity but also its self-transparency. See also Braunstein 2007: 66–67.

52. Beauvoir 1976 [1947].

53. Ibid., 7–8.

54. Claudia Card, "Introduction," in Card 2003: 14–15.

55. The "Hegel renaissance" in France is the subject of several accounts that I will not retrace here; see Butler 1987; Jarczyk and Labarrière 1996. On the sense of danger to the self, see also Hyppolite 1971, 1: 233; Roth 1988: ch. 4; also chs. 2–3, 189; Baugh 2001; Jay 1980: ch. 9.

56. *BN*, 315–39.

57. Such was, e.g., Sartre's critique of Bataille in "Un nouveau mystique" [1943], in Sartre 1947.

58. Geroulanos 2011a: 536–43.

59. Bataille 1997: 132. See Geroulanos 2011a: 531–60.

60. Bataille 1997: 140.

61. BnF, Département des manuscrits occidentaux, Fonds Bataille, Env. 52, "Les guerres sont pour le moment les plus forts stimulants de l'imagination" [1939]. The titular reference to Marinetti and Ernst Jünger is clear if implicit. Other such stimulants, according to this text, are revolutions and religious ecstasy.

62. Bataille 1988a: 12.

63. Ibid., 28.

64. Bataille 1988b.

65. In his later writing, Bataille explicitly reinterpreted sovereignty as true heterogeneity, something experienced in an instant (and hence not exactly experienced at all). See "Sovereignty" in Bataille 1993.

66. Bataille 2009: 58, 167–68, 170–74.

67. Mascolo 1993 [1946]: 21–22.

68. Kendall 2007: 11.

69. Levinas 1969: 42.

70. Ibid., 58.

71. *HM*, 183.

72. L-*S1*, 108.

73. L-*S2*, 7–8. See also Lacan's discussion of the problems that a conception of consciousness as transparent to itself brings up: there Lacan points back to Descartes but clearly hints at existentialism (ibid., 6).

74. In 1954, Lacan was appreciative of this line, but also critical of its slogan-

eering quality. Until 1948, he had been much more approving. See "Aggressiveness in Psychoanalysis" (1948), in L-*E*, 118/96.

75. Lacan, "The Mirror Stage as Formative of the I Function as Revealed in Psychoanalytic Experience," in L-*E*. Note also Lacan's introductory note that "the experience psychoanalysis provides us [on the I function] . . . sets us at odds with any philosophy directly stemming from the cogito (ibid., 93/75).

76. Ibid., 94/76; also 96/77.

77. Lacan 1938.

78. On the language of Umwelt, which formed a particular way of refracting the problem of "external reality" (and which is traditionally associated with the work of the biologist Jakob von Uexküll from the late 1920s on), see Lacan, "The Mirror Stage," in L-*E*, 96–97/78; also SLP, 280/232.

79. Lacan, "The Mirror Stage," in L-*E*, 97/78. See also L-*S2*, 50.

80. Lacan, "Presentation on Psychical Causality" [1946–47], in L-*E*, 188/153.

81. Lacan, "The Mirror Stage," in L-*E*, 98/79.

82. Lacan, "Psychoanalysis and Its Teaching," in L-*E*, 454/379.

83. L-*S2*, 43.

84. Ibid., 43.

85. Lacan, "Psychoanalysis and Its Teaching," in L-*E*, 439/366; SLP, 265/219.

86. L-*S2*, 6.

87. Ibid., 177; emphasis added.

88. See the discussion with Mannoni after Lacan's presentation, ibid., 188.

89. Ibid., 246. See also "The Freudian Thing" (1955–56), in L-*E*, 431/358, and "Psychoanalysis and Its Teaching," in L-*E*, 442/369: "It is only owing to the place of the Other that the analyst can receive the investiture of the transference that qualifies him to play his legitimate role in the subject's unconscious and to speak there in interventions that are suited to a dialectic whose essential particularity is defined by the private realm."

90. Lacan, "The Freudian Thing" (1955–56), in L-*E*, 430/358.

91. See L-*S2* 246; "The Freudian Thing" (1955–56), in L-*E*, 416–17/347, 426/354; "The Instance of the Letter in the Unconscious," ibid., 524/435; "The Subversion of the Subject," ibid., 801/678; and "Science and Truth," ibid., 864–65/734.

92. Ibid., 524/435.

93. Michel de Certeau, "Lacan," in Certeau 1986: 50.

94. L-*E*, 442/369.

95. See Glissant 2006 [1990], esp. 189–92.

CHAPTER 12: THE NORM AND THE SAME

1. Internationally, the best known antipsychiatrists and anti-medicine thinkers were R. D. Laing and Ivan Illich; in France, see the contributions of Jean Oury, Félix Guatarri, and Fernand Deligny. See also Bourg 2007, Dosse 2008, and the recent work of Camille Robcis.

2. Goblot 1901: 365–66.

3. *VTC*, 2: 691.

4. Ibid., 688–89.

5. Ibid., 689.

6. More curious (if not quite relevant to the present discussion) is a second quotation, from an 1851 socialist work that that refers to capitalism as an overturning of the "normal" hierarchy of needs.

7. Ibid., 690. See also Lalande's own (largely affirmative) engagement with normative sciences in Lalande 1893: 201 and 1911: 527–32.

8. Wundt 1897: 1.

9. Lévy-Bruhl 1927: 2, 8, 21; see pp. 8 and 19, where sociology is recommended for the study of "morals." On Lévy-Bruhl's distance from Durkheim, see Deprez 2010: 51–56.

10. It is precisely sociology's refusal of idealism's tendency to universality that philosophers were unwilling to treat as constitutive of the concepts of norm and normal. Some philosophical sociologists, notably Célestin Bouglé, who was partly formed in the Durkheim school, but in the 1920s moved in a new direction, aimed to bridge the two concepts by insisting on the dependence of norms on values (Bouglé 1922: ch. 9). A few more notes are in order here on Durkheim, particularly on the organicism essential to his definition of the norm. In his view, the formation of society took priority over the particularities exhibited by individuals in it. For Sartre, Levinas, Lévi-Strauss, and Lacan (not to mention Bataille), this posed significant problems for thinking separation and for developing a sense of the other as other. Rather than a shift, the development of the other and the norm could be viewed as an evolution that assumes Durkheim's argument and sees that a religious communion is completely missing in the present world. The phenomenological and then the structural emphasis on interpersonal separation suggests a profound refusal of the possibility of being swept up by a community, or a shared experience that renders the self ecstatically transparent to this community and vice versa. Mauss engaged with the debates between sociology and philosophy (pointing specifically to Bergson and Brunschvicg) in "La Sociologie en France depuis 1914" (1933), in Mauss 1969: 436.

11. Durkheim 1982 [1919]: ch. 3.

12. Quételet 1835. On Quetelet, see Hacking 1990: ch. 13.

13. Halbwachs 1912: 156. Halbwachs's book is discussed by Canguilhem in *NP*, 156–62.

14. The "average man" is not (Halbwachs concedes) ontologically "normal" in Quetelet; however, he is "firmly founded" in a fashion that approximates such ontologization. See Halbwachs 1912: 159.

15. Ibid., 175.

16. Sociology also treated the normal as a matter for discussion and explanation, not a given, or so he argued: ibid., 157–58.

17. Ibid., 158.

18. Ibid., 178–79.

19. Fiss 2009: 73.

20. Cited in Rydell 1993: 103.

21. Fiss 2009: 73–75.

22. Leriche, 1936.

23. *MT*, 408.

24. Ibid., 402–3.

25. Ibid., 407.

26. Ibid., 409–10.

27. Ibid., 410.

28. Early reviews to the book recognized this: Lagache, "Le Normal et le pathologique d'après G. Canguilhem," in Lagache 1977: 439–56; and Starobinski 1953.

29. *KL*, xvii.

30. Ibid., 127.

31. A long list of examples could follow here, and in some ways Canguilhem can even be said to underplay Comte's emphasis on progress and normality. From the very beginning of the *Course on Positive Philosophy* (lesson 2), Comte argued that positivism offered the only proper educational system that included instruction in physiological matters: it went from the simple to the complex and rearticulated all human knowledge, putting deep trust in its political promise.

32. Canguilhem 1983: 135–36.

33. Among his articles and books on the subject, see Leriche 1927a and 1927b.

34. *NP*, 91, 92, 101, 118, 243; *KL*, 129.

35. *NP*, 100–101.

36. Ibid., 91.

37. Ibid., 98.

38. See the accounts of Goldstein's interwar work in Harrington 1999; Geroulanos and Meyers 2014. Canguilhem would rely on Goldstein from *NP* until his very last essays.

39. *NP*, 185, 188.

40. Canguilhem took detailed notes from Lagache's course "Psychologie pathologique"; he even wrote down conversations with patients. See CAPHÉS GC.II.I.5.

41. *KL*, 126, 132. The operation here was essentially the same as that proposed by Jurgis Baltrušaitis (1984 [1969]: 8) as regards anamorphic art: anamorphosis shows the reduced, structured, formalized but also overwrought character of the linear perspective that reduces all other forms of sight and representation to monstrosity.

42. *NP*, 137.

43. Ibid., 200.

44. Canguilhem discussed Comte's theory of progress in his 1926 *mémoire*—(a type of dissertation) written under the guidance of two doyens of the secular, progressivist education that was official policy in the Third Republic: his mentor Alain and Lucien Lévy-Bruhl, whose *La Philosophie d'Auguste Comte* had just been published.

45. Canguilhem and Planet, *Traité de logique et de morale* (1939), in Canguilhem 2011: 791.

46. Ibid., 801–2.

47. CAPHÉS GC.11.2.2, "Les Normes et le normal," 8.

48. Ibid., 7; emphasis added.

49. Maurice Blanchot's (1996 [1948]) metaphors of disease in novel *Le Très-Haut* (*The Most High*) are in many respects germaine to Canguilhem's discussion. In *Le Très-Haut*, it is disease, not the complexity of everyday life or historical existence in general that clouds the transparency of the law, confuses the state's capacity to operate according to the reduction that Blanchot's protagonist-narrator Henri Sorge evokes when he writes that "everyone seemed to be acting only in their own interests, everyone performed obscure acts, and yet there was a halo of light around these hidden lives." Conversely, one could use Canguilhem's terminology to call the result of Blanchot's epidemic a transformation of the state of the "State" from normal to pathological. See Bruns 1997: 30–31; Geroulanos 2007: esp. 1077 n. 20.

50. *NP*, 89.

51. Ibid., 125–50.

52. Ibid., 156.

53. CAPHÉS GC.11.2.2, "Les Normes et le normal," 98. See also GC.12.1.9, "Agrégation 1947, Durkheim," 17.

54. Lecourt 2008.

55. By contrast, a rather uncomplicated philosophical explanation of Canguilhem's *résistance* effort has been suggested by Roudinesco 2008: 11.

56. See, e.g., Burleigh and Wippermann 1993: 181, and more generally their chapter on hereditary illness, homosexuality, and asociality (136–95).

57. CAPHÉS GC.11.2.2, "Les Normes et le normal," 98.

58. Sartre 1989a: 309–10. Lagache suggested a proximity between Sartre and Canguilhem in his "Le Normal et le pathologique d'après Canguilhem" (Lagache 1977: 455).

59. Canguilhem, "The Problem of Regulation in the Organism and in Society" (Canguilhem 2012: 67–77).

60. Pieron 1951: 190. Pieron wrote both definitions himself and retained them unchanged in the expanded 1963 edition, then added normalisation in a basically positive tone.

61. *KL*, 132; emphasis added.

62. Lagache, "Le Normal et le pathologique d'après G. Canguilhem" (Lagache 1977: 453).

63. Lacan 1975 [1932].

64. Lagache, "Les hallucinations verbales et la parole," in Lagache 1977: 1–133.

65. Minkowski 1926, 1927.

66. Lacan criticizes Ey's "organo-dynamism" in *L-E*, 151–193/123–158; see Allendy 1934; Nin 1994; and also the discussion of Allendy's influence of Canguilhem in Lecourt 2008: ch. 1.

67. *L-S3*, 19; also 20.

68. Ibid., 20.

69. Ibid., 154.

70. Ibid., e.g., 48.

71. Ibid., 74; also 123.

72. Ibid., 35.

73. Lacan's note on the fragmented body derives from "The Mirror Stage as Formative of the I Function," *L-E*, 97/78.

74. *L-S3*, 87; emphasis added.

75. *L-S3*, 189.

76. *L-S2*, 49.

77. Ibid., 43; emphasis added.

78. Ibid., 41.

79. E.g., *L-E*, 849/720.

80. See the discussion of the Oedipus complex above, and also Lacan's comments on the "pacifying" effect of the ego ideal in "Aggressiveness in Psychoanalysis," *L-E*, 117/95.

81. *L-S2*, 19.

82. Lacan, "The Direction of the Treatment," *L-E*, 641/536.

83. Lacan, "Variations on the Standard Treatment," *L-E*, 362/300.

84. SLP, 244/203.

85. Lacan, "Response to Jean Hyppolite's Commentary on Freud's 'Verneinung,'" *L-E*, 394/328.

86. The remark on analysts' opacity can be found in Lacan (1957: 92), in a response to Jean Wahl. See also "Variations on the Standard Treatment" (esp. 340/282) and "The Situation of Psychoanalysis and the Training of Psychoanalysts," both in *L-E*.

87. *OT*, 328.

CHAPTER 13: THE THIRD ORDER, OR, THE STRUCTURAL "SYMBOLIC"
AS EPISTEMOLOGICAL INTERFACE

1. Foucault begged anglophone readers to reject the term "structuralism," forced on him, he claimed, by "half-witted commentators" (*OT*, xiv).

2. Gilles Deleuze, "How Do We Recognize Structuralism," in Deleuze 2004: 171.

3. Many of the accounts and histories of structuralism have offered either a

biography of a movement (Dosse 1998) or a history of its growth from linguistic roots (e.g., Seriot 2014). Other, more systematic accounts have sought to address the matter of what exactly thinkers labeled as "structuralists" shared: in an intriguing 1971 article, Gilles Deleuze attempted one such interpretation and offered six principal criteria for structuralism. I focus here on the first criterion that Deleuze offers: the invention of the symbolic. But this of course is not to judge the merits of these different approaches.

4. For two recent examples from historians of philosophy, see Worms 2009: 483 (with reference to Derrida), and Bourg 2007: 162. In discussing the difficulties of the term "transparency" in the work of Roland Barthes, whom I do not consider here, Marie-Jeanne Zenetti (2011) emphasizes: "In Barthes, transparency points to an other utopia, that of a 'neutral and inert state of form' . . . transparency becomes the 'fashion in which a silence exists' across 'a style of absence which is almost an ideal absence of style.'"

5. Roman Jakobson's intermediary role in Lévi-Strauss's "structuralization" is well known (see Wilcken 2010: 142–48). The transposition of structural linguistics in ethnology is confirmed in *ESK*, 493, 496.

6. Ibid., 8. Lévi-Strauss extends the Durkheimian tradition here by identifying cultures specifically with their *norms* and treats the normal as non-universal and relative.

7. Ibid., 8–9.

8. Ibid., 24.

9. Ibid., 24–25.

10. Ibid., 489.

11. Lévi-Strauss, "Structural Analysis in Linguistics and Anthropology," in Lévi-Strauss 1974: 33. See also Keck 2005: 62–67.

12. Lévi-Strauss, "Language and the Analysis of Social Laws," in Lévi-Strauss 1974: 56–57.

13. Ibid., 65.

14. In this regard, Georges Bataille (1986: 214) was inexact when he stated: "When Lévi-Strauss talks about nature and culture he is setting one abstraction beside another; while the transition from the animal to man implies not only those states as such but also their movement into opposite camps." In his criticism, Bataille adopts as his own a part of Lévi-Strauss's goal.

15. Lévi-Strauss 1987 [1950], and Merleau-Ponty, "From Mauss to Lévi-Strauss" in Merleau-Ponty 1964b: 114–25. See Breckman 2013: 15–18.

16. See Jakobson's letters to Lévi-Strauss in BnF, Fonds Lévi-Strauss, NAF 28150.193, which reference the two men's friendship with Lacan.

17. *L-E*, 98/79.

18. On the symbolic, besides the standard-setting book by Breckman (2013), see also Fabre 1996 and Dews 2002.

19. *L-E*, 92/74.

20. Ibid., 96/78.

21. On Lacan working with a totalized conception of the psyche in the aftermath of Georges Politzer's critique of Bergsonian/spiritualist psychology, see Worms 2009: 477.

22. L-*S1*, 66. On the limitation of the Real, see also SLP, 284/235, where Lacan writes that "reality in analytic experience often . . . remains veiled in negative forms."

23. On the different genres of Lacan's work, see Milner 1995: ch. 1. Milner, by the way, begins with the exclamation "Lacan is a crystalline author" (7).

24. Lacan notes his proximity to Lévi-Strauss and his adoption of "structure" and other concepts from him in L-*E*, 648/542.

25. SLP, 285/236.

26. Ibid., 275/227.

27. Ibid., 286/237; see also 284/235 for Lacan's attack on positivism's prioritization of the hard sciences.

28. Ibid., 279/231.

29. See the identification of the other with the symbolic, e.g., in "Psychoanalysis and Its Teaching," L-*E*, 454/379.

30. SLP, 277/229.

31. Ibid., 277–78/229–30.

32. Ibid., 277/229.

33. Ibid., 283/235.

34. L-*S2*, 29. Specifically presenting Lévi-Strauss as trying to avoid a situation where "having shown God out of one door . . . [he would] bring him back in by the other," Lacan appealed to conversations with him in order to make clear their shared hostility to allowing nature ("a masked transcendentalism") to appropriate "the symbolic register" or elementary structure (ibid., 35).

35. Ibid., 33.

36. Ibid., 20.

37. Ibid., 33.

38. Lacan 1998: 34.

39. Deleuze, "How Do We Recognize Structuralism?" in Deleuze 2004: 172. The point about the symbolic being "deeper" is on p. 173.

40. Hallward, "Theoretical Training," in Hallward and Peden 2012, 1–56.

41. Ibid., 11.

42. Serres and Badiou, "Model and Structure," in Bianco and Tho 2013: 106.

43. Ibid., 111.

44. Foucault 1957; Foucault 1976.

45. Souloumiac 2004.

46. Han, "The Analytic of Finitude and the History of Subjectivity," in Gutting 2006: 176–209.

47. *OT*, xxiii.

48. Ibid., xx; emphasis added.

49. Ibid., xxi–xxii.

50. Foucault 1972: 55.

51. *OT*, xx.

52. Descartes 1970: 5–6; quoted by Derrida, *OG*, 330–31.

53. Leibniz 1989 [1679].

54. Mill 1874: 13. No less typical is, of course, utilitarianism's opposition to confusion and uncertainty; see Mill 1863: 2; Mill 1861: ch. 7.

55. *PC*, §368.

56. Bouglé and Gastinel 1920: 4, 12, 39, 51–52.

57. Febvre 1944: 120–21.

58. Cf. Heidegger's famous remark that the French, "when they begin to think, they speak German, being sure that they could not make it with their own language" (Heidegger 1976 [1966]: 282). Heidegger had expressed a similar disdain for French to French thinkers at least as early as his first letter to Jean Beaufret of November 23, 1945.

59. For the implicit Koyré–Beaufret debate on Heidegger and truth, see Koyré 1946 and Beaufret 1947; also Janicaud 2001: 1: 113.

60. Evans 1979: 387.

61. Culler and Lamb 2003.

CHAPTER 14: LÉVI-STRAUSS'S WORLD OUT OF SYNC

1. Claude Lévi-Strauss, "The Work of the Bureau of American Ethnology" (1965), in Lévi-Strauss 1976: 59.

2. The much celebrated figure of the disappearing native, so central to *Tristes tropiques*, had long been a trope in anthropological writing. Adolf Bastian and Lewis H. Morgan probably originated it—see Morgan 1877, vii–viii; Steinberg 1995: 60. Bronislaw Malinowski (1932) opened his magnum opus *Argonauts of the Western Pacific* with an image highly similar to Lévi-Strauss's, albeit one more concerned with the suffering of ethnology than with that of its subjects: "Ethnology is in the sadly ludicrous, not to say tragic, position that at the very moment when it begins to put its workshop in order, to forge its proper tools, to start ready for work on its appointed task, the material of its study melts away with hopeless rapidity. Just now, when the methods and aims of scientific field ethnology have taken shape, when men fully trained for the work have begun to travel into savage countries and study their inhabitants these die away under our very eyes" (xv). In the same year as that of Malinowski's paradigm-setting work, a collection titled *Essays on the Depopulation of Melanesia* also appeared (Rivers 1922). W. H. R. Rivers made colonial depopulation and violence his direct target, decrying "apologists for the effects of their own civilization"; they "give reasons for the supposed original decadence, [that] often bear their own refutation on the face," and "in some parts the decline is taking place so rapidly that at no distant date the islands will wholly lose their native inhabitants unless something is

done to stay its progress" (84; see also 87). What is particular here to Lévi-Strauss (or to his generation) is the argument on the homogenization and singularization of human culture.

3. On "hot" and "cold" societies, see Lévi-Strauss, "The Scope of Anthropology," in Lévi-Strauss 1976: 29. On Western progress as resulting in homogenization and entropy, and on anthropology as "entropology," see *TT*, 413–14. Georges Bataille understands homogenization as involving a loss of the uncontrollable element of excess and waste that sustains humanity.

4. See the famous review by de Beauvoir 1949; Georges Bataille's repeated discussions of *The Elementary Structures of Kinship* in Bataille 1986; Bataille 1993: 2: 29–56; and Wilcken 2010: ch. 5.

5. *TT*, 149.

6. Ibid., 386–87.

7. Ibid., 38.

8. Lévi-Strauss 1975: 133–34.

9. *TT*, 38; also 414.

10. Ibid., 391; emphasis added.

11. For a discussion of Lévi-Strauss's interpretation of Western history as hinging on an interpretation of thermodynamics and as tending toward inertia, see Canguilhem 1987: 451–52. See also *TT*, 414, where Lévi-Strauss suggests that anthropology "could, with advantage, be changed into entropology."

12. *TT*, 39.

13. Ibid., 392.

14. A few paragraphs earlier, Lévi-Strauss speaks in more or less the same terms—of a quest "to look beyond abuses and crimes to find the unshakable basis of human society. To this quest, anthropological comparison can contribute in two ways. It shows that the basis is not to be discovered in our civilization: of all known societies ours is no doubt the one most remote from it. At the same time, by bringing out the characteristics common to the majority of human societies, it helps us to postulate a type, of which no society is a faithful realization, but which indicates the direction the investigation ought to follow" (ibid., 391).

15. Lévi-Strauss, "Les trois humanismes" [1956] in Lévi-Strauss 1973: 320. See also Lévi-Strauss 1956: 384–85, where Lévi-Strauss repeats the three humanisms motif and states that "black writers and artists" are representatives of their respective cultures.

16. See *TT*, 55 and 383 on the anthropologist's "mental disorder."

17. Lévi-Strauss 1955: 1214.

18. Lévi-Strauss, "History and Dialectic," in Lévi-Strauss 1966: 245–70.

19. Lévi-Strauss, "Les trois humanismes," in Lévi-Strauss 1973: 320.

20. Lévi-Strauss, "The Scope of Anthropology," in Lévi-Strauss 1976: 30, 32; translation amended.

21. See the note on Mauss in ibid., 5.

22. Lévi-Strauss, "Une Science révolutionnaire, l'ethnographie," lecture delivered on January 29, 1938 (or 1939) at the Federated Center for Workers' Education: BnF, Fonds Lévi-Strauss, NAF28150: 82/3.

23. A typescript of the thesis, dated June 1930, can be found in BnF, Fonds Lévi-Strauss, NAF 28150 (1).

24. Lévi-Strauss, "Une Science révolutionnaire, l'ethnographie" (cited n. 22 above), 6; see also 7–8.

25. Ibid., 17.

26. Ibid., 16, 11–12, 17, 18.

27. Ibid., 26, 31–32, 33. Lévi-Strauss closely echoes the argument made by André Leroi-Gourhan and others in Rivet 1937.

28. Lévi-Strauss 1966: 249.

29. Marcel Mauss to Lévi-Strauss, Bibliothèque du Collège de France, Fonds Marcel Mauss, MAS 19.

30. *TT*, 389.

31. Lévi-Strauss, "Une Science révolutionnaire, l'ethnographie," 9; see also 5.

32. *TT*, 375–76 emphasis added; see also 383–84. This phrase is characteristic of other texts by Lévi-Strauss as well, and Alfred Métraux (1978: 517) even notes that Lévi-Strauss discussed this element of the ethnographer's paradoxical situation at dinner (entry of July 29, 1953).

33. See the quotation from Chateaubriand (*TT*, 44) and the argument about living in, and studying, one's own mind rather than one's surroundings (ibid., 376, 378, 385–86).

34. Ibid., 87. See also the classic critique of Lévi-Strauss's treatment of time offered in Fabian 1983: 52–69.

35. *TT*, 87, 85, 95.

36. Ibid., 55.

37. Ibid.

38. This is also why Paul Ricœur's judgment of Lévi-Strauss as offering merely a "Kantianism without a transcendental subject" amounted to a criticism of Lévi-Strauss—but one that Lévi-Strauss himself did not oppose. See Ricœur, 1963: 618.

39. See Lévi-Strauss, "Structural Analysis in Linguistics and Anthropology" (1945), in Lévi-Strauss, 1974: 40; and *ESK* 493–94.

40. From a manuscript of *Tristes tropiques*, p. 79bis, BnF, Fonds Lévi-Strauss, NAF 28150.10; see *TT*, 57 for the published English version.

CHAPTER 15: THE ETHNOGRAPHER, *CINÉMA-VÉRITÉ*, AND THE DISRUPTION OF THE NATURAL ORDER

1. BnF, Fonds Paul Valéry, NAF 19176, CLXXVI F.130–33. The letter, with its nonchalant expressions of racism front and center, is too complex to be analyzed here.

2. Jean Rouch with Lucien Taylor, "Life at the Edge of Cinema and Anthropology," *CE*, 136.

3. Rouch, "Cinq regards sur Vertov," in Sadoul 1971: 13; also *CE*, 31, 32–33.

4. Edgar Morin, "Chronicle of a Film," *CE*, 248, cited in DiIorio 2007: 39.

5. *CE*, 325–26.

6. Edgar Morin, "Chronicle of a Film," *CE*, 252.

7. Contrasting his own participation with Richard Leacock's passive camera presence, Rouch (*CE*, 144) later said: "In our films we intervened brazenly; Morin was there in front of the camera, speaking to the people, provoking everyone he met."

8. Mauss 2002: 35.

9. Griaule advanced a proposal for a joint ministerial project (Ministry of National Education and Ministry of Air) that would require the involvement of aviation in ethnographic research (see the minutes of a meeting of the Office de la recherche scientifique coloniale on October 20, 1945, in LAS/FML.B.S03.03.04.025): see Griaule 1937; 1946; 1948. See also Mauss 2002: 34, and Rouch's discussion in "The Cinema of the Future?" in *CE*, 269.

10. Aliette Armel (1997) suggests that the rift between Leiris and Griaule was caused by Griaule's unacknowledged use of Leiris's (at the time unpublished) study on masks and not just by Leiris's mention of the *kono* theft. For Griaule's work on Dogon masks, see Griaule 1994: 773–818. Leiris finally published his shortly after Griaule's death (Leiris 1958).

11. Clifford 1988: 74, 76.

12. Griaule 1957b: 27; Clifford 1988: 83–84. Lévi-Strauss, too, had no compunction about resorting to trickery, notably in the scene in *Tristes tropiques* where he persuades the children to reveal to him the secret names of the tribe's members.

13. Mauss was mistrustful of the ethnographic encounter (2002 [1947]: 38); see also the instructions in chs. 8–9 of his *Manuel d'ethnographie* on the various other methods available to the ethnographer for studying moral and religious phenomena.

14. Griaule 1957b: 59. See also his "critique" of the informant (92–94).

15. "Yes. I prefer not to be a scientist but to participate. I often used to discuss the matter of one's form of participation with Griaule" (Rouch with Taylor, "Life at the Edge of Cinema and Anthropology," *CE*, 141).

16. Rouch published his dissertation (Rouch 1960) the year that he filmed *Chronique d'un été*.

17. Clifford 1988: 68, 71, 75, 83–84. For the relation to Rouch, see Henley 2010: 12–15, 315.

18. Sadoul 1971: 126; emphasis added.

19. Jean-Luc Godard, "From Critic to Filmmaker," in Hillier 1992: 65.

20. "Morin was a member of the Communist Party, along with Marguerite Duras and others, but he was a militant. While I on the other hand advocated

anarchy without militancy. The card-carrying militants were quite blind" (Rouch with Taylor, "Life at the Edge of Cinema and Anthropology," *CE*, 139). Rouch also discusses his indifference to Griaule's politics (ibid., 109).

21. EDC; Rouch's presence is noted in Armel 1997. It is important to note that Griaule had similar views on the power of ethnography to ameliorate colonialism, if not quite to annul it, although he believed that France was "protective" of its colonies; see Griaule 1939, 1952.

22. Rouch 2008: 242.

23. Ibid., 247.

24. Jacques Rivette, in Hillier 1992: 320.

25. Jean-André Fieschi, "Neo-neorealism," in Hillier 1992: 271.

26. Louis Marcorelles, "The Leacock Experiment," in Hillier 1992: 265.

27. Godard 1986: 129; translation amended.

28. Deleuze 1989: 153.

29. EDC, 106.

30. Rothberg 2004: 1231–46.

31. Ibid., 1238.

32. *CE*, 341, partially quoted in Rothberg 2004: 1239.

33. *CE*, 327.

34. DiIorio 2007: 43.

35. Fried 1980. DiIorio (2007: 43) reframes Fried's central concepts so that "the Bazinian era of absorption starts to give way to a new emphasis on a theatricality of process: in its wake, the truth of the real was no longer a simple matter of sound and vision."

36. Rouch 1958: 92–94, esp. 93–94.

CHAPTER 16: RETURN TO ROUSSEAU

1. Starobinski, "Rousseau et la recherche des origines" [1962], in Starobinski 1988 [1971]: 319.

2. *OG*, 338 n. 1.

3. *TT*, 390; translation modified. For his identification with Rousseau and his "temperament," see FSM, 35.

4. In 1963 and 1969, respectively in *UNESCO Courier* 16 (3): 10–15 and 22 (8–9): 61–63.

5. FSM, 35.

6. Ibid., 40–41.

7. Ibid.37.

8. Ibid., 35.

9. Ibid., 40.

10. BnF, Fonds Lévi-Strauss, NAF 28150: 86/1, "Discours prononcé à Genève lors des cérémonies célébrant le 250e anniversaire de la naissance de Rousseau," note on an unnumbered page.

11. BnF, Fonds Lévi-Strauss, NAF 28150: 86/1, notes on two consecutive, unnumbered pages.

12. The similarity between certain passages of FSM and *Tristes tropiques* is often astonishing; much of the argument of the latter is reprised here. The close parallels include the discussion of the anthropologist's displacement, guilt, and suspension between worlds (cf. *TT*'s chapter "The Apotheosis of Augustus" with FSM, 35–36, a paragraph-long section); the refusal of the ego (cf. the concluding page of *TT*, with the discussion of Descartes in FSM, 36); the extensive attack on humanism (restricted to philosophy in FSM, 40); the sense of the present as a time irreversibly compromised by homogeneity and false unity.

13. FSM, 38.

14. Ibid., 39–40.

15. *TT*, 390.

16. FSM, 40.

17. Ibid., 41–42.

18. Ibid., 43; translation modified.

19. Ibid., 37.

20. Starobinski 1988, 11.

21. Starobinski 1964: 101.

22. FSM, 39; translation modified.

23. The critique of Lévi-Strauss was originally published as "Nature, culture, écriture," in *Cahiers pour l'analyse* 4 (September–October 1966), 7–49; Lévi-Strauss wrote a short letter protesting that Derrida was applying to his work a too rigorous reading, more appropriate for philosophers, and sneered that Derrida was imposing his reading and philosophical priorities "with the delicacy of a bear" (Lévi-Strauss 1967: 89–90).

24. *OG*, 340; emphasis added. Quotations are from Starobinski 1988 [1971].

25. At least one aim of Starobinski's *Rousseau* is not captured in Derrida's note. Starobinski was pushing to the extreme an existentialist argument that presented ethical transparency as a desideratum that could help make the world a better place and found a new humanism.

26. See Starobinski's review of Canguilhem's work in Starobinski 1953: 777–91.

27. *OG*, 115.

28. Ibid., 157.

29. See also Derrida's reading of Lévi-Strauss's conclusion in "A Little Glass of Rum," where Lévi-Strauss searches for "the unshakeable basis of human society" (ibid., 115).

30. Ibid., 119; emphasis added.

31. Ibid., 137. A similar description, not cited by Derrida, is offered by Lévi-Strauss in "The Scope of Anthropology," his inaugural lecture at the Collège de France (Lévi-Strauss 1976 [1973]: 32).

32. *OG*, 125, 135.

33. Lévi-Strauss to Marcel Mauss, July 7, 1936, Bibliothèque du Collège de France, Fonds Marcel Mauss, MAS 8.3.

34. The thesis was originally published as Lévi-Strauss 1947.

35. For the alterations, see BnF, Fonds Lévi-Strauss, NAF 28150.10, "*Tristes tropiques*, vol. 3 de la dactylographie." This passage is on p. 327; compare to the finalized version in *TT*, 302. Lévi-Strauss repeatedly removes words like "adversary" and "aggression"; similar revisions can be found on the cut-and-pasted p. 328 of the typescript, which corresponds to the heavily reworked pp. 93–94 of "La Vie familiale et sociale des Indiens Nambikwara" (these pages contain elaborate references to declarations and songs of war removed on *TT*, 302–3, again without reference to the earlier thesis). One further example is the long final paragraph of chapter 27 of *Tristes tropiques*, marked as deriving directly from his notebooks (*TT*, 293; more pronounced in the original French), the only memory Lévi-Strauss would like to retain of the Nambikwara. Lévi-Strauss cut up and pasted much of this passage from his dissertation, rather than from field notes (though the passage might originate in notes), then completed it by rewriting the remainder by hand (BnF, Fonds Lévi-Strauss, NAF28150.10, "vol. 3," p. 315).

36. *OG*, 138.

37. Ibid., 139, 140.

38. See also ibid., 113.

39. Ibid., 112. See also the discussion of proper names (and of the secret of the proper names among the Nambikwara) on 109. There again, Derrida sees Lévi-Strauss acceding to the "original myth of transparent legibility" in his adoption of the Nambikwara anxiety over the revelation of proper names.

40. Ibid., 112.

41. Ibid., 106; see also 127, on the ineluctable link of writing and knowledge to the intersubjective violence.

42. Ibid., 137.

43. Ibid., 112.

44. Ibid., 114–15.

45. *TT*, 383.

46. *FSM*, 39.

47. On Derrida's early ambivalence regarding Algeria, see Baring 2010.

CHAPTER 17: RETURN TO DESCARTES

1. Lacan, "The Instance of the Letter in the Unconscious," *L-E*, 516/429; translation amended.

2. *OT*, 322.

3. *OG*, 97–98.

4. The list of discussions of Descartes and transparency in the period is of course far more complex than could be represented here. See, notably, Hans Blu-

menberg's critique and historicization of Descartes on "clarity," particularly the clarity of concepts, in Blumenberg 2010: 1–4.

5. "This last tribunal of the Cogito" is a phrase used by Jacques Derrida (CHM 32).

6. Glucksmann 1977, 1987. See Pierre Macherey's (2002) response, where Macherey concluded with "Non, Descartes c'est pas la France!"

7. Against that revisionism, see, e.g., Badiou 2002: 2.

8. This congress marked an important moment for the tensions seething within Cartesian studies during interwar France; see Bayer 1937; Valéry 1937 and Valéry's notebooks on Descartes in the Fonds Valéry (BnF, NAF 19056 [MF22241–22242]).

9. Valéry 1961: 13.

10. Quoted in Bouglé 1926: 148–49; translation modified.

11. For some, e.g., Paul Ricœur, this would remain a major concern to the end of their work; Ricœur's phenomenology, for example, was profoundly concerned with the status and problems of the cogito. See Ricœur 1996: 57–66, and 1992, "Introduction."

12. Husserl 1975.

13. Most significant in this regard was Jean Cavaillès, whose criticisms of Husserl were spread and insisted upon by Canguilhem. See Cavaillès 1976 [1947]; Canguilhem 2004: 27; and the critiques of the return to a transcendental ego in Sartre 1957 [1937] and Gurwitsch 1966: 287–300 (esp. 295, where Gurwitsch all but endorses Sartre 1957 [1937]).

14. I am using "derealization" as an English equivalent of Alquié's (1950) *déréalisation*.

15. Peden 2011: 366. This seems to me to go too far; although convincing in the case of Jean-Luc Marion, and perhaps also in that of Michel Henry, Peden's argument ignores both Husserl's own influence (particularly through the *Cartesian Meditations* and the *Crisis*) and the cases of Sartre and Ricœur; the parallel between Alquié and Lévinas is not altogether adequate.

16. Merleau-Ponty 2007b: 98.

17. Boutroux 1897: 315.

18. Koyré 1990 [1948]: 114–15.

19. Heidegger's anti-Cartesianism has often been credited with giving shape, in France, to the anti-subjectivist and antihumanist impulse that would define much of philosophy in the 1950s and 1960s. As Jacques Derrida and Knox Peden have emphasized, even a Cartesianism as deep-seated as that of Alquié was not without existentialist and Heideggerian affinities; this was visible in Alquié's emphasis on a "nostalgia for being" in Descartes that grounded his effort to organize subjectivity and to ground it in the modern era. See Peden 2011 and "Jacques Derrida" in Janicaud 2001: 2: 92–93. While the broader account is largely correct, it still remains unclear quite how well Heidegger knew the French context itself when composing the "Letter on Humanism." *Pace* Tom Rockmore and Richard

Wolin (and others who write of French intellectuals as Heidegger's disciples), these thinkers, with the exception of Jean Beaufret's minor coterie, made use of Heidegger's argument for positions very different from his own and advocated a version of modernity similar to Heidegger's for reasons different from his. Excellent accounts of Heidegger's reception are offered in Kleinberg 2005; Janicaud 2001, vol.1; Pettigrew and Raffoul 2008.

20. On Foucault and technique, see Behrent 2013: 54–104.

21. Axelos 1976: 156. Histories of technological bourgeois domination were already undertaken in the interwar period; see Canguilhem's discussion of Franz Borkenau and Henryk Grossman in *KL*, 82.

22. Peden 2011.

23. Colloque philosophique de Royaumont 1957, 486.

24. Merleau-Ponty 1973: 96.

25. Canguilhem, "L'Œuvre scientifique de Descartes et la science du 17e siècle, 1959–1960," CAPHÉS GC.13.5.1, 92.

26. Lacan 1998: 222.

27. Lacan, "Seminar on 'The Purloined Letter,'" L-*E*, 20/14.

28. SLP, 270/224.

29. Lacan, "Science and Truth," L-*E*, 866/736. Here Lacan reuses the prosopopoeia of the truth at L-*E*, 409/340 and 411/342.

30. See his note on personae and masks in the critique of Lagache (L-*E*, 671/562).

31. See "The Freudian Thing" [1955], L-*E*, 406/338.

32. Baring 2012: 194–96.

33. *HM*, 45–46.

34. E.g., to contrast Descartes to the eighteenth-century understanding of the alterity of the mad (ibid., 181).

35. Ibid., 157; emphasis added.

36. Ibid., 156.

37. On the delivery of Derrida's paper and Foucault's "really rather positive" reaction, see Peeters 2013: 131–32.

38. CHM, 42–43. Foucault makes this point repeatedly, first in a well-known, forceful passage (quoted by Derrida in CHM, 42) on "*the necessity of madness throughout the history of the West . . . [madness] is, in short, linked to the possibility of history*" (*HM*, xxxii; see also 372 and, notably, 377–78).

39. CHM, 47.

40. Ibid., 54–55.

41. This is one point that Foucault would refuse outright and against which he would argue insistently in his "My Body, this Paper, this Fire," his aggressive 1972 response to Derrida's reading. For him Derrida's assumption of the mask amounted instead to a full-throttled distinction between Descartes and "an interlocutor" who would speak in his stead.

42. CHM, 56, 55. See also the discussion in Peter Fenves, 2002: 275–76.

43. *OG*, 98.

44. *OT*, 322.

45. Canguilhem 2005.

46. Canguilhem writes: "Whether [Foucault] is working in Bachelard's wake or not . . ."; but the implication is as obvious as the genealogy he is promoting (ibid., 92).

47. *OG*, 97–98.

48. Derrida continues in this direction, emphasizing that this transparency of the cogito is not even disturbed by the introduction of God as a mediator, himself conceived of as "the name and the element" of what enables this transparency (*OG*, 98).

49. Badiou 2006: 431. Badiou is referring here to Lacan's 1946 call to return to Descartes in "Presentation on Psychical Causality" (L-*E* 163/133), where Lacan also discusses the madness argument of the First Meditation.

50. Lacan, "The Instance of the Letter in the Unconscious," L-*E*, 516/429; translation amended.

51. L-*E*, 516/429; translation amended.

52. L-*S2*, 6.

53. It is worth noting that Lacan's formulation bears remarkable similarities to Sartre's treatment of the separation between consciousness and ego in his 1936 phenomenological essay "The Transcendence of the Ego," though of course Sartre left little to no space for the unconscious.

54. L-*E*, 856/727.

CHAPTER 18: "SPEAK NOT OF DARKNESS, BUT OF A SOMEWHAT BLURRED LIGHT"

1. Foucault 1994 = *OT*.

2. Ibid., 328.

3. Ibid., 36.

4. Ibid., 35.

5. Ibid., 34; emphasis added.

6. Ibid., 35.

7. Ibid., 34.

8. Ibid., 79; emphasis added; also 84.

9. Ibid., 29–30.

10. Ibid., 56, 79.

11. Ibid., 62; also 64, 65–66, 208.

12. Ibid., 79.

13. Ibid., 79; also 76.

14. Ibid., 311.

15. Ibid., 329; also 81 and 117.

16. Ibid., 206.

17. It is worth noting Martin Jay's claims on Foucault's supposed celebration of opacity (J-*DE*, 407, 415); I am suggesting that something very different from "celebration" occurred in Foucault's texts, notably in *OT*.

18. See Foucault's discussion of coinage in *OT*, 170, where he argues that the sign that coins bear is "merely the exact and transparent mark of the measure they constituted." Compare this to Foucault's contrast of David Ricardo and the "decisive importance" of his analysis (vs. Adam Smith's), for which "Men's activity and the value of things were seen as communicating in the transparent element of representation" (*OT*, 253; see also 229, 228).

19. Ibid., 232–33.

20. Ibid., 298.

21. Ibid., 283; see also 293 and 299.

22. Ibid., 242; see also 210, where Foucault twice interprets the understanding of desire and the "table of representation" again by way of transparency.

23. Ibid., 247.

24. See also Paul Rabinow's (1989) reformulation—"the unifying medium has lost its transparency"—and related passages, e.g. on p. 8.

25. Deleuze, 2009: 67, also 65–66; in English in Deleuze 2004: 91; translation modified.

26. *OT*, 303.

27. Gusdorf 1960, 1966–67.

28. Gusdorf 1963: 5. Gusdorf calls for a fundamental anthropology based on the human sciences (ibid., 81).

29. A contrast between Foucault and Gusdorf was offered by Jean-Claude Margolin in his review of *The Order of Things* (Margolin 1967: 324).

30. This was, of course, not a new problem; in Germany it had characterized debates on the status of different sciences in the mid-nineteenth century, psychology being a particularly significant case; see, e.g., the case of Wilhelm Wundt, in Wundt 1907: 2, and in Ash 1980: 396–421. In France, these problems played out in part thanks to Auguste Comte and positivism.

31. Ricœur 1960a: 273; 1960b.

32. In 1957, the Société française de philosophie had organized the ninth Congress of the Philosophical Societies in the French Language, titled "Man and His Works." Gaston Berger announced the main sections of the conference—"creative activity; scientific and technical works; aesthetic works; and social works"—in 1957, in *Bulletin de la Société française de philosophie* 49 (2): 67.

33. Benveniste 1966.

34. See the later pushback, notably Pierre Clastres's critiques of Marxist anthropology in Clastres 1987: 202, and Clastres, "Marxists and Their Anthropology," in Clastres 1994. On Clastres, see also Moyn 2004. In *Arguments*, see nos. 12–3, 18, 21, 22.

35. See Geroulanos 2010: ch. 8; Bianco 2013; Hyppolite 1952; Vuillemin 1954.

36. For Foucault's debt to Hyppolite, see F-*DE*, 1: 785. For Deleuze, see "Jean Hyppolite's Logic and Existence," in Deleuze 2004: 15–18.

37. Hyppolite 1952: 187.

38. Vuillemin 1954: 306.

39. Vuillemin 1948: 309–15.

40. Because of the prominence of a specifically French Neokantian tradition (the Lachelier–Renouvier–Brunschvicg line), Hermann Cohen and the Marburg School had a negligible presence in French philosophy (except for Bréhier 1932: ch. 12). Ernst Cassirer was better known and had visited the Société française de philosophie.

41. Kant 1988 [1800]: 29.

42. Foucault, "Problèmes de l'anthropologie," course at the École normale supérieure in 1954–55, IMEC, Fonds Foucault, C.2.1/FCL 2. A03–08 (notes by Jacques Lagrange), 23–25.

43. Ibid., 35.

44. Ibid., 48–49.

45. *OT*, 341.

46. See Foucault's oft-quoted sentence: "Only those who cannot read will be surprised that I have learned such a thing more clearly from Cuvier, Bopp, and Ricardo than from Kant or Hegel" (*OT*, 307). In more public presentations he could articulate much the same argument in philosophical terms, but in *OT* he pursued the "death of the human" without centering on philosophy (except for its unappreciated herald, Nietzsche), and also with virtually no reference to contemporary philosophy.

47. Ibid., 348.

48. According to Didier Eribon, Foucault and Vuillemin became "close friends" during Foucault's years in Clermont-Ferrand; Vuillemin was instrumental in proposing and presenting Foucault's candidacy at the Collège de France. See Eribon 1991: 131, 217.

49. *OT*, 262.

50. Ibid., 342–43.

51. Ibid., 348.

52. Ibid., 342.

53. Ibid., 387.

54. Ibid., 379.

55. Ibid.

56. Ibid., 382.

57. Ibid.

58. Ibid., 340.

59. Ibid., 342.

60. Ibid., 322.

61. As Foucault responded to Hyppolite in a televised conversation led by Badiou and Dina Dreyfus: "but the anthropological too . . . is precisely a transcendental that would wish to be true as natural . . . which it cannot be!" (Hyppolite et al. 1965: 13–14).

62. Canguilhem 2005: 71–91. Foucault expanded on this issue in *The Archaeology of Knowledge* (1972), 55.

63. *OT*, 383.

64. Ibid., 385.

65. Ibid., 384.

66. Ibid., 385.

67. Ibid.

68. Ibid., 384.

69. Ibid., 386; emphasis added.

70. Habermas 1987: 248.

CHAPTER 19: CYBERNETIC COMPLEXITY

1. But see Stiegler 1998. Johnson 2015 covers a different strand of the French tradition in cybernetics from the one that is significant for my argument here.

2. On the notion of "history of life," see *OG*, 84, 131, 165, 166.

3. For a history of the rise and decline of a cybernetic imagination, see Dupuy 2000.

4. In addition to works cited elsewhere in the present chapter, see Couffignal 1952; Ducasse 1958; Moles 1962.

5. For accounts of the complex, messy development of the major concepts of information and communication, see Aspray 1985; Geoghegan 2008; Galison 1994.

6. Louis de Broglie, "Préface" in Broglie 1951. (Couffignal 1953 is another proceedings volume for a similar conference of the same period, held in January 1951 under the auspices of the Centre national de la recherche scientifique.)

7. See Geoghegan 2011: 96–126. On Lacan, see Johnston 2008: ch. 2; Liu 2010: 288–320.

8. Ruyer 1954: 5; 1962.

9. See Canguilhem's critique in "The Problem of Regulation in the Organism and in Society" (1955), in Canguilhem 2012. Canguilhem's opinion would change; see his "Le Concept et la vie" (1966) in Canguilhem 1983: 335–64, and his later works on regulation, including Canguilhem 1977.

10. Simondon's 1959 theses on individuation and technics were frequently phrased in cybernetic terminology. Simondon also introduced Wiener at the 1962 Royaumont conference; see Couffignal 1965.

11. Guillaumaud 1971.

12. Leroi-Gourhan 1943, 1945.

13. *MT* 435–38 and ch. 6; note Leroi-Gourhan's discussions of how technology affects the "inner environment" and hence evolutionary transformations.

14. Leroi-Gourhan 1962: 31–45.

15. Ibid., 39–41.

16. Ibid., 44.

17. Ibid., 43.

18. *GS*, 8.

19. Ibid., 10–11, 14. Leroi-Gourhan makes this point over and over in *GS*: the human is not linked to the monkey, which is no "staging post" in the evolution from fish to man (19; see also 116). The entire chapter 3, where Leroi-Gourhan establishes the criteria for the evolution of the genus *Homo*, emphatically states that the particular properties of humans "[bear] no relation to the monkey": members of the genus *Archanthropus* were "inheritors of a long human past" whose "humanness remains disconcerting," and who "are no longer seen as the half-monkeys we once believed them to have been."

20. It was especially the discovery of *Paranthropus boisei* in 1959 that, in Leroi-Gourhan's judgment, finally refuted the line of thought according to which all the species that seem less than human can be aligned on pathway from ape to fully human form—"a line of thought that had persisted without weakening" since the early nineteenth century (*GS*, 18).

21. *GS*, 106, repeated at 239; emphasis added. On the parallel "evolution" of language and technics, see ibid., 215.

22. Ibid., 113; see also the next quotation.

23. Ibid., 107.

24. Ibid., 115.

25. Ibid. This, he writes, already occurs with *Paranthropus boisei*.

26. "Their journey will be not so much a matter of biological development as of freeing themselves from the zoological context and organizing themselves in an entirely new way, with society gradually taking the place of the phyletic stream" (ibid., 116).

27. Ibid., 148; emphasis added.

28. Ibid., 114, and chs. 7–8.

29. Ibid., 225, 230.

30. Ibid., 230.

31. Ibid., 227.

32. Ibid., 231.

33. Ibid., 232.

34. Ibid., 237.

35. Ibid., 245.

36. Ibid., 184–85.

37. Ibid., 129–130.

38. Ibid., 5–6, 141–44.

39. See Johnson 2011.

40. *GS*, 139, 238, 247, 252–53, 349, 405–6.

41. With the exception of the highly political Lysenko affair, which galvanized biologists like Jacques Monod to strongly defend natural selection. On Lysenko, see Lecourt 1977.

42. On neurophysiology, see Fessard 1953 and 1970 (Alfred Fessard was chair of general neurophysiology at the Collège de France, 1949–71); Cahn 1962: 187–95.

43. For Jacob's contempt of Canguilhem's writing on genetics, see his 2004 interview in Jacob 2016.

44. Georges Canguilhem, "La nouvelle connaissance de la vie: Le Concept et la vie" (1965), in Canguilhem 1983: 360, also 359–61.

45. "Vivre et parler" 1968.

46. *LL*, 1–2.

47. "Any organized system can be analyzed in terms of two concepts: message and feedback regulation" (*LL*, 251–52). Jacob also cites Wiener in support of his claim (ibid.) that even "the organism can be understood as a message."

48. Ibid., 299, 300.

49. Ibid., 295.

50. Ibid., 300.

51. Ibid., 247.

52. Ibid., 276.

53. Ibid., 278.

54. Ibid., 286.

55. Ibid., 281–82.

56. *OG*, 11.

57. Ibid., 98. See also the remarkable opening of "The Exorbitant," where Derrida points to Rousseau's argument against mediation and then installs the "supplement" at the heart of his method: "The intermediary is the mid-point and the mediation, the middle term between total absence and the absolute plenitude of presence. It is clear that mediacy is the name of all that Rousseau wanted opinionatedly to efface . . . the supplement occupies the middle point between total absence and total presence" (ibid., 157; also 353 n. 31 and 338 n. 1).

58. Ibid., 65.

59. Ibid., 9; also 10, 84. Céline Lafontaine (2007: 37) records Derrida's affirmation about cybernetics without examining it. Johnson 1993: 6 finds no more than an allusive reference to cybernetics, but in a footnote he places Leroi-Gourhan front and center in Derrida's argument (*OG*, 216 n. 19). In more recent work, he returns in greater detail to the question.

60. *OG*, 9.

61. Ibid., 84.

62. Ibid., 10. See also Derrida's (1978: 102) reference to cybernetics in his critique of Levinas's views on originary speech.

63. Baring 2012: 291. It is worth emphasizing, with Baring, Derrida's double-edged effort to destabilize but reinscribe "the program" by means of an ingenious interpretation of "pro" and "gramme," namely by explaining the former as a combination of "pretension" and "retention" and the latter as a reference to "writing" (Greek *graphein*).

64. *OG*, 70.

65. Ibid., 4.

66. Ibid., 83.

67. Martin Heidegger, "The End of Philosophy and the Task of Thinking" (1966), in Heidegger 1977: 376–77, 391.

68. See a remarkable passage in *OG* (332 n. 35) on the constitution of linear writing and sonic inscription. The words "general phenomenon of manual regression . . . and of a new 'liberation'" there clearly allude to Leroi-Gourhan.

69. Ibid., 131.

70. "Leroi-Gourhan shows it well; to refuse the name of man and the ability to write beyond its own proper community, is one and the same gesture" (ibid., 83, 84). For the same reason, Derrida could probably also interpret Leroi-Gourhan's argument as reinforcing his own critique of Husserl by making the point that there is no community in which writing has not been inscribed already.

71. Ibid., 85. Leroi-Gourhan's approach (in which tools and language precede writing but are somehow analogous and proximate to it) supports a notion of *archē* writing by pointing out the ways in which linear or phonetic writing "took over" rather than appearing from nothing, as it were.

72. Ibid., 9.

73. Ibid., 85.

74. Ibid., "The End of the Book and the Beginning of Writing" (ch. 1) and "The Program" (a subchapter).

75. Ibid., 87.

76. Derrida, "Différance," in Derrida 1982: 19.

77. See the reference in Derrida 1987: 259; see also the discussion of the "biogenetic" in Johnson 1993: 165–66.

78. Derrida pursues the textual dimension more pointedly than Jacob. Jacob does point out that, "by analogy, this linear sequence [of the protein] is often compared to the arrangement of the letters of the alphabet in a text" (*LL*, 274) and that mutations can be understood by analogy with changes of letters in a text, but the text is not a major or self-sufficient component of his concept of language.

79. VM, 4: 1.

80. Ibid., 11.

81. Ibid., 5, quoted in Garrido 2012: 72.

82. VM, 4: 16.

83. Ibid., 12.

84. That is, the place of biology according to both Jacob and his contemporaries (ibid., 1).

85. Ibid., 9, 12. Francesco Vitale (2014) studies Derrida's treatment of cybernetic biology in the context of Hegel's reliance on botanical metaphors.

86. VM 4: 10–11.

87. The interpretation proposed above does not preclude a literalist reading of life along the lines proposed by Henry Staten and Martin Hägglund. It should nevertheless raise the question whether these authors' reliance on "Darwinism" gets anywhere close to the field Derrida aimed to cover. Hägglund (2011) in particular uses Daniel Dennett's Darwinism with little concern for Dennett's broader work, or Darwin's original texts.

CHAPTER 20: THE PRESENT TIME AND THE AGENT OF HISTORY
BEFORE AND AFTER MAY 1968

1. Deleuze, "How Do We Recognize Structuralism?" in Deleuze 2004: 170.

2. Cited in Wolin 2010: 264.

3. *PP*, 3: ch. 2.

4. See L-*S2*, 1 and 13 and the critique of the metaphor at 224; see also Lacan's repeated invocations of the theme at L-*E*, 401/335; 516/429; 796–97/674.

5. The claim to psychoanalytic radicalism was hardly isolated at the time; see Erich Fromm, "The Present Crisis in Psychoanalysis," in Simmel 1968: 241–42.

6. SPL, 283/235.

7. L-*E*, 859/730.

8. SPL, 292/242.

9. Lacan's metahistorical account in the second seminar contains references to Canguilhem, Koyré, and Husserl for the modern sciences and to Heidegger for the history of ontology. He posited there that a version of the self, not articulated in terms of "the individual," could be dated to Plato (L-*S2*, session 1). After Galileo and Descartes, the scientist-subject has postulated her own transparency, as well as that of the objects before her, as premises for a knowledge of the world that would be certain, pure, and exact. Scientificity was equated with knowledge determined over determinable things—the kind of knowledge that discarded everything beyond its limits. Science created a hierarchy that prioritized the natural sciences and turned the human sciences into sciences of human application of knowledge.

10. Lacan 1997: 8–11.

11. *OT*, 385.

12. *OG*, 4.

13. Ibid.

14. Ibid., 4–5.

15. See also Zakariya 2017.

16. House and MacMaster 2006.

17. Sartre, "Preface" in Fanon 2004: lxii.

18. Rancière 1998: 28; emphasis added.

19. Bourg 2007, 2011; Wolin 2010; Robcis 2012, 51–69; Christofferson 2004; Montag 2013.

20. See thesis 4 of an unsigned article "Résolution politique de la Ire session du Ier Congrès de l'UJC (ml)" in *Les Cahiers marxistes-léninistes* 15 (1967).

21. Robcis 2012: 63.

22. Althusser 1966: 8, cited in Robcis 2012: 61.

23. ISA, 137.

24. Ibid., 144.

25. Ibid.

26. Ibid., 175.

27. Ibid., 133; also 145.

28. Ibid., 165.

29. Ibid., 176.

30. Debord 1967 [1994], §§4, 1.

31. The spectacle was absent from Debord's writings between *Potlatch* and the last issues of the journal *L'Internationale situationniste*. Of Debord's nine signed articles in the latter, only one centered on the "spectacular character of modern industrial society," and that one was the opening of his 1967 book *La société du spectacle* (*The Society of the Spectacle*); see *L'Internationale situationniste* (1958–69) 11: 43–48.

32. Debord 1967 [1994], §§1–8, 60, 72, and esp. 18. See also Clark 1999: ix.

33. Clark links Debord to Rousseau (ibid., viii).

34. Debord 1967 [1994], §221.

35. See, e.g., Clastres 1987 [1974]: 204; on private property, ibid., 212.

36. Ibid., 203.

37. Dosse 1997, 1: 161–62.

38. *SAS*, 200.

39. Ibid., 60.

40. Ibid., 212.

41. Sahlins 1972, discussed in Clastres 1994: 105–18; also *SAS*, 196.

42. *SAS*, 198.

43. Ibid., 200, 198.

44. Ibid., 124–25.

45. Ibid., 207, 209–12.

46. Quoted in Moyn 2004: 72.

47. Ibid., 65; on Rousseau, ibid., 73–74. This would be Miguel Abensour's takeaway from Clastres, to whom he devoted several publications; Clifford Geertz, "Deep Hanging Out," in Geertz 2001: 117.

48. *DP* 293–308.

49. Foucault 2008: 77.

50. Ibid., 216.

51. Ibid., 200, 202.

52. Ibid., 201.

53. Ibid., 317 n. 4.

54. Ibid., 206.

55. Ibid., 217; J-*DE*, 411. On Foucault and Debord more broadly, see J-*DE*, ch. 7, and Geroulanos 2006.

56. E.g., *DP* 213. My thanks to Luca Provenzano for discussing his as yet unpublished work on "state apparatuses" in Foucault and Althusser with me.

57. Foucault, "The Eye of Power,'" in Foucault 1981: 152; translation modified.

58. See also the 40-page analysis of philosophies of the contemporary state in Châtelet and Pisier-Kouchner 1981.

CHAPTER 21: THE MYTH OF THE SELF-TRANSPARENCY OF SOCIETY

1. Habermas 1991 [1961]: 203, 144, 188–89.

2. Habermas 1985: 92 and passim. See also his discussion of "obscure expressions" (ibid., 54–55) and Habermas 1987: 263.

3. Rawls 2005 [1993]: 66–69; Rawls 1999 [1971]: 15, 49, 115, 153, and (on Kant) 115 n. 8.

4. Lefort and his group have been the subject of extensive research in recent years. See Moyn 2012a: 37–50 and Breckman 2013: chs. 3–4. Charles Taylor, "Hegel's Philosophy of Mind," (1983) in *Philosophical Papers*, vol.1 *Human Agency and Language* (Cambridge: Cambridge University Press, 1985), 85–88, quotation on 86.

5. Rosanvallon, "Marx and Civil Society" [1978–79], in Rosanvallon 2006: 186.

6. Lefort 1978: xii. On Lefort and Lacan, see Breckman 2013: 152–58.

7. Lefort 1966: 767 (reprinted in Lefort 1979 [1971]: 345).

8. Similarly, transparency was at best marginal, if not untheorized, in Lefort's book on Machiavelli (1972), which discusses symbolic division.

9. See Abensour 2011: 104.

10. Textures, 1972, 2/3: 4.

11. *PFM*, 207 ("Outline of the Genesis of Ideology in Modern Societies" [1974]).

12. Ibid., 222.

13. Ibid., 216.

14. See the highly similar view of the mass party in Châtelet and Pisier-Kouchner 1981: 243.

15. Lefort 1976: 114.

16. Ibid., 174; see also an interview in *L'Anti-mythes* 14 (April 19, 1975), reprinted in Lefort 2007 [1975]: 235.

17. Lefort 1976: 174–75.

18. "Social relations, woven as they are into production, can become transparent to its agents" (ibid., 185; see also 189–90).

19. *PFM*, 270 ("Politics and Human Rights" [1980]).

20. Ibid., 160 ("Marx: From One Vision of History to Another" [1978]).

21. Lefort, "Rereading the Communist Manifesto," in Lefort 1989: 150.

22. Lefort 1979: 10–11, quoted in Abensour 2011: 104.

23. *PFM*, 297–98; also 305 ("The Image of the Body and Totalitarianism" [1979]). Cf. a similar passage in Lefort 1989: 13–14 ("The Question of Democracy" [1983]).

24. But see Nancy and Lacoue-Labarthe 1983.

25. In "The Logic of Totalitarianism," e.g., Lefort emphasized that the representation of society's transparency to itself "emerges from the depths of modern democracy, but more remarkable is its transformation in the context of totalitarianism" (*PFM*, 288; see also "The Image of the Body and Totalitarianism," ibid., 305)

26. Abensour 1968, 1966; Castoriadis 1992; RTS; Baczko 1989.

27. RTS, 24; see also ibid., 11.

28. Ibid., 31.

29. Ibid.

30. Ibid., 39; 40.

31. Ibid., 15.

32. Baczko 1974 [1964]. From p. 1 on, Baczko cites Starobinski's work repeatedly and approvingly, as that most relevant to his own study (see ibid., 50 n. 3).

33. Baczko 1989: x.

34. Ibid., 147, 118.

35. Moyn 2008.

36. *IFR*, 19.

37. Ibid., 16. Lefort would adopt this contrast of Michelet to Tocqueville almost verbatim: see "Interpreting Revolution within the French Revolution" [1980], in Lefort 1989: 96. He was more careful about Tocqueville's account of the history of America, "transparent" to Tocqueville insofar as, for him, "the birth of the nation is visible" ("From Equality to Freedom," in Lefort 1989: 184). Lefort's argument that the instituting and instituted moments of political action need to be kept separate, as do history and institution, revolve around this problematic reduction.

38. *IFR*, 74; translation amended.

39. Ibid., 60 and 50; translation substantially modified.

40. Ibid., 27, 74, etc.

41. Lefort 1989: 99 ("Interpreting Revolution within the French Revolution" [1980]).

42. Gauchet and Swain 1999; see also Pierre Rosanvallon's disregard for Foucault in Rosanvallon 1993. Despite Furet's and Gauchet's (1980) hostility to Derrida

(Gauchet, cited in Peeters 2013: 314), the case seems rather more complicated, not least because Lefort contributed to efforts by Derrida's students Jean-Luc Nancy and Philippe Lacoue-Labarthe to rethink the political in the early 1980s. He also offered a chapter in a multicontributor volume edited by these two (Nancy and Lacoue-Labarthe 1983).

43. *PFM*, 288–89 ("The Logic of Totalitarianism" [1980]).

44. On Gauchet's relationship to Lefort (and Richir) and his role in *Textures* and *Libre*, see Lefort and Gauchet 1971; also Moyn 2012b, and Dosse 1999: 55–57.

45. For Lefort's critique of Castoriadis, see Lefort 2007 [1975]: 245; Châtelet and Pisier-Kouchner (1981: 631) formulate a similar suspicion. On Lefort and Castoriadis, see Breckman 2013: chs. 3–4.

46. Habermas 1987: 318.

47. Rosanvallon 1979: 1.

48. Abensour 2011: 19, 62.

49. Rosanvallon 1999.

50. Rosanvallon 2000: 33–34.

51. Lévy 1979: 144–45.

52. Fabius 1990: 183.

CHAPTER 22: *NINETEEN EIGHTY-FOUR*

1. Lefort 2000: 13.

2. Lyotard 1985: 433–43.

3. Lyotard 1985: 441.

4. Schneider 2013: 12.

5. Ellul 1954. See also Cornelius Castoriadis, "Dead End" [1987], in Castoriadis 1991: 270–71.

6. Lefort 1966: 761.

7. Lemoine 1974 (signing as Jean-Philippe Faivret).

8. Habermas 1978.

9. Habermas 1987.

10. Ricœur 2004: 244; see also Ricœur's critique of Tzvetan Todorov in Ricœur 2003: 171, 268.

11. Ricœur 2004: 314, 287. See also Ricœur's discussion of Gerard Genette in Ricœur 2003: 165, 406 n. 11.

12. David Linge, "Editor's Introduction," in Gadamer 1976: xxvi.

13. Ricœur, 1986: 120–21.

14. Dosse 1999: 13.

15. Foucault 1978, 1: 86; emphasis added.

16. Péan 1985.

17. Bourg 2007: 343.

18. See the rhetoric of the Barre years in Wubbels 1979: 23–27.

19. Nivat 1983: 63.

20. Rocard 1986: 152, 168. For Rocard's influence on the Left, see Chabal, 2015: 240.

21. Rocard 1987: 154–55, 247.

22. Lasserre, Lenoir, and Stirn 1987; Rangeon 1988.

23. Servan-Schreiber 1990: s.v. "Transparence"; Baudrillard 1985; and 1990: 56, 75; Le Goff 1993. On Le Goff's politics, see Bourg 2007: 34–35.

24. Conseil de l'Europe 1988: 88, etc.

25. Lyotard 1993b, 139.

26. Ligue des droits de l'homme 1990.

27. Lyotard 2011: 82.

28. Ibid., 101, 112, 169, 172. See also J-*DE*, 564. Jay's concluding passages on Lyotard and opacity (ibid., 582–86) are uncharacteristically unfair.

29. *OG*, 158.

30. Lyotard 1993a; on philosophies of desire, see Bourg 2007: chs. 8–14.

31. Scott 2007: chs. 3–4. Robcis 2013: ch. 6 and epilogue, passim.

32. Lyotard 1985: 441 (quoted on p. 00 in this chapter).

33. Lyotard 1978, 4–9.

34. Lyotard 1985: 441 (quoted on p. 00 in this chapter).

35. Lyotard, 1984: 6.

36. Ibid., 5–6.

37. Lyotard 1992: 24–25; also Lyotard 1984: 81–82.

Bibliography

ARCHIVES AND ARCHIVAL MATERIALS

Archives nationales de France
    Series: F/7, F/17, F/23, F/44
Bibliothèque nationale de France, Département des manuscrits occidentaux
    Fonds Georges Bataille
    Fonds Alexandre Kojève
    Fonds Claude Lévi-Strauss
    Fonds Paul Valéry
    Fonds Jean Rouch
    Fonds Maurice Merleau-Ponty
Bibliothèque Éric-de-Dampière, Université de Nanterre
    Fonds Marcel Griaule
Collège de France
    Fonds Marcel Mauss
École normale supérieure, Centre d'Archives en Philosophie, Histoire et Édition
    des Sciences, Archives de Georges Canguilhem
    Fonds François Jacob
Institut Mémoires de l'Édition contemporaine (IMEC)
    Fonds Michel Foucault
    Fonds Jean Wahl
Laboratoire de l'anthropologie sociale, Collège de France
    Fonds Michel Leiris (LAS.FML)
    Fonds Alfred Métraux (LAS.FAM)
London School of Economics Special Collections
    Bronislaw Malinowski Archive
Muséum national d'histoire naturelle
    Papiers Marcel Mauss, 2 AP4 2B 2b R

JOURNALS

Les Allobroges, 1948
Arguments, 1956–62
L'Aurore, 1944, 1946–48
Aux Écoutes, 1947
Bulletin de la Société française de Philosophie, 1920–69
Cahiers de la nouvelle époque, 1945
Les Cahiers marxistes-léninistes, 1964–67
Combat, 1947–49
Critique, 1946–68.
Davoser Revue: Zeitschrift für Literatur, Wissenschaft, Kunst und Sport, 1928
Dieu Vivant, 1945
L'Époque, 1945, 1947–48
France-Dimanche, 1947
France-Soir, 1945
L'Humanité, 1948
L'Internationale situationniste, 1958–69
Le Libertaire, 1946
Littéraire, 1947
Minotaure 2, 1933
Paroles, 1947
Le Pays, 1945
Police de France, 1954
Résistance, 1945
Le Réveil, 1948
Socialisme ou barbarie, 1949–65
Les Temps modernes, 1945–53
Textures, 1971–72
La Voix policière, 1945–46

FILMS

L'Armée des ombres (*Army of Shadows)* (dir. Jean-Pierre Melville, 1969)
Le Chagrin et la pitié (*The Sorrow and the Pity)* (dir. Marcel Ophuls, 1969)
Rififi (dir. Jules Dassin, 1955)
Sous les masques noirs (dir. Marcel Griaule, 1939), in *Jean Rouch: Une Aventure af-
    ricaine* (DVD, Éditions Montparnasse, 2010)
Tirez sur le pianiste (*Shoot the Piano Player)* (dir. François Truffaut, 1960)
Les Yeux sans visage (*Eyes without a Face)* (dir. Georges Franju, 1960)

PUBLISHED PRIMARY AND SECONDARY LITERATURE

Abensour, Miguel. 1966. "La Philosophie politique de Saint-Just." *Annales historiques de la Révolution française* 38 (183): 1–32.

———. 1968. "La Théorie des institutions et les relations du législateur et du peuple selon Saint-Just," In *Actes du Colloque Saint-Just, 25 juin 1967*, 239–90. Paris: Société des études robespierristes.

———. 2011 [1997]. *Democracy against the State: Marx and the Machiavellian Moment.* Translated by Max Blechman and Martin Breaugh. Malden, MA: Polity Press.

Affron, Mirella Jona. 1998. "Bresson and Pascal, Rhetorical Affinities." In James Quandt, ed., *Robert Bresson*, 165–98. Toronto: Cinematheque Ontario.

Allendy, René. 1934. *Essai sur la guérison.* Paris: Denoël & Steele.

Alloa, Emmanuel. 2008. "Architectures de la transparence." *Appareil* 1. https://appareil.revues.org/138 (accessed August 4, 2016).

———. 2011. *Das durchscheinende Bild: Konturen einer medialen Phänomenologie.* Zurich: Diaphanes.

Alquié, Ferdinand. 1950. *La Découverte métaphysique de l'homme chez Descartes.* Paris: Presses universitaires de France.

Althusser, Louis. 1966. "Sur la révolution culturelle." In *La grande révolution culturelle prolétarienne*, special issue of *Cahiers marxistes-léninistes* 14: 5–16.

———. 1971a. "Ideology and Ideological State Apparatuses" [= ISA]. In Althusser, 1971b, 127–86.

———. 1971b. *Lenin and Philosophy and Other Essays.* New York: Monthly Review Press.

———. 1990 [1965]. *For Marx.* London: Verso.

Althusser, Louis, and Étienne Balibar. 2009 [1968]. *Reading Capital.* London: Verso.

Anderson, Benedict. 1983. *Imagined Communities.* London: Verso.

Aristotle. 1993a. *De anima.* Translated by David Hamlyn. Oxford: Oxford University Press.

———. 1993b. *Politics.* Translated by David Hamlyn. Oxford: Oxford University Press.

Armel, Aliette. 1997. *Michel Leiris.* Paris: Fayard.

Ash, Mitchell G. 1980. "Wilhelm Wundt and Oswald Külpe on the Institutional Status of Psychology." In Wolfgang G. Bringmann and Ryan D. Tweney, eds., *Wundt Studies: A Centennial Collection*, 396–421. Toronto: C. J. Hogrefe.

Aspray, William. 1985. "The Scientific Conceptualization of Information." *Annals of the History of Computing* 7 (2): 117–40.

Aucouturier, Michel. 1998. *Le Réalisme socialiste.* Paris: Presses universitaires de France.

Augustine, Saint. 1992. *Confessions.* Oxford: Oxford University Press.

Aumont, Jacques. 1992. *Du visage au cinéma*. Paris: Étoile.

Axelos, Kostas. 1969. *Arguments d'une recherche*. Paris: Minuit.

———. 1976. *Alienation, Praxis, and Technē in the Thought of Karl Marx*. Austin: University of Texas Press.

Bachelard, Gaston. 1949 [1938]. *La Psychanalyse du feu*. Paris: Gallimard.

———. 1957. "Préface." In Roland Kuhn, *Phénoménologie du masque à travers le test de Rorschach*, 7–14. Bruges: Desclée de Brouwer.

———. 2002 [1938]. *The Formation of the Scientific Mind: A Contribution to a Psychoanalysis of Objective Knowledge*. Manchester, England: Clinamen Press.

Baczko, Bronisław. 1974 [1964]. *Rousseau: Solitude et communauté*. Translated from the Polish by Claire Brendhel-Lamhout. Paris: Mouton.

———. 1989 [1979]. *Utopian Lights: The Evolution of the Idea of Social Progress*. New York: Paragon House.

———. 1994 [1989]. *Ending the Terror: The French Revolution after Robespierre*. Translated by Michel Petheram. Cambridge: Cambridge University Press.

Badiou, Alain. 2002. *Ethics*. London: Verso.

———. 2006. *Being and Event*. London: Continuum.

Balibar, Etienne. 2012. "Postscript." In Graham Hammill and Julia Reinhard Lupton, eds., *Political Theology and Early Modernity*, 299–306. Chicago: University of Chicago Press.

Balla, Giacomo, and Fortunato Depero. 2009. "Futurist Reconstruction of the Universe." In Lawrence Rainey, Christine Poggi, and Laura Wittman, eds., *Futurism*, 209–11. New Haven, CT: Yale University Press. Originally published as *Ricostruzione futurista dell'universo* (Milan: Direzione del Movimento Futurista, 1915).

Baltrušaitis, Jurgis. 1984 [1969]. *Anamorphoses ou "Thaumaturgus opticus."* Paris: Flammarion. Updated English translation as *Anamorphic Art* (New York: Harry N. Abrams, 1977).

Baring, Edward. 2010. "Liberalism and the Algerian War." *Critical Inquiry* 36 (2): 239–61.

———. 2012. *The Young Derrida and French Philosophy*. Cambridge: Cambridge University Press.

Barnstone, Deborah. 2005. *The Transparent State: Architecture and Politics in Postwar Germany*. London: Routledge.

Barthes, Roland. 1972. *Mythologies*. London: Paladin.

Baruch, Marc-Olivier. 1997. *Servir l'État français*. Paris: Fayard.

Bataille, Georges. 1973. *Œuvres complètes*. Vol. 5: *La Somme athéologique*, 1, *L'Expérience intérieure; Méthode de méditation; Post-scriptum 1953; Le Coupable; L'Alleluiah*. Paris: Gallimard.

————. 1985. *Visions of Excess: Selected Writings, 1927–1934*. Minneapolis: University of Minnesota Press.

————. 1986 [1957]. *Erotism: Death and Sensuality*. San Francisco: City Lights. Originally published as *L'Erotisme*.

————. 1988a [1944]. *Guilty*. Venice, CA: Lapis Press. Original title: *Le Coupable*.

————. 1988b [1943]. *Inner Experience*. Albany: State University of New York Press. Originally published as *L'Expérience intérieure*.

————. 1991 [1965]. *Trial of Gilles de Rais*. Los Angeles: Amok. Original title: *Le Procès de Gilles de Rais*.

————. 1993 [1949]. *The Accursed Share*. Vols. 2 and 3. New York: Zone Books. Originally published as *La Part maudite*.

————. 1997. "The Psychological Structure of Fascism." In *The Bataille Reader*, ed. Fred Botting and Scott Wilson, 122–46. Oxford: Blackwell.

————. 2009. *The Cradle of Humanity: Prehistoric Art and Culture*. Edited by Stuart Kendall. New York: Zone Books.

Baudrillard, Jean. 1985. *La Gauche divine*. Paris: Grasset.

————. 1990. *La Transparence du mal*. Paris: Galilée.

Baugh, Bruce. 2001. *French Hegel*. New York: Routledge.

Bayer, Raymond, ed. 1937. *Travaux du 9ème congrès international de philosophie (Congrès Descartes)*. 2 vols. Paris: Hermann.

Bazin, André. 1958–62. *Qu'est-ce que le cinéma?* 4 vols. Paris: Cerf.

————. 1971. *What Is Cinema?* Berkeley: University of California Press. Partial translation of Bazin 1958–62.

Beaufret, Jean. 1947. "Martin Heidegger et le problème de la vérité." *Fontaine* 62–63: 758–85.

Beauvoir, Simone de. 1949. "Les Structures élémentaires de la parenté par Claude Lévi-Strauss." *Les Temps modernes* 5: 943–49.

————. 1976 [1947]. *The Ethics of Ambiguity*. New York: Citadel Press.

————. 1999 [1954]. *The Mandarins*. London: Norton.

————. 2006 [1943]. *She Came to Stay*. London: Harper Perennial.

Behrent, Michael C. 2013. "Foucault and Technology." *History and Technology* 29 (1): 54–104.

Bell, David A. 2003. *The Cult of the Nation in France*. Cambridge, MA: Harvard University Press.

Ben-Ghiat, Ruth. 2001. *Fascist Modernities: Italy, 1922–1945*. Berkeley: University of California Press.

Benedict, Ruth. 1941. "Race Problems in America." *Annals of the American Academy of Political and Social Science* 216: 73–78.

————. 1942. "Nature Builds No Barriers." *Asia*, 42: 697–99.

————. 1983 [1940]. *Race and Racism*. London: Routledge & Kegan Paul.

Benjamin, Walter. 2005. *Collected Works*. Vol. 2. Edited by Michael W. Jennings. Cambridge, MA: Harvard University Press.

Bennett, Jane. 2010. *Vibrant Matter*. Durham, NC: Duke University Press.

Bentham, Jeremy. 1834. *Deontology, or the Science of Morality*. Vol. 1. Edited by John Bowring. London: Longman.

Benveniste, Émile. 1966. *Problèmes de linguistique générale*. Paris: Gallimard.

Bergeron, Louis. 1981. *France under Napoleon*. Princeton, NJ: Princeton University Press.

Berlière, Jean-Marc. 2001. *Les Policiers français sous l'Occupation*. Paris: Perrin.

Bernot, Lucien, ed. 1988. *André Leroi-Gourhan ou les voies de l'homme*. Paris: Albin Michel.

Bertholet, Denis. 2003. *Claude Lévi-Strauss*. Paris: Plon.

Bianco, Giuseppe. 2009. "La Réaction au bergsonisme." PhD diss., Université de Lille-III.

———. 2012. "Deleuze before Deleuze: Humanism and Anti-Humanism." MS.

———, ed. 2013. *Jean Hyppolite*. Paris: Presses universitaires de France/Ulm.

———. 2015. *Après Bergson*. Paris: Presses universitaires de France.

Bianco, Giuseppe, and Tzuchien Tho, eds. 2013. *Badiou and the Philosophers*. London: Bloomsbury.

Blanchot, Maurice. 1995. *The Work of Fire*. Stanford, CA: Stanford University Press.

———. 1996. *The Most High*. Translated and with an introduction by Allan Stoekl. Lincoln: University of Nebraska Press. Originally published as *Le Très-Haut* (Paris: Gallimard, 1948).

Blümlinger, Christa, and Karl Sierek, eds. 2002. *Das Gesicht im Zeitalter des bewegten Bildes*. Vienna: Sonderzahl.

Blumenberg, Hans. 1987. "An Anthropological Approach to the Contemporary Significance of Rhetoric." In Kenneth Baynes, James Bohman, and Thomas McCarthy, eds., *After Philosophy*, 429–48. Cambridge, MA: MIT Press.

———. 2010. *Paradigms for a Metaphorology*. Ithaca, NY: Cornell University Press.

Boccioni, Umberto. 2009. "Futurist Sculpture." In Lawrence Rainey, Christine Poggi, and Laura Wittman, eds., *Futurism*, 113–19. New Haven, CT: Yale University Press.

Bocquet-Appel, Jean-Pierre. 1989. "L'Anthropologie physique en France et ses origines institutionnelles." *Gradhiva: Revue d'anthropologie et d'histoire des arts* 6: 25–26.

Bommart, Jean. 1951. *Monsieur Scrupule, gangster*. Paris: Horay.

Bouglé, Célestin. 1926. *The Evolution of Values*. New York: Henry Holt.

Bouglé, Célestin, and P. Gastinel, eds. 1920. *Qu'est-ce que l'esprit français?* Paris: Garnier Frères.

Boulez, Pierre. 1984. "On New Music." *New York Review of Books*, June 28.

Bourg, Julian. 2007. *From Revolution to Ethics*. Toronto: McGill-Queen's University Press.

Bourg, Julian. 2011. "The Moral History of 1968." In Julian Jackson, ed., *May 68*, 17–33. London: Palgrave.

Boutroux, Émile. 1897. *Études d'histoire de la philosophie*. Paris: Félix Alcan.

———. 1927. *Des vérités éternelles chez Descartes*. Paris: Félix Alcan.

Brattain, Michelle. 2007. "Race, Racism, and Antiracism." *American Historical Review* 112 (5): 1386–413.

Braunstein, Jean-François, ed. 2007a. *Canguilhem*. Paris: Presses universitaires de France.

———. 2007b. "Psychologie et milieu." In Braunstein, ed., *Canguilhem*, 63–89. Paris: Presses universitaires de France.

———. 2008. "Deux philosophies de la médecine: Canguihem et Fleck." In Anne Fagot-Largeault and Claude Debru, eds., *Philosophie et medicine*, 63–80. Paris: Vrin.

Breckman, Warren. 2013. *Adventures of the Symbolic: Post-Marxism and Radical Democracy*. New York: Columbia University Press.

Bréhier, Émile. 1932. *Histoire de la philosophie*. Vol. 4. Paris: Alcan.

Broglie, Louis de. 1929. "Déterminisme et causalité dans la physique contemporaine." *Bulletin de la Société française de philosophie* 29 (4): 372–419.

———, ed. 1951. *La Cybernétique, theorie du signal et de l'information*. Paris: Éditions de la Revue d'optique théorique et instrumentale.

Bruns, Gerald L. 1997. *Maurice Blanchot*. Baltimore: Johns Hopkins University Press.

Brunschvicg, Léon. 1921. "L'Intelligence est-elle capable de comprendre?" *Bulletin de la Société française de Philosophie* 21 (3–4): 35–67.

———. 1950. *Héritage de mots, heritage d'idées*. Paris: Presses universitaires de France.

———. 1953. *Le Progrès de la conscience dans la philosophie occidentale* [= *PC*]. 2 vols. Paris: Presses universitaires de France.

Buraud, Georges. 1948. *Les Masques*. Paris: Seuil.

Burleigh, Michael, and Wolfgang Wippermann. 1993. *The Racial State: Germany, 1933–1945*. Cambridge: Cambridge University Press.

Butler, Judith. 1987. *Subjects of Desire*. New York: Columbia University Press.

———. 2005. *Giving an Account of Oneself*. New York: Fordham University Press.

———. 2006. "Merleau-Ponty and the Touch of Malebranche." In Taylor Carman and Mark B. N. Hansen, eds., *Cambridge Companion to Merleau-Ponty*, 181–205. Cambridge: Cambridge University Press.

Cahn, Théophile. 1962. "Modèles électroniques et fonctionnement de l'organisme." *Revue philosophique* 152: 187–95.

Caillois, Roger. 1954. "Illusions à rebours." *Nouvelle Nouvelle Revue française* 24 (December): 1010–24.

———. 1955. "Illusions à rebours (fin)." *Nouvelle Nouvelle Revue française* 25 (January): 58–70.

———. 1964. *The Mask of Medusa.* New York: C. N. Potter. Originally published as *Méduse et Cie* (Paris: Gallimard, 1960).

Camus, Albert. 1948. *The Plague.* New York: Modern Library.

Canales, Jimena. 2015. *The Physicist and the Philosopher.* Princeton, NJ: Princeton University Press.

Canguilhem, Georges. 1930. "De l'introspection." *Libres propos*, November, 522–23.

———. 1943a. "Commentaire au troisième chapitre de *l'Evolution créatrice.*" *Bulletin de la Faculté de Lettres de Strasbourg* 7: 126–43; 8: 199–216.

———. 1943b. *Essai sur quelques problèmes concernant le normal et le pathologique.* Clermont-Ferrand: La Montagne.

———. 1960. "L'Œuvre scientifique de Descartes et la science du 17e siècle, 1959–1960." Unpublished lecture series. CAPHÉS, GC.13.5.1, 92.

———. 1963. "The Role of Analogies and Models in Biological Discovery." In A. C. Crombie, ed., *Scientific Change*, 507–21. London: Heinemann.

———. 1964–65. "Philosophie et science." Interview with Alain Badiou. *Revue de l'enseignement supérieur* 15 (2): 10–17.

———. 1968. *Le Normal et le pathologique.* 2d ed. of Canguilhem 1943b. Paris: Vrin.

———. 1977. "La Formation du concept biologique de régulation." In André Lichnerowitz, François Perroux, and Gilbert Gadoffre, eds., *L'Idée de régulation dans les sciences*, 25–39. Paris: Maloine.

———. 1983. *Études d'histoire et de philosophie des sciences.* Paris: Vrin.

———. 1987. "La Décadence de l'idée de progrès." *Revue de métaphysique et de morale* 92 (4): 437–54.

———. 1991 [1943b, 1968]. *The Normal and the Pathological* [= *NP*]. New York: Zone Books.

———. 2004. *Vie et mort de Jean Cavaillès.* Paris: Allia.

———. 2005. "The Death of Man, or Exhaustion of the Cogito?" In Gary Gutting, ed., *The Cambridge Companion to Foucault*, 71–91. Cambridge: Cambridge University Press.

———. 2008a. "The Brain and Thought." *Radical Philosophy* 148 (7): 7–18.

———. 2008b. *Knowledge of Life* [= *KL*]. Translated by Stefanos Geroulanos and Daniela Ginsburg. New York: Fordham University Press.

———. 2011. *Œuvres complètes.* Vol. 1. Paris: Vrin.

————. 2012. *Writings on Medicine*. New York: Fordham University Press.

Canguilhem, Georges, and Camille Planet. 1939. *Traité de logique et de morale*. Marseille: F. Robert et fils.

Card, Claudia, ed. 2003. *The Cambridge Companion to Simone de Beauvoir*. Cambridge: Cambridge University Press.

Cassin, Barbara, ed. 2014 [2004]. *Dictionary of Untranslatables: A Philosophical Lexicon* [*Vocabulaire européen des philosophies: Dictionnaire des intraduisibles*]. Edited by Emily Apter, Jacques Lezra, and Michael Wood. Princeton, NJ: Princeton University Press.

Castoriadis, Cornelius. 1988. *Political and Social Writings*, vol. 1: *1946–1955*. Minneapolis: University of Minnesota Press.

————. 1991. *Politics, Philosophy, Autonomy*. Oxford: Oxford University Press.

————. 1992. *Political and Social Writings*, vol. 3: *Recommencing the Revolution: From Socialism to the Autonomous Society, 1961–1979*. Minneapolis: University of Minnesota Press.

Cavaillès, Jean. 1976 [1947]. *Sur la logique et la théorie de la science*. Paris: Presses universitaires de France.

Centre national de formation et d'études de la protection judiciaire de la jeunesse. 1963a. *500 jeunes délinquants: Résultats d'une pré-enquête sur les facteurs de la délinquance juvénile entreprise par l'équipe des chercheurs de Vaucresson*. Vaucresson: Centre de formation et de recherche de l'éducation surveillée.

————. 1963b. *La délinquance des jeunes en groupe: Contribution à l'étude de la société adolescente*. Vaucresson: Cujas.

Certeau, Michel de. 1986. *Heterologies*. Minneapolis: University of Minnesota Press.

Césaire, Aimé. 2001. *Discourse on Colonialism*. New York: Monthly Review Press. Originally published as *Discours sur le colonialisme* (Paris: Réclame, 1950).

Chabal, Émile. 2015. *A Divided Republic: Nation, State and Citizenship in Contemporary France*. Cambridge: Cambridge University Press.

Chambost, Léon. 1950. "Réflexions sur l'orientation médicale de l'hygiène scolaire et universitaire." *Archives de médecine sociale* 6 (5): 156–67.

Chapman, Herrick. 2008. "Shopkeepers and the State." In Sylvie Guillaume and Michel Lescure, eds., *Les PME dans les sociétés contemporaines, de 1880 à nos jours*, 277–88. Brussels: Lang.

Châtelet, François, and Évelyne Pisier-Kouchner. 1981. *Les Conceptions politiques du XXe siècle*. Paris: Presses universitaires de France.

Chimisso, Cristina. 2008. *Writing the History of the Mind, 1900 to the 1960s*. Aldershot, England: Ashgate.

Chombart de Lauwe, Marie-José. 1959. *Psychopathologie sociale de l'enfant inadapté*. Paris: Centre national de la recherche scientifique.

Christie, D. A., and E. M. Tansey. 1998. "Making the Human Body Transparent: The Impact of Nuclear Magnetic Resonance and Magnetic Resonance Imaging." In E. M. Tansey, D. A. Christie, and L. A. Reynolds, eds., *Wellcome Witnesses to Twentieth Century Medicine*, 2: 1–72. London: Wellcome Trust.

Christofferson, Michael Scott. 2004. *French Intellectuals against the Left*. New York: Berghahn Books.

Clark, T. J. 1999. Foreword to Anselm Jappe, *Guy Debord*. Berkeley: University of California Press.

Clark-Taoua, Phyllis. 2002. "In Search of New Skin: Michel Leiris's *L'Afrique fantôme*." *Cahiers d'études africaines* 167: 479–98.

Clastres, Pierre. 1987 [1974]. *Society against the State: Essays in Political Anthropology* [= *SAS*]. New York: Zone Books. Originally published as *La Société contre l'État: Recherches d'anthropologie politique* (Paris: Minuit).

———. 1994. *Archeology of Violence*. New York: Semiotext(e).

Clifford, James. 1988. *The Predicament of Culture: Twentieth-century Ethnography, Literature, and Art*. Cambridge, MA: Harvard University Press.

Cohen, Françoise, ed. 1995. *La Transparence dans l'art du XXe siècle*. Le Havre: Musée des Beaux-Arts.

Cohn, Dorrit. 1978. *Transparent Minds: Narrative Modes for Presenting Consciousness in Fiction*. Princeton, NJ: Princeton University Press.

Colangelo, Carmelo. 2004. *Jean Starobinski*. Genève: Éditions Zoé.

Colloque philosophique de Royaumont. 1957. *Descartes: Cahiers du Royaumont*. Paris: Minuit.

Conklin, Alice. 2007. "L'Ethnologie militante de l'entre-deux guerres." In Tzvetan Todorov, *Le Siècle de Germaine Tillion*. Paris: Seuil.

Conseil de l'Europe. 1988. *Secret et transparence: L'Individu, l'entreprise et l'administration: Actes du dix-septième Colloque de droit européen*. Strasbourg: Conseil de l'Europe.

Constant, Benjamin. 1992 [1815]. *De l'esprit de conquête et de l'usurpation dans leurs rapports avec la civilisation européenne*. Paris: Imprimérie nationale éditions.

Couffignal, Louis. 1952. *Machines à penser*. Paris: Minuit.

———, ed. 1953. *Les Machines à calculer et la pensée humaine*. Paris: Éditions du Centre national de la recherche scientifique.

———, ed. 1965. *Le Concept de l'information dans la science contemporaine*. Paris: Gauthier-Villars.

Culler, Jonathan, and Kevin Lamb, eds. 2003. *Just Being Difficult? Academic Writing in the Public Arena*. Stanford, CA: Stanford University Press.

Cupers, Kenny. 2014. *The Social Project*. Minneapolis: University of Minnesota Press.

Darnton, Robert. 1984. *The Great Cat Massacre and Other Essays.* New York: Basic Books.

———. 1988. "A Star Is Born." *New York Review of Books,* October 27.

Daston, Lorraine. 1991. "Historical Epistemology." In James Chandler, Arnold I. Davidson, and Harry D. Harootunian, eds., *Questions of Evidence: Proof, Practice, and Persuasion across the Disciplines,* 282–89. Chicago: University of Chicago Press.

Davidson, Arnold. 2002. *The Emergence of Sexuality: Historical Epistemology and the Formation of Concepts.* Cambridge, MA: Harvard University Press.

Davis, Allison. 1943. "Race Status and Personality Development." *Scientific Monthly* 57: 354–62.

"Le Débat de l'UNESCO: Le racisme est né du colonialisme, a déclaré le professeur Leyris [*sic*]." 1951. *L'Écho du centre,* February 11. LAS/FML.B.S03.03.05.017.

Debord, Guy [unsigned]. 1966. "L'Historien Lefebvre." *L'Internationale situationniste* 10: 73–75.

———. 1967. *La société du spectacle.* Paris: Buchet-Chastel, 1967. Translated as *The Society of the Spectacle* (New York: Zone Books, 1994).

Debû-Bridel, Jacques. 1947. *Histoire du marché noir, 1939–1947.* Paris: Jeune Parque.

Delaporte, François. 1989. *Disease and Civilization.* Cambridge, MA: MIT Press.

———. 2008. *Anatomy of the Passions.* Stanford, CA: Stanford University Press.

Delaporte, François, Bernard Devauchelle, and Emmanuel Fournier. 2010. *La Fabrique du visage.* Turnhout, Belgium: Brepols.

Delbo, Jacques. 1946. "Le Contrôle dit 'économique.'" *L'Aurore,* April 13.

Deleuze, Gilles. 1989 [1985]. *Cinema 2: The Time-Image.* Translated by Hugh Tomlinson and Robert Galeta. Minneapolis: University of Minnesota Press.

———. 1995. *Negotiations.* New York: Columbia University Press.

———. 2003. *Francis Bacon.* London: Continuum.

———. 2004. *Desert Islands and Other Texts.* New York: Semiotext(e).

———. 2009. "L'Homme, une existence douteuse." In Philippe Artières, ed., *Les Mots et les choses de Michel Foucault: Regards critiques, 1966–68,* 63–71. Caen: Presses universitaires de Caen.

Deleuze, Gilles, and Georges Canguilhem. 2006. *Il significato della vita: Letture del 3. capitolo dell'Evoluzione creatrice di Bergson.* Edited by Giuseppe Bianco. Milan: Mimesis.

Deprez, Stanislas. 2010. *Lévy-Bruhl et la rationalisation du monde.* Rennes: Presses universitaires de Rennes.

Derrida, Jacques. 1966. "Nature, culture, écriture." *Cahiers pour l'analyse* 4: 7–49.

———. 1967. "Cogito et Histoire de la folie." In *L'Écriture et la différence.* Paris: Seuil. Translated as "Cogito and the History of Madness" [= CHM] in Derrida 1978.

———. 1975. "La Vie la mort" [= VM]. Unpublished seminar. UC Irvine Critical Theory Archive, Jacques Derrida Papers, Seminar, 1975, MS-C01, box 12, folder 10/29.

———. 1978. *Writing and Difference*. Translated by Alan Bass. Chicago: University of Chicago Press.

———. 1982. *Margins of Philosophy*. Chicago: University of Chicago Press.

———. 1987. *The Post-Card*. Chicago: University of Chicago Press.

———. 1990. *Du droit à la philosophie*. Paris: Galilée.

———. 1992. *The Other Heading: Reflections on Today's Europe*. Translated by Pascale-Anne Brault and Michael B. Naas. Bloomington: Indiana University Press. Originally published as *L'autre cap. Suivi de La Démocratie ajournée* (Paris: Minuit, 1991).

———. 1997. *Of Grammatology* [= OG]. Revised ed. Translated by G. C. Spivak. Baltimore: Johns Hopkins University Press. Originally published as *De la grammatologie* (Paris: Minuit, 1967).

———. 2005. *Rogues: Two Essays on Reason*. Stanford, CA: Stanford University Press.

Derrida, Jacques, and Maurizio Ferraris. 2001. *A Taste for the Secret*. Malden, MA: Polity Press.

Descartes, René. 1908. *Cogitationes privatae*. In *Œuvres de Descartes*, ed. C. Adam and P. Tannery, 10: 213–58. Paris: Cerf.

———. 1970. *Philosophical Letters*. Oxford: Oxford University Press.

———. 1972. *Treatise of Man*. Cambridge, MA: Harvard University Press.

———. 1984–91. *The Philosophical Writings of Descartes* [= PWD]. Edited by John Cottingham et al. Cambridge: Cambridge University Press.

Descombes, Vincent. 1979. *Le Même et l'autre: Quarante-cinq ans de philosophie française (1933–1978)*. Paris: Minuit. Translated under the title *Modern French Philosophy* (New York: Cambridge University Press, 1980).

Dews, Peter. 2002. "Imagination and the Symbolic: Castoriadis and Lacan." *Constellations* 9 (4): 516–21.

Diderot, Denis, and Jean Le Rond d'Alembert. 1751–65. *Encyclopédie; ou Dictionnaire raisonné des sciences, des arts et des métiers*. Paris: Briasson.

DiIorio, Sam. 2007. "Total Cinema." *Screen* 48 (1): 25–43.

Doquet, Anne. 1999. *Masques Dogon*. Paris: Karhala.

Donaldson, Megan. 2016a. "Textual Settlements: The Sykes–Picot Agreement and Secret Treaty-Making." 110 *AJIL Unbound* 127 (2016).

Donaldson, Megan. 2016b. "From Secret Diplomacy to Diplomatic Secrecy: Secrecy and Publicity in the International Legal Order, c.1919–1950." JSD thesis, New York University School of Law.

Dosse, François. 1998. *History of Structuralism*. 2 vols. Minneapolis: University of Minnesota Press.

———. 1999. *Empire of Meaning*. Minneapolis: University of Minnesota Press.

———. 2008. *Gilles Deleuze, Félix Guattari*. Paris: La Découverte.

Ducasse, Pierre. 1958. *Les Techniques et la philosophie*. Paris: Presses universitaires de France.

Ducoulombier, Romain. 2013. "L'Histoire obscure de la transparence." *Fragments sur les temps présents*, September 9. https://tempspresents.com/2013/09/19/romain -ducoulombier-transparence-histoire-socialisme (accessed August 4, 2016).

Dugléry, D. 1996. "L'Adaptation des stratégies policières." *Cahiers de la Sécurité intérieure* 23: 110–20.

Duhem, Pierre. 1954. *The Aim and Structure of Physical Theory*. Princeton, NJ: Princeton University Press.

Dupuy, Jean-Pierre. 2000. *The Mechanization of the Mind*. Princeton, NJ: Princeton University Press.

Durkheim, Émile. 1982 [1919]. *Rules of the Sociological Method*. New York: Free Press. Originally published as *Les Règles de la méthode sociologique* (Paris: Alcan, 1895).

Edelstein, Dan. 2009. *The Terror of Natural Right*. Chicago: University of Chicago Press.

———. 2017. "Revolution in Permanence and the Fall of Popular Sovereignty." In Zvi Ben-Dor Benite, Stefanos Geroulanos, and Nicole Jerr, eds., *The Scaffolding of Sovereignty: Global and Aesthetic Perspectives on the History of a Concept*. New York: Columbia University Press.

Ellul, Jacques. 1954. *La Technique: L'enjeu du siècle*. Paris: Armand Collin.

Eribon, Didier. 1991. *Michel Foucault*. Cambridge, MA: Harvard University Press.

Eribon, Didier, and Claude Lévi-Strauss. 1988. *De près et de loin*. Paris: Odile Jacob.

Evans, Martha Noel. 1979. "Introduction to Jacques Lacan's Lecture." *Psychoanalytic Quarterly* 48: 386–404.

Évolution de la délinquance juvénile (Période d'après-guerre). 1959. Vaucresson: Cujas.

Fabian, Johannes. 1983. *Time and the Other*. New York: Columbia University Press.

Fabietti, Elena. 2015. "A Body of Glass." *symploke* 23 (1–2): 327–40.

Fabius, Laurent. 1990. *C'est en allant vers la mer*. Paris: Seuil.

Fabre, Daniel. 1996. "Le Symbolique." In Jacques Revel and Nathan Wachtel, eds., *Une école pour les sciences sociales*, 229–50. Paris: Éditions du CERF.

Falasca-Zamponi, Simonetta. 2011. *Rethinking the Political*. Montréal: McGill-Queen's University Press.

Fanon, Frantz. 2004. *The Wretched of the Earth*. New York: Grove Press. Originally published as *Les damnés de la terre* (Paris: F. Maspero, 1961).

———. 2008. *Black Skin, White Masks*. London: Pluto Press. Originally published as *Peau noire, masques blancs* (Paris: Seuil, 1952).

Favez-Boutonier, Juliette. 1957. "Le Rôle des conflits familiaux dans l'inadaptation de l'enfant et de l'adolescent." Lecture delivered at the Seine Police Prefecture, April 10, 1957 (BnF 8-R-58185–17).

Faye, Jean-Pierre. 1985. "Inlassable questionnement: Collège philosophique," In Pascal Ory, ed., *Mots de passé*, 70–72. Paris: Autrement.

Febvre, Lucien. 1944. "Le Génie de la langue française." *Mélanges d'histoire sociale* 6: 120–21.

———. 1945. "L'Europe et le bon Européen: Mythe ou réalité?" *Annuaire du Collège de France, 1944–1945*: 151–52.

———. 1946. "Face au vent." *Annales: Economies–Sociétés–Civilisations* 1 (1): 1–4.

———. 2009 [1937]. "Le Progrès." In Febvre, *Vivre l'histoire*, 982–85. Paris: Armand Colin.

Febvre, Lucien, Émile Tonnelat, Marcel Mauss, Adfredo Niceforo, and Louis Weber. 1930. *Civilisation: Le mot et l'idée*. Paris: La Renaissance du livre.

Fenves, Peter. 2002. "Derrida and History." In Tom Cohen, ed., *Jacques Derrida and the Humanities*, 271–94. Cambridge: Cambridge University Press.

Féraud, Jean-François. 1787–88. *Dictionnaire critique de la langue française*. Marseille: J. Mossy.

Fessard, Alfred. 1953. "Points de contact entre neurophysiologie et cybernétique." *Structure et évolution des techniques* 35–36: 25–33.

———. 1970. *Cybernétique et biologie*. Paris: Encyclopædia Universalis.

Fiemeyer, Isabelle. 2004. *Marcel Griaule*. Paris: Actes Sud.

Fishman, Sarah. 2002. *The Battle for Children: World War II, Youth Crime, and Juvenile Justice in Twentieth-Century France*. Cambridge, MA: Harvard University Press.

Fiss, Karen. 2009. *Grand Illusion: The Third Reich, the Paris Exposition, and the Cultural Seduction of France*. Chicago: University of Chicago Press.

Fitzpatrick, Sheila. 2005. *Tear off the Masks! Identity and Imposture in Twentieth-Century Russia*. Princeton, NJ: Princeton University Press.

Fogg, Shannon L. 2008. *The Politics of Everyday Life in Vichy France*. Cambridge: Cambridge University Press.

Foucault, Michel. 1957. "La Psychologie de 1850 à 1950." In D. Huisman and A. Weber, eds., *Histoire de la philosophie européenne*, 2: 591–606. Paris: Fischbacher.

———. 1970. "Theatrum philosophicum." *Critique* 282: 885–908.

———. 1972. *The Archaeology of Knowledge*. New York: Pantheon Books. Originally published as *L'Archéologie du savoir* (Paris: Gallimard, 1969).

———. 1976. *Mental Illness and Personality*. Berkeley: University of California Press.

———. 1978. *History of Sexuality*. Vol. 1. New York: Vintage Books.

———. 1980. "Le Philosophe masqué." *Le Monde*, 10945 (April 6): i and xvii.

————. 1981. *Power/Knowledge*. New York: Pantheon.

————. 1991. "Life: Experience and Science." In Georges Canguilhem, *The Normal and the Pathological*, 7–24. New York: Zone Books.

————. 1994 [1971]. *The Order of Things: An Archaeology of the Human Sciences* [= *OT*]. New York: Vintage Books. Originally published as *Les Mots et les choses: Une Archéologie des sciences humaines*. Paris: Gallimard, 1966.

————. 1994a. *Dits et écrits* [= *F-DE*]. Edited by D. Defert and Fr. Ewald. Vol. 1: *1954–69*. Vol. 3: *1976–79*. Paris: Gallimard.

————. 1994b. "L'Œil du pouvoir." In F-*DE*, 3: 190–207.

————. 1995 [1975]. *Discipline and Punish: The Birth of the Prison* [= *DP*]. New York: Vintage Books. Originally published as *Surveiller et punir: Naissance de la prison*. Paris: Gallimard, 1975.

————. 2006. *History of Madness* [= *HM*]. Translated by Jonathan Murphy. London: Routledge. Originally published as *Folie et déraison. Histoire de la folie à l'âge classique*. Paris: Plon, 1961.

————. 2008. *Psychiatric Power*. Translated by Graham Burchell. New York: Picador.

————. 2009. *Security, Territory, Population*. Translated by Graham Burchell. New York: Picador.

François-Unger, Claude. 1957. *L'Adolescent inadapté*. Paris: Presses universitaires de France.

Freud, Sigmund. 1955. "Notes on a Case of Obsessional Neurosis." In *The Standard Edition of the Complete Psychological Works of Sigmund Freud*, 10: 155–250. London: Hogarth Press.

Fried, Michael. 1980. *Absorption and Theatricality*. Berkeley: University of California Press.

Fried, Michael. 1998. *Art and Objecthood*. Chicago: University of Chicago Press.

Friedland, Paul. 2002. *Political Actors*. Ithaca, NY: Cornell University Press.

Friedmann, Georges. 1936. *Machine et humanisme*. Vol. 1: *La Crise du progrès: Esquisse d'histoire des idées, 1895–1935*. Paris: Gallimard.

————. 1946. *Machine et humanisme*. Vol. 2: *Problèmes humains du machinisme industriel*. Paris: Gallimard.

Fuchs, Wilhelm. 1923. "Experimentelle Untersuchungen über das simultane Hintereinandersehen." *Zeitschrift für Psychologie*, 91: 145–235.

Furet, François. 1981 [1978]. *Interpreting the French Revolution* [= IFR]. Cambridge: Cambridge University Press.

Gadamer, Hans-Georg. 1976. *Philosophical Hermeneutics*. Berkeley: University of California Press.

————. 2013. *Truth and Method*. London: Bloomsbury.

Galison, Peter. 1994. "The Ontology of the Enemy." *Critical Inquiry* 21: 228–68.

Galletti, Marina. 1989. "Masses: A Failed 'College'?" *Stanford French Review* 12 (1): 49–73.

Garrido, Juan Manuel. 2012. *Of Time, Being, and Hunger: Challenging the Traditional Way of Thinking Life*. New York: Fordham University Press.

Gauchet, Marcel. 1980. "Les Droits de l'homme ne sont pas une politique." *Le Débat* 3: 3–21.

Gauchet, Marcel, and Gladys Swain. 1999. *Madness and Democracy*. Princeton, NJ: Princeton University Press.

Geertz, Clifford. 1973. *The Interpretation of Cultures: Selected Essays*. New York: Basic Books.

———. 2001. *Available Light: Anthropological Reflections on Philosophical Topics*. Princeton, NJ: Princeton University Press.

Geoghegan, Bernard. 2011. "From Information Theory to French Theory." *Critical Inquiry* 38 (1): 96–126.

———. 2008. "The Historiographic Conceptualization of Information." *Annals on the History of Computing* 30 (1): 66–81.

Geroulanos, Stefanos. 2006. "Theoscopy: Transparency, Omnipotence, Modernity." In Hent de Vries and Lawrence Sullivan, eds., *Political Theologies: Public Religions in a Post-Secular World*, 633–51. New York: Fordham University Press.

———. 2007. "Transparency Thinking Freedom." *Modern Language Notes* 122 (5): 1050–78.

———. 2010. *An Atheism That Is Not Humanist Emerges in French Thought*. Stanford, CA: Stanford University Press.

———. 2011a. "Heterogeneities, Slave-Princes, and Marshall Plans." *Modern Intellectual History* 8 (3): 531–60.

———. 2011b. "Russian Exiles, New Scientific Movements, and Phenomenology." *New German Critique* 113: 89–128.

———. 2013. "Postwar Facial Reconstruction: Georges Franju's *Eyes without a Face*." *French Politics, Culture, and Society* 31 (2): 15–33.

Geroulanos, Stefanos, and Todd Meyers. 2014. *Experimente im Individuum*. Berlin: August Verlag.

Giraud, H. 1975. *L'Enfant inadapté à l'école*. Toulouse: Privat.

Glissant, Édouard. 2006 [1990]. *Poetics of Relation* [*Poétique de la relation*]. Ann Arbor: University of Michigan Press.

Glucksmann, André. 1977. *Les Maîtres penseurs*. Paris: Grasset.

———. 1987. *Descartes, c'est la France*. Paris: Flammarion.

Goblot, Edmond. 1901. *Vocabulaire philosophique*. Paris: Armand Colin.

Godard, Jean-Luc. 1986. *Godard on Godard: Critical Writings*. Edited by Jean Narboni and Tom Milne. New York: Da Capo Press.

Goffman, Erving. 1959. *The Presentation of Self in Everyday Life*. New York: Doubleday.

Goldstein, Jan. 2005. *The Post-Revolutionary Self: Politics and Psyche in France, 1750–1850*. Cambridge, MA: Harvard University Press.

Greeff, Étienne de. 1947. *Introduction à la criminologie*. Brussels: Vandenplas.

Grenard, Fabrice. 2008. *La France du marché noir, 1940–49*. Paris: Payot.

Griaule, Marcel. 1937. "L'Emploi de la photographie aérienne et la recherche scientifique." *L'Anthropologie* 47: 469–74.

———. 1939. "Connaitre l'indigène." *Questions du jour* 9: 47–51.

———. 1946. "Aviation and Scientific Research." *Nature* 157 (June 22): 848–49.

———. 1948. "L'Homme et le milieu naturel." In Paul Henry Chombart de Lauwe, *La découverte aérienne du monde*, 177–208. Paris: Horizons de France.

———. 1952. "La Connaissance de l'homme noir." In *La Connaissance de l'homme au XXe siècle*, 147–66. Neuchâtel: La Baconnière.

———, ed. 1953. *L'Originalité des cultures, son role dans la compréhension international*. Paris: UNESCO.

———. 1957a. *Marcel Griaule, conseiller de l'Union française*. Paris: Nouvelles éditions latines.

———. 1957b. *Méthode de l'ethnographie*. Paris: Presses universitaires de France.

———. 1994. "Remarques sur le role de l'institution des masques." In Marcel Griaule, *Masques dogons*, 773–818. Paris: Musée de l'homme.

Groys, Boris. 1992. *The Total Art of Stalinism*. Princeton, NJ: Princeton University Press.

Guérin, Daniel. 1946. *La Lutte des classes sous la première république*. 2 vols. Paris: Gallimard.

Guignon, Charles. 1993. *Heidegger and the Problem of Knowledge*. Indianapolis, IN: Hackett.

Guillaumaud, Jacques. 1971. *Norbert Wiener et la cybernétique*. Paris: Seghers.

Gurwitsch, Aron. 1966. *Studies in Phenomenology and Psychology*. Evanston, IL: Northwestern University Press.

Gusdorf, Georges. 1960. *Introduction aux sciences humaines*. Paris: Belles Lettres.

———. 1963. "Les Sciences humaines et la philosophie." *Bulletin de la société française de philosophie* 56: 5–112.

———. 1966–67. *Les Sciences humaines et la pensée occidentale*. 2 vols. Paris: Payot.

Gutting, Gary, ed. 2005. *The Cambridge Companion to Foucault*. Cambridge: Cambridge University Press.

Habermas, Jürgen. 1961. *Strukturwandel der Öffentlichkeit: Untersuchungen zu einer Kategorie der bürgerlichen Gesellschaft*. Frankfurt a/Main: Suhrkamp.

———. 1978. *L'Espace public: Archéologie de la publicité comme dimension constitutive de la société bourgeoise*. Paris: Payot. A translation of Habermas 1961.

————. 1985. *Theory of Communicative Action*. Vol. 1. Boston: Beacon Press. Originally published as *Theorie des kommunikativen Handelns* (Frankfurt a/ Main: Suhrkamp, 1981).

————. 1987. *The Philosophical Discourse of Modernity: Twelve Lectures*. Translated by Frederick Lawrence. Cambridge, MA: MIT Press. Originally published as *Der philosophische Diskurs der Moderne: Zwölf Vorlesungen* (Frankfurt a/Main: Suhrkamp, 1985).

————. 1991 [1989]. *The Structural Transformation of the Public Sphere: An Inquiry into a Category of Bourgeois Society*. Cambridge, MA: MIT Press. A translation of Habermas 1961.

Hacking, Ian. 1990. *The Taming of Chance*. Cambridge: Cambridge University Press.

————. 1998. "Canguilhem amid the Cyborgs." *Economy & Society* 27: 2–3.

————. 2002. *Historical Ontology*. Cambridge, MA: Harvard University Press.

Hagglund, Martin. 2011. "The Arche-Materiality of Time." In D. Attridge and J. Elliott, eds., *Theory after "Theory,"* 265–77. London: Routledge.

Halbwachs, Maurice. 1912. *La Théorie de l'homme normal*. Paris: Félix Alcan.

Halfin, Igal. 2000. *From Darkness to Light: Class, Consciousness, and Salvation in Revolutionary Russia*. Pittsburgh, PA: University of Pittsburgh Press.

Hallward, Peter, and Knox Peden, eds. 2012. *Concept and Form*. Vol. 1. London: Verso.

Han, Byung-Chul. 2013. *Transparenzgesellschaft*. Berlin: Matthes & Seitz.

————. 2015. *The Transparency Society*. Stanford: Stanford Briefs, an imprint of Stanford University Press.

Hand, Séan. 2002. *Michel Leiris: Writing the Self*. Cambridge: Cambridge University Press.

Harcourt, Bernard. 2015. *Exposed: Desire and Disobedience in the Digital Age*. Cambridge, MA: Harvard University Press.

Harrington, Anne. 1999. *Reenchanted Science: Holism in German Culture from Wilhelm II to Hitler*. Princeton, NJ: Princeton University Press.

Hartog, François. 2003. *Régimes d'historicité: Présentisme et expériences du temps*. Paris: Seuil.

Heidegger, Martin. 1976 [1966]. "Only a God Can Save Us: The *Spiegel* Interview." *Philosophy Today* 20: 267–84.

————. 1977. *Martin Heidegger: Basic Writings*. Edited by David F. Krell. San Francisco: Harper.

Hellbeck, Jochen. 2000. "Self-Realization in the Stalinist System: Two Soviet Diaries of the 1930s." In David Hoffmann and Yanni Kotsonis, eds., *Russian Modernity: Politics, Knowledge, Practices*, 221–42. New York: St. Martin's Press.

Henley, Paul. 2010. *The Adventure of the Real*. Chicago: University of Chicago.

Herf, Jeffrey. 1997. *Divided Memory*. Cambridge, MA: Harvard University Press.

Heuyer, Georges, and Jean Pinatel, eds. 1953. *L'Examen médico-psychologique et social des délinquants*. Paris: Ministère de la Justice.

Hillier, Jim, ed. 1992. *Cahiers du cinema*. Vol. 2: *1960–1968*. Cambridge, MA: Harvard University Press.

Hoffmann, Stanley, with Michel des Accords, Serge Hurtig, Jean du Rostu, and Jean-Michel Royer. 1956. *Le Mouvement poujade*. Paris: Armand Collin.

Hollier, Denis, ed. 1988. *The College of Sociology*. Minneapolis: University of Minnesota Press.

House, Jim, and Neil MacMaster. 2006. *Paris 1961*. Oxford: Oxford University Press.

Huisman, Denis. 1962. *Les grands courants de la pensée contemporaine et l'avenir de la liberté*. Paris: Fédération nationale des syndicats d'ingénieurs et de cadres supérieurs.

Husserl, Edmund. 1975. *The Paris Lectures*. Translated by Peter Koestenbaum. The Hague: Martinus Nijhoff.

Huxley, Julian, Alfred C. Haddon, and A. M. Carr-Saunders. 1936 [1935]. *We Europeans: A Survey of "Racial" Problems*. New York: Harper. Translated by Jules Castier as *Nous, Européens* (Paris: Les Amis des Éditions de Minuit, 1947).

Hyppolite, Jean. 1952. *Logique et existence*. Paris: Presses universitaires de France. Translated as *Logic and Existence* (Albany: State University of New York Press, 1997).

———. 1971. *Figures de la pensée philosophique*. Paris: Presses universitaires de France.

Hyppolite, Jean, Georges Canguilhem, Michel Foucault, et al. 1965. "L'Enseignement de la philosophie et la television." *Revue de l'enseignement philosophique* 15 (4): 11–21.

Institut national de la statistique et des études économiques [INSEE]. 1947. *Statistique de médecine préventive universitaire*. Paris: INSEE.

Jackson, Julian. 2001. *France: The Dark Years*. Oxford: Oxford University Press.

Jacob, François. 1982. *The Logic of Life: A History of Heredity* [= *LL*]. New York: Pantheon Books. Originally published as *La logique du vivant: Une Histoire de l'hérédité* (Paris: Gallimard, 1970).

———. 2016. Interview, Georges Canguilhem segment. www.webofstories.com/play/francois.jacob/68 (accessed January 10, 2017).

Jamin, Jean. 1989. "L'Anthropologie et ses acteurs." In *Les Enjeux philosophiques des années 50*, 99–115. Paris: Centre Georges Pompidou.

———. 1992. "L'Homme du secret discret." *Magazine littéraire* 302: 16–24.

Janicaud, Dominique. 2001. *Heidegger en France*. 2 vols. Paris: Albin Michel.

Jankowski, Paul. 2008. *Shades of Indignation: Political Scandals in France, Past and Present*. New York: Berghahn.

Jarczyk, Gwendoline, and Pierre-Jean Labarrière. 1996. *De Kojève à Hegel*. Paris: Albin Michel.

Jaspers, Karl. 2001. *The Question of German Guilt*. New York: Fordham University Press.

Jay, Martin. 1980. *Marxism and Totality*. Berkeley: University of California Press.

———. 1993. *Downcast Eyes: The Denigration of Vision in Twentieth-Century French Thought* [= J-*DE*]. Berkeley: University of California Press.

Jobs, Richard. 2007. *Riding the New Wave: Youth and the Rejuvenation of France after the Second World War*. Stanford, CA: Stanford University Press.

Johnson, Christopher. 1993. *System and Writing in the Philosophy of Jacques Derrida*. Cambridge: Cambridge University Press.

———. 2011. "Leroi-Gourhan and the Limits of the Human." *French Studies* 65 (4): 471–87.

———. 2015. "French Cybernetics." *French Studies* 69 (1): 60–78.

Johnston, John. 2008. *The Allure of Machinic Life: Cybernetics, Artificial Life, and the New AI*. Cambridge, MA: MIT Press.

Jolly, Eric. 2001. "Marcel Griaule, ethnologue." *Journal des Africanistes* 71 (1): 149–90.

Judt, Tony. 1992. *Past Imperfect: French Intellectuals, 1944–56*. Berkeley: University of California Press.

Kafka, Ben. 2012. *The Demon of Writing*. New York: Zone Books.

Kant, Immanuel. 1988 [1800]. *Logic*. Translated by Robert S. Hartman and Wolfgang Schwarz. New York: Dover.

Keck, Frederick. 2005. *Claude Lévi-Strauss*. Paris: La Découverte.

Kedward, H. R. 1999. *In Search of the Maquis*. Oxford: Clarendon Press.

Kendall, Stuart. 2007. *Georges Bataille*. London: Reaktion Books.

Kleinberg, Ethan. 2005. *Generation Existential: Heidegger's Philosophy in France, 1927–1961*. Ithaca, NY: Cornell University Press.

Kline, Ronald R. 2015. *The Cybernetics Moment, or, Why We Call Our Age the Information Age*. Baltimore: Johns Hopkins University Press.

Kluckhohn, Clyde. 1949. *Mirror for Man*. New York: Whittlesey House.

Koreman, Meghan. 1999. *The Expectation of Justice: France, 1944–46*. Durham, NC: Duke University Press.

Koselleck, Reinhart. 1985. *Futures Past*. Cambridge, MA: MIT Press.

Kotkin, Stephen. 1995. *Magnetic Mountain*. Berkeley: University of California Press.

Kotsonis, Yanni. 2014. *States of Obligation: Taxes and Citizenship in the Russian Empire and Early Soviet Republic*. Toronto: University of Toronto Press.

Koyré, Alexandre. 1922. *Essai sur l'idée de Dieu et les preuves de son existence chez Descartes*. Paris: Leroux.

———. 1946. "L'Évolution philosophique de Martin Heidegger." *Critique* 1: 73–83; 2: 161–83.

———. 1963. Intervention in "Commémoration du cinquantenaire de la publication des *Étapes de la philosophie mathématique* de Léon Brunschvicg" (among several speakers). *Bulletin de la Société française de philosophie* 57 (2): 10–14.

———. 1990 [1948]. "Philosophers and the Machine" ["Les philosophes et la machine"], in Sabayasachi Bhattacharya and Pietro Redondi, eds., *Techniques to Technology*, 112–60. New Delhi: Orient Longman.

———. 1998. "Present Trends in French Philosophical Thought." *Journal of the History of Ideas* 59 (3): 521–48.

Kracauer, Siegfried. 1997. *Theory of Film.* Princeton, NJ: Princeton University Press.

Krell, Jacob. 2011. "An Attempt in All Directions: The Concept of *Technique* in French Thought, 1900–1968." Honors thesis, New York University.

Kuhn, Roland. 1957. *Phénoménologie du masque à travers le test de Rorschach.* Bruges: Desclée de Brouwer.

Lacan, Jacques. 1938. "Le Stade du miroir." In "La Famille," in Henri Wallon, ed., *L'Encyclopédie française*, 8: 8.40.3–8.42.4. Paris: L'Encyclopédie française.

———. 1957. "La Psychanalyse et son enseignement." *Bulletin de la Société française de Philosophie* 49 (2): 65–101.

———. 1975 [1932]. *De la psychose paranoïaque dans ses rapports avec la personnalité.* Paris: Seuil.

———. 1991. *Seminar I: Freud's Papers on Technique* [= *L-S1*]. Translated with notes by J. Forrester. New York: Norton.

———. 1988. *Seminar II: The Ego in Freud's Theory and in the Technique of Psychoanalysis, 1954–1955* [= *L-S2*]. Translated by S. Tomaselli. New York: Norton.

———. 1993. *Seminar III: The Psychoses, 1955–56* [= *L-S3*]. Translated with notes by Russell Grigg. London: Routledge; New York: Norton.

———. 1997. *Seminar VII: The Ethics of Psychoanalysis.* New York: Norton.

———. 1998. *Seminar XI: The Four Fundamental Concepts of Psychoanalysis.* New York: Norton.

———. 2001. *Autres écrits.* Paris: Seuil.

———. 2006 [1966]. *Écrits: The First Complete Edition in English* [= *L-E*]. Translated by Bruce Fink. New York: Norton.

Lacroix, Jean-Paul. 1954. *Le Gangster aux étoiles.* Paris: Calmann-Lévy.

Lacroix, Jean. 1957. "Cheminement vers les philosophies contemporaines." In Gaston Berger, ed., *L'Encyclopédie française*, vol. 19: *Philosophie, Réligion*, 19.04.1–19.04.5. Paris: L'Encyclopédie française.

Lafontaine, Céline. 2007. "The Cybernetic Matrix of French Theory." *Theory, Culture & Society* 24 (5): 24–46.

Lagache, Daniel. 1977. *Les Hallucinations verbales et travaux cliniques.* Paris: Presses universitaires de France.

———. 1979. *Le Psychologue et le criminel.* Paris: Presses universitaires de France.

Lalande, André. 1893. *Lectures sur la philosophie des sciences.* Paris: Hachette.

———. 1898. "Le Langage philosophique et l'unité de la philosophie." *Revue de métaphysique et de morale* 6 (5): 566–88.

———. 1911. "Du parallélisme formel des sciences normatives." *Revue de métaphysique et de morale* 19 (4): 527–32.

———. 1988 [1926–32]. *Vocabulaire technique et critique de la philosophie* [= *VTC*]. 2 vols., 16th ed. Paris: Presses universitaires de France.

Lambert, Maurice. 1950. *Le Gangster aux yeux bleus.* Paris: Janicot.

Lasserre, Bruno, Noëlle Lenoir, and Bernard Stirn. 1987. *La Transparence administrative.* Paris: Presses universitaires de France.

Laurent, Sébastien. 2009. *Politiques de l'ombre. État, renseignement et surveillance en France.* Paris: Fayard.

Lawall, Sarah. 1968. *Critics of Consciousness.* Cambridge, MA: Harvard University Press.

Le Clère, Marcel. 1957. *Histoire de la police.* Paris: Presses universitaires de France.

Le Corbusier. 1946 [1923]. *Towards a New Architecture* [= *TNA*]. London: Architectural Press.

———. 1971. *The City of Tomorrow and Its Planning.* London: Architectural Press.

Le Goff, Jean-Pierre. 1993. *Le Mythe de l'entreprise.* Paris: La Découverte.

Le Sueur, James D. 2005. *Uncivil War: Intellectuals and Identity Politics during the Decolonization of Algeria.* Lincoln: University of Nebraska Press.

Lebovici, Serge. 1953. "La Psychologie de groupe." In Georges Heuyer and Jean Pinatel, eds., *L'Examen medico-psychologique et social des délinquants,* 165–70. Paris: Ministère de la Justice.

Lebovici, Serge, Pierre Male, and Francis Pasche. 1951. "Psychanalyse et criminologie." *Revue française de psychanalyse* 15 (1): 30–61.

Lecourt, Dominique. 1977. *Proletarian Science? The Case of Lysenko.* Atlantic Highlands, NJ: Humanities Press. Originally published as *Lyssenko: Histoire réelle d'une "science prolétarienne,"* with a foreword by Louis Althusser. Paris: F. Maspero, 1976.

———. 2008. *Georges Canguilhem.* Paris: Presses universitaires de France.

Lefaucheur, Nadine. 1994. "Psychiatrie infantile et délinquance juvénile." In Laurent Mucchielli, ed., *Histoire de la criminologie française,* 313–32. Paris: L'Harmattan.

Lefebvre, Henri. 1947–62. *Critique de la vie quotidienne.* 2 vols. Paris: l'Arche.

———. 1965. *Proclamation de la Commune.* Paris: Gallimard.

———. 1992 [1974]. *The Production of Space.* London: Wiley Blackwell.

———. 1995 [1962]. *Introduction to Modernity.* London: Verso.

———. 2002 [1962]. *Critique of Everyday Life.* Vol. 2. London: Verso.

Lefort, Claude. 1966. "Pour une sociologie de la démocratie." *Annales: Economies–Sociétés–Civilisations* 21 (4): 750–68.

———. 1972. *Le Travail de l'œuvre Machiavel.* Paris: Gallimard. Translated by Michael B. Smith as *Machiavelli in the Making* (Evanston, IL: Northwestern University Press, 2012).

———. 1976. *Un homme en trop: Réflexions sur "L'Archipel du Goulag"* [= *UH*]. Paris: Seuil.

———. 1978. *Sur une colonne absente.* Paris: Gallimard.

———. 1979 [1971]. *Éléments d'une critique de la bureaucratie.* Paris: Gallimard.

———. 1983. "La Question de la démocratie." In Jean-Luc Nancy and Philippe Lacoue-Labarthe, eds., *Le Retrait du politique*, 71–88. Paris: Galilée.

———. 1988. *The Political Forms of Modern Society: Bureaucracy, Democracy, Totalitarianism* [= *PFM*]. Cambridge, MA: MIT/Polity Press.

———. 1989. *Democracy and Political Theory.* Minneapolis: University of Minnesota Press.

———. 2000. *Writing, the Political Test.* Durham, NC: Duke University Press. Originally published as *Écrire: À l'épreuve du politique* (Paris: Calmann-Lévy, 1992).

———. 2007 [1975]. Interview with *L'Anti-mythes*, April 19, 1975, reprinted in Lefort, *Le Temps présent: Écrits 1945–2005*, 223–60. Paris: Belin.

Lefort, Claude, and Marcel Gauchet. 1971. "Sur la démocratie: Le Politique et l'institution du social." *Textures* 2–3: 7–78.

Leibniz, Gottfried Wilhelm. 1989 [1679]. "On the Universal Characteristic." In Leibniz, *Philosophical Essays*, trans. Daniel Ariew, 5–10. Indianapolis, IN: Hackett.

Leiris, Michel. 1934. *L'Afrique fantôme.* Paris: Gallimard. Translated by Brent Hayes Edwards as *Phantom Africa* (Calcutta and London: Seagull Books, 2017).

———. 1949. "Note sur le problème des échanges culturels entre peuples autonomes et peuples non-autonomes." MS. June 24. Bibliothèque du Laboratoire d'anthropologie sociale CNRS–EHESS–Collège de France, Paris. LAS/FML.B.S03.04.04.021.

———. 1950. "L'Ethnographie devant le colonialisme" [= EDC]. In Leiris, *Cinq études d'ethnologie*, 83–112. Paris: Gallimard, 1988.

———. 1953. "Les Nègres d'Afrique et les arts sculpturaux." In *L'Originalité des cultures, son role dans la compréhension internationale*, 336–73. Paris: UNESCO.

———. 1958. *La Possession et ses aspects théâtraux chez les Éthiopiens de Gondar.* Paris: Plon.

———. 1975 [1950–51]. "Race and Culture" ["Race et civilisation"]. In Leo Kuper, ed., *Race, Science and Society*, 135–72. New York: Columbia University Press.

Lemoine, Philippe [as Jean-Philippe Faivret]. 1974. "Le Socialisme = autogestion + ordinateur?" *CFDT Aujourd'hui* 10: 40–50.

Leonelli, Sabina, Brian Rappert, and Gail Davies. 2017. "Data Shadows: Knowledge, Openness, and Absence." *Science, Technology, & Human Values* 42, 2: 191–202.

Leriche, René. 1927a. "La Chirurgie de la douleur." *Presse médicale* 32 (April 20): 497–99.

———. 1927b. "Résultats de la chirurgie de la douleur." *Presse médicale*, 36 (May 4): 561–64.

———, ed. 1936. *L'Être humain*. Vol. 6 of *Encyclopédie française*. Paris: Société de gestion de l'Encyclopédie française.

Leroi-Gourhan, André. 1943–45. *Évolution et techniques*. 2 vols. Vol. 1: *L'homme et la matière*; vol. 2, *Milieu et techniques*. Paris: Albin Michel.

———. 1945. "Leçon d'ouverture du cours d'ethnologie coloniale." *Les Études rhodaniennes* 20: 1–2.

———. 1952. "Sur la position scientifique de l'ethnologie." *Revue philosophique* 142: 506–18.

———. 1955. "Où en est l'ethnologie?" In Jean Ladrière, ed., *La Science peut-elle former l'homme?* 141–46. Paris: Fayard.

———. 1962. "L'Ethnologie et l'élaboration d'un nouvel humanisme." In Denis Huisman, ed., *Les grands courants de la pensée contemporaine et l'avenir de la liberté*, 31–45. Paris: Fédération nationale des syndicats d'ingénieurs et de cadres supérieurs.

———. 1965. "L'Ethnologie." *Revue de l'enseignement supérieur* 3: 5–10.

———. 1968. "Anthropologie et ethnologie." *La Vie de la recherche scientifique* 218: 5–6.

———. 1973 [1943]. *L'Homme et la matière*. Paris: Albin Michel.

———. 1975 [1943]. *Milieu et techniques* [= *MT*]. Paris: Albin Michel.

———. 1983. *Le Fil du temps*. Paris: Fayard.

———. 1993. *Gesture and Speech* [= *GS*]. Translated by Anna Bostock Berger. Cambridge, MA: MIT Press. Originally published as *Le Geste et la parole* (2 vols., Paris: A. Michel, 1964–65).

Leroy, Maxime. 1929. *Descartes: Le philosophe au masque*. Paris: Rieder.

Letteron, Rosaline. 1987. "L'Administré et le droit à l'information." PhD diss., Université de Lille–III.

Levin, Thomas Y., Ursula Frohne, and Peter Weibel, eds. 2002. *CTRL [SPACE]: Rhetorics of Surveillance from Bentham to Big Brother*. Cambridge, MA: MIT Press.

Levinas, Emmanuel. 1969. *Totality and Infinity*. Pittsburgh, NJ: Duquesne University Press.

———. 1996. *Proper Names*. Stanford, CA: Stanford University Press.

———. 1998. "Questions and Answers." In Levinas, *Of God Who Comes to Mind*, 79–99. Stanford, CA: Stanford University Press.

————. 2001 [1947]. *Existence and Existents*. Pittsburgh, PA: Duquesne University Press.

Lévi-Strauss, Claude. 1948. "La Vie familiale et sociale des Indiens Nambikwara." *Journal de la Société des Américanistes* 37: 1–132.

————. 1949. "Histoire et ethnologie." *Revue de métaphysique et de morale* 54 (3–4): 363–91.

————. 1953. "Panorama de l'ethnologie (1950–1952)." *Diogène* 2: 96–123.

————. 1954. "Place de l'anthropologie dans les sciences sociales." In *Les Sciences sociales dans l'enseignement supérieur*, 102–34. Paris: UNESCO.

————. 1955. "Diogène couché." *Les Temps modernes* 110: 1–34.

————. 1956. "Lettre au Premier Congrès d'artistes et écrivains noirs." *Présence Africaine* 8–10: 384–85.

————. 1960. "L'Anthropologie devant l'histoire." *Annales: Economies–Sociétés–Civilisations* 15 (4): 625–37.

————. 1961a. "La Crise moderne de l'anthropologie." *UNESCO Courier* 14 (11): 12–17.

————. 1961b. "Le Métier d'ethnologue." *Annales: Revue française de lettres françaises* 129: 5–17.

————. 1961–62. "1. Les Fondements philosophiques de l'anthropologie; 2. Recherches sémiologiques." In *Annuaire de l'École pratique des Haute Études* 40–42.

————. 1963. "Rousseau, the Father of Anthropology." In *UNESCO Courier* 16 (3): 10–15.

————. 1964. *Mythologiques*. Paris: Plon.

————. 1966. *The Savage Mind*. Chicago: University of Chicago Press.

————. 1967. "À propos de 'Lévi-Strauss dans le XVIIIe siècle.'" *Cahiers pour l'analyse* 8: 89–90.

————. 1969. *The Elementary Structures of Kinship* [= *ESK*]. Boston: Beacon Press. Originally published as *Les Structures élémentaires de la parenté* (Paris: Presses universitaires de France, 1949).

————. 1973. *Anthropologie structurale deux*. Paris: Plon.

————. 1974. *Structural Anthropology*. New York: Basic Books.

————. 1975. "Race and History." In Leo Kuper, ed., *Race, Science and Society*, 95–134. Paris: UNESCO. Originally published as "Race et histoire" in *Le Racisme devant la science*, 9–53 (Paris: UNESCO, 1953), and republished as Lévi-Strauss 1987.

————. 1976. *Structural Anthropology*. Vol. 2. Chicago: University of Chicago Press.

————. 1987. *Introduction to the Work of Marcel Mauss*. London: Routledge & Kegan Paul. Originally published as *Introduction à l'œuvre de Marcel Mauss* (Paris: Presses universitaires de France, 1950).

———. 1983. "Jean-Jacques Rousseau, Founder of the Sciences of Man" [= FSM]. In Lévi-Strauss, *Structural Anthropology*, trans. Monique Layton, 2: 33–43. Chicago: University of Chicago Press.

———. 1987. *Race et histoire*. Paris: Folio/Essais.

———. 1992 [1955]. *Tristes tropiques* [= *TT*]. Translated by John Weightman and Doreen Weightman. New York: Penguin Books.

———. 2008. "How the Social Sciences Have Humanized Technical Civilization." *UNESCO Courier* 5: 25–28. Originally published in 1956 as "Les trois humanismes" and republished in Lévi-Strauss 1973: 319–22.

Levitt, Theresa. 2009. *The Shadow of Enlightenment: Optical and Political Transparency in France, 1789–1848*. Oxford: Oxford University Press.

Lévy, Bernard-Henri. 1979. *Barbarism with a Human Face*. New York: Harper & Row.

Lévy-Bruhl, Lucien. 1927 [1903]. *La Morale et la science des mœurs*. Paris: F. Alcan.

Leys, Ruth. 2010. "Navigating the Genealogies of Trauma, Guilt and Affect." *University of Toronto Quarterly* 79 (2): 137–49.

Ligue des droits de l'homme. 1990. *La Liberté de l'information en France*. Paris: Éditions Ouvrières.

Littré, Émile. 1883. *Dictionnaire de la langue française*. Paris: Hachette.

Liu, Lydia. 2010. "The Cybernetic Unconscious." *Critical Inquiry* 36 (2): 288–320.

Locard, Edmond. 1918. *La Police, ce qu'elle est, ce qu'elle devrait être*. Paris: Grasset.

———. 1923. *Manuel de technique policière*. Paris: Payot.

———. 1934. *La Police et les méthodes scientifiques*. Paris: Rieder.

Loubet del Bayle, Jean-Louis. 2006. *Police et politique*. Paris: L'Harmattan.

Lowenstein, Adam. 2005. *Shocking Representation: Historical Trauma, National Cinema, and the Modern Horror Film*. New York: Columbia University Press.

Lowie, Robert Harry. 1920. *Primitive Society*. New York: Boni & Liveright. Translated by E. Métraux as *Traité de sociologie primitive* (Paris: Payot, 1935).

Lubac, Henri de, S.J. 1950 [1945]. *The Drama of Atheist Humanism*. New York: Sheed & Ward.

Luhmann, Niklas. 1998. *Observations on Modernity*. Stanford, CA: Stanford University Press.

Lyotard, Jean-François. 1954. *La Phénoménologie*. Paris: Presses universitaires de France.

———. 1971. *Discours, figure*. Paris: Klincksieck.

———. 1974. *Economie libidinale*. Paris: Minuit.

———. 1979. *La Condition postmoderne: Rapport sur le savoir*. Paris: Minuit.

———. 1984. *The Postmodern Condition: A Report on Knowledge*. Minneapolis: University of Minnesota Press. A translation of Lyotard 1979.

———. 1985. "Une Ligne de résistance." In Jean-Louis Weissberg, ed., *"1984" et les présents de l'univers informationnel: 34 auteurs pour un colloque*, 433–43. Paris: Centre Georges Pompidou.

———. 1986. *Le postmoderne expliqué aux enfants: Correspondance, 1982–1985*. Paris: Galilée.

———. 1992. *The Postmodern Explained to Children*. London: Turnaround. A translation of Lyotard 1986.

———. 1993a. *Libidinal Economy*. Bloomington: Indiana University Press. A translation of Lyotard 1974.

———. 1993b. *Political Writings*. Minneapolis: University of Minnesota Press.

———. 2011. *Discourse, Figure*. Minneapolis: University of Minnesota Press. A translation of Lyotard 1971.

Lyotard, Jean-François, with Jean Papineau. 1978. "De la fonction critique à la transformation." *Parachute* 11: 4–9.

Macherey, Pierre. 1996. "Georges Canguilhem." *Cahiers philosophiques* 69: 47–56.

———. 2002. "Descartes, est-ce la France?" *Methodos* 2. http://methodos.revues. org/94 (accessed October 29, 2015).

Malinowski, Bronislaw. 1932. *Argonauts of the Western Pacific*. London: Routledge.

Margolin, Jean-Claude. 1967. "L'Homme de Michel Foucault." *Revue des sciences humaines* 128: 497–523. Reprinted in Philippe Artières, ed., *Les Mots et les choses de Michel Foucault: Regards critiques, 1966–68*, 303–43 (Caen: Presses universitaires de Caen, 2009).

Marin, Louis. 1977a. Interview. *Diacritics* 7 (2): 44–53.

———. 1977b. "Puss-in-Boots: Power of Signs–Signs of Power." *Diacritics* 7 (2): 54–63.

———. 1989. "The Body-of-Power and Incarnation at Port Royal and in Pascal." In Michel Feher, Ramona Naddaff, and Nadia Tazi, eds., *Fragments for a History of the Human Body*, 1: 421–47. New York: Zone Books.

Maritain, Jacques. 1946. *The Dream of Descartes*. London: Editions Poetry.

Marrati, Paola. 2008. *Gilles Deleuze: Cinema and Philosophy*. Baltimore: Johns Hopkins University Press.

Marx, Karl. 1976 [1887]. *Capital*. Vol. 1. London: Penguin Books.

———. 1988. *Economic and Philosophical Manuscripts of 1844*. Amherst, NY: Prometheus.

Mascolo, Dionys [as Jean Gratien]. 1946. "Si la lecture de Saint-Just est possible." In Louis-Antoine-Léon de Saint-Just, *Œuvres de Saint-Just*, 9–54. Paris: Cité universelle.

Mascolo, Dionys. 1953. *Le Communisme*. Paris: Gallimard.

———. 1993. *À la recherche d'un communisme de pensée*. Paris: Fourbis.

Maurel, Chloé. 2010. *Histoire de l'Unesco*. Paris: L'Harmattan.

Mauriac, François. 1951. Review of Bresson's *Journal d'un curé de champagne*. *Le Figaro*, February 27.

Mauss, Marcel. 1950. *Sociologie et anthropologie*. Paris: Presses universitaires de France.

———. 1974. *Œuvres*. Vols. 2 and 3. Paris: Minuit.

———. 2002 [1947]. *Manuel d'ethnographie*. Paris: Payot.

Mazower, Mark. 2001 [1993]. *Inside Hitler's Greece: The Experience of Occupation, 1941–44*. New Haven, CT: Yale Nota Bene.

McGrath, Larry. 2014. "The Bergsonian Moment: Science and Spirit in France." PhD diss., Johns Hopkins University.

Mekeel, Scuder. 1944. "Concerning Race Prejudice." *Phylon* 4: 305–13.

Merleau-Ponty, Maurice. 1947. *Humanisme et terreur: Essai sur le problème communiste*. Paris: Gallimard.

———. 1955. *Les Aventures de la dialectique*. Paris: Gallimard.

———. 1960. "L'URSS et les camps." In Merleau-Ponty, *Signes*, 330–43. Paris: Gallimard. Originally published as "Les Jours de notre vie" (1949–50).

———. 1962. *Phenomenology of Perception* [= *PP*]. New York: Humanities Press.

———. 1963. *The Structure of Behavior*. Boston: Beacon Press. Originally published as *La Structure du comportement* (Paris: Presses universitaires de France, 1942).

———. 1964a. *Sense and Non-Sense*. Translated by Hubert L. Dreyfus and Patricia Allen Dreyfus. Evanston, IL: Northwestern University Press.

———. 1964b. *Signs*. Evanston, IL: Northwestern University Press.

———. 1964c. "The War Has Taken Place" [= *WTP*]. In Merleau-Ponty 1964a: 139–52. Originally published as "La Guerre a eu lieu," *Les Temps modernes*, no. 1 (October 1945).

———. 1973. *The Prose of the World*. Evanston, IL: Northwestern University Press. Originally published as *La Prose du monde* (Paris: Gallimard, 1969).

———. 1973. *Adventures of the Dialectic*. Translated by Joseph Bien. Evanston, IL: Northwestern University Press. Originally published as *Les Aventures de la dialectique* (Paris: Gallimard, 1955).

———. 2001. *The Incarnate Subject: Malebranche, Biran, and Bergson on the Union of Body and Soul*. Amherst, NY: Humanity Books.

———. 2007a [1951]. Presentation of Michel Crozier's article "Human Engineering: The New 'Human' Techniques of American Big Business." In *The Merleau-Ponty Reader*, ed. Ted Toadvine and Leonard Lawlor, 185–89. Evanston, IL: Northwestern University Press. Originally published in *Les Temps modernes* 7 (69): 44–48.

———. 2007b. "The Primacy of Perception and Its Philosophical Consequences." In *The Merleau-Ponty Reader*, ed. Ted Toadvine and Leonard Lawlor, 89–118. Evanston, IL: Northwestern University Press.

Métraux, Alfred. 1950. "Race et civilization." *UNESCO Courier* 3: 6–7.

————. 1957. "One Man's Meat Is Another Man's . . . Taboo." *UNESCO Courier* 10: 10–11.

————. 1958. "The Rise of the New Elites." *UNESCO Courier* 11: 8–9.

————. 1978. *Itinéraires. 1, 1935–1953.* Paris: Payot.

Meyran, Régis. 2000. "Races et racismes: Les Ambiguïtés de l'antiracisme chez les anthropologues de l'entre-deux-guerres." *Gradhiva. Revue d'anthropologie et d'histoire des arts* 27: 63–76.

Michaud, Eric. 2004. *The Cult of Art in Nazi Germany.* Translated by Janet Lloyd. Stanford, CA: Stanford University Press.

Michaux, Henri. 1997. *Darkness Moves: An Henri Michaux Anthology, 1927–1984.* Translated by David Ball. Berkeley: University of California Press.

Michaux, Léon, and Didier-Jacques Duché. 1957. *L'Enfant inadapté: Rôle médico-social du médecin.* Paris: G. Doin.

Mill, John Stuart. 1861. *Considerations on Representative Government.* London: Parker, Son, and Bourn.

————. 1863. *Utilitarianism.* London: Parker, Son, and Bourn.

————. 1874. *Three Essays on Religion.* New York: Henry Holt.

Miller, J. Hillis. 1966. "The Geneva School." *Critical Quarterly* 8 (4): 302–21.

Miller, James. 2000. *The Passion of Michel Foucault.* Cambridge, MA: Harvard University Press.

Milner, Jean-Claude. 1995. *L'Œuvre claire: Lacan, la science, la philosophie.* Paris: Seuil.

Minkowski, Eugène. 1926. *La Notion de perte de contact vital avec la réalité.* Paris: Jouve.

————. 1927. *La Schizophrénie: Psychopathologie des schizoïdes et des schizophrènes.* Paris: Payot.

Moles, A. 1962. "Machinisme et philosophie." *Revue philosophique* 152: 249–60.

Monet, J.-C. 1991–92. "Le Système policier français: Un Modèle à revisiter." *Cahiers de la Sécurité intérieure* 7: 41–64.

Montag, Warren. 2013. *Althusser and His Contemporaries.* Durham, NC: Duke University Press.

Morgan, Lewis H. 1877. *Ancient Society.* New York: Henry Holt.

Morin, Gilles. 2000. "Les Problèmes de la reconstruction de la police, 1944–1960." In Jean-Marc Berlière and Denis Peschanski, *La Police française, 1930–1950,* 219–34. Paris: Documentation française.

Mornet, André. 1949. *Quatre ans à rayer de notre histoire.* Paris: Self.

Mouré, Kenneth. 2010. "Food Rationing and the Black Market in France (1940–1944)." *French History* 24 (2): 262–82.

Moyn, Samuel. 2004. "Of Savagery and Civil Society." *Modern Intellectual History* 1 (1): 55–80.

————. 2005. *Origins of the Other*. Ithaca, NY: Cornell University Press.

————. 2008. "On the Intellectual Origins of François Furet's Masterpiece." *Revue Tocqueville* 29 (2): 59–78.

————. 2012a. "Claude Lefort, Political Anthropology, and Symbolic Division." *Constellations* 19 (1): 37–50.

————. 2012b. "The Politics of Individual Rights." In Raf Geenens and Helena Rosenblatt, eds., *French Liberalism from Montesquieu to the Present Day*, 291–310. Cambridge: Cambridge University Press.

Mucchielli, Laurent, ed. 1994. *Histoire de la criminologie française*. Paris: L'Harmattan.

Nancy, Jean-Luc. 1979. *Ego sum*. Paris: Flammarion.

Nancy, Jean-Luc, and Philippe Lacoue-Labarthe, eds. 1983. *Le Retrait du politique*. Paris: Galilée.

Neuville, Henri. 1933. "L'Espèce, la race, el le métissage en anthropologie." *Archives de l'institut de paléontologie humaine* 11: 469–70. Paris: Masson.

Newton, Isaac. 1718. *Opticks, or, A Treatise of the Reflections, Refractions, Inflections, and Colours of Light*. 2nd ed. London: W. and J. Innys.

Nin, Anaïs. 1994. *The Diary of Anaïs Nin*. Vol. 1. Orlando, FL: Harcourt.

Nivat, Maurice. 1983. *Savoir et savoir-faire en informatique: Rapport remis à Laurent Fabius, ministre de l'Industrie et de la Recherche et Alain Savary, ministre de l'Éducation nationale par la Mission "Informatique fondamentale et programmation" placée sous la présidence de Maurice Nivat*. Paris: Documentation française.

Nizan, Paul. 1971. *Pour une nouvelle culture*. Paris: Grasset.

Nogueira, Rui. 1996. *Le Cinéma selon Melville*. Paris: Étoile.

Ozouf, Mona. 1966. "L'Image de la ville chez C. N. Ledoux." *Annales: Economies–Sociétés–Civilisations* 6: 1273–304.

Pace, David. 1991. "Old Wine—New Bottles: Atomic Energy and the Ideology of Science in Postwar France." *French Historical Studies* 17 (1): 38–61.

Parro, Philippe, and Monique Gueneau. 1959. *Les Gangs d'adolescents*. Paris: Presses universitaires de France.

Paxton, Robert. 2005. *The Anatomy of Fascism*. New York: Vintage Books.

Péan, Pierre. 1985. *Secret d'état: La France du secret, les secrets de la France*. Paris: Fayard.

Peden, Knox. 2011. "Descartes, Spinoza, and the Impasse of French Philosophy." *Modern Intellectual History*, 8 (2): 361–90.

Peden, Knox. 2014. *Spinoza contra Phenomenology: French Rationalism from Cavaillès to Deleuze*. Stanford, CA: Stanford University Press.

Peeters, Benoît. 2013. *Derrida: A Biography*. Malden, MA: Polity Press.

Pétonnet, Colette. 1979. *On est tous dans le brouillard*. Paris: Galilée.

Pettigrew, David, and François Raffoul, eds. 2008. *French Interpretations of Heidegger*. Albany: State University of New York Press.

Peukert, Detlev. 1991. *The Weimar Republic*. New York: Hill & Wang.

Piaget, Jean. 1947. *La Psychologie de l'intelligence*. Paris: Armand Colin.

———. 1971. *Psychologie et pédagogie*. Paris: Denoël.

Piaget, Jean, and Bärbel Inhelder. 1955. *De la logique de l'enfant à la logique de l'adolescent*. Paris: Alcan.

Picabia, Francis. 1978. *Écrits*, 2 vols. Paris: Belfond.

Picard, Max. 1929. *Das Menschengesicht*. Munich: Delphin. Translated as *The Human Face* (New York: Farrar & Rinehart, 1930); translated by J.-J. Anstett as *Le visage humain* (Paris: Buchet-Chastel, 1962).

Pieron, Henri, ed. 1951. *Vocabulaire de psychologie*. Paris: Presses universitaires de France.

Pinel, Alain. 2004. *Une Police de Vichy*. Paris: L'Harmattan.

Pollard, Miranda. 1998. *Reign of Virtue: Mobilizing Gender in Vichy France*. Chicago: University of Chicago Press.

Ponge, Francis. 1998. *Soap*. Stanford, CA: Stanford University Press.

Poster, Mark. 1975. *Existential Marxism in Postwar France*. Princeton, NJ: Princeton University Press.

Poulet, Georges. 1969. "Phenomenology of Reading." *New Literary History* 1 (1): 53–68.

Proust, Marcel. 2002 [1919]. *In the Shadow of Young Girls in Flower*. New York: Penguin Books.

———. 2003 [1927]. *Finding Time Again*. London: Penguin Books.

Pudal, Bernard. 2003. "Récits édifiants du mythe prolétarien et réalisme socialiste en France." *Sociétés et représentations* 15: 77–96.

Quételet, Adolphe. 1835. *Sur l'homme et le développement de ses facultés*. Paris: Bachelier.

Rabinbach, Anson. 1993. *The Human Motor*. New York: Basic Books.

Rabinow, Paul. 1995. *French Modern*. Chicago: University of Chicago Press.

Rajsfus, Maurice. 1995. *La Police de Vichy*. Paris: Cherche Midi.

Rancière, Jacques. 1998. "The Cause of the Other." *Parallax* 4 (2): 25–33.

Rangeon, François. 1988. *Information et transparence administratives*. Paris: Presses universitaires de France.

Rawls, John. 1999 [1971]. *A Theory of Justice: Revised Edition*. Cambridge, MA: Harvard University Press.

Rawls, John. 2005 [1993]. *Political Liberalism: Expanded Edition*. New York: Columbia University Press.

Redfield, Robert. 1943. "What Do We Know about Race," *Scientific Monthly* 57: 193–201.

———. 1944. "Race and Human Nature." In *Half a Century Onward: Report of the Jubilee Meeting of the Conference of Foreign Mission Boards in Canada and in the United States . . . January 3–7, 1944*, 179–86. New York: Foreign Missions Conference of North America.

Redondi, Pietro. 1986. Introduction to Alexandre Koyré, *De la mystique à la science: Cours, conférences et documents, 1922–62*, 21–40. Paris: Éditions EHESS.

Revel, Jacques. 1975. "Une France sauvage." In Michel de Certeau, Dominique Julia, and Jacques Revel, *Une politique de la langue*, 136–54. Paris: Gallimard.

Rheinberger, Hans-Jörg. 2005. "Gaston Bachelard and the Notion of 'Phenomenotechnique.'" *Perspectives on Science* 13 (3): 313–28.

———. 2010. *On Historicizing Epistemology*. Stanford, CA: Stanford University Press.

Richir, Marc. 1974. "Révolution et transparence sociale" [= RTS]. In J. G. Fichte, *Considérations destinées à rectifier les jugements du public sur la Révolution française*, 3–74. Paris: Payot.

Richman, Michèle. 2002. *Sacred Revolutions: Durkheim and the Collège de Sociologie*. Minneapolis: University of Minnesota Press.

Ricœur, Paul. 1960a. "L'Antinomie de la réalité humaine." *Il Pensiero* 5 (3): 273–80.

———. 1960b. *Finitude et culpabilité*. Vol. 1. Paris: Aubier-Montaigne.

———. 1963. "Structure et herméneutique." *Esprit* 31 (11): 596–627.

———. 1969. *Le Conflit des interprétations: Essais d'herméneutique*. Paris: Seuil.

———. 1986. *Lectures on Ideology and Utopia*. New York: Columbia University Press.

———. 1992. *Oneself as Another*. Chicago: University of Chicago Press.

———. 1996. "The Crisis of the Cogito." *Synthese* 106: 57–66.

———. 2003 [1975]. *The Rule of Metaphor*. London: Routledge.

———. 2004. *The Conflict of Interpretations*. London: Continuum. A translation of Ricœur 1969.

Rivers, W. H. R., ed. 1922. *Essays on the Depopulation of Melanesia*. Cambridge: Cambridge University Press.

Rivet, Paul, ed. 1937. *L'Espèce humaine*. Vol. 7 of *L'Encyclopédie française*. Paris: L'Encyclopédie française.

Robcis, Camille. 2012. "China in Our Heads." *Social Text*, 30 (1): 51–69.

———. 2013. *The Law of Kinship*. Ithaca, NY: Cornell University Press.

Robespierre, Maximilien. 2007. *Virtue and Terror*. Edited by Jean Ducange. London: Verso.

Rocard, Michel. 1986. *À l'épreuve des faits*. Paris: Seuil.

———. 1987. *Le Cœur à l'ouvrage*. Paris: Odile Jacob.

Rorty, Richard. 1979. *Philosophy and the Mirror of Nature*. Princeton, NJ: Princeton University Press.

Rosanvallon, Pierre. 1979. *Le Capitalisme utopique: Critique de l'idéologie économique*. Paris: Seuil.

———. 1993. *L'État en France.* Paris: Seuil.

———. 1999. *Le Capitalisme utopique: Histoire de l'idée de marché.* 2nd ed, of Rosanvallon 1979. Paris: Seuil.

———. 2000. *The New Social Question: Rethinking the Welfare State.* Princeton, NJ: Princeton University Press. Originally published as *La nouvelle question sociale: Repenser l'État-providence* (Paris: Seuil, 1995).

———. 2006. *Democracy Past and Future.* Edited by Samuel Moyn. New York: Columbia University Press.

Ross, Kristin. 1995. *Fast Cars, Clean Bodies: Decolonization and the Reordering of French Culture.* Cambridge, MA: MIT Press.

Rostand, Jean. 1963. *Aux frontières du surhumain.* Paris: Grasset.

Roth, Michael S. 1988. *Knowing and History.* Ithaca, NY: Cornell University Press.

Rothberg, Michael. 2004. "The Work of Testimony in the Age of Decolonization." *PMLA* 119 (5): 1231–46.

Rouch, Jean. 1958. "L'Africain devant le film ethnographique." In Luc de Heusch, *Le Cinéma et l'Afrique au sud du Sahara,* 92–94. Brussels: Rencontres internationales.

———. 1960. *La Religion et la magie Songhay.* Paris: Presses universitaires de France.

———. 2003. *Ciné-ethnography* [= *CE*]. Edited by Steven Feld. Minneapolis: University of Minnesota Press.

———. 2008. *Alors le Noir et le Blanc seront amis: Carnets de mission, 1946–1951.* Paris: Mille et une nuits.

Roudinesco, Elisabeth. 2008. *Philosophy in Turbulent Times.* New York: Columbia University Press.

Rousselet, Jean. 1956. *L'Adolescent, cet inconnu.* Paris: Flammarion.

Rousso, Henry. 1994. *The Vichy Syndrome.* Cambridge, MA: Harvard University Press.

Ruyer, Raymond. 1954. *La Cybernétique et l'origine de l'information.* Paris: Flammarion.

———. 1962. "Les Informations de présence." *Revue philosophique* 152: 197–218.

Rydell, Robert W. 1993. *World's Fairs.* Chicago: University of Chicago Press.

Sadoul, Georges. 1971. *Dziga Vertov.* Paris: Champ Libre.

Safranski, Rüdiger. 1998. *Martin Heidegger.* Cambridge, MA: Harvard University Press.

Sahlins, Marshall. 1972. *Stone Age Economics.* Chicago: Aldine.

Sanders, Paul. 2001. *Histoire du marché noir, 1940–46.* Paris: Perrin.

Sangline, Guy-Marc. 1955. "Contribution à l'étude de la dissociation familiale." PhD diss., Paris.

Sartre, Jean-Paul. 1947 [1944]. "The Republic of Silence." In A. J. Liebling, ed., *The Republic of Silence,* 498–500. New York: Harcourt, Brace.

———. 1947. *Situations I*. Paris: Gallimard.

———. 1957 [1937]. *The Transcendence of the Ego: An Existentialist Theory of Consciousness*. New York: Noonday Press.

———. 1962. *The Imagination*. Ann Arbor: University of Michigan Press.

———. 1970 [1939]. "Visages." In *Les Écrits de Sartre*. Edited by Michel Contat and Michel Bibalka, 560–64. Paris: Gallimard.

———. 1970. "La Libération de Paris: Une Semaine d'apocalypse." In Michel Contat and Michel Rybalka, eds., *Les Écrits de Sartre*, 659–63. Paris: Gallimard.

———. 1989a. "Existentialism Is a Humanism." In Walter Kaufmann, ed., *Existentialism from Dostoyevsky to Sartre*, 345–69. New York: Meridian.

———. 1989b. *No Exit and Three Other Plays*. New York: Vintage Books.

———. 1992 [1943]. *Being and Nothingness* [= *BN*]. New York: Washington Square Press.

———. 2004. *The Imaginary*. London: Routledge.

———. 2007. *Nausea*. New York: New Directions.

Scheerbart, Paul. 1914. *Glasarchitektur*. Berlin: Der Sturm.

Schneider, Manfred. 2013. *Tranzparenztraum: Literatur, Politik, Medien und das Unmögliche*. Berlin: Matthes & Seitz.

Schrift, Alan. 2006. *Twentieth-Century French Philosophy*. Oxford: Blackwell.

Schrödinger, Erwin. 1945. *What Is Life?* Cambridge: Cambridge University Press.

Schuhl, Pierre-Maxime. 1938. *Machinisme et philosophie*. Paris: Alcan.

Scott, Joan W. 2007a. *The Politics of the Veil*. Princeton, NJ: Princeton University Press.

———. 2007b. "History-Writing as Critique." In Keith Jenkins, Sue Morgan, and Alun Munslow, eds., *Manifestos for History*, 19–38. London: Routledge.

Sériot, Patrick. 2014. *Structure and the Whole: East, West and Non-Darwinian Biology in the Origins of Structural Linguistics*. Boston: De Gruyter Mouton.

Servan-Schreiber, Jean-Louis. 1990. *Le Métier de patron*. Paris: Fayard.

Sheehan, James. 2006. "The Problem of Sovereignty in European History." *American Historical Review* III (I): 1–15.

Shepard, Todd. 2011. "Algeria, France, Mexico, UNESCO." *Journal of Global History* 6: 273–97.

Shklar, Judith. 1988. "The Paranoid's Paradise." *New Republic* 198 (26): 38–40.

Siegfried, André. 1949. "Taylor et Descartes." *Le Figaro*, December 16, 1 and 9.

Simmel, Marianne L., ed. 1968. *The Reach of the Mind*. New York: Springer.

Simondon, Gilbert. 1959. *Du mode d'existence des objets techniques*. Paris: Aubier.

Singer, Charles. 1931. *A History of Biology*. New York: Abelard.

Solzhenitsyn, Aleksandr. 1974–76. *L'Archipel du Goulag, 1918–1956: Essai d'investigation littéraire*. 2 vols. Paris: Seuil.

Sontag, Susan. 1966. *Against Interpretation*. New York: Farrar, Straus & Giroux.

Souloumiac, Julien. 2004. "La Norme dans l'*Histoire de la folie.*" *Traces* 6: 25–47.

Starobinski, Jean. 1946. "Interrogatoire du masque." *La Suisse contemporaine* 2: 153–59; 3: 209–21; 4: 358–76.

———. 1953. "La Connaissance de la vie." *Critique* 75–76: 777–91.

———. 1958. "Des taches et des masques" [= TM]. *Critique,* 135–36: 792–804.

———. 1971 [1957]. *Jean-Jacques Rousseau: La Transparence et l'obstacle.* Paris: Gallimard.

———. 1964. *The Invention of Liberty, 1700–1789.* Geneva: Skira.

———. 1970. *La Relation critique.* Paris: Gallimard.

———. 1982. *1789: The Emblems of Reason.* Charlottesville: University Press of Virginia.

———. 1988. *Jean-Jacques Rousseau: Transparency and Obstruction.* Translation by Arthur Goldhammer of Starobinski 1971 [1957]. Chicago: University of Chicago Press.

———. 1989. *The Living Eye.* Cambridge, MA: Harvard University Press.

———. 2012. *L'Encre de la mélancolie.* Paris: Seuil.

Steinberg, Michael. 1995. "Aby Warburg's Kreuzlingen Lecture." In Aby M. Warburg, *Images from the Region of the Pueblo Indians of North America,* 59–114. Ithaca, NY: Cornell University Press.

Stiegler, Bernard. 1998. *Technics and Time 1.* Stanford, CA: Stanford University Press.

Stoczkowski, Wiktor. 2008. *Anthropologies rédemptrices.* Paris: Hermann.

Surkis, Judith. 2012. "When Was the Linguistic Turn?" *American Historical Review* 117 (3): 700–22.

Tétry, Andrée. 1948. *Les Outils chez les êtres vivants.* Paris: Gallimard.

Tiles, Mary. 1994. *Bachelard.* Cambridge: Cambridge University Press.

Trilling, Lionel. 1972. *Sincerity and Authenticity.* Cambridge, MA: Harvard University Press.

Valéry, Paul. 1937. "Discours prononcé à la Sorbonne" (July 31). *Revue de métaphysique et de morale,* 4: 693–710.

———. 1960. *Œuvres.* Paris: Bibliothèque de la Pléiade.

———. 1961 [1941]. *Les Pages immortelles de Descartes, choisies et expliquées par Paul Valéry.* Paris: Buchet/Chastel.

———. 1973 [1927]. *Monsieur Teste.* Princeton, NJ: Princeton University Press.

Van Kley, Dale. 1999. *The Religious Origins of the French Revolution.* New Haven, CT: Yale University Press.

Vasiliu, Anca. 1997. *Du diaphane.* Paris: Vrin.

Vattimo, Gianni. 1992. *The Transparent Society.* Baltimore: Johns Hopkins University Press.

Veyne, Paul. 1983. *Did the Greeks Believe in Their Myths?* Chicago: University of Chicago Press.

Vidal, Fernando. 2001. "La fine peau de l'apparence." In Murielle Gagnebin and Christine Savinel, eds., *Starobinski en mouvement*, 216–27. Paris: Champ Vallon.

Vidler, Anthony. 1990. *Claude-Nicolas Ledoux*. Cambridge, MA: MIT Press.

———. 1992. *The Architectural Uncanny*. Cambridge, MA: MIT Press.

Vieillard-Baron, Jean-Louis. 2000. *Philosophie française*. Paris: Armand-Colin.

Virgili, Fabrice. 2002. *Shorn Women: Gender and Punishment in Liberation France*. New York: Berg.

Vitale, Francesco. 2014. "The Text and the Living." *Oxford Literary Review* 36 (1): 95–114.

"Vivre et parler." 1968. *Les Lettres françaises* 1221: 3–7; 1222: 4–5.

Vuillemin, Jules. 1948. *Essai sur la signification de la mort*. Paris: Presses universitaires de France.

———. 1954. *L'Héritage kantien et la révolution copernicienne: Fichte, Cohen, Heidegger*. Paris: Presses universitaires de France.

Wahl, Jean. 1932. *Vers le concret*. Paris: Vrin.

———. 1950. "The Present Situation and Present Future of French Philosophy" [= PSF]. In Marvin Farber, ed., *Philosophic Thought in France and the United States*, 35–54. Buffalo, NY: University of Buffalo Publications.

Watson, James, and Francis Crick. 1953. "A Structure for Deoxyribose Nucleic Acid." *Nature* 171: 737–38.

Watts, Philip. 1998. *Allegories of the Purge: How Literature Responded to the Postwar Trials of Writers and Intellectuals in France*. Stanford, CA: Stanford University Press.

Weindling, Paul. 1989. *Health, Race, and German Politics*. Cambridge: Cambridge University Press.

Wilcken, Patrick. 2010. *Claude Lévi-Strauss*. New York: Penguin Books.

Wittgenstein, Ludwig. 1986. *Philosophical Investigations*. Translated by G. E. M. Anscombe. London: Blackwell.

Wolin, Richard. 2010. *The Wind from the East: French Intellectuals, the Cultural Revolution, and the Legacy of the 1960s*. Princeton, NJ: Princeton University Press.

Worms, Frédéric. 2009. *La Philosophie en France au XXe siècle: Moments*. Paris: Gallimard.

———, ed. 2016. *Les 100 mots de la philosophie*. Paris: Presses universitaires de France/Que sais-je?

Wubbels, Rolf E. 1979. "The French Economic Miracle." *Financial Analysts Journal* 35 (4): 23–27.

Wundt, Wilhelm. 1897. *Ethics*. New York: Macmillan.

———. 1907. *System der Philosophie*. Vol. 1. Leipzig: Engelmann.

Zakariya, Nasser. 2017. *A Final Story: Science, Myth, and Beginnings.* Chicago: University of Chicago Press.

Zambelli, Paola. 1998. Introduction to Alexandre Koyré, "Present Trends of French Philosophical Thought." *Journal of the History of Ideas* 59: 521–29.

Zenetti, Marie-Jeanne. 2011. "Transparence, opacité, matité dans l'œuvre de Roland Barthes, du *Degré zéro de l'écriture* à *L'Empire des signes.*" *Numéros/Appareil* 7. https://appareil.revues.org/1201?lang=en (accessed August 10, 2016).

Index

Cultural Memory | *in the Present*

Jonathan Culler and Kevin Lamb, eds., *Just Being Difficult? Academic Writing in the Public Arena*

Jean-Luc Nancy, *A Finite Thinking*, edited by Simon Sparks

Theodor W. Adorno, *Can One Live after Auschwitz? A Philosophical Reader*, edited by Rolf Tiedemann

Patricia Pisters, *The Matrix of Visual Culture: Working with Deleuze in Film Theory*

Andreas Huyssen, *Present Pasts: Urban Palimpsests and the Politics of Memory*

Talal Asad, *Formations of the Secular: Christianity, Islam, Modernity*

Dorothea von Mücke, *The Rise of the Fantastic Tale*

Marc Redfield, *The Politics of Aesthetics: Nationalism, Gender, Romanticism*

Emmanuel Levinas, *On Escape*

Dan Zahavi, *Husserl's Phenomenology*

Rodolphe Gasché, *The Idea of Form: Rethinking Kant's Aesthetics*

Michael Naas, *Taking on the Tradition: Jacques Derrida and the Legacies of Deconstruction*

Herlinde Pauer-Studer, ed., *Constructions of Practical Reason: Interviews on Moral and Political Philosophy*

Jean-Luc Marion, *Being Given That: Toward a Phenomenology of Givenness*

Theodor W. Adorno and Max Horkheimer, *Dialectic of Enlightenment*

Ian Balfour, *The Rhetoric of Romantic Prophecy*

Martin Stokhof, *World and Life as One: Ethics and Ontology in Wittgenstein's Early Thought*

Gianni Vattimo, *Nietzsche: An Introduction*

Jacques Derrida, *Negotiations: Interventions and Interviews, 1971-1998*, ed. Elizabeth Rottenberg

Brett Levinson, *The Ends of Literature: The Latin American "Boom" in the Neoliberal Marketplace*

Timothy J. Reiss, *Against Autonomy: Cultural Instruments, Mutualities, and the Fictive Imagination*

Hent de Vries and Samuel Weber, eds., *Religion and Media*

Niklas Luhmann, *Theories of Distinction: Re-Describing the Descriptions of Modernity*, ed. and introd. William Rasch

Johannes Fabian, *Anthropology with an Attitude: Critical Essays*

Michel Henry, *I Am the Truth: Toward a Philosophy of Christianity*

Miryam Sas, *Fault Lines: Cultural Memory and Japanese Surrealism*

Peter Schwenger, *Fantasm and Fiction: On Textual Envisioning*

Didier Maleuvre, *Museum Memories: History, Technology, Art*

Jacques Derrida, *Monolingualism of the Other; or, The Prosthesis of Origin*

Andrew Baruch Wachtel, *Making a Nation, Breaking a Nation: Literature and Cultural Politics in Yugoslavia*

Niklas Luhmann, *Love as Passion: The Codification of Intimacy*

Mieke Bal, ed., *The Practice of Cultural Analysis: Exposing Interdisciplinary Interpretation*

Jacques Derrida and Gianni Vattimo, eds., *Religion*

Lightning Source UK Ltd.
Milton Keynes UK
UKOW04f0604230917
309710UK00002B/41/P